PROMISED LANDS

Promised Lands

THE BRITISH AND THE OTTOMAN MIDDLE EAST

Jonathan Parry

PRINCETON UNIVERSITY PRESS
PRINCETON & OXFORD

Published by Princeton University Press
41 William Street, Princeton, New Jersey 08540
6 Oxford Street, Woodstock, Oxfordshire OX20 1TR

press.princeton.edu

All Rights Reserved
ISBN 978-0-691-18189-9
ISBN (e-book) 978-0-691-23145-7

British Library Cataloging-in-Publication Data is available

Editorial: Ben Tate and Josh Drake
Production Editorial: Jenny Wolkowicki
Jacket design: Layla Mac Rory
Production: Danielle Amatucci
Publicity: Alyssa Sanford and Charlotte Coyne
Copyeditor: Maia Vaswani

Jacket art: *Mahmoudie Canal*, c. 1850. Watercolor on paper heightened with white bodycolor. © P&O Heritage

This book has been composed in Miller

Printed on acid-free paper. ∞

Printed in the United States of America

10 9 8 7 6 5 4 3 2 1

England, it is usually supposed, regards her Eastern possessions with apathy and indifference. . . . But it is very certain that the same apathy and indifference does not extend to the interesting countries by which India is surrounded; the very name of Arabia, the country of Abraham, Isaac, and Jacob, calls up an echo from every bosom.

—J. RAYMOND WELLSTED, *TRAVELS TO THE CITY OF THE CALIPHS* (1840)

CONTENTS

MAPS

Places and Provinces

The maps at the end of this preface aim to show all the places mentioned in the book. In the text, I have sometimes called the main administrative divisions of the Ottoman Empire by their official name, *eyalet* (*vilayet* from the 1860s), and sometimes instead used "pashalik," which the British preferred, or simply "province." I have followed the universal British practice of referring to the provincial Ottoman governors as "pashas." *Eyalet*s were divided into districts called *sancak*s, which were administered by pashas of lesser rank.

This book covers the years from 1798 to 1854. Provincial and district boundaries were altered at several points during this period, and contemporary maps are not consistent in depicting them. The maps do not show these boundaries, except in the case of two of the Syrian *eyalet*s (for the 1840s).

By "Syria," I mean the whole region between the Egyptian border at al-Arish and the province of Adana in Anatolia. From the seventeenth century, there were four *eyalet*s in Syria: one, Aleppo, in the north, and the other three created out of the historic province of Damascus. Its coastal area was divided between the northern *eyalet* of Tripoli, and the southern one of Sidon, which began just north of Lebanon. Damascus was left as essentially an inland *eyalet* based around the city and its highway to north and south. The pashalik of Sidon increased in importance in the eighteenth century because of the growth of trade, and Cezzar moved its capital to Acre and built up its fortifications. He sought to dominate Damascus as well, but managed this only intermittently. His influence in mountainous Lebanon was always limited, as the book will show; Bashir sought to establish a semi-independent position there through alliances with other local landowners. His local primacy was reflected in the title of amir, but Lebanon was not formally autonomous until the 1860s. When the Egyptians governed Syria in the 1830s, they restored the dominance of Damascus over Sidon. In 1841, the capital of Sidon was switched to Beirut, reflecting the transfer of commercial primacy to it from Acre, as well as the political importance of Lebanon and of communication with Damascus. After that, Sidon consisted of four *sancak*s, Beirut, Acre, Nablus, and Jerusalem. In 1841, the Jerusalem *sancak* was enlarged and its governor given some autonomy and special responsibilities for managing the affairs of the local Christians, as a result of the diplomatic tensions of 1840. It became a separate *eyalet* in 1854. What the West called Palestine was never an Ottoman district as such.

The region of Baghdad (or Turkish Arabia, or Iraq) was made up of the three *eyalet*s of Mosul, Baghdad, and Basra, whose relationship is explained at the beginning of chapter 3. Though normally ruled by the pasha of Baghdad, the small Basra *eyalet* was important to the Porte because its jurisdiction was regarded as extending along the western Persian Gulf coast, as far as Qatar and even Muscat. However, Britain did not recognise Ottoman sovereignty over Kuwait, let alone the coastal shaykhdoms beyond it.

I have used the term "Kurdistan" as shorthand for all the mountainous regions that the Kurds dominated. I use it simply for convenience, and have no precise boundaries, or any other implication, in mind. Chapters 7 and 8 discuss the Kurd-swayed mountains north of Mosul that became the (short-lived) Ottoman administrative province of Kurdistan from 1848. Chapters 3 and 10, on the other hand, focus on the Kurdish stronghold of Sulaimaniya further south and east, which fell within the Baghdad pashalik. For Claudius Rich, the British agent at Baghdad in the 1810s, "Koordistan" really meant Sulaimaniya, which the British tended to see as conceptually a separate problem from the more northerly Kurdish provinces.

The Ottoman province of Hijaz on the east side of the Red Sea was controlled by the Egyptian government until 1841 and was then restored to the control of Constantinople. Though there was a pasha, based on the coast at Jeddah, the hereditary sharif of Mecca, the steward of the Holy Cities, was usually the dominant local force. Ottoman/Egyptian ability to control Mocha and Massawa, the main Red Sea ports south of the Hijaz, fluctuated a great deal in this period and is best traced through the index entries for each place. Further south, the Ottomans claimed sovereignty over the harbours on each side of the mouth of the Red Sea, but Britain did not recognise it. As explained in the text, the sharif of Abu Arish dominated some of them, and the sultan of Lahej controlled Aden. Like the British, I have sometimes called him the sultan of Aden.

I have used the term "Wahhabi" to describe the religiopolitical Arab movement that spread outwards from central Arabia to its western and eastern coasts, and into the Baghdad pashalik, at the beginning of the nineteenth century, because the many British observers of it invariably used that name. I have reverted to "Saudi" to refer to those members of the House of Saud who revived this Wahhabi power from the mid-1820s, and to the second Saudi state that they established in central and eastern Arabia, though in fact most Britons continued to refer to them as Wahhabi.

Names and Spellings

Since this is a book about British views and activities in the Middle East, rather than a history of the region itself, it is not easy to adopt a consistent approach to using and spelling names and titles, especially since I quote extensively from contemporary writings.

I have followed general nineteenth-century Western practice in calling the Ottoman capital Constantinople rather than Istanbul, because it is an important argument of the book that its politics were viewed in a European context, and that the leading British officials saw it as a long way from the Middle East.

Though "Turk" was universally used by the British, I have, outside quotations, almost always used "Ottoman" to denote the Constantinople regime, though I have occasionally resorted to "Turk" for effect, usually in contrast to "Arab." I have, however, followed the British in talking about Persia and Abyssinia rather than Iran and Ethiopia.

I have used modern spellings for place names rather than the variants commonly used by British people at the time (e.g., Basra, rather than Bussorah). I have adopted Western variants where these are familiar (Jeddah, Mecca, Mocha). When writing about the Red Sea port at which most Indian travellers to Egypt arrived until at least the 1830s, I have followed the contemporary British usage of Kosseir, rather than today's Quseer (or Quseir or Qoseir).

In spelling Arabic place names, and all other Arabic terms, I have generally followed the transliteration principles of the *International Journal of Middle Eastern Studies*. I have omitted Arabic diacritical marks, and have hardly used the letters *'ayn* and *hamza*: exceptions include Qur'an and Shi'a.

My aim (I hope achieved) has been to give Ottoman officials Turkish names, with modern spelling (hence Mehmet Ali), and Arabs Arab ones. However, I have made no attempt at accurate full names, so most people have just a single shorthand name. There are two figures in this story whom the British called Reshid. I have used the Turkish Reşid for the grand vizier and military commander Reşid Mehmet Pasha, but have left Koca Mustafa Reşid Pasha, the leading Anglophile of the 1840s and 1850s, as Reshid. Likewise, his ally Mehmet Emin Ali Pasha remains Ali Efendi, which was how the British first encountered him, though he was promoted pasha in 1847.

I have kept the use of Ottoman official titles to a minimum, as they do not seem necessary for my argument. So I have talked about "local authorities" and "local officials" more than some readers may like. I have used Turkish terms for a handful of official posts: *defterdar* (state collector of provincial revenue); *kaymakam* (governor of a provincial district); *mütesellim* (governor of an individual town before the Tanzimat); *wakil* (deputy or legal administrator). I have occasionally referred to the grand vizier, the sultan's chief minister, the kapudan pasha, the senior Ottoman minister who was in charge of the fleet, and the reis efendi. The last was the title used until 1836 to describe the minister at the Porte who was responsible for dealings with foreign ambassadors; from then on, he was known as foreign minister.

As usual, I have used ulema to refer to the local guardians and teachers of Islamic religious traditions, and qadi to refer to shari'a law judges.

Rayas, Millets, *and Franks*

As is normal, I have used the term "raya" to describe a subject of the sultan who was not a Muslim. Rayas were regarded as inferior subjects, were liable for special taxes in return for not serving in the army of the faithful, and were often subject to abuse, but they also had certain rights. Well before the beginning of this period, the main non-Muslim religions within the empire had established the privilege of managing the judicial and administrative affairs of their rayas. The heads of the religion organised justice within each sect, collected the taxes due to the sultan by the members, and in return expected their religious practices to be tolerated and respected. This organisation was known as the *millet* system. The original *millet*, the *millet-i Rûm* or Roman nation, was the Greek Orthodox community, under the authority of the Greek patriarch of Constantinople. The Porte always reserved the power (by firman) to nominate the patriarch, usually by confirming elections made by the bishops. (At points in this period, the British ambassador at Constantinople sought to defend the Porte's right of election against suspected Russian interference in the process.) A similar arrangement applied for the Armenians and the Jews. The chief rabbi, like the Greek and Armenian patriarchs, had a place in Ottoman ruling councils. In the provinces, the local religious leaders had considerable power over their communities. The affairs of the Syrian Orthodox Church (sometimes called Jacobites) were formally managed by the Armenian patriarch, but in practice were delegated to the Syrian patriarch.

The rayas who belonged to other Christian denominations were not protected by the *millet* system at the beginning of this period, nor did they have episcopal representatives at Constantinople. The Nestorians in the Kurdish mountains were used to defending their own interests within local power structures. Communities within each of the Eastern Churches had been converted to Roman Catholicism by Jesuit or Lazarist missionaries; traditionally they relied on the European Catholic powers to protect them. When the European representatives were forced to leave Constantinople during the Russo-Ottoman war in 1828, Armenians who had converted to Romanism found themselves without patrons. The Armenian *millet* leaders promptly banished them from Constantinople and forced them to sell their property. Once the representatives returned, they secured a firman in 1831, by which Armenian Catholics were allowed to organise themselves under a separate patriarch holding authority direct from the pope. This creation of an official Armenian Catholic community encouraged pressure for something similar among other "Latins" and among Greek Catholics. Then in 1841 tighter regulations required Ottoman subjects to have a *tezkere* for internal travel in the empire, which meant that formal representation of these raya communities at Constantinople was practically necessary. In the 1840s, most of the Catholic communities were given *millet* status, with an agent at the Porte who obtained the necessary paperwork for them.[1] In 1850, the same status was given to the Protestant communities that had converted from the Armenian and other Churches. The Maronites also had a lay agent at the Porte in the 1840s, while their patriarch stayed in Lebanon.

The status of rayas must be distinguished from that of those residents of the Ottoman Empire who were subjects not of the sultan, but of the European powers—often called "Franks." The historic capitulations negotiated between the Ottomans and the European powers in the seventeenth and eighteenth centuries conceded special taxation and justice arrangements to such residents, as well as preferential export and import duties for their trade. Certain local Ottoman subjects connected with the European consulates also secured these privileges, by virtue of being given protected status. In the nineteenth century, the Ottoman state sought to restrict the number of local merchants who enjoyed this protection. On the other hand, British possession of Malta from 1800 and the Ionian Islands from 1815 meant that British consuls in many parts of the empire found themselves responsible for the behaviour of their Maltese and Ionian subjects who had emigrated to their areas. Many Jews who were European subjects also emigrated to Palestine, relying on the protection of the European consuls against ill treatment by members of other religions—and could not expect membership of the Jewish *millet*. All these developments caused difficulties that this book will trace.

The East India Company

The East India Company (EIC), whose charter gave it a monopoly of British trade with India and China throughout the seventeenth and eighteenth centuries, acquired significant political and military power in large parts of the Indian subcontinent between 1745 and 1761. It had three main centres, or presidencies—in Bengal, Madras, and Bombay—each of which had a president (or governor) and small council. Of these the most powerful was Bengal, and in 1773 the British government established the post of governor-general of Bengal, to reside at Fort William in Calcutta, with some powers over the other presidencies. These principally related to war and foreign policy, until they were expanded in 1833 to include most other matters, from which point the post holder became formally known as governor-general of India.

In 1800, the presidency of Bombay had much less territory than the other two, and relied for revenue largely on the trade of Bombay and Surat merchants with ports in western Asia and eastern Africa. As this book will explain, from 1686 it had a small navy, the Bombay Marine, to help to protect its territory and trade and to secure merchant rights. As primarily a trading

1. On this process, see the memo by Charles Alison (June 1847, FO 78/682, National Archives).

company, the EIC established "factories" or warehouses in many foreign ports to protect its goods; these required resident factors, such as the one periodically appointed at Mocha. It also established residents, or political agents, at the courts of the Indian princes with whom it had alliances. In the eighteenth century, the term "resident" was already generally used to describe the EIC factors/agents at Basra and at Bushehr, and the EIC's Secret Committee appointed Harford Jones as "resident at Baghdad" in 1798. In 1812, Claudius Rich was given the formal title of "political agent in Turkish Arabia," but continued to be generally known as resident, as did Robert Taylor after him. Stafford Haines was made the political agent of the Bombay presidency in Aden from 1839; Aden became a residency in the 1850s.

The British government in London had direct responsibility for relations with European countries and the Ottoman Empire, through the Foreign Office. Those relations were a major preoccupation of all British cabinets and especially of each prime minister and foreign secretary. They had a more distant relationship with India. In the 1770s and 1780s, the problem of how to get some control over the affairs of the East India Company was nearly as contentious in Britain as the government of North America. In 1784, the 1773 Regulating Act, which had established the post of governor-general, was superseded by new legislation that gave the London government stronger authority in principle over the EIC. A Board of Control was established (generally known as the India Board) with a president who was from now on usually a member of the British cabinet. He had considerable power over EIC appointments, and was able to set EIC policy if he could reach agreement with the Secret Committee of three senior members of the company's Court of Directors, who operated out of its base, India House in Leadenhall Street. The Secret Committee was responsible for sending instructions to India on important matters. However, the ability of the men in London to control the decision making of the governor-general and the presidency governors was necessarily very limited, in view of the severe delays in communicating with India before regular steam communication was established in the 1830s.

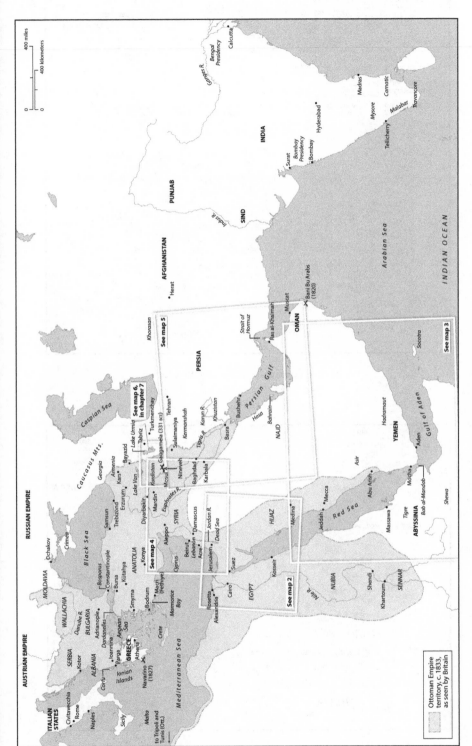

MAP 1. The Ottoman Empire and Eurasia

AUSTRIAN EMPIRE
RUSSIAN EMPIRE
ITALIAN STATES

Naples
Rome
Civitavecchia
Sicily
Malta
to Tripoli and Tunis (Ott.)

SERBIA
WALLACHIA
MOLDAVIA
BULGARIA
Danube R.
Adrianople
ALBANIA
Kotor
Parga
Ioannina
Corfu
Ionian Islands
Navarino (1827)
GREECE
Athens
Aegean Sea

Crimea
Ochakov
Black Sea
Caucasus Mts.
Georgia
Armenia
Kars
Bayazid
Erzurum
Trebizond
Samsun

Caspian Sea

RUSSIAN EMPIRE

Constantinople
Bosporus
Dardanelles
Bursa
Kütahya
ANATOLIA
Smyrna
Bodrum
Marid (Fethiye)
Marmarice Bay
Konya
Cyprus
Mediterranean Sea

Lake Urmia
Tabriz
Turkmenchay
See map 6, in chapter 7

Lake Van
Kurdistan
Mardin
Diyarbekir
SYRIA
Aleppo
Lebanon
Beirut
Damascus
Acre
Jerusalem
Jordan R.
Dead Sea
See map 4

Mosul
Nineveh
Gaugamela (331 BC)
Baghdad
Karbala
Euphrates R.
Sulaimaniya
Kermanshah
Tigris R.
Karun R.
Khuzistan
Basra
Bushehr
Hasa
Bahrain
Persian Gulf

PERSIA
Tehran
Khorasan
See map 5

AFGHANISTAN
Herat

PUNJAB
Indus R.
SIND

Bengal Presidency
Ganges R.
Calcutta

INDIA
Surat
Bombay Presidency
Bombay
Hyderabad
Madras
Mysore
Carnatic
Tellicherry
Malabar
Travancore

Arabian Sea

INDIAN OCEAN

Strait of Hormuz
Ras al-Khaimah
Muscat
Bani Bu Arabs (1820)
OMAN
See map 3
Socotra

NAJD
Hadramaut
YEMEN
Aden
Gulf of Aden
Bab al-Mandab
Shewa

Suez
Cairo
EGYPT
Rosetta
Alexandria
Nile R.
Kosseir
See map 2
NUBIA
Shendi
Khartoum
SENNAR

HIJAZ
Medina
Mecca
Jeddah
Red Sea
Abu Arish
Asir
Mocha
Massawa
Tigre
ABYSSINIA

Ottoman Empire territory, c. 1833, as seen by Britain

400 miles
400 kilometers
0
0

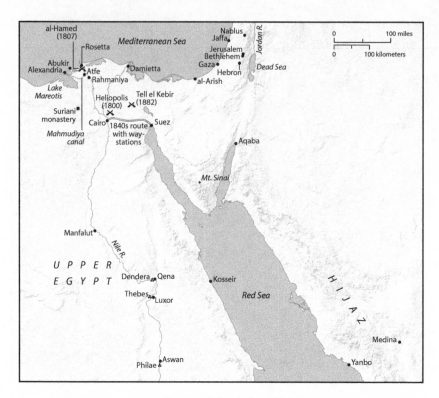

MAP 2. Egypt and the northern Red Sea

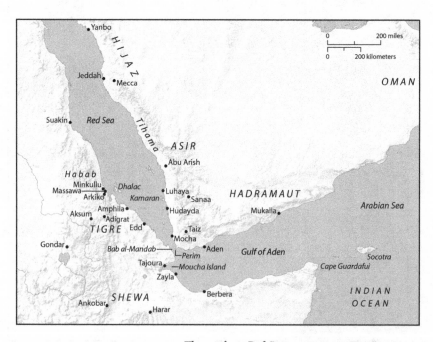

MAP 3. The southern Red Sea

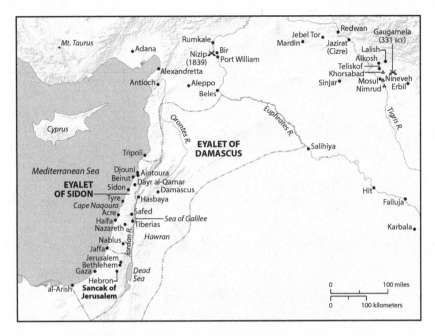

MAP 4. Syria and western Kurdistan

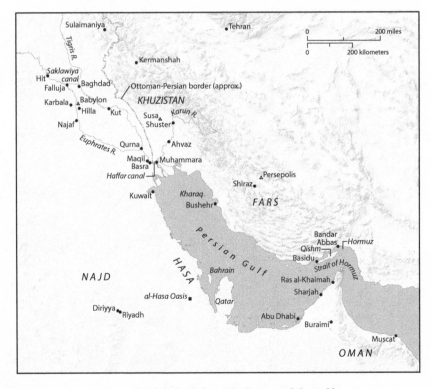

MAP 5. Baghdad, southern Kurdistan, and the Gulf

PROMISED LANDS

Introduction

The Lands, Their Rulers, and Their Aggressors

Early on March 8, 1801, fifty British soldiers sat huddled with their muskets between their knees in each of fifty-eight flat-bottomed boats off the Egyptian Mediterranean coast at Abukir. Each wore a belt containing three days' rations of food and water and sixty rounds of ball cartridge. They were the first wave of an assault on the shore from the offshore fleet, made up of five thousand soldiers in all. As their boats approached the beach, they came under shell attack from the French artillery on top of the sandhills. This was followed by a hailstorm of grape shots to which they had no means of responding. Three boats were sunk; some soldiers drowned wearing their heavy belts. On landing, many more were immediately dispatched by French bayonets, but replacements continued to arrive. The men on the right clambered up a steep sandhill, panicking the French artillerymen into retreat. On the left, the resisting enemy was soon outnumbered. The traveller Edward Clarke, who arrived soon afterwards, was told by survivors that "a spectacle more horrible than the landing of the troops was never seen." They "had been taught to expect no quarter, and therefore none was given. . . . [A]ll was blood, and death, and victory."[1] Within twenty minutes, the British army found itself in secure possession of a small pocket of land—the first step in the first British occupation of Egypt, and the first modern British military encounter with what we now know as the Middle East.[2]

The soldiers' mission was to reconquer Egypt from the twenty-five thousand French troops who had occupied it ever since Napoleon's invasion in 1798. This took five months, during which at least 1,600 British soldiers died, and probably as many more were permanently maimed, including 160 blinded

---

1. Otter, *Edward Daniel Clarke*, 2:102–3; E. Clarke, *Travels in Various Countries*, 1:279.
2. For the landing, see T. Walsh, *Journal of the Late Campaign*, 74–78; Mackesy, *British Victory in Egypt*, 71–75.

by ophthalmia. They had to live in their clothes day and night, exposed to sear-
ing heat, thirst, flies, fleas, sand lice, and sirocco-whipped sandstorms.[3] Once
the two main bodies of French troops in Cairo and Alexandria surrendered,
the British army found itself in possession of Egypt. But then what? It had had
persistent angry arguments with its allies, the Ottoman military commanders,
who thought that the British were there to help them to liberate their own
country. The British army had made commitments to the Mamluk leaders
who had governed Egypt for many years before 1798, and who bitterly distrusted the Ottomans. It relied for provisions on local Arab chiefs who disliked
both groups. Its continuing presence was an affront to Napoleon, who held the
upper hand in the European war, and who planned to renegotiate the future
of Egypt in a peace settlement. It was also an irritant to Russia, Britain's only
significant ally, which could see that a long-term British occupation might
alter the global balance of power. These factors all helped to force the British
army to evacuate Egypt in 1803. However, it reinvaded the country in 1807,
determined to keep France out.

Why did Egypt matter so much to the British, and to Napoleon? Egypt
was an obvious route to India, and India was the cornerstone of Britain's new
empire. It seemed essential in view of the humiliating loss of the thirteen
American colonies in 1783. Britain had recently begun to expand the amount
of Indian territory that it governed directly, and remained alarmed at possible internal and external challenges there. Napoleon threatened a global war
against Britain. He originally hoped to ally with Indian princes to subvert British authority; moreover, the occupation of Egypt would weaken the British
navy by forcing it to spread itself thinly across the world. Napoleon's challenge
to British power was never forgotten. Every prime minister until 1868 and
most of the wider political elite spent their formative or adult years living
through his war. Nor was Egypt the only route that Napoleon could take. In
1799, it was widely assumed that he would move up through Syria, east to the
Tigris, and then down past Baghdad to the Persian Gulf, as Alexander the
Great had done on his march to the East. After 1810, the French threat to India
disappeared, but within twenty years the Russians had begun to threaten it
instead. When they penetrated Kurdistan in 1828, the Russians showed how
they might be able to send an invasion force down the Mesopotamian rivers.
In planning against French or Russian aggression, Britain's strategy involved
thinking geopolitically—about how to define, defend, and develop these
two crucial routes from Europe to India, through Egypt and the Red Sea, or
through Syria, Mesopotamia, and the Gulf.

The main purpose of this book is to discuss how Britain went about securing these lands and waterways from its rivals. The book argues that to all
intents and purposes it had done this by the time of the Crimean War in 1854,

---

3. See Daniel Nicol's diary in Macbride, *With Napoleon at Waterloo*, 52–56.

when the account ends. So this can be seen as an important imperial story. Yet there has been astonishingly little interest from historians in considering this region as a British problem and British opportunity in the first half of the nineteenth century. There is no large-scale analysis of British policy to it, and in the general histories of the British Empire it hardly features.[4] One reason is because the region is almost never seen as a unit. I have used the term "Middle East," which is of course anachronistic, simply as the best shorthand description for the territory with which the book is concerned, the Asian and Egyptian lands of the Ottoman Empire south of the Anatolian plateau.[5]

These were lands of many diverse cultures, and it will become clear that the British response to them appreciated at least some of that diversity. Nonetheless, there are four reasons for treating them as a coherent region, from a British perspective. First, these territories were essential in keeping the European powers from British India. Second, Britain had to think seriously about how to manage and cultivate their inhabitants, which meant mainly the Arabs. Third, they were lands of enormous historical and religious importance—the bases of three great religions, and formerly provinces and empires of immense fertility. The contrast between their present state and their past glory was obvious to anyone who knew their Bible and classical literature, yet this very contrast raised the question of what the region might become if it were wisely governed. Finally, and most problematically, they were all owned by another ruler—the sultan of the Ottoman Empire.[6]

---

4. Robert Harrison's *Britain in the Middle East* is a valiant recent exception, though it naturally focuses on later periods. Edward Ingram's articles and books contain stimulating insight: see, for instance, some of the essays in his compilation *In Defence of British India*. Some valuable material can still be found in Temperley's *England and the Near East*.

5. As this book's subject is the parts of the nineteenth-century "Middle East" that were recognised to be Ottoman, it excludes Persia and, for most purposes, the Gulf. The term "Middle East" became fairly widely used between 1896 and 1903. "Near East" and "Far East" already existed; "Near East" continued for some time to be applied to discussion of the Balkan and Levantine Ottoman lands from a European perspective. The "Middle Eastern problem" was defined as the defence of India from the west, so most uses of the term in the early twentieth century prioritised the regional importance of Persia and even Afghanistan. But Huseyin Yilmaz has shown that Goethe used "Middle East" in 1819, again primarily with reference to Persia and its neighbourhood, and that others followed his usage. So it seems reasonable to use the term "Ottoman Middle East" in a book that argues that the British thought seriously about the region from the beginning of the nineteenth century, in relation to Indian defence. See Koppes, "Captain Mahan," and Yilmaz, "Eastern Question," 24.

6. The reason for focusing on the *Ottoman* Middle East in this book is partly to aid clarity in discussing British policy and attitudes, and partly because I see this region as neglected in historical accounts of this period, compared with Persia and the Gulf. However, the issues of Persia and the Gulf were often very relevant to the politics of Baghdad and Basra, so I discuss both at certain points. For the Gulf, I have relied mostly on the classic account by J. B. Kelly, *Britain and the Persian Gulf*. This is now updated by the

These four aspects mean that this is a geopolitical story, about routes and strategy, but it is also a cultural story, about histories, religions, and races, and thirdly it is a diplomatic story, about European great power tactics. One issue immediately arises: whether this third element can help to explain British policy to the extent that the old accounts of the "Eastern question" suggested.

The sparse coverage of British policy to the Middle East in the first half of the nineteenth century is mostly due to diplomatic historians viewing British concern with Ottoman lands through the lens of an "Eastern question" that was managed by European governments. For a long time, diplomatic narratives, concentrating on the dispatches of aristocratic ministers and their conversations in European drawing rooms, reduced Britain's objectives to a fixed policy or "system": the maintenance of the Ottoman imperial state and its territorial integrity.[7] Yet this perspective does not get us very far in understanding British actions, for three reasons. First, the other European powers also, in general, attached importance to the principle of Ottoman territorial sovereignty. Second, Britain was as willing as other powers to compromise it in practice. Third, British officials always needed to consider the range of regional issues—geopolitical, economic, religious—that this book explores. In fact, recent scholarship on the Eastern question has started to recognise that all the European powers had diverse and shifting priorities and visions, and that diplomacy was not a static system involving fixed rules and principles, but a dynamic and interactive process, in which the Ottoman Empire also participated actively. This is a very helpful shift of perspective, which this book hopes to take further.[8] It is part of the wider recent realisation that international relations were not just a matter of diplomatic negotiation; they involved clashing conceptions and assumptions.[9]

The status of the Ottoman Empire was a fundamental problem of European diplomacy. In 1683, its army reached as far west as the gates of Vienna.

---

important work of Guillemette Crouzet: *Inventing the Middle East*. For British strategy regarding Persia, see Yapp's *Strategies of British India* and Ingram's *Britain's Persian Connection*.

7. The best classic account is Schroeder's *Transformation*. M. Anderson's *Eastern Question* is a good example of the old thematic treatments. An incisive general survey of British foreign policy that nonetheless adopts this very Eurocentric approach is Paul Hayes's *Nineteenth Century*, chap. 9. John Clarke's *British Diplomacy*, another very intelligent overview, almost entirely omits the Middle East, though it discusses the Americas, India, and the Far East as well as Europe.

8. See Šedivý, *Metternich, the Great Powers*; Frary and Kozelsky, *Russian-Ottoman Borderlands*; Ozavci, *Dangerous Gifts*.

9. Three stimulating recent reinterpretations of nineteenth-century international history from an ideological and geographical perspective have been Lauren Benton's *Search for Sovereignty*, Mark Mazower's *Governing the World*, and Barry Buzan and George Lawson's *Global Transformation*.

Since then, it had been in retreat, but a sultan who was the caliph of Sunni Islam still ruled most of the Christian populations of the Balkans. To most Europeans, Ottoman governing practice appeared offensively barbarous and its military and economic power in terminal decline. It was generally assumed throughout this period that the empire could not survive. Only the Crimean War of 1854–56 made the powers guarantee its independence. The extent of Ottoman territory in Europe, in Asia, and along the North African seaboard naturally led many Europeans to dream of capitalising on its demise. In the sixty years after 1798, Napoleonic France and then Russia seemed to pose major threats to it.

Moreover, French and Russian interest in Constantinople had massive historical ramifications. Constantine, the first Christian emperor of Rome, had founded his new capital—a second Rome—on the straits between Europe and Asia in 330 CE, and called it after himself. This decision reflected the enormous size of the Roman Empire, its natural division into Latin and Greek realms, and the pressing need to combat challenges from Persians and others in central Asia. Within 150 years, the Roman Empire had collapsed in the Latin West, but it was revived as the Holy Roman Empire when the pope crowned the Frankish king Charlemagne in 800. The Byzantine Empire continued in the East, but lost most of western Asia to Arab invaders in the seventh century. These two empires promoted rival styles of Christianity, which each claimed to be the only true religion. In 1054, a formal split occurred between Roman Christianity and the Eastern Orthodox Church. From 1095, the Catholic powers in the West began Crusades against the Muslim rulers of their claimed Holy Land. In 1204, however, the Fourth Crusade diverted to attack Constantinople instead, and all but destroyed Byzantine power. By 1400, the Byzantines were struggling to hold off the Ottomans, the latest anti-Christian invaders from Asia, who overran Constantinople in 1453. In the eighteenth century, France and Austria continued to vie for the leadership of European Catholicism, while Russia emerged as the new standard-bearer for Orthodoxy. In the nineteenth century, finally, the whole of Europe assumed that the Islamic empire to its east was dying. Was it the destiny of the Christian powers to take over its lands, and regenerate Christianity in its very birthplace? If so, could France and Russia, and the Churches that they represented, cooperate in this project any more easily than in the past, or would they end up fighting for it?

Napoleon and the Russian empress Catherine (who died in 1796) both seemed very tempted by Ottoman partition. Yet it was never clear throughout this period whether either France or Russia really wanted to dismantle the empire. Though partition continued to have its advocates, the dominant view was usually that war over such a large territory would be devastating; besides, for any power there was huge risk that rivals would gain relatively more from the regime's collapse. An alternative strategy was to exploit Ottoman weakness and dependency, and to offer the sultan protection. France, Russia, and Austria had a history of seeking influence at his court—against the others. France's economic and naval power in the Mediterranean had given it a favoured position at the Ottoman capital since the sixteenth century. In the eighteenth century, Russia used its military weight, its extensive common border with the empire, the threat of war, and occasional real conflict to bully the sultan into recognising its growing power. Sometimes the Ottomans accepted this; sometimes they turned to Austria or France to protect them from it. Napoleon's occupation of the semi-independent Ottoman province of Egypt in 1798 could be seen as a new way of putting French pressure on Constantinople—as the European powers called it. The use of such a historic Christian name reflected the fact that though the sultan and his ministers might not be a formal part of the European diplomatic network, the pursuit of ascendancy at their court was an integral aspect of the struggle for power across the whole of eastern Europe. This remained the case after 1815. The continental powers knew that a new war over the Ottoman Empire, after twenty-two years of European fighting, would be catastrophic. They were all deeply conservative in their attitude to European politics, and worried that further conflict would unleash liberal, nationalist, and even revolutionary sentiments across the continent, destroying the propertied order. Moreover, conscious of the importance of legitimacy and legal rights in national and international affairs, they appreciated the dangers of undermining Ottoman sovereignty claims, and remained very reluctant to do so.

This existing French and Russian influence at Constantinople posed a much greater problem for Britain than the old diplomatic histories recognised. Britain's fundamental aim was to stop French or Russian aggression in Middle Eastern territory, and so naturally it had to claim to defend Ottoman sovereignty against invasion. Yet France and Russia both seemed adept at promoting their interests at the heart of Ottoman government—at the ministerial offices of the Sublime Porte. This book shows time after time that Britain could never trust the Porte to pursue British interests in a coherent and sustained way, rather than French or Russian ones. In 1798, Britain had no tradition of asserting itself at Constantinople, and few obvious means of browbeating the ministers there. This sense of Ottoman vulnerability to French, and later to Russian, pressure created an inherent suspicion between Britain and the Ottoman regime. Britain had to pursue its own aims in the Middle East irrespective of the desires of that regime, even while it was upholding Ottoman sovereignty. A major theme of this book is that the British ambassador at Constantinople, who was usually struggling against the odds to maintain good relations with the Porte, had a different perspective from the British agents and officers in the main cities of the Middle East.

Britain had to neutralise the danger that the Ottoman Empire would act as a pawn of France or Russia, if either of them sought to attack British

India.[10] There were two potential ways of doing this. One was the geopolitical approach already mentioned, which focused on securing practical influence over the lands and waterways of the Middle East without bothering much about the fact that the Ottomans nominally ruled them. This was the main policy before 1840, and the most successful. The second, more ambitious, goal was to challenge other powers at Constantinople itself, and to ally with Ottoman ministers who might promote British perspectives.

The powers' general preference for propping up the Ottoman Empire did not translate into agreement about its future needs. There were differences of opinion about the conditions on which it should be allowed to survive, and about the governance of its territories.[11] Diplomats spent much effort in trying to find common approaches. In the years after 1815, Russia, Austria, and Prussia worked together to prioritise the interests of conservative Christianity in Europe, in what the tsar called the "Holy Alliance." Yet they had more difficulty deciding how to manage the problem of Greece, once it became clear, in the 1820s, that its current position within the Ottoman Empire was unsustainable. The process by which these powers, Britain, and France worked out a future for an independent Greece was tortuous and hesitant.

British governments were always in two minds about this post-1815 Concert of Europe. It was a valuable security mechanism for the maintenance of European peace, but it did not look very congenial to a parliamentary, Protestant, global naval empire. In the 1820s, the conservative European powers tried to resist representative liberalism and to promote Catholic and Orthodox religion. By the 1840s, moreover, it was clear that continental peoples, as well as governments, tended to view the Ottoman lands through the prism of supporting Christian interests there. If the Ottoman Empire really was collapsing, and Islam was attacked by Catholic and Orthodox power, was this progress? Was it better to try to reshape the empire? Or was that not feasible? There was never a united British position on that thorny question.

Strategies and Visions

This book explores the strategies and visions adopted by British officials and commentators towards the Ottoman Middle East—towards the lands themselves, and towards the empire that had ultimate authority over them. There were diverse perspectives on most key issues. This diversity was partly ideological and partly geographical: the view was usually different from London,

10. Edward Ingram is one of very few historians to stress the need to write about British policy to Baghdad and Persia from this perspective. See particularly *Beginning of the Great Game* and *Britain's Persian Connection*.

11. On Russia particularly, see Edward Ingram's essays in *British Empire as a World Power*, pt. 1. Caquet's *Orient* and Ozavci's *Dangerous Gifts* both shed significant light on the perspectives of all the powers.

Bombay, and Constantinople. More importantly still, British officials in Egypt, Syria, and Baghdad all had different outlooks and agendas from those of the Constantinople embassy with which they had to communicate. So at many points this is a story of competing opinions about national interests and the best ways of promoting them. There may be parts of the nineteenth-century world for which simple, uniform generalisations about British "imperialism" are sustainable, but the Middle East was not one of them. The policy of the Foreign Office emerged out of a dialogue between centre and locality—a dialogue in which the Indian government's voice also featured inconsistently. The foreign secretary was most comfortable in imposing policy on British ambassadors and consuls when that policy was not simply "British," but had been agreed with representatives of some of the continental powers. When this was not the case, local men were usually given more latitude. Often they took it whether they were given it or not.

Some of these visions involved the application of coherent principles. On the other hand, one sub-theme of the book is that individuals frequently talked up British objectives in one or other remote part of the Middle East in order to secure a posting, and a career, for themselves. The risk of French invasion or Russian aggression may at times have been real, but there was also great scope for British representatives to exaggerate the threat in order to demonstrate their own utility. The national interest was also often a personal interest. As a result, this is a story of individuals much more than it is of abstract economic forces—which came to matter seriously in Middle Eastern policy only after 1860.

The first disagreement, in 1798, was about how much Egypt mattered in a war for control of Europe. Britain's international position in 1798 was not attractive. The government was preoccupied with finding European allies against Napoleon. This Eurocentric strategy meant downplaying British interests in the Middle East. But Britain lost all its European allies anyway—not an unusual occurrence—and in 1800 the cabinet realised that it was essential to get France out of Egypt. This was done by a strategically unprecedented two-pronged attack, from the Mediterranean, but also from India into the Red Sea. For the next thirty years, the defence of the Middle East, Ottoman and beyond, was left mainly to Indian officials, and in particular to the presidency of Bombay. The Bombay government's navy, the Bombay Marine, was used to protecting Indian commerce in the Gulf and around Arabia, so it was a natural extension of its function to safeguard these waters against potential European threats. After Britain took Mauritius from France in 1810, these threats greatly diminished anyway. So all the fundamental assumptions about how to defend the Middle East from Britain's rivals were developed in India, or by the civil servants of the East India Company in London. Until the 1830s, the Foreign Office had not thought much about the Middle East, or indeed India, because it continued to be preoccupied with Europe and with other regions where European powers might challenge British might.

In the 1830s, Indian interests continued to dominate thinking about the Middle East, but perceptions were changed by the introduction of steam power in the Indian Ocean and on the rivers of Mesopotamia. In the latter case, one explicit aim was to pre-empt the threat that Russia might take that route towards India. The other reason for investing in steam in Mesopotamia was the search for a new route for the transport of people, mail, and goods between Britain and India, because of the great practical difficulty of the Red Sea route. In the late 1830s, however, more advanced steam technology made possible the conquest of the Red Sea. Around 1850, plans for a railway across Egypt made the Red Sea route yet more attractive. By the 1850s, reliable and swift communication had brought nineteenth-century material culture to the narrow corridor that the British used for the transit across Egypt. In addition, the ships of the Bombay Marine (renamed the Indian Navy in 1830) secured dominance in the Gulf and maintained a presence on the Mesopotamian rivers.

Steam power extended British visions of the region in several ways, which were imported from India in the hope that they could work among the Arabs. Improved communication networks made it easier to move troops and guns about, and thus to use technology to flaunt Britain's military and economic superiority over feudal Russia or the Ottoman sultan. Steam also promised to help Britain in assisting local authorities to secure order and the rule of law, including the protection of property. As a result, the process of strengthening British authority on the waterways of the Middle East can be compared to the "rage for order" described by Lauren Benton and Lisa Ford for other parts of the early Victorian empire.[12] Some commentators also hoped to persuade the inhabitants to settle by riverbanks and to grasp the mutual benefits of commerce with the passing steamers.

An important group of British politicians, led by William Huskisson and Lord Palmerston, developed a more ambitious link between steam power and commercial development. They were enthusiasts for the idea of freeing British trade from monopolies, prohibitions, and extortionate tariffs, and wanted to apply this to Ottoman lands. In 1825, this had led to the abolition of the Levant Company, the venerable body that had monopolised Anglo-Ottoman trade and had employed local consuls. The hope was that free enterprise and capital investment could revive old land trade routes like the one between Syria and the Gulf. Egypt seemed less promising, because of the bargain that the monopolist pasha Mehmet Ali had made with the remnants of the Levant Company to build up a protectionist economic system. As it happened, Mehmet Ali was himself a great enthusiast for British steam power, and it further entrenched his rule in Egypt. By the 1840s, many British people regarded Egypt as a model for the future economic development of the region. The British now tried to enhance their commercial presence in Baghdad as well.

12. Benton and Ford, *Rage for Order*.

The same tensions emerged, between those who favoured cooperation with powerful local vested interests and those who hoped for transformative capital investment from outside. In Baghdad, unlike in Egypt, both groups were disappointed.

Thus there was never only one economic policy aim for the Middle East. In the same way, there had been a division of opinion during the Napoleonic Wars, between those who believed that the best way to enhance local respect for Britain was by destructive bombardments of uncooperative Arab trading settlements, and those who hoped instead to build friendship and respect through mutually beneficial commerce. Both were tried in the Red Sea in 1799–1802, but the first was quickly abandoned. The Indian government faced a similar issue in relation to the Gulf, where "pirate" shaykhdoms were shelled in the desperate wartime conditions of 1809, but also in the much less desperate ones of 1819.[13]

The ancient equivalent of steam had been irrigation, which had turned deserts into gardens, until human neglect turned them back again. Most British residents and travellers thought about the future of these lands through the prism of their past. Those who had had a classical education remembered particularly the way in which the Greeks and Romans had united Europe and western Asia into prosperous civilisations under the rule of law, and the accounts they had left of the history and geography of these lands. The modern world was the result of the fusion of those classical empires with the Christian religion. The British could not avoid thinking about the Middle East through the same historical lens as the French and Russians. They dreamed of the return of civilisation as they defined it. They regarded Britain as the natural successor and best interpreter of those ancient civilisations. Nearly all were Protestants, and saw the Catholic and Orthodox versions of Christianity as intolerant perversions.

In Britain, one body had a particularly religious perspective on the history of the Middle East: the Church of England. The Church regarded itself as the purest exponent of historical Christianity and the body best suited to reunite other Christian communities, around Anglican Protestantism. In the 1830s and 1840s, leading bishops pressed for Church missions to the "primitive" Churches of the East, which had spent centuries courageously defending their independence from Catholic, Orthodox, and Muslim aggressions. Well-funded evangelical societies also eyed the region because they believed that Islam was about to fall, allowing the word of God to be spread freely. They looked to history to suggest alliances with small groups that could spearhead this

---

13. Crouzet, in *Inventing the Middle East*, provides the first major discussion of the debates in India about how best to secure British interests in the Gulf in the first half of the nineteenth century. I consider the bombardment of 1819–20 briefly below in chapter 3, as part of my discussion of Britain's policy to Baghdad.

evangelism. One of the "primitive" Churches, the Nestorians of Kurdistan, had successfully evangelised across Asia in the past; perhaps they could reprise this role? Alternatively, one approach to reading the Bible suggested that the resettlement and conversion of Jews in their Old Testament lands would usher in the Second Coming of Christ. This book argues that these explicitly Christian domestic visions had little purchase among British officials in the Middle East itself, where there was usually much more tolerance towards Muslim culture. Nonetheless, their power in Britain gave them a brief political impact.

Finally, there were divisions in domestic politics. Until 1830, Britain was governed by a succession of Tory governments. They were concerned to avoid revolution in Europe and to keep down defence spending. So they saw the value of cooperation between the conservative European regimes to maintain the peace. They had no particular plans for the Ottoman Empire, but they hoped that the powers' aversion to a European war over it would provide adequate security for the defence of India. Tories who had a Eurocentric outlook usually sympathised with the explicit institutional Christianity of continental conservatives, including the Russians. When the Church of England became actively involved in the region around 1840, it, likewise, tentatively sought common ground with the Orthodox Churches, against Roman Catholicism. In the 1830s, a series of Liberal governments had very different attitudes to domestic politics and to Russia, which they treated as an ideological as well as a geopolitical foe. They used steam and trade to assert British technological modernity in Asia as a way of warning Russia not to advance towards India. This meant a more active approach in the Middle East, as noted above.

In all these calculations, there was rarely much emphasis on upholding the status of the Ottoman Empire. Only the Constantinople embassy was consistently concerned with that. The army and the Indian Navy were much more interested in the practicalities of winning local influence, sometimes in challenging conditions, by gaining the confidence of contending factions and trying to mediate between them. So they were concerned to secure a balance between Ottoman state interests and those of local groups, primarily for political reasons, and sometimes also for moral ones.[14]

No British government in this period ever guaranteed the Ottoman Empire unilaterally, and before 1840 none attempted a special relationship with it. They assumed that common European action was the only way of securing the empire, while they doubted its capacity for independence in the face of Russia's use of pressure to win influence at the Porte. The European diplomatic

14. Hutchinson, the British army commander in Egypt in 1801, had very negative views about the morals of his Ottoman counterparts, which might be described as "Orientalist" or alternatively as "humanitarian." Both terms have been used so indiscriminately as to become problematical, and I have tried to avoid them. My policy throughout the book has been to quote British comments at some length rather than to seek to pigeonhole them. Readers can judge them for themselves.

crisis of 1839–40 over the future of the Ottoman Empire improved its security, and therefore its prospects, but did not resolve the issue of whether it could be saved from dominant Russian influence.

The Tory government of 1841–46 still preferred to pursue stability in the East by getting the five European powers to agree to any adjustments in Ottoman ruling arrangements. This meant working with Russia and Austria to a much greater degree than Liberal governments wanted to do. It also aimed at cooperation with France, on a joint policy to press the Porte to keep its word to look after all oppressed religious minorities. One aim of this policy was to restore good relations with France after the 1839–40 crisis. The other aim was to position both countries behind a group of ministers at Constantinople who had recently unveiled their own vision of law-based government founded on the principle of security for all interests and religions, usually known as the Tanzimat. This was also how the British thought they governed India.

When the Liberals returned to power in 1846 they dramatically increased the stakes, arguing that the Ottomans should remove the bias in their legal system that favoured Muslims over others. They hoped that this would remove most grievances of Orthodox Christians, and undercut the Russian strategy of exploiting those grievances in order to maintain primacy at the Porte. Therefore, a strategy emerged that tried to unite Britain, France, and Tanzimat-minded Ottoman ministers behind the principle of legal equality among religions. In advocating it, Palmerston and Lord John Russell had wider ambitions: to reshape the European Concert around Anglo-French liberal values. That would help to pen in Russia across Eurasia. The aftermath of the 1848 revolutions made this approach doubly attractive. The Ottoman Empire now became a liberal project, and we can begin to talk of a liberal approach to empire. There were two difficulties with this strategy. One was that France was still tempted by its old policy of prioritising the interests of the Catholic Church at times of crisis; Napoleon III's international aspirations increased French assertiveness. The other was that Russia seemed determined still to support the grievances of the Ottomans' Orthodox subjects. The Crimean War emerged from this situation. It was only the war's outcome that allowed the the British liberal project to develop, for the next few years at least.

The Claims of Chronology

This is a British story—a story about the pursuit of British political objectives. The book approaches political history in the way I have always tried to write it, by taking into account the mentalities of those who sought to shape policy. I wanted to understand how they conceived of Britain's role in the Middle East, what they did there, and how far particular ideas—about geography, history, trade, and religion—may have affected them. This volume is based almost entirely on British sources, and confines itself to British viewpoints, aspirations, and prejudices. It is a history of how the British saw the Middle East, not of the Middle East itself, though I hope that students of that subject will find some interest in the evidence presented here about British views of Ottomans and Arabs. There are many fine works on particular parts and aspects of the Middle East from which I have benefited, but many others that I have not been able to consult. There are many non-English archives that seem not yet to have been fully used by anyone. I have made no attempt to explore the effects of British activities on local societies. My instinct is that usually they were not very significant, but it would take a lot more specialised knowledge than I possess to reach convincing conclusions about that. Generalisation about the impact of European interventions on existing complex trading relationships is problematical, as Sarah Shields has shown so persuasively.[15] I see this book as complementing the important recent work on the Ottoman regime's role in, and response to, these European interventions, from which I have learned a good deal.[16] Several of these works have emphasised Ottoman agency in these relationships, and have usefully qualified entrenched assumptions about the role of European powers in modernising or subjugating the empire, which Edward Said's *Orientalism* did so much to establish.[17]

Said's writings have had a crucial impact on the investigation of British attitudes to the Middle East over the last forty years. A rich body of secondary literature has examined an array of British works and value judgments on eastern themes—on attitudes to gender and sexuality, and to travel, archaeology, architecture, literature, and the other arts.[18] This literature has introduced essential theoretical sophistication, while emphasising how many of the

15. Shields, *Mosul before Iraq*, 8–12. She warned specifically against making sweeping judgments on the impact of the 1838 commercial treaty. R. T. Harrison, on the other hand, confidently attributes Egypt's ills after 1841 to the treaty and its mastermind Palmerston. Ignoring the constraints imposed by Egyptian economic patterns and interests, the Ottomans, and the other powers, he blames Palmerston's free-trade imperialism for checking tendencies to independence, turning Egypt into a "glorified vegetable garden," and destroying the ambitions of industrialisers and young intellectuals alike: *Britain in the Middle East*, chap. 7. As Aaron Jakes has recently pointed out, Mehmet Ali himself bears most responsibility for focusing the Egyptian economy on cotton exports and on the lucrative intercontinental transit trade: "World the Suez Canal Made."

16. Aksan, *Ottoman Wars*; Anscombe, *State, Faith, and Nation*; Ateş, *Ottoman-Iranian Borderlands*; Aydin, *Politics of Anti-Westernism in Asia*; Deringil, *Conversion and Apostasy*; Douwes, *Ottomans in Syria*; Ozavci, *Dangerous Gifts*; Philipp, *Acre*; Toledano, *Ottoman Slave Trade*; Yaycioglu, *Partners of the Empire*; Yurdusev, *Ottoman Diplomacy*.

17. For recent work on the Ottoman Empire and modernity in this period, see Ze'evi: "Back to Napoleon?"; Bouquet, "Ottoman Modernisation"; McDougall, "Sovereignty, Governance"; Zanou, *Transnational Patriotism*.

18. Bar-Yosef, *Holy Land in English Culture*; Bohrer, *Orientalism and Visual Culture*; Crinson, *Empire Building*; Laisram, *Viewing the Islamic Orient*; Lockman, *Contending Visions*; Melman, *Women's Orients*; Moser, *Wondrous Curiosities*; Ziter, *Orient on the Victorian Stage*.

British arguments about Ottoman and Arab governance and culture were stereotypical, negative, and self-interested. My aim here is not to challenge any of those works, except occasionally at the margins. However, my perspective differs in one sense, because a fundamental concern of a political historian must be to make distinctions across time, whereas many of these works, from Said onwards, have sought to underplay those distinctions in a search for general explanatory models.

This book operates on the principle that context and chronology are essential tools in explaining the purchase of particular strategies and ideas, since the political process is always in flux. I argue, for example, that British moves to protect the Jews in Palestine had different meanings in 1838, in 1841, and in 1849, and that bold explanations like the influence of Christian Zionism are greatly overdrawn.[19] I suggest that British attitudes to Islam were determined not by abstract reactions to its theology, but by reasoned assessments of the likely impact of specific instances of Islamic fervour. I criticise the very common assumption that British policy to Mehmet Ali between 1807 and 1840 can be reduced to a simple choice as to whether to support or oppose him. In fact, he was almost irrelevant to the decision to invade Egypt in 1807; in 1839–40, Britain demonised his ambitions for its own purposes; between those years, he seemed an irremovable presence, usually for the better.

The art of political history—perhaps the art of all history—is to know when to make connections and when to make distinctions. Historians have lacked a coherent overview of British activity in Ottoman lands in different decades, which would provide a framework for those who seek to contextualise individual events or texts. As a result, for instance, David Katz's recent book, *The Shaping of Turkey in the British Imagination, 1776–1923*, can claim that a handful of famous writers (Gibbon, Byron, and Disraeli) "set the horizon of expectations about Turkey" for British readers.[20] The shortage of general overviews has meant that I have had to supply my structure myself. My hope is to show that our understanding of the Middle East from a British perspective is helped enormously when local stories that historians have treated separately— when they have treated them at all—are connected up. This book is written from primary sources: from contemporary memoirs, but primarily from the Foreign Office and India Office archives in London—particularly the thousand or so volumes in FO 78 alone of original correspondence with British representatives in the Ottoman Empire in this period, and the more fragmented but still vast India Office collections.

19. My argument supports, and extends, Abigail Green's contention that in practice British support for the Jews in the Middle East should be seen in terms not of Christian Zionism but of what she calls an "imperialism of human rights" that applied to other faiths as well: "British Empire and the Jews."

20. Katz, *Shaping of Turkey*, 7.

I have focused on the period before 1854, because Britain's activities in the Middle East then are much less well covered by historians than they are for later decades. Writing about comparatively uncharted episodes brings rich opportunities as well as challenges. One of my claims is that a large proportion of the things the British ever thought about the Middle East had already been thought by 1854. T. E. Lawrence was obviously a figure of political significance and charisma, but there was little new in his fascination with the elemental spiritual significance of the desert and the deeply venerable qualities and defects of its spartan, virile Arab tribes. Jonathan Duncan tried to organise an Arab revolt against the French in 1801. However, some of the perspectives of imperial historians of a later period cannot be applied here so easily.[21] Subjugating the Arabs themselves was just not practical. I underline the uncertainty and pragmatism that affected Palmerston's policy for the Ottoman Empire between 1833 and 1850, as it went through at least four phases. Political strategies are not always imposed with imperial arrogance; they are often pursued hesitantly, against the odds, and fail. Ideas on what the region needed mattered. It is curious that, despite all the writing on the 1839–40 diplomatic crisis, there has been no attempt to uncover the British government's ideas of what Syria should look like after the Egyptian evacuation that it enforced. In the light of Iraq since 2003, this is not an uninteresting question to ask.

The limits to Britain's power in the region were always important. Its freedom of manoeuvre can easily be exaggerated if one ignores the role of local political forces with which British officials had to interact. The Ottoman Empire was a much more durable and significant presence than the Saidian model recognised. An assumption is often made that Britain aimed to impose constitutionalism on it.[22] Here, I side with those who have always insisted that, until the 1840s, British policy was merely to make the Ottoman army and taxation system function better.[23] The central principles of the Tanzimat programme of 1839 were designed by Ottoman bureaucrats, not British liberals, and Britain's policy for Syria in 1840 was Reshid's as much as it was the British embassy's. Likewise, the 1838 Commercial Convention was primarily a simplification of existing trading principles, of greater political than economic significance; there is no evidence that it was a British capitalist plot to

21. Shawn Malley imaginatively asserts that Layard's vision of Arab agricultural settlement by the Mesopotamian rivers resembled a "concentration camp replete with gun towers": *From Archaeology to Spectacle*, 40.

22. Caquet argues that Britain made a fixed decision to support the Ottomans against Mehmet Ali from 1832–33, and that it did so on condition that the Turks embraced "adaptive constitutionalism": *Orient*, 19–22, 111–13, 243–45. See also Figes, *Crimea*, 53–56, and Charmley, "Britain and the Ottoman Empire," 73. Caquet asserts, oddly, that the future of Islam in the East "preoccupied . . . almost no one" in 1839–41: *Orient*, 249.

23. Temperley, "British Policy"; Bailey, *British Policy*, 153–54.

destroy Egyptian industry.[24] Major political forces within the empire—Reshid, Bashir, Mehmet Ali—exploited Britain's presence for their own gain.[25] The Porte was a great beneficiary of the military assistance that Britain gave it in Egypt in 1801 and Syria in 1840, which increased Ottoman prospects of dominating local elites. It was these military alliances, and the destruction that they caused, that generated an impulse in British official circles to accept more responsibility for the future of the territory concerned. Nowadays we are instinctively wary of any Western impulse to intervene in foreign lands, but the historian should also recognise the political potency of that concept of responsibility. British embarrassment at the killing of Mamluk leaders in 1801, or at the Lebanese civil war of 1841, created a consensus in favour of further intervention, just as domestic guilt at Britain's role in the Crimean War prompted the popular agitation twenty years later demanding that Ottomans should no longer be allowed to misgovern the Balkans. They were two sides of the same coin.

Similarly, care is required in applying generalisations about "West" and "East." A number of area studies have done important work in uncovering local political and economic realities, and in contrasting those realities with the limited understanding shown by British and French observers. Rubenson's superb study of Ethiopia is a model of the genre, in revealing the activity of both sets of officials in a superficial and sometimes ridiculous light.[26] The West can easily be seen as a unitary interfering force, incompetently imposing itself on the East. This tendency has been noticeable especially in discussing British and French attempts to protect local religious sects; both powers are often blamed for promoting a damaging sectarianism. Certainly their interventions could sharpen local factional disputes, and be exploited by actors in them.[27] What is more doubtful is whether support for particular sects was Britain's intention: nearly all the examples used by Makdisi for Lebanon, or Shields for Mosul, are in fact of French activity.[28] In chapter 7, I argue that British policy in both places took a sectarian form only briefly and tentatively, and for particular reasons. Britain deprecated the extent to which the French

24. For assertions to the contrary, see R. Harrison, *Britain in the Middle East, chap. 7*; Marsot, *Egypt*, 239, 259–60.

25. Ozavci, *Dangerous Gifts*, epilogue, esp. 360–62.

26. Rubenson, *Survival of Ethiopian Independence*.

27. It is clear, for example, from Rose's consular reports from Syria throughout 1842 and 1843, that Ottoman and Maronite leaders, the Russian consul, and Druze rivals, all of whom disliked the high profile of the Jumblatts in Lebanon, spread rumours about the latter's supposed connection with Britain in order to damage them. It was the allegation of British bias, rather than the reality, that became politically important.

28. Makdisi, *Culture of Sectarianism*; Shields, *Mosul before Iraq*. It should be noted that Makdisi's study is impressively sophisticated in its handling of political contingency and change over time.

pursued sectarianism, not least because it exploited the local power of the Catholic Church, a body that most Britons feared on several grounds, but with which they knew they could not compete.

In this period, most of the time, the British saw their function in the Middle East as being to defend it from other European rivals. They were inherently suspicious of French and Russian Christian imperialism. Many local representatives also criticised Turkish imperialism over the Arabs, and aimed to gain credit with them by protecting them from its consequences. On the whole, the British imagined that they would manage western Asia more sensitively than the Russians or the Ottomans, who, for most of this period, seemed the only alternatives. Of course, there was a lot of self-deception in these arguments; if readers wish to see this account as a straightforward British imperial story, they are free to do so. One repeated theme is how swiftly Britain moved to pre-empt threats that were almost invariably exaggerated. There is much truth in Gladstone's remark of 1859: "the English piously believe themselves to be a peaceful people; nobody else is of the same belief."[29] Nonetheless, as long as the region was threatened by rivals, including France, it is not appropriate to think of a united "West" as against an "East."

To my knowledge, the first Briton to use "Western" in relation to the future of the Ottomans was David Urquhart in 1838, who employed it to denote sinister French and now Russian religious and commercial imperialist pressures on the East. These, he argued, could be defeated by an Islamic patriotic reform movement founded on decentralising, low-tax principles that British liberals should admire and encourage.[30] In the 1830s and 1840s, many people talked of "West" and "East," but they defined both in a suggestive variety of ways. Some writers envisaged a "civilising" project towards the "East," but this did not mean that they agreed on the nature of that "civilisation."[31] Some offered a historical perspective, imagining the re-establishment of law and order across the lands of the Roman Empire, or the recreation of an interactive Mediterranean culture.[32] When Layard wrote about the social failings of "eastern nations," he implied that Russia was one of them. When the French philosopher Auguste Comte envisaged a "West," founded on the principles of humanity, ruling Eurasia, this was to expunge the baleful influence of Eastern Orthodox Christianity. He wanted to build a future republican basis for the Ottoman Empire, to

29. Quoted in Parry, *Politics of Patriotism*, 238.

30. Urquhart, *Spirit of the East*, 1:xxxi. He blamed Colbert's protection system for originating this commercial rivalry in the 1660s (1:358).

31. The shallowness of one of the most famous "civilising" visions—that of Alphonse de Lamartine—was already noted at the time: C. Miller, "Orientalism, Colonialism," 701–2.

32. Hegel insisted in *The Philosophy of History* that the Mediterranean was the centre of world history, the origin of its main civilisations and religions, the sea that gave the Old World its unity—cited in Yapp, "Europe in the Turkish Mirror," 135. On visions of the Mediterranean, see Isabella and Zanou's *Mediterranean Diasporas*, 9–10.

rescue it from war and Russian imperialism. In fact, he hoped to extend this to India, defeating British imperialism there.[33] Some British commentators were similarly tempted to include India in a future vision of this Eurasian region, though others were frightened off by traditional concerns about its corrupting effects on British politics. Whether India was added or not, it seemed clear that Egypt was an essential first step. In 1847, John Stoddart, the consul in Alexandria, set out a plan for Britain to secure Egypt and make it happy and wealthy, in order to realise the plans of both Alexander and the Caesars for a dominion spanning Europe and Asia. In his view, Alexandria was destined to be the capital of a great transcontinental empire "full of hope and of progress," combining vast commercial prospects with protection of the Muslim religion and its Holy Cities.[34] I hope to convince future scholars to explore more fully the richness and diversity of these various visions.[35]

On the level of practical diplomacy, Britain's strategy after 1846 was to bend France to its purposes. This was an extension of Britain's European policy after 1830, which, as Paul Schroeder has shown, was an attempt to keep France in line as a junior partner in a cautiously liberal coalition to counterbalance Russia and Austria.[36] There was always a risk that an alternative France might emerge: an aggressive France, a Catholic France—particularly under Napoleon III in the 1850s, who had his own ambitions in Italy and the East—seeking especially to work with Russia towards a mutually acceptable revision of the European settlement. A very large amount of British international policy in the nineteenth century ultimately turned on the question of which was the real France: the France of the rational Enlightenment or the France of restless expansionism. British cooperation with France always aimed to encourage the former and to restrain the latter.

This is a useful perspective if we are to understand the ambiguity of Anglo-French relations in the Middle East. France was never wholly trusted, but, after 1815, it was trusted more than it was distrusted.[37] Holger Hoock has argued that British and French cultural rivalry over antiquities was a major and neglected theme of the period, manifest particularly in the excavations of Henry Layard and Paul-Émile Botta near Mosul.[38] This has been a valuable insight, but I argue here that our perspective on Mosul affairs benefits from

33. For Layard, see chapter 9 below. Varouxakis, "Godfather of 'Occidentality.'"

34. Stoddart to Palmerston, Feb. 9, 1847, FO 78/710.

35. See Arsan's "France, Mount Lebanon" for some interesting French visions.

36. Schroeder, *Transformation*.

37. David Todd's account of French informal imperialism in the Middle East in the 1850s and 1860s is strong on this collaboration: *Velvet Empire*.

38. Hoock, *Empires of the Imagination*, 243–51. The same is true of Maya Jasanoff, who sees Britain and France competing in Egypt for cultural ascendancy after 1815 because the peace debarred them from conquering it: *Edge of Empire*, 216.

"putting the politics back in." His main actors on both sides were intensely political figures with a political agenda, while their archaeological inquiries were driven at least as much by the spirit of shared Enlightenment enthusiasm for knowledge as by national rivalry. The same combination—superficial competition, limited by an underlying cooperation in pursuit of a liberal project—was the driver of their political behaviour in Kurdistan as well. The problem of interpreting French behaviour also explains the ambiguity of the Crimean War. On the one hand, it was a traditional struggle for dominance at Constantinople between a Catholic and an Orthodox power, exploiting a row over the Holy Places of Jerusalem. On the other, it was a liberal war fought by France and Britain to force Russia to respect the territorial integrity of a reformed Ottoman Empire—if that empire could be dragooned into ruling its own peoples by law and principles of civil equality.

A Tale of Two Obelisks

What had the British achieved by 1854? In terms of reforming Ottoman governance, not a great deal. In terms of practical influence in the Middle East, it was almost inconceivable that France or Russia could challenge Britain's presence in Egypt, in Aden and its hinterland, in the Gulf shaykhdoms, or on the Mesopotamian waterways. In the decade before 1854, the troublesome regime that the British worked hardest to subdue throughout this region, again successfully, was the Ottoman Empire itself. By 1854, Britain had staked a strong claim—under the carapace of Ottoman sovereignty—to nearly all the parts of the Middle East that it governed after 1918. As this was the case, Britain had no interest in actually governing them, which would be diplomatically explosive, extremely expensive, and bound to incite awkward local tensions. But that did not reflect a lack of ambition or influence. Between 1815 and the 1870s, there was (outside India) little interest in expensive territorial acquisition anywhere. This was the period of the Pax Britannica, when British dominance rested on commercial, naval, and technological pre-eminence, globally, and specifically in the waters around Arabia.

So this Middle Eastern story can be seen as a typical one of the period after 1815: of stealthy rather than overt imperialism, of quietly growing world dominance rather than bombastic celebration. These priorities also explain the disappearance of the British campaign in Egypt from the historical memory. Edward Clarke, who arrived there in April 1801, was confident that "the laurels acquired by our army in Egypt can never fade."[39] The officers and men expected a permanent memorial to their achievement. Lying in the sand at Alexandria was a seventy-foot-long Egyptian obelisk that seemed perfect

39. E. Clarke, *Travels in Various Countries*, 1:271.

for the task. The troops christened it "Cleopatra's Needle," though in fact it predated Cleopatra by at least fourteen hundred years. In 1802, Lord Cavan, the commander of the British army in Egypt, set up a subscription to transport it to London for permanent public display. Robert Wilson, one of the officers, hoped that it would "animate with pride and emulation" the rising generation.[40] The army itself subscribed £7,000, but politics intervened; the price of peace with France at Amiens in 1802 was Britain's evacuation from Egypt the next year, which meant that such glorification suddenly seemed inappropriate.[41]

The obelisk remained in the sand. In 1819, Mehmet Ali gave it to Britain as a symbol of his friendship. The British were happy to accept his friendship, but they were less happy with the expense of transporting home such an unwieldy object in the post-war economic depression, so it stayed where it was. In the 1830s, more obelisks were identified and Mehmet Ali, still looking for friends, offered them to Britain and France. In 1836, the French erected theirs with great fanfare in the middle of the Place de la Concorde, where it continues to stand, projecting to generations of passers-by the impression of a unique French cultural affinity with, or power over, Egypt.[42] The British, now even more concerned with cutting government costs, did nothing. In 1851, the Great Exhibition in Hyde Park celebrated the stages of human civilisation with lavish mock-ups in a great glass greenhouse known as the Crystal Palace, and a commercial company was formed to re-erect the "palace" as a permanent display in south London. Some directors planned to pay to bring over the British Needle as one of the main attractions, but they were overruled by those who argued that a cleaner and cheaper reproduction of antiquity would attract more customers. Besides, the Crystal Palace had been built as a hymn to international cooperation, so military memorials seemed out of place: the building implied that British global domination and peace went hand in hand. The Crimean War was fought in alliance with France, and Anglo-French cooperation became even more desirable after that.

The British never doubted that they owned the Needle and, more importantly, that they had supreme reserve power in Egypt, because they had the only military force capable of removing the regime. Finally, in 1877–78, at the dawn of a new era of imperial competition, Erasmus Wilson, a rich and philanthropic dermatologist, decided to redress this long-standing neglect after the abandoned obelisk was brought to his attention by a veteran army officer with Eastern interests, Sir James Alexander. Wilson's navy surgeon father had taught him to worship Nelson and Abercromby for combatting Napoleon in Egypt; more recently, he had developed interests in oriental skincare and

---

40. R. Wilson, *History of the British Expedition*, xiii.
41. The money was returned: Head, *Eastern and Egyptian Scenery*, 54–55.
42. For this episode, see Porterfield, *Allure of Empire*, 13–41.

Egyptology. He paid the £10,000 needed to bring the Needle to London—a hazardous project, on which six sailors died in a Biscay storm. In September 1878, it was erected in its current position on the Thames Embankment, carrying appropriate memorials to the men of 1801 and to Nelson.[43] Less than four years later, British troops invaded Egypt. This time, they did not leave for seventy-four years.

43. See E. Wilson, *Cleopatra's Needle*, 182–83, 190, 205; J. Alexander, *Cleopatra's Needle*. For the prehistory, see the dedicated volume of correspondence in FO 78/2116, and below, chapter 11, p. 339, n.19.

CHAPTER ONE

Napoleon, India, and the Battle for Egypt

ON MAY 9, 1798, the ambitious young general Napoleon Bonaparte stood before his soldiers at Toulon, France's Mediterranean naval base, and told them that they were the heirs of the Roman legions whose discipline and prowess had subdued the African power of Carthage. Ten days later, his army sailed, like the Romans, across the Mediterranean—not to Carthage but to Alexandria, the Egyptian port built, as he later reminded them, by Alexander the Great himself.[1] Once reinforced from Corsica and Civitavecchia, this was an immense expedition: 31,000 men, seventeen warships and frigates, nearly four hundred transports, plus 167 men of letters who were to record its benefits for human civilisation. They landed at Alexandria on July 1, and had taken Cairo and the main arteries of Egypt by the end of the month.[2]

British spies had observed the expedition assemble, but were unclear where it was headed. Was it Sicily, Syria, or, as the Russians believed, the Balkans? The British government was preoccupied with the risk of a French invasion of Ireland or Britain. Admiral Nelson had been sent into the Mediterranean to prevent this great fleet moving west and north. He failed to find it en route; he finally discovered the ships moored in Abukir Bay and destroyed nearly all of them in early August. Even so, the greatest general of the age had succeeded in occupying the crucial strip of fertile land along the Nile that connected the Mediterranean to the Red Sea and to India. He had indicated that France was now fighting not just a European and Caribbean battle, but one for world

1. Bonaparte, *Proclamations, Speeches and Letters*, 37–40. Many British and French people at this time referred to Britain as the successor of Carthage, the great classical sea power: see Lambert, "Tory World View," 125–29.

2. For Napoleon in Egypt, see Bierman, *Napoleon in Egypt*; J. Cole, *Napoleon's Egypt*; Strathern, *Napoleon in Egypt*.

domination. For the British, the French Wars had always been about colonies, trade, and wealth as much as about continental alliances, but mostly so far in the West Indies. Now, suddenly, the new British Empire in the East was at stake.

In invading Egypt and displacing the ruling regime of Mamluks, Napoleon was also invading the Ottoman Empire. Since the 1770s, the Mamluk leaders Murad and Ibrahim had consistently managed to resist Ottoman power in Egypt, as had their recent predecessors. Nonetheless, they recognised the sovereignty of the sultan, and the sultan was naturally horrified by a European invasion of his lands. The British government had to consider how far to ally with the Ottomans, as well as the Russians, in order to oppose him. Britain had not thought seriously about Ottoman territory previously. Most British policymakers assumed that a Eurocentric strategy was needed to defeat France's military expansion. Diplomacy and subsidies would persuade Austria, Prussia, and others to do most of the fighting. This continued to be the approach of the foreign secretary, Lord Grenville. For Grenville, the East was relevant only insofar as it affected the European military balance. By 1800, his approach had failed. His cabinet rival Henry Dundas had an alternative strategy, which involved seeking military help from India rather than unreliable Europeans. It also involved cultivating local Arabs and Mamluks in order to build a coalition against France on the ground. In 1801, Dundas's approach succeeded in getting the French out of Egypt. Their departure was followed by peace talks, but if the French resumed the war, it was easy to see how they might return. This was partly because British officers never trusted the Ottomans to fight effectively. The war of 1799–1801 revealed enormous tensions between the British and their supposed allies. Was it safe, or honourable, to hand Egypt back to them?

Grenville, the Eurocentric Approach, and Sidney Smith

In the late eighteenth century, the Ottoman Empire was not a formal part of the European political system. A Christian diplomatic representative to the Porte was treated as an infidel intruder and forced to walk backwards in the presence of the sultan, deprived of his sword.[3] Though the empire had informal contacts with European powers, it did not have resident ambassadors in their capitals before the 1790s, and was not expected to engage in international conferences or to participate in alliances. These traditions were being eroded by the growing threat to the empire, particularly from Russia in the Black Sea region. Russia secured access to the Black Sea in 1774 and annexed the Crimea, including significant numbers of Muslims, in 1783. Russia had also occupied the Ottomans' Danubian Principalities (Moldavia and Wallachia) in

3. Barker, *Syria and Egypt*, 1:7–9; Turner, *Journal of a Tour*, 1:58–60.

the war of 1768–74; then, in return for handing them back, it secured some rights to protect Orthodox Christians there against misrule. In 1772, Russia and Austria combined to take some of Poland's territory, and in further partitions of 1793 and 1795 Poland was swallowed completely by these two powers and Prussia. It seemed likely that the Ottoman Empire would be partitioned in the same way. Under Catherine II, Russia seemed to have bent Prussia and Austria to its will, securing itself from attack, swinging the balance of power in Europe to the east, and making France and the Ottomans more insecure. In return, the Ottomans cultivated the protection of France, continuing a historic link going back to the sixteenth century. So in 1793, when France began its war with most of Europe, the Ottomans had no incentive to join in.[4]

British interests at Constantinople were much more limited than French or Russian ones. The role of British ambassador to the Ottoman Porte had grown out of the Levant Company's need to protect its trading arrangements. The company had been created in 1592 by merging existing trading entities with Venice and Turkey. It paid the salary of a representative at Constantinople, and was still funding the bulk of this salary in the 1790s, together with generous gifts to Ottoman officials. By now, this arrangement seemed anomalous, since from the 1690s the Crown had appointed the ambassador, recognising that the role was political as well as commercial. Even so, most embassy business was still bound up with the affairs of the Levant Company's three trading bases at Constantinople, Smyrna, and Aleppo. These affairs remained healthy for most of the eighteenth century, but had declined by the 1790s, especially in Aleppo, which depended on the trade between western Asia and the Mediterranean. This trade was increasingly being routed through either the Persian Gulf or the Black Sea, while the direct commerce between England and India round the Cape now dwarfed it altogether. Meanwhile the trade from the Syrian ports to the Mediterranean was now dominated by France. Moreover, in 1753 the Levant Company in effect lost its monopoly on the trade between the Levant and England, and was often undercut. The company's profits fell significantly, and from the 1760s Parliament often needed to subsidise its embassy costs. Most "ambassadors" were also involved in commerce: in the 1780s, Robert Ainslie supplemented his salary by exporting wine and by charging commissions on money changing.[5]

Before the 1790s, British diplomacy focused on the European balance and on America, not on the eastern Mediterranean. Ainslie was told to be neutral in the Russo-Ottoman war of 1788. Britain tended to be relaxed about Russia's

4. See Yurdusev, *Ottoman Diplomacy*.

5. Berridge, *British Diplomacy in Turkey*, 28–30. For the Levant Company, see Laidlaw, *British in the Levant*; Masters, "Levant Company"; A. Wood, *Levant Company*. For an excellent recent treatment of the embassy's commercial culture, see Talbot's *British-Ottoman Relations*.

expansion in that region, because checking French power was a greater anxiety. Not until 1791 did Britain first challenge it, when William Pitt's government sent Russia an ultimatum to evacuate the Black Sea port of Ochakov, which it had occupied since taking it from the Ottomans in 1788. Even so, this threat was not couched in terms of defending the integrity of the Ottoman Empire, showed no interest in Constantinople as an ally, was widely criticised in the House of Commons, and was quickly abandoned. It was a failed attempt to hold together Britain's alliance with Prussia, which feared Russian expansion in the Balkans.[6] The Ottomans' further defeat at Russia's hands in 1792 prompted the Porte to send a diplomatic mission to Britain for the first time, in 1793—but also to recognise the new French republic in 1795. The Ottomans needed all the friends they could get.

Until 1798, the war hardly impinged on Ottoman territory. In 1796, Robert Liston, Ainslie's successor at Constantinople, was allowed to leave for a post in America, unhappy at the poor salary and lack of influence.[7] In the same year, the British fleet was withdrawn from the Mediterranean for the first time in centuries, because a French-Spanish alliance increased the fear of invasion and made home defence a priority. Then a peace treaty with Austria in October 1797 gave France the old Venetian territories of Corfu and the other Ionian islands: these could be bases for an invasion of the sultan's Balkan territories. Within a few months, Napoleon invaded Ottoman Egypt—and underlined his strength in the Mediterranean by occupying the strategic island of Malta en route, which was previously governed by the Order of Saint John. The invasion of Egypt by a Christian power inevitably forced the sultan to declare war against France in September 1798. Moreover, Russia offered him a treaty of mutual defence, in the hope of replacing French influence at Constantinople with its own. From now on, whenever France or Russia overtly threatened the enfeebled Ottoman regime, the other power would promise it protection in the hope of achieving dominance by stealthier means. In fact, France's invasion of Egypt did not mean that it had given up hope of wooing the Ottomans itself. The move was a warning to the sultan not to let Russia take control of the straits between the Black Sea and the Mediterranean. It was a demand to play a part in all future diplomatic discussions in the region—a response to the unwillingness of the three eastern powers to consult France over the partition of Poland. So it was a statement against unbridled Russian dominance in the Balkan region. But it was also clearly an attempt to control the Mediterranean and its shores, a great springboard from which to challenge British dominance in Asia.

Napoleon's invasion had a dramatic effect on British strategy. It immediately forced Britain to abandon the attempt to take Manila and Java (owned

6. Cunningham, *Anglo-Ottoman Encounters*, chap. 1.
7. For the best account of Liston's embassy, see Cunningham, chap. 3.

by France's Spanish and Dutch allies) and to concentrate on the defence of the seas around India.[8] Napoleon claimed solidarity with Tipu of Mysore in his fight against British expansion on the Indian subcontinent, and this in turn gave the new governor-general Lord Wellesley an incentive to increase British control across southern India, especially in Hyderabad and the Carnatic, claiming that only this would prevent serious local instability. For the first time, Britain had to consider European objectives and the defence of India simultaneously, and try to make them compatible.

The British cabinet was profoundly unprepared to meet this crisis. News of Napoleon's success arrived at a bad time, when the leading ministers had dispersed to their country houses for the summer. Of the three members of the war cabinet, Prime Minister Pitt was ensconced at Walmer Castle, Grenville was enjoying his new house at Dropmore in Buckinghamshire, and Henry Dundas's health had broken down in Scotland. No one seemed able to force a policy on the others. William Huskisson, Dundas's bright young undersecretary at war, tried from the latter's Wimbledon house to broker some agreement, but complained that Grenville "sees nothing beyond the Rhine and never stirs from Dropmore."[9] Grenville opposed the Ottomans' request for a treaty of defence with Britain, alarmed at where such a commitment might lead. In fact, he had taken hardly any notice of the Ottomans' new London embassy since 1793.[10] Had Tsar Paul not taken the initiative by offering the Ottoman sultan a defence treaty so quickly, Britain might not have done anything. News of this allowed Huskisson to confront Pitt in late September during his "fortunate visit to London." Pitt now ordered the British embassy in Constantinople to offer to be a party to that treaty.[11] Grenville was keen to encourage Russia to take the lead against Napoleon: he approved Russia's plan for its fleet to sail through the straits into the Mediterranean, and for Austrian and Russian soldiers to be dispatched into the Ottoman Balkans to guard against a French attack. Russo-Ottoman treaty negotiations took a long time, because many officials at the Porte were unhappy at the idea of admitting eighty thousand Russian troops to its territories, fearing future ramifications. Britain's willingness to underwrite the treaty provided some reassurance that the Russians would not exploit this massive protection.[12]

Britain's accession as third party to the Russo-Ottoman defence pact in January 1799 did not imply a close understanding with the Ottomans. Britain's offers of military support were insignificant compared with those of Russia and Austria; nor were they well received at Constantinople. A detachment

8. Ingram, *British Empire as a World Power*, 39.
9. Huskisson to Dundas, Sept. 11, 1798, DPNS, GD 51/1/769/1.
10. Cunningham, *Anglo-Ottoman Encounters*, 57–60.
11. Huskisson to Dundas, Sept. 26, 1798, DPNS, GD 51/1/768/83.
12. Grenville to Spencer Smith, Sept. 14, 1798, FO 78/20 28; Sidney Smith to Grenville, Jan. 5, 1799, FO 78/21 3.

of under a hundred gunners and engineers was sent there to help to train Ottoman troops in the use of European instruments. It was led by General George Koehler, who had helped to survey Ottoman defences in 1791–93, but he soon complained of being marginalised by anti-European elements at court; his men spent their time on fortification works at the Dardanelles and on an inconsequential expedition to Anatolia.[13] Two more officers, Villettes and Broderick, were sent into Albania on a mission to raise local troops, with little more effect. However, the Admiralty also sent three ships to the Ottoman coast to support the military operations (the rest of the Mediterranean fleet was needed to protect Naples). The ships were under the local command of a thirty-four-year-old Royal Navy commodore. The Ottomans may have wished to marginalise him as well, but he was determined to grab the spotlight.

Sidney Smith was chosen for this mission by Grenville, for diplomatic reasons rather than naval ones. His brother, John Spencer Smith, was the main British diplomatic representative at Constantinople after the departure of Liston, whose private secretary he had been. He and his brother were family connections of Grenville, and Spencer Smith shared Grenville's Eurocentric view that the Ottoman conflict was just one aspect of a necessary cooperation with Russia and Austria aimed at defeating Napoleon's plans for Europe. Spencer had just married the daughter of the Austrian minister at Constantinople, the internuncio, Baron Herbert (who was in fact Irish). Grenville promoted him to minister plenipotentiary in 1798, so that he could act for Britain in the discussions over the Russo-Ottoman treaty. The attraction of selecting Sidney for the naval mission was that they would enforce it together. Sidney arrived at Constantinople in thirty-one days from Plymouth, and was a joint signatory to the treaty in January 1799. Grenville saw the Smith brothers as special agents who would help to impose an orderly cooperation on the unreliable Ottomans. Though they had agreed to commit a hundred thousand men to this conflict, Grenville feared that they lacked the courage and organisation to fight France unless kept up to the mark.[14] In April 1799, Sidney boasted that he had the Ottoman fleet and army under his orders by virtue of the arrangements agreed at Constantinople, and that his goal was to check their "insubordination."[15] Admirals St. Vincent and Nelson, the two senior naval officers in the Mediterranean, quickly became angry at the way that Sidney exploited his diplomatic position to claim an independent authority as he cruised off the coast of Syria on HMS *Tigre*.

Sidney Smith's egocentric, swashbuckling, and well-publicised activity in the eastern Mediterranean over the next three years gave him the status of a national hero, plus a special coat of arms from the king, a vote of thanks and

13. Elgin to Grenville, Nov. 25, 1799, FO 78/24 74.
14. Grenville to Spencer Smith, Oct. 1, 1798, FO 78/20 96.
15. Barrow, *William Sidney Smith*, 1:256–57.

£1,000 from Parliament, and the freedom of the City of London. He projected independence of mind and manly decisiveness, suffering neither fools nor bureaucracy gladly. He was irresistibly attracted to fame; his dashing exploits somehow always found their way into the prints back home. He was the first Englishman who defined his heroic status in terms of defending the Ottoman Empire: when he returned to Britain in 1801, he wore Turkish dress and the special Order of the Crescent given him by the sultan, and a turban was included in his coat of arms. In 1802, Caroline, Princess of Wales, commissioned him to redecorate a room at Montagu House in the style of a "Turkish tent"—requiring a series of late-night meetings that embarrassed them both when her extramarital affairs became public knowledge in 1820.[16] But for all Smith's sartorial flamboyance, he loathed and despised Ottoman officials, and sought at every turn to bully and if possible ignore them. He was the first man to realise that Britain's key allies in promoting its interests in the Middle East were not Ottoman ministers, but were instead the local chiefs of various races and religions whom he could encourage, cajole, and bribe into working together against Napoleon. Caroline's "Turkish tent" was modelled on that of the Ottomans' bitter foe, and Smith's correspondent, the Egyptian Mamluk leader Murad. The politicians at the Porte could not make their warring peoples a nation capable of driving out the French; Smith was confident that he could.

In particular, Smith found himself working with Cezzar Ahmet (known to most Britons as Djezzar or Gezzar), the pasha of the two key Syrian *eyalets* of Sidon and Damascus. Cezzar's base was the coastal port of Acre, which boasted a formidable Crusader fortress and had recently become an economic power through European demand for local cotton and grain. The allies' plan was for Cezzar to make an initial attack on Egyptian territory, so he seized the border fort of al-Arish. Napoleon counter-attacked, and moved into Syria with thirteen thousand men in February 1799. Napoleon's aim in invading Syria was to intimidate Constantinople, to overwhelm Cezzar, to control the Syrian ports on which the British ships relied for supplies, and perhaps to open a land route to Baghdad, the Gulf, and then India. British forces had intercepted promises of French help sent to Tipu, the ruler of Mysore who was resisting British power in India (until killed in battle in May 1799).

Having conquered Jaffa in early March, Napoleon began a two-month siege of Acre, which controlled the region's food supplies. His comment to Murat from a nearby hill—that "the fate of the East depends on yonder petty town"—became a staple of subsequent British memorialisation of the struggle.[17] On the fourteenth day, he breached the walls, only to discover further fortifications within. Cezzar held out, helped by naval bombardment from

16. For his arrival, see *The Times*, Nov. 11, 1801. J. Nightingale, *Queen Caroline*, 268.
17. See, e.g., *Description of a View of the Bombardment*, 7.

Smith's battleships. Smith's control of the sea enabled him to capture some siege artillery that Napoleon had sent by boat from Egypt. After eleven failed attempts on Acre, and with troops suffering from plague, Napoleon was forced to raise the siege on May 20 and retreat to defend Egypt from an impending attack. By October 1799, Napoleon had left the Middle East altogether for adventures in France, leaving Jean-Baptiste Kléber in charge of the Egyptian army. At home, Smith was elevated into the man whose heroic leadership of his plucky seamen had stopped the conquest of Asia by "the future Alexander," as Grenville called Napoleon in Parliament.[18] On his new coat of arms, Smith included the phrase "Coeur de Lion," reflecting Crusader Richard's seizure of Acre in 1191, but also the Lionheart's greatest enmity—with France.

Smith's apotheosis in Britain massively underplayed the role of Cezzar, and plague, in defeating Napoleon at Acre. This was Western bias, but it also reflected Smith's insistence that Cezzar's rule was more of a problem than a solution, and that Britain must discipline, not glamorise, him. Cezzar was the first of the semi-independent Ottoman provincial governors with whom the British had to deal, and amply confirmed the stereotype of the brutal oriental ruler. His nickname meant "butcher." Observers were fascinated by his ruthlessness and cruelty. This was represented most clearly by the servants who waited on him, "some without a nose, others without an arm, with one ear only, or one eye"—"marked men" whom he had disfigured for some breach of trust, but kept around him to show his absolute power. He had apparently put seven wives to death with his own hand when he returned from Mecca to discover that his janissary soldiers had taken advantage of his absence from his harem. During a rage, he stabbed an unfortunate gardener who was standing by. Such a man "'out-Herod's Herod', whose seat he occupies."[19] Smith defined his manly heroism in terms of bending the power of "Herod Gezzar" to British rather than inhumane ends—to frustrate a modern Massacre of the Innocents. Cezzar was known for his fierce Islamic rhetoric, and his persecution of Greek and Maronite Christians. He talked of cleansing Jerusalem and Nazareth of its Christians; Smith in return threatened to burn Acre to the ground.[20]

In particular, Cezzar was waging a semi-permanent struggle for influence on Mount Lebanon. At the height of the crisis at Acre, Smith decided that Cezzar's open hostility to the inhabitants was damaging the unity of the struggle against the French invader; some mountaineers were sending gunpowder to Napoleon. Writing as a "Christian knight," he therefore offered British protection to Bashir, the amir (or prince) in Lebanon, and to the other Christian and

18. Barrow, *William Sidney Smith*, 1:322, 328.

19. E. Clarke, *Travels in Various Countries*, 1:363 (first quotation); Spilsbury, *Picturesque Scenery*, 11–13 (final quotation at 13); Spencer, *Private Papers*, 4:95.

20. Historical Manuscripts Commission, *Manuscripts of J. B. Fortescue*, 5:480; Burckhardt, *Travels in Syria*, 340.

Druze Lebanese chiefs.[21] Bashir was near the beginning of his long and successful attempt to consolidate power on the mountain into his own hands, and Smith's intervention had important future consequences, because it brought him to British attention as an underdog deserving of support. Towards the end of 1799, Cezzar tried to remove Bashir as prince of the mountain. Smith gave Bashir refuge on HMS *Tigre*, and took credit for restoring him.[22] Moreover, Bashir, though the most formidable of Cezzar's rivals, was not the only one; the latter's attempts to consolidate his position also required him to sustain long and hard battles for influence in Nablus and Jaffa. In 1801, Cezzar complained that Smith had supported his rebel chiefs against him, in order to prevent him from becoming a regional power.[23]

So Smith saw himself as arbiter of the local power balance. Nor was he shy about displaying British might. After Acre was relieved, he twice visited Jerusalem with his marines, claiming that as the sultan's diplomatic representative he had authority to protect the Christian religious establishments there from oppression by local governors (a claim that caused much annoyance at Constantinople).[24] His troops approached it with colours flying and drums beating, took up residence in the Franciscan convent, and unfurled the British standard on the walls. This symbolised their protection of the friars, from whom the governor wanted more taxes, now that the historic French protection had ended after the revolution. He presented the convent with an English translation of the bible; "Jerusalem, 1799" was to form part of his crest. His men spread the rumour that Napoleon had threatened, if he reached Jerusalem, to trash the Christian Holy Places by burying a French soldier in Christ's tomb and planting the revolutionary tree of liberty where the cross of Calvary had reputedly stood.[25]

The explorer John Lewis Burckhardt claimed that he had often heard local Muslims and Christians compare a pledge by Smith to "God's word—it never failed."[26] Smith certainly liked creating alliances with the Arabs—not only in Syria but also in Egypt, through elaborate and surreptitious chains of communication with the Mamluks and tribal chiefs. Using "faithful Arabs," he was in touch throughout 1799 and 1800 with the Mamluk leader Murad in Upper Egypt, and with potential allies in the Red Sea area—the British

21. Barrow, *William Sidney Smith*, 1:298, 308 (quotation).

22. R. Wilson, *History of the British Expedition*, 240n.

23. E. Clarke, *Travels in Various Countries*, 1:370–71. For Cezzar and the local balance of power, see Philipp, *Acre*, 77–88.

24. Smith to Elgin, Jan. 24, 1800, FO 78/29 20. On Ottoman annoyance, see Spencer, *Private Papers*, 4:90–91.

25. E. Clarke, *Travels in Various Countries*, 1:526–27; Spilsbury, *Picturesque Scenery*, 69; Wittman, *Travels in Turkey*, 157. [Jolliffe], *Letters from Palestine*, mentions the Bible that he presented (131).

26. Burckhardt, *Travels in Syria*, 340.

naval captains, but also locals. He claimed some credit for the Arab expedition that sailed across from Yanbo in the Hijaz to force the French to evacuate the Upper Egyptian port of Kosseir.[27] Once the British had landed in Egypt itself in 1801, he coached the young army officer Robert Wilson in the value of Arab communication networks. Wilson claimed that "the Arabs regarded him as a superior being. To be the friend of Smith, was the highest honour they coveted."[28] Smith exemplified a particular sort of patriotic masculinity, priding himself on his friendship with men of all classes and races on a relatively democratic basis. Smith, Wilson, and others contrasted the British treatment of Arabs with that of the French, who did not dare to befriend locals or to pay them fairly, and who instead skulked in their tents, enervated by their isolation as well as by the climate.[29] Ideally, a British officer should be as much at ease with the Arabs as among his own men: both groups would then respond to his confidence and determination never to accept defeat however unpromising the surroundings. Smith was "loved for his uncommon courage by every soldier." A subaltern reminisced that "he was most handsome when there was the most to do," his head like "a flash of lightning rolled up into a ball."[30] Wilson modelled his subsequent political career on Smith's virile patriotism.

Smith's respect for local fighters was in stark contrast to his increasing contempt for the Ottoman officials whom he encountered daily through 1799. He sought activity and energy; he found incompetence, corruption, fatalism, and duplicitousness. The Ottoman army charged with the recovery of Egypt was put together from many parts of the empire and seemed to lack cohesion and training.[31] Its attacks were ill-advised and fruitless. The first attempt at reconquering Egypt in July 1799 was a disaster: sixteen thousand Ottoman troops, transported from Cyprus by an Anglo-Ottoman fleet, were routed by the French on trying to land at Abukir, and thousands then drowned trying to re-embark. A naval attack on Damietta at the end of October failed as well. The grand vizier finally arrived at Jaffa in the autumn of 1799 with the main Ottoman army (and Koehler's detachment), but in the eyes of all British commentators his camp was a disorganised abomination. It was a "confused and crowded fair" of different races and tribes; there were no guards to stop enemy spies; unproductive hangers-on and "commodious sophas" proliferated; animals roamed freely through the camp, copulating enthusiastically; dead horses and camels were left unburied; sanitation practices were horrendous;

27. Barrow, *William Sidney Smith*, 2:38–44; Smith to Mornington, Nov. 9, 1799, FO 78/23 188. See Strathern, *Napoleon in Egypt*, 290–91.

28. R. Wilson, *History of the British Expedition*, 65.

29. R. Wilson, xi, 221.

30. Frederick Adam, in *Brougham and His Early Friends*, 1:59–60; [Howard], *Sidney Smith*, 1:279.

31. See the critique by the Member of Parliament and former Indian officer William Fullarton, August 25, 1798, at FO 78/19 284.

the filth led to plague, from which Koehler and his wife died in December.[32] Mutual suspicion between the grand vizier's officials and local governors like Cezzar prevented cooperation. After attempting to work with the various Ottoman army and navy chiefs throughout 1799, Smith believed that they were characterised by "breach of faith, want of humanity and a thirst of plunder." He feared that many of them wanted only to secure their lucrative posts, and were willing to make deals with the French in order to avoid conflict.[33] Nor was this illogical, with Napoleon dominant in Europe and capable of destroying the Ottoman Empire. Either the Porte, or local pashas like Cezzar, might well make bargains with the French.[34]

By contrast, Sidney had no doubts that, with Bonaparte out of the picture, the French officers under Kléber were men of their word. In late 1799, Kléber sent him a proposal to negotiate the French evacuation of Egypt; Smith leapt at the prospect. As another man of integrity, he would offer them safe passage back to France, and would ensure that the Ottomans cooperated. Now that India was safe from the threat of Tipu, surely the home government would accept the logic of an honourable French retreat. Negotiations between the French and the Ottomans began—on HMS *Tigre*—in December. The convention agreeing the terms of evacuation was signed in late January 1800 at the border fort at al-Arish, which the Ottoman grand vizier had just retaken, and in front of which were camped forty-five thousand Ottoman troops.

The Convention of al-Arish shows just how far Smith had moved towards a nuanced understanding of the realities on the ground—but also how far he had departed from the pleasant fantasies of Grenville, the Foreign Office, the Admiralty, and opinion at home. No one in London knew much of the state of the Ottoman army, but they did know about the heroics of Acre, the cowardly departure of Napoleon from Egypt, the British domination of Mediterranean food supplies as a result of the conquest of Malta, and the propaganda stories about French troops enduring deserved, miserable, providential deaths in Egypt, like locusts.[35] The particular problem was that the convention allowed the French to retire with their arms, and with passports for a safe return to France. This was anathema to European diplomatic circles, especially in Austria, which feared that these troops would swiftly be sent out to extend French gains in continental Europe. Moreover, Whitworth, the British ambassador in Russia, feared, as did many Russians, that the Ottomans would now join the French side. Led by Grenville, the cabinet rejected the idea of a French

32. Morier, *Memoir of a Campaign*, 7–41 ("commodious sophas" at 41); T. Walsh, *Journal of the Late Campaign*, 54 (quotation 1); Mackesy, *British Victory in Egypt*, 22, 179.

33. Sidney Smith to Elgin, Dec. 17, 1799, FO 78/23 160, and Jan. 18, 1800, FO 78/29 14.

34. For Smith's fears relating to Cezzar, see Smith to Elgin, Dec. 17, 1799, FO 78/23 160. For his fears of a Franco-Ottoman alliance, see Spencer, *Private Papers*, 4:97.

35. For some views expressed to Spencer, see *Private Papers*, 4:30, 63. For Grenville, see Buckingham and Chandos, *Court and Cabinets of George III*, 46.

evacuation before the convention was even agreed. They also considered it an underhand Ottoman plot, because of a rumour that the Ottomans would after all kill the French troops as they departed, in revenge for Napoleon's atrocities against their own troops at Jaffa in early 1799. Responding to this horrified veto from London, the British naval commander in the Mediterranean, Lord Keith, offended Kléber by demanding that his soldiers could not evacuate on convention terms, but should surrender themselves and their arms if they wished to leave. The result was a resumption of war and another Ottoman military humiliation when the French defeated thirty thousand troops of the grand vizier at Heliopolis in March 1800. Only then did the commanders in the Middle East receive the news that the cabinet, having heard about the convention, had decided that it had to honour it. This news had come too late, and the conflict continued. Smith was furious at being condemned to carry on planning a war that he felt the Ottomans could not be relied on to fight. By June 1801 he was referring to them as our "ill-informed, illiberal, cruel, avaricious, perfidious, allies."[36]

Smith's policy of honourable French evacuation was further undermined by the new player that the Foreign Office introduced on the scene in 1799, a high-status and fully diplomatic ambassador at Constantinople, rather than a Levant Company relict. The logic of this new appointment was to build up British influence there and check current Russian dominance—on the assumption that the Ottomans must be grateful for Britain's naval support. The new mission was reinforced by extra ceremonial and extra presents, in the hope of appealing to Ottoman ministers' private interests. Yet the logic was still a Eurocentric one: the ambassador would persuade the Porte to continue a European alliance with Russia and Austria against Napoleon. So the ambassador chosen was Lord Elgin, who, though only thirty-two, had extensive experience of European diplomacy in Vienna, Brussels, and Berlin. He was another Grenville protégé, and was well placed at court (his mother was the infant Princess Charlotte's tutor); the king personally encouraged him to take the post. Elgin's role was to befriend the Ottomans in order to keep them signed up to the war alliance, but also to intimidate them by stressing his dignity.

Unfortunately, when Elgin arrived at Constantinople in November 1799, he encountered an immediate challenge from a source that Grenville had not anticipated: Sidney's brother Spencer Smith and the Levant Company. Grenville had hoped that Spencer, who was only thirty and owed him career loyalty, would accept Elgin's arrival as the Crown's ambassador in return for demotion to the subordinate post of secretary of embassy in charge of the consular, commercial business of the Levant Company. Spencer, however, made up in vanity and affectation what he lacked in age and common sense, and

36. Barrow, *William Sidney Smith*, 1:429. For the cabinet and the convention, see Ingram, *Commitment to Empire*, 355–66.

whipped up the company merchants against Elgin's arrival and his war policy. They cared little for the war, which had severely damaged their Mediterranean trade from Constantinople and Smyrna, for the sake of a place, Egypt, that offered them almost nothing. They also loathed the Russian-Ottoman alliance, fearing that Russian merchants would use it to strengthen their existing Black Sea trading privileges. In 1800, Elgin and Spencer Smith had a series of increasingly unseemly spats about their relative powers. Smith asked the company to remove Elgin's dragoman Bartolomeo Pisani from his company position, and then claimed that all Elgin's staff except Pisani and his young secret agent John Philip Morier were company employees not answerable to the ambassador. Elgin retorted that, in opposing the war, the company merchants in Constantinople were selfish and dangerous republicans, with too many French ties.[37] Ottoman ministers were faced with a divided and squabbling embassy, damaging British influence.

Elgin naturally extended his suspicion to Sidney, who had as much reason as his brother to resent Elgin's arrival at Constantinople. He was still claiming his own diplomatic authority from the sultan, and using it in ways that the Ottomans themselves found offensive. In asserting his status against the Smith brothers, Elgin found an ally in the Porte. Ottoman ministers made clear that they would deal only with the ambassador on all matters, diplomatic or commercial, and could never accept any separate consular authority. Elgin sent Morier as his personal representative to the Ottoman army camp in Syria, in a vain attempt to rein in Sidney's independent diplomacy. Moreover, after the ratification of the Convention of al-Arish, Elgin (who had tipped off the cabinet about Sidney's negotiation plans) adopted the indignant Foreign Office line at home, condemning any solution that allowed Frenchmen back home with their arms. Elgin argued that by preserving French dignity, the convention would allow them to return to Egypt in future, while it prevented the British from getting full credit with the Ottomans for their permanent defeat. He criticised Sidney for his closeness to French royalists, and Spencer for his wife's connections with the Austrian internuncio; both men, he implied, lacked the patriotism to see that British interests dictated respect for and alliance with the Porte. Elgin supported the Porte against Smith's instinct to elevate the influence of local chiefs against the centre. The result was the eventual recall of both brothers. Grenville, having given Spencer one warning in early 1800, was finally forced to accept his recall on leave of absence in January 1801. Sidney was not given the independent command in the Egyptian campaign in 1800–1801 that he expected. He was told off for freelancing with Cezzar and with the Mamluks, and was eventually removed from Egypt

37. Elgin to Grenville, July 10 and 11, 1800, FO 78/29 384, 390, 398. On the views of the merchants, see Cunningham, *Anglo-Ottoman Encounters*, 75–77; on Egypt, Elgin, *Letters of Mary Nisbet*, 215–16.

shortly after the British landed in April 1801. Elgin was convinced that Baron von Hammer—a friend of the brothers, an oriental scholar, and interpreter to the British army in Egypt—was their Austrian spy.[38]

In other words, Elgin and Sidney Smith had both quickly gone native, but whereas Smith had shown a bias towards the local chiefs against Ottoman misrule, Elgin had become an Ottoman apologist. Elgin gave the Ottomans every reason to think that Britain would support them governing Egypt and Syria themselves after the French were removed. This reflected the traditional Foreign Office view that the internal government of the empire was not a British matter.

Unfortunately, the Grenville strategy, of fighting on with the Ottomans in order to strengthen the wider continental alliance against France, crashed to the ground in the course of 1800. This was because Britain lost all its allies while being confronted again with the Ottomans' military unreliability. In late 1799, an Anglo-Russian campaign in the Netherlands failed. In 1800, Austria was driven out of Italy, humiliated at the Battle of Hohenlinden, and forced to accept peace with France. Meanwhile Russia and Britain fell out badly. The British occupation of Malta in September was a major blow to Tsar Paul's strategy, as he had hoped to use his ties there to exert influence in the Mediterranean. Meanwhile there was a serious crisis in the Baltic, where the British tried to blockade the ports to stop them from supplying France. Paul ordered the seizure of British vessels in Russian ports and formed an anti-British Baltic League of Armed Neutrality. In March 1801, Britain, short of grain, timber, and other naval supplies, made more enemies by bombarding Copenhagen. Meanwhile, the defeat of the grand vizier's great Ottoman army by the French at Heliopolis in March 1800 damaged Anglo-Ottoman relations so badly that Morier, in the Ottoman camp, detected three attempts to poison him. The Ottomans complained that Britain's inconsistency over the al-Arish Convention had left them in the lurch. Anglo-Ottoman military relations never fully recovered, while Cezzar was now less likely than ever to commit his forces to the feeble Ottoman side.[39] Victory at Heliopolis also showed that the French troops had an effective Egyptian supply chain; their military successes gave local Arab tribes more and more reason to respect and cooperate with their new rulers. After Kléber was killed by a janissary sent from Syria, his replacement Abdallah Menou, a Muslim convert, advocated a policy of long-term French colonisation. This seemed increasingly plausible. With Russia veering towards an understanding with France in 1800–1801, there was a risk of an agreement to divide Ottoman spoils between them.

38. Grenville to Spencer Smith, Jan. 31, 1801, FO 78/31 121; R. Wilson, *History of the British Expedition*, 65–66; Elgin, *Letters of Mary Nisbet*, 100–102, 121–22. This was Baron Joseph Freiherr von Hammer-Purgstall (1774–1856).

39. Elgin to Grenville, July 22, 1801, FO 78/30 3; Barrow, *William Sidney Smith*, 1:398, 413.

So in the autumn of 1800 Britain faced isolation globally and regionally. Peace with France was essential, but if peace negotiations began with the French still in Egypt, they would require major British concessions elsewhere as the price of withdrawal. They would also have put down a marker for a future reoccupation if war resumed, while the peace terms would probably give them a stronger attacking position in the Mediterranean and in the Indian Ocean. There seemed no option but to increase efforts to remove the French army. This could be done only by using the military and naval resources of India—by approaching Egypt from the Red Sea and working with the Mamluks in Upper Egypt. This was the high-risk strategy that Grenville's cabinet rival Henry Dundas had been promoting since 1798, on the strength of his many Indian connections.

Dundas, India, and the Blue Water Strategy

In 1798, Dundas was only fifty-six, but his health was already half broken from the strain of an extraordinarily successful but punishing political career. No one before him had risen from the Edinburgh law courts to a position of such power in the British Empire. His family were influential Scottish lawyers; his control over Scottish patronage gave him his initial base. In 1782, he connected himself with Lord Shelburne, who made him treasurer of the navy, and then Pitt, who made him a member of the Board of Control. He used this position to build up an Indian political network, in particular destroying his rival Warren Hastings along the way. His energy, assertiveness, and ruthlessness were invaluable to Pitt, as was his ability to use his patronage to deliver votes in the House of Commons. These strengths more than compensated for his coarse language, heavy drinking, broad Scottish accent, and what George III considered his "ungentlemanlike" handwriting.[40] From 1794, he was secretary for war and simultaneously president of the Board of Control. In other words, he was in charge not just of the war effort but also of relations with the East India Company (EIC) and the governors of the Indian presidencies. This pluralism ensured a massive extension of Dundas's power. His influence over military and Indian appointments was invaluable to the many Scottish families who sought to advance themselves in the service of the imperial war state.[41]

For both ideological and self-interested reasons, Dundas favoured a traditional blue water strategy. For him, the main benefits of war for an island country like Britain lay in colonial acquisitions and their concomitant commercial benefits for the officials, sailors, and merchants who were posted there. Specific continental alliances might be necessary at times, but Britain's interests were fundamentally different from those of the European powers.

40. Quoted in Hutton, *Sir James Bland Burges*, 88.
41. For the best account, see Fry, *Dundas Despotism*.

They lay in extending her naval, political, and commercial clout through the world, particularly by taking rich French, Dutch, and Spanish colonies. This meant giving much more attention to the West and East Indies, and to staging posts like the Cape and Ceylon, than Grenville ever had. It was global trade that gave Britain "all the means of strength and pre-eminence by which we have been enabled to perform . . . miracles of exertion" during the war.[42]

Information arriving from the French base of Mauritius in mid-June 1798 made Dundas think that Napoleon aimed to attack India. On June 16, he told Indian governor-general Wellesley that the cabinet was sending him European troop reinforcements. He alerted Wellesley to a potential French move from Mauritius, towards the Red Sea or the Gulf, and asked him to intercept it.[43] Fearing that Napoleon might launch an attack on India from the Egyptian Red Sea ports, he sent one of his contacts, Admiral John Blankett, from Britain, in his ship *Leopard*, to take charge of Red Sea naval operations. Another, Harford Jones, was sent to Baghdad, as discussed in chapter 3. One of Jones's roles would be to get the support of the local pasha for these planned naval activities in the Gulf and the Red Sea. Blankett, Jones, and other members of Dundas's network mulled over tactics at his Wimbledon house in the summer of 1798.[44]

Dundas's connections were mostly EIC men with great experience of trading or travelling in the Middle East (Blankett was an exception, which largely explains his subsequent failure). They had a familiarity with Arab communication networks, and an interest in geopolitical strategy and mapping. The EIC mail between India and Britain was generally sent along what was called the "desert route" from Basra at the head of the Gulf to the Levant Company base at Aleppo; it relied absolutely on the employment of trustworthy local couriers with camels, who usually made the nine-hundred-mile journey in thirteen to fifteen days.[45] It did not go via the Red Sea, because of the difficulty of navigation and the hostility of the Ottomans to Western interference there. Alexander Dalrymple, the EIC's hydrographer for nearly twenty years, now urged the Red Sea's significance and the importance of mastering its navigability.[46] He worked with William Vincent to produce a modern edition of the *Periplus of the Erythrean Sea*, the account by a first-century Alexandrian merchant of the Red Sea as a conduit of Indo-European trade, which was dedicated to George III on its publication in 1800. James Rennell, a former surveyor in Bengal who was now head of the Geographical Department at India House, also helped to professionalise Middle Eastern geographical study.

42. Dundas to Grenville, Nov. 24, 1799, DPNS, GD/51/1/548/3.

43. Fortescue, *British Army*, 4:718–20; Ghorbal, *Beginnings of the Egyptian Question*, 63.

44. Jones Brydges, *Account*, 2:177–78.

45. Carruthers, *Desert Route to India*.

46. See Dalrymple's observations, May 16, 1798, in DPNS, GD 51/1/768/4.

Another Dundasite, Alexander Maitland, proposed himself for a mission to work up Arabs and Mamluks on the Red Sea coast to fight against Bonaparte's invasion of Egypt. Maitland argued that though the Red Sea area was nominally Ottoman, it was pointless trying to influence it through Constantinople; it was the various local chiefs whose loyalty would determine France's fate in Egypt. They had discordant interests, but could be brought together by British money. He should go as a roving ambassador "empowered by our Government to purchase the services of any of the chiefs. . . . Our purse, I fairly confess, I consider as the sole engine by which Bonaparte's ruin can be secured." Huskisson and Dundas took up this idea, as did David Scott, Dundas's right-hand man at the EIC, a veteran and very successful merchant with experience of the Gulf trade. One ulterior purpose of Maitland's intended mission was to see if the promise of military help from India might make the Arabs and Mamluks commit to Britain. Dundas therefore proposed to ask Wellesley to keep five thousand men ready at Tellicherry in southern India, in case of need.[47]

Dundas asked the Foreign Office to appoint Maitland as a formal Crown envoy. This allowed Grenville to slap the idea down, as likely to inflame regional tensions and complicate relations with the Ottomans.[48] Dundas did not make that mistake again. He never considered it necessary to get the permission of the Foreign Office or the Ottoman Empire for the appointments of Blankett or Jones, despite the notorious reluctance of the Porte to allow foreigners any official position on Ottoman territory. Dundas's circle all had a low view of the Ottomans' reliability and efficiency, and did not believe that they could be trusted to fight France. Only the locals could be persuaded to do so.[49]

Another Dundas strategy, proposed by one of his secret agents, William Eton, was to establish a temporary base at the mouth of the Red Sea, in case the French built a navy capable of getting out of it. So the Bombay government was ordered to occupy Perim, an island in the straits of Bab al-Mandab; Bombay appointed Colonel Murray commissioner in the Red Sea and sent him there in May 1799 with three hundred men. By September, Murray had decided it was too barren, lacking water, and too far from the navigation channel to obstruct an enemy. He withdrew to Aden, struck up good relations with the local sultan, and argued that the British should take it as a base. This would stop the French from ever using it as a depot, while the Ottomans could not object as it was outside their territory. However, the general view was that a new permanent base would be an unnecessary complication. Blankett, who arrived in the Red Sea in April 1799, argued that it would require constant

47. Maitland to Huskisson, Nov. 13, 1798, DPNS, GD 51/1/770/1; Dundas to Grenville, Dec. 13, 1798, DPNS, GD 51/1/772/1.

48. Grenville to Dundas, Dec. 13, 1798, DPNS, GD 51/1/772/2.

49. William Eton, memo, Aug. 16, 1798, and to Dundas, Sept. 20, 1798, DPNS, GD 51/1/768/39 and 79; Fullarton, Aug. 25, 1798, FO 78/19 284 (also in DPNS); Jones to Dundas, Aug. 24, 1798, FO 78/20 114.

protection and that his ships would be more effective on patrol. By 1800, it was clear that the French had not managed to construct a navy at Suez, which in any case was fourteen hundred miles away from Perim.[50]

The main question was how to use Britain's roving Red Sea naval force to weaken France's position in Egypt. Blankett brought three ships with him, reinforced by two others already supplied by Admiral Rainier, Britain's naval commander in the Indian Ocean. He spent the next two summers patrolling the length of the Red Sea, going back to Bombay for the winter months on account of the vicious seasonal monsoons, which played havoc with navigation. His squadron's initial strategy was to damage French morale by bombarding the main ports and destroying the trade between Egypt and the Hijaz. The hope was that this would break the alliance between the French in Egypt and the sharif of Mecca, the most influential of the Arab chiefs. Mecca and Jeddah relied heavily on Egyptian grain and on the revenues from Muslim pilgrims from Egypt, and exported coffee through Egypt in return. The sharif had gained great influence in the Red Sea, especially over the Upper Egyptian port of Kosseir. Blankett had failed to persuade either the sharif or the chiefs further down the coast at Mocha to take sides against France; they did not seem moved by his revelation that the French were not good Muslims.[51] So a number of voices argued that the trade to Suez and Kosseir could never be beneficial to Britain, and that both ports should be destroyed, forcing the sharif to send his coffee through Aleppo and Damascus instead.[52] The French had seized Kosseir in order to stop the Mamluks in Upper Egypt from getting help from the Hijaz. Blankett attacked it for three days in August 1799. HMS *Fox* and HMS *Daedalus* badly damaged the castle, but an amphibious landing to destroy the drinking wells failed. Two years later, the invading Indian army came across the bodies of half a dozen British marines whitening in the sun at a spring sixteen miles from Kosseir, identifiable from their uniforms and buttons.[53] The French never regarrisoned Kosseir, but Suez was a more difficult proposition for the British to attack, as it was well garrisoned and the water approach too shallow; in 1800 Murray managed to take it only briefly with his three hundred men.[54] Meanwhile the sharif continued to be uncoopera-

50. Eton, memo, Aug. 16, 1798, DPNS, GD 51/1/768/39. Parkinson, *War in the Eastern Seas*, 140–54.

51. Blankett to Harford Jones, June 15, 1799, FO 78/24 41.

52. Blankett to Duncan, Aug. 7, 1800, WP, IOR H/473 319; memo, DPNS, GD 51/1/800/2. Ingram's complex narrative implies that the bombardment policy was a reflexive initial strategy that was adopted in the face of several criticisms, including from Blankett himself. See *Commitment to Empire*, 311–15, 323–35, and *British Empire as a World Power*, chap. 9.

53. [Hook], *David Baird*, 1:360. For the bombardment, see Parkinson, *War in the Eastern Seas*, 152.

54. Murray to Morier, Apr. 20, 1800, FO 78/29 339.

tive. He knew that his base as a semi-independent regional power was better guaranteed by his current understanding with France than by encouraging the return of the Ottomans and their British ally. From then on, Blankett was reduced to impotent outbursts of anger that the situation was not more promising; he died of fever at Mocha in 1801.

The policy of damaging the Red Sea trade was quickly abandoned, because it became apparent that it would win no hearts and minds. Governor-General Wellesley vetoed the idea of attacking the Mecca trade, arguing that anything that undermined the hajj would turn Muslims against Britain.[55] If the aim was to win over the sharif of Mecca, it was better to build up his revenues; healthy pilgrimage receipts would also help him combat the threat to his position from the Wahhabi in central Arabia. The Bombay government opposed the destruction policy because it depended financially on local merchants who traded between Jeddah and western India. A party within the EIC had been trying to build up the Red Sea trade for twenty-five years. The main obstacle had been Ottoman opposition to allowing European ships into the northern half of the sea, near the Islamic Holy Cities (and the rebellious Egyptian Mamluks), on political and religious grounds. In 1786, George Baldwin, a former British merchant in Cairo, had been appointed EIC consul in Egypt, in an attempt to supersede a French commercial arrangement with the Mamluks, but had had little impact.[56] Now, David Scott and others in the Dundas circle argued once more for the commercial potential of the region, and hoped that the new British flotilla would allow a local entry point.[57] The Smith brothers were also keen on building up British trade in the Red Sea in order to persuade local chiefs to put their political trust in Britain rather than France. In August 1798, Spencer Smith got the Porte to overturn its prohibition of British merchant ship activity there, while Sidney urged the British to take possession of Kosseir in order to develop a thriving and mutually beneficial commerce with Murad, the Mamluk leader.[58]

The capitulation of Murad to the French in March 1800 pushed British thinking decisively in this direction. Kléber now made him governor over most of Upper Egypt. Murad claimed that the failure of the Ottoman attempt to remove the French from the country had strengthened their hold and given him no choice but to make a formal submission to them.[59] Murad implied that he might secretly prefer a British victory, if that would allow his reinstatement as ruler of Egypt, but would work for it only if the British seemed strong enough for it to be worth the gamble. It was also clear that Murad, like the

55. Parkinson, *War in the Eastern Seas*, 153.

56. Zahlan, "George Baldwin."

57. For Scott's arguments, see the memos of Dec. 4, 1800, and Aug. 20, 1801, at IOR G/17/7 98 and (Popham) 158.

58. Spencer Smith to Grenville, Nov. 30, 1800, FO 78/30 288.

59. Strathern, *Napoleon in Egypt*, 290.

sharif of Mecca, had no faith in Ottoman pretences of goodwill towards him.[60] If Britain wanted to get the French out of Egypt, it would have to rely on its own influence with the local chiefs, which meant projecting more military and commercial power than the French.

In the attempt to intimidate locals into cooperation and the French into surrender, Britain's major card was its ability to invade Egypt from north and south simultaneously. The fear of such a pincer movement had helped to persuade Kléber to negotiate evacuation in late 1799. The Indian army had expanded greatly in the 1780s and 1790s.[61] Wellesley had suggested a Red Sea campaign in May 1799. Elgin had also mooted it in 1800, reflecting his Russophobia: he feared that Russia would propose Ottoman partition to France.[62] The continental setbacks of 1800 meant that peace negotiations between Britain and France could not be far off. A successful pincer movement on Egypt would transform the negotiations, while a half-successful one, dividing Egypt into two spheres, would increase Britain's options. Even if France still controlled Cairo, British power at Suez, Kosseir, and Alexandria would mean a strong bargaining position.[63] Moreover, every success in India, and every failure in Europe, tilted public perception of the British interests that were at stake in the war. Pitt was aware of popular expectation that Britain must secure its existing possessions in Asia and the Caribbean.[64]

Even so, it took several cabinet meetings in September and October 1800 before Dundas defeated the Eurocentrics and got approval for his plans for a campaign to make "a Bengal Sepoy shake hands with a Coldstream guardsman on the banks of the Nile."[65] This was a four-pronged strategy, with two elements on each side. In the north, there would be a landing of troops from British ships to take and hold Alexandria. This recognised its strategic significance for future talks and—nearly as important—that the British must hold it alone, not cede it to unreliable Ottomans. Meanwhile, the Ottoman army in southern Syria would make its own way to Cairo, helped by Koehler's small cadre of British artillery advisers, now led by Charles Holloway. On their own, Ottoman soldiers might be of limited use, but their tradition of giving no quarter in battle might terrify the French into surrender.[66] Thirdly, an Indian army of three to five thousand men would be transported from Bombay up the Red Sea to Kosseir, from where it would defeat any local French forces. By showing British power to the local chiefs, the army should be able

60. Huskisson to Abercromby, Dec. 23, 1800, WO 1/345 475.

61. Edward Ingram discusses its effectiveness in *In Defence of British India*, chap. 4.

62. Ingram, *Commitment to Empire*, 382–85.

63. Dundas to Abercromby, Oct. 6, 1800, DPNS, GD 51/1/774/19.

64. Ingram, *Commitment to Empire*, 381.

65. As Popham later put it to Dundas, Mar. 19, 1802, DPNS, GD 51/1/805. For the cabinet discussions, see Ingram, *British Empire as a World Power*, 165.

66. Dundas, memo for cabinet, Oct. 2, 1800, DPNS, GD 51/1/777/1.

to "prevail upon the Arabs, the Mamelukes, and other troops in that part of the country, to act against the French . . . with union and vigour."[67] It would meet up with Murad, secure Upper Egypt, sail down the Nile, and block the French retreat from Cairo. Finally, there would be a mission to court the leading chiefs in the Red Sea. This would be entrusted to the naval captain Home Popham, another Dundas connection, who would be sent from Britain and pick up some troops at the Cape on the way. If he arrived in the Red Sea before the Indian army, Popham proposed to cultivate the local chiefs around Kosseir, in case the French had already retreated to Upper Egypt. Once the troops arrived, Popham's main function would be commercial: to use British naval power to make treaties with the sharif of Mecca, with the chiefs at Mocha, and if possible with the Mamluks in Upper Egypt through Kosseir. He would thus revive the Red Sea trade, make these chiefs dependent on Indian imports and British naval goodwill, and ensure the French got no foothold in the Hijaz.[68] (The Popham enterprise is discussed in chapter 2.)

As his many detractors could have predicted, Dundas's plans were neither accurate nor prudent. He greatly underestimated the time that it would take to coordinate a campaign from India. He also underestimated the number of French troops in Egypt (there were over twenty-five thousand fit ones, twice his estimate), and the ease with which they could get supplies. He put enormous faith in, and responsibility on, his cousin Sir Ralph Abercromby, who had just become commander of the army in the Mediterranean. Abercromby was able to collect only fifteen thousand men, far fewer than Dundas hoped. When he reached Marmorice Bay, hoping to coordinate with the Ottomans, he was held up by their failure to organise adequate numbers of troops, magazines, or boats. The British had to send missions to Cezzar, to the Mamluks, and to other local chiefs in search of supplies and reinforcements, but the old antagonisms remained: neither the central government ministers nor their local counterparts would do anything that might strengthen the position of the other. When Abercromby finally sailed from Marmorice on February 18, he and other British officers remained pessimistic about Ottoman reliability in the forthcoming attack. He had enough boats to land only six thousand men, and lacked an adequate cavalry. When he arrived at Alexandria on March 1, a gale prevented an early assault, allowing the French time to bring up reinforcements. Moreover, in urging a beach landing, Dundas had given inadequate thought to supplying the invasion force with drinking water in a hot climate.[69]

67. Dundas, Oct. 6, 1800, cited in [Hook], *David Baird*, 1:270.
68. Popham suggested himself for this role: Sept. 19, 1800, DPNS, GD/51/1/775. See Home Popham, *Concise Statement*, 84–85, and Spencer, *Private Papers*, 4:127–28.
69. Anstruther to Elgin, Jan. 2, 1801, FO 78/31 69; Abercromby to Huskisson, Feb. 16, 1801, DPNS, GD 51/1/774/37; Fortescue, *British Army*, 4:808–10; Mackesy, *British Victory in Egypt*, 25, 45–47.

In the circumstances, the landing at Abukir Bay on March 8 went better than could have been predicted, owing to British planning and French miscalculation. Even so, the two subsequent battles of March 13 and 21 around Alexandria seemed indecisive: thirteen hundred British soldiers were killed or wounded in the first, and thirteen hundred more in repulsing a French counter-attack in the second, including Abercromby, who succumbed to a gangrenous thigh wound, and died believing that the assault on Egypt had reached stalemate at best.[70] Alexandria remained in French hands, while the British camped on the outskirts frequently came across human remains on the sandhills, and dead bodies coming ashore from the hospital ships moored off the coast.[71]

The British invasion was saved by three developments. One was the four thousand reinforcements that arrived on March 25, which the new commander John Hely-Hutchinson used to march on Rosetta, forcing the French to evacuate it, and opening the Nile supply route to the British. A second was the decision to isolate Alexandria by cutting a dyke and inundating a local lakebed, making it more vulnerable to naval attack, depriving the French of drinking water, and facilitating British contact with Arabs to the west. The third was the number of Arab collaborators that the British found as they then marched down the Nile, leaving a force behind to besiege Alexandria. John Moore, one of the generals, ascribed this to the British army's wish to "treat the inhabitants well, and pay them." Alexander Cochrane, one of Dundas's men, reported back that the Arabs "touch the hard cash from us while the French gave them little or nothing and this seems to be the keystone of friendship in most countries."[72] On the march to Cairo, many British troops, overpowered by the heat, would "have perished but for their assistance." In the same way, later in 1801 when the Indian army traversed Upper Egypt and sailed down the Nile in ten days, it was because of the readiness of the local people to supply them with provisions, "for which, to their astonishment, they were immediately paid."[73]

Hutchinson's decision to march on Cairo was controversial, because his instructions were to confine himself to the taking of Alexandria, which he had not yet done. He was aware of the suffering that it would cause his soldiers. They were already afflicted by blindness, disease, and low morale (a thousand of them were sick by early June); their supply chain was very fragile; they were at risk of attack from a superior French force. When he decided to move south, there were protests and a foiled plot against him from other officers.[74] He did

70. T. Walsh, *Journal of the Late Campaign*, 92, 103.

71. E. Clarke, *Travels in Various Countries*, 1:292–93; R. Wilson, *History of the British Expedition*, 53.

72. Moore, *Life*, 2:383; Cochrane to Dundas, Apr. 18, 1801, DPNS, GD 51/1/790.

73. R. Wilson, *History of the British Expedition*, 107–8, 208.

74. R. Wilson, 97–98, 136–37, 259; Mackesy, *British Victory in Egypt*, 175–76.

so because the army was now aware of the broader significance of Egypt as a whole, not just the harbour of Alexandria, for British strategy. Advancing towards Cairo would achieve several connected objectives. It would encourage the Mamluks to join the fight. Murad had just died of plague in Upper Egypt, but his son Osman seemed on the verge of committing to Britain.[75] It was essential to get their participation, since otherwise the French troops outnumbered the British. Secondly, a British advance would encourage the Ottoman army to move on Cairo from the east: the British and Ottoman forces met up north of Cairo in late May, forming a more intimidating phalanx. This combination also kept the Ottomans subordinate to British command. Hutchinson feared that, unchecked, Ottoman soldiers would plunder Cairo when they arrived, and exact brutal revenge on the French soldiers and their local collaborators—especially the Muslim women who had become their mistresses and prostitutes.[76] Finally, the threat of attack from both sides would encourage the French in Cairo to surrender, rather than decamp into Upper Egypt where they might be more difficult to prise out. When he decided to march south, Hutchinson had already heard that Murray had arrived at Kosseir and had secured camels to transport the main Indian army, which would follow behind.

Owing to these various pressures, the 11,000 French troops in Cairo surrendered on June 28, and the 8,000 in Alexandria followed on September 1. The surrender was on the same terms as the Convention of al-Arish—including the right to take their weapons back to France. David Baird, in charge of 5,800 soldiers from India, arrived too late to play more than a psychological role in facilitating this surrender, as he landed at Kosseir only on June 8, and had to wait there for news that Hutchinson had got Osman's cooperation before proceeding to the Nile. He spent most of July at Qena before sailing down the river in August, meeting up with the other troops near Cairo and going on to garrison Alexandria once the siege was lifted. If the overall operation had not succeeded, there would have been much criticism of the overambitious nature of the double-sided attack. As it was, there was wonderment at the unprecedented merging of forces from different continents and cultures. Several writers were fascinated by Baird's march, as well as by the traverse of the desert from Suez to Cairo undertaken by a separate advance party of Colonel Lloyd and his 320 men, twenty-three of whom died en route owing to lack of food and water.[77] When the dishevelled, exhausted British troops who had marched from Alexandria to Cairo finally met up with their Indian counterparts, they were astounded. Even the sepoys had cooks, and they had brought flocks of sheep, goats, and poultry with them. The officers sat down to

75. Barrow, *William Sidney Smith*, 2:46–47.
76. R. Wilson, *History of the British Expedition*, 73, 135, 149–50, 175.
77. R. Wilson, 161–66.

a celebratory dinner on their polished mahogany tables in a gorgeous marquee with green silk hangings, lit by glass lustres. Roasted pigs, port, claret, and madeira were served by waiters in smart muslin jackets.[78]

⁌══⁍

The 1801 campaign had two significant effects on British thinking. The first was the importance of the Red Sea and its chiefs. Control of it could prevent a future French attack on India, while in conjunction with the Mediterranean it seemed to promise the British a unique doubled-edged influence in Egypt.[79] A great weakness in France's strategy had been its inability to dominate Upper Egypt. By operating as a Eurasian power, Britain had achieved a significant military victory without relying on any European allies. Eurocentric thinking continued to dominate in the Foreign Office, but it would never be so unchallenged again, especially since most people assumed that France, still the major victor of the war to date, would seek to return to Egypt at some point.

Secondly, no British army or navy officer who served in the eastern Mediterranean between 1798 and 1801 regarded the Ottomans as satisfactory allies. They seemed at best grotesquely inefficient, and at worst duplicitous and untrustworthy, since their objectives seemed fundamentally different from Britain's. The traditional Eurocentric assumption was that, insofar as the Ottoman war theatre mattered at all, it was only to the extent that it facilitated alliances with Austria or Russia, or other European objectives. It followed that there was no point in intervening in the internal government of Ottoman provinces. Yet British officers doubted the viability of the Ottoman plan to resume direct government of Egypt after 1801. Could they prevent the disorder that would give the French a cast-iron reason to reoccupy the country? In addition, British deaths, killings, and pledges of protection all created a sense of responsibility for the region's future.

78. E. Clarke, *Travels in Various Countries*, 2:55–57; Mackesy, *British Victory in Egypt*, 225.

79. In May 1800, Morier was already excited about the strategic and commercial benefits that Britain would gain from working with a friendly regime in Egypt, given its naval power in the Mediterranean and the Indian Ocean: to Elgin, May 17, 1800, FO 78/29 322.

CHAPTER TWO

Sealing off Egypt
and the Red Sea

AFTER 1801, BRITISH officials were preoccupied with stopping the French from reinvading Egypt. Napoleon had justified his original invasion by stressing the extortionate and tyrannical rule of the Mamluks, so it became a priority to seek stability there, in order to deprive him of a similar argument in future. The search for principles of good government in Egypt concerned the British army of occupation, the British government, and travellers and writers, some of whom hoped that Roman history might supply answers. These British discussions about Egypt were alarming to the Ottomans, who saw the campaign of 1801 as a means of strengthening their own hold on it. Relations between Ottoman and British soldiers were extremely bad until the British army evacuated the country in early 1803, as a condition of the wider European peace agreed at Amiens in 1802.

Egypt then fell into the destabilising civil war that the British army had predicted. War also returned to Europe in 1803, and by 1806 Napoleon seemed more powerful than ever. The British government's anxiety to prevent a French conquest led it to invade Egypt itself, in 1807. Ministers assumed that the Ottoman Empire was under French influence, was terminally unreliable, and might well collapse soon. Russia was Britain's only plausible ally in 1806–7, and had signalled that Egypt was a legitimate British sphere of interest within the empire. Politicians at home accepted this Russian interpretation. At this time, few of them had a good understanding of the East. Dundas was a shadow of his former self even before he fell from power spectacularly in 1805. The ambassadors in Constantinople lacked weight, and there was no one else with authority on the spot. The Egyptian campaign of 1807 was incoherent and a failure. Nonetheless, it underlined that Britain had no intention of ever ceding Egypt to France.

The same applied to the Red Sea. The initial British strategy for the sea was the Dundas-Popham one of Arab trading alliances. Once the French were forced out of Egypt in 1801, local Arab chiefs had less incentive to pursue these, as did the East India Company (EIC). In the absence of French power in the region, there was little risk of the chiefs taking up Napoleon's cause, while Britain would incur Muslim hostility if it tried to interfere in the politics of the Hijaz and its Holy Cities. When the French became a theoretical threat again in 1805–7, it seemed much more plausible that they would seek allies at the southern end of the Red Sea. Abyssinia and Mocha now became a British interest, despite backing from London and from Bombay that was half-hearted at best.

The Search for Stability in Egypt, 1801–3

For the Ottoman Porte, the evacuation of the Christian interlopers from Egypt meant the rightful return of lost Muslims to the caliphate, the restoration of the unity of the sultan's dominions, and a great fillip to his pride. The celebrations were on a grand scale. For a week, the Bosporus was illuminated; rockets, guns, and cannons were fired repeatedly; there was great feasting; the ulema called the sultan "Selim the Conqueror." A considerable part of this lavish expenditure went to British representatives to thank them for helping the Ottomans' military achievement. The brother of Hutchinson, the army commander, strutted around Constantinople wearing a gold medal and a handsome pelisse. Ambassador Elgin was given three exquisite pillars of porphyry, and new land for an embassy building. The sultan also freed 136 slaves from Malta into his protection, indicating approval of Britain's acquisition of so strategic an island.[1] Elgin coveted an even better present from the Ottoman regime, stimulated by the agents whom he had sent to Ottoman Greece to make copies and plaster casts of the great works of Athenian art. Since many were in bad repair, he asked to take away sculptures on the citadel at Athens that were of no value for the city's defence. The sultan issued a firman allowing him extensive rights there.[2] Its words were ambiguous, but Elgin's men persuaded local officials to allow them to transport the Parthenon marbles back to Britain. This, he hoped, would make his name.

To Ottoman ministers, the loss of some ancient stones was a price worth paying. The unspoken bargain between them and Britain's vain ambassador was that they would be left to govern their historic empire themselves, while the Foreign Office got on with its European war. The ministers did not want

---

1. Elgin, *Letters of Mary Nisbet*, 105, 111–13, 119, 134–35, 158, 162–65, 227. For the Maltese slaves, see Elgin to Hawkesbury, Jan. 25 and 28, 1802, FO 78/35 86, 110.

2. Elgin, *Letters of Mary Nisbet*, 97–98; St. Clair, *Lord Elgin and the Marbles*, 88–91.

the British to stay in Egypt for long. They expected to assume direct control there, claiming that the past disobedience of the Mamluk chiefs made them inherently unsuitable representatives of Ottoman power.[3] Elgin accepted this perspective: his priorities were to maintain the regional status quo and for Britain to be the Porte's most valued European friend. He thought that the way to prevent a future French invasion of Egypt would be for Ottoman rule there to be confirmed.[4]

For the army commanders in Egypt, however, these celebrations and gifts were a lavish charade to disguise the reality of the Egyptian situation. Parading a reconquest did not make it true. The Ottomans had no chance of governing Egypt effectively. Abercromby went to his death depressed that Britain was fighting their battles "without their assistance, or cooperation in any one article," and that the return of such feeble and selfish rulers would leave Egypt "a prey either to Russia or France, [which] no means in our power can prevent."[5] His successor Hutchinson sent home the same warning repeatedly: allowing the Ottomans to misgovern Egypt would give the French the perfect incentive and opportunity to return. They would probably come by invitation rather than reconquest, since the Mamluks, the Arabs, the Copts, the Greeks, "every description of man in this country, looks upon the [Turks] with horror."[6] The Earl of Cavan, who succeeded him, said the same: the Turk was "a being replete with tyranny and treachery."[7]

These views were derived from talking to Egyptians, but they also reflected a common perception that the Ottoman Empire was at death's door. The publication of J. P. Morier's account of his stay in the chaotic, filthy Ottoman camp at Jaffa caused considerable shock in Britain.[8] Hutchinson and his colleague John Moore both called their troops "banditti."[9] When the British and Ottoman armies met up north of Cairo, the soldier Donald Nicol was appalled to see the latter's commanders distributing money to every Turk who brought them a Frenchman's head from the battlefield, and the glee with which they kicked the heads about.[10] Enforced familiarity with Ottoman soldiers and officials between 1798 and 1801 created the lasting stereotype that, as Edward

3. See the sultan's letter to George III, Nov. 23, 1801: *LPM*, 1:137.

4. Elgin to Hutchinson, Nov. 18, 1801, FO 78/33 225. This remained the embassy view; for Drummond in 1803, see Ghorbal, *Beginnings of the Egyptian Question*, 218.

5. Abercromby to Huskisson, Feb. 16, 1801, DPNS, GD 51/1/774/37.

6. To Hobart, June 2 (quotation) and Sept. 21, 1801, WO 1/345 253, 467; to Elgin, Apr. 25, 1801, FO 78/32 40.

7. To Hobart, May 5, 1802, WO 1/346 53.

8. E.g., Charles Burney, cited in Windham, *Papers*, 2:181.

9. Hutchinson to Hobart, Sept. 21, 1801, WO 1/345 467; Moore, *Life*, 2:381. Conversely, Elgin's successor Drummond thought the Mamluks were the "banditti": Ghorbal, *Beginnings of the Egyptian Question*, 218.

10. Macbride, *With Napoleon at Waterloo*, 49–50.

Clarke wrote in 1802, "Turkey is at its last gasp, and waits only for some potent state to put an end to its insignificance."[11] A Persian visitor to London felt that the invasions of Egypt by France in 1798 and Britain in 1801 had destroyed the illusion of Ottoman military vigour that persisted from its earlier incursions into Europe.[12]

The British army commanders argued that stability in Egypt required the restoration of the status quo of Mamluk rule under nominal Ottoman sovereignty. This was not because they romanticised the Mamluks as a noble feudal aristocracy, though Elgin's successor Drummond thought they did.[13] They were just as likely to see them as pretentious medieval survivals concerned more with absurd uniforms, jewelled sabres, and caparisoned horses than with military efficiency. The army officer Robert Wilson had a low opinion of their energy and vigour, whose lack he blamed on their traditions of slavery and sodomy.[14] The main point was simply that they were the existing ruling class, whose displacement by France had created a vacuum. Moreover, British officers had no choice but to rely on them. The military threat they posed had been crucial in forcing the surrender of 1801; without them, French soldiers outnumbered the British. In order to get that collaboration, the army had given the Mamluks promises of protection. Dundas's protégé Huskisson, at the War Office, had told Abercromby to persuade them to ally with the invading British force despite their legitimate distrust of the Ottomans. Ottoman objections to the reinstatement of their privileges should be overruled ("we must serve the Turks in spite of themselves"). Abercromby had opened negotiations with Murad when still at Malta on his way to Egypt. Baird and Murray clearly had understandings with Murad's court. In May 1801, an emissary from his son Osman came to Rosetta and secured from Hutchinson an agreement that the Mamluks would be reinstated in authority, under Ottoman sovereignty, if they cooperated in the march on Cairo, which they duly did.[15] Nor could Baird's army have got to Qena and then so quickly down the Nile without the cooperation of Murad's local officials, who secured provisions for them. Unless this cooperation continued, it would also be very difficult to get out again, to the Red Sea at any rate.[16]

11. Otter, *Edward Daniel Clarke*, 2:180.

12. Mirza Abu Taleb, *Westward Bound*, 173.

13. Ghorbal, *Beginnings of the Egyptian Question*, 163.

14. R. Wilson, *History of the British Expedition*, 123, 246; Marlowe, *Anglo-Egyptian Relations*, 22. For a recent exploration of this very ambivalent view, see Quinn's "British Military Orientalism."

15. See the diary of Hutchinson's brother Christopher, Donoughmore papers, T3459, E/10 A; Hutchinson to Osman, May 5, 1801, FO 78/37 7; Anstruther to Hobart, May 8, 1802, WO 1/346 101. For Huskisson's letter to Abercromby, see *LPM*, 1:83–85 (quotation at 84).

16. [Hook], *David Baird*, 2:6–7; T. Walsh, *Journal of the Late Campaign*, 193.

A particular reason why the British respected the Mamluks was their power in Upper Egypt, which was fertile, gave access to the Red Sea, and was an area of French and Ottoman weakness. Upper Egypt quickly became an area of British fascination, especially because of the French discoveries of the ancient, Ptolemaic, and Roman temples of Luxor, Dendera, and Philae in 1798–99. In January 1802, William Hamilton, Elgin's secretary, celebrated his twenty-fifth birthday descending the Nile, after an exploration with the British army officer Martin Leake. They had got as far south as Aswan and Philae before admitting defeat at the Nubian border, like the Romans and Herodotus before them.[17] Hamilton and Leake were curious antiquarians, but they were also interested in the commercial and strategic possibilities of the region for the British government and army. Hamilton collected material on Egyptian history, and on the Mamluks, the Arabs, and modern commercial routes. He sought information on how to manage the Nile water supply, introducing irrigation and preventing flooding. He wanted to understand the causes of the unpopularity of the French with the local Arab population, and how to win the latter's cooperation and promote commercial development.

In other words, Hamilton—a promising civil servant who became permanent under-secretary of the Foreign Office between 1809 and 1822—wanted to learn how to govern the historic heartlands of Egypt. His view was that recent governments had short-sightedly mistreated the Arabs. They should be given farming land, protected by law, and given "the privileges and rights of citizens." This would create a loyal army to be "turned against the enemies of the country," and would also begin to restore Egypt's "ancient splendour."[18] The regeneration of Upper Egypt depended on commerce with the Red Sea by the road between Qena and Kosseir. Hamilton approved of the British policy of 1800–1801, of facilitating Arab trade to the Hijaz, rather than Blankett's destructive gambit of starving the French into submission.[19]

Like most Western travellers at this time, Hamilton viewed Egyptian geography and history through the prism of classical accounts of the country. He urged more understanding of the Hellenistic and Roman governments of Egypt. In a book he published in 1809, he urged that "we should now read with avidity every fragment that could throw light on the political economy of these governments: the modes they adopted to encourage population, to promote commerce, to collect their revenues, to administer justice, and to preserve the public peace." This was because "the dismemberment of the Turkish empire, should it take place, will bring Egypt, with several other Eastern provinces, into the sphere of European politics. When that barrier, which seems now to separate the West of Europe from Asia, is once broken, the new connection

17. See Hamilton's report, July 2, 1802, FO 78/36 194.
18. Hamilton's report, July 2, 1802.
19. Hamilton, *Remarks*, 186–88.

between the two extremities of the Mediterranean must give rise to new interests and new projects, and perhaps may lead to the foundation of new empires."[20] These lands were not some oriental "other"; they had once been part of a greater Europe and should be again. In 1801 he, together with Edward Clarke, helped Hutchinson and the army to secure for the British Museum the most significant cultural artefact discovered by the French invaders—the Rosetta Stone, a physical example of the Hellenistic administration of Egypt, and the key to the decipherment of Egyptian hieroglyphics.[21] So the British Museum's two greatest attractions for the next forty years both derived from the Egyptian campaign of 1801. Whereas Elgin's Marbles reflected his Eurocentrist classicism, the Rosetta Stone symbolised the army's—and increasingly the wider British elite's—interest in learning lessons from the governance of Egypt itself.

There was considerable pleasure at home in the British occupation of Egypt. The philosopher Jeremy Bentham, despite disliking the arrogant ignorance of most British imperial administration, thought that in Egypt Britain's ability to provide "a government of universal and perpetual security" would be "an advantage, beyond all price," because it would reverse population decline.[22] Another progressive voice extolling its merits was Henry Brougham, the prodigiously verbose Edinburgh lawyer and future Whig politician, who at the age of twenty-four wrote a thousand-page treatise in defence of the history of European colonialism, stimulated by the struggle with France for possession. Brougham argued that colonial expansion was a natural historic impulse that tended to benefit commerce, capitalism, and peace. He was excited by the way in which Egypt was being drawn into the ambit of the West. Its new rulers would harness the great natural resources and climate of the country and create a major commercial hub. It would naturally expand to be a significant regional power, civilising Arabia and Syria. This would be more likely to benefit British India commercially than to threaten it politically. Once the barbarous Ottomans were dismissed, Egypt would produce grain, sugar, flax, cotton, and coffee, especially if Europeans relied on the "quiet and natural industry of the Arabs" and allocated them land on a rational basis. Arabs would be enlightened farmers, as they were a free people who had never been enslaved. So Egyptian commercial development would make the odious Dutch, French, and British slave colonies in the West Indies uncompetitive. Egypt would become such a global powerhouse that the other colonial powers would try to fight whichever of Britain or France acquired it.[23] In his *History* of the Brit-

20. Hamilton, 225–26. For the role of classical accounts in perceptions of Egypt, see Ahmed, *Edward W. Lane*, 52–54.

21. Downs, *Discovery at Rosetta*.

22. Bentham, *Economic Writings*, 3:356–57.

23. Brougham, *Inquiry*, 2:333–99 (quotation at 378).

ish campaign in Egypt, Robert Wilson developed a similar argument about Egypt's fertility and commercial prospects, if well governed.[24]

In July 1801, the British government also tried to shape the future of Egypt. Pitt, Grenville, and Dundas had fallen from power in March, and the foreign secretary in Henry Addington's new administration was Lord Hawkesbury, the future Lord Liverpool, who was trying to secure an honourable peace with France. He and the new war secretary, Lord Hobart (a former governor of Madras), quickly became alarmed by Hutchinson's reports to the War Office about the state of Egypt and the risk that this posed to India. In late July, Hawkesbury sent Elgin "some ideas which have occurred to H.M.'s ministers" on how Egypt should be governed.[25] Hawkesbury's intervention skilfully took advantage of an approach that the reis efendi, the Ottoman foreign minister, had made to Elgin in June. On behalf of the Porte, he formally requested that the army should remain in Egypt for a while after the French evacuation, fearing that otherwise it could not be defended. The reis did not ask the British government for its opinion on how Egypt should be governed. Nonetheless Hawkesbury sent it, having discussed the matter in cabinet but also with Morier, whom Elgin had sent to London.[26]

Hawkesbury's intervention recognised that the French had set Egypt on an improved course by securing the rights of local communities and exposing the weaknesses, arbitrariness, and cruelty of the Mamluks as a governing caste. They had protected the agricultural and commercial activities of Copts, Greeks, and Arabs from ruling-class oppression, knowing that this would boost political stability and prosperity. The only way to stop the French from reinvading was to continue this progress. France would hope to exploit the "divisions amongst the different sects and parties there" that the rapacity of the governing elites would reintroduce. The British must ward off this disintegration by instilling in all Egyptian social groups "confidence in the British government, and by making them feel that they have a common interest in concerting together the most effectual means of providing for the security of their respective rights." While Britain must support Ottoman sovereignty in principle, it must act as France had acted, as "mediators between the different parties."[27] The aim must be slowly to reduce the adverse influence of the

24. R. Wilson, *History of the British Expedition*, 234–36.

25. Hawkesbury to Elgin, July 28, 1801, FO 78/32 190.

26. The government's original view was that the only object of the campaign was the restoration of Ottoman sovereignty, not the government of Egypt. Its shift in June and July, in response to Hutchinson's letters, can be observed from the timing of the various letters that it received from and sent to Constantinople and Egypt, set out in *LPM*, 1:8–54. I had independently reached the same conclusion as those editors, that the unsigned and undated memo in WO 1/345, cited below, is the one that Hawkesbury sent. For evidence, see Hawkesbury to Elgin, Jan. 27, 1802, FO 78/35 92.

27. Hawkesbury to Elgin, July 28, 1801, FO 78/32 190.

Mamluks, secure "privileges and rights to all classes," and therefore restore "some degree of that prosperity and greatness [that Egypt] formerly enjoyed." The key was to "establish a coercive military force under regular and strict discipline," in order to enforce popular rights and duties. Hawkesbury set out nine "Principles" to achieve this, including fixed rules for government tax exactions on land and trade, a budget for an efficient army "under the direction and control of British officers," and control of the garrison of Alexandria by British troops. In other words, the British army would hold the ring between Ottomans, Mamluks, Arabs, Greeks, and Copts, and establish some basic principles of fair government. He hinted that this solution would be needed only until the Ottomans were capable of ruling Egypt for themselves. Surely, he wrote, the Ottomans would be willing to accept "whatever measures we should propose for the consolidation of their powers in Egypt."[28] The War Office assured Hutchinson that its hope was for Britain's name to become "reverenced by all descriptions of the people of Egypt."[29]

These ideas may have seemed rational in London, but they were not at all acceptable in Constantinople.[30] Meanwhile the army of occupation had independently planned a rough-and-ready version of these aims, concentrating on mediation between the various local forces, protection of the Mamluks, and the prevention of gross abuses on any side. An immediate question arose about the control of Alexandria, once the French were driven out of it at the end of August 1801. The British army insisted on garrisoning it itself, for fear that the unpopularity of the Ottomans would otherwise see it fall to France.[31] In October, the army refused to allow Ottoman troops into the garrison.

Exasperated by the Mamluks and the British, the kapudan pasha, the Ottoman naval minister, and his men took affairs into their own hands on October 21. Five of the senior Mamluk chiefs had been invited to dinner on the boat of the British naval commander Sir Richard Bickerton, moored off Alexandria. The kapudan pasha offered to escort them but, as they were being rowed across Lake Mareotis, a message arrived for him and he left their boat. It was then fired on and they panicked, assuming—probably correctly—that they were being hijacked and deported. In the ensuing scuffle, three, including Murad's son Osman, were killed and the other two badly injured.[32] The British officers were appalled, because of the pledge they had given to protect Osman and the Mamluks from the Ottomans. So was the government: Hawkesbury felt that the kapudan pasha and grand vizier would never have

28. WO 1/345 309, also in *LPM*, at 1:50–54.

29. *LPM*, 1:37–38.

30. As Elgin hinted to Hawkesbury, Oct. 19, 1801, FO 78/33 43.

31. Hutchinson first argued this on April 3, 1801, and by June 2 was suggesting a garrison of five to six thousand troops: WO 1/345 151, 253.

32. R. Wilson, *History of the British Expedition*, 244–45; [Hook], *David Baird*, 1:428–30.

risked alienating the local population by this act, if the British army had not been keeping the peace.[33] Hutchinson—conscious of his pledge to protect Osman—told the grand vizier that he should feel "shame and opprobrium." Relations between them became extremely frosty; each demanded the surrender of those Mamluks who were in the camp of the other. The British secured the release of those in Ottoman hands, who departed to Upper Egypt in January 1802, underlining the effective partition of the country.[34] Hutchinson returned to Britain, was given a peerage, and publicised the murder of the Mamluks. He thought that the Hawkesbury plan for Egypt gave too much power to Ottoman leaders who would never secure stability and property. Moreover, the Albanian troops that they had brought with them to keep order in Cairo seemed unruly and bloodthirsty, "the wildest of all human beings." If the British facilitated Ottoman government in Egypt, they would be selling out the Arabs and Copts, and driving them into the hands of the French. Britain's only hope must be "the downfall of their Empire."[35]

The army's new commanders, the Earl of Cavan and then Major-General John Stuart, were left trying to broker some understanding on the ground. Both men, like Hutchinson, assumed that the ferocity of the Albanian troops would make the Ottomans too unpopular to govern Egypt, and that the French would be welcomed back. Their solution was to reinstall the Mamluks, while Britain would guarantee an increased tribute from them to the Porte.[36] The commanders assumed that the army's presence could force the Ottomans to accept this compromise, and Stuart went to Constantinople to promote it. It got nowhere: Ottoman ministers insisted that the Mamluks should retire from the country with pensions. Back in Egypt, Stuart was ashamed by his inability to interfere to prevent "perpetual carnage and slaughter almost at our very gates between parties whom we call reciprocally our friends."[37] Elgin, meanwhile, had tried in his own way to smooth relations between the Porte and the army commanders. Embarrassed that the latter had not reciprocated the Ottomans' lavish present giving, he made up for it by gifts to ministers amounting to £3,000, including for the kapudan pasha "a very handsome snuff box set in brilliants."[38]

The Ottomans' intransigence was rational, however, because they regarded the British army as their main obstacle, and judged, correctly, that it could not remain for long. By late 1801, the French and Russians were already working

33. Hawkesbury to Elgin, Jan. 27, 1802, FO 95/327.

34. [Hook], *David Baird*, 1:432–36.

35. To Hobart, Jan. 9, 1802, WO 1/346 1.

36. Stuart to Hobart, Apr. 29, 1802, WO 1/346 33.

37. Stuart to Hobart, Nov. 24, 1802, WO 1/346 291. See Ghorbal, *Beginnings of the Egyptian Question*, 175–77.

38. Elgin to Hawkesbury, Jan. 28, 1802, FO 78/35 130.

together at Constantinople against Britain.[39] The Peace of Amiens, signed in March 1802, accepted the integrity of the Ottoman Empire and committed the British army to leave Egypt. The Bonapartist diplomat Horace Sébastiani arrived there later that year, ostensibly on a trade mission to the region, but with secret instructions to inspect the fortifications of Alexandria. He demanded to know why the British troops were still there, and offered to negotiate between the Mamluks and the Ottomans himself. Elgin was clear that Britain must evacuate Egypt in order to secure its position at Constantinople, and prevent Russia and France from resuming their monopoly of influence there. For him, the British occupation of Malta was the most effective way to prevent French aggression on Egypt, as well as underlining British protection of Constantinople itself.[40] The Treaty of Amiens specified that Britain would abandon Malta too, to the Knights of Saint John. However, evacuation from Egypt could be a smokescreen to delay that, on the grounds that time was needed to establish the workable arrangements for Maltese neutrality that would have to precede it.

Elgin, with the approval of Hawkesbury in London, negotiated a final treaty with the Porte in January 1803 that was designed to allow the army to evacuate Egypt with dignity and him to leave Constantinople with honour. It allowed some Mamluks to stay in the Aswan province, while others would take pensions and leave. They were allocated much less than the amount of Upper Egypt that they actually held, since the Ottomans coveted Kosseir and the corn country nearby. Elgin's successor as ambassador, William Drummond, felt that he had secured them merely a "ridge of rocks" in the far south, without the means of subsistence, whereas in practice they were within two days' march of Cairo.[41] In fact, the treaty's content was of little significance, as neither side was likely to observe it once the army left. Stuart, embarrassed by Mamluk complaints at being abandoned, gave them 8,000 dollars and some sabres and muskets in order to persuade them to retreat to Upper Egypt.[42] Meanwhile, his last act as commander was to leave three British representatives in Alexandria and Cairo, to the displeasure of the Constantinople embassy. These were his secretary, relative, and fellow army officer Ernest Missett, to liaise with the Ottoman administration; Captain Hayes of the Royal Engineers, to advise on improving the fortifications at Alexandria; and the merchant Samuel Briggs, who had come to Egypt as an army contractor in 1801. Briggs was to look after commercial interests and communication, on behalf of the EIC and the Levant Company, while Stuart made clear to Missett that his aim should be to support the agreement between the Ottomans and the Mamluks, ensure

39. Elgin to Hawkesbury, Dec. 12, 1801, FO 78/33 396.

40. See Ingram, *British Empire as a World Power*, 254–63.

41. See Elgin, Jan. 15, 1803, FO 78/38 63, and Drummond, June 7, 1803, FO 78/40 33.

42. Ghorbal, *Beginnings of the Egyptian Question*, 183n3.

the repair of the fortifications, send the War Office military intelligence, and counter French influence in Egypt, in the shape of their new diplomatic representatives Mathieu de Lesseps and Bernardino Drovetti.[43]

Except for the ennobled Hutchinson and a few others, the British soldiers in Egypt never gained official renown. The campaign to erect Cleopatra's Needle in London in their honour fell foul of politics: if the Peace of Amiens was to survive, there could be no memorial to their gruelling labours. In any case, if they were handing Egypt back to the Ottomans, what was there to celebrate? There were, however, other memorials. As the British prepared to leave Alexandria, the naval officer John Shortland twice climbed Pompey's Pillar, the eighty-eight-foot-high Roman triumphal column that was ancient Alexandria's main landmark, hoisted the Union Jack, toasted the king, and ate a beefsteak.[44] A pillar that had been erected to mark Roman rule in Egypt, and that Napoleon had intended to use for celebrations of France's success, had finally been scaled by a Briton. When the plan to bring the Needle home was scuppered, the army commanders engraved an inscription on its pedestal, celebrating Nelson at Abukir, Smith at Acre, and Abercromby's landing.[45] In 1803, the Great Egyptian Gun, a large cannon captured at Alexandria, was exhibited in St. James's Park with a special carriage depicting Britannia pointing towards the Pyramids, a sphinx, and a crocodile.[46] Southey noted the fashion for crocodile earrings, and for men to venture on the streets of London wearing green eyeshades and arm slings in honour of the blinded and maimed soldiers.[47] When Nelson died in 1805, the first memorial to him was a publicly funded obelisk in Glasgow, whose foundation stone was laid in 1806 on the anniversary of his defeat of Napoleon at Abukir, with eighty thousand people present.[48]

In 1803, Thomas Walsh produced a handsome account of the British campaign, paid for by subscribers, including many high-quality maps and plates, expressing the hope "that it will not easily be forgotten, either by our enemies, or by our friends."[49] It was published a few months after Robert Wilson's history of the same campaign. Wilson was plainly wrong-footed by the enforced evacuation: his book, like that of Henry Brougham, published later in 1803, was composed on the assumption that Britain must continue to have influence in Egypt. His downbeat conclusion lamented that the country could not yet be rescued from slavery, and hoped for the best from an alliance between Britain and the Ottomans.[50] Brougham argued that if the Russians

43. See the letters of Stuart, Missett, and Straton in *LPM*, 2:1–7.

44. "Pompey's Pillar."

45. R. Wilson, *History of the British Expedition*, 387.

46. Curl, *Egyptomania*, 141, 144.

47. Southey, *Letters from England*, 3:274–75.

48. King, *People's Palace*, 23.

49. T. Walsh, *Journal of the Late Campaign*, 223.

50. R. Wilson, *History of the British Expedition*, 242, 248–51.

and the French ganged up and put the French back into Egypt, then the British would have to take Syria in compensation and develop that instead, making a French Egypt strategically harmless.[51]

Egyptian Chaos, the French Threat, and the British Response, 1803–7

In January 1803, the French government newspaper *Le moniteur universel* published Sébastiani's report advocating a new French invasion of Egypt, which he declared would need only six thousand men because its defences were in a poor state. The report also mooted the partition of the Ottoman Empire, which French diplomats were independently broaching in discussions with Russia. The aim was clearly to use the Peace of Amiens to drive a wedge between Britain and Russia.[52] To the British government, it seemed obvious that France had not abandoned its ambitions in Egypt and Asia. This in turn stiffened resistance to the evacuation of Malta. Ministers had been willing to leave Egypt in order to justify holding Malta for the foreseeable future. Malta provided security for the whole eastern Mediterranean, the Ottoman lands, and the route to India: to Nelson, it was "the most important outwork of India."[53] Later in 1803, in another media sensation, the British government arranged for the publication of Leibniz's memoir of 1670, presented to Louis XIV but since hidden away in a Hanoverian library. It argued not only that France should conquer Egypt, but that the possession of Malta could be crucial to such a project.[54] The British refused to evacuate Malta. The result was that Britain and France resumed their war in May 1803.

Crucially, despite internal divisions on the issue, the Russian government was willing to tolerate the British occupation of Malta, in the short term.[55] But at the outset this was one of the few areas of common ground, as Russia was not willing to break with France. This meant that there was no chance of a new Anglo-Russian coalition, or of any significant British influence over the Ottomans. Hawkesbury feared that unless Britain and Russia acted together to browbeat the Porte to do their bidding, the Ottomans would submit to French pressure.[56]

The marginality of British influence at Constantinople was shown by one issue that indicated a suggestive cultural difference between the behaviour of the British embassy and those of its rivals. One crucial way in which Russia

51. Brougham, *Inquiry*, 2:396–99.

52. Saul, *Russia and the Mediterranean*, 175–76; Schroeder, *Transformation*, 241.

53. Ingram, *Empire-Building*, 94.

54. Leibniz, *Summary Account*.

55. Schroeder, *Transformation*, 241.

56. Hawkesbury to Drummond, May 31, 1803, FO 95/327.

and France demonstrated and exploited their power at Constantinople was through the protection system. Each embassy enjoyed special privileges under the diplomatic capitulations agreed by each power with the Ottoman Porte in the seventeenth and eighteenth centuries. The capitulations confirmed that embassy diplomats and staff, and resident local merchants who were European subjects, could be liable to European laws rather than Ottoman ones, especially in matters of taxation and justice. This system was easily abused, because the definition of "staff" was left to each ambassador, subject only to their not being Muslims. He granted *berat*s confirming the right of such people to conduct legal business in the ambassadors' courts and to be taxed like the embassy's European subjects. Many non-Muslims who were not subjects of the European power in question could benefit from this exemption, especially if they were merchants, so they were willing to pay high sums for *berat*s. The European embassies thus acquired substantial revenues from their sale, and a large list of hangers-on.[57] In 1803, the British embassy declared against the *beratli* system and promised to limit the number of those that it would protect, restricting the right to genuine British subjects and their direct households. In making these declarations, ambassadors were trying to please the Porte, to increase Britain's standing, and to check the power of French and Russian financial networks.[58] In the peace treaty of 1809, the British formally agreed with the Ottomans not to grant *berat*s to any trader or banker.[59] The Porte had asked all the embassies to reduce the number of protected dependents, which damaged its revenues. In practice, however, Ottoman ministers were not willing to offend France or Russia on the issue, in case this made them less willing to protect the Ottoman Empire's territory against hostility from the other. In other words, both sorts of "protection system" were intimately connected.

By exposing embassy officials to local commercial pressures, the system of *berat*s was one of several ways in which Constantinople diplomats became enmeshed in embarrassing financial obligations. Local dragomans, who communicated in Turkish between the embassies and the Porte, had a lot of power because European ambassadors could not check what they said; they had

---

57. Van den Boogert, *Capitulations*. For a good general introduction to the capitulations and their consequences for legal relations with the European powers, see Özsu, "Ottoman Empire."

58. Drummond to Hawkesbury, June 22, 1803, FO 78/40 72. According to dragoman Pisani, Elgin had granted only five *berat*s: July 11, 1803, FO 78/40 149. Straton, secretary of embassy, had granted none in eighteen months: June 26, 1803, FO 78/40 108. Soon after he arrived in 1805, Drummond's successor Arbuthnot claimed that he "might have already gained several thousand pounds" if he had followed the example of other powers: August 25, 1805, FO 78/45 247. Liston had complained about the system in the mid-1790s: Cunningham, *Anglo-Ottoman Encounters*, 89–91.

59. Hurewitz, *Diplomacy*, 83.

their own networks of favoured merchants, and it was widely assumed that they took bribes from them and from rival embassies. Moreover, court culture insisted on frequent and elaborate present giving, as Elgin had found. He and subsequent ambassadors tried to distance themselves from this web of mutual obligations, as far as was politically possible. Drummond and his friend Hawkesbury were also conscious of pressure from reformers in Britain to reject patronage politics for a more disinterested official culture.

All this made the British government anxious to distinguish between the diplomatic and commercial functions of the embassy, and to underline the disinterestedness expected of British diplomats. In 1804, it was agreed that the ambassador would now be paid by the Crown. There would be a separate consul-general paid by the Levant Company to manage its commercial concerns—a role given to the long-serving and much-respected dragoman Isaac Morier (father of Elgin's secret agent John Philip Morier). Only the ambassador would award *berat*s, on political not commercial grounds. Presents would be refused except on great ceremonial occasions.[60] The Levant Company would continue to employ its own commercial consuls in the empire's main ports. Two new consuls would also be created who, though ostensibly its appointees, were in fact to be diplomats paid by the Crown: Charles Lock and John Philip Morier. Morier, proud of becoming a state servant, ostentatiously refused to take any orders or fees from the Levant Company that might infringe his independence.[61]

Tellingly, these two diplomatic consuls were appointed specifically to reside in the most politically sensitive regions of the empire: Lock in Egypt, and Morier in Albania and Greece. These new posts, which had been planned since the resumption of war in 1803, show that the government realised British influence required a local presence. The ambassador at Constantinople had no influence in Egypt, or the Balkans. Only representatives on the ground would be able to mediate effectively, and to report back on the meddling of rival powers.[62] When the new appointments were announced in December 1803, Hawkesbury told the unwilling Constantinople embassy that Britain's policy remained mediation to secure a compromise between the Porte and the Mamluks that would stabilise Egypt against France.[63] The probabil-

60. Memo by Drummond and William Hamilton, June 13, 1804, FO 78/42 303. Neither Arbuthnot nor Stratford Canning liked the loss of contact between the ambassador and the commercial consuls, and the link was restored well before the abolition of the Levant Company in 1825: Berridge, *British Diplomacy in Turkey*, 33.

61. For the resulting spat in 1805 between Morier and the Levant Company, see FO 78/47 190, 198.

62. As Straton acknowledged, July 1, 1804, FO 78/42 369.

63. See Hawkesbury's letters, Dec. 20, 1803, and Jan. 30, 1804, in *LPM*, 2:70–73, 91–94. The Porte rejected this offer of mediation in March 1804, and again in 1806: see *LPM*, 2:113–15, 277.

ity of a new war made a British presence essential in areas that were vulnerable to foreign activity. The lack of a strong voice at Constantinople made this approach all the more necessary. After Drummond's resignation, there was a hiatus; Charles Arbuthnot was appointed in June 1804, but did not arrive at Constantinople until June 1805. At home, meanwhile, the Addington government fell in May 1804 and Hawkesbury left the Foreign Office. Pitt returned to power and Dundas with him, but the latter was brought down by his enemies in 1805 and impeached in a corruption case, while Pitt spent the year before his death in January 1806 trying to hold together a European coalition. Almost all London officials felt that there were more pressing concerns than the eastern Mediterranean. The result was that Egyptian policy drifted.

Unfortunately, the plan to send Lock to Egypt was foiled by his death from plague at Malta in September 1804. He was not replaced until mid-1805, because of the lack of policy grip in London, but mainly because Egypt collapsed into civil war. In 1802, the Ottomans sent in thousands of Albanian troops. In spring 1803, they mutinied against the Ottoman governor, Hüsrev, and his janissaries, and took up another candidate. This fractured Ottoman power at the same time as divisions among the Mamluks burst into the open. The Wahhabi reached Mecca in April 1803 and installed a new ruler there, beginning two years of struggle for dominance in the Holy Cities of the Hijaz. The caliphate, the greatest support for Ottoman authority in Egypt, seemed to be tottering. In Egypt, Albanian leaders made a temporary pact against the janissaries with Osman Bardisi, leader of one Mamluk faction. Then in March 1804, one of the Albanian military chiefs, Mehmet Ali, exploited ill feeling in Cairo at the regime's heavy taxes and engineered a coup. First Hüsrev and then another Ottoman governor was reinstalled, but Mehmet Ali was increasingly the dominant force and in July 1805 he got himself named governor of Cairo, though he still struggled to get all the Albanian troop factions under control. Meanwhile the Mamluks had succumbed to petty divisions. Already by 1804, Osman Bardisi had little following in Cairo, while his rival Alfi, hoping instead to rally support in Britain, returned with nothing more than ten dozen bottles of milk punch, having encountered much less admiration for his feudal noblesse than he expected.[64]

In this unpromising situation, hope for British influence in Egypt through local mediation gave way to the more basic concern of the War Office with defence of the Mediterranean coastline of Egypt against possible French invasion. Its analysis continued to be, as in 1801, that anarchy and factionalism in Egypt would facilitate that invasion, and it continued to propose a British garrison at Alexandria to prevent it. When Lock was finally replaced as consul in 1805, the job was given not to a diplomat but to Ernest Missett, the army officer left behind there by Stuart in 1803. His posting had been renewed by

64. Fortescue, *British Army*, 6:10. See Mikaberidze, *Napoleonic Wars*, 403.

the War Office—despite Ottoman opposition and Lock's appointment—so that he could report on the military situation. His appointment as consul was due to lobbying by Stuart, and the support of the war secretary Lord Camden.[65] By this stage, still with no breakthrough in the war against Napoleon, the idea of a military occupation of Alexandria was pressed increasingly. Drummond and Alexander Straton (Drummond's deputy and interim replacement) had both suggested it in 1803, and Lock in 1804. Sir Alexander Ball, the British commissioner in Malta, proposed a British resident at Alexandria who would supply the local governor with funds for four thousand soldiers, to be commanded by a non-Turk.[66] British officials pressed the Ottomans to legitimise this occupation. Lock and Missett both asked the Constantinople embassy to get permission for it, and Straton tried to persuade the reis efendi to take it up, only to be told that it was politically impossible and would destroy Anglo-Ottoman friendship. To force the issue would certainly have encouraged the Porte into the arms of France. British diplomats convinced themselves that, despite their protests, the Ottomans would not oppose an occupation of Alexandria in practice. In October 1804, Straton wondered if "perhaps our being in actual possession of Alexandria would as essentially consolidate [our influence at Constantinople] as the proposal to do so would lower it."[67] In 1805, Missett persuaded the Ottomans to issue a firman that Alexandria's defence should be entrusted to a naval officer independent of the regime in Cairo.[68]

Alexandria was also an important tool in the delicate negotiations to bring Russia into the war against Napoleon. The cabinet's recall of Wellesley from India, and the abandonment of his forward policy there, helped to smooth Anglo-Russian relations. In early 1805, the anti-French party headed by Czartoryski became dominant at Saint Petersburg. A draft Anglo-Russian treaty was ready in April, and the new coalition against France was cemented in the summer when Napoleon invaded Genoa. Russia and Austria had agreed to defend Ottoman integrity late in 1804, an important moment in increasing Ottoman confidence in Russia. The Anglo-Russian understanding of 1805 was on the same basis, plus the defence of Naples. British ministers were convinced that a concert with Russia was necessary in order to stop the French invading the Ottomans' vulnerable possessions in Greece and Egypt. But Russian ideas of "defence" of the Ottoman Empire included military bases on Ottoman territory, increased pressure in the Caucasus, and dominance at the Porte. Czartoryski was interested in expanding Russian influence in the Balkans, especially

65. See WO 1/347 17, 317, and, for Ottoman opposition, *LPM*, 2:133.

66. Drummond to Hawkesbury, June 7, 1803, FO 78/40 33; Straton to Hawkesbury, July 1, 1804, FO 78/42 369; Straton to Harrowby, July 24, 1804, FO 78/43 19. For Ball, see Ghorbal, *Beginnings of the Egyptian Question*, 215.

67. Pisani to Straton, July 17, 1804, FO 78/43 32A; Straton to Harrowby, Oct. 24, 1804, FO 78/43 154.

68. Missett to Mulgrave, Jan. 1, 1806, in *LPM*, 2:255.

once the Serbian revolt began in 1804, and expected the empire to collapse soon. Russia, still annoyed by the British retention of Malta, hoped for an Adriatic naval base in compensation.[69] So the Anglo-Russian understanding was on the basis that Russia would take the lead in defending Corfu and the western Balkan coast, while Britain would do the same with Alexandria.

In other words, Anglo-Russian cooperation was founded on an assumption of spheres of influence within an enfeebled empire, with Egypt in Britain's sphere. Both powers would use the threat of a French invasion to justify their own military consolidation. Britain would sign up to Russia's policy of heavy-handed military protection of Ottoman provinces. The Russians, like the British, tried to get the Ottomans to legitimise these defensive arrangements. In May 1805, they proposed to add a secret clause to a Russo-Ottoman treaty permitting the occupation of Parga and Alexandria by the Russians and the British respectively in case of French attack. The Ottomans continued to find these proposals "repugnant to our laws and to the nature of our government," and the treaty was agreed in September 1805 without them.[70] Everyone knew that in practice Russia and Britain would occupy these key bases in a war, and that the Ottomans would have to accept that as the price of survival.

Between autumn 1805 and early 1806, the war went well for France and badly for Russia. After the battles of Ulm and Austerlitz, Austria had to make peace with Napoleon, and the French invaded Naples. The Neapolitan court crossed to Sicily under British protection, and so Britain found itself occupying a second strategic Mediterranean island, which did not improve the mood in Russia. Meanwhile, Austria ceded its Adriatic possessions to France, making a French attack on the Ottoman Balkans easier; in March, Russia seized one of those ports, Kotor, claiming to forestall that threat. The Ottomans, already angry at overbearing Russian pressure, increasingly turned to France for protection. They refused to ratify the Russian treaty, recognised Napoleon's imperial title, and approved the appointment of French consular agents in their provinces. Napoleon pledged to respect Ottoman integrity. Sébastiani and his agents mooted a French triple alliance with Persia as well as the Ottomans; this suggested a fresh French design on India. Sidney Smith felt that Napoleon was on the verge of controlling Constantinople and thus the road to the East.[71]

So in 1806, Britain had little choice but to acquiesce in Russia's assertive policy, in order to keep a mutual understanding alive. It seemed essential not to encourage the alternative Russian faction that was advocating peace with France (one rogue Russian envoy signed a draft treaty in June 1806). When a

69. Schroeder, *Transformation*, 249–50, 255, 259–64, 275–76; Saul, *Russia and the Mediterranean*, 183–86; Ghorbal, *Beginnings of the Egyptian Question*, 199–200.

70. Ghorbal, *Beginnings of the Egyptian Question*, 206.

71. Windham, *Papers*, 2:293.

dispute emerged about the government of Moldavia and Wallachia, the British ambassador Arbuthnot sympathised with Russia's complaints, while France, led by Sébastiani, encouraged the Ottomans to ignore the agreement about the two principalities made in 1802. The Russians invaded Moldavia, and the Ottomans declared war against them in December 1806, in an atmosphere made worse by Napoleon's victory over Prussia at Jena. Britain and Russia blamed the Ottomans' behaviour on Sébastiani's underhand tactics, and demanded his removal from Constantinople as well as a return to the status quo in Moldavia and Wallachia. A small British squadron arrived, in an attempt to persuade the sultan to listen to these demands, but he ignored them. Arbuthnot evacuated the British residents from Constantinople. Strengthened to seven battleships, the squadron sailed through the Dardanelles in February 1807, and managed to reach the approaches to Constantinople after several difficulties. Without troops, a landing was pointless, and the Ottomans had no incentive to make concessions to it. When it retreated again in March 1807, it encountered heavy firing and twenty-nine sailors were killed. For the rest of 1807, Sébastiani remained dominant at Constantinople, and Britain and the Ottoman Empire were technically at war.[72]

More importantly, Britain attacked Alexandria. In the light of all the discussions since 1801, this seemed to the cabinet—now headed by Lord Grenville—a logical pre-emptive strike against a Franco-Ottoman alliance. Five thousand men were sent, "for the purpose of preventing the French from regaining a footing in that country." It was acknowledged that some involvement in the internal affairs of Egypt might well be necessary, but the invading forces were given no guidance on what this might be.[73] The troops landed at Alexandria in mid-March 1807; the weather created difficulties, but the town surrendered on March 20. British consul Missett, alarmed that Alexandria might be blockaded as in 1801, and aware that the Arab farmers would not immediately support an invader, cautioned that the British must also secure Rosetta and Rahmaniya in order to ensure food supplies.

Rosetta had been taken easily in 1801, but when the British arrived on March 31 they foolishly neglected a reconnaissance and were ambushed by hidden Albanian troops. They lost 185 men, including wounded captives beheaded by the Albanians in full view. A second attempt on Rosetta was no more successful, as the Albanians had brought in reinforcements and the British siege eventually had to be raised; meanwhile 280 troops were killed in a battle at al-Hamed, and hundreds taken prisoner.[74] Individual heroics

72. Ghorbal, *Beginnings of the Egyptian Question*, 235–47; Shupp, *European Powers*, 359–86.

73. The quotation is war secretary William Windham's, in Shupp, *European Powers*, 361. For the general instructions, see Fortescue, *British Army*, 6:5–6.

74. Fortescue, *British Army*, 6:16–17, 24.

were in vain: "seven Albanians were slain in succession by the claymore of Sergeant John MacRae of the 78th ere his head was cloven from behind by a yataghan."[75] By the time the news of the army's struggles got back to Britain, the Grenville government had been replaced. The new war secretary, Viscount Castlereagh, had already decided against sending reinforcements to prolong the occupation, which seemed merely to be strengthening French influence at Constantinople.[76] Over one hundred British prisoners were taken to Cairo, along with a hundred British soldiers' heads. Mehmet Ali, who had now been confirmed as pasha by Constantinople, arranged for most of the prisoners to be liberated (though some converted to Islam and stayed behind). He reached an agreement with the British commanders, by which their army evacuated Alexandria in September.

The invasion of Egypt in 1807 was undoubtedly mismanaged, but it reveals a great deal about British priorities. The Constantinople embassy and the Levant Company, which valued good relations with the Ottoman Empire, had been marginalised. The overriding calculation instead was a fear of French domination of Europe and the Ottoman court, leading to another French occupation of Egypt with Ottoman backing, or else a Franco-Russian partition of the Ottoman Empire. If the status quo meant French predominance at Constantinople, it was not acceptable. The only alternative was to support the Russian strategy: an overbearing protection of the Ottomans in the hope of pressuring them to follow Anglo-Russian interests. This strategy tipped over into a war that alienated the Ottomans even more, and left Sébastiani victorious on the ramparts at Constantinople against Arbuthnot sitting impotently in a boat. The Porte had no reason to trust Britain, which was less able to protect it than either France or Russia. The French did not need to attack Egypt in 1807 and open a new war front; instead they secured a peace deal with Russia at Tilsit in July 1807. This paved the way for the other British horror, a Franco-Russian agreement about dividing up the East. Britain had failed to find enough common ground with Russia to prevent that happening. The coalition against Napoleon had ended in failure and in Anglo-Russian recrimination, since Britain failed to use the occupation of Sicily to attack the French in Italy. Britain once again had no continental allies, and would have to rely solely on naval and imperial power.

Geopolitically, the invasion of Alexandria revealed that the government understood that Britain, isolated in Europe, was a power with global interests that had to force France and Russia to acknowledge its claim on Egypt in the event of Ottoman collapse. Prime Minister Grenville now accepted the imperial perspective that he had been so reluctant to grasp in 1800. The French

75. Grant, *Scottish Soldiers of Fortune*, 111.

76. See Edward Cooke's note on Egypt, Castlereagh Papers, D3030/2582, and Ghorbal, *Beginnings of the Egyptian Question*, 255–57.

never attacked Egypt again. Nor did they press for Ottoman partition: ultimately, neither France nor Russia was willing to set in train a course of events that might create limitless chaos. Since neither the attack nor the partition took place, the British invasion of Egypt looked foolish, but that does not mean that the French were unimpressed by Britain's move. Nor was the speedy evacuation of Alexandria ignominious. It was the result of the Franco-Russian agreement at Tilsit, which made it essential for Britain's ships and troops to regroup for the defence of Sicily, a major prize that had fallen into Britain's lap in 1806.[77] Conceding Alexandria was the price of not terminally offending France and Russia, and therefore of keeping Sicily as well as Malta, which in turn made it much easier to protect Alexandria. Though Russia was unlikely to remain a reliable supporter of British interests in the Mediterranean, the Treaty of Tilsit benefited those interests, since the tsar, more concerned with central and eastern Europe, agreed to abandon Corfu, and evacuated his whole Mediterranean fleet.[78] Britain was left with only France to worry about in the Mediterranean.

However, the Alexandria manoeuvre showed that Grenville and his cabinet had not had a proper education in Dundas's world view, for they had a poor grasp of Eastern power structures and cultures. The move on Egypt was driven by the logic of previous discussions with Russia, and by the War Office's narrow priority to secure a military base. An uninvited, unjustified Western invasion, by an army one-fifth the size of France's in 1798, was bound to arouse opposition from Muslims, and to give the local regime an overwhelming propaganda advantage in combatting it. It had been difficult enough to take Egypt in 1801 in defence of Ottoman sovereignty and in alliance with many Arab chiefs fighting a similar Western intrusion. Of course the government did not intend to occupy Egypt, just to secure the harbour and town of Alexandria, and the military historian of the 1807 campaign pinned the blame on Missett for encouraging the army commanders to think that they needed to expand their operations to the Nile in search of food supplies and communication chains.[79] Missett's perspective was no doubt muddled by four years' immersion in complex, factional, and unstable local politics, and he was paranoid that Drovetti, his French consular rival, might plot conspiracies against the British troops unless they could consolidate their position. Nonetheless, his assumptions were strategic, and shared by the army of 1801—that Alexandria was not enough of a fortress to be secured if its hinterland was hostile, that the Nile as well as Alexandria must be protected from a French invasion force, and that the Arab chiefs would cooperate only once they had seen real

77. Ghorbal, *Beginnings of the Egyptian Question*, 255–57; Shupp, *European Powers*, 549.

78. Saul, *Russia and the Mediterranean*, 222.

79. Fortescue, *British Army*, 6:16–27. See also Bunbury, *Narratives*, 290–92.

British military success.[80] If experienced military commanders had planned the Alexandria assault, they would have insisted on the need for British power to appear indomitable, yet sympathetic to local interests. The lesson of 1801 was that British influence in Egypt depended on conciliating local chiefs, and on shows of power, preferably in the Red Sea as well as the Mediterranean. The French had probably already learned that lesson, explaining their coolness towards another invasion. In comparison, Grenville's government showed a failure of vision about the East.

The other person who had learned the lesson of 1801 was Mehmet Ali, who was keen to treat fairly with the British officers, and for them to leave Alexandria amicably. He recognised the status of the British prisoners of war, and helped to secure their good treatment and return.[81] There were still eight thousand British troops in Alexandria at that point, while Britain's actual and potential economic and naval power on both sides of Egypt could not be ignored. Several historians have argued that Britain invaded Egypt not because of the European wartime tensions discussed here, but, rather, from dislike of Mehmet Ali or in support of the Mamluks. However, the latter had now repeatedly shown they could not unite Egypt; by early 1807 they were also leaderless, following the deaths of Alfi and Osman Bardisi. Before that, Missett's strategy had been, like the British government's, to mediate between Alfi and Mehmet Ali, not to take sides, which would have been pointless.[82]

80. In 1801, Hutchinson had made it clear that in order to control food supplies, the Nile must be held, as well as Alexandria: Apr. 25, 1801, FO 78/32 40, and Aug. 16, 1801, WO 1/345 385. On May 2, 1807, Missett reiterated that the Arabs would not support Britain "until they see us acquire a superiority in the field": to Isaac Morier, IOR G/17/7 474.

81. Sir Henry Bunbury credited him with being the first Ottoman ruler to recognise these norms: *Narratives*, 305–6. The French consul Drovetti helped to protect the prisoners, though was later annoyed by Mehmet Ali's determination to treat the evacuating British officers so well: Ridley, *Bernardino Drovetti*, 46–50.

82. R. Harrison (*Britain in the Middle East*, 33) sees the invasion in terms of hostility to a pro-French Mehmet Ali. Ridley (*Bernardino Drovetti*, 45) claims that it was driven by Missett's support for the Mamluks. It is true that Missett occasionally made encouraging remarks to Mamluk leaders in the hope of checking their dissensions and retaining influence with them. But by late 1806, he placed no reliance on any Mamluk leader: see the letters to Windham at WO 1/347 357, 374, 393, 409. In principle, he continued to prefer the Mamluks to the "foreign" Albanian soldiers who were making stability impossible, but only if they magically reunited: to Arbuthnot, Mar. 22, 1806, FO 24/2 115. In September 1806, he proposed to mediate between Mehmet Ali and Alfi, hoping to boost Britain's standing with the former, and in November 1806 he reported that Mehmet Ali seemed agreeable to this, but Alfi had foolishly rejected it: to Arbuthnot, Sept. 28 and Nov. 17, 1806, FO 24/2 132, 138. No doubt he imagined that a successful British invasion might rally the Mamluk cavalry and the local Arabs against France. But the reason for the invasion was the London government's concern to check French power and maintain the Russian alliance, not Missett's dispatches. Marlowe (*Anglo-Egyptian Relations*, 32–35) appreciates that the British had given up on the Mamluks, but argues that instead of invading Egypt, they should have

The British government may have feared that Mehmet Ali, like the Ottomans, would soon succumb to French power, but if so, the invasion was a warning shot in his direction. Hardly any Briton yet imagined a rosy future for the Albanian adventurer who had managed to play off individual shaykhs, Turks, and Mamluks to gain a precarious hold over limited territory around Cairo. No one foresaw that he would retain his role as pasha (or viceroy, as he called himself) permanently—still less that he would reconquer the whole of Egypt, destroy the Mamluk threat completely (in 1811), re-establish the stability and the Ottoman tribute payments for which Britain had aimed since 1801, and create the greatest power in the Middle East for centuries.[83] If they had, they would surely have thought it an enormous improvement on the messy reality of 1807.

The Red Sea: Popham and Valentia, Arabs and Abyssinians

The Indian army's voyage towards Egypt in 1801 required an accommodation with the Arab chiefs along the Red Sea coast. Two were regarded as particularly important: the sharif of Mecca and the imam of Sanaa. The sharif of Mecca was the hereditary guardian of the Holy Cities, the most important political influence in Jeddah, Mecca's port, and the most powerful local embodiment of Ottoman sovereignty over the Hijaz. At the southern end of the Red Sea, the independent imam of Sanaa rather than the Ottoman sultan exercised sovereignty over Yemen and the Yemeni ports, of which the most significant was Mocha. Indian merchants, especially the Banyan, had had trading links with Jeddah and Mocha for centuries, which the French occupation of Egypt had badly damaged.[84] Overwhelmingly, British interest in 1801 focused on the eastern shore of the Red Sea. On the western coast, the two main harbours south of Kosseir, at Suakin and Massawa, still owed the Ottomans allegiance.

As Britain had learned in the 1770s and 1780s, Muslim concern to safeguard Mecca and Medina gave Red Sea politics its distinctive flavour. From 1798, British policymakers stressed that their pursuit of influence in the Red Sea would rest on defence of Islam—against the French soldiers from a revolutionary secularist regime who were now so near the Holy Cities of the Hijaz.

---

had faith in Mehmet Ali against the French and Ottomans in 1807. This probably exaggerates Mehmet Ali's power and his scope for independence.

83. The title of viceroy was an anglicisation of Khedive. Mehmet Ali and his descendants used it, although the Ottomans did not formally bestow it until 1867.

84. Henry Rudland reported in 1808 or 1809 that the trade with Jeddah and Mocha had typically remitted 2.1 million rupees per year to India before 1798, but only four hundred thousand since: IOR F/4/290/6518.

In July of that year, Spencer Smith pledged to the Porte that British ships there would show the "most exact and scrupulous respect" for Islam, and for "religious institutions of every persuasion," just as Britain did in India.[85] In 1801, Baird's army brought presents from Governor-General Wellesley for the sharif of Mecca, the imam of Sanaa, and the sultan of Aden, together with letters reassuring them that the British troops were there "to provide for the security of the Mahomedan possessions on the Arabian side of the Red Sea." On landing at Kosseir in Upper Egypt in 1801, Murray made the same pledge, urging the inhabitants to "fulfil the sacred precept of the Koran which teaches 'you must put to death your enemies wherever you may find them, and rout them out from places from whence they have driven you', for the loss of your religion is more to be dreaded than death itself."[86] This was shrewd politics, but it was not original. Napoleon had initiated this game by sending warm letters in early 1799 to the sharif and to the imam of Muscat, at the same time as to Tipu Sultan in Mysore, urging mutual cooperation to defeat "the Iron yoke of England." These letters were intercepted by Captain Wilson at Mocha, and alerted Bombay to the urgent need to woo the Arab chiefs.[87]

Jonathan Duncan, governor of Bombay, had a more ambitious plan to mobilise Arab Muslim sentiment. He sent Mahdi Ali Khan, a financially astute Persian Muslim and long-time associate of his, to Jeddah and Mecca to lead an Arab revolt against the French, to coincide with the arrival of Baird's army.[88] Mahdi Ali Khan had made the pilgrimage to Mecca twenty-five years before and claimed that, by repeating it, he could rouse an independent Arab army. His formal function would be to recruit camels and horses for Baird's impending invasion of Egypt, but his underlying objective would be to find "7 or 8 principal people among the Arabs to send them as agents among the different tribes of the wild Arabs to bring these last into the interest of our government," and ideally to begin an Arab land march up the eastern Red Sea coast into Egypt.[89] Duncan allowed any "reasonable expense" for this mission, and Mahdi Ali Khan set off with 61,000 rupees, plus a pearl rosary, muskets and pistols, mirrors, a watch, fine cloths and spices for the sharif of Mecca. After arriving at Jeddah in May 1801, he claimed to have arranged that the sharif would supply the cause with six thousand Arabs. Within a couple of months, he expected also to assemble, from desert tribes, a force of potentially

85. Spencer Smith to Manesty, July 28, 1798, FO 78/19 249.

86. For the letters, see [Hook], *David Baird*, 1:299–302; Murray to Duncan, June 5, 1801, WP, IOR H/477 111, 120.

87. See Nicolini, *Makran, Oman, and Zanzibar*, 87–90 (quotation at 88).

88. For Duncan's connection with Mahdi Ali Khan, see Onley, *Arabian Frontier*, 87–91. In 1798, in order to promote negotiations with Persia and Muscat, Duncan made him resident at Bushehr, ignoring complaints from Nicholas Hankey Smith, the incumbent, at the appointment of a Muslim to the position. See Onley and *PGP*, 1:350–52.

89. Duncan to Wellesley, Mar. 5, 1801, WP, IOR H/475 215.

one hundred thousand, "some thro motives of gain, and others influenced by religious zeal."[90]

Mahdi Ali Khan's plan was probably always fanciful, but any initial warmth that the sharif may have displayed to the enterprising pilgrim dissipated once he realised his connection with the impending arrival of over five thousand Indian troops under Baird, seeking to replace the French in Egypt with a revived Ottoman sovereignty. The sharif was dependent for corn on the French regime in Egypt; he also enjoyed great practical independence from the sultan in Constantinople, which Baird seemed to threaten. When Baird arrived at Jeddah with this army, the sharif became hostile to all his British visitors. He complained about an outrage inflicted on one of his merchants who had been arrested at Bombay, and demanded a more beneficial customs arrangement for his coffee there. Baird realised that it was prudent to leave Jeddah as soon as possible, and sail to Kosseir, taking the gamble that Murray, whom he had sent ahead, could get camels and horses there.

The negotiations between the British and the sharif at Jeddah were led by the naval officer Home Popham, who was accompanying Baird. He had arrived in the Red Sea in order to pursue the trade mission to the sharif, the imam, and the sultan of Aden that he had planned with Dundas in 1800. Popham's aim was to knit these chiefs, and the Mamluks in Upper Egypt, into a network of commercial allies. None would become too powerful; all would be bound into British trade; there would be no reason for them to side with French agents instead. Popham claimed that his mission was in the interests, and in the name, of the sultan.[91]

The sharif, however, successfully disputed Popham's claim to speak for the sultan, asserting his own loyalty to his caliph and understanding of his interests. Popham's attempt to intimidate him with British power was a failure.[92] Moreover, Popham had to rescue Mahdi Ali Khan, whom the sharif had effectively imprisoned, and to pay his debts. Mahdi Ali Khan had not helped himself by supporting the party of the sharif's rival Abdullah. Popham had likewise hoped—albeit more subtly—to help the local faction opposed to the sharif's rapacity, confident that replacing him would boost British popularity.[93] Wellesley, however, vetoed any British challenge to the guardian of Mecca, on the grounds that it risked inflaming "every Mussulman state in India."[94] As it happened, from 1803, Sharif Ghalib's local power was seriously

90. See the letters from Duncan and from Mahdi Ali Khan, WP, IOR H/475 295, 311 (first quotation), 477; IOR H/476 239, 259 (second quotation).

91. Popham to Wellesley, Aug. 20, 1801, and July 26, 1802, IOR G/17/7 158, 241.

92. Popham to Elgin, June 26, 1801, WP, IOR H/477 68.

93. See the letters of Mahdi Ali Khan and Popham in WP, IOR H/477 58, 68, 77.

94. Wellesley to Popham, Oct. 16, 1801, IOR G/17/7 177.

compromised, not by Britain, Constantinople, or local enemies, but by the Wahhabi, and eventually by Mehmet Ali.[95]

Popham was no more successful on the western side of the upper Red Sea, where he faced a similar problem in deciding how far to distance himself from the Ottoman interests that he was in principle sent to uphold. His main aim was a treaty with the powers of Upper Egypt, which would get the corn of Kosseir into British hands.[96] In April 1802, when he returned to Kosseir to escort Baird's troops home, he tried to make a trade arrangement directly with the Mamluk leaders there. This was, naturally, vetoed by the Ottomans, and also by Wellesley, who insisted that any arrangements for Egyptian trade must be made only with those who had been authorised to do so by Constantinople.[97]

Popham was left with nothing to show for his efforts in the northern Red Sea. Once the French had been removed from Egypt, Arab chiefs had no incentive to pursue his offers of alliance. British assertiveness now risked appearing alien and threatening. Once again, it was clear that Europeans interfered in the Hijaz at their peril. There was less and less urgency on the British side as well. From 1803, civil war in Egypt and Wahhabi incursions in the Hijaz underlined regional instability. The Red Sea remained almost impossible to navigate in the monsoon season.

However, the sea's southern end was more promising. There had twice been an EIC factory at Mocha, reflecting its historic importance as a coffee trading port, though in recent decades most coffee had been taken north by Ottoman traders. Since the seventeenth century, Mocha had owed allegiance to the imam of Sanaa, rather than to the Ottomans. Murray had been based there when Red Sea commissioner, and had left behind a Bombay surgeon, John Pringle, as acting resident. American merchants from Salem had started buying coffee there in 1801 as an alternative to Java, which suggested that an international market could be re-established there.[98] In 1801, Baird and Popham sent Pringle to Sanaa to court the imam, with Wellesley's letter, and he agreed to allow the British expedition to use Mocha as a base for their expedition up the sea. Popham returned in 1802, invested by Wellesley as ambassador to Arabia and commissioner for the Red Sea (replacing Murray), in order to underline his authority to make commercial treaties. Popham's idea was to resurrect the Mocha trade on such a large and lucrative scale that the imam and the local chief, the dola of Mocha, would become dependent on British wealth rather than Ottoman or French.[99]

95. Abir, "'Arab Rebellion,'" 189, 195–97.

96. Popham to Wellesley, July 26, 1802, IOR G/17/7 241.

97. Wellesley to Popham, June 20, 1802, IOR G/17/7 222.

98. Oliver, *American Travelers on the Nile*, 51.

99. See Popham to Wellesley, Sept. 15, 1801, IOR G/17/7 167; Playfair, *Arabia Felix*, 123–24.

His planned treaty making failed. Popham and his guard got only a quarter of the way inland to Sanaa, encountering many indignities en route. They were waylaid and tricked by a "hoary villain"; some of the party had their buttons torn off by Arabs looking for gold; their surgeon was lucky not to be judged guilty of killing a dying man by giving him an opium pill. Where they had hoped to encounter commercial potential, they found grinding poverty and hostility.[100] Moreover, the imam had little power in Mocha itself, where the local chief, the dola, treated Popham's party with "every insult."[101] This was perhaps because he saw no reason to disrupt the existing trade links, especially in view of the promising new connection with Massachusetts. Popham left Pringle in Mocha and appointed him resident—an appointment resented by Bombay, which had to pay for it. Popham fell back on Aden, and in September 1802 signed a treaty of amity and commerce with its ruler, Sultan Ahmed, securing a low duty of 2 per cent for British goods for ten years, which would then rise to a maximum of 3 per cent.[102] Popham hoped thereby to make the imam jealous of Aden's trade benefits. He was also aware of Aden's strategic potential, just as Murray had been, and anxious to stop France taking it.[103]

Soon after Popham's mission, Mocha, like most of the Red Sea's east coast, became vulnerable to a new threat—the expansionist Wahhabi Arabs from the centre of the peninsula. They had taken Mecca briefly in 1803, and forced the sharif to recognise their interpretation of Islam. Over the next few years, they imposed heavy tolls on the hajj, took effective control of Medina, and raided the Yemeni ports. Wellesley sent his own man to report on the area in 1804, partly in order to find out more about their threat and their popularity. This was Viscount Valentia, an Irish peer and political connection of his, who had arrived in Calcutta from Britain in early 1803, fascinated with Wellesley's new Indian empire, but also seeking to reinvent himself. He had left home after his wife had had a child by another man, alleging his preference for male servants: these affairs were aired in two court cases, which gripped society.[104] In Calcutta, Wellesley and Valentia hatched a plan for the latter to explore and chart the Red Sea and its peoples, an adventure with clear geographical, anthropological, and strategic benefits. Valentia had been inspired by William Vincent's 1800 edition of the *Periplus*. He believed that Britain and India could learn valuable lessons from its account of the Roman-era Red Sea trade route, its peoples, and its navigation difficulties. He sought to make a name for

100. "Sir Home Popham's Embassy," 252 (quotation), 445, 446; Playfair, *Arabia Felix*, 125–26.

101. Home Popham, *Concise Statement*, 201.

102. Aitchison, *Treaties*, 13:75–78.

103. Popham to Wellesley, July 25, 1802, IOR G/17/7 231. See Murray to Duncan, Feb. 1, 1800, WP, IOR H/470 353.

104. See Leask, *Curiosity*, 181–82, and Trumbach, *Sex and the Gender Revolution*, 420–22.

himself as intellectual and patriot, by applying modern science to supplement the ancient Alexandrian author's observations. Wellesley agreed to give him a Bombay cruiser, the *Antelope*, and a captain to go with it. Armed with the *Periplus*, he left Bombay for the Red Sea in March 1804.

Valentia found his trip very frustrating. Captain Keys did not want to sail hundreds of miles up an uncharted coast under the orders of a vain, camp, and headstrong Irish peer—who seized much of the cabin as his private space. Keys preferred the security of Mocha, which Valentia hated because there was much less respect for Britain, and himself, than he had imagined. This was typified by the behaviour of the dola, who ran a system of kidnapping sailors off boats, getting them drunk, forcing them to convert to Islam, and selling them into slavery as "renegadoes." Valentia blamed the upstart American traders for tolerating this practice, and exploiting Arab avarice in other ways, in order to get preferential access to local coffee. He was even more annoyed that neither Keys (who acquired two boy slaves) nor the resident, Pringle, seemed willing to challenge this system. Pringle had succumbed to drink, leaving Valentia to fight to liberate the sailors on his own. Valentia's contempt for the dola extended to the seventy-eight-year-old imam of Sanaa, a debauchee preoccupied with his "sooty harem." Valentia prophesied that neither man could resist the oncoming Wahhabi, who would subdue and purify the area as Muhammad had swept away previous dissolute Arabian rulers. There was no point in relying on existing authorities. Britain's future relationship would probably have to be with the Wahhabi.[105]

Valentia drew the same conclusion as Murray and Popham: the best local port was Aden, which was independent of the Ottomans and could become free of Sanaa if the British induced the Yemeni coffee trade to switch there from Mocha. The *Periplus*'s account of its history and harbour confirmed his conclusion.[106] But the Bombay government wanted no territory in this confused part of the world, nor to make a deal with the Wahhabi; it worried that their recent victories so far from their base at Diriyya might be contested and temporary. It recalled Pringle in 1805 and Mocha was once again left without a resident.

The British might have given up on the Red Sea, had the European situation not got progressively worse. In 1805 and 1806, it seemed that the war with France would probably spread to the East again, and several rumours arose about French activities in the Red Sea and the Indian Ocean, instigated from their Mauritius base. One fear was that France would exploit local tensions over the island of Kamaran near the mouth of the Red Sea, between the Yemeni ports of Luhaya and Hudayda. In late 1805, a powerful merchant,

105. Valentia, *Voyages and Travels*, 2:76–78, 212–15, 370–93 (quotation at 381). Valentia to Mackintosh, Feb. 4, 1806, MPBL, 78765.

106. Valentia, *Voyages and Travels*, 2:83–87, 380.

Sayyid Muhammad Aqil, bought the island from the sharif of Abu Arish, who had established an independent position in northern Yemen. Aqil probably did so in order to assert himself against the Wahhabi, but three French naval officers from Mauritius visited the island with him, apparently seeking to restore a French factory in the area. Pringle and Valentia both reported that Aqil was courting French support in order to safeguard his position, and would offer them Kamaran. In April 1806, his "pirate" followers boarded an American ship from Salem, the *Essex*, and killed all but one of the crew. This showed his power and ruthlessness, but also justified a British intervention. In July 1806, two warships were sent from Bombay to force him from the island, though in fact he had already left. This intimidating military expedition had the side benefit of impressing the local Arab chiefs. Sharif Hamud of Abu Arish now confirmed that the sale of the island had been a mistake, pledged peace with Britain, and promised to supply the EIC with two thousand bales of coffee.[107] This arrangement passed the test of Jonathan Duncan in Bombay—that visiting British naval officers could make deals with Arab coastal chiefs as long as they did not offend the Wahhabi, or the imam.[108]

Valentia planned a second journey from India to the Red Sea. He justified this by the French threat, and the strategic importance of the lower west coast of the sea—especially the port of Massawa and the mysterious independent kingdom of Abyssinia beyond it. The main lesson that he took from the *Periplus* was that the ancients had chosen to sail and trade along the sea's western, not eastern, side, allowing Roman Egypt to benefit from the wealth of the African interior.[109] A number of British gentleman-explorers had been interested in Abyssinia for years. In the fifteenth and sixteenth centuries, Portuguese adventurers popularised the idea that the legendary spiritual warrior Prester John had ruled a great and hidden Christian kingdom there. Stories of its astounding wealth seemed to be borne out by the samples of ivory and gold from central Africa that appeared in the Red Sea ports. To the Greeks, the Ethiopians had been "the first of all men"; the Romans noted their invulnerability to conquest. Milton drew on seventeenth-century explorers' accounts and maps for his picture of Abyssinia as a way station to paradise in *Paradise Lost*, and Coleridge used Milton's vision of it in *Kubla Khan* (1797).[110] James Bruce became a major celebrity through his travels in Egypt, down the Red Sea to Massawa, and into Abyssinia in 1768–73, in the hope of finding the source of the Blue Nile. He also had talked of myrrh and frankincense coming from Africa. The long memoir that he published in 1790 excited much interest and controversy. Some of his wilder claims—that Abyssinians got their steaks by

107. See the papers at IOR F/4/257/5648, and Baldry, "Kamaran."
108. Duncan to the governor-general, July 21, 1806, IOR F/4/257/5648.
109. Valentia, *Voyages and Travels*, 2:3–5.
110. Clark, "Milton's Abyssinian Paradise," 136–37, 142 (quotation at 136).

cutting them out of live cows before stitching them up again—seemed fantastic, while his anecdotes of Abyssinian primitivism jarred unconvincingly with his over-elaborate praise of its court manners and with received understandings of its riches.[111] The African Association, founded in 1788 by the explorer and scientist Joseph Banks, and originally preoccupied with understanding West Africa and the problem of the slave trade, saw the benefit of collecting more reliable information about the region.

The French invasion of 1798 then consolidated this interest. One Dundasite proposed taking the ports of Massawa and Suakin on the African Red Sea coast, in the name of the Ottoman Empire, in order to shelter a British fleet and to build up local support against the French in Egypt.[112] In 1801, a Foreign Office memo proposed that if the French would not tolerate a permanent British garrison of Egypt, an armed force should instead be kept at Massawa, ready to invade Egypt or defend Abyssinia and the Red Sea as necessary.[113] Massawa had the best harbour on the lower west coast of the sea, and looked an excellent gateway into Abyssinia. Bruce had found 370 man-made cisterns on Dhalac Island off Massawa, which he thought the Ptolemies had used to support a thriving local economy, but which had more recently been neglected in favour of Turkish "violence and injustice."[114] Valentia sought to rival Bruce's fame and to build on his research, though also to correct his mistakes as a geographer.

So Valentia spent most of 1805 in the southern Red Sea, with the two slave boys liberated from Captain Keys, plus four Englishmen: his servant (William Coffin), a renegado liberated from the dola of Mocha in 1804 (Nathaniel Pearce), a Bombay soldier trying rather circuitously to get home (Henry Rudland), and his long-time travelling companion Henry Salt, a family friend and accomplished artist. Valentia charted a lot of the west coast, identified its safe passages, and named an island and bay near Massawa after himself (something that later map-makers conveniently forgot). He looked assiduously for sources of wood and drinking water. He investigated the prospects of Massawa as a British base, but the local ruler, the naib of Arkiko, was uncooperative, and it was bound up in the power struggles between the Wahhabi, the sharif of Mecca, and the Ottomans.

Abyssinia itself seemed more promising, especially since the French had not yet made inroads there. Wolde Selassie, the ras of Tigre, the Abyssinian

111. Mitsein, "Abyssinian Liar." For Valentia on myrrh and frankincense, see *Voyages and Travels*, 2:15.

112. See the unsigned "sketch" on the Red Sea, focusing on Abyssinia, at FO 78/23 328. Fullarton's memo of Aug. 25, 1798 (FO 78/19 284), also envisaged getting Abyssinians to fight against the French.

113. Oct. 4, 1801, Liverpool Papers, BL Add. MSS 38357 124. This memo reworked the sketch mentioned in the footnote above, which seems to date from 1800 or early 1801.

114. Bruce, *Travels and Adventures*, 69, noted in Valentia, *Voyages and Travels*, 2:4.

province most accessible from Massawa, apparently wanted to make contact. So Salt, Rudland, Pearce, and Coffin journeyed to Tigre between July and October 1805. Rudland pretended to be a doctor, and cured bad eyes and other minor ailments: "a hot mixture of coffee and curry powder does a lot."[115] It transpired that there were limits to the ras's friendliness: he forbade them from venturing further inland to see the nominal Abyssinian emperor, in Gondar, and seemed unenthusiastic about their hints on commercial links. Salt nonetheless promised that he would send him gifts from Britain and return soon. In anticipation of further contact, Pearce stayed behind for employment with the ras, not realising that the EIC had decided to withdraw the Mocha resident, who was their intended link to India and British power. As a two-time deserter who had accidentally killed a man, Pearce saw no advantages in returning to Britain.[116]

Once back in London, Valentia presented a letter to George III that Salt had brought back from the Abyssinian emperor, and began a political career, becoming a Wellesleyite Member of Parliament in 1808. In 1807, he argued that as France had made peace with Russia and was exploring alliances with the Ottomans and Persians, Britain could no longer rely on Persia and the Persian Gulf region to protect India. It must instead build up influence in the Red Sea against the risk of French attack from Mauritius. His claim to Dhalac and the island of "Valentia" and Salt's mission to Abyssinia were valuable initial achievements, on which Britain must capitalise in order to court Abyssinia and shut France out of the region.[117] Now that the Ottomans were the enemy, their trade with Abyssinia should be turned into a new channel; the British should develop a rival port near Massawa. Britain should also support Abyssinian Christianity by arranging for a new head (abuna) to be sent from Egypt to lead the local Church. He further proposed that Britain should restore its agent at Mocha. This would help the development of the Abyssinian trade, and counter the risk of Red Sea piracy by Aqil and other Arab chiefs with whom France was "forming the strictest union."[118]

Valentia put these arguments to George Tierney, during the Grenville ministry, and then to George Canning, foreign secretary from 1807. As no one in London had any better ideas, they were taken up. Valentia persuaded William Jacob, a merchant and African Association Member of Parliament, to send a ship round the Cape to Massawa in search of trade opportunities in the Red

115. Salt to Valentia, July 30, 1805, VPBL, 19347 5.

116. There are some excellent accounts of the Abyssinian missions of Salt, Pearce, and Coffin, in addition to Valentia's *Voyages and Travels*, though their focus is obviously not on geopolitical visions: Manley and Rée, *Henry Salt*; Rée, *Paire of Intelopers*; Rubenson, *Survival of Ethiopian Independence*. The liberated slave boys were named George after Valentia and Harry after Salt.

117. Valentia, *Voyages and Travels*, 3:263–64, 272.

118. The quoted phrase is actually Salt's, to Valentia, June 1, 1809, VPBL, 19347 62.

Sea. He convinced the government that Jacob's voyage was an ideal opportunity for a government mission to the Abyssinian emperor in reply to his letter to George III. He successfully suggested Salt as the king's representative; the African Association gave him £500 travel money; Coffin went with him, together with presents that cost the government nearly £2,000, also chosen by Valentia.[119] Salt set off early in 1809, and arrived at Mocha in November, where he discovered Rudland, who had been made British resident there, also ultimately through Valentia's influence.

Rudland had been appointed at the insistence of the new Indian governor-general, Lord Minto, in the teeth of opposition from the Bombay governor Jonathan Duncan. Duncan disliked another costly attempt to win influence at Mocha, suggested by people with much less experience of its problems than he had. He had no faith in the visionary talk of trade benefits in Abyssinia, and feared that British assertiveness at Massawa would antagonise the Arab Red Sea chiefs. Minto's decision was dictated by concerns of French activity; he cited the Kamaran episode. He renewed Rudland's appointment in 1810 for the same reason, noting France's influence in Persia and continuing military strength in Europe.[120] In fact, a new French representative arrived at Mocha in April 1810.[121] Rudland and his friends proposed a series of initiatives to justify his appointment. The first—which helped to sway Minto's decision—was to set up a line of communication from India through Mocha and Egypt to Malta and Britain, while the war made the line through Constantinople unavailable. This would require using his expertise with the local Arab tribes, whose independence of spirit, he claimed, "was ready always at the call of the British Govt."[122] Salt and Pearce planned to work on the ras to consider a new trade route from Tigre to the sea, avoiding Ottoman Massawa; Rudland suggested that Britain should buy land at nearby Amphila and create a rival port. Bombay was horrified at plans that would offend every power in the region, and slapped them down.[123] It also rejected the attempt of Rudland's assistant John Benzoni to make a trade treaty with Mehmet Ali in Egypt to accompany the idea of a through postal route. This risked upsetting the Porte by implying the Egyptian ruler's virtual independence. Moreover, a vibrant through trade with Europe would challenge the EIC's own monopoly on local British commerce. Samuel Briggs, the main British merchant in Alexandria, who was coming to

119. For the planning of the mission, see the correspondence in FO 1/1 1–57. See also Rubenson, *Survival of Ethiopian Independence*, 42–44; Halls, *Henry Salt*, 1:136–46.

120. See the letters in IOR F/4/290/6518 and IOR F/4/416/10286, and Rudland to Valentia, May 16, 1809, VPBL, 19347 54.

121. Rudland to Valentia, Apr. 18, 1810, VPBL, 19347 95.

122. For the quotation, Rudland to Valentia, May 16, 1809, VPBL, 19347 54. The proposal is discussed at IOR F/4/290/6518.

123. Rudland proposed this in February 1810 and Bombay ruled it out in May: see the letters in IOR F/4/416/10286.

be on good terms with Mehmet Ali, clearly aimed at this very outcome, which Valentia also supported.[124] Rudland then annoyed Bombay further by suggesting, as an alternative, Benzoni's idea of enticing merchants to carry the produce of the Red Sea around the Cape, thus avoiding duties at Jeddah or Suez, but equally undermining the EIC's monopoly.[125]

It was no surprise that in 1811 the Bombay regime recalled Rudland, on the grounds of his political activities and failure to keep proper accounts, and instructed his successor, Theodore Forbes, to confine himself to strictly EIC-related commercial activities. By late 1810, the French had been removed from their Indian Ocean naval base on Mauritius. Moreover, the cross-country mail route to India via Constantinople and Baghdad had been re-established. So there seemed no further need for British political activity in the Red Sea. Rudland left for India, wisely leaving behind the pet lion that Coffin had sent him. After a torrent of "almost cracked" claims about the malevolence of Bombay officials, he died in 1814.[126] Meanwhile Salt returned home in 1812. He had discovered that local politics at Massawa were even more fraught and unpromising than before. He had made a brief visit to Tigre, was once again prevented from going on to see the emperor, and left the presents behind with the ras, whose letter back to George III made clear that any British contact should be with himself. The ras implied that he might do business with the British if they won control of the coast from the Ottomans, but would do nothing to help them. Nonetheless, the government paid Salt £2,000 for his mission, a generosity perhaps influenced by the fact that Wellesley was foreign secretary at the time.[127]

There was more brief talk of seizing Massawa and developing British trade in the Red Sea in 1813, at the time of the decision to abolish the EIC's monopoly over Indian trade, which some people expected to create new commercial opportunities.[128] Salt's account of his expedition, which appeared in 1814, was dedicated to the Prince Regent, with the aim of giving it "additional sanction as a public mission."[129] He urged that at least one west coast port should be brought under British protection, in order to counter the powers at Jeddah and Mecca.[130] His plan was that a permanent British resident at Mocha would work with the independent sharif of Abu Arish and the imam of Sanaa to take Massawa and Suakin from the sharif of Mecca and the sultan. Thus Britain

124. IOR F/4/416/10288.

125. IOR F/4/416/10287.

126. Salt to Valentia, Apr. 13, 1815, VPBL, 19347 135. For the lion, see Pearce to Salt, Nov. 1812, VPBL, 19347 99.

127. For Salt's mission, see Rubenson, *Survival of Ethiopian Independence*, 44–48, and Salt's report, Mar. 4, 1811, FO 1/1 78. For the money, see FO 1/1 219, 225.

128. Rivaz, *Proposal*.

129. Salt to Valentia, July 16, 1813, VPBL, 19347 103.

130. Salt, *Voyage to Abyssinia*, 496–98.

would shut the Ottomans and Mehmet Ali as well as the French out of the Red Sea.[131] However, the French threat had now faded from view, and interest in Abyssinia faded with it, except in philanthropic and academic circles.[132] Pearce and Coffin stayed behind in Abyssinia, maintained by the ras, through an arrangement negotiated between him and Salt. They were given several tasks, including the keeping of a journal for the African Association. As Abyssinia descended into civil war, they began to realise that Valentia's hopes of spearheading its transformation had been abandoned, and they with it.

The story of Mocha, and the other southern Red Sea ports, is a story of tension between the cautious, economical Bombay government and the utopian visions of Popham, the other Dundasites, and Valentia. If there were to be a station at all, Bombay wanted it to be a purely commercial one, preferably staffed by a local agent familiar with trading traditions. Bombay was not uninterested in commercial development, but would support it only as long as it did not threaten the EIC's limited economic interests. It was opposed to interference in local politics, which it regarded as dangerous and expensive. It had a particular anxiety not to alienate the Wahhabi: Rudland was told not to take sides once Mehmet Ali attacked them.[133] Bombay's main concern was to manage the politics of the Gulf, where the commercial stakes were much higher and the Wahhabi were a lot more influential (as discussed in chapter 3). Jonathan Duncan found most British plans for the Red Sea impractical. He was quite right. After the fall of Dundas, there was little government expertise about the area, and those who appeared to have it, such as Valentia, had considerable influence. Extra pressure for intervention came from merchants like Briggs who hoped for trade benefits, and from philanthropists. None of the visionary plans for the Red Sea succeeded. They had no impact on the threat from the French, which disappeared when they were forced out of Mauritius in 1810. Shortly afterwards, France's defeat in Spain consolidated British naval superiority in the Mediterranean, and therefore on the northern Egyptian coast. Almost everyone now forgot about Abyssinia and Mocha.

One person who did not forget was the ambitious Henry Salt.[134] After 1812, he burnished his contacts with the African Association and the Bible Society, and encouraged talk of Christian missions to Abyssinia.[135] With the backing of Valentia, Joseph Banks, and the religious-minded former cabinet minister Charles Yorke, he was appointed British consul-general in Egypt on Missett's retirement in 1815, with a salary of £1,700 a year. In future years, he told Mehmet Ali several times that Britain would object to his expansion towards

131. As his memo of September 1811 for Wellesley explained: FO 1/1 191, 193.

132. E.g., Salt's discussions with Alexander Murray, Bruce's editor and professor of oriental languages at Edinburgh University, in Halls's *Henry Salt* (1:279–80, 331–40).

133. IOR F/4/416/10290.

134. For his drive for fame, see Jasanoff, *Edge of Empire*, 234–35.

135. See Halls, *Henry Salt*, 1:391–92, 444.

Abyssinia or Aden.[136] In saying this, Salt did not speak for the Foreign Office, but this did not matter, since the Foreign Office never spoke about Abyssinia at all. By the 1830s, Salt and his successors in Egypt had made British "interest" in Abyssinia and its coastal outlets a fact. Nor could the British ever abandon a preoccupation with Mocha and Aden on the other side of the Red Sea. The enthusiasms of Valentia and Salt cast a long shadow over future policy.

136. See chapter 10, pp. 327–28.

CHAPTER THREE

Striving for Leverage in Baghdad

WHEN LORD ELGIN left Constantinople in 1803, one reason was to alert badly informed ministers in London to "the increasing interest we daily acquire in the eastern provinces of Turkey and Persia."[1] The main eastern Ottoman province was the pashalik of Baghdad. Its capital city was the centre of road and river communications to the Persian Gulf, Persia, Syria, and Kurdistan, and a great Asian commercial mart. No Ottoman town east of the Levant could match Baghdad's strategic, political, and economic importance. It was only a few miles from the site of the great historic civilisation of Babylon. Alexander the Great had swept past Babylon during his war against the Persians, before his victories at Susa and Persepolis, on his way to India. When the French took Egypt in 1798, many expected them to follow his route through Syria to the upper Tigris and down the river towards the Gulf. Henry Dundas, brooding on Alexander's example, was persuaded by a member of his network, Harford Jones, that Jones should go to Baghdad in 1798 as a government agent, to turn local opinion against the French. France had recently sent agents and a consul to the city.[2] As already noted, Dundas's men were realists, for whom money and power were the best tools for winning friends in the East. Jones knew Baghdad and its Indian trading links well; he had been assistant East India Company (EIC) agent at Basra at the head of the Gulf for a decade from 1783. His new mission aimed to engage "the secret efforts of the Arabs and Pashaws on the eastern and southern frontiers of the empire. These from their connection with India may be brought, some by money, some by threats and some by

1. Ingram, "From Trade to Empire," 298.
2. Jones Brydges, *Account*, 2:177–78. For Dundas on Alexander, and for the French, see J. Kelly, *Britain and the Persian Gulf*, 64–65.

promises heartily to enter into our cause."[3] Dundas and Jones were confident that British commercial and naval power could overawe local factions and build a lasting influence by mediating judiciously between them. This would be easier in the Gulf region than in Egypt, because no European rival matched Britain's naval position in the Indian Ocean.

British officials in Bombay, meanwhile, valued the Gulf mainly for its extensive trade, on which their revenues relied. The EIC stationed agents on the Gulf coast at Persian Bushehr and Ottoman Basra, and sometimes also at Muscat just to the east of the Gulf. It had founded a factory at Basra in 1763, its first in Ottoman territory, in order to develop the Gulf trade and the overland government mail route from there to Aleppo and the Mediterranean. Its main resident at Basra from 1784 to 1806 was Samuel Manesty, son of a Liverpool slave trader, who became the dominant British figure in the Gulf by building extensive trade networks with Bombay and marrying into the local Armenian merchant community (his wife was a date-plantation heiress). Manesty was an enthusiastic operator of the *beratli* protection system that Britain's Constantinople ambassadors found distasteful, but which he used to extend his patronage empire among wealthy locals. Manesty epitomised the policy of prioritising commercial advantages for himself and his Armenian friends, and so made a lot of enemies, including Ambassador Liston at Constantinople, and his erstwhile assistant, Jones.[4] Nonetheless, his hard-headed approach to making the British residency a financial power facilitated political understandings with those who mattered in the region—including the Wahhabi and other Arab tribes.

The Indian government in Calcutta was also concerned about the region, and especially the potential role of Persia in any European attack on India—by France or by Russia, which was manifestly extending its informal influence in northern Persia. India consistently tried to counter European influence in Persia by its own diplomacy there.[5] This diplomacy was often as preoccupied with the Gulf as with Persia itself. In 1799, Governor-General Wellesley appointed his protégé Captain John Malcolm as envoy to the court of Persia, hoping to bind the shah to Indian objectives. On his way, Malcolm visited Muscat, where he courted the local imam, and then the Bushehr residency, from where he reported on the state of trade with India in February 1800. He argued for a permanent British military and commercial presence in the Gulf, preferably on the island of Qishm, by the straits of Hormuz.

The idea of possessing an island in the Gulf—Qishm, or Hormuz, or Kharaq further north, near Bushehr—was to be a demand of the "Malcolmite"

3. Jones to Dundas, Aug. 24, 1798, FO 78/20 114.

4. See Cunningham, *Anglo-Ottoman Encounters*, 83; Mirza Abu Taleb, *Westward Bound*, 279–81.

5. See Yapp, *Strategies of British India*; Ingram, *Britain's Persian Connection*.

school of British Indian strategists for the next half-century. Though this island strategy was always contentious, the underlying argument for a strong British naval presence in the Gulf was not. Malcolm's argument was commercial, but more fundamentally political. The commerce between India and the Gulf, for foodstuffs and manufactures, was so great and promising that it was indispensable for Indian prosperity and stability. The EIC must protect it, develop it, and "excite a liberal spirit of commercial enterprize and adventure" in its Indian population. For the same reasons, that commerce was bound to be attractive to France and Russia. France's conquest of Egypt had shown the inability of the Ottoman Empire to act as "a barrier between India & Europe." The British needed to become the dominant power in the Gulf, in order to apply counter-pressure on Persia, and on Basra and Baghdad, which were "more immediately dependent on the trade with India . . . for their very existence." The pasha of Baghdad must be told that to take sides against Britain would be to sacrifice "the trade on which [his] prosperity depended." EIC protection of lives and property should be more attractive to local merchants, rulers, and tribal chiefs than the capricious and venal rule of Ottoman or Persian overlords.[6] After the 1807 Treaty of Tilsit suggested that France or Russia or both were likely to move against Britain in the East, this argument became more urgent.

Between 1798 and 1821, British policy in this region was in the hands of the Dundasite Jones and then the Malcolmite Claudius Rich at Baghdad, and Samuel Manesty at Basra, together with a succession of figures at Bushehr and Bombay who worried about the security of British trade in the Gulf, which seemed threatened by "pirate" tribes in alliance with the Wahhabi. Their subtly different perspectives help to explain occasional variations in policy. Yet those differences were greatly outweighed by their agreement—that strengthening Britain's presence was a priority strategically, and for their own careers. Moreover, this must be done irrespective of any concerns of the Ottoman ministers at Constantinople, who were of only slightly more importance in Baghdad than they were in Egypt. Britain must use naval and commercial power, and a reputation for fair dealing, to build up influence with local chiefs and become indispensable to the regional political balance.

Harford Jones: Failure of the Dundas Strategy

The *eyalet* of Baghdad was the largest, wealthiest, and most powerful of three Ottoman administrative provinces that spanned the territory between Kurdistan and the Gulf. British officials usually called this area Turkish Arabia, and sometimes Mesopotamia, which was more accurately the space between its two great rivers, the Tigris and Euphrates. Sometimes they called it Iraq, a

6. Feb. 26, 1800, *PGP*, 1:442–55 (quotations at 446, 448, 449, 449).

local name that drew on its Sumerian and Babylonian heritage. The northern-most of the three *eyalet*s, Mosul, extended into Kurdistan, and until 1834 was governed by Jalili pashas who sometimes tried to make trouble in Baghdad. In this period, the small southerly *eyalet* of Basra was assumed to be incapable of functioning independently of Baghdad, so was governed by its pashas.[7] Since 1704, Baghdad had been ruled by a Mamluk caste originally from Georgia. These Mamluks were never quite as independent from Constantinople as those in Egypt, which is why the Porte had a residual confidence that the regime would do the sultan's bidding in an emergency. Nonetheless, the distance from Constantinople, and competing political pressures from the Gulf and Persia, meant that the Baghdad Mamluks had every expectation of retaining their titles (which were nominally in the sultan's gift) and their day-to-day self-government.

In 1798, the pasha of Baghdad was Sulayman, who had taken power in 1780 and become the most formidable of the Mamluk rulers. Jones hoped that he would be amenable to British requests, since he had benefited from EIC support in establishing his rule. Jones, Dundas, and Manesty in Basra all aimed to ensure that Sulayman would remain on Britain's side, even if the French became the dominant power at Constantinople. No one in 1798 sought the sultan's permission for Jones's appointment; he had no official diplomatic status in the Porte's eyes until Elgin took advantage of a brief warming of relations to get it legitimised in 1802.[8] The EIC had never had an agent in Baghdad before, and much preferred Basra, where British naval and commercial power was more obvious. It, and Manesty, were reluctant to accept the Dundas-Jones argument that Baghdad would be a good place to organise the government mail between India and the Mediterranean, and that the patronage involved would help to buy the loyalty of the Arab tribes.[9]

The direct French threat to Baghdad ended with their retreat from Acre in May 1799, though Jones continued to help the war effort by facilitating the transfer of Baghdad's surplus revenue to subsidise the grand vizier's march on Egypt. After the end of that campaign in 1801, he needed to find another way of justifying his presence in Baghdad. So he focused on the internal problems of the pashalik, which were numerous. In the mountains of the north and east, the Kurdish tribes were impossible to subjugate, and on the Persian border they had a vested interest in playing the Ottomans and Persians against each other. The Persians could use border disputes, Kurdish grievances, or national honour as reasons to invade Ottoman territory. Shi'i Muslims were strong

7. For the first time in a century, the governor of Basra appointed in 1850 was allowed to correspond directly with Constantinople, but was still subordinate financially and militarily to Baghdad: *PGP*, 6:26–27.

8. Jones Brydges, *Account*, 2:186–91; Castlereagh, *Correspondence*, 170.

9. For the debate about mail routes, see Ingram, "From Trade to Empire," 282–84.

numerically in Iraq, and the Persians had ruled Baghdad for a time before the Ottoman conquests, recaptured it between 1623 and 1638, and threatened it again in 1743. Baghdad remained a Persian aspiration, especially since gains here could compensate for ongoing territorial losses to Russia on their northern frontier.[10] Another potential Persian grievance was the treatment of Shiʻa who made annual pilgrimage to the holy sites of Karbala and Najaf south of Baghdad. The Arab tribes were also a constant problem, particularly because of their reluctance to pay tribute to the pashalik. The powerful Muntafiq and Kaʻb, which controlled most of the fertile ground around Basra and the Gulf, were more of a headache than most, but their support was needed if the pashalik was to defeat incursions from the puritanical Wahhabi tribes of Arabia, who had their eyes on rich Baghdadi territory. The Wahhabi particularly detested the veneration of Muslim saints on which Karbala's status rested. If they attacked it, the Persians would have an incentive to invade.

The difficulty lay in knowing how to try to discipline these contending elements without revealing the pashalik's weakness and making it more vulnerable to the Persians, the Wahhabi, the French, or the Russians. The doom-laden letters of Jones, and his successors in Baghdad over the next fifty years, constantly asserted that the regime was so weak that this problem was almost insoluble. However, the situation also offered opportunities for Britain to strengthen its position, and for Jones to promote his career, by offering protection, advice, and threats to the various parties, and by mediating between them.

As soon as he arrived in Baghdad, Jones impressed on Sulayman that he must husband the resources of the pashalik and avoid counterproductive campaigns against its enemies, which would expose its weakness and assist French attack. The immediate problem was the Wahhabi on the southern flank of the province, in Hasa, against whom Sulayman had sent forces. Jones urged a peaceful settlement with them, as he did again when there was renewed tension in 1800 and 1801 over money that the Wahhabi claimed from Sulayman. Jones asserted that the British representatives in Basra—he, Manesty, and previously William Digges Latouche—had all managed to cooperate with them. They had sent their leaders small presents from Basra so as to prevent interference with the EIC mail; they also emphasised British power in order to impress them. Jones told Sulayman to try to persuade the Wahhabi to be allies in the campaign to defend Muslim Egypt from the French. He also hoped for an agreement between Baghdad and Persia, to defend the Shiʻi holy places in Karbala and Najaf against the risk of Wahhabi attack. This agreement would, naturally, be brokered by himself, and would show the ability of the British to bring peace to the region.[11]

10. [McNeill], "Invasion of India," 278.
11. Jones Brydges, *Account*, 2:15; Jones letters, 1801, WP, IOR H/475 509, 513, 605.

Jones urged Sulayman, and the British and Indian governments, to understand the seriousness of the Wahhabi threat. If Sulayman tried to fight them, he would lose, because they represented a more vital force than he did, and might easily overwhelm the pashalik. Since their campaign of 1798–99, the Wahhabi now "prevail from Medina to Damascus from Damascus to Bussora [Basra] from Bussora to Muscat." They had "immense resources and means of injury" and a determination to promote them. Like Muhammad, they had come out of the Arabian Desert, where they had lived face to face with God, far from the trappings of civilisation. They understood Islam better than the self-interested ulema of Constantinople, who wrongly criticised them for fabricating new superstitions. Their appeal was simple and their moral code unwavering: they stood for the essence of Islam, "the same temper of mind [that] overturned in 632 on the banks of the Tigris a power better established and more formidable than that of the Pasha of Bagdad." They stood against Ottoman ruling class amorality; they exposed the emptiness of the sultan's claim to defend Islam as its caliph. So they imperilled the whole basis of the Ottoman Empire.[12] Jones's view that the Wahhabi represented a genuine spiritual force, an elemental type of Islam, and a bracing challenge to modern corruptions, was shared by the idiosyncratic traveller Thomas Hope, who almost certainly met Jones in Iraq in 1794 and later set out similar opinions in his fantastical but quasi-biographical novel *Anastasius*.[13]

Rather to Jones's surprise, Sulayman seemed to listen to him and sent a peace embassy to the Wahhabi.[14] However, Sulayman was now old and ill, and in the course of 1801 surrendered control of the pashalik to forces led by his son-in-law Ali, of whom Jones disapproved. As a result, Jones lost what influence he had. The Baghdad regime was annoyed by Jones's failure to support its conflict with Muscat, and by his closeness to Persia. In 1801, Malcolm returned from Persia via Baghdad and told Jones to be more assertive, so he celebrated the visit of the queen mother of Persia by having two fifers and drummers accompany the parade of his sepoy guards twice daily. The pasha's ministers—apparently egged on by the French consul—forbade this noise, on the grounds that it disturbed Muslim prayers. Jones, fearing a revival of French influence in Baghdad, retaliated by unwisely trying to get Sulayman's French doctor removed. All Jones could offer the aged pasha instead was three pairs of fleecy stockings "made purposely to come up to the top of the thighs"; they seem not to have done the trick. In June 1801, Sulayman asked

---

12. Jones to Willis, early 1801, WP, IOR H/475 513 (quotations). In November 1802, he assumed that the Empire would collapse: Castlereagh, *Correspondence*, 173–77. For similar views expressed in retirement, see Jones Brydges, *Account*, 2:8–9, 107–14.

13. Hope, *Anastasius*, 3, chaps. 5–8; Jones Brydges, *Account*, 2:193–94, on the book.

14. Jones to Duncan, Mar. 1, 1801, WP, IOR H/475 509.

for Jones's removal from Baghdad to Basra, a request that Jones blamed on Ali's influence.[15]

In April 1802, what Jones feared came to pass. The Wahhabi overran Karbala, sacked the Shi'i holy sites and massacred five thousand inhabitants and pilgrims.[16] This spelled disaster on several fronts. It was a mortal blow for old Sulayman Pasha, and Ali won the struggle to succeed him. Jones toyed with supporting his rival, who played his hand very badly, and left Jones with little choice but to support Ali; in fact he helped in the forwarding of Ali's bribe of £60,000 to Constantinople.[17] Meanwhile, the ulama in Persia pressed for immediate war against the Ottomans, which only a crisis in Khorasan averted.[18]

Over the next three years, the threats from the Wahhabi and Persians grew. The Wahhabi attack on Mecca and Medina in May 1803 made Jones fear the collapse of the empire. In 1805, he estimated that Baghdad had lost 40 per cent of its commercial revenue in seven years, owing to the damage to confidence resulting from successive Wahhabi incursions.[19] In July 1804, they threatened Basra, a provocation designed to humiliate Ali. He insisted on revenge, as did the Porte. In late 1804, the long-planned attack finally happened, and predictably was a failure, leaving Jones all the more critical of Ali's vulgarity, stupidity, and venality. He was now even more convinced that the Wahhabi would bring the empire down. He also expected a Persian invasion under the pretence of guarding the sacred tombs, or else a Wahhabi conquest of Basra and then an attack on Persia.[20]

The main aim of these warnings was to get his superiors to make a commitment to the region and to himself. In 1802, he asked for a British military force to protect Baghdad so as to deter an attack from the Wahhabi, the Persians, or anyone else.[21] After all, "if the passage of the Euphrates had been properly guarded Darius might have been saved" from Alexander at Gaugamela (near Mosul) in 331 BCE.[22] Whether the ultimate enemy was to be France from the west or Russia from the north, "India one day or other will be fought for on the banks of the Tigris or Euphrates; and the victory most

15. Jones to Inglis, Oct. 23, 1800, WP, IOR H/474 502; Jones to Elgin, June 7, 1801, WP, IOR H/477 263; Jones to Duncan, Aug. 30 and Sept. 10, 1801, WP, IOR H/478 193, 239; Elgin to Hawkesbury, July 6, 1801, FO 78/32 139; Elgin to Jones, Aug. 3, 1801, IOR G/17/7 395.

16. For some responses, see Bonacina, *Wahhabis*, 61–62, 67, 70n. Authorities, including those cited by Bonacina, differ on the year of the massacre, but Jones's letters indicate that it was 1802, not 1801.

17. Jones Brydges, *Account*, 2:28–29, 204–10.

18. Ingram, "From Trade to Empire," 298.

19. Castlereagh, *Correspondence*, 402.

20. Castlereagh, 309–12, 364, 393; Jones Brydges, *Account*, 2:182–84.

21. Castlereagh, *Correspondence*, 173–77.

22. Jones, 1802, quoted in Ingram, "From Trade to Empire," 295.

probably will rest with the enemy or us, according as this government shall be managed by us in the interim."[23] Failing to get anywhere with these strategic arguments, he thought that the EIC might listen to economic ones. He suggested that a Wahhabi empire would damage the Bombay revenue, since "a people whose whole dress consists in a dirty, greasy clout about their heads, and a homespun woollen cloak on their backs" would not buy Indian goods.[24] No one in London or Bombay took the bait: Britain could certainly not declare a protectorate over Baghdad during the Peace of Amiens, while between 1803 and 1806 the need to woo Russia meant avoiding any aggressive British moves in Baghdad or Persia.[25]

Jones had no friends, only a surfeit of enemies. Neither Ali nor the Porte saw the need for a European presence in Baghdad. Ali also disliked Jones's attempts to persuade Constantinople to interfere with his independence of action. The ulema in Baghdad were suspicious of Jones's appeasement of the Wahhabi. In London, Dundas left office in 1801, and few others saw the point of an agent in Baghdad, especially since Jones's rows with Ali jeopardised the harmonious operation of the mail, the formal reason for his appointment.[26] The cautious, economy-minded Bombay government was quite content with having a man at Basra. Nor did the vain Wellesley see the value of a Baghdad position, since his own genius had secured an understanding with the shah, who was surely a more significant figure in protecting India from attack. Jones's most formidable enemy was probably Manesty in Basra, who resented and tried to ignore his appointment, and continued direct contact with Ali himself. In 1804, Manesty felt that Jones had not supported him during his own difficulties with Ali, which he smoothed over with judicious bribes. Meanwhile, Jones lost the support of the influential Baghdad Armenians over a testamentary dispute. Manesty appointed a powerful Armenian as his agent in Baghdad, and Ali encouraged the latter's pretensions to be the EIC representative instead of Jones; he gave him public distinctions and help with the mail.[27] By early 1805, Jones was practically confined to his house; in February 1806, he left Baghdad for good, after Ambassador Arbuthnot advised that the Porte could not protect him.[28]

The failure of Jones's mission shows that Britain lacked the respect in either Baghdad or Constantinople that was necessary to secure his position. There was no history of British influence in this great Muslim city; nor was there yet much agreement in Britain or India on its strategic significance.

23. Jones, quoted in Ingram, 299.

24. Castlereagh, *Correspondence*, 292–93.

25. Ingram, *Britain's Persian Connection*, 77.

26. On the problems with the mail, see Yapp, "East India Company Residency," 333–35.

27. For this dispute, see Yapp, 331–33, and Jones to Duncan, Mar. 16 and 24, 1805, WP, IOR H/479 501, 527.

28. Arbuthnot to Mulgrave, Nov. 16, 1805, FO 78/46 211.

Nonetheless, when Britain and the Ottoman Empire went to war in 1807, Ali in Baghdad made clear that his pashalik would not follow the Porte. This was a triumph for the cynical but effective Manesty at Basra, who noted that, with his help, the sultan's order directing Ali to seize British property and prevent British commerce within the pashalik remained a dead letter.[29] Baghdad saw itself as a separate entity with discrete economic interests, and it did not want a British bombardment of Basra. Britain kept a strong naval squadron in the Gulf throughout 1807, consisting of HMS *Fox* and eight EIC cruisers.[30] Malcolm had not been wrong to argue that naval and commercial power in the Gulf would shape Baghdad's policy. British regional influence was potentially a lot more significant than the unfortunate experience of Harford Jones suggested.

Claudius Rich: Pomp and Mediation in an Indian Outstation

The collapse of British relations with the Ottoman Empire in 1806–7, followed by the Franco-Russian Treaty of Tilsit, made diplomacy at Constantinople impossible. In any case, between 1806 and 1808, there was an unprecedented internal political crisis in the Ottoman capital. Two sultans and five grand viziers were overthrown in three major changes of government; there was no coherent foreign policy. It took until January 1809 even to sign a peace treaty between Britain and the sultan, and that was achieved only by threats that British naval power in the Mediterranean might cut Ottoman connections with their Balkan and Egyptian territories, leading to successful revolutions in both.[31] After that, the Foreign Office continued to encourage Russia to split with France, and so would do nothing to support the Ottomans, who were now in renewed conflict with Russia, which in turn continued to moot partition schemes. When British representatives returned to Constantinople in 1809, they tried to get the Ottomans and Persians to combine against France, a strategy that was doomed to fail, given their visceral enmity, and Britain's simultaneous attempts to pacify Russia.[32] Despite endless fears and conspiracy theories on all sides, eastern diplomacy had reached stalemate, with no power wishing to make a decisive move against any other. The only reassurance for Britain was the continued inability of France and Russia to work together to any effect.

So Britain had to pursue its interests in the Middle East by direct action. In 1807, France had signed a draft treaty with Persia that, if ratified, would

29. Manesty to Bombay, Sept. 20, 1807, IOR F/4/259/5659.

30. C. Low, *Indian Navy*, 1:318–19.

31. Adair, *Negotiations*, 1:43.

32. Adair, 1:249; 2:72, 169, 179.

allow France to occupy two Gulf islands—Qishm and Kharaq—in the event of an Anglo-Persian war. A twenty-nine-strong French mission headed by General Gardane spent 1808 in Persia trying to consolidate these ties. The fear of a French alliance with Persia led Britain to strengthen its Gulf residency at Bushehr: Nicholas Hankey Smith and the young soldier-linguist Robert Taylor were sent there in 1807. It also led to the competing missions of Jones and Malcolm to Persia between 1807 and 1809, one sent by London and the other by Calcutta, without consultation. They cost a great deal of money, and generated much mutual hostility and recrimination between the British and Indian governments. Malcolm hoped to intimidate the Persians into giving the British concessions, including a Gulf island, whereas Jones pursued an Ottoman-Persian common front against Christian imperialist threats from France or Russia. Neither achieved anything of note—though Jones secured a draft treaty—and Anglo-Persian relations remained in flux for some years. Nonetheless, both missions grasped the importance of the pasha of Baghdad. Jones was given permission to guarantee him against a French attack, and to explore the willingness of the Wahhabi to cooperate in repelling a French invasion. Malcolm was similarly authorised to offer him an alliance against a French or Russian attack, if the shah had sided with either of those powers.[33]

Britain's lack of allies, or of influence at Constantinople, underlined the importance of a local political presence. The region was now more vulnerable than the Red Sea, given the risk of French or Russian aggression, and the rumours of French influence in Baghdad as well as Persia. It was agreed in London and India that Jones's vacant post must be filled. There was a hope that Manesty at Basra wished to retire, but if he did not, he needed to be reined in. He had damaged his standing in Bombay by ignoring its—as ever cautious—instruction of neutrality in the crisis at Baghdad that had followed the assassination of Ali in August 1807 (an instruction given in order not to damage the peace talks at Constantinople). He had supported the successful claim of Ali's nephew Sulayman because he had assurances that the latter would maintain Ali's policy of support for British interests and neutrality in the Ottoman war. This meant opposing the party that planned to impose a figure from Constantinople, Yusuf, whom Manesty assumed must necessarily have French support. (Formerly grand vizier, Yusuf had commanded the Ottoman assault on Egypt in 1800–1801.)[34]

In replacing Jones, Bombay looked for someone unconnected with Manesty's local network, and more easily controlled from India. In January 1808,

33. For the missions, see Ingram, *Britain's Persian Connection*, chaps. 5–6, and J. Kelly, *Britain and the Persian Gulf*, 86–93. For Jones on the Muslim front, see Jones Brydges, *Account*, 1:xix–xx. When he returned to Constantinople, Ambassador Adair also formed the view that it was essential for Britain to cultivate Baghdad: Adair, *Negotiations*, 2:298.

34. See IOR F/4/259/5659. For background, see Nieuwenhuis, *Politics and Society*, 77.

Claudius Rich was chosen. Rich was only twenty-three, and an illegitimate son, probably of the Irish soldier Sir James Cockburn. He had demonstrated extraordinary linguistic talents during his upbringing in Bristol, including learning Arabic from a local library and a visiting Turkish merchant. Recommended to the EIC by the missionary Joshua Marshman, his precocity was recognised first by a cadetship and then by the post of oriental secretary to the non-Arabist Lock on his appointment as consul in Egypt in 1804. Rich, even more than Lock, symbolised the new British approach to the East—one that prioritised an intelligent understanding of local political realities, and disdained Levant Company mercantilism and protection rackets. After Lock's death, he sent himself to college at Smyrna to perfect his Turkish, copied the Qur'an, and spent time in Alexandria in 1806 with Missett and Briggs, where he learnt horsemanship and the use of the scimitar. During the war of 1807, he travelled undercover in the empire, impersonating a Georgian Turk at Damascus so charmingly that (he claimed) an eminent local merchant offered him his daughter in marriage.[35] Arriving at Bombay, his linguistic and antiquarian orientalism won him a similar success at the home of the resident liberal intellectual there, the eminent Whig historian Sir James Mackintosh. Mackintosh had gone to Bombay as recorder in an attempt to erase his debts, and presided over the town's cultural life. Within weeks, Rich was engaged to marry Mackintosh's eighteen-year-old daughter Mary, while Mackintosh, as ever a consummate fixer, had secured his appointment to Baghdad. Mackintosh convinced Bombay's governor Jonathan Duncan that Rich would be a cultured, intelligent diplomat, not a corrupt merchant; his terms of appointment forbade him to trade.

Mackintosh imbued Rich with his grand Whiggish historical perspective. He saw Baghdad and India as major players in a desperate world-historical struggle for the preservation of liberty. At Tilsit, Tsar Alexander had sold the West into slavery and allowed Bonaparte to sweep towards India in his attempt to establish a universal monarchy that would crush freedom. Mackintosh regarded the Jones and Malcolm missions to Persia as foolish, because Persia, like Constantinople, was lost to tyranny.[36] The Persians and the French were partners in crime; Britain must make Baghdad a place of British influence against them. It should be an independent outstation of India. If the Persians took Baghdad and Basra, as Mackintosh feared, they would dominate the Gulf. The pashalik must be kept independent, nominally subject to the Ottomans but in practice, given their death spiral, reliant on British naval power and trade. In 1808, Mackintosh articulated the principle that became a

35. [Burgess], *Motives*, 52–54; Rich, *Narrative of a Residence*, 1:xv–xxiii. Rich is usually supposed to have been born in 1786 or 1787, but on March 11, 1811, his wife recorded him completing his twenty-seventh year: Mary Rich to Maitland Erskine, RPBL, 80751 245.

36. Mackintosh, *Memoirs*, 1:376–78, 391.

cornerstone of British regional policy for decades to come: Baghdad must be held by a weak chief whom the British could influence, rather than by a strong ruler with ambitions.[37] As the young couple ascended the Tigris towards Baghdad, he compared their journey to the inspiring voyage of Alexander's general Nearchus against the Persians of old. Mixing his historical metaphors, he hoped that Mary, on arrival in the city, would take the seat of the Assyrian queen Semiramis, another scourge of Eastern tyrants.[38]

Claude and Mary shared Mackintosh's assumption that the collapse of Ottomanism was imminent.[39] Moreover, when they arrived at Baghdad there was no proper British representation at Constantinople, and therefore no hope of persuading the Porte to sway young Sulayman. So Rich aimed to treat him as an independent ruler, and overawe him by pomp and expenditure, as the British did with Indian princes. At the heart of Rich's policy in Baghdad for the next thirteen years was desperately magnificent spending, on lavish presents and public display. After his row with Sulayman in 1809, when he was forced out of Baghdad to live in a tent, he spent 80,000 piastres on presents to recover his position.[40] In August 1809, Mary asserted that "a good deal of show and state is needed among the Turks; if a person brings you a plate of fruit as a present you cannot offer him less than six rupees." "A certain number of mounted servants are essential for going out" as it "dazzles and pleases" the inhabitants; Rich insisted, therefore, on a guard of European hussars as well as Indian sepoys.[41] A visitor, James Silk Buckingham, noted that "every thing belonging to the Residency was calculated to impress ideas of great respect on the minds of the inhabitants," owing to Rich's bodyguard, "large and commodious yacht," and substantial stud of "choice" horses.[42] Mary insisted on getting the best Irish linen for Claude's outfits, well-made shoes from China, a piano from Calcutta, the latest patent flute, and for herself "a fine antelope, two herons of different kinds [and] a beautiful greyhound . . . I am also looking out for a young lion."[43] The Bombay government, headed by its parsimonious governor Jonathan Duncan, was shocked and appalled by this extravagance. Already by 1811, relations with Rich were irredeemably bad because of it: every subsequent attempt to get his finances on an even keel failed, and he was £2,000 in debt after ten years in Baghdad.[44]

37. Mackintosh, 1:422, 433.

38. Mackintosh, 1:424–25.

39. Mary Rich to Maitland, Mar. 18, 1810, RPBL, 80751 147.

40. Turner, *Journal of a Tour*, 3:491–92.

41. Mary Rich to Maitland, Aug. 17, 1809, and June 27, 1811, RPBL, 80751 100, 292.

42. Buckingham, *Travels in Mesopotamia*, 2:210–11.

43. Mary Rich to her family, Dec. 26, 1808, RPBL, 80751, 63. For the clothes, see M. Finn, "Material Turns in British History," 13–14.

44. See, e.g., Rich to Erskine, June 26, 1811, RPBL, 80751, 288.

Rich felt assertion was necessary in order to defeat a great French threat at Baghdad. He thought that Manesty, whom he despised as a self-interested merchant dependent on Armenian loans and corruption, was far too complacent about Sulayman's friendliness. Rich feared that the pasha owed his appointment mainly to Sébastiani's influence at Constantinople. In 1809, he was aghast that the French agent, "a contemptible bankrupt native of Aleppo," was allowed to celebrate Napoleon's birthday with a dinner, whereas Sulayman was so annoyed by Rich's own dinner for George III's birthday that he threatened to behead Rich's dragoman.[45] Rich became very alarmed by French plans to build up a proper consulate at Baghdad; in November 1809, he noted the presence of four French agents in the city. As an assertive Malcolmite, he was also annoyed by Jones's unwillingness to threaten the shah of Persia, and Minto's refusal to occupy Kharaq in pursuit of the same object; this appeasement policy seemed to leave French influence dominant in Tehran.[46] Once a British ambassador, Robert Adair, returned to Constantinople in 1809, Rich managed to get a firman from the sultan reprimanding Sulayman for his ill treatment of him, and permitting the Baghdad residency to beat drums and celebrate the king's birthday. Accordingly, the celebration of June 1810 became an extraordinary junket for the whole town, with three separate dinners for Ottomans, Persians, and Arabs, and "Jugglers Dancers Wrestlers and Singers amusing a court full of people." Mary was now in danger of getting carried away. "If ever we wish to make them our own subjects . . . the Resident has prepared them to love their new Padshah—as long as we secure them feasting and stuffing every king's birthday, they will be some of the best subjects under the Crown."[47]

From 1810, Rich's influence and mood dramatically improved. All his rivals disappeared. The appeasing Jones was removed from Persia. Rich, Mackintosh, and the economy-minded Bombay government conspired to arrange the dismissal from Basra of the "madman" Manesty and his wife, the "dirty Armenian drab" with a "bad skin little colour and a face the size of a full moon."[48] Once the Anglo-Ottoman peace treaty was signed, it was agreed that Britain needed only one representative in Turkish Arabia, and the EIC dismissed Manesty after a review of his various mistakes over twenty-five years. Failing to adjust to life in Britain, he killed himself in 1812 while staying in the house of Sir Charles Forbes.[49] Meanwhile, the designated French consul Corançez never turned up at Baghdad, and his brother died of dysentery shortly after arriving. Though the Corançez brothers were eventually replaced, and French

45. Rich to Adair, Aug. 2, 1809, IOR L/P&S/9/74 68.

46. See Mary Rich to Maitland, Oct. 30, 1808, and Oct. 27, 1809, RPBL, 80751 47, 115.

47. Mary Rich to Maitland, June 1 and 4, 1810, RPBL, 80751 166.

48. Mary Rich letters, Feb.–Mar. 1808, Dec. 26, 1808, and March 11, 1811, RPBL, 80751 7, 63, 245.

49. See Wright, "Samuel Manesty," 159.

representatives at Baghdad occasionally caused trouble thereafter, the combination of the loss of Mauritius in 1810 and the all-consuming struggle with Russia in 1811–12 meant that France never subsequently threatened British dominance at Baghdad. One French consul admitted that the pashas of Baghdad were "princes of India."[50] James Silk Buckingham claimed that "Mr Rich was universally considered to be the most powerful man in Bagdad, next to the Pasha."[51] When Rich was made sole British resident in Turkish Arabia in 1810, he had the choice of stationing himself in Basra or Baghdad. Naturally, the Bombay government hoped he would choose Basra. Naturally, he chose Baghdad.[52]

Rich now reversed his feelings about the Porte. In 1809, he had been so weak locally that he had had to apply to Adair in Constantinople to force Sulayman to take him seriously. In 1810, he realised that only through bullying the Porte might France get enough influence in Baghdad to undermine his own local dominance. The result was a comical misunderstanding, which turned serious. The Porte disliked Sulayman's pretensions to independence and his remissness in settling Ali's debts in Constantinople, and decided to replace him with someone more compliant. Adair, having only recently received copious accounts from Rich of Sulayman's preference for France, was keen to cooperate. He helped Halet Efendi, who was now emerging as the most powerful minister at the Porte, when Halet decided to go to Baghdad and remove Sulayman. On arrival there, Halet proposed to Rich that they should agree on an alternative to Sulayman, only to discover that Rich now wanted to support him. This was because he feared that Britain and the Ottomans would soon be at war again. If so, he was confident that Sulayman would remain friendly to Britain, while a nominee of Constantinople might do the bidding of France, which "by a simple word might at any time procure our entire expulsion from Western Asia."[53] So Rich remained aloof. Halet set to work with Sulayman's local rivals, the Baban Kurdish leader Abdurrahman and the Jalili pasha of Mosul, and with Halet's Jewish finance network in Baghdad. They arranged for Sulayman to be waylaid and beheaded by Shammar Arabs.[54]

The murder of Sulayman, immediately after Rich had spent so much money and time courting him, had a lasting effect on him. He never trusted the Porte again, and opposed its subsequent attempts to interfere in Iraqi politics. Ottoman ministers wanted the pashalik to be dependent on Constantinople, but he felt that this was in no one's interests except their own short-term one. The problem was apparent from the way that Halet had operated.

50. Nieuwenhuis, *Politics and Society*, 82.

51. Buckingham, *Travels in Mesopotamia*, 2:211.

52. [Malet], *Précis*, 104–5.

53. Rich narrative, Sept. 1, 1810, IOR L/P&S/9/77 248.

54. Nieuwenhuis sees the involvement of the Jalili as revenge for Sulayman's meddling in Mosul: *Politics and Society*, 106–7. For Halet's network in Baghdad, see Philipp, *Acre*, 92.

He had practised the old policy of divide and rule, encouraging the pashalik's rivals to strengthen themselves at Sulayman's expense. In particular, he had played on the aspirations of Abdurrahman, who hoped that by working with the Porte he could get security for his Kurdish fiefdom in Sulaimaniya. Abdurrahman appears to have toyed with taking the pashalik of Baghdad himself, but instead agreed with Halet to nominate the *kaymakam*, Abdullah Aga, who was appointed. Rich was despondent, feeling that this outcome gave the Baban Kurds, and by extension the Persians, more power over Baghdad than they had ever had, thus weakening the independence, revenues, and power of the pashalik.[55]

This was Rich's introduction to the politics of Kurdish Sulaimaniya, which were to become his major preoccupation. The province of Sulaimaniya lay just inside the border with Persia, 165 miles north-east of Baghdad, and was ruled by the Baban clan. The town of Sulaimaniya was a recent foundation, built as his capital by the new Baban leader Ibrahim in 1784. It was named in honour of Sulayman of Baghdad, but in fact it was nearer the Persian regional centre of Kermanshah. The Sulaimaniya province was rich and fertile. Baghdad needed to control it on account of its wealth as well as the hardy mountain troops that it might supply for external campaigns; in 1813, it was thought able in principle to contribute half the revenues of government, and a body of four thousand horsemen.[56] However, these same troops could easily defend themselves against Baghdadi aggression, and the Babans had become expert at playing off the Ottoman and Persian regimes in order to maintain their independence from both. In return, Baghdad and the Persians both encouraged factionalism within the extended Baban family, and took up exiled siblings who could then return to Sulaimaniya to lead a revolt. An early task for any new Baghdad pasha was to try to discipline the Baban leadership into submission, yet too much pressure on them would force them into the hands of Persia. In 1802, Ali Pasha of Baghdad had deposed Ibrahim in favour of one rival, but shortly afterwards another, Abdurrahman, built up support from a base in Persia. After Ali's unsuccessful skirmish with Persia in 1806, Abdurrahman took power in Sulaimaniya. His aggressive pursuit of independence forced Sulayman to attack him in late 1808, forcing him back into Persia. When he returned in 1810, it was with the connivance of Persia as well as the Porte. After the overthrow of Sulayman, therefore, Rich feared that Abdurrahman, and Persian interests, might become too powerful in the pashalik.

The conundrum of Sulaimaniya was almost insoluble, given the weakness of Baghdad. The saving grace was that it gave Rich the chance of influence

---

55. Rich, in *Narrative of a Residence* (1:95–97), quotes Abdurrahman as prudently declining the offer, though he appears earlier to have sought it: see Atmaca, "Negotiating Political Power," 66. See Mary Rich to Maitland, Sept. 11, 1811, RPBL, 80751 305.

56. Hine to Nepean, Dec. 10, 1813, IOR L/P&S/9/77 285.

by mediation. It was a manifest British interest to secure peace on the border and to establish a workable relationship between the pasha and Abdurrahman that would minimise the threat of war with Persia—and prevent Russia or France from using its influence in Tehran to affect the local balance of power. Rich was pleased to note that Abdullah and Abdurrahman both seemed anxious to seek his own advice. In fact, Abdullah attacked and briefly deposed the latter in 1812, and the Persians counter-attacked on Abdurrahman's behalf, but this was a half-hearted affair, and an agreement was reached in autumn 1812, brokered by Rich, by which Abdurrahman was reinstated in Sulaimaniya and peace was secured with Persia. Abdurrahman's death the following year allowed peace to last for the time being.[57]

However, the south of the pashalik was also endangered—by the continuing incursions of the Wahhabi and the growth of piracy in the Gulf. These threats diverted trade from Basra to Bushehr and further diminished revenues. Moreover, the Muntafiq Arabs claimed that dealing with the Wahhabi threat was so demanding that they could not also pay tribute to Baghdad. In late 1812, Abdullah's charismatic young rival Said left Baghdad to live and plot with the Muntafiq. Said was the handsome twenty-one-year-old son of the revered Sulayman the Great; he had a popular following in Baghdad because he promised to restore the stability and prosperity of the 1780s and 1790s. Claude and Mary had developed close personal ties—rather too close—with Said's mother and other family members. Early in 1812, Abdullah had tried to have Said murdered, but his life and property were saved by Rich's intervention, at the request of his mother. When Rich brought him back to the British residency, the popular clamour for Said and "his preserver" was such that Mary thought "we might do what we liked with the people, this one action has so gained their hearts." Bombay took a different view, telling Rich off for his partisanship.[58] He also brokered a treaty between Abdullah and Said in which he personally guaranteed Said's pledge of loyalty to the regime. Shortly afterwards, Said broke the pledge to Abdullah and Rich, and decamped to the Muntafiq. In early 1813, Abdullah led an expedition against Said and the Muntafiq, depleting treasury resources further. Abdullah was captured, strangled, and decapitated, and Said became pasha.[59]

A few months later, Rich felt that, though Said's power remained very fragile, the major threats to regional stability were under control. French influence had been decimated, especially after Napoleon's humiliating retreat from Moscow, while enough local balance had been secured among Said, the Babans, and the Muntafiq to minimise the dangers of interference from the Porte or Persia. In autumn 1813, he took three months' leave on health grounds. To the

57. Rich to Bombay, June 29 and Sept. 20, 1812, IOR L/P&S/9/77 262, 267.
58. Mary Rich to Maitland, May 19, 1812, and Mar. 10, [1813], RPBL, 80752 11, 62.
59. Rich to Liston, Feb. 27, 1813, IOR L/P&S/9/77 269.

further anger of Bombay, he managed to stretch this to over two years, during which he enjoyed the fine society and musical sophistication of Constantinople, Vienna, Italy, and Paris. He returned to Baghdad in spring 1816, not because he wanted to, but because Bombay would not give him the promotion at home that he had expected (Mackintosh had long since left for home).

He came back to discover that Said had dissipated his popularity by incompetence, cronyism, and inability to manage the endless local tensions. He had failed to discipline the Shammar Arabs in northern Mesopotamia, which led to widespread brigandage, creating merchant hostility to his government. He had lost the support of the Muntafiq, because he could not continue the financial benefits that he had promised them. He had failed to challenge Persia's increasing control over the new Baban leader in Sulaimaniya, Abdurrahman's son Mahmud. In September 1816, Rich thought that either the loss of Sulaimaniya to Persia, or a war over it, was almost inevitable.[60] Not surprisingly, the Porte turned against Said and ordered his removal. In February 1817, his brother-in-law Davut took up arms against him, recreating the same alliance of the Baban Kurds, the pasha of Mosul, Halet in Constantinople, and the Persians that had seen off Sulayman in 1810. Said was beheaded, along with some other members of Sulayman's family, and Davut took his place as pasha. This was a highly distressing business for Rich and Mary, given their continuing ties to the "unfortunate women throwing themselves at our feet and beseeching us to save a husband, son or brother from death and the most horrible torture." Rich had to stay neutral during the coup, but his dislike of Davut was common knowledge.[61]

Rich's main concern was that Davut seemed to be the nominee of the Porte, and governed in its interests, in contravention of the proudly independent Mamluk tradition that Said had inherited from his father Sulayman. This was indicated by Davut's rapid betrayal of the Babans and Arabs on whom he had depended for his coup. He appointed minions who would do his bidding, and seemed to have no interest in managing the delicate balance of forces in the pashalik. Instead, he made it a priority to find money for the Porte by whatever means came to hand. Rich—and his new assistant Robert Taylor at Basra—felt that whereas previous Mamluk pashas hoped to build up trade with India and the British in order to preserve their practical independence, Davut subordinated this to a policy of iniquitous taxation on any wealthy group "with the sole view of satisfying the rapacious demands of the Porte."[62] This alienated

60. Rich to London, Sept. 29, 1816, IOR L/P&S/9/77 291.

61. Mary Rich to Erskine, Mar. 12, 1817, RPBL, 80752 229. For some background to Davut's coup (based on French reports), see Nieuwenhuis, *Politics and Society*, 16–22.

62. The best statement of this is Taylor's retrospect to Warden, Nov. 9, 1821, IOR F/4/706 471.

all the elements on which the power of the pashalik depended—Kurds, Arabs, and Indian merchants. They expected government to treat them fairly and protect their security. If it did not, then they would seek protection elsewhere, including from the Wahhabi or the Persians. Rich was still concerned that Russia or France could take up Persia, which seemed so resistant to British influence, and then support Persian interests against Baghdad.

Though there was some plausibility to this analysis, Rich was letting his hostility to Davut and the Porte go to his head. His criticism was really of any attempt to manage the Arab and Kurdish tribes without relying on Britain as mediator. In March 1817, Mary asserted—of her husband's influence in Baghdad—that "all parties equally pay court to him."[63] After nine years in Baghdad, Rich had developed a supreme confidence that only British influence could keep the pashalik intact by holding the ring between the various forces within it. He, not Constantinople, understood best what the regime needed. Baghdad would either survive as an Indian outstation, or collapse as a slave of a mercenary and short-sighted Porte.

So Rich set himself the task of conciliating both the Wahhabi and the Baban Kurds, even though he knew it would incur the opposition of Davut. He started with the Wahhabi. In early 1817, he made contact with the Wahhabi leader Abdullah through their secret agents. Abdullah proposed an understanding by which the British would not interfere with his war against the Egyptians. For Abdullah, this would continue his father's friendship with the British; for Rich, the idea of a "permanent alliance" with the Wahhabi was a tantalising prospect, as Abdullah was "undisputed lord of all the interior of Arabia, who possesses a line of coast extending from the Euphrates to the Indian Ocean and the influence of whose power is more or less felt from the Persian Gulf to the shores of the Mediterranean." In September 1817, Rich settled the terms of his proposed alliance with Abdullah. He asked for permission to go as ambassador to Diriyya to make the treaty. It would be a "glorious" personal achievement.[64]

Rich had spectacularly misjudged the situation, and appalled Bombay once more. Abdullah was trying to strengthen himself against an increasingly successful attack from Mehmet Ali of Egypt, which was to destroy his power within a year. The Indian authorities certainly did not want to commit themselves to him. Rich had thought that they might, in order to stop the attacks on British shipping by the Wahhabi's Qasimi allies in the Gulf. Bombay officials were thinking of tackling that problem in a very different way.

63. Mary Rich to Erskine, Mar. 12, 1817, RPBL, 80752 229.

64. Rich to Nepean, Apr. 4, 1817, IOR L/P&S/9/77 297; to London, Sept. 28, 1817, IOR L/P&S/9/77 300; to Erskine, Apr. 10, 1817, RPBL, 80752 237.

The Wahhabi, the Qawasim, and British Sea Power in the Gulf

The Bombay authorities had been concerned about "pirate" attacks on Gulf shipping for over fifteen years. These attacks were generally blamed on the Qawasim (usually called Joasmees by the British), the trading Arabs based at Ras al-Khaimah and Sharjah on the south-eastern Gulf coast, who in the 1760s had also taken territory on the opposite, Persian shore. There was a history of rivalry between the major tribes engaged in trade within and outside the Gulf, and the Qawasim's main aim was to take trade away from the independent port city of Muscat, which had become the major commercial force on the western Indian Ocean seaboard on account of Omani trading connections with India and the East African coast. How far this trade warfare deserved the name "piracy" is a moot point, but Bombay used the term in justifying action to protect its merchants who traded with the Gulf. Since 1686, the EIC had operated a naval force, the Bombay Marine, primarily to safeguard merchant shipping. This was not easy, since the Marine had only a dozen ships, and Bombay was very reluctant to get drawn into disputes between Arab tribes.[65]

After 1798, two problems complicated the politics of the Gulf from Bombay's perspective. One was fear that France might seek to build up local influence, particularly in Muscat, which Napoleon had openly courted in 1799. The other was that the Qawasim began to pay tribute to the Wahhabi and accept their protection, making the latter a force in Gulf politics. The imam of Muscat was determined to keep his independence from all parties, and could see the benefits of playing Britain and France off against each other. Moreover, the climate there was appalling for Britons: four residents died between 1800 and 1809. From 1810, the idea of a permanent agent in Muscat was abandoned in favour of hoping that, now that France had been deprived of its Mauritius naval base, the lucrative trade between Muscat and Bombay would keep the imam sufficiently loyal to Britain. From 1803 onwards, the growth of Wahhabi and Qasimi power on Muscat's borders had offered Britain—or potentially France—the chance to protect it against its rivals. British agents toyed with offering Muscat this protection from time to time, but Bombay decided it did not want to take sides against the Wahhabi. It gravitated instead towards the idea of trying to secure a regional balance between the previously dominant Muscat and its new challengers, which would give the Bombay Marine a recognised role in the Gulf. This became its default policy in the years to come. In 1799, Duncan in Bombay, Jones, and Manesty had already cooperated to apply British pressure to settle a dispute between Baghdad and Muscat.[66] The reso-

65. The best history of the "piracy" issue is Davies's *Blood-Red Arab Flag*.

66. *PGP*, 1:352–57; Kelly, *Britain and the Persian Gulf*, 66, 70; Bhacker, *Trade and Empire*, 41; Seton, *Journals*.

lution of the dispute allowed the imam to turn his attention to another of his objectives—an attack on the wealthy island of Bahrain.[67] This was a reminder that local enmities were almost impossible to suppress entirely.

The imam of Muscat was killed in battle against the Wahhabi in 1804. This increased Qasimi power in the Gulf: they now took Hormuz and Bandar Abbas as well as Qishm, and so controlled its entrance. In December 1804, they captured two ships belonging to Manesty. In Bombay, Duncan ordered his resident in Muscat, David Seton, to cooperate with the new ruler of Muscat against the Qawasim only if he was sure that it would not offend the Wahhabi. Seton coordinated his tactics with Manesty, who was keen to reach an understanding with the Wahhabi, not least to protect his own trading fleet. In February 1806, Seton secured a treaty with the Qawasim in which they pledged to respect EIC property and restore one of Manesty's ships.[68] The presence of a British Gulf squadron during the crisis of 1807 also helped to keep the peace locally. However in late 1808, the Qawasim—now hunting in flotillas of up to twenty vessels—increased their activities, and attacked over a dozen merchant vessels from Bombay, as well as the *Sylph*, a Bombay Marine ship. It was ceremonially purified with rose water and a number of crew members were killed before the rest were rescued. In May 1809, Manesty's country ship *Minerva* was intercepted after a fierce battle. Since some of the attackers were killed, forty-five of the (mostly Lascar Indian) crew had their throats cut in revenge, to the cry of "Allah Akbar." The women on board—the young Armenian wife of Robert Taylor, then stationed at Bushehr, her female servant, and her baby—were taken to Ras al-Khaimah, but then bought by a contact friendly to the British, and finally rescued.[69]

Now Bombay could no longer ignore demands for reprisals, owing to merchant anger and to a concern that the regional balance had swung so far towards the Wahhabi that Muscat's survival was endangered.[70] This was also the period of maximum concern about French influence in Persia, and potential French regional dominance. All this explains the attempt to show British might by bombarding Ras al-Khaimah in November 1809. Even so, Bombay did not want to antagonise the Wahhabi, especially as they seemed likely to become the major regional player if the Ottoman Empire collapsed. The expedition was a purely naval one to teach the Qawasim a lesson: Ras al-Khaimah was badly damaged, but the soldiers then withdrew, in order to avoid clashes with land forces supposedly coming to reinforce it. Though several dozen

67. For the conflict over Bahrain, see Risso, "Competition for Bahrain."

68. Bhacker, *Trade and Empire*, 47–54; Seton, *Journals*, 36, 77; Hawley, *Trucial States*, 99–100.

69. Davies, *Blood-Red Arab Flag*, 349n66; Wellsted, *Travels in Arabia*, 1:247–48; on the rescue of Mrs. Taylor, see Bruce to Bombay, Oct. 17, 1809, IOR P/383 10783.

70. Kelly, *Britain and the Persian Gulf*, 115; Hawley, *Trucial States*, 102.

Qasimi dhows were destroyed, this was only a small percentage of the fleet; the rest had been hidden.[71]

The Wahhabi leader Saud urged a truce and promised not to molest British ships. The truce continued uneasily for six years. Saud died in 1814. By 1815, Qasimi attacks on other traders en route to India, in the Gulf and Indian Ocean, were so frequent that Bombay's naval authority seemed in peril. Moreover, in 1816, the Qasimi chief announced that only English Christians would henceforth be exempt from his attacks, not Indian merchants; this was plainly unacceptable to the traders of Surat and Bombay.[72] In 1818, planning began in India for a major attack on Qasimi strongholds.

This bold step was possible because several things had changed. The Napoleonic Wars had ended without the Ottoman Empire collapsing. Instead, the local balance of forces between the Ottomans and the Wahhabi had shifted in the former's favour, because since 1810 Mehmet Ali of Egypt had been reducing Wahhabi power in the Hijaz and central Arabia. Mehmet Ali had been ordered to attack the Wahhabi by Sultan Mahmud, who probably hoped that a tough struggle in inhospitable climes would preoccupy both sides for many years and limit the danger to the Porte from either of them. By 1816, the Wahhabi were penned into their Arabian heartland, and had no capacity for aggression for the foreseeable future. In view of their new weakness, the greater danger was that continuing disorder in the Gulf would damage Britain's prestige and her local commercial relationships. A continuation of disruption would damage "our interests in Egypt and in the Pachalic of Bagdad but also at the Ottoman Court."[73] In 1818, finally, Mehmet Ali's son Ibrahim reached Diriyya and captured the Wahhabi leaders, including their new chief Abdullah. He was sent to Constantinople with two followers, where they were forced to listen to the lute, against all their principles, and then beheaded. Rich's idea of an alliance with Abdullah was, to the benefit of his reputation, lost to history. Harford Jones later suggested that the "atheist Turk" Mehmet Ali had been able to suppress the Wahhabi threat, temporarily, only by betraying his word on several occasions, and by repeatedly bribing Bedouin tribes.[74]

The destruction of the Wahhabi threat gave the Indian government the chance to strike at the Qawasim, while the end of the Mahratta wars freed up enough soldiers for a powerful expedition. In October 1819, 2,800 European and Indian troops set sail in three warships and seventeen transports under Sir William Grant Keir. They completely destroyed Ras al-Khaimah in December, and the fortifications and larger ships in most of the nearby

71. Hawley, *Trucial States*, 103–4; see the declarations of friendship to the Wahhabi by Seton and Duncan in *PGP*, 5:7.

72. Kelly, *Britain and the Persian Gulf*, 131–35.

73. Evan Nepean, governor of Bombay, 1815, quoted in Kelly, 132.

74. Jones Brydges, *Account*, 2:113–14.

ports, with the loss of five British soldiers and four hundred killed or wounded Qawasim. A garrison of 800 troops was left at Ras al-Khaimah. A treaty was negotiated with the Qawasim, which in the course of 1820 was broadened into a "General Treaty" on Gulf piracy signed by most of the Arab chiefs. This outlawed piracy and bound the chiefs to register their trading ships under the same flag. If they kept the terms of the treaty, they would be free to trade with British ports. Britain would, if necessary, coordinate the punishment of any pirate attacks. This was the beginning of the Trucial system of British protection of the Gulf chiefs, which was to make Britain dominant there. However, the initial intention was for only a limited intervention. The treaty gave the Bombay Marine no right of search; it was implied that tribes would resolve their petty disputes themselves, because of the "state of equilibrium" between them secured by the British.[75]

The general treaty was the idea of Keir's Arabic interpreter, Thomas Perronet Thompson, whose vision for the Gulf went beyond the intimidating bombardments on which his colleagues relied. Thompson was a man of intelligence and sensibility who was looking for a life mission. He aspired to cultivate an Anglo-Muslim friendship built on mutual religious and legal respect. He was the son of a rich Hull merchant in William Wilberforce's network, went to Cambridge, and was then appointed governor of Sierra Leone in 1807 by Wilberforce's evangelical anti-slave-trade friends. He fell out with them over strategy, joined the army, and transferred to India in 1815. He had befriended many Muslims in Sierra Leone, and became an enthusiast for their culture. From 1812, he learned Arabic, because he was convinced that Britain would gain politically and morally from good relations with the peoples of the Middle East as well as North Africa. His studies were influenced by his brother, an enthusiast for bringing steam technology to Egypt, who was killed in Spain in 1813.[76] As a burgeoning radical and strong opponent of Russia, Thompson saw the Arabs as an important support for British liberal power. After the fall of Ras al-Khaimah, he was charged with negotiating the terms on which the shaykhs would agree to British protection. His aim was to create a local "Arab power, owing its existence and continuation to the British government"—through which Britain could keep the existing regional interests (Ottoman, Egyptian, and Qasimi) in check.[77] He drew up the general treaty, and included in it a clause defining the slave trade between Africa and the Gulf as a species of the "plunder and piracy" that the signatories now renounced. The shaykhs signed it in "high mirth," since the main slave trader

75. T. Perronet Thompson to Wilson, Feb. 26, 1820, TPTP, DTH 2/5. For the campaign, see Kelly, *Britain and the Persian Gulf*, 143–66, 208–9.

76. Johnson, *T. Perronet Thompson*, 91–92; Thompson to Lincoln Stanhope, Nov. 5, 1818, TPTP, DTH 2/1. His brother Charles presented a steam engine and engineer to Mehmet Ali in 1810: see Johnson, *T. Perronet Thompson*, 72–73, and chapter 5, p.153.

77. Thompson to Wilson, Feb. 26, 1820, TPTP, DTH 2/5.

in the Gulf was their rival, the imam of Muscat. Thompson anticipated that the treaty would lead to "the pacification of the Persian Gulf, the suppression of piracy, and the introduction of a gallant race of men, the Wahabees, to an improved commercial intercourse with other nations."[78]

When Keir returned to India, he left Thompson in charge of the British garrison, as political agent to the Arab tribes. The garrison was moved to Qishm, reflecting the hope in India that Britain would develop a Gulf island base. Unfortunately, Thompson's hopes for a new era of Arab goodwill were destroyed by a disastrous failure of communication in late 1820. The Bani Bu Arabs of Oman were in conflict with the imam of Muscat, who accused them of piracy in contravention of the treaty and proposed an attack on them. Under pressure from the imam, and lacking instructions from Bombay, Thompson agreed to British troops joining in Muscat's attack, but only after a series of ultimatums to the tribe, which were not answered because they never arrived. Almost four hundred sepoys and European soldiers accompanied the imam's force inland, but were waylaid by the Bani Bu; nearly all were killed. India, aware that it was an "empire . . . of opinion" dependent on British prestige, insisted on a revenge expedition into the interior in January 1821, which left five hundred Arabs dead.[79] Thompson was blamed for the embarrassment and was subjected to an (unsuccessful) court martial trial. His post of political agent to the Arab tribes was abolished, at the insistence of the civil servants of Bombay.

Bombay used the Bani Bu affair for years afterwards to reiterate its traditional policy of not taking sides in Arab tribal conflicts, and of not sending soldiers inland. Such a policy would infallibly create "confederacies against us" by local forces.[80] In 1822, Britain abandoned the Qishm garrison, reluctantly, after a cholera outbreak: the climate was dreadful. Persia had also claimed sovereignty over it, but this was ignored. The navy clung on to a supply depot at Basidu (Bassadore) on the north-western tip of the island, which was treated as British territory.[81] So Britain was forced back on naval power for influence in the Gulf. At first, this meant just occasional maritime patrols. The

---

78. Johnson, *T. Perronet Thompson*, 98. For the "high mirth," see Thompson in 107 Parl. Deb. (3d ser.) (1849) col. 1033. The treaty is in Aitchison, *Treaties*, 12:172–76.

79. See Johnson, *T. Perronet Thompson*, 100–111; Kelly, *Britain and the Persian Gulf*, 159–63, 174–76; Wellsted, *City of the Caliphs*, 1:34–42 (quotation at 34).

80. Warden to Thompson, Jan. 10, 1821, TPTP, DTH 2/13. Crouzet, in *Inventing the Middle East*, discusses Indian thinking about the Gulf in subsequent decades in proper detail.

81. In 1833, Jessop Hulton found there "about fifty hovels, where filth, laziness, and depravity are in high cultivation": Hulton, *South Arabia*, 15. But in 1838, Lt. Whitelock thought that the facilities built for British officers were impressive, though decaying because they were so busy on patrol that they were hardly ever there: Whitelock, "Descriptive Sketch," 178.

1820 treaty had not specified a permanent British naval presence. Only slowly did it become the logical conclusion. Britain was determined to defend the Gulf against France, Russia, Baghdad, Persia, Muscat, and anyone else. The policy of mediating local disputes became entrenched. In 1819, for example, there were renewed discussions in India about making an alliance with the imam of Muscat and allowing him to take Bahrain, but this was shot down as a provocative disruption of the status quo. The implication of the 1820 general treaty was that Britain would take a strong interest in preserving the independence of Bahrain, which was periodically threatened by both Muscat and Persia (and later by the Saudis). As there were no permanently reliable local allies in the Gulf, there was no way of securing a balance of forces, except by active British intervention.

Notwithstanding his previous overtures to the Wahhabi, Claudius Rich was naturally pleased at Britain's naval assertiveness in the Gulf in 1819–20, which strengthened British commercial influence at Basra. Moreover, the removal of the Wahhabi threat left the Muntafiq and Ka'b as the major Arab tribes in southern Iraq, both of which were used to working with British officers at Basra. By the beginning of 1820, therefore, Rich considered that he was in an even stronger position to negotiate a rational balance of power throughout the pashalik of Baghdad—and particularly to reach a humane settlement in its most problematic region, Baban Kurdistan.

"Our Koordistan": The Extraordinary Ambitions of Claudius Rich

On May 8, 1820, Mary Rich had just settled into her tent, which had a beautiful view over the Kurdish city of Sulaimaniya, and was enjoying the sun, the mountains, the linnets, the graceful willows, and the sweet-smelling rose bushes, when the messenger arrived with the post from India and Britain. The packets contained no shortage of improving reading—the *Quarterly* and *Edinburgh* reviews, the *Journal des savans*, the *Journal des dames et des modes*—but above all she was thrilled by the *Evening Mails* from February 1820 reprinting her father's impassioned parliamentary protest at the Libel and Stamp Acts, the latest outrages in the "tyrannical career of our present un-English ministers."[82] Lord Liverpool's repressive measures in London excited her Whiggish indignation as much as they had Sir James Mackintosh's. The desire to fight the battle of liberty was one reason why she was in the tent, accompanying Claude on his mission to the border province.

By early 1820, Claudius Rich was deeply weary of Baghdad politics and desperate to escape to a suitably distinguished post in India, while contemptuous of the small minds who unfortunately decided such things. His health was

82. Rich, *Narrative of a Residence*, 1:364–65.

not good and the idea of another stifling summer in the city seemed insupportable. He conceived instead the idea of escaping to Sulaimaniya to enjoy the mountain air, flowers, and fine natural scenery, and he informed the pasha accordingly. Davut was suspicious, given his own lack of interest in flowers and mountains, and the central significance of Sulaimaniya to the politics of his pashalik, to the acute border tensions between the Ottoman and Persian Empires, and, therefore, to the ability of Britain or other powers to interfere in the region. Moreover, Mary's interest in Kurdistan had been stimulated by her Baghdad friend Salkha Khanum, an influential Baban exile who was the widow of wise old Sulayman Pasha, and who seemed to symbolise a much more measured approach to the Babans than Davut had in mind.[83]

Rich's Sulaimaniya trip led his thoughts in directions that were most uncongenial to Davut. He spent five months in and around the province, during which he fell in love with it and the Baban princes' way of life, which he compared to that of the Scottish clans. Mary's father was a son of Clan Mackintosh who often reminisced about his upbringing on a farm by Loch Ness. In truth, his nostalgia for the Highlands was intermittent, overlaid by a Whiggish taste for worldly and imperial success. Nonetheless, he admired mountain folk, such as the Swiss, as brave and honest defenders of their freedoms.[84] Rich similarly saw something admirable in the Kurds' fighting courage, devotion to feudal princely rank, and love of family. The princes' respect for their (sole) wives and children set them apart from the polygamous, patriarchal Turks. Their pasha Mahmud "loves his wife and children as ardently as the best European could do," rising above the degrading doctrines of Islam that despised "excess of feeling for a woman or child." Kurdish women danced freely and enjoyed domestic comforts rather than the subjection of Baghdad, while sons were at ease before their fathers. Even the mountain lamb was less greasy.[85] By contrast, a trip across the border exposed Rich to the distressing rapacity and vindictiveness of Persia's "ruffian dandies." He felt enormous relief to return to the Alpine purity of "*our* Koordistan": "The very soil seemed to have changed its nature and tint—everything was a mixture of the grand and beautiful." "It will be long ere I again live among people who treat me with so much real kindness and hospitality wherever I may go."[86]

Rich was annoyed by Davut's hostility towards Mahmud, and Mahmud's inability to handle it. The bigger issue was the tension between Davut and Muhammad Ali Mirza Dowlatshah, his Persian equivalent as prince-governor of the Kermanshah region, whose ambitions to succeed his father as shah

83. Rich, 1:3, 331–32.

84. Mackintosh, *Memoirs*, 1:2–3; 2:302, 308. See Gust, "Remembering and Forgetting."

85. Rich, *Narrative of a Residence*, 1:89–90, 117–18, 280–86, 303–4, 325–26 (quotations at 304, 325).

86. Rich, 1:243, 259, 305. Cf. "my own Koordistan': 2:204.

rested on pursuing a virile border policy. He was hoping to tempt Davut into attacking him, which would give him an incentive for a war on Baghdad that he would probably win. Mahmud, all too aware of superior Persian military power along his border, was pursuing his father's general approach of keeping close to Persia and paying tribute to Kermanshah, and Davut was trying to overturn this policy and get the tribute himself. He bestowed patronage on two rival members of Mahmud's family, encouraging their pretensions to Mahmud's position. The Persians responded by sending troops to the border, in case Mahmud needed support. By early 1820, Davut claimed to want peace, but continued to exploit rivalries within the Babans. Mahmud decided to submit to this politicking and to pay Davut subsidy in return for the promise of military support—until the Persians took up one of his rivals. By autumn 1820, Mahmud was spurning Davut and paying tribute to Kermanshah again, and had to send his seven-year-old son there as a hostage.[87]

Rich was clear what the Babans should do. They should form a united family front, and force Davut to take them seriously. Davut should then give Mahmud his unqualified protection. Once the Baban aristocracy had security of land tenure, the fertile country could be rapidly developed. Instead, Davut was able to exploit Baban factionalism, helped by the pious Mahmud's reverent subservience to him as the appointee of the Sunni caliph.[88] Davut's insistence on playing the Babans against each other in the hope of short-term financial gain—tribute money—seemed absurdly short-sighted. As Sunnis, the Babans were natural allies of the Ottomans, but Davut's policy was likely to lead to a Persian attack on the Ottoman Empire, and behind Persia lay potentially Russia and France.[89] Rich was sure that the Porte, unwisely, was pressing Davut to stand up to the hated Persians. In June 1821, Davut sent troops to Sulaimaniya, and in the autumn the Persians invaded.

While Rich was still in Sulaimaniya, Davut and his ministers moved against him and against European influence in the pashalik. The pasha tore up the capitulations that allowed the handful of European merchants in Baghdad—who were under British protection—to trade at lower duties than locals. One, Sturmy, was charged 11.75 per cent instead, while in November the goods of Anton Svoboda, a young Croatian merchant, were seized at the customs house when he refused to pay the increased duties. Davut also instructed his subordinate at Basra to seize goods loaded on the boats of merchants under British protection, claiming that they were destined for Arab tribes in rebellion against the pasha's authority. Hostility to Rich's political interference was

87. Rich to Bombay, Oct. 25, 1819, IOR L/P&S/9/77 306; to Bombay, Sept. 15, 1820, IOR F/4/695/18918.

88. Rich, *Narrative of a Residence*, 1:95–97, 313–15, 323–24.

89. Rich to Bombay, May 20, 1819, IOR F/4/695/18918; to Bombay, Oct. 26, 1819, IOR L/P&S/9/77 306.

generally assumed to be the cause of these announcements, though it may also be relevant that Davut and his treasurer Haji Taleb Aga, "a dark fanatic, and peculiarly inimical to Europeans," were devoted Muslims wary of the social impact of European influence. Davut was to end his life as custodian of the shrine at Medina. Rich also blamed a "Jewish cabal" of merchants who aimed at a local monopoly.[90] Rich had gone out of his way to enhance Davut's suspicions of his activity, by spending four months in Mosul after the five in Sulaimaniya. He visited ancient sites, including the Nineveh mounds, but also the local Jalili pasha, whose loyalty to the Baghdad regime was inherently suspect. Additionally he spent time with the sturdily independent Yazidi, attracted by their liveliness and bravery, so reminiscent of the Kurds. He remarked, rather oddly, that "under the British government much might be made of them."[91] Davut alleged to Constantinople that Rich was in league with the Babans and Persians against him and had now gone to Mosul in order to concert an attack on him with its pasha.[92]

For Rich, however, Davut's anti-British gestures were a pointless protest at his own lack of power. He could get nowhere in Sulaimaniya without British help, nor could he prevent the Muntafiq from controlling Basra and its waterways. In September 1820, when still in Sulaimaniya, and anticipating the seizure of Svoboda's goods, Rich ordered his assistant Robert Taylor at Basra to respond to the seizure by refusing to allow any ship under British colours to land goods at the customs house there until the proclamation was withdrawn. If it was not withdrawn, all those ships were to return to India without unloading. If Indian warships arrived at Basra, they were to help Taylor enforce these orders and protect British property. Taylor implemented this policy. He planned to strike his flag and move the British residency across the Shatt al-Arab to Persian Muhammara, where the shaykh of the Ka'b Arabs had offered him his protection, but the *mütesellim* of Basra begged him to stay. Ships from India started to arrive; Taylor ordered them to anchor off Muhammara and wait. The Baghdad government became alarmed and sent messages to Rich urging a compromise and inviting him to return from Mosul to Baghdad. He did so, demanding the removal of the treasurer, but still felt that Davut was uninterested in recognising Britain's full rights, only in tricking him into lifting the trade embargo. The Basra *mütesellim* who had befriended Taylor was removed and replaced by an assassin of "atrocious character," forcing Taylor to go to Muhammara after all.[93]

90. Unless indicated otherwise, all the material in this and the next three paragraphs comes from the large volume of correspondence on the 1821 crisis at IOR F/4/706. I have footnoted direct quotations separately below. These ones are from Rich to Elphinstone, Nov. 10, 1820, and Mar. 22, 1821, 121, 205.

91. Rich, *Narrative of a Residence*, 2:87.

92. Rich, 2:179–80; C. Alexander, *Baghdad in Bygone Days*, 296.

93. Rich to Elphinstone, Mar. 22, 1821, IOR F/4/706 205.

Unable to get full satisfaction from Davut, Rich declared that he would remove the residency from Baghdad. Before this could happen, one of Davut's officials entered the residency building and told Rich that he was under house arrest, "then rose and standing in the middle of my divan demeaned himself before all my servants in a manner which it was impossible further to tolerate." Rich lost his temper and "snatched up a mace which usually lays by me, at sight of which the offender made a most precipitate retreat."[94] He organised his sepoys and attendants into a house guard and barricaded himself in, comforted by reports that large parts of the town, including a large force of armed Arabs on the other side of the riverbank, would take his side in the event of hostilities. Ottoman soldiers appeared outside the house, though how far he was ever under threat was much disputed.[95] Negotiations ensued: Davut consented in writing to the return of all seized merchant property, and Rich in return lifted the embargo at Basra. However, he remained under watch by Baghdad troops, until a rumour of his appointment to a post in India allowed him to leave Baghdad in May, for Bushehr.

Rich wrote to Bombay that his treatment was "an outrage unprecedented in the annals of Diplomacy" and hoped that "every civilized nation" would support his case in order to "secure their servants employed in distant lands from the malignity of unprincipled barbarians."[96] The Bombay Council, however, was astonished by Rich's decision to declare an embargo at Basra on the basis of an incident involving a Croatian merchant. It was normal to deal with such abuses by reference to Constantinople and retrospective restitution. Nor should he have demanded the removal of the treasurer. Once Rich left Baghdad, Taylor prudently did not reimpose the embargo, which—it became clear—was illegal. Several merchants demanded compensation for the stoppage of their trade and for costs incurred in a pointless voyage. Bombay's legal counsel attempted a tortured defence of Rich's behaviour by assuming that Baghdad was "an Indian state" with which the EIC could go to war. The advocate-general in Calcutta demolished this case, pointing out that it was no such thing, and that as war had not been declared, merchants were entitled to sue Rich for any damages incurred.[97]

The Bombay lawyer's mistake was illuminating, for Rich surely did see Baghdad as an Indian dependency. At heart, the crisis was about the relative influence of Britain and Constantinople on the pashalik. Rich and Taylor believed that Davut had misgoverned it by following the Porte's short-sighted interests. A properly independent ruler would have worked intelligently with

94. Rich to Elphinstone, Mar. 29, 1821, IOR F/4/706 221.
95. Davut denied that he was, to Elphinstone, Jan. 5, 1822, IOR F/4/706 577.
96. Rich to Elphinstone, Mar. 29, 1821, IOR F/4/706 221.
97. Advocate-General Spankie to Swinton, Oct. 2, 1821, IOR F/4/706 435, correcting Woodhouse, Bombay advocate-general, Aug. 9, 1821, 375.

the Babans and the Arabs, and supported Indian and European merchants in order to boost revenues. Davut had oppressed and overtaxed them in order to enrich himself and send tribute to Constantinople. This policy was destroying Baghdad's regional power and leaving it vulnerable to Persia. Since Davut was already at the mercy of Persian troops on the border, stopping the Basra trade was intended to make him submit to India's interests.

In the autumn of 1821, Taylor set out an audacious new plan to secure those interests. He proposed that the British residency should move permanently out of Ottoman territory. A British base should be established elsewhere in the northern Gulf, probably at Kuwait. It would be a "secure and independent entrepot for the Indian trade and a nursery for its ... advantage." "Western Asiatic trade" would be diverted to it. Merchants would arrange with the Arab tribes, especially the Muntafiq, to convey goods direct by cross-country caravan to various ports of Syria and Egypt, in order to avoid the ordeal of submitting to the customs officials of Baghdad and Basra who would not respect the capitulations. British Indian merchant claims could be dealt with swiftly and fairly, rather than be imperilled by a capricious and distant Ottoman government. The merchants of Iraq would prefer it to their own corrupt authorities. This "commanding station in their vicinity, independent of their control," would force the Ottomans to respect British power. The station would be the equivalent of the Gulf island for which Malcolm had been calling for twenty years. Central to Taylor's plans were the Arabs and Armenian merchants, with whom he had worked in Bushehr and Basra since 1807. He claimed that the British had so many supporters locally that they could "overawe the puny power of this government." The Arabs, the "sole masters" in the region, were "our friends," and "unquestionably well disposed" to the idea.[98] Taylor was particularly confident in them after the defeat of the Wahhabi, whose plundering philosophy he blamed for the deterioration of Arab morals in the Gulf. In 1818, he had authored a detailed report on Arab culture there, which helped persuade the Bombay government of the case for the 1819 attack.[99]

The full audacity of this vision was obscured because Rich unexpectedly fell victim to virulent cholera. Finding Bushehr in summer suicidally steamy, he decided to go further into Persia, to Shiraz, so that he could explore Persepolis, while Mary went back to Bombay. He was about to return to Bushehr in early October when he was taken ill and died within days.

Rich's Legacy

Rich's final struggle with Davut and sudden death left several legacies. Mary and her ever-active father made him a cultural icon, emphasised his scholarly interests, and hid his politics. She returned to England with the ancient

98. Taylor to Warden, Nov. 9, 1821, IOR F/4/706 471.
99. Hughes Thomas, *Arabian Gulf Intelligence*, 39.

manuscripts that he had collected on his various trips; in 1825, the Trustees of the British Museum bought them for £7,500.[100] She got Thomas Phillips to paint a posthumous picture of him, which still hangs at the entrance of the Asian and African Studies Room in the British Library. In 1836, she edited and published the diaries of their journeys of 1820 to Kurdistan and Mosul. These lively volumes greatly stimulated future British interest in Nineveh, in the Christian monasteries of Kurdistan, and in the habits and culture of the Kurds and the Yazidi.

Rich's apotheosis as a man of learning disguised his ambitious and controversial policies. He had tried to use Britain's commercial and naval power to sway the pasha and build up connections with Arabs and Kurds. He wanted Britain rather than the Porte to be the indispensable regional arbiter, securing peace and strengthening the economic and political resources of the pashalik. As Mackintosh had written in 1808, Britain's interest in Mesopotamia was for "a weak chief . . . whom we could, according to circumstances, easily overawe or effectually support."[101]

Rich's overzealous behaviour made Bombay determined that his successor, Taylor, should remain at Basra rather than live in Baghdad (or in Kuwait, where he had fled). Bombay had long wanted to abolish the Baghdad agency, having had no say in Dundas's original plan. There had been a logic to it in 1798, and again in 1808–10, the two periods of maximum French threat, but now surely an agent at Basra would suffice. However, this did not mean that Bombay thought about the Gulf just in commercial and not in political terms. It expected to exercise political power, but cheaply, from the coast. This would avoid wasting resources and goodwill on inland disputes, in Arabia or in Kurdistan. In 1821, Britain still had its Gulf island base on Qishm. When it was abandoned on climate grounds, the Bombay government told its Marine that, while remaining neutral between the local powers, it must still maintain "maritime control over the piratical ports."[102] In the 1820s, accordingly, the Marine conducted a detailed survey of Gulf waters, in order to enhance its knowledge of local geography, and to improve its day-to-day relations with the coastal Arab tribes. The sailors held athletic competitions with the locals, who excelled at "wrestling [and] leaping."[103] Bombay disliked the idea of Kuwait as a base because the independent Arabs there would need to be kept in order by active use of military force, which, as the Bani Bu affair had shown, would create complication and opposition. Taylor himself abandoned the idea after encountering some local hostility. The main advantage of Basra over Kuwait

---

100. J.R.F. Thompson, *Rich Manuscripts*, 18–23; "Report of a Committee of the House of Commons."

101. Mackintosh, *Memoirs*, 1:422.

102. Instructions to Macleod at Bushehr, Nov. 9, 1822, IOR L/P&S/5/369 135.

103. Wellsted, *Travels in Arabia*, 1:258–59.

was that it gave Britain more influence over Ottoman customs authorities and therefore over the pashalik—just as Malcolm had argued in 1800.[104]

The history of the 1820s bore this judgment out. Taylor accepted Davut's apology and moved back to Basra on his own initiative; an amicable settlement was reached in 1822. By the late 1820s, Davut had a good working relationship with Taylor, who admired the pasha's ruthless efficiency and modernising instincts.[105] He now governed as a typical Mamluk, with little affection for the Porte. The loss of Sulaimaniya revenues made him all the keener to encourage British trade. Rich had overreached himself, but the core tactic of maintaining an active local British presence independent of a weak Ottoman Empire remained. For British India, the Gulf region remained more important than the Red Sea, because of the latter's navigational difficulties. Taylor in Basra and the men of the Bombay Marine invested a lot of their time in cultivating the local Arab chiefs. When Russia started to threaten the Ottoman and Persian Empires after 1828, the value of this investment became clear, and these efforts grew into a sustained strategy.

104. See Warden to Taylor, Jan. 7, 1822, IOR F/4/706 515, and Taylor to Warden, Jan. 18, 1822, IOR F/4/706 561.

105. E.g., Taylor to Norris on Davut as "the animating soul, the reflecting mind of the body politic of the country": July 14, 1830, IOR L/P&S/9/92 21.

CHAPTER FOUR

Filling the Arabian Vacuum

STEAM, THE ARABS, AND THE
DEFENCE OF INDIA IN THE 1830S

THE EUROPEAN PEACE of 1815 ended Napoleon's dreams and left the Ottoman Empire intact. However, increased Western familiarity with its manners and customs had bred increased contempt. Russia seemed best placed to capitalise on its weaknesses. The Greek crisis that dominated the 1820s underlined the problematic fragility of Ottoman rule and exposed Russian ambition. In 1828–29, conflicts in the Balkans and the Caucasus showed that the Ottoman and Persian Empires were vulnerable to Russian pressure. The defence of India against Russian aggression became a major concern throughout the 1830s. As the Russians had penetrated Kurdistan in 1828, the fear developed that they could seize the Tigris-Euphrates region south of the Caucasus, and threaten the Persian Gulf beyond it. Almost no one thought that the Ottomans themselves could stop them. In Mesopotamia, there was a glaring power vacuum.

Steam-powered ships emerged as Britain's main weapon in strengthening its position there, as well as in the Gulf and along the Arabian coast. It was hoped that these would demonstrate Britain's military reach, and potentially bring commercial benefits, as in India. Steam power was a way of extending the cooperation with local Arab chiefs that had become the practice of the Bombay Marine in the Gulf, and the residents at Bushehr and Basra. In the 1830s, the Marine, renamed the Indian Navy, further increased its influence over the Gulf shaykhs. Its surveys of the Arabian shoreline culminated in the annexation of Aden at the mouth of the Red Sea in 1839. This was a remarkable extension of Britain's practical power in a region that it claimed to have no desire to govern. It was done in the name of preventing other powers from interfering with Ottoman independence. The more influence Britain secured in the Ottoman Middle East, the more attractive the maintenance of the empire became. Even if it could not be saved, these initiatives seemed effective in shutting out Russian and French competition.

One benefit of cultivating the Arabs was to address the concerns of some commentators that Mehmet Ali of Egypt might otherwise create an Arab empire. Mehmet Ali had some successes in Arabia in the 1830s, in the name of the sultan. In reality, his intermittent activities gave Britain a convenient excuse to pursue policies that were primarily aimed against a threat not from Egypt, but from Russia.

Ottoman Collapse and Russian Threat

Between 1827 and 1830, the powers of Europe were confronted with Ottoman decay and showed that they had no solution to it. The Greek insurrection, which had begun in 1821, proved so sustained and so well supported in the West that European governments had to accept some form of self-government, and then, in 1830, independence, for Greece. Publicity for the Greek cause, particularly in the British and French media, helped to demonise the Ottomans as barbarous and tyrannical interlopers in Europe. In 1826–27, George Canning tied Britain, together with Russia and France, to a plan of brokering a settlement between Greeks and Ottomans. His original hopes, crystallised in the Treaty of London in July 1827, were to try to limit the fallout for the Ottoman Empire. He wanted to lock Russia into a joint policy of peace and cooperation, to prevent France from experimenting with Ottoman partitionist ideas, and to satisfy Western supporters of Greece while restricting the new Greek regime both territorially and jurisdictionally.[1] However, Britain could not control the course of events. The Ottomans resisted the attempt of the three powers to get them to submit, leading to the disaster of the Battle of Navarino when the allied powers destroyed their fleet. Ottoman pride and weakness then brought on a Russo-Ottoman war in 1828, and Ottoman defeat in it in 1829. France, not to be outdone, sent troops to Greece to put further pressure on the Ottomans to reach a settlement. By 1830, the Ottomans had to accept the humiliation of Greek independence, on top of Russian intrigue in their other Orthodox Balkan territories. The Russians invaded Moldavia, Wallachia, and Bulgaria in 1828, and in August 1829 were 130 miles from Constantinople. The peace treaty of Adrianople in October strengthened self-government in Serbia, gave Russia control of the mouth of the Danube, and legitimised its influence in Moldavia and Wallachia. Ottoman power in Europe was never the same again.

For Britain, the effects of the crisis of 1827–30 were most striking further east. In 1827–28, the Russian general Paskevich comprehensively defeated a Persian attempt to reverse previous losses in the Caucasus. The Russo-Persian

1. Schroeder, *Transformation*, 647–53.

Treaty of Turkmenchay then established Russian control of modern Armenia and Azerbaijan. Paskevich's army immediately joined in the attack on the Ottomans, advancing through the western Caucasus and taking Bayazid and the Ottoman strongholds of Kars in 1828 and Erzurum in June 1829. Though the Treaty of Adrianople agreed the return of the latter three places, it strengthened the Russian presence in the Caucasus by giving Russia important border forts, as well as extending its territory along the eastern coast of the Black Sea. It was clear that Russia could have forced more gains, but preferred to use its new power to exert continuous pressure on both Ottomans and Persians.

The strengthening of the Russian position in the Black Sea, and the ability of the Russian army to penetrate as far south as Erzurum, Bayazid, and Kars, had profound effects on British thinking. Erzurum was near the source of the western branch of the Euphrates. It was easy to imagine—and Paskevich had imagined—how an army could move southwards down the Euphrates valley towards Mesopotamia and the Persian Gulf. Equally, Bayazid and Kars, further east, allowed the Russians to put more pressure on Persia and northern Kurdistan.[2] Armenians in northern Turkey could act as facilitators for these Russian advances. The Treaty of Turkmenchay had already given Russia great power in northern Persia, not least through the exclusive right to maintain a navy on the Caspian Sea. From now on, Britain could never be sure that Persian chiefs in Tabriz and Tehran would not cave in to Russian demands. In April 1829, Lord Ellenborough, the cabinet minister responsible for India, thought that Russia would persuade Persia to bully the Ottomans and probably to go to war with them to give Persia Baghdad. The Ottoman Empire, like Persia, now seemed completely vulnerable to future Russian pressure.[3]

In 1830, the almost universal British view was that the Ottoman Empire could not be saved. Its internal and external positions seemed equally bleak. The barbarities against the Greeks showed the savagery but also the failure of the regime. An army officer, George de Lacy Evans, made his name with a book foretelling Russia's conquest of Constantinople and its subsequent designs on India.[4] Sir Robert Gordon, the ambassador in Constantinople, explained the Russian military victories in terms of the disappearance of Ottoman patriotic enthusiasm and religious feeling. Factionalism among local governors had created parties willing to let the Russians into Adrianople, Erzurum, and Trebizond. Erzurum had been lost by the "treachery of the Janizaries," the traditional Ottoman military class whose central power base had been overthrown by Sultan Mahmud in 1826 in an attempt to create

2. Robert Taylor cited Paskevich's dispatch to the tsar from Erzurum about this: to Norris, July 14, 1830, IOR L/P&S/9/92 21.

3. For concern by Ellenborough and others on these points, see Ellenborough, *Political Diary*, 1:224; 2:92, 95, 102–3. See Ingram, *Beginning of the Great Game*, 48–57.

4. Evans, *Designs of Russia*.

a loyal and disciplined European-style army.[5] When British commentators discussed Mahmud's reforms, the consensus tended to be that they were necessary but half-hearted measures that underlined the incoherent weakness of modern Ottoman despotism. The historic strength of the Ottomans had been their fierce military zeal, allied to their religious fervour. Both were now on the wane in the face of Western influence, yet powerful groups like the janissaries and the ulema were still trying to keep them alive, and the regime was unable to build up popular patriotic feeling on a different basis.[6]

Mahmud commanded his officials to abandon traditional costume for the fez and the frock coat, but did not tackle the empire's fundamental economic problem, of depopulation owing to misgovernment. Large swathes of the Balkans and the Middle East supported a fraction of their previous population. Pashas aimed to overtax the land for their private benefit, instead of investing in agricultural improvement (such as irrigation techniques) for long-term public gain. This was because they were in post for only a year or two before being moved to another part of the empire. Their interest was in private peculation, not in planning for eventual higher revenues.[7] These institutionalised political failings exacerbated the underlying cultural reasons for Ottoman economic stagnation that Europeans had identified since at least the eighteenth century: the lack of private property and a middle class, and a fatalistic outlook on life.[8]

Externally, there was no international agreement on how far to defend the empire. After Canning's death in August 1827, succeeding Tory governments abandoned his activist policy, and took few initiatives. When Prime Minister

5. Ellenborough, *Political Diary*, 2:88–89.

6. Mackinnon, like Gordon, used the periodic revolts of the janissaries to warn about the excessive power of armed Ottoman factions: Mackinnon, *History of Civilisation*, 2:47, 180. Chesney also believed they were using the crisis of 1828–29 in order to re-establish themselves: *Russo-Ottoman Campaigns*, 253–54. John Bowring thought Mahmud's reforms "frivolous and useless": "Anglo-Turkish War," 211. Bulwer assumed that the old Ottoman spirit was gone, and that the question at issue was whether the reformers would succeed in creating a new regime melding Muslim and Western influences or whether the regime would collapse: June 28, 1838, FO 78/334 7. For the tendency of reforms (Mahmud's, and the Tanzimat) to erode popular religious loyalty by "mixing up the spirit of Voltaireism with the forms of Mahometanism," see Macfarlane, *Turkey and Its Destiny*, 1:72; see also Ponsonby's worry about the Tanzimat, chapter 6, p. 197, below, and Bowring on Mehmet Ali's more efficient and secure despotism, in chapter 5, p. 159.

7. This analysis was set out at length in Robert Walpole's "Preliminary Discourse: The Causes of the Weakness and Decline of the Turkish Monarchy," which introduced his collection of scholarly travel accounts: *Memoirs*, 1–31. For similar analyses, see Jowett, *Christian Researches in the Mediterranean*, 57–58; Mignan, *Travels in Chaldaea*, 312; Addison, *Damascus and Palmyra*, 1:390–95; Wellsted, *City of the Caliphs*, 1:248–49; Mackinnon, *History of Civilisation*, 2:207–13.

8. See Yapp, "Europe in the Turkish Mirror," 149–50, 153–54, and, e.g., Addison, *Damascus and Palmyra*, 1:399–402; J. Reid, *Turkey and the Turks*, 66–69.

Wellington asked his cabinet colleagues in June 1829 whether they would permit Ottoman ruin, they pointed out that this was not in Britain's power, a view that Wellington came to share. It was too late to prevent dissolution if the Russians pressed for it. The continental powers had different objectives in the Balkans, so it seemed unlikely that they would combine to guarantee Ottoman integrity. Later that year, the conservative French foreign minister, Prince Jules de Polignac, suggested partition of the empire and the extension of the new Greek state to include Constantinople.[9] In any case, there was no appetite in Britain for a war in the East, especially given economic depression and taxpayer discontent. Ellenborough, the most hawkish Russophobe in the cabinet, accepted that it would be absurd to fight for an empire "dissolved in its own weakness."[10] After the Treaty of Adrianople, Foreign Secretary Aberdeen believed that there was no chance of "any European sympathy with a system founded upon ignorance and ferocity," and so the best option was to make Greece into a "substantive state, which may hereafter receive the *débris* of the Ottoman Empire." If Greece were strong enough to take the place of the defunct empire in European power relations, it could help to secure a regional balance between Russia, Austria, and France. For Aberdeen, as for Polignac, a Christian Greece could play a significant part in a Christian diplomatic system. Independence for a small Greece became cabinet policy.[11]

In the Balkans, French and Austrian influence offered a chance that Russian power could still be checked. In Asia, however, this would be Britain's responsibility. Britain had gained more by the war and settlement of 1815 than Russia had, though Russia had done more of the fighting. Would there not now be a reckoning? Russia had an incentive to attack India, for its wealth and as the only way of checking British commercial dominance in Asia. It would probably do so by establishing control of Persia first.[12] In 1828–29, Ellenborough, the president of the Board of Control (the India Board), led the campaign for an assertively anti-Russian policy in the Ottoman lands and in central Asia. He considered the Russian occupation of Erzurum as "a victory gained over me, as Asia is *mine*." However, most of the cabinet, led by Aberdeen, retained a Eurocentric and peace-loving view, which Ellenborough regarded as foolish appeasement of the Russians. In October 1829, he complained that the British government, "chained by European politics, would hardly move if they entered Cabul."[13] This was a paralysing split.

9. Price, "Our Aim Is the Rhine," 84–85.

10. Ellenborough, *Political Diary*, 2:49, 82–85, 87, 107–9, 118 (quotation at 107).

11. Gordon, *Aberdeen*, 85–87 (first quotation at 86); Ellenborough, *Political Diary*, 2:105–6, 113 (for the second quotation, Ellenborough's summary of the cabinet's agreed position).

12. [McNeill], "Invasion of India."

13. Ellenborough, *Political Diary*, 2:88, 122.

Ellenborough represented an India-centred Tory Russophobia, as did John Malcolm, now governor of Bombay. But a policy of standing up confidently to Russia also became a defining cause for a group of Liberal Tories, led by Dundas's ex-assistant William Huskisson after Canning's death in 1827. They abandoned Wellington's government in May 1828, took up the centre ground in Parliament, and began to attack its feeble inaction. The Huskissonite most responsible for this attack was Viscount Palmerston, who used it to make his name as a foreign policy expert, in opposition to Aberdeen's cautious Tory conception of Britain's global role. Palmerston came to the idea of an independent Greece before the Tories, and wanted it to have larger borders. He urged Britain to protect it with a strong naval presence. For him, the cases of Greece and Portugal signified liberty, as against the despotism of the Holy Alliance powers that he accused Wellington and Aberdeen of favouring. He suggested that the liberal side was bound to win this struggle through the support of public opinion and the press, which reactionary despots could not match. In June 1829, he declared that the future would lie with "those statesmen who know how to avail themselves of the passions, and the interest, and the opinions of mankind"—an intended insult not only to Russia and conservative Europe but also to Wellington's timid, divided, and unpopular government.[14] In 1830, both British and French politics were reshaped by groups that won power by adopting the mantle of liberalism. A coalition government of Whigs and Huskissonites took power in Britain in November 1830, and held it almost continuously for a decade, becoming the first Liberal government in British history. It had a common interest with Louis Philippe's new Orléanist regime in France in presenting Russia as an ideological foe, the enemy to progress and civilisation. Palmerston became its foreign secretary.

In 1828–30, meanwhile, Ellenborough at the India Board already had a degree of freedom to pursue a vigorous anti-Russian policy in Asia, as opposed to Europe. This was partly because Wellington shared his concern with India, but mainly because he saw eye to eye with John Malcolm, who used his position in Bombay to marginalise his cautious colleagues. Ellenborough revived Malcolm's idea that if Russia started to move down through the Baghdad pashalik to the Gulf, Britain should seize Kharaq, control the Gulf, and "seal the Euphrates."[15] Both men emphasised the importance of Baghdad and the Gulf for British strategy. The attraction of Baghdad was the vigour and semi-independence of the local pasha Davut, one of the few who had not been enfeebled by the decadence of Ottoman central government. In November 1827, he had asked for British military supplies and training to help consolidate his power, and Malcolm had supported the idea. However, Governor-General Amherst had opposed it, fearing that Davut might use them to declare independence from the sultan. In

14. Bourne, *Palmerston*, 298–99; Parry, *Politics of Patriotism*, 150–51.
15. Ellenborough, *Political Diary*, 2:93.

December 1828, Ellenborough in turn overturned that decision, arguing that Davut would be an asset if the Russo-Ottoman war spread to the south, and that he needed supporting against a likely attack from Persia. Britain should build up a friendship with him in order to stop any other European power creating an influence in Baghdad. He ordered Robert Taylor, the political agent in Turkish Arabia, who was based in Basra, to move the residency to Baghdad and cultivate him.[16] So Taylor went to live in Baghdad in May 1829, brought his son from India to take charge of the Residency Guard, and trained up five hundred bodyguards and a brigade of cavalry. Davut dismissed his other foreign advisers.[17] Taylor, who shared the fear that the Russian army might sail down the Mesopotamian rivers from Anatolia, claimed that these reforms "had made rapid advances towards the establishment of a military and political bulwark impregnable to Russia."[18]

Steam and Plague: Progress and Decay

For Taylor, Ellenborough, and Malcolm, the defence of Baghdad and the Gulf from a Russian attack was inextricably mixed up with another great enthusiasm of the late 1820s—the potential of steam technology as an agent of naval and imperial power. Steam-powered shipping promised to annihilate distance—to make communication between Britain and Asia much quicker and more certain than before.

As far as the security and defence of India were concerned, this would have three connected benefits. The first was that it would be quicker to send official dispatches, information, money, goods, and equipment between the two. If the London government wanted to have significant influence over India, steam was essential.[19] Steamer services already ran between London and Marseilles and the eastern Mediterranean; the challenge was to develop an equally rapid, and connecting, service onwards to India. Secondly, steamers on the navigable rivers of Asia—the Ganges, the Indus, but also the Tigris and Euphrates— would allow the rapid transport of troops to meet local crises and foreign invasions, and thus help to spread precious military resources more efficiently across a vast subcontinent. Thirdly, steam might increase influence over local communities, through impressing them with British power and potentially introducing them to Western knowledge. Those who sought to "civilise" indigenous tribes were particularly enthusiastic about the last option. As Daniel Wilson, the new bishop of Calcutta, wrote in 1833, steam was a "highway cast

16. See [Malet], *Précis*, 121–27.

17. Khan, "British Policy in Iraq," 177–81; Ingram, *Beginning of the Great Game*, 149–60.

18. Stocqueler, *Fifteen Months' Pilgrimage*, 53–54; Taylor to Norris, July 14, 1830, IOR L/PS/9/92 21.

19. Wellsted, *Travels in Arabia*, 2:292–94.

through the wilderness of waters; the entrance and forerunner of all education, missions, commerce, agriculture, science, literature, policy, legislation,
everything."[20] All three calculations applied to British India itself, while the
initial concern in the Middle East was most clearly with the first. However,
the second and third also applied there, in the minds of some influential proponents of steam, especially as there were so few other levers of British power.
Between 1828 and 1837, intense discussion of the role of steam power in link-
ing the Mediterranean and India led to hopes that it could also check Russian
influence and enhance respect for Britain among Middle Eastern chiefs.

Not everyone was keen on trying to communicate with India through the
Middle East. The East India Company (EIC) would have been content with
the traditional lengthy journey around the Cape, because this avoided any
need to tangle with local chiefs, and because of the known difficulties of Red
Sea navigation, especially during the seasonal monsoons.[21] If steamers were
introduced on the Cape route, they would probably sail direct to Calcutta, mar-
ginalising Bombay. So John Malcolm and the Bombay government needed to
develop Middle Eastern steam options as an alternative policy. Against the
opposition of the parsimonious EIC, Malcolm sent his first steamer, the *Hugh
Lindsay*, from Bombay to Suez in thirty-three days in April 1830. In 1828, he
had got his brother Charles appointed head of the Bombay Marine, the naval
force in the Bombay presidency that was traditionally responsible for protecting its commercial activities in the Gulf and Arabian Sea. Charles Malcolm
was a zealous supporter of exploration (he founded the Bombay branch of the
Royal Geographical Society in 1831) and developed the Marine as a professional surveying force on a larger scale than before, renaming it the Indian
Navy in 1830. It was a priority for him to transfer to the Red Sea the surveying expertise that its officers had shown in charting the Gulf in the 1820s. In
1829, a detailed survey of its navigable channels was launched: the sea was
divided between Thomas Elwon in the *Benares* and Robert Moresby in the
Palinurus.[22] This was also a "moral and political survey of the tempers of the
ruling powers" along the coasts.[23] The survey focused on the political and
economic as well as physical obstacles to British naval influence: the officers
explored the availability of water and fuel supplies, and the willingness of local
tribes to cooperate in securing them. The crew of the *Palinurus* used to play
cricket and other games on shore; the locals were happy to join in if they had
had previous encounters with Europeans, though the Mecca pilgrims were less

20. D. Wilson, *Journal Letters*, 8.

21. The early steamers required 380 tons of coal to cope with the journey up the Red
Sea: Searight, *Steaming East*, 8.

22. Elwon was promoted commander in the Gulf in 1833 and Moresby took over the
Benares to finish his work, releasing the *Palinurus*, which had finished in the northern
part, for the southern Arabian coast.

23. [St. John], "Surveys of the Indian Navy," 462.

keen. One of its officers, Raymond Wellsted, admitted to a local chief that the survey would ensure that, if the French invaded Egypt again, the British could secure the Red Sea and drive them out more easily than in 1801.[24]

Entrepreneurs in India and elsewhere had been trying to raise money for an integrated steam service to London since 1823. Two in particular, the merchant James Taylor (brother of Robert Taylor of Basra), and Thomas Waghorn, a marine pilot, were developing potentially lucrative schemes to convey mail across Egypt from Alexandria to Suez. In 1829, encouraged by the new survey of the Red Sea, both men made experimental journeys overland across Egypt with mail, in the hope of getting financial backing for their ventures. James Taylor won the support of the Court of Directors for an official steamer service from London to the eastern Mediterranean, but could not get the matching funds in Bombay for the onward journey.

Mulling over the problems with the Red Sea route, Thomas Love Peacock, a senior civil servant at the India Board in London (and part-time novelist), proposed complementing the survey of the Red Sea with an investigation of steam navigation of the Euphrates from the Gulf to northern Syria. The land route from Basra to the Mediterranean was the traditional one for the India mail. Now that steamers plied the major rivers of America and Europe, why could they not also traverse the 1,100-mile length of the Euphrates from Basra to Bir, from which only a short land journey of 120–170 miles would be needed to the Mediterranean coast? Like Ellenborough, who supported him, Peacock was alarmed at the Russians' military successes in Kurdistan, and concerned that they might descend the Euphrates to the Gulf. A classical enthusiast, he knew the river's history: Herodotus's account showed that it had supported trade, while Trajan and Julian had used it for invasion. Its decline seemed due to the decay of local commerce and the rise of vagabondage.[25] The Euphrates route was several hundred miles shorter than the Red Sea one, and a steamer from Bombay would find it much easier to reach Basra than Suez. Peacock sent the local British consuls a detailed questionnaire on the two routes. In Alexandria, this questionnaire was seen by a restless Royal Artillery officer, Francis Rawdon Chesney, who was touring the area on behalf of the Constantinople ambassador, having arrived there too late to organise an Ottoman rocket corps to fight against Russia in the Balkans in 1829. Chesney, four feet nine inches tall, frequently rejected in love, and anxious to rescue a stalling military career, decided to answer the questions by an assiduous on-the-spot survey of both options, which might give him fame. In 1830, he examined the northern Red Sea; he then travelled through Syria to Baghdad, which he reached in January 1831.

24. Wellsted, *Travels in Arabia*, 2:118, 192.
25. Peacock, in *PP* (1834), 5–6; [Peacock], "On Steam Navigation," 462. For interest in steam on the Indus and Ganges, see Ingram, *Beginning of the Great Game*, 73–76, 85.

Chesney, however, had been pre-empted by Robert Taylor and his brother James. Having failed in his Red Sea plan, James met with his brother in Baghdad in the spring of 1830, and the two developed the idea of a steamer route up the Euphrates to connect to the Mediterranean. Robert had already been discussing with Davut a local steamer operation. From his years of managing the mail and trade at Basra, he was confident that he could get the local Arab tribes to cooperate with a Euphrates steam venture. By July, Davut had granted James the right to run a tolled steam service on the rivers. He also offered him thirty miles of land along the banks, for indigo and rice production, at a low rent. James agreed to introduce "machinery of the latest and most approved invention" for the "cultivation and irrigation of the soil." Davut also agreed to cut a canal between the Tigris and Euphrates to help these developments.[26]

Robert told the India Board that steam navigation would be "a political lever of inestimable power and consequence" to defeat Russia. He did not say that it would also enrich his own brother.[27] Realising that a detailed survey of the Euphrates would be essential, he recruited William Bowater, a Bombay Marine lieutenant with experience of the Red Sea, but recently court-martialled for insubordination. Bowater's first report in June 1830 advocated the superiority of the Euphrates route over the Red Sea, particularly because it would allow a flow of information between British representatives in Baghdad, the Gulf, Persia, Constantinople, and London.[28] Bowater and James Taylor set off to survey the upper Euphrates in August 1830. Near the Sinjar hills, they were threatened by Yazidi highwaymen. They foolishly killed one of them, the one thing no British traveller in the East should ever do: they were murdered on the spot.

Undeterred by his brother's death, Robert continued to press the Euphrates steam project on the many British visitors to the palatial Baghdad residency that he inherited from Rich. He also exploited the Indian Navy's interest in Arab culture. He found another Bombay Marine veteran to continue Bowater's survey of the river: Henry Ormsby, who had dropped out of naval life to live among the tribes. Taylor linked Ormsby up with Bowater's Arabic interpreter William Elliot, who had been a London medical student and a surgeon in the Turkish navy, had converted to Islam, and had then lived as a wandering dervish called Ali. Ormsby also brought another Arabophile Bombay Marine officer to Baghdad, William Henry Wyburd, interpreter to the Gulf squadron. Wyburd was practising living in Basra in full Arab disguise under the title of Rustem Beg, while preparing for a secret mission to the Saudis.[29] Ormsby and

26. Robert to James Taylor, July 11, 1830, IOR L/P&S/9/91 201; Groves, *Journal of a Residence*, 3–4, 9–11, 17, 54; F. Newman, *Personal Narrative*, 99–101.

27. Taylor to Auber, July 14, 1830, IOR L/P&S/9/91 169.

28. June 17, 1830, IOR L/PS/9/92 55.

29. In 1840, another Indian Navy officer, Raymond Wellsted, published the story of Wyburd's perfect adoption of the street Arab lifestyle in Basra, and his coy self-reveal to his

Elliot began by descending the Tigris and exploring the lower Euphrates as far upstream as Hilla. When Chesney arrived in Baghdad, Taylor, presumably not rating him very highly in view of his lack of Arabic, suggested he should broadly follow in their footsteps, which he did. (Taylor himself had a dozen oriental languages.)

The main blow to the project followed quickly afterwards: the devastating plague that swept through the Baghdad province in the spring of 1831. It prevented the completion of both surveys, driving Ormsby and Elliot to Damascus, and Chesney to Persia and then Syria. It forced Taylor and the residency out of Baghdad to Basra. Most importantly, it led to the fall of Davut. After Sultan Mahmud's humiliation at Adrianople, Davut had been openly contemptuous of him, and had murdered one of his messengers who had asked for increased tribute. In 1831, Mahmud sent Ali Rida from Aleppo with an army to force Davut to submit to Ottoman power, in alliance with the pasha of Mosul and the Shammar Arab chief Suffuq. The Arabs and the Mosul pasha besieged the famine-struck city for three months. Davut eventually surrendered, only because of the desperate circumstances of the plague. For long periods in 1831, there was no government to speak of. Only four of the hundred Mamluks in the pasha's palace survived the epidemic, and only one of Davut's thousand English-trained troops.

The Baghdad plague added to the Western narrative that these were doomed lands, in which the effects of acts of nature—or divine punishment—were aggravated by chronic misgovernment and barbaric human sinfulness. When plague was first predicted, Taylor had urged Davut to impose medical precautions, such as quarantine, but had been ignored. British travellers usually ascribed the Ottomans' lack of interest in such policies to Islamic notions of predestination.[30] The resulting disaster was chronicled remorselessly for a British religious audience in the journals sent home by Anthony

---

narrator friend. Thus was born one of the great tropes of Arabophile fiction: it was surely the inspiration for John Buchan's Sandy Arbuthnot. Wellsted's book noted that Ormsby, likewise, was marked by "the facility with which he filled up the variety of characters it was necessary he should assume": *City of the Caliphs*, 1:v (quotation), 150–51. This is a curious book, in which Wellsted mashed up the narrative that Ormsby had given him with his own adventures, so that it is not clear who experienced what. Both men were in Basra at some time in 1830–31, and either could have had this encounter with Wyburd, but the real point is the close-knit relationship among these officers and their shared enthusiasm for mingling with local Arabs. It is sometimes assumed that Wellsted took Ormsby's notes because he had died, but in fact he lived until 1857, latterly in Weston-Super-Mare. Wyburd was lost in central Asia, probably decapitated by the amir of Bokhara. Taylor found Elliot's preference for living as an Arab very useful and employed him to reconnoitre the route taken by the retreating ten thousand Greek mercenaries after fighting at Cunaxa (seventy miles north of Babylon) in 401 BCE. Having cured a local girl of ophthalmia, he was given her as a spouse, but asked for a donkey instead: Ainsworth, "Termination of the Transport," 241.

30. E.g., Jowett, *Christian Researches in the Mediterranean*, 57.

Norris Groves, a publicity-conscious missionary from the Plymouth Brethren who had chosen Baghdad for his mission in 1829 (with the encouragement of Taylor's Armenian wife, who had met him while visiting England and had returned with him across Russia). Groves had declined to leave Baghdad with the Taylors, putting his trust in God. One day he ventured out and brought back the disease—his wife and baby daughter died; he survived, with his sons. Taylor had had to leave by boat because robber Arabs were circling the city stripping naked those who tried to escape. In April, the plague claimed two thousand people per day. Ormsby, who also stayed until late April, noted that with the onset of death all around, survivors resorted to barbaric hedonism: "All moral feeling appeared extinguished. . . . Every evil passion which attends human nature burst forth unrestrained." Soon the only people seen in the streets were either infected or carrying their dead. Then came floods: the rising Tigris inundated the Jewish quarter and swept away two hundred houses in one go. Half of Groves's own house disappeared. The waters took weeks to subside; then the resulting stagnant pools produced a deadly fever. By the end of May, the plague had lost its force, but the lack of provisions led to famine. This was intensified by the Arabs' blockade. Then the sultan's men entered the city, but after the fall of Davut, anarchy intensified; mobs attacked Jews and Christians and stole the possessions of Groves's family tutor John Kitto. Groves believed that two-thirds of the population died; Ormsby estimated that over four-fifths died or left.[31]

At home, the dramatic painter John Martin's *Fall of Babylon* (1819) was reissued as a popular print. Groves—and surely most of his evangelical readers—saw this affliction as the wrath of God delivered to "the literal Babylon," in divine punishment of the "antichrist."[32] After all, Jeremiah had prophesied that the sea would cover Babylon with "tumultuous waves," its "broad wall shall be levelled" and it would become a "land of drought."[33] One religious army officer, Thomas Skinner, visiting a "wretched" Baghdad in 1833, felt that its affliction was "a judgment against the power of Mohammed, which surely must fall, dwindled to a shadow as it now is." Returning briefly in 1832, Ormsby inspected the town's deserted banquet halls, and imagined scenes of indulgence cut short by death, just as at Belshazzar's Feast.[34] Even Groves left, for more promising terrain in India.

The dream of English-assisted progress had given way to confirmation of epic Ottoman misrule. Ali Rida's was a pyrrhic victory; government authority

31. Most of this paragraph is taken from Groves, *Journal of a Residence*. For Ormsby's views, see Wellsted, *City of the Caliphs*, 1:288 (quotation), 295.

32. Groves, *Journal of a Residence*, 122.

33. Jeremiah 51:42–58. The Plymouth Brethren defined their own religious purity, against other Christian sects, by identifying them with the "Whore of Babylon" in the Book of Revelation. See Harding, *Babylon and the Brethren*.

34. Skinner, *Adventures*, 2:134, 137; Wellsted, *City of the Caliphs*, 1:296–97.

beyond the city walls was in tatters, and Arabs periodically blockaded the city, fleecing traders at will. In 1834, Taylor lamented that the Tigris between Baghdad and Basra was completely under Arab control and that fleets of boats were regularly attacked. He expected an Arab revolt, ending the sultan's authority in Baghdad.[35] In the same year, James Baillie Fraser arrived on a British government investigation of the region, and reported on the complete disorganisation of the pashalik, though it boasted some of the most fertile country in the world. He recounted massive official peculation, and favouritism in the grant of land and monopoly rights, but noted that revenues could amount to a million pounds per year with good government. Taylor insisted that the only long-term solution was steam navigation, securing order on the riverbanks and boosting revenues. Though some members of the India Board in London had criticised his closeness to Davut, Fraser's report vindicated him and advocated a return to their joint plan of economic improvement. Fraser agreed that Baghdad's urgent need was for more efficient and just government; the resulting prosperity and stability would help to discipline the Arabs and to gain Britain the "permanent influence" that it needed, whether the Ottoman regime survived or not.[36]

Steamers and Arabs in Mesopotamia

Mehmet Ali's conquest of Syria in 1831–32, and the fallout from it, confirmed all these views: that the Ottoman Empire was moribund, that it was entirely at Russia's mercy, and that only by steam power could Britain secure its position in Mesopotamia. In December 1832, the sultan's army was defeated at Konya and the Porte requested Russian military aid at Constantinople in case of Egyptian attack. The Russian fleet arrived in the Bosporus on February 19, 1833. In July, Russia and the Ottomans signed the Treaty of Hünkar İskelesi, which secured Russian assistance in the case of a defensive war, in return for closing the Dardanelles against foreign warships—in other words, against Britain and France.

With Russia dominant at Constantinople, Ali Rida in Baghdad seemed friendlier to Russia than to Britain. In 1833, the Baghdad residency suffered several humiliations: a British merchant and Taylor's gardener were both unjustly fined, and one of the residency yacht crew was badly beaten for telling a naked swimmer to cover up.[37] Some influential Baghdadis, despising

35. Taylor to Ponsonby, Mar. 31, 1834, FO 195/113 99. For the India Board's instructions on preserving neutrality in that event, see FO 78/250 70.

36. Fraser, "Present Condition of the Pachalic of Bagdad" (quotation at xliv). I have discussed the criticism and vindication of Taylor more fully in my "Steam Power," 153–54.

37. Taylor to Ponsonby, June 25, July 30, Aug. 23, and Oct. 25, 1833, and Mar. 31, 1834, FO 195/113, 42, 51, 60, 73, 99; Taylor to London, Mar. 14, 1834, IOR L/P&S/9/96 193. A garbled version was reported in The Times, Jan. 14, 1834, 4.

the Ottomans, expressed a preference for Russian rule, which Taylor attributed to intrigue and bribery.[38] Meanwhile, Persia increased its claims on the border province of Sulaimaniya. Sir John Campbell, British minister in Persia, feared that the only way that the sultan could stop a Persian invasion of the pashalik would be by allowing the Russians to occupy Baghdad, something that Britain must stop at all costs. The sultan sent a military commander, the former grand vizier Reşid, to try to shore up Ottoman rule over Kurdistan in response to Mehmet Ali's presence in Syria, but Taylor feared that he would ask for Russian help.[39]

Britain's answer was an experiment for steam travel down the Euphrates. The Euphrates Expedition was Peacock's brainchild, and the result of his earlier questionnaire. The idea, funded by a parliamentary grant of £20,000, was developed in a select committee established in June 1834, chaired by the current president of the India Board, the evangelical Huskissonite Charles Grant. Peacock, giving evidence to the committee, insisted that Britain needed to respond to Russia's clear new policy of controlling the sultan. Russia would surely seek exclusive privileges in Mesopotamia, shutting Britain out. Russia could also follow Trajan and Julian by building fleets in Armenia and sending them downriver. British steamers on the Mesopotamian rivers would foil this, keeping the trade open and giving Britain "a right to interfere."[40] Peacock's only concern was about the cooperativeness of the local Arab tribes, but other witnesses insisted that this was not a problem. Taylor's son, who was conveniently in England at the time, explained that his father always paid them a regular tribute for safe passage of British goods and mail, and bought their sheep and other articles. He claimed that the Muntafiq near Basra and the Anaza near Bir were particularly reliable; moreover, by developing commerce, river steamers opened the prospect of "civilizing the Arabs."[41]

The organisation of the expedition was divided between Peacock at India House and Chesney, who was made its commander, having devoted eighteen months to publicising himself and the project among influential people, from King William IV downwards.[42] The two men approved the design of two steamers, to be built by Macgregor Laird at Birkenhead and sent in parts to the Syrian coast, then floated up the Orontes before being conveyed to Bir (now Birecik). Chesney's appointment was significant in shaping the expedition's priorities, because he knew little of the Arabs or of regional politics and was primarily interested in the military defence of the Ottoman Empire against Russia and Mehmet Ali. His view was the view of the Constantinople

38. See Taylor to London, Aug. 3, 1833, IOR L/P&S/9/95 535.

39. Campbell to Taylor, Feb. 2, 1834, FO 78/245 169; Taylor to London, Sept. 5, 1834, FO 78/250 337.

40. *PP* (1834), 6–7.

41. *PP* (1834), 107–9.

42. The best account of the expedition is Guest's *Euphrates Expedition*.

embassy, which had employed him on his visit to Alexandria in 1830, and whose influence he used to promote himself. This influence disguised his lack of local knowledge: in a couple of months in early 1832, he had inspected only a small portion of the upper Euphrates around Bir and Rumkale, to add to the section between Hilla and Falluja that it had been possible to visit in 1831. Crucially, he had not proved the navigability of the Euphrates above Hit, just north of Falluja. Like the new Constantinople ambassador Ponsonby, he saw the issue in terms of defending Ottoman power. Already in 1832, he had drawn up plans for a military attack on Mehmet Ali, and reverted to this idea in 1836.[43] His other priority was to prevent a Russian descent of the Euphrates, by repairing the old castles on the river and building Martello towers at the historic Crusader strongholds of Bir and Rumkale. He stressed that these would be valuable, even assuming Arab hostility.[44] He saw the Arabs as "lawless and predatory," though potentially effective fighters against Russia and Mehmet Ali.[45] When he eventually made a formal agreement with the Anaza in 1836, his main objective (which failed) was for them to make up their differences with their Shammar rivals so that they could fight together against the Russians and Mehmet Ali. As theirs was to get aphrodisiacs, it was not a meeting of minds.[46]

In December 1834, after many fears of Russian vetoes, British diplomats at Constantinople got official sanction for the application to run two steamers on the Euphrates for commercial purposes. This firman involved a significant infringement of the sultan's sovereignty, and his willingness to grant it reflected his fury at Mehmet Ali's continuing occupation of Syria.[47] The components of the steamers reached the Syrian coast in April 1835, but no work had then been done on a dock or roads for them, because of obstructions imposed by Mehmet Ali's son Ibrahim. Naturally, Ibrahim did not want a British military expedition camped at Bir in eastern Syria, which might threaten his power. Mehmet Ali tried to tempt Britain with an alternative idea, of a railway across Egypt, which his engineer Thomas Galloway had proposed. He was publicly blamed for the delays to the expedition by Chesney and some other members. The reality was more complicated, because the Porte refused to order Mehmet Ali to cooperate with Britain, fearing that he would decline and reveal its own lack of power. Consul-General Campbell in Egypt led the efforts to get Mehmet Ali on side, and felt that Chesney was his own worst

43. See his memos in FO 78/250 299, 414, and 78/273 249.

44. Guest, *Euphrates Expedition*, 36; Chesney in *PP* (1834), 22.

45. Campbell and McNeill felt that Chesney lacked an understanding of how to handle Arabs: Dec. 1831, IOR L/P&S/9/92 819, 837.

46. Chesney to Hobhouse, Apr. 30, 1836, FO 78/299 67, includes the agreement; for the aphrodisiacs, see Ainsworth, *Euphrates Expedition*, 1:267.

47. FO 78/240 143, 180.

enemy, alienating everyone with his demands.[48] His greatest mistake was not to notice that the Orontes was unnavigable, so the steamer parts had to be lugged overland using twenty-seven carts, while eight men died of fever. In July, the party finally arrived at the assembly point on the Euphrates, which they named Port William for the king. At this point, Chesney was debilitated first by sunstroke and then by malaria, so there were great delays in buying transport and equipment. Reşid, now in the region commanding Ottoman troops, imposed further obstacles to the completion of the Port William settlement throughout the winter of 1835–36.[49] It was not just the Egyptians who found the ambition of this British project disturbing.

The vessels finally started downstream in March 1836, but ran aground several times. On May 21, the *Tigris* capsized in a hurricane below Salihiya, drowning twenty of the crew. The surviving ship, the *Euphrates*, reached Basra in June, after encountering many river Arabs, who were impressed by the power of its swivel guns when fired into the river.[50] They also received presents, usually of British-made clothes.[51] At the end of September, it arrived in Baghdad, creating a sensation. The population treated it as "a new prophet . . . sent into the world."[52] However, an attempt to ascend the Euphrates in October—the main point of the experiment—failed, owing to engine pump failure. By December 1835, Chesney had spent over £30,000; the eventual cost reached £43,197. He seemed uncontrollable. John Hobhouse, now president of the India Board, decided he was "not a safe man," and not to be employed again in Mesopotamia.[53]

It fell to Hobhouse to decide the future of the steam experiment on the Euphrates. He quickly accepted that steamers were not quick or reliable enough to help with the Indian mail, especially in view of the simultaneous improvements being made to Red Sea navigation. However, bearing in mind continuing uncertainty about the latter, the India Board agreed to turn the existing overland mail route between Basra and Syria through Baghdad into a regular monthly dromedary postal service. It was initially run by Alexander Hector, the expedition's storekeeper and purser, who now stayed behind to set up as a Baghdad merchant.[54] It was not entirely successful either: the

48. Campbell to Palmerston, Dec. 24, 1835, FO 78/258 180; see Guest, *Euphrates Expedition*, 134–36.

49. Guest, *Euphrates Expedition*, 54–55, 66, 70.

50. Chesney to Hobhouse, Apr. 30, 1836, FO 78/299 67.

51. Chesney to Hobhouse, June 19, 1836, Broughton, F213 4; J. Jones, *Memoirs*, 271. This practice had inestimable benefits, but had to be concealed from the bureaucrats in charge of the Indian Navy accounts.

52. Chesney to Grant, Oct. 16, 1836, Broughton, F213 5.

53. Hobhouse to Auckland, Apr. 1, 1837, Broughton, F213 5. See Guest, *Euphrates Expedition*, 141.

54. There is a file on the dromedary post 1837–44 at FO 618/4.

post was lost for two successive months during the 1838 monsoon after being attacked by desert raiders or saboteurs, paralysing London's ability to respond to the Herat crisis.[55]

In 1837, Hobhouse also decided that the steam presence in Mesopotamia should continue permanently, taking advantage of the sultan's firman of 1834. Whereas the Indian government assumed that the surviving steamer, the *Euphrates*, would be reallocated to an Indian river, Hobhouse insisted that it should stay in Iraq and that the deputy commander of the expedition, Henry Blosse Lynch, should command it. He should also take over the dromedary post, so that it could in theory benefit from steam power at some future point. It became clear that Hobhouse was planning a flotilla of steamers, under Indian Navy command. Lynch, a long-time Indian Navy officer, had learned Persian and Arabic while engaged on the naval survey of the Gulf in the 1820s, and had become the interpreter to the Gulf squadron. So he had years of experience of talking with the Arab tribes there. On the expedition, he was noted for his "successful intercourse with the natives, for which he is well fitted by his general knowledge of their customs, manners, language etc."[56] His instructions were to command the *Euphrates* and "any other steam vessel or vessels" that might be employed there, to work with Taylor to establish with the tribes of the rivers "such relations as may be serviceable" to British interests, to help with the new mail service, and to survey the rivers.[57] Arriving in Baghdad in August 1837, his opinions quickly became indistinguishable from those of Taylor. In August 1838, he married Taylor's daughter Caroline.

The replacement of Chesney by Lynch and Taylor as directors of the steamer operation signalled a switch of priorities. The main aim would now be to extend British influence by conciliating local chiefs. Hobhouse hoped it would "silently obtain that influence with the Arab tribes which will more than half ensure our permanent predominance."[58] Lynch claimed that the Arabs were "the finest band of soldiers, by land or sea, on our Indian frontier." They would defend Mesopotamia much better than the Turks. In November 1838, he expressed the hope that, whatever happened to Ottoman rule, the British would be able to arrange things locally "as our interests dictate, without any violent measures likely to attract attention." Within a few years, the province might be made safe for travel and commerce, but "should on the contrary these countries be destined to sink, as they are sinking under a weight of anarchy and misrule . . . England must still be here to watch. . . . Her power must be increased to scare those who are now [waiting for] the time to seize their

55. Hobhouse to Taylor, May 14, 1839, Broughton, F213 7.
56. Chesney to Hobhouse, Dec. 14, 1836, Broughton, F213 5.
57. [Malet], *Précis*, 133–34.
58. To Lynch, Dec. 26, 1838, Broughton, F213 7.

prey. To be as it is now, the resort of the Arab in his hour of need."[59] Lynch's fellow Indian Navy officer Raymond Wellsted described the aim of the steam flotilla as to "attain . . . a political ascendancy over the several tribes on the basin of the Euphrates . . . command the whole fertile and inhabited districts, and consequently every portion of the country over which it might be necessary to extend our influence."[60] Taylor envisaged that steam would strengthen British influence over the local factions and turn all the "latent energy" of the pashalik in Britain's direction.[61]

British influence would be used to secure a better balance between the misgoverning Turks and the misgoverned Arabs. In May 1838, Lynch suggested that "the Turks look upon [steam power] as a means of consolidating their power here. The Arabs as their only chance of protection from the ravages of the Turks. We must look to it to civilize both."[62] The Turk was responsible for depopulation, demoralisation, and devastation, by fleecing the land with arbitrary and excessive taxes for the pasha's personal gain. "Shortsighted, all-decaying despotism" was forcing the Arabs to revert to primitive "robber-barbarism."[63] But they could be led in other directions. When they had encountered the Euphrates Expedition, they had shown an avidity for British goods—handkerchiefs, shawls, cutlery, guns—which might encourage them to become traders and farmers.[64] Over a two-year period, the expedition men had paid them to transport letters, money, and other items, and noted "the decided honesty of the Arabs, who were intrusted with many valuable things, . . . unattended by any European, . . . almost invariably without loss."[65] Because of the weakness of Ottoman rule, the Muntafiq were already having to settle on land in lower Mesopotamia in order to protect it, and would surely learn the benefits of cultivating it.[66] Stereotypes of Arab lawlessness were wrong: they would prove energetic, intelligent farmers, "the most tractable people in the world" according to Lynch's brother, who later in the century employed many of them to grow grain, cotton, and tobacco.[67] Primitive civilizations had made Mesopotamia the richest, most fertile country known to man, the granary of the world, simply by irrigation and good government. Herodotus claimed that Mesopotamia grew one-third of Asian produce.

59. Lynch to Hobhouse, Nov. 12, 1838, and May 28, 1839, Broughton, F213 9; Lynch memo, Aug. 1837, IOR L/P&S/9/103 245.

60. Wellsted, *Travels in Arabia*, 2:298–99.

61. Taylor to London and Bombay, Aug. 15 and 21, 1837, IOR L/P&S/9/103 179, 213.

62. Lynch to Hobhouse, May 31, 1838, Broughton, F213 6.

63. Taylor, cited in F. Newman, *Personal Narrative*, 104.

64. Three members of the expedition argued this: Chesney, *Expedition for the Survey*, 2:686–99.

65. Chesney, "Special Meeting of the Society," xiv.

66. Fraser, *Travels in Koordistan*, 2:97–98.

67. T. Lynch, *Across Mesopotamia to India*, 18.

Settlement and irrigation together would improve the agricultural yield 250 times.[68]

This confidence that Arabs would respond beneficially to the chance of a relationship with British ships was also shaped by the Indian Navy's increasing familiarity with the Gulf.[69] In 1834, W.M.G. Colebrooke, a member of the 1819-20 expedition there, claimed that piracy had emerged only because political turbulence had disrupted the pearl trade, and that once the Bombay Marine had regulated relations between the tribes, commercial habits had returned. "Whenever you hold out to the Arabs the means of profitable employment for their industry, they seem ready to engage in such pursuits"— for they were "an intelligent, enterprising, and highly-improvable race."[70]

As it happened, the state of the Gulf also became a significant British concern again in 1834. The Saudi leader Turki had reasserted Wahhabi power in recent years. He drove the Ottoman forces out of Riyadh in 1824, making it his new capital, and took most of Najd thereafter, acquiring the Hasa oasis in 1830, and increasing his influence over Buraimi in Oman. So Turki became a regional player, with allies along the Gulf coast. However, he seemed amenable to negotiation and might be a natural counter to the regional power of Muscat, especially as he evinced a striking degree of toleration to Shiʻi Muslims, and "good sense and talents for Government," according to Indian officials. Bombay reiterated to Turki that Britain sought his friendship. Samuel Hennell, the resident in the Gulf, pressed Muscat to make a peace treaty with him. In 1834, the Indian government continued to take the view that, unless disorder became severe, it would not take the side of Muscat against the Saudis, "a free and powerful people." Their two leaders must reach an accommodation by themselves.[71]

Unfortunately, the assassination of Turki in May 1834 by a disaffected kinsman weakened Saudi power and raised again the issue of regional instability. At the same time, concern about Russia and the new focus on Mesopotamia drew attention to the strategic significance of the Gulf. In 1833-34, there had been serious maritime conflict between the Qawasim and the Bani Yas over the pearl fisheries of Abu Dhabi, which also threatened the livelihood of the divers and made a forced return to piracy more likely. It became clear to Hennell, and several of the shaykhs, that these disputes could be checked only by the imposition of a maritime truce during the entire pearl fishing season. This was drawn up by Hennell at the Bushehr residency, and signed by the contending parties in August 1835. The truce was renewed annually under the

68. J. Jones, *Memoirs*, 42, 133, 240-41; Chesney, *Expedition for the Survey*, 2:602-3; Fraser, "Present Condition of the Pachalic of Bagdad," xxviii–xxxii, xl–xlii.

69. See Onley, "Politics of Protection."

70. *PP* (1834), 134.

71. J. Kelly, *Britain and the Persian Gulf*, 235-38; Winder, *Saudi Arabia*, 77-82; PGP, 5:11 (quotation).

authority of the Indian Navy. Hennell toured the Gulf with gifts for shaykhs and the offer of medical treatment by the residency surgeon. From now on, Hennell and his Gulf residency ran an independent fiefdom directly answerable to Bombay. Old talk of a forged merger with the Basra agency on economy grounds was dropped, while on most matters Hennell no longer needed to report to the British mission in Persia (which was transferred from India to the Foreign Office in 1836).[72]

So British dominance in the Gulf was strengthened at much the same time as the arrival of the steamers at Baghdad. Both stemmed from the variety of factors traced here, all fundamentally caused by anxiety about Russia. The Euphrates Expedition was much more useful to Britain as a failure than it would have been as a success: a navigable route would have made Mesopotamia much more desirable to other powers. In retrospect, one other leader also seemed to have ambitions in Arabia: Mehmet Ali. From autumn 1836, he began to take advantage of the assassination of Turki to try to reassert Ottoman rule in Najd, though Britain could not object to this in principle, any more than in the 1810s. In the late 1830s, some British policymakers began to claim that Mehmet Ali *was* the problem in Arabia. Whether this claim should be taken at face value is much more dubious—either in the Gulf, or in the Red Sea and the Hijaz, where he was also active.

Steam, the Red Sea, and Southern Arabia

In the mid-1830s, technological progress was conquering the Red Sea and revealing it as the best route for steam navigation to India. The question was how to provide for the security of British shipping there, since it had traditionally been so inaccessible. The overriding problem was an alarming lack of effective authority.

After the 1834 select committee report, there was investment in all parts of the route to India. The Admiralty funded six new steamers for the Mediterranean service, and by 1837 there was a sophisticated postal arrangement for that part of the route, aided by Anglo-French collaboration. Under Hobhouse, the India Board became much more willing to spend money on the Red Sea service. This was the result of increased government control over the EIC under the new charter of 1833, in addition to pressure from cotton manufacturers, and general scepticism about the Euphrates route among senior Indian administrators. In summer 1835, Hobhouse got the EIC to pay for two large new steamers on the Suez–Bombay route, the *Atalanta* and *Berenice*. They were better equipped to confront the seasonal monsoons (though not perfect, and passengers disliked the coal smuts). From early 1837, they provided a monthly service. In April 1837, the Treasury agreed to pay half the cost of this

72. J. Kelly, *Britain and the Persian Gulf*, 256–59, 357–65.

expanded steamer service, and another vessel was added in 1838. Plans were laid for the Indian Navy to convert to a steam flotilla.[73]

These were necessary changes, but they involved optimistic assumptions about the route itself. Steamers would require at least one secure coaling station and store depot en route, yet the Indian Navy's Red Sea surveys under Elwon and Moresby had not found the right location. So in 1834 the *Palinurus* was sent back to the region under Stafford Haines, specifically to survey the southern Arabian coast, and the island of Socotra to its south (which Leibniz in the 1670s had proposed as an essential component of a French seaborne commercial empire in the Indian Ocean).[74] In October 1834, shortly after it sent back its first accounts of Socotra, the Indian government asked Haines to negotiate for possession of the island. This failed, partly because of the opposition of the ruler on the mainland (which Haines tried to ignore), but mainly on account of the deadly climate.[75] There were few alternatives. In 1837, in explaining the new arrangements for the Red Sea service, Hobhouse airily remarked that Mocha was to be the depot.[76] Yet Mocha was a problem on several levels: previous failures to get local authorities there to respect a British residency; the decline of the direct coffee trade; above all, uncertainty about who exercised effective sovereignty over it.

The attempts of Popham, Pringle, and Rudland to strengthen Britain's position in Mocha during the Napoleonic Wars had come to nothing. Bombay replaced Rudland with a new resident in 1812 on condition that he confined himself to commercial affairs. EIC interest in the Red Sea declined after the abolition of its trading monopoly in 1813; merchants from London as well as from the United States were now buying coffee themselves. In 1817, an officer of the Bombay Marine visiting Mocha was dragged naked from his bed and spat on, and the residency pillaged, after a rumour that the sepoys on guard were part of a planned British attack on Mecca. Bombay was reluctant to respond until after the end of the Wahhabi threat on the Arabian Peninsula, but was then emboldened by the signing of the 1820 Gulf treaty. A squadron was sent in August 1820 to demand reparations, and bombarded the fort twice. The British then imposed a treaty that secured the resident's rights and lowered export duties to 2.25 per cent (the sum paid by the French since bombarding Mocha themselves in 1737).[77] Britain treated with the imam of

73. For this paragraph, see Hoskins, *British Routes to India*, 210–22; Searight, *Steaming East*, 48–49.

74. Baruzi, *Leibniz*, 33.

75. Wellsted's first brush with literary fame derived from his detailed and charming account of Socotra's natural features and hospitable and naturally law-abiding tribes: "Island of Socotra."

76. *PP* (1837), 21.

77. Playfair, *Arabia Felix*, 135–40; C. Low, *Indian Navy*, 1:299–307; India Board, Sept. 5, 1822, FO 78/112 256.

Sanaa, regarding him as the sovereign authority over the local ruler, the dola of Mocha. However, the imam had little power over his petty chiefs, and so there was no remedy for continuing ill-treatment of traders. Mehmet Ali's son had briefly taken Luhaya and Hudayda in the 1810s, but had given both ports to the imam in return for tribute payments in coffee.

The pasha of Egypt had a similar problem of getting his rights enforced. For most of the 1820s, the British consul-general in Egypt, Henry Salt, argued that Britain and Mehmet Ali had a common interest in encouraging Ottoman/Egyptian influence over Mocha, despite the fact that since the 1630s it had been under the nominal sovereignty of the imam and not the Ottomans. Jeddah was increasingly a safer commercial bet, showing the benefits of Mehmet Ali's control.[78] Once the Red Sea surveys began in 1829, the British resident in Mocha was withdrawn. The hope now was that British naval power, together with Mehmet Ali's name, would secure respect there.

A crisis in 1832–33 then exposed the limits of Mehmet Ali's control of the Hijaz, let alone the coastal strip (the Tihama) of the Asir and Yemen to the south, which included the ports of Luhaya, Hudayda, and Mocha. Six thousand Ottoman troops at Jeddah revolted under Muhammad Agha, a Georgian cavalry commander who acquired the nickname Turkçe Bilmez. The cause was lack of pay, but also Turkçe's view that Mehmet Ali had overreached himself in invading Syria. Mehmet Ali had to send a new army to reconquer the Hijaz, and this drove Turkçe south along the Tihama to Mocha. In late 1833, he and his force were attacked there by twenty thousand men from the Yemeni mountains; they ransacked the mosques and sold the women of the harems to the highest bidder, on average for twenty or thirty dollars apiece. Turkçe was given sanctuary on board an Indian Navy vessel, while the British supported Mehmet Ali's successful blockade against the mountain tribes, in the hope of restoring peace.[79]

Patrick Campbell, now British consul-general in Egypt, and the India Board in London both condoned the resulting Egyptian occupation of Mocha, because it would benefit commercial stability.[80] Commercial stability, however, was difficult to achieve, because of the tribes in the mountains behind the Tihama, who were strongly anti-Egyptian, impossible to conquer, and pro-Wahhabi. Mehmet Ali sent more troops under his nephew Ibrahim Küçük to deal with them in 1835, but the conflict quickly reached stalemate. These reinforcements were draining his treasury, in Campbell's view. Moreover, in an attempt to reduce his losses, Mehmet Ali was buying up as much of the coffee

78. Marston, *Red Sea*, 40–41. Robert Harrison, in *Britain and the Middle East* (18), exaggerates the stability and permanence of the British position at Mocha in the 1800–1830 period.

79. Hulton, *South Arabia*, 74–75.

80. See Campbell to Palmerston, Oct. 27, 1833, FO 78/228 232, and Palmerston to Campbell, May 12, 1838, FO 78/342 23.

at Mocha as possible and channelling it towards Egypt for sale. When pressed, he agreed to uphold Britain's 1821 treaty securing low duties on its own coffee exports.[81]

So the new steam arrangements for the Red Sea announced in 1837 relied on Mehmet Ali's control of the Hijaz, and an anticipation of the same in the Yemeni ports. In June 1837, Thomas Waghorn (who in 1835 had established himself in Egypt as an agent for the transporting of mail, goods, and passengers between Alexandria and Suez) was made Campbell's deputy, in charge of the new postal service across the country and down the Red Sea. Waghorn got Britons appointed as packet agents and vice-consuls in Suez, Kosseir, and Jeddah, to superintend the service.[82] Thus Archibald Ogilvie, a young Cambridge graduate, was permitted to reside as the first British agent at Jeddah, despite its proximity to Mecca, replacing a local EIC agent, a Baghdadi Armenian (himself established there in 1821–22 under Mehmet Ali's protection).[83] Waghorn's mail system assumed British cooperation with Mehmet Ali throughout the Red Sea.

But while British officials in Egypt took the position that Britain's Red Sea interests depended on good relations with the Cairo government, an alternative, more assertive view was emerging from the decks of the *Palinurus*, the Indian Navy survey vessel. This view was most strongly held by its commander, Stafford Haines, and reflected the same navy enthusiasm for steam power and Arab commerce that was simultaneously driving forward Henry Blosse Lynch's thinking in Mesopotamia and the Gulf. Haines had joined the Bombay Marine at fifteen, had seen action against the Gulf shaykhs in 1819, and had become assistant surveyor in the Gulf in 1826. He shared Lynch's assumptions about the potential of steam to educate the Arabs as trading partners and potential allies. He was also inspired by Popham's earlier attempts to establish a regional commercial naval presence independent of the Ottomans. Haines was determined to uphold the 1821 Mocha treaty with the imam of Sanaa, and to restrict Mehmet Ali's interference in an area of historic British influence, especially as Haines saw him as an unfriendly trade monopolist who would damage British commercial hopes. In 1836, Haines produced a long historical paper insisting that Mocha was independent of the Ottomans—a view shared by Lynch.[84]

In the same way that Lynch and Taylor looked back to the time when Mesopotamia was an economic powerhouse, the Indian Navy explorers drew

81. Marston, *Red Sea*, 47–51. Haines and India complained about Mehmet Ali's apparent infringement of the 1821 treaty, but Campbell had already dealt with the issue in October 1836: see FO 78/319 48, 59.

82. FO 78/322 187 and 78/344 26.

83. See the list at FO 78/214 469. For Ogilvie in Jeddah, see Freitag, "Helpless Representatives," 359–64.

84. Waterfield, *Sultans of Aden*, 34–35; Lynch to Cabell, Mar. 30, 1835, FO 78/269 210.

inspiration from the ancient trading history of southern Arabia and its African hinterland. They suggested that once the Red Sea resumed its place as a great trade route, displacing the Cape, any of the ports at the southern tip of Arabia—Mocha, Aden, or Mukalla—could have a prosperous future. The first of them to popularise this theme was Raymond Wellsted, who had been Charles Malcolm's secretary at the Bombay Marine in 1829, and was ambitious for literary fame as an intrepid explorer and chronicler of the geography, history, and culture of Arabia. One aim of his two books of 1838 and 1840 was to convince a domestic public of the historic—and perhaps future—significance of the region, especially the fertile Hadramaut region of southern Arabia. This had been the Arabia Felix of the Romans, and was believed to be the home of the Queen of Sheba (Saba); it might also have been the first human settlement after the deluge. This was where commerce with India and Africa began, in spices, silk, and gold. Wellsted discovered some important Himyaritic inscriptions in 1834 and planned to use the expedition of Mehmet Ali's troops against the Asiri as his chance of exploring the interior of Hadramaut in 1835, before the latter were beaten back.[85]

Most people could see that Mehmet Ali was making no inroads into Asir and Yemen. Campbell assumed that the Arabs would soon drive him out. By 1839, his customs house officials in the Yemeni ports were owed twenty months' arrears of pay.[86] Haines, however, had failed in his independent bid to secure Mocha as a steam depot for Britain. In 1836 he sent one of his officers, Charles Cruttenden, to Sanaa to discover if the new imam, in power since 1834, could help Britain there, but was appalled by his drunkenness and debauchery—his penchant for raw spirits tasting like "bad whiskey," and his dancing girls. Such a man, he claimed, would be easy prey for Mehmet Ali.[87]

Britain urgently needed a secure local base, and there seemed only one remaining choice: the port of Aden, with which Britain had signed a treaty in 1802. Reflecting that historic tie, even the consuls in Egypt made a distinction between Aden and Mocha: Mehmet Ali was beneficial in the latter, but Salt had warned him against taking an interest in the former in 1825.[88] In 1835, Haines argued that it was of the "first mercantile importance," and convinced the men of the *Palinurus* that the possession of Aden might allow Britain to

85. Wellsted, *Travels in Arabia*, 1:2, 355, 431–32, and 2:436; *City of the Caliphs*, 2:33–39. Another reason for his planned explorations of the interior of southern Arabia was that he fell out with Haines and had to leave the *Palinurus*. It was while in Muscat in 1837, in a delirium caused by fever, that he shot himself through the mouth. Never mentally or physically the same again, he was sent home to a gentleman's asylum in London and died in 1842.

86. Campbell to Palmerston, Nov. 1, 1837, FO 78/321 66, and Mar. 20, 1838, FO 78/342 111; Marston, *Red Sea*, 98–99.

87. Hulton, *South Arabia*, 174; Waterfield, *Sultans of Aden*, 36.

88. Gavin, *Aden*, 26.

divert the coffee trade there from Mocha.[89] In June 1837, James Mackenzie of the Bengal Light Cavalry warned the Indian government that Mehmet
Ali could control land only about a mile inland of the Yemeni Red Sea ports,
but that this heightened the risk that he might decide to take Aden as well,
which he could then sell to the highest European bidder. Britain must secure
it, because it offered "a power and consequence and commercial advantages"
in Arabia, Abyssinia, and north Africa.[90]

The potential for anarchy in a region that seemed so important to Britain
was highlighted by the attack on the *Daria Dowlat*, a ship owned by the nawab
of the Carnatic and flying the British colours, when it ran aground near Aden
in early 1837. The freight was stolen (a concerted move between the super-
cargo and a local gang), and Indian ladies of high rank were raped; it became
a cause célèbre in Bombay.[91] Robert Grant, governor of Bombay, led the drive
for measures of reparation, but also to take this chance to possess Aden's excellent harbour. The aim would be to restore regional stability, protect the new
monthly steamer service, and spread Indian produce "through the rich provinces of Yemen and Hadhar-el-mout." Grant was confident that Mehmet Ali
would not object, as his real interest lay in the development of British Red
Sea steam travel.[92] Campbell supported its acquisition as a coaling station
because he was pessimistic that Mehmet Ali could maintain much authority
in the Yemen. He also thought that his war was imperilling the coffee trade,
which might be attracted by a secure outlet at Aden. Aden was independent—
Mehmet Ali had no claim there, nor did the imam of Sanaa; Britain was fully
entitled to come to an arrangement with Aden's ruler, the sultan of Lahej,
about it.[93]

Grant sent Haines to make an agreement with the sultan about establishing a depot there, building on the treaty that his father had signed with Britain
in 1802. The sultan wanted to attract Indian trade and bolster his authority
against his troublesome neighbours, especially the Fadhli and the Egyptians.
However, he aimed for a limited arrangement by which the British would
pay an annual tribute for access to a coal depot, while he would maintain his
independent powers over non-British residents. His son suspected the British, and did not want an agreement at all. In January 1838, this suspicion led
to an apparent plot to kidnap Haines. Haines, looking for a grievance, suggested that this was an insult to the British flag. As his ultimate aim was the

89. Waterfield, *Sultans of Aden*, 29. Haines's enthusiasm was picked up by Hulton
(*South Arabia*, 177) and Wellsted (*City of the Caliphs*, 2:157).

90. Marston, *Red Sea*, 51–53.

91. Reese, *Imperial Muslims*, chap. 2.

92. Hoskins, *British Routes to India*, 198–99; Grant to Hobhouse, Feb. 27, 1838,
Broughton, F213 9.

93. Campbell letters, Nov. 1, 1837, Jan. 18 and March 22, 1838, FO 78/321 66 and
FO 78/342 45, 122.

region's commercial development, he aspired to control the port's trade duties as well as the depot. He now argued that the ruling family was unreliable, and that Britain should secure the town by force if necessary. In autumn 1838, the Bombay government sent a small expedition, which it claimed was a mission of peace to encourage the sultan to make a treaty. As the sultan's son was now in command in the town, no compromise was possible. After some skirmishes, seven hundred British troops landed from three warships and took the territory in January 1839.

Haines was installed as governor, and spent the first eighteen months dealing with potential insurrections from the local tribes. He kept briefing Bombay to be on its guard against Mehmet Ali's encroachments and claims over the coffee trade, in order to promote his own design to attract the trade to Aden. Mehmet Ali toyed with an alliance with the imam of Sanaa against Aden, but this foundered on mutual distrust and on Mehmet Ali's lack of money and unwillingness to antagonise Britain. In early 1840, he announced that he was withdrawing his troops from the Yemen, leaving the coastal ports to the leading local shaykh, Sharif Husayn of Abu Arish, in return for annual tribute. Haines became Bombay's representative all over the southern Red Sea.[94]

The manoeuvre that secured Aden for Britain provided a coaling station for the monthly steamships and a presence at the mouth of the Red Sea. It also made the tension between Mehmet Ali and the Asiri tribes irrelevant to Britain. However, even at the time, it was seen as discreditable.[95] In the past, the local obstacles might have deterred the cautious Bombay government from persevering with it, especially once Robert Grant died suddenly in July 1838. The difference now was that there was clear and repeated backing for the acquisition in London. The acting governor of Bombay sanctioned the expedition of autumn 1838 because Foreign Secretary Palmerston's correspondence with Campbell suggested that the government attached "very great importance" to the possession of Aden, and that Bombay must pre-empt any risk of Mehmet Ali taking it.[96] Though Haines's personal ambitions explain a lot about the acquisition, its ultimate cause was pressure from the British government. This was part of an expansionist strategy for the whole Middle East, and India, in 1838–39.

Hobhouse, Palmerston, the Middle East, and India

In 1838, instability seemed to be increasing throughout western Asia. Several wars were raging, and authority was in question across Arabia, Baghdad, Persia, and Afghanistan. The Ottoman sultan's power was minimal south of

94. For these two paragraphs, see Waterfield, *Sultans of Aden*, 51–130.
95. [Holme], "Occupation of Aden." For EIC criticism, see Gavin, *Aden*, 362n126.
96. Waterfield, *Sultans of Aden*, 55–58.

Anatolia, while Persia was in turmoil after the death of Fath Ali Shah in 1834. This might be an ideal situation for Russia to exploit. In 1838, and again in 1840, Hobhouse and Palmerston claimed that Russia and Britain were in contention for an empire of the East; the stakes could not be higher. Both men determined on a forward policy to defeat "Russian schemes" and demonstrate Britain's global reach and strength.[97]

For some time, Persian specialists had worried that a Russian-dominated Persia might advance to its east, threatening the border with Afghanistan, and potentially India. In late 1837, the Persians, aided by Russian loans and a Russian advisor, besieged Herat, the westernmost Afghan state. Meanwhile, instability within Persia after the shah's death encouraged the pasha of Baghdad to attack the growing port town of Muhammara on the Shatt al-Arab, which Persia wished to build up as a potential rival to Basra. As before, Britain deprecated these border aggressions by a weak pasha, which opened up the risk of a counter-attack on Baghdadi territory.

One fear was that Mehmet Ali might exploit this turbulence and invade the pashalik. The rumour arose because Mehmet Ali had sent troops into Najd in response to the tensions in the Saudi heartlands after the assassination of Turki. Mehmet Ali upheld the claim of Khalid (brother of the former Wahhabi leader Abdullah), who had become an Egyptian puppet during long residence in Cairo. Khalid was installed in Riyadh in 1837, and Mehmet Ali's proconsul Hurşit arrived with an army in 1838, to strengthen his position. Turki's son Faysal was captured and taken to Cairo in late 1838. Mehmet Ali's initial priority in attacking Najd had probably been to prevent further instability in the Hijaz and the Holy Cities, but he was now able to claim that the chiefs of Najd recognised his authority. His first expression of interest in independence from the Ottoman sultan, in May 1838, accompanied the news of Faysal's subordination to him.[98] He could persuasively claim to be the best leader of the Arabs and defender of Islam. Moving further east to possess Baghdad and Basra would strengthen that claim enormously, as well as multiplying his revenues and making him the dominant regional force.

The possibility that Mehmet Ali might create a powerful Arab empire was welcomed by some British commentators, who wanted to check the Russian threat to the Middle East. In 1839, for example, Adolphus Slade, a Mediterranean naval officer with a strong interest in Middle Eastern politics, argued that an Islamic state founded on the Holy Cities in Mehmet Ali's possession—Mecca, Medina, and Jerusalem—could revive the spirit of the caliphate,

97. In February 1840, Palmerston foretold to Hobhouse that "the Cossack and the Sepoy, the man from the Baltic and he from the British islands, will meet in the centre of Asia," but Hobhouse had wanted to write something similar to Auckland in 1838, which the cabinet regarded as too incendiary: Russell to Hobhouse, Oct. 14, 1838, and Palmerston to Hobhouse, Oct. 29, 1838, and Feb. 14, 1840, Broughton, F213 6, 7.

98. J. Kelly, *Britain and the Persian Gulf*, 292–94.

regenerate the region, and prevent Russia conquering western Asia—in a way that the enfeebled sultan could not do. The beating heart of the empire was "Arabian not Ottoman."[99] The same idea had occurred to Consul-General Campbell, and appears to have been openly discussed by British and Austrian representatives in Cairo in 1833–34, in consequence of Russian power over the Porte.[100] On the other hand, Russia had also teasingly indicated in 1834 that it might welcome the idea of Mehmet Ali as caliph of Arabia. This was a reminder that, geopolitically, a strong pan-Arab empire would uproot the status quo in completely unpredictable ways, and create the potential for new alliances, allowing Russia or France new chances to expand.[101] Moreover, the most likely outcome, as the veteran Indian and Persian expert Henry Ellis argued in 1833, was that an ambitious Arab ruler would destabilise British rule in India, by appealing to Muslim sympathies. It was not in Britain's interest for "a powerful Mahomedan state to be placed at the mouth of the Euphrates." It was far better for Britain if Mesopotamia remained subject to a weak figurehead with no interest in expanding eastwards. Palmerston quickly adopted Ellis's argument.[102]

Better still would be for the weak rulers of the region to seek British protection against any threats to their territory, real or exaggerated. As soon as Lynch arrived in Baghdad in the summer of 1837, he and Taylor started to bombard London and Ambassador Ponsonby in Constantinople with evidence that Baghdad's position was so perilous that Britain must increase its presence there—by expanding the flotilla under Lynch's control, and strengthening their influence with the pasha and the Arabs. These jeremiads prompted Palmerston to warn Mehmet Ali in late 1837 that Britain would not tolerate an attack on Baghdad.[103]

Palmerston was concerned about Baghdad, but he was also very interested in the Gulf. If Britain wanted to put pressure on Persia—as it did because of Persia's aggression on Herat—the Gulf was the natural place to do so. A statement of British power in the Gulf would make a point to Persia, to Russia, and to Mehmet Ali at the same time. It might also defuse tension over Bahrain, the richest island in the Gulf, which had long been claimed by Persia and Muscat. If Persia withdrew from Herat and sought domestic prestige by

99. Slade, *Sultan and Mehemet Ali*, 30–31.

100. Campbell to Ponsonby, Aug. 21, 1834, FO 78/246 75; to Palmerston, Oct. 1 and Nov. 27, 1838, FO 78/343, pt. 3, 6, 85.

101. As Broughton warned Werry, Aug. 4, 1840, Broughton, F213 7. For Russia's views in 1834, see Guest, *Euphrates Expedition*, 141–42.

102. Ellis's memorandum of 1833 is in J. Kelly, *Britain and the Persian Gulf*, 838–39. For Palmerston, see Bulwer, *Palmerston*, 2:145. Britain's new consul-general in Syria, J.W.P. Farren, also argued that if Mehmet Ali created an Arab empire it would be a destabilising force: to Palmerston, May 23, 1832, IOR L/P&S/9/93 497.

103. J. Kelly, *Britain and the Persian Gulf*, 291–92.

some aggression elsewhere, Bahrain was a likely choice. Britain had several options for retaliating against Persia's move on Herat. It could invade by land from the residency at Bushehr, or up the Karun river from Muhammara into Khuzistan. However, to do either would probably weaken the shah, whose hold over southern Persia was very fragile, and increase his dependence on Russia, as well as creating an international crisis. Instead, it was agreed to occupy the Persian island of Kharaq off Bushehr—a clear challenge to Persian dignity, and easily held. Kharaq was only a hundred miles from the mouth of the Euphrates, and just over two hundred from Bahrain.

In May 1838, Lord Auckland, the Indian governor-general, ordered Bombay to send a squadron and five hundred troops to occupy Kharaq until Persia lifted the siege of Herat. Though he did so without instruction from London, he must have known that Palmerston and Hobhouse would support it, as did Grant in Bombay. All four agreed that Britain must use its strength in the Middle East as well as India to push forward against Russia and Persia. In February 1838, Grant argued that Britain must take Kharaq and Aden as "advanced posts" to meet a possible challenge to India from Russia through Persia and, potentially in the future, France through Egypt. In May 1838, Hobhouse and Palmerston asked that Britain should obtain both these stations. For Palmerston, the attraction of Kharaq was that Britain could keep it, securely and cheaply, for as long as was diplomatically necessary. Hobhouse wanted to buy it from the shah after the crisis was over. Sir James Carnac, Grant's successor in Bombay, also wanted to keep it permanently, while Auckland saw it as the "Singapore of the Persian Gulf." Similarly, in late 1839, after Aden was taken, Palmerston and Hobhouse insisted on retaining it, even when Bombay expressed doubts about the expense.[104]

The British government was also anxious to show its presence in the pashalik of Baghdad. It was obvious that Britain could not occupy an Ottoman province without provoking a massive diplomatic furore. However, an expanded Indian Navy flotilla on the rivers required only an imaginative reinterpretation of the sultan's firman of 1834. In June 1838, Hobhouse told Grant that he wanted to see "the British flag on the Mesopotamian rivers" along with the occupation of Kharaq and Aden.[105] In May 1838, Lynch made his inaugural voyage in the *Euphrates*, down the Tigris, up the Euphrates to Hit, and then back to Baghdad along the Saklawiya canal. He and Taylor sent enthusiastic reports to London about this penetration of a region "so long lost to our commercial interests."[106] When these letters arrived in London in

104. Grant to Hobhouse, Feb. 27, 1838; Hobhouse to Grant, May 10, 1838; Hobhouse to Auckland, June 9 and Dec. 5, 1838; Palmerston to Hobhouse, Aug. 27, 1838, and Dec. 14, 1839; Carnac to Hobhouse, Oct. 5, 1839; Auckland to Hobhouse, Aug. 15, 1840; all in Broughton, F213.

105. Hobhouse to Grant, June 9, 1838, Broughton, F213.

106. Lynch and Taylor to London, June 20 and 25, 1838, IOR L/P&S/9/106 419, 435.

late August, Hobhouse, his secretary Cabell, and Peacock (now the chief civil servant at India House) used them to get permission for three new steamers, which arrived in Basra in early 1840. The creation of this flotilla of four ships then allowed the cabinet to reject envoy McNeill's request to send five thousand more men to the Gulf, since an invasion of mainland Persia would be too inflammatory.[107] However, another convenient symbol of British military power was at hand: a detachment of British troops had been in Persia helping to train the shah's army, until diplomatic relations were suspended in June 1838. It was sent home via Baghdad, where it stayed between February and late October 1839—with instructions to be on public display. Throughout 1839, Palmerston continued to warn Mehmet Ali against attacking Baghdad or Basra, even though the latter continued to deny any interest in doing so.[108]

In December 1838, Hobhouse expressed confidence that Mehmet Ali would do what Britain told him.[109] Nonetheless, it was irresistible to exploit the uncertainty about his intentions, in order to justify British assertiveness across the region. Palmerston became exercised about Hurşit's attempts to meddle in the politics of the Gulf, especially in Bahrain. Hurşit proposed an arrangement with its ruler, Abdullah, by which he would restore tribute payments to Riyadh (which the Wahhabi had periodically been able to enforce), and Abdullah agreed this in April 1839. Implicit in this arrangement was the idea that the sultan had some sovereignty over the Gulf coast, which Mehmet Ali and Hurşit were now loyally enforcing. Palmerston told the Porte that Britain would not accept Mehmet Ali taking a naval station on the Gulf in the sultan's name, claiming once again that this would help him to attack Baghdad and Basra. The Indian government agreed that its navy would protect Bahrain against an Egyptian attack.[110] Once the Ottoman sultan died in June 1839, and the European diplomatic crisis over the East began, Palmerston's warnings about Mehmet Ali's supposed expansion had even more merit, in constructing an idea of him as a universal aggressor against whom Europe must unite. Britain could be portrayed as asserting itself in the Gulf not for selfish reasons, but as the local enforcer of a status quo. It was upholding the sultan's authority against Mehmet Ali—even though Mehmet Ali also claimed to be upholding it.[111]

107. See Cabell and Peacock notes, Aug. 30 and Sept. 14, 1838, IOR L/P&S/3/4; Hobhouse to Auckland, Oct. 27, 1838, Broughton, F213 6. See J. Kelly, *Britain and the Persian Gulf*, 297–98.

108. Hobhouse to Taylor, June 13, 1839, Broughton, F213 7; Rawlinson, *Memoir*, 69–70; J. Kelly, *Britain and the Persian Gulf*, 320.

109. To Taylor, Dec. 26, 1838, Broughton, F213 7.

110. J. Kelly, *Britain and the Persian Gulf*, 302, 317–19; Palmerston to Campbell, June 15, 1839, FO 78/372 32.

111. Hobhouse hoped that the "four powers" of Europe would prevent Mehmet Ali from advancing on the Gulf: to Auckland, Sept. 16, 1839, Broughton, F213 7.

While Palmerston was increasingly concerned to turn Mehmet Ali into a useful enemy, the Indian Navy was more preoccupied with maintaining British prestige over the Gulf Arabs. If Hurşit were allowed to emerge as a new regional force, Britain would look weak, and the shaykhs could play off Britain and Hurşit against each other. Lynch regarded the presence of Mehmet Ali's proconsul on the Gulf coast as a "very great embarrassment" to Britain's traditional ability to "treat with every petty Chief, and force them to respect our views and interests with little trouble."[112] In this situation, Samuel Hennell, the resident in the Gulf, had to try to organise the Gulf shaykhs himself—having moved to Kharaq, with troop reinforcements, after Persian hostility drove him out of Bushehr. In July 1839, he secured a written agreement from the Trucial shaykhs to oppose any Egyptian attack. In the autumn, Hurşit told Hennell that he wished to assert Ottoman sovereignty over Buraimi. In response, Hennell gave an informal promise of protection to the ruler of Buraimi, being unable to do more by the uncertainty about the availability of ships, given the simultaneous crises in China and Persia. He pressed the chiefs in Muscat and the Trucial territories to organise their own protection. Using offers of rice, currency, and ammunition, Hennell got the shaykhs to agree a united front for the protection of Buraimi against the Egyptians. He also made clear that his squadron would obstruct any Egyptian naval excursion to the Trucial territories. He had to operate mostly alone, because of the Indian government's traditional reluctance to make formal commitments for the defence of petty shaykhdoms, especially in such an uncertain situation. Auckland would have been willing to give the Trucial shaykhs naval protection, in the last resort, if they were swiftly overrun by the Egyptians, though he did not think that Britain could or should commit to protect Oman. He preferred to wait and to react to events. This was wise, because Hurşit's strategy for the Gulf was never clear; he was always vulnerable to endemic tribal factionalism, which his heavy taxation exacerbated. There was also an underlying confidence that Britain could rectify any coastal gains he made, if really necessary. In retrospect, it seems likely that the interest in Buraimi was driven by a local subordinate of Hurşit's, while the latter's probings in Bahrain arose from overestimating its financial potential and underestimating its political complexity.[113]

This judgment was confirmed when Mehmet Ali ordered Hurşit to withdraw from the Gulf coast in February 1840. Ever since he had defeated Sultan Mahmud's forces at Nizip in June 1839, Syria had become the place that would determine his future. Maintaining an army in Arabia was an expensive luxury, and there were many local Arab revolts against Hurşit's exactions. France was also urging him to be cautious, fearing that Britain was looking for an excuse

112. To Hobhouse, Mar. 31, 1839, Broughton, F213 9.

113. J. Kelly, *Britain and the Persian Gulf*, 309–11, 330–36, 352; Winder, *Saudi Arabia*, 128–31.

to occupy Basra as well as Aden and Kharaq.[114] Palmerston wished it to be thought that Mehmet Ali was showing his hostility to Britain by threatening Baghdad and Basra; in fact, he backed away from threatening them because he wanted to avoid being the enemy of Britain. Palmerston wanted to portray Mehmet Ali as an Islamic imperialist, but his experience in Arabia between 1836 and 1840 showed instead the impossibility of uniting the Arabs.

One by-product of the shift of interest towards Syria in 1840 was that Lynch's three new Mesopotamian steamers were not as useful as expected. They created a minor sensation when they arrived at Basra in early 1840, in parts for local assembly. As the bits were converted into ships, and eventually floated one after the other, it seemed to the wondering Arabs that they had reproduced themselves.[115] The hope had been that, by sailing up and down the Tigris and on the lower Euphrates, they would help to maintain the authority of the Baghdad pasha, and build the loyalty of the Muntafiq and the other powerful tribes against any threat from Hurşit in Arabia. But by 1840, if there was a threat to the pashalik, it came from the west and north, not the south. The battle of Nizip that inaugurated the Eastern crisis in June 1839 took place only a few miles from Port William, where the original steamers had been assembled. So the ships might be useful for strengthening Ottoman and British authority in the upper Euphrates and Tigris regions as well. However, this depended on proving the navigability of the upper reaches of the rivers. It was frustrating that the steamers could not get far enough up the Tigris to reach Kurdistan: in March 1839, in the *Euphrates*, Lynch had to stop twenty miles short of Mosul.[116] The navigability of the upper Euphrates was even more sensitive because Lynch feared that any failure there would weaken British prestige among Arab tribes, vis-à-vis the Egyptian army in Syria. He demanded large crews in order to assert his power, worried that the steamers would get stuck in the shallows. He also worried that Ibrahim might capture the vessel. These reasons explain his refusal to try the ascent to Beles in 1838. In 1840, he abandoned the flotilla and travelled to London to lobby for more money and men.[117]

This was a self-defeating trip, which exposed the boats' irrelevance in this new situation, and in retrospect its logic seems baffling. However, in the spring and summer of 1840 it was possible to believe that Mehmet Ali was now a permanent enemy of Britain and that the Egyptian transit might well be jeopardised. Moreover, if the British government were going to put money and resources into a project to remove him from Syria, it might support a case

114. J. Kelly, *Britain and the Persian Gulf*, 320n.

115. Lynch to Hobhouse, Jan. 25, 1840, Broughton, F213 10.

116. Lynch to Ponsonby, Mar. 22, 1839, PPD, E370 34.

117. Lynch to Maddock, Aug. 23, 1839, IOR L/P&S/9/112 365; to Ponsonby, June 5, 1840, PPD, E370 55.

for longer-term investment in Syrian transport links afterwards. This might be the moment, finally, for the Syria–Euphrates route to India to prove its reliability, to the benefit of British interests in Baghdad—and, not least, the Lynch-Taylor family. During his trip home, Lynch persuaded his two young brothers to come out to establish a family merchant operation in Baghdad. Lynch underestimated the continuing strength of Anglo-Egyptian commercial and political ties, but his family continued to urge the importance of the Euphrates Valley connection on British governments for decades to come.

In fact, the crisis of 1838–41 allowed Britain to secure greater control over both key routes between Europe and India. By 1841, its power was evident at the mouth of the Red Sea, in the Gulf, and in lower Mesopotamia. Steam communication was established between Egypt and India, and Aden was becoming a garrison. The Trucial system had been set up in the Gulf. The British had sent clear signals that they would defend Baghdad if anyone threatened it, which no one did. Their regional naval supremacy was undisputed. Whether steam might civilise the Arabs was a question for the long term, but they generally behaved well to the officers who dealt with them. All these objectives had been pursued independently of Constantinople. But they were compatible with the maintenance of the fig leaf of Ottoman sovereignty, and if this were what was meant by "the independence and integrity of the Ottoman Empire," it seemed an attractive proposition. When Britain declared against Mehmet Ali's rule in Syria in July 1840, it was already six months after Mehmet Ali had acknowledged that he could not subdue either the Yemen or eastern Arabia. He had failed to create an Arab empire, if he had ever seriously tried to do so. Britain and Mehmet Ali fell out in 1840, but they fell out over Syria not because the latter seriously threatened British interests in Arabia. Britain extended its power in and around Arabia in order to counter the effects of a lack of local authority and security; Mehmet Ali's manoeuvres helpfully justified some of its actions. This was clearly a forward policy. In 1840, the British press tried to imply that France had aggressive ambitions in the Middle East, even though France claimed no new territory. Not surprisingly, the French press had already had something to say about Britain's rather more blatant aggression in seizing Aden and Kharaq.[118]

118. See, for example, the article in the *Journal des débats* of May 23, 1839, quoted in Rodkey, *Turco-Egyptian Question*, 94n74.

CHAPTER FIVE

Britain, Egypt, and Syria
in the Heyday of Mehmet Ali

MEHMET ALI HAD GOVERNED EGYPT for over a quarter of a century before he invaded Syria in 1831–32. The Convention of Kütahya of 1833 that established his legitimacy there was brokered by France and Britain, and allowed his men to rule it for over seven years before international political pressures removed them in 1840. Yet owing to the lack of studies of British relations with Egypt, there is a default assumption that because Britain took the lead in opposing his tenure of Syria in 1840, it must have been critical of Mehmet Ali's economic and political ambitions all along, viewing them as a proxy for French imperialism.[1] This is not the case. In Egypt, there was a lot of positive British engagement with Mehmet Ali, who seemed both a necessary and a beneficial figure. It was less flamboyant than the French courting of him, but it achieved three essential British aims. One was safe travel through the country, which was crucial in reaching India—and in exploring Egyptian history, which became fashionable after 1815. Another was political influence: Mehmet Ali was the strongest military leader in the Ottoman Empire, probably the only man keeping it alive, and a key figure in resolving the Greek crisis. A third was economic gain for well-placed individuals. By the 1830s, there were a lot of British "Mehmetists."

When Mehmet Ali conquered Syria as well, there was a vigorous debate about whether his regime—which relied on state monopolies over most

1. In 1931, Dodwell was already aware that Mehmet Ali was "the traditional hero of French and villain of English writers": *Founder of Modern Egypt*, vii. His book tried to challenge the stereotype, but did not get very far (see, e.g. 55, 143–44): it does not even mention Briggs. Fine recent books such as Jasanoff's *Edge of Empire* continue the theme of the "special relationship" between France and Mehmet Ali (230, 281–86), as does Caquet in *Orient* (chap. 3). John Clarke hardly considers the issue of Mehmet Ali, regarding him as "too identified with France to be suitable for British purposes": *British Diplomacy*, 203.

produce—was suited to the economy and culture of the Syrian Levant, especially the old Phoenician seafaring littoral and the Lebanese mountains. This was because the British had diverse visions of Syria, as they did of Egypt. The debate about Mehmet Ali was in part between schools of thought—between Benthamite utilitarians, most of whom saw Mehmet Ali's strong rule in Egypt as the best model for the region, and Liberal Tories like Huskisson and Palmerston who sought economic expansion all over the world on a policy of freeing trade from restrictive tariffs. They hoped to promote British trade in order to pre-empt Russian dominance in western Asia. To this end, the Liberal Tories had already, in 1825, abolished the Levant Company, the long-established body for British trade with the Ottoman Mediterranean, which they saw as a lethargic vested interest. However, Levant Company culture survived, in the form of Samuel Briggs, to exercise considerable power in Mehmet Ali's monopolistic Egypt. The debate came to turn on whether Mehmet Ali's statist regime was suited to a potentially European space like Syria, or just to "African" Egypt, which most people in Britain still regarded as an Old Testament land of slavery. Until at least 1838, Palmerston's criticism of Mehmet Ali's rule in Syria was only half-formed and was driven by visionary free-trading aspirations. In the late 1830s, the growth of Christian tourism to Palestine, made possible by Mehmet Ali's rule itself, created a new vision of the potential of the "Holy Land," which was even more unrealistic. Moreover, as we shall see in chapter 6, Palmerston's interest in Syria was, until 1839, much more of a political strategy to challenge Russian dominance over the Ottomans than it was a concern about anything that the French might achieve by wooing Mehmet Ali. Most observers continued to be confident that Britain would secure its objectives in his Egyptian fiefdom.

Samuel Briggs and the Afterlife of the Levant Company

In 1803, a twenty-seven-year-old trader set up Briggs & Company in Alexandria. For the next sixty years, it was the rock on which British commercial and political interests in Egypt stood. There was hardly a pie in which it did not have a finger—hardly a commercial initiative, political agitation, or transit arrangement in which the name Briggs & Company was not prominent. Samuel Briggs remains an underdiscussed figure because of a dearth of material, but also because of the perception, developed by Palmerston in the late 1830s, that his company represented a mere vested interest.[2] In fact, it is the breadth of Briggs's connections that is significant. He represented continuity with the military occupation and hopes of 1801–3; he was intimately associated with the Levant Company and kept its influence alive after its abolition in

2. Rodkey, "Attempts of Briggs and Company."

1825. Above all, he represented the strategic and economic reality that Britain and Mehmet Ali had essential common interests whether Palmerston liked it or not. With every technological breakthrough, the importance of Egypt in securing trade and communications with India grew, and the money and power bound up in that transit ensured cooperation and good understanding. Briggs outlived Palmerston by three years, dying at ninety-two in 1868, but well before then it was obvious that he had had the clearer vision of Britain's relationship with Egypt all along.

Briggs arrived in Alexandria as a contractor for army supplies after the British invasion of 1801. In early 1803, when the army left, General Stuart, assuming the authority of the War Office, appointed him temporary proconsul at Alexandria in charge of British commercial needs (probably at Briggs's own suggestion). In this role, he showed enterprise and patriotism, priding himself on developing an unofficial mail channel across the desert, which allowed India to receive early news of the resumption of the war, and later of the Battle of Trafalgar.[3] He sympathised with the army officers, and blamed the War Office's poor reconnaissance for the failure of the 1807 invasion. It was Briggs's idea that Mehmet Ali should give Cleopatra's Needle to Britain as a memorial of the 1801 campaign.[4] Briggs worked well with Ernest Missett, Stuart's secretary, who became consul for Egypt in 1805. After peace with the Ottomans was resumed, Missett re-established the consulate in Egypt in 1811, though handicapped by the complete loss of use of his legs and arms. He was popular with British travellers, "a perfect specimen of an Irish gentleman, courageous and chivalrous to the last degree, an ardent admirer of the fair sex, a *bon vivant* of great refinement, . . . an excellent singer of after-dinner songs."[5] For the conduct of diplomatic business, Missett relied heavily on his secretary Robert Thurburn, whom Briggs chose as his business partner after Missett retired. From 1818 to 1839, Thurburn was manager of Briggs & Company in Alexandria, allowing Briggs to move back to Britain.

Stuart's temporary appointment of Briggs in 1803 was beneficial to him, even though the home government never ratified it. This was because it allowed the Levant Company, of which Briggs's kinsman Ebenezer was already a freeman, to set him up as its own consul, paid from local consular and customs fees. Briggs held this appointment until 1810, when he moved back to the Levant Company hub at Smyrna for a while (he had married the daughter of the former consul there, but she soon died). However, the company realised the continuing need for a commercial consul at Alexandria, and appointed Peter Lee, a company merchant from Smyrna who was also local agent for

3. For his activities in 1803–6, see IOR G/17/7 426–57.

4. See Briggs's various letters on the subject, 1820–51, in FO 78/2116 1, 20, 45, 184, 188.

5. Buckingham, *Autobiography*, 2:152–53.

Briggs & Company. This began a tradition that the Alexandria consul was closely connected to Briggs's firm. When the Levant Company was abolished in 1825, and its consuls became Foreign Office appointees, the other merchants successfully challenged this policy, but the result was an appointment popular with neither them nor Mehmet Ali. So in 1833, Thurburn was made consul at Alexandria, as deputy to the new Egyptian consul-general Patrick Campbell. This reflected the widespread wish for a British representative of "high character and influence" in the post.[6] In 1839, Thurburn was succeeded by John Wingfield Larking, who was related by marriage to both Thurburn and Briggs. After the hiatus of the Eastern crisis, Briggs's network was re-established in the 1840s. The Egyptian transit was managed first by Thurburn and then by Richard Lee Green, another old Smyrna Levant Company hand and, it so happened, the brother-in-law of Larking and the second Mrs. Briggs.

These appointments did not just please Briggs; they were also designed to satisfy Mehmet Ali, who several times pressed for Briggs or Thurburn to be made consul through the 1820s and 1830s. At some point in the 1810s, Briggs became Mehmet Ali's commercial agent in England—which is why he moved back to Britain. Briggs had won this role by appreciating Mehmet Ali's power and potential significance, after returning to Alexandria on the resumption of peace in 1809. In 1810, Briggs was the main organiser of a project for a commercial treaty between Mehmet Ali and the Indian government, which would have boosted British trade in the Red Sea. Briggs also secured Mehmet Ali's word that he would remain neutral if war resumed between Britain and the Ottomans.[7] Through the 1810s, Briggs continued to explore, in conjunction with Mehmet Ali, the development of commerce between Egypt and India.[8] More importantly, he was among the merchants who took advantage of the enormous demand for grain to feed the British regiments in Malta, Sicily, and Spain between 1810 and 1813. Most of this grain came from Egypt, where Mehmet Ali's government increasingly monopolised the stocks, because between 1808 and 1814 he took every opportunity to revoke previous land grants to private individuals, leaving the state in direct control of most land. The profits from government sales to British merchants funded Mehmet Ali's military campaigns against the Mamluks and the Wahhabi—defying the Constantinople regime, which prohibited sales outside the empire. From 1810, Mehmet Ali allowed British merchants access to the sheltered western harbour at Alexandria, which had previously been reserved for Ottoman traders.[9]

6. Foreign Office memo, Nov. 1836, FO 78/295 358.

7. Briggs to Wellesley, May 30, 1810, FO 24/3 75. This treaty project is discussed in chapter 2 above, pp. 76–77.

8. Buckingham, *Autobiography*, 2:418–20; Burckhardt, *Travels in Syria*, 469n.

9. Cotton to Croker, Feb. 8, 1811, FO 24/4 105; Dodwell, *Founder of Modern Egypt*, 30–31. See Marsot, *Egypt*, 145–47.

From 1820, Mehmet Ali and Briggs developed a mutual economic interest in the commercial development of long-staple cotton, another government monopoly. In 1824, Mehmet Ali gave Briggs right of sale in Britain, and he discovered great demand for this high-quality cotton at Liverpool. As a result, 111,000 bales were imported in 1825, the beginning of a thriving trade. Campbell estimated that Briggs made £20,000 from the cotton trade in 1832.[10] Briggs developed extensive contacts in the British manufacturing districts. This is revealed, inter alia, by the opportunities he gave to a bright Armenian boy, Joseph Hekekyan, whose dying father, a civil servant of Mehmet Ali's, had asked Briggs to arrange his education in England. In order to prepare him for a useful career in Egypt, Briggs also arranged for him to visit leading cotton-spinning factories in Manchester and Glasgow, of which he left a valuable record.[11]

Briggs's role as Mehmet Ali's agent in Britain necessarily took on a political aspect. In 1828, he claimed that he had been "for many years . . . the organ of his confidential communications" to the British government.[12] Throughout the 1820s and 1830s, he bombarded the Foreign Office with information about Egypt, and suggestions about Eastern policy. Briggs's view—which was shared by most British people with experience of Egypt—was that Mehmet Ali was committed to protecting the Anglo-Indian thoroughfare through Egypt, and was, if well treated, Britain's most reliable friend in the East. He was also the best bet for the future of the Ottoman Empire, on account of his military efficiency, interest in economic modernisation, and ability to control the Holy Cities of Islam. Briggs insisted that he did not want to overthrow the sultan, just to ensure hereditary possession of Egypt and the Hijaz for his family under Ottoman suzerainty. The Foreign Office recognised that there was a self-interested element to Briggs's letters, but still saw them as providing essential knowledge about an important figure. In February 1829, it was Briggs who urged the Foreign Office to remember that it must not treat Mehmet Ali as an independent ruler, because it would offend the sultan.[13]

Before and after 1830, it was natural for British officials to appreciate Mehmet Ali's military and economic achievement—in the Greek wars, and then in rapidly rebuilding his navy after Navarino—and his political influence, including in Constantinople, where there was always a well-funded lobby in his favour. Patrick Campbell quickly came to admire the vigour of his regime, and his value as a potential opponent of Russian aggression. By 1831, Mehmet Ali had collected a disciplined army of sixty thousand men, supported by

10. Campbell to Palmerston, Oct. 12, 1833, FO 78/228 177. See Owen, *Middle East*, 66–68, and *Cotton and the Egyptian Economy*, 37. For merchant complaints at Briggs's role in the monopoly system, see Barker to Dudley, Aug. 24, 1827, FO 78/160 334.

11. See the autobiography, Hekekyan Papers, BL Add. MSS 37448, 163.

12. To Aberdeen, June 4, 1828, FO 78/177 289.

13. To Bidwell, Feb. 7, 1829, FO 78/186 109.

foundries, armouries, and a naval arsenal at Alexandria modelled on France's at Toulon. This remarkable feat showed the extent of his resources, and offered a glaring contrast to Ottoman decline.[14] Was he wrong to claim that he had the best chance of stabilising Syria and consolidating Ottoman power there? Would the sultan do himself any favours by trying to attack him? Nor was it likely that Mehmet Ali would combine with Russia: his "only chance of permanent security is from England and France."[15]

Economic and Cultural Exchanges

Briggs's respect for Mehmet Ali was almost universally shared by Britons who spent any length of time in Egypt—by merchants, travellers, and explorers. It rested on the remarkable security that they enjoyed while there, so different from elsewhere in the region. Mehmet Ali ruthlessly stamped out brigandage and Bedouin plunder; in the towns, murder and robbery were penalised harshly. In 1818, at Kosseir, which remained the port at which most British travellers from India arrived, George Fitzclarence was told that "gold might be placed on the road, and none would touch it." In 1841, Richard Madden wrote that no European country was safer for the traveller.[16] A system of quarantine was introduced in 1817, followed by a rigorous public health policy in the 1820s. In his conversations with visiting Britons, Mehmet Ali constantly boasted that his priority was to make Egypt safe for their persons and property. He insisted that, even if the sultan and Britain were at war, he would continue to uphold "justice and liberality" to all British subjects in Egypt. When, after the Battle of Navarino, diplomatic relations collapsed at Constantinople and the ambassadors withdrew from there, no British merchant left Alexandria.[17] Even at the nadir of Anglo-Egyptian relations in 1841, Mehmet Ali kept his pledge that British money, mail, and commercial goods would be conveyed safely across Egypt. By the late 1830s, more than seventy Arab tribes were employed in the transit.[18]

Mehmet Ali also associated his regime with Christian rights. His long-standing chief minister and adviser, Boghos Yusufian, was an Armenian Christian (and former Levant Company dragoman in Smyrna), as were many other high government functionaries. By the mid-1820s, the law protecting Christian communities from attack by other religions was strictly applied, and the local Coptic and Armenian churches were allowed to ring their bells. This was at a time when, elsewhere in the empire, Greek Christians were being attacked

14. Barker, *Syria and Egypt*, 2:154–58.

15. Campbell to Ponsonby, May 21, 1834, FO 78/245 148.

16. Fitzclarence, *Journal*, 360; Madden, *Egypt and Mohammed Ali*, 25–26. For other examples: Salibi and Khoury, *Ottoman Syria*, 3:211; [Wilkinson], *Three Letters*, 28–31.

17. Barker, *Syria and Egypt*, 2:59, 72.

18. [Platt], *Journal of a Tour*, 2:73.

and the circulation of European Bibles was forbidden.[19] In the late 1830s, the Coptic bishop boasted that he walked the streets of Cairo wearing his cross and carrying his episcopal staff, invariably "without any molestation whatever."[20] Even at Jeddah, once Mehmet Ali governed it, Christians in European dress could walk freely in public, and in 1833 the local governor bastinadoed those responsible for plundering a shipwrecked British vessel, the *Nautilus*.[21] The mixed courts set up in Alexandria and Cairo to settle commercial cases contained only a minority of Muslims.[22] In 1838–39, Mehmet Ali permitted the British merchants to establish Saint Mark's in Alexandria, the first Anglican church built outside consular property anywhere in the Ottoman Empire, and granted the land for it; a chaplain arrived in 1841. He also engaged Alice Holliday, one of the Anglican missionaries in Cairo, to provide an education to the women in his harem, thus signifying his support for the principle of female education, which the missionaries believed was an essential first step in undermining superstition and ignorance in Islamic societies. Naturally, this emphasis on toleration and civil rights ensured very favourable publicity for Mehmet Ali in the British religious press. His heavy investment in a scientific and European education for his elites, in order to improve the functioning of his bureaucracy and army, was also widely praised, and contrasted with Ottoman ignorance.[23] In 1833, his son Ibrahim pleased a British diplomat by telling him—with reference to Sultan Mahmud's reforms—that "it is not by giving epaulettes and tight trousers to a nation that you begin the task of regeneration," but by education.[24]

Egypt became the most valuable market in the Middle East for British merchants, notwithstanding the special favours granted to the Briggs network. Mehmet Ali's economy was based on his landownership, and his police power to ensure that peasants sold produce to him at a price of his choosing.[25] In a bid to maximise revenue for his wars, produce was often seized by government warehouses, cutting out local traders. The export of grain, cotton, rice, and tobacco by foreign merchants contributed a large proportion of his annual revenue, which rose from eight million francs in 1805 to fifty million in 1821. British exports to Egypt, meanwhile, increased from £49,377 in 1827 to £237,444 in 1840; three-quarters were cotton goods.[26] To aid communica-

19. Burckhardt, *Travels in Arabia*, 206; Halls, *Henry Salt*, 2:199–202; Salibi and Khoury, *Ottoman Syria*, 3:211–12; Mansel, *Levant*, 58. For the firman on the circulation of the Bible, see chapter 7, p. 214.

20. Bowring, "Report on Egypt and Candia," 149.

21. Burckhardt, *Travels in Arabia*, 207–8; Gobat, *Life and Work*, 155–56.

22. Dodwell, *Founder of Modern Egypt*, 229.

23. Salibi and Khoury, *Ottoman Syria*, 3:212; Society for Promoting Female Education, *History of the Society*, 97–125.

24. Bailey, *British Policy*, 172.

25. Hunter, *Egypt under the Khedives*, 15.

26. Fahmy, *All the Pasha's Men*, xxviii, 267.

tion, Mehmet Ali had a new canal dug between Alexandria and the Nile, the Mahmudiya Canal, between 1817 and 1820. He then built up Alexandria as a place of European business. A smart European area was created around the Place des Consuls in the decade after 1834. The houses (owned by Ibrahim and rented out to foreign merchants) were built "as regularly as in Park Crescent," with green Venetian shutters. European tailcoats and round hats predominated, while "carriages of every description, filled with smartly dressed ladies, are to be seen driving about at all hours."[27] The town's population rose tenfold between 1806 and 1840; there were sixty-nine European firms there in 1837, against twenty-three in 1822.[28] Already in 1816, more than one-third of the ships in Alexandria's harbour were British. Some of the merchants complained at the high prices they had to pay for goods, but, as Consul Salt noted, "they are all making money." Visiting in 1831, John Malcolm noted how Mehmet Ali, Boghos, and Briggs worked together to promote commercial development.[29] In 1817, Thomas Jolliffe felt that Britain was bound to inherit responsibility for Egypt, and that with enlightened government it could be "one of the finest colonies in the world, and become eventually the centre of universal commerce."[30]

Mehmet Ali's cultivation of Britain included cultural diplomacy. In 1826–27, he arranged for a giraffe (usually then called a camelopard) from Nubia to be sent to London for George IV. France also received a specimen, and in both countries there followed a craze for giraffe-shaped candlesticks and for women's hair to be piled high "à la girafe." George IV's failure to show it to his people contributed to his unpopularity. The sickly creature died in 1829, was stuffed, and was presented to the new London Zoo, founded in 1828. A race ensued to get live specimens, which were viewed as essential publicity for the zoo's wider scientific purpose. The Egyptologist James Burton journeyed back to Britain with one in 1835, hoping that it would be the star of his intended menagerie, but it died slipping on ice at Calais. The Surrey Zoo, established in 1831 as a rival to the London establishment, captured three in Egypt. London Zoo paid £2,000 to beat them by chartering a steamer for four specimens that a member of its network had procured and sent to Malta. Their exhibition attracted unprecedented numbers of visitors, 260,000 over the year, even though until 1847 there were complex restrictions on public entry.[31] This episode is a reminder that, for a lot of people, Egypt in the early nineteenth century was seen as primarily an "African" and wild space. The Egyptian Hall, founded in Piccadilly in 1812, originally housed stuffed elephants, zebras, and

27. Griffith and Griffith, *Journey across the Desert*, 2:37–39.

28. Mansel, *Levant*, 71.

29. Halls, *Henry Salt*, 1:452, 469 (quotation); Malcolm to Palmerston, Mar. 23, 1831, FO 78/207 37.

30. [Jolliffe], *Letters from Palestine*, 240–41.

31. Ito, *London Zoo*, 63–69; Cooke, "James Burton," 91–92; Majer, "*La Mode à la Girafe.*"

other curiosities brought back from far-flung parts of the world and assembled for public display by William Bullock.

As the affair of the giraffes demonstrated, Mehmet Ali kept cultural ties with France, and French intellectuals maintained a strong interest in Egypt, as shown by Champollion's successful decipherment of hieroglyphics in the 1820s. Mehmet Ali used French experts to help him improve Egyptian administration, especially Soliman Pasha (Joseph Sève) who helped to train his army, and Clot Bey (Antoine Clot) who managed the public health system. Some young Egyptians intended for the civil service were sent to Paris for a suitable education.[32] Such visible signs of French influence in Egypt were naturally cultivated by a French state that continued to be extremely sensitive about the failure of the 1798 occupation, and that still presented itself as a Mediterranean power, especially after it took Algiers in 1830. In 1836, the obelisk from Luxor that Mehmet Ali had given to France a few years earlier was erected in the middle of the Place de la Concorde, while the British ignored theirs.[33] At any time in the nineteenth century, resident Englishmen could be found expressing anxiety at these various signs of Franco-Egyptian concord and urging more state activity by Britain to counteract them.[34] But this anxiety had limits. In 1816, Consul Salt remarked that Mehmet Ali's regime was dependent on revenue from commerce and hence was "entirely at our mercy." Ten years later, he was still confident that the friendship of Britain was more important to the pasha than that of any other country.[35]

Every shrewd commentator understood that Britain's power in Egypt rested on the thing that Mehmet Ali most feared, naval force, and the thing that he most needed—money. Mehmet Ali never forgot the lesson of the invasion of 1801: that the British, uniquely, could attack him simultaneously from the Mediterranean and the Red Sea. He was candid to several interviewers about his overriding fear of such an attack.[36] His emerging policy of independent diplomacy, separate from the Porte, was designed to appeal to Britain at a time when French influence at Constantinople seemed overwhelming. His discussions with Briggs and Benzoni in 1810 about a commercial treaty were founded on his dislike of Ottoman support for Napoleon's blockade. The money he made from selling grain to British troops in 1810–13—and the ammunition he procured in return—were fundamental to his political-military

32. Jasanoff, *Edge of Empire*, 275–77.

33. Porterfield, *Allure of Empire*, 13–41.

34. Waghorn, *Egypt as It Is*, 24; Campbell to Palmerston, June 12, 1837, FO 78/319 165. For W. H. Russell on this theme, see chapter 11, p. 353.

35. Dodwell, *Founder of Modern Egypt*, 58; Salt to Foreign Office, Dec. 4, 1826, FO 78/147 140.

36. Burckhardt, *Travels in Arabia*, 79; John Malcolm, Mar. 23, 1831, FO 78/207 37; Campbell to Palmerston, Oct. 27, 1833, FO 78/228 232.

strategy.[37] In the 1820s, despite Colonel Sève's help with training, his army remained modelled on Ottoman more than French practice, its activities in Greece alienated pro-Greek French public opinion, and a lot of the foreign adventurers who flooded into Alexandria offering to supply Mehmet Ali with Western technology were merely chancers, "the refuse of France and Italy" offering irrelevant gimmicks. French trade with Egypt remained inconsequential.[38] Consul John Barker could not understand why France even bothered to court Mehmet Ali, when Britain would triumph just by arousing his fear. As late as December 1838, Campbell believed that Mehmet Ali cared more for British support than French, and would make any sacrifice to get it.[39]

At least until the late 1830s, few Englishmen who experienced Egypt gave any thought to alternatives to Mehmet Ali's rule. They regarded him as a given, as a permanent regional presence, entrenched in power through his command of the government and military machine, and they appreciated the benefits of his rule. However, in some quarters there was also a moral debate about the nature of Egyptian government. Was it a model for the region, or troublingly inhumane?

Steam and the Two Faces of Mehmet Ali's Egypt

The steam revolution promised to underline Egypt's importance to Britain, as a communications channel, a commercial partner, and an orderly regime. The advocates of a Red Sea steam link between Britain and India assumed that a secure and powerful Mehmet Ali would be integral to the arrangement.[40] In 1838, John Bowring explained France's restlessness over the state of *Syria* in terms of "the obvious preponderance of English interests in Egypt which the steam navigation has created."[41]

Mehmet Ali's own evident fascination with steam and technology was part of his appeal to modernisers. He doubled the number of waterwheels in the country, in order to promote irrigation, and increased the cultivated acreage of Egypt by 30 per cent. At several times after 1810, he asked the British government to send him an engine and steam pump to help with irrigation and other improvements. One finally arrived in 1815, but his aides were unable

37. Ridley, *Bernardino Drovetti*, 46–56.

38. For the army, see Fahmy, *All the Pasha's Men*, 46–47; Rogan, *Arabs*, 91–92. For the adventurers: Jason Thompson, *Sir Gardner Wilkinson*, 45. On French trade: Caquet, *Orient*, 5.

39. Barker, *Syria and Egypt*, 2:51–52; Campbell to Palmerston, Dec. 12, 1838, FO 78/343 pt. 3, 89.

40. Waghorn, *Egypt as It Is*; [Wilkinson], *Three letters*, 22; [Dawson-Damer], *Question of the East*, 12.

41. To Palmerston, May 22, 1838, FO 78/345 130.

to operate it.[42] In November 1814, one of his agents was at Malta looking for European engineers who could be tempted to Egypt to provide similar help. He found an Anglophile Italian, Giovanni Battista Belzoni, who had been trained in mechanics but had drifted into work as a circus strongman in Britain. Belzoni came to Egypt, brought a better pumping machine, and later built a waterwheel, though his initial hopes were defeated when the wheel broke his assistant's thigh in front of Mehmet Ali himself, terrifying his courtiers. Similarly, James Burton arrived in Egypt in 1822 because Mehmet Ali advertised for mineralogists to work on a geological survey of Egypt in the hope of finding iron and coal (a hope that was also to drive Mehmet Ali's interest in Syria).[43]

Burton, and especially Belzoni, featured extensively in the British-led excavation of ancient Egypt after 1815, and Belzoni's story in particular is a reminder that the origins of what we now call Egyptology were a consequence of modernity, not an escape from it. Popular interest in his exploits created "Egyptomania" in Britain in the early 1820s, but this interest was less about the past, at least in any very systematic way, than about the ingenious application of "British" skill and technology to achieve a sensational result. Belzoni started by working for Consul Salt and then sought fame on his own. He achieved success by using his engineering brain to work out the location of hidden entrances to tombs, organising their excavation, and transporting over long distances enormous ancient Egyptian sculptures and other artefacts. The most spectacular of these was the seven-ton statue of Ramses II, known as the Young Memnon. The renown that Belzoni acquired for this technological feat gave Briggs, one of his financial backers, the idea that Mehmet Ali should donate Cleopatra's Needle to Britain, since Belzoni could advise the government on transporting it home.[44]

When Belzoni exhibited his collection at the Egyptian Hall in 1820 and 1821, his skill, enterprise, and flair made him a great success. So soon after the defeat of Napoleon, he was seen as a patriot for securing Ramses for Britain rather than France. His show was also immersively theatrical, focusing on the thrill of penetrating subterranean mysteries and wandering through a half-lit full-size reconstruction of Seti's burial chambers. He unwrapped an Egyptian mummy in order to publicise the show, a practice that the surgeon Thomas Pettigrew developed into a crowd-pulling autopsic art in the 1830s. The "Egyptomania" of the 1820s played on a taste for the spectacular, the magical, and the strange. London theatrical productions featured arcane sorcery,

---

42. For figures on waterwheels and land cultivation, see Dodwell's *Founder of Modern Egypt* (211) and Marlowe's *Anglo-Egyptian Relations* (50). For British initiatives to supply Mehmet Ali with a steam engine in 1810–12, see FO 24/4 12, 97, and Johnson's *T. Perronet Thompson* (72–73). For its arrival in 1815, see Mayes, *Great Belzoni*, 82–96.

43. Mayes, *Great Belzoni*, 83, 96, 109; Cooke, "James Burton," 88–89.

44. Briggs to Bloomfield, Apr. 11, 1820, FO 78/2116 20. For Belzoni's activities in Egypt, see Jasanoff, *Edge of Empire*, 247–55.

underground treasures, and heroines imprisoned in pyramids.[45] Similarly, the Egyptian relics in the British Museum tended to be seen as "curiosities," unlike the classical antiquities displayed nearby, which were proper objects of imitation for aspiring artists. Cuneiform began to be deciphered in the late 1820s, but it took years of further study before it was possible to know enough about ancient Egyptian society to allow an informed analysis of the objects on display. For a long time, therefore, Egypt remained a mysterious place associated mostly with buildings of immense size. In the 1830s and 1840s, the main context in which architects in Britain, and America, used ancient Egyptian designs was in very bulky constructions that served the new industrial economy, such as suspension bridges and railway stations.[46] This underlined a general view that, whatever else the ancient Egyptians may have been, they were technologically skilful, and that Mehmet Ali's modernising instincts made him a fitting inheritor of their throne.

However, there was another, less attractive side to this coin, which applied alike to ancient and modern Egypt. The pyramids symbolised inhumane working practices; they were "reared by slaves for tyrants to moulder in."[47] The colossal figures of Thebes seemed to William Jowett reminders of the gross idolatry of ancient tyrannies.[48] Modern Egyptians similarly seemed crushed in spirit and not full men. Soldiers forced peasants to accept poor prices for their crops; merchants similarly had to accept government terms of trade; there was no concept of freehold property. Wealth was siphoned into state military projects; the people had no chance of eventual affluence.[49] Used to an economy that left them exploited and hopeless, they could see no economic or moral advantage in working by themselves. Belzoni boasted of his unique insight into the manners of the Egyptians because, unlike dilettante travellers, his function had been to "persuade these ignorant and superstitious people to undertake a hard task."[50] Two other pioneers of Egyptian excavation, Charles Irby and James Mangles, described how they had to teach locals the meaning of useful labour by taking off their shirts and digging in the hot sun themselves.[51] Egyptians seemed always to be treated like brutes and kept on the verge of starvation.

45. Mayes, *Great Belzoni*, 260–75; Moshenska, "Unrolling Egyptian Mummies"; Ziter, *Orient on the Victorian Stage*, 77–79.

46. Curl, *Egyptomania*, 167–69; Carrott, *Egyptian Revival*, 105–7. For the reception of the Egyptian antiquities at the British Museum in the 1820s, see Moser's *Wondrous Curiosities* (114–20).

47. "Antiquity," 308.

48. Jowett, *Christian Researches in the Mediterranean*, 135.

49. Fitzclarence, *Journal*, 415; Irby and Mangles, *Travels in Egypt*, 50–51; [Jolliffe], *Letters from Palestine*, 296–97.

50. Belzoni, *Narrative of the Operations*, vii.

51. Irby and Mangles, *Travels in Egypt*, 15.

Two aspects of Mehmet Ali's Egypt brought this fact home to contemporary travellers. The first was the horrific loss of life—supposedly twenty-five thousand men—in the digging of the Mahmudiya Canal in the late 1810s. The second was his conscription policy from 1821, which he used to build up his army. If the government needed men for either construction or conscription, it raided villages of their menfolk, and left them depopulated and the land uncultivated. Men might never see their families again unless they fled to the desert, or mutilated themselves to make them unattractive as soldiers. "Six out of every ten men we meet have deprived themselves of the forefinger of their right hand, their front teeth, and even the right eye."[52] To run a country like this was not only bad policy; it was soul-destroying. It was slavery in all but name. Fitzclarence wrote that Mehmet Ali "treats Egypt as a planter does his West India estate." "When a Briton considers the happiness of those under British rule in India, contrasted with the state of these slaves, he will feel his country rise higher than ever in his estimation."[53] John Brine, the first Englishman invited to run a factory in Egypt in the 1810s, a sugar and rum operation near Manfalut, had been overseer of a West Indian sugar plantation, and claimed that "it was often impossible to make these Africans work without blows."[54]

The idea that Egypt had always been a land of slavery was very familiar in the British imagination. The theme in Egyptian history that was even better known than the construction of the pyramids was the oppression of the Israelites in Old Testament Egypt before their exodus under Moses. In 1827, the Jewish philanthropist Moses Montefiore, passing through the country on his way to Palestine, recoiled at such a "horrible land of misery and plague, the hand of God still being upon it." The American Protestant missionary Eli Smith, in the same year, found it "a land of darkness and of the shadow of death."[55] The artists Francis Danby and David Roberts both treated the Israelites' departure from Egypt on canvas, in 1825 and 1829, and for both the painting was an important breakthrough in their career; each was reproduced for popular consumption as a wood-engraved frontispiece in the widely read *Christian Magazine* in the early 1830s. This was at just the time when parliamentary reform and the immediate abolition of slavery had become the two most popular political demands in Britain. Moses could be hailed as the first political reformer, a natural legislator who refused to accept a system of government that did not recognise law and justice, and who therefore rejected the principle of slavery. Roberts's picture emphasised the small individual scale—but inexorable collective force—of the departing Israelite masses, in the shadow of the forbidding tyrannical architecture that they had been forced to build.[56]

52. Leech, *Letters*, 203 (quotation); Searight, "Naval Tourist," 144.

53. Fitzclarence, *Journal*, 416.

54. In Carne, *Letters from the East*, 115.

55. Montefiore, *Diaries*, 1:39; Salibi and Khoury, *Ottoman Syria*, 1:98.

56. Coltrin, "Picturing Political Deliverance."

Was Mehmet Ali just a despotic pharaoh with good public relations skills? His ruthless entrapment and murder of dozens of his Mamluk opponents in the Cairo citadel in 1811 was one of the best-known stories about him. Or did his enlightened despotism offer something genuinely better than Egypt had ever known, and perhaps something of merit across the wider Middle East? Britain's economic and political influence in Egypt suggested that it could not escape some responsibility for how the country would develop. The question that William Hamilton had posed in 1809 now recurred. Egypt was being drawn into the sphere of the European empires, as it had been under the Romans; its resources were being integrated into the global economy. More understanding was needed of Egyptian society and its real needs, in order to understand how far British influence could improve it.

So a group of experts emerged who claimed to go beyond lazy stereotypes about biblical slavery and oriental despotism and fanaticism. Instead, they offered "useful knowledge" on the "manners and customs" of the people. In 1836, the Society for the Diffusion of Useful Knowledge published Edward Lane's *Account of the Manners and Customs of the Modern Egyptians*, which, the title page explained for added veracity, had been "written in Egypt in the years 1833, 34 and 35." Lane stressed that his knowledge of Arab life came from two residences there, lasting four years in total, while he was learning Arabic. (He later married the Greek mistress whom he had acquired there.) He had quickly learned to converse with the locals and had "associated, almost exclusively, among Mooslims, of various ranks in society." His book presented a compendium of information about the behaviour and beliefs of the Egyptian common man, stressing particularly the way in which Islamic customs and assumptions were woven into daily life. It was full of detail about Egyptians' houses, dress, decorations, food and drink, leisure and musical habits, legal arrangements, and funeral rights. It stressed their benevolence, charity, cheerfulness, temperance, and industry, though also their superstition and their libidinousness (which he explained by reference to a combination of climate and ancient Egyptian debauchery, as condemned in the Qur'an). To a modern reader, its remaining prejudices jar, but it was praised by reviewers for offering a newly intimate and deliberately balanced account of Egyptian life, in contrast to travellers' hackneyed accounts of pyramids and mummies. It blamed several bad habits, such as avarice, on rapacious Ottoman government rather than on Islamic culture itself.[57]

Lane's book was an ethnographic tool to understand the Egyptian people. It did not stand alone for long. The following year, John Murray published John Gardner Wilkinson's *Manners and Customs of the Ancient Egyptians*. Wilkinson was the most productive of the group of young men who, inspired by the excavations of Belzoni and others, settled in Egypt in the 1820s in order

---

57. Lane, *Manners and Customs*, 1:iii–vii (quotation at vi), 154–57, 376 (on debauchery), 397. See Ahmed, *Edward W. Lane*, chap. 5.

to gain a better understanding of historic Egyptian culture and artefacts—who included also Burton, Robert Hay, and Joseph Bonomi. A gentleman scholar, Wilkinson spent twelve years there and got himself circumcised, though never became a Muslim and made a financial settlement with his local mistress rather than marrying her. He was a defender of Mehmet Ali in the 1840 Eastern crisis, and, like Belzoni, he was no escapist from modernity: he argued for steamers on the Nile to transport British travellers from Qena to Cairo, which would also provide employment for Arabs.[58] In the three volumes of *Manners and Customs*, and his earlier book *Topography of Thebes* (1835), Wilkinson exhibited the understanding that he had acquired from his visits to the newly uncovered Egyptian sites and his copious careful studies of inscriptions and drawings. This seemed remarkable scholarship, and earned him a knighthood.

Though Wilkinson used his knowledge of the earlier pharaohs to great effect, the bulk of his book was actually a celebration of Egyptian culture as it had developed by the time of the Roman era. Wilkinson's primary intellectual inspiration was Sir William Gell, who lived in Rome and Naples, had published *Topographies* of Troy and of Rome, and was one of the earliest to study the Greco-Roman government of Egypt and its pharaonic inspirations.[59] *Manners and Customs* stressed the economic and military organisation of the state, its great resources, and its system of laws. While acknowledging its repressive tax system and elements of cruelty, he insisted that it had a fundamental respect for "justice and humanity." Wilkinson brought the Egyptians of classical times to life as real people with comprehensible needs and hopes. He described their chairs, beds, kitchen utensils, flutes, harps, guitars, vases, vegetables, chess, and children's toys. The overwhelming impression given was that these people were not miserable or starving but industrious and happy, with a moral code, and opportunities for beer, wine, and dancing.[60]

Benthamism, Islam, and the Pursuit of Good Government in Egypt

What chance was there of using this information to improve the government of Egypt? In the decade before his death in 1832, the philosopher Jeremy Bentham became preoccupied with the problem of governing Islamic societies. Bentham regarded a rational judicial code as the sine qua non of good government. However, he had always opposed British rule in India. Human behaviour, he argued, was determined by environment. In an Islamic culture, justice and fair rule would not be achieved by imposing the prejudices

58. Wilkinson, *Topography of Thebes*, 589–92.

59. Jason Thompson, *Sir Gardner Wilkinson*, 11–43.

60. Wilkinson, *Manners and Customs*, vol. 2, esp. chap. 4 (quotation at 36); Jason Thompson, *Sir Gardner Wilkinson*, 141–53.

of British interest groups: it was essential to adapt to "the local situation, the climate, the bodily constitution, the manners, the legal customs, the religion, of those with whom they have to deal."[61] Nonetheless, strong, purposeful central government was also essential, otherwise it would not be respected and successful. In 1822, Bentham drafted a set of guidelines for Hassuna D'Ghies, who aspired to rule Tripoli (Libya) and had declared himself a Benthamite: Bentham's model code for D'Ghies aimed to deliver justice for the many while emphasising executive authority and a legal framework that accommodated Islamic religious principles.[62]

To Bentham and several followers, the centralising, modernising Mehmet Ali sent out the right signals, especially in contrast to the miserable, incompetent Constantinople regime. In 1828, imagining that Mehmet Ali was about to follow the Greeks in declaring independence from the sultan, Bentham wrote to him proposing a constitution and offering to bring up his eventual heir Abbas himself.[63] After Bentham's death, his executor and early biographer John Bowring made himself into an expert on Egypt and Syria, in the hope of continuing Bentham's project. Bowring insisted that the East must avoid direct Ottoman rule, which was a nonsense dreamed up by Europeans (especially Russians) for their own destabilising purposes. The Ottomans had shown that they did not understand modern government. Their lack of education, their corruption, and their other character flaws ensured failure. Wherever they had tried to rule, the result was misallocation of resources, depopulation, tribal warfare, rampant brigandage and "boundless rapine."[64] Insofar as the Ottoman Empire had any future, it rested on the sultan's abandonment of temporal power: he should be a quasi-pope exercising nominal authority, while power was delegated to local men with more understanding of their local circumstances. Ottoman rule meant "anarchy," which was "far more fatal" than the "despotism" of Mehmet Ali. In Egypt, and Syria, the latter's tyranny was "severe but equalizing"—a point also made by Wilkinson when he justified Mehmet Ali's Egyptian police regulations as benefiting rich and poor equally, and preventing the corrupt rule supplied by the Ottoman elite elsewhere. He had imposed order, developed the resources of the country, increased productivity, and boosted commerce. This was the basic aim of any regime that called itself a government, because it maintained the population.[65] Bentham had justified the British occupation of Egypt in 1801 on similar grounds, that it would prevent the insecurity and consequential depopulation that accompanied Ottoman or

61. Bentham, "Influence of Time and Place," 180.

62. Bentham, "Securities against Misrule," 555–600. For D'Ghies, see Coller, "Ottomans on the Move."

63. Bentham, *Correspondence*, 468–75.

64. Bowring, "Anglo-Turkish War," 192–94.

65. Bowring, 206; Wilkinson, *Three Letters*, 28–34.

Mamluk misrule.[66] Bentham's philosophy, after all, sought not just the greatest happiness, but also the greatest number.

Bowring suggested that Mehmet Ali's strong rule also offered the best chance of religious toleration and stability. Ottoman governance could function only by setting sect against sect, guaranteeing bloodshed. Mehmet Ali's order prevented such discord and made the position of Christians secure. Bentham had insisted that superseding misrule by good government was the way to make Christians and Muslims "grateful and steady allies."[67] Toleration for Christianity under law was not just compatible with the Ottoman idea of the caliphate; it strengthened it. Once Mehmet Ali took Syria and controlled the Holy Cities of Islam, his reliable rule on the sultan's behalf allowed Muslims to worship in peace, underpinning social order. Unlike Sultan Mahmud, he did not offend the prejudices of his Muslim subjects by bringing in an ostentatiously European style of military uniform when reforming his army. The caliphate would survive only if Muslims believed that their rulers were authentic, rather than visibly weak puppets of the Russian or indeed the English infidel. Mehmet Ali's rule showed the way for a modern Islamic empire. He was the best defender of the Qur'an against the forces that were attacking it—which, whatever bien pensant Englishmen might think, were at root Russian and illiberal.[68] The argument that strengthening popular Arabian Islam was the best way of checking the advance of Russian political despotism in Asia was also advanced by Thomas Perronet Thompson, who after his return from the Persian Gulf became Bowring's co-editor at the *Westminster Review*.[69]

So Islam was not hostile to modernity. Bowring was particularly pleased when Mehmet Ali told him that "there is not a word said against steamers in the Koran"—to take pilgrims to Mecca.[70] Bentham approached Mehmet Ali in 1828 through his friend the radical deist machine-maker Alexander Galloway, whose son Tom had gone out to Egypt and become Mehmet Ali's favourite engineer, superintending a metal foundry at Bulac, proposing a railway from Cairo to Suez in 1834, and earning the title "Galloway Bey."[71] The Benthamites hoped that economic progress would create its own dynamic. So would education, naturally percolating more and more widely in society. Bowring very much approved of Mehmet Ali's encouragement for female education, and of sending his young bureaucrats to pursue the rational French curriculum.[72] For Bowring, Mehmet Ali's most striking trait was his thirst for information. "He

66. See p. 51 above.
67. To Blaquiere, 1823, cited in Rosen, *Bentham, Byron, and Greece*, 88–89.
68. Bowring, "Anglo-Turkish War," 189–90, 207–12; Wilkinson, *Three Letters*, 18–20, 57–58.
69. T. Thompson, "Arabs and Persians."
70. Bowring, *Autobiographical Recollections*, 181.
71. For Galloway, see N. Green, *Love of Strangers*, 263–65.
72. Bowring to Palmerston, Mar. 27, 1838, FO 78/345 100.

has had translated for his own use a great portion of the works published by the Society for the Diffusion of Useful Knowledge."[73]

The British government dispatched Bowring to Egypt and Syria in 1837–38 to report on Mehmet Ali's economic regime, and he made useful contacts with several of those Westernised young men, especially Joseph Hekekyan, Briggs's former protégé (educated at Ampleforth), and Edhem Bey, the education minister. Bowring hoped that his visit would lead to an ongoing dialogue with the Egyptian regime, and its further improvement. He was impressed that Mehmet Ali apparently grasped the benefit of stamping out the Nubian slave trade, on realising how much it was damaging him with European public opinion.[74] Bentham's hopes of the 1820s, to become the intellectual godfather of Islamic reform, might now be realised. Bowring aimed to convince Mehmet Ali of the inefficiencies in his economy: his monopolies, his impractical investments in manufacturing equipment and factories, his diversion of resources to the army and navy, and the poor bookkeeping of his officials.[75] This was a great opportunity for England. "Egypt is in the political market. . . . [W]e may influence her—we may govern her—we may consolidate her happiness . . . [as she] daily becom[es] more the great highway between the East and the West!"[76] On his return to Britain in 1838, Bowring toured industrial and mining districts to build up support for Mehmet Ali, accompanied by Edhem Bey, who arrived at one Cornish country house "dressed in a large blue pelisse with loose sleeves, and full blue trousers, with scarlet gaiters and slippers, a gold waistband a foot and a half in width, and on his right breast . . . uncommonly large diamonds, said to be worth £50,000!"[77]

Syria, Liberalism, and the Russian Threat to Asia

Foreign Secretary Palmerston had not expected that Bowring's investigation would make him such a "Mehmetist." Bowring had undertaken several similar official inspections, which had advocated the extension of free trade in and with other countries. Palmerston wanted his reports to expose the error of monopolistic policies in Syria and to promote commercial liberalism there.[78] Palmerston had been one of a group of ministers interested in the potential of Syrian trade for a decade. That interest changed and developed over time. At first, it was not about Mehmet Ali at all, but about the benefits of free trade in challenging Russian illiberalism.

73. Bowring, "Report on Egypt and Candia," 146.
74. Bowring, *Autobiographical Recollections*, 177–79.
75. Bowring to Campbell, Dec. 17, 1837, FO 78/342 pt. 1, 42.
76. Bowring to Granville, Mar. 27, 1838, quoted in Bartle, "Bowring," 766–67.
77. Fox, *Memories of Old Friends*, 1:63.
78. Palmerston cut over twenty-five pages of political opinion from Bowring's report before the government published it: see Rodkey, "Colonel Campbell's Report," 102n.

In the mid-1820s, as the post-war depression lifted and the full extent of British global maritime dominance became apparent, few ideas had more resonance in British economic debate than that of freer world trade. Lowering high tariffs promised to increase consumer demand and prosperity. Local monopolies on production and transportation, whether imposed by British or other governments, seemed to restrict international commerce, mainly for the benefit of vested interests. This was the message of Foreign Secretary George Canning, President of the Board of Trade William Huskisson, and Huskisson's deputy Charles Grant. It was also attractive to Palmerston, then their little-known junior colleague. They formed a clique in the Tory governments of the 1820s (usually known as Liberal Tories by historians). Between 1823 and 1826, Huskisson established new arrangements for British and colonial trade, removing most of the protections for national shipping, and greatly reducing tariffs on most imported items.[79] Capitalists poured money into potential markets, particularly in newly independent South America, in the hope of high returns.

The Levant Company, which had controlled British trade in Ottoman lands since the sixteenth century, was sacrificed to this trend. It was undeniably in decline, though aspects of its trade benefited from the Napoleonic Wars, and Smyrna remained a successful factory. The two hundred company merchants were notoriously cautious, keener to preserve their privileges and limit the market than to speculate and expand. Most of its Ottoman consulates were funded by consulage, which imposed an extra tax on trade, estimated to be 2 per cent of the whole. The existing arrangements created significant political problems. The increasing strategic importance of Ottoman territory made the government anxious to control the appointment and behaviour of the ambassador and his consuls in the eastern Mediterranean. Many consuls were Levantine merchants, not British, with little loyalty to British policy, and swayed by commercial interests. They lacked the wider diplomatic experience to make judgments in charged political circumstances. Britain's wartime Mediterranean acquisitions left consuls with responsibility for local Maltese and Ionian residents, who often had complex legal needs. After 1821, the Greek crisis raised more difficult questions of international law.[80] In 1825, Canning and Huskisson abolished the company and its consulage, and its consuls throughout the Ottoman Empire were transferred to Foreign Office control.

Huskisson and Grant (who succeeded him as president of the Board of Trade in 1827) now hoped for growth throughout the Levant region. They pointed to the Egyptian cotton trade and the prospects of Greece, but they also focused on Syria. Syria's appeal owed a certain amount to Beirut, where

79. Brady, *Huskisson and Liberal Reform*.

80. A. Wood, *Levant Company*, 198–201; Huskisson, *Substance of Two Speeches*, 67–68; Robert Walsh, *Levant Company*, 59–64.

existing French networks had been damaged by the war. The Levant Company had established a consul there in 1820 in the hope of attracting trade, and twenty British ships had docked there in 1823. However, it was not yet clear that Beirut was about to become the most flourishing port in Syria. The Levant Company thought its growth prospects were limited.[81] As it happened, Beirut captured a lot of trade from Acre in the course of the 1820s, because the latter town persisted with monopoly pricing of cotton and other goods for European markets, whereas the merchants at Beirut were able to be much more flexible.[82] In fact, Huskisson and Grant's main Syrian interest was neither in Acre nor in Beirut, but in inland Damascus. In 1826 and again in early 1828, they urged a new consular appointment there as an experiment. On the second occasion, they produced a blistering memo complaining at the government's failure to respond to the Board of Trade's earlier initiative and to promote trade through consular expansion in western Asia.[83]

The case for Damascus was that it was a political centre and a trading hub for all the Asian Ottoman lands. It was a way of joining up British interests in Europe with those in India. Huskisson and Grant were anxious to promote Britain's position throughout Asia Minor, to Kurdistan, Armenia, and the Gulf. Here there were nine million commercially minded people in "large, wealthy, and luxurious towns," of whom a great number were Christian. Damascus was the starting point for the Syrian hajj route. It could also be one end of a British postal service to Baghdad and India. It was a centre of Ottoman power, in the same way as Baghdad further to the east. (After Cezzar's death in 1804, and especially after 1812, the Porte managed to re-establish Damascus as a rival Syrian power base to Acre.) More consuls should follow further east, in Trebizond, Erzurum, and Diyarbekir.[84]

In other words, this was an argument based on the potential of the land mass of western Asia for British imperial and commercial communication. The primary threat was from Russia in the Caucasus, as the Russo-Persian war was just revealing. A Syrian strategy would also counter French local interests there. The Ottoman Empire seemed to be collapsing. The steam revolution of the 1830s had not yet happened, and so this landmass seemed essential to the promotion of British interests in Asia. The Huskisson-Grant proposal was in fact a renewal of Dundas's strategy in sending Harford Jones to Baghdad

81. See the memos by Cartwright and Liddell, FO 78/135 38 and 78/177 104.

82. Philipp, *Acre*, 131–35.

83. Grant, Sept. 25, 1826, FO 78/149 320; March 1828, FO 78/171 138. Huskisson sent this second memo to the Foreign Office.

84. Grant, March 1828, FO 78/171 138. In 1830, a consulate was established at Trebizond, in response to Russian gains in Armenia and Azerbaijan in 1828: see Ingram, *In Defence of British India*, 157–58. Posts in Erzurum and Diyarbekir followed in 1836 and 1852. For Cezzar's struggles with the Porte in Damascus, see Douwes, *Ottomans in Syria*, 86–88.

in 1798, when Huskisson had been Dundas's subordinate. It was a restatement of the idea that Britain had a global reach, not just the narrow eastern Mediterranean one of the Levant Company—and its last president Grenville. Grant—together with his brother Robert, later governor of Bombay—was the son of Charles Grant the elder, one of the dominant figures in the East India Company for thirty years from 1790. Dundas and the elder Grant had both been very interested in the relation between trade and power. Britain's changed circumstances in the 1820s made it possible for their protégés now to develop a more dynamic, expansive, and liberal idea of the global potential of trade relations.

Huskisson and Grant had a man in mind for the Damascus consulship, John William Perry Farren, who had suggested himself in 1826 owing to an existing friendship with Grant; they shared evangelical sympathies as well as Indian interests. Farren had connections with the merchants of Manchester and of Liverpool (Huskisson's constituency).[85] He claimed to have travelled for three years in Syria and learned Arabic. He seemed knowledgeable about economic matters, and had edited a commercial paper, the *British Traveller*. Huskisson and Grant proposed that he, like Jones in 1798, should be a special agent with direct government authority, independent of the old consular networks. He could then expose the corruptions of other countries' consuls.[86] The appointment was opposed by the former secretary of the Levant Company, and was then frustrated by the resignation of the Huskissonites in 1828. It was only in autumn 1830, amid heightened anxiety about Russian activity in western Asia, that Farren was appointed, having now ingratiated himself with Foreign Secretary Aberdeen. By this point the case could be linked to the hopes for the Euphrates route, which were being developed by Peacock at India House: Farren proposed, and in due course implemented, the establishment of an official dromedary postal service between Damascus and Baghdad. Before setting off, he toured the industrial centres of England and Scotland in late 1830, and claimed to have stimulated £40,000 of business ready for export to Syria and further east.[87]

---

85. Farren remains an elusive figure. For his friendship with Grant, see *Appendix to the Report from the Select Committee*, 1024–25, 1029–30, and Lindsay, *Letters on Egypt*, 2:338. For his links with two merchants with Syrian ambitions, Alfred Clegg and Campbell Christie, which ended badly, see the papers at FO 78/232 131, 147, et seq. Unlike the Huskissonites, Farren remained a Tory in the 1830s.

86. Grant to Planta, Sept. 29, 1826, FO 78/149 324. In proposing a new Anglo-Ottoman trade treaty in the 1830s, David Urquhart was similarly critical of Levant Company networks: see chapter 6, section "David Urquhart, Islam, and Free Commerce."

87. See the letters in FO 78/194 and 78/206 22. For the post and the Euphrates route, see Farren, Aug. 1, 1834, IOR L/P&S/9/96 481, and J. Kelly, *Britain and the Persian Gulf*, 268.

In retrospect, the Liberal Tories' plan for Syria appears a hopelessly optimistic project deriving from an abstract faith in British world trade prospects and an immediate panic about Russian dominance in western Asia. The old trading route through Aleppo had virtually collapsed, as most trade went through the Black Sea or the Gulf. Because of ulema power, Damascus was one of the least accessible cities in the world to Westerners. Though its Christian rayas were protected by *millet* status, no Christian had been seen there in European dress for decades. In late 1831 there was a rebellion, instigated by janissaries, against tax impositions, which they alleged were funding Westernising corruptions. The governor, Selim, was overthrown and murdered.[88] In March 1831, Palmerston, now foreign secretary, nearly cancelled Farren's appointment because he doubted that the venture would succeed.[89] This reflected his worldly realism, but perhaps also his awareness of the growing risk that Mehmet Ali would shortly seize Damascus along with the rest of Syria. When Farren arrived at Beirut in June 1831, the government of the region and the management of its economy were about to be transformed.

When Mehmet Ali's son Ibrahim invaded Syria in late 1831, Britain's response showed how little influence it possessed there.[90] After a long siege, Ibrahim captured Acre in May 1832 and swept into Damascus in June. When the sultan sent his grand vizier and fifty thousand men to stop his advance, they were defeated at Konya in December. The prospect that Ibrahim would march on Constantinople (fifteen days away) forced the sultan to agree to a Russian naval presence in the Bosporus in February and the subsequent Treaty of Hünkar İskelesi. A settlement between Ibrahim and the sultan's forces was reached in April at Kütahya, brokered mainly by the French, after neither Britain nor France had offered the sultan the naval support that he needed in order to force a compromise on Mehmet Ali. Britain played a passive role: Prime Minister Grey doubted that the Ottoman Empire could survive and saw no merit in offending Mehmet Ali, while public opinion was preoccupied with domestic issues and extremely averse to increasing defence spending.[91]

The final settlement of May 1833 allowed Mehmet Ali to rule all Syria and Adana, much more than the sultan had originally been willing to give—though Mahmud regarded this as merely a temporary forced concession. Ibrahim stayed on in command of the troops. Mehmet Sharif, a connection of Mehmet Ali's by marriage, was appointed governor-general of all the Syrian pashaliks, ruling from Damascus, indicating a newly centralised approach to government. His remit included Mount Lebanon, though Bashir, a supporter of the Egyptians, was given extended powers there. Sharif and Ibrahim imposed

88. Burns, *Damascus*, 248.
89. FO 78/206 3, 21.
90. For the background, see Douwes, *Ottomans in Syria*, 188–90.
91. Webster, *Foreign Policy of Palmerston*, 1:279–83.

Egyptian principles throughout Syria—an emphasis on order and strong government, combined with protection for religious minorities. They abolished local customs that had discriminated against Christian Europeans, such as the one forbidding them to ride horses through the streets of Damascus (they had occasionally been allowed the indignity of a jackass). They promised tax reductions, though it was not clear how they were to pay for their large standing army.[92]

Only this strong military rule and religious toleration policy made it possible for Farren to leave the safety of Mediterranean Beirut for Damascus, which he entered in February 1834, on a fine Arabian horse and accompanied by local soldiers and a detachment of Lancers. His uniform resplendent, topped by a hat "studded with diamonds and topped with white and red feathers," he headed a cortège of five hundred, including English merchants. They paraded before a subdued, intermittently hostile Muslim crowd that he estimated at one hundred thousand. Farren insisted on the right to walk on passageways formerly restricted to Muslims; he moved around with an escort of eight guards, to indicate Christian power. Soon afterwards, the arriving traveller Alexander Kinglake felt that "Damascus was safer than Oxford" for a European; his servant horse-whipped the only Muslim to insult him.[93] Farren wanted it to be known that his position rested not on Egyptian sufferance but on "the moral influence of [British] national power."[94]

Farren refused to acknowledge his reliance on Ibrahim because he aimed to resist the imposition of Mehmet Ali's economic principles in Syria, which would undermine the free-trading capitalist vision of himself and his backers. He consistently argued that British trade would increase much faster "if the resources of the country and industry of the people were not so crippled by . . . the Pacha." From the beginning of his tenure, Farren identified three bad principles of Egyptian government in Syria: excessive taxation, the attempt at commercial monopolies, and the resort to conscription in order to threaten the sultan. The greatest symbol of increased taxation was the head tax, the *ferde*, on all adult males. In 1838, he estimated that the Egyptians had increased direct taxation by 50 per cent.[95] In 1833, and again in 1835, the government tried to secure a monopoly on the production and export of silk, claiming precedents from the previous regime, but the farmers refused to cooperate. Conscription of particular groups was attempted from 1834, but the fear of it

92. Douwes, *Ottomans in Syria*, 194–205.

93. Farren to Palmerston, Feb. 7, 1834, FO 78/243; Kayat, *Voice from Lebanon*, 93; Tibawi, *Modern History of Syria*, 85 (first quotation); Addison, *Damascus and Palmyra*, 2:97, 450; Kinglake, *Eothen*, 259–60.

94. Farren to Palmerston, Feb. 7, 1834, FO 78/243.

95. Farren to Palmerston, June 1836, FO 78/291 192 (quotation); Lindsay, *Letters on Egypt*, 2:278. Douwes estimates that in Hama it may have tripled in eight years: *Ottomans in Syria*, 202–3.

anticipated its widespread implementation, because of the publicity given to the stories of Egyptians cutting off their fingers and blinding themselves in order to avoid it. The first significant revolt against Egyptian rule came in Nablus in 1834, starting with Bedouin resistance to the tax demands and hostility from local notable families to the conscription idea. These revolts, afforced by those of the Ansari (Alawites) in the northern mountains, led Ibrahim to start disarming the tribes. This in turn facilitated the extension of conscription: by the summer of 1836 there were 36,100 conscripts in Syria. Attempts to disarm and then conscript the Druze created particular problems for stability. They were already alarmed by the improved status which the Egyptian governors had conferred on their Christian rivals in Lebanon.

Farren quickly decided that Egyptian rule over Syria was unsustainable. Mehmet Ali had promised the Syrians lighter taxes and better government, but his system required the repression and harshness that had built the pyramids. Heavy taxation and attempted monopolies were reducing economic demand, whereas investment in agriculture was needed to build it up. Levies for the army depopulated the land and further damaged agricultural production; they also inflated wages and prices. The country was being ruined to make Syria "a great nursery of war" and to allow Mehmet Ali to defy the sultan. His policy required him to incur the hatred of the Syrian people. He disrespected the laws of political economy, and the more fundamental principle that the security of government required laws that reflected "a people's interests and affections." Already in 1834, Farren insisted that the Egyptian system could not fit a territory like Syria, which possessed hereditary and powerful local chiefs, a great variety of religions, a mountainous terrain, and a historic preference for the subdivision of property. Farren was particularly struck by the alienation of the Druze, whose neutrality under Bashir had allowed Ibrahim to take Acre in 1832. Egyptian "despotism and monopoly" could not work in Syria. After the initial crises of Lebanon and Nablus in 1834, Farren prophesied that Mehmet Ali would learn too late "that the interests and sentiments of a people should form some part, at least, of the political system of their rulers."[96]

In other words, Farren's critique of Mehmet Ali's rule in Syria was rooted in an Enlightenment sociological analysis (rather grandiloquently expressed) that went far beyond the specific problem of economic monopolies. As it happened, British pressure forced the Egyptians to abandon their monopoly plans in Syria. Palmerston, receiving complaints from merchants, instructed Ambassador Ponsonby to get a firman from the sultan ordering Mehmet Ali to avoid them. Obtained and sent in January 1836, it directed Mehmet Ali to remove

96. For these two paragraphs, see Farren to Foreign Office, Mar. 10, 1832 (quotation 2); Feb. 27, 1833 (quotation 1); May 26 (quotations 3 and 4) and May 29, 1834; Sept. 20, 1834; Jan. 30, 1835; May 2, 1835; Oct. 23, 1837: FO 78/215 199; 78/229 280; 78/243 47, 53, 192; 78/262 25, 131; 78/315 268.

all the new obstacles on British trade that infringed the capitulations. Mehmet Ali never challenged the order thereafter, to the satisfaction of Consul-General Campbell in Egypt. In March 1836, Campbell himself came to Syria, with Mehmet Ali's commissioner Colonel Sève, in order to underline Britain's insistence that monopolies had no place there.[97] So Palmerston and Campbell neutralised the immediate threat posed by Egyptian rule to British economic interests in Syria. The broader difficulties, however, were not so easy to tackle.

New Voices on Syria: Embassy Ottomanists and Christian Tourists

Campbell's visit to Syria was also a response to Farren's insubordination to him. Farren never accepted the Foreign Office demand of 1833 that, with Mehmet Ali in control of Syria, he should now be junior to, and report to, the British consul-general in Egypt. He was sacked by Palmerston in late 1837, after a series of rows with Campbell. Farren was desperately status driven—Campbell thought him "eaten up with pride, vanity and pomp and self-love."[98] He persistently refused to treat Campbell, Ibrahim, or Sharif with diplomatic respect. He ended by defending all the rights of the old Levantine consuls in Syria, especially their large-scale protection of local raya merchant networks, even when individuals committed criminal offences. The Egyptians were determined to root out this protection system, in order to increase tax receipts, and Campbell and the Foreign Office agreed.[99] In theory, the removal of Farren should have lessened the impact of his argument that Egyptian rule was inappropriate for Syria. In fact, his views had a significant afterlife after 1837, because two groups of people were inspired by them.

The first was the British embassy at Constantinople. It began meddling in Syria in order to encourage the popular resistance that Farren claimed to discern. In May 1835, Farren wrote to Ponsonby that the Porte could "easily overthrow" the Egyptian regime in Syria. In September 1835, the new consul in Beirut, Niven Moore, suggested that if an invasion force appeared on the coast, the Syrians would rise against the Egyptians.[100] Moore, who had just been appointed to succeed the late Peter Abbott, a Levant Company man, had spent thirteen years in the Constantinople embassy, where he had imbibed the Porte's hostility to Mehmet Ali. So had his brother-in-law Richard Wood, who

97. Palmerston to Campbell, Oct. 5, 1835, FO 78/258 3; Campbell to Palmerston, Sept. 5, 1835, Jan. 23, 1836, and Mar. 30, 1839, FO 78/258 12, 78/282 3, 78/376 69.

98. Campbell to Thurburn, July 27, 1836, FO 78/295 369. In 1834, Ibrahim's confidential secretary had told Campbell that Farren was "a very strange man and not so agreeable as he could wish an English agent to be, with whom he had to transact public business": FO 78/245 59.

99. Campbell to Palmerston, Oct. 6 and 9, 1837, FO 78/320 154, 166.

100. May 31, 1835, FO 78/254 17; Moore to Campbell, Sept. 9, 1835, FO 78/258.

was Ponsonby's trusted English dragoman. Encouraged by Farren's remarks, Ponsonby sent Wood to Syria over the winter of 1835–36 to investigate the state of the country under Egyptian rule. When Campbell arrived from Egypt, he was appalled to discover Moore and Wood plotting together in Beirut to spread invented stories that Ibrahim had burnt thirty villages in the course of implementing his disarmament.[101] Farren was not replaced as consul-general; of the other Syrian consuls, Moore in Beirut became the most power-ful, as he was able to channel information to Constantinople, strengthening Wood's emerging claim to be an expert on the region.

The second group was the British travellers to Syria who started to arrive in significant numbers to see the Christian sites, as a result of the security provided by Egyptian rule. Farren gave them hospitality and the benefit of his analysis of the Syrian situation. Most of these travellers were socially well connected; several of them published accounts of their journeys on returning to Britain, beginning with Lord Lindsay and Charles Addison, both in 1838. Lindsay's book included a hundred-page letter to him from Farren, written after his dismissal, warning British people of the damage done by the Egyp-tians in Syria. Addison repeated these views, which received much wider pub-licity than a letter from a British resident of Damascus that skewered Farren's allegations.[102] Lindsay's book was favourably reviewed by Lord Ashley, who like Lindsay was a young Anglican Tory nobleman, part of a group anxious to promote the Church of England's standing in Britain and abroad. Such travel-lers naturally viewed Palestine through the lens of the Bible, and measured its current situation by reference to its past and potential future.

These two groups were responsible for the emergence of a very strong consensus that the Egyptian occupation was inappropriate for Syria, econom-ically, politically, morally, and historically. Wood's official report of 1836 set out the basic case that Farren, Lindsay, and Addison repeated in 1838: that Mehmet Ali's high and unpredictable taxes, attempts to interfere with the sale of produce, and widespread conscription were all draining the land of men and of any incentives for capital investment. There was no stimulus to agricul-ture and commerce.[103] "You may be carried away for a soldier, or pillaged by a rapacious governor. You have no secure laws to appeal to; for equity and jus-tice are unknown in the land. . . . Thus it is that we see the land lie waste, the fertile plains untilled and devoid of inhabitants." Syria used to export grain; it now had to import it. One merchant told Addison that, under good govern-ment, British trade with Syria might be trebled in ten years, but at present it

101. Campbell to Palmerston, July 31, 1836, FO 78/283 1.

102. The letter, published in the *Morning Chronicle* under only the initial "G." ("British Subjects in Syria and Mr Farren," Nov. 2, 1838), refuted the suggestion that Egyptian rule in Syria had either damaged British economic interests or persecuted Christians.

103. Wood's "Report on the Political and Moral State of Syria and the Egyptian Govern-ment" is reproduced in R. Wood, *Early Correspondence*, 78–88.

was impeded by Mehmet Ali's personal vendetta against the sultan.[104] This was a "selfish despotism," a military occupation that was failing the test of civilisation at any level—efficiency, productivity, humanity. Three-quarters of Syrian revenue was spent on a military occupation of the land, in order to threaten the Ottomans, rather than on civil administration. Egyptian government was a war machine that "follows no guide but caprice, and no fixed laws whereby to restrain its influence." There was no legal code, in defiance of the basic principle of just government.[105] Ibrahim already had a reputation in Europe for inhumanity, on account of the atrocities perpetrated by his Ottoman troops in Greece in the mid-1820s.

Some of the language used in these reports suggests an underlying religious perspective. Wood depicted Syria degenerating into "a wilderness" that would "end by becoming a vast necropolis." Addison felt that a storm of destruction had passed over the land.[106] For the devout Christian Lindsay, the condition of Egypt and Syria during his time was a "literal accomplishment of prophecy"—of the destruction of prosperity and happiness that resulted from ignoring God's laws. When he left Egypt, the land of slavery, for Syria, he climbed Mount Sinai on the way, and imagined hearing the voice of God utter "that fiery law—holy, and just, and good." He then entered "the Land of Promise"; he tasted cow's milk for the first time in weeks. Yet this promise had been betrayed by Muslim misgovernment. Everywhere Lindsay went in Syria, he noted the natural fertility of the soil, yet the irresponsible failure to cultivate it. The deliberate underinvestment and resulting depopulation were not just ego-driven crimes, but sins. Lindsay hoped for a "great moral revolution" guided by English "Protestants, entrusted with the revealed will of God." Lebanon, which he next visited, might point the way: the vale of Eden (Ehden) was indeed a "garden of Eden," with church bells ringing every morning and evening. "We *felt* ourselves in a Christian country, and almost among brethren."[107]

In January 1838, a severe Druze rebellion began in the Hawran, in response to Ibrahim's conscription policy: several thousand Egyptian troops were killed. Wood heard that great cruelty had been required to suppress it: "long strings of Ears are to be met with everywhere hanging about, indicating the number of persons found guilty and beheaded."[108] Ibrahim had had to appeal for Maronite armed support, a decision that indicated Muslim ambivalence about Egyptian rule and that was bound to increase sectarian tensions. The rebellions seemed to be destroying the basic case for Mehmet Ali, that he

104. Addison, *Damascus and Palmyra*, 2:473–74, 480, 483 (quotation).

105. Farren in Lindsay, *Letters on Egypt*, 2:274, 309–10; R. Wood, *Early Correspondence*, 78–80.

106. R. Wood, *Early Correspondence*, 87–88; Addison, *Damascus and Palmyra*, 2:484.

107. Lindsay, *Letters on Egypt*, 1:vi, 358; 2:51,190, 222, for the quotations, and 2:73, 77, 90, for the neglected fertility.

108. R. Wood, *Early Correspondence*, 131.

could secure order. N. W. Werry, acting consul in Damascus, discerned a loss of respect for him among Arabs, which was affecting the safety of the post and British commercial hopes.[109] In fact, the whole Liberal Tory vision of Damascus as a gateway to western Asia had collapsed. It was just as well that the steamer routes had developed in the meantime.

In 1840, Egyptian misgovernment of Damascus was exposed dramatically. Thirteen prominent members of the Jewish community were imprisoned and tortured for their alleged part in the disappearance of a Catholic priest, Father Tommaso. The Catholic missions and the French consul claimed that Jews had killed Father Tommaso because they needed Christian blood for their rituals. The Egyptian local government accepted the case against them and proposed their execution, before an international outcry forced Mehmet Ali to order an investigation; those Jews still in prison were eventually freed. Many European Jews and Protestants were convinced that the Egyptian local governor had given into French pressure, in order to win France's support for the retention of Syria. The Egyptians and the French Catholic Church seemed to be allied in support of barbaric religious intolerance. A number of newspaper articles interpreted the Damascus affair to show that papists still retained their taste for persecution, and that they justified it by medieval falsehoods.[110] The drama was also exploited by Ponsonby in Constantinople: his client journalist Churchill, running a pro-Ottoman English-language paper in Smyrna, felt that "the affair of the Jews is a trump card."[111] Ponsonby's dragoman Pisani, visiting England, met the leading Jewish financiers and merchants and told them that Mehmet Ali's persecution of their fellow religionists in Damascus was driven by greed for their money, and typical of his approach to government.[112] Palmerston consistently supported the Anglo-French Jewish campaign to get justice for the Damascus Jews, which was led by Moses Montefiore and Adolphe Crémieux. He was appalled to discover that the local consul Werry, a former Levant Company employee, was inclined to believe the allegations.[113]

Palmerston had become noticeably hostile to Mehmet Ali over the winter of 1837-38, in reaction to the "frightful atrocities" committed by Egyptian soldiers in Syria when trying to enforce conscription. He observed that they followed no law or system; they treated the people "much in the manner in which a given number of wild animals would be caught out of a herd in the desert." It was Mehmet Ali's inhumane behaviour to his fellow man, his disrespect for justice, his taste for plunder and military force, that mainly drove

109. Farren in Lindsay, *Letters on Egypt*, 2:306-8; Werry to Palmerston, Aug. 3, 1838, FO 78/341 119. For the problems caused by postal disruption, see pp. 126-27 above.

110. Feldman, "Damascus Affair," 137-39.

111. W. N. Churchill to Ponsonby, summer 1840, PPD, GRE/E/134 28.

112. Alexander Pisani to Ponsonby, June 17, 1840, PPD, GRE/E/477 38.

113. See the letters in FO 78/410, especially the summary "Memorandum on the Persecution of the Jews at Damascus," Nov. 23, 1840, at 176.

Palmerston's criticism of his regime from then on.[114] In June 1839, he declared "I hate Mehemet Ali . . . as great a tyrant and oppressor as ever made a people wretched."[115]

As the Eastern crisis developed in 1839–40, the idea that Mehmet Ali was a tyrant naturally became much more common in books and newspapers, affecting views of Egypt as well as Syria. Traditionally, most British visitors to Egypt had been en route to or from India, and their perspective on his rule was influenced by hard-headed military and geopolitical assumptions about Britain's regional interests, together with an ingrained acceptance of Eastern governing practices. From the late 1830s, a different tone was set by the Constantinople embassy on the one hand and the proliferation of Christian tourist accounts on the other. The embassy sent Charles Alison to Egypt in 1840: he duly reported that Mehmet Ali's rule presented a façade of modernity to deceive progressive travellers, but that the real Egypt was cruelly impoverished and neglected. He claimed that locals regarded Alexandria as "an embroidered veil drawn on the gate of a charnel house" and that Mehmet Ali's only supporters were vested interests complicit in a policy of starving the people.[116] When Lord Ashley reviewed Lindsay's book, he compared Mehmet Ali to the "cruel lord" that Isaiah had prophesied would be sent to rule Egyptians in punishment for their false religion.[117] In 1841, Richard Madden, who had been part of the mission to secure justice for the Jews of Damascus in 1840 and who had a track record as a campaigner against West Indian slavery, published a fierce critique of Mehmet Ali's support for the slave trade.[118] The journalist James St. John expressed the view that the Egyptian *fallahin* were now, as before, "demoralised and degraded by a thousand years of political servitude": they were not fully human, never exposed to improving influences, and incapable of more than a sensual existence. He regarded Mehmet Ali as a typical Egyptian despot. The first edition of his book, published in 1834, had been deliberately ambivalent about whether Mehmet Ali's attempts to borrow ideas and machinery from the West might allow him to regenerate his people. His second edition, in 1845, gave the answer: he was a vain, misguided adventurer who had done nothing to improve Egyptians' happiness.[119] In 1845,

114. Palmerston to Campbell, Dec. 8, 1837, and March 16 and 29, 1838, FO 78/318 42, 78/342 7, 9. See his critique of Mehmet Ali in 1840, in Rodkey, "Colonel Campbell's Report."
115. Bourne, *Palmerston*, 576.
116. Therefore he could easily be overthrown in Egypt as well: Alison to Ponsonby, Jan. 5, 1840, PPD, GRE/E/14 20. This was also the implication of Ponsonby's reports: to Palmerston, Oct. 4 and Nov. 9, 1840, FO 78/397, 109, 78/398 148.
117. Isaiah 19:4. He quoted Joseph Wolff's comparison of the two: [Ashley], "Lord Lindsay's Travels," 171.
118. Madden, *Egypt and Mohammed Ali.*
119. St. John, *Egypt, and Mohammed Ali,* 1:viii (quotation)–xii, 2:181, 373–76; *Egypt and Nubia,* 47–48.

Eliot Warburton's *Crescent and the Cross*—which was in large part a dextrous compendium of other writers' opinions—claimed that the Egyptians were the "most miserable nation under heaven," prophetically doomed to be "trodden down and abased, a nation that should ever be under the rule of foreigners," of whom Mehmet Ali was the latest.[120]

Charles Napier remarked in 1842 that Mehmet Ali's "Eastern despotism" was inappropriate for Syria.[121] The implication was that it deserved better. There were various reasons why British observers might take that view: a biblical perspective; the coastal towns' historic ties with Mediterranean trade; admiration for the independent-minded Lebanese mountaineers and their property rights.[122] All these arguments contributed to the notion that the Egyptians' government in Syria lacked the legitimacy conferred by popular approval. Crucially, however, there was still no consensus in 1839 about how to remove them, or what should replace them. Mehmet Ali was after all an Ottoman pasha: Farren himself admitted that his despotism was based on "the embodying of Turkish principles in European forms."[123] What he had done in Syria was only what the Ottomans were accused of in other parts of the empire: overtaxing the land rather than investing in its improvement, and governing by favouritism rather than justice. Few people—outside the Constantinople embassy—thought that the Ottoman regime was the answer to the Syrian problem. In any case, the brutal fact was that the sultan had no power to remove him. The crucial argument for driving Mehmet Ali from Syria was not that his government was less acceptable than that of the Ottomans. It was that the stand-off between him and the sultan was making the whole region ungovernable by diverting valuable resources on both sides to unproductive military expenditure, weakening both regimes, and increasing the risk of collapse and great-power conflict.

120. Warburton, *Crescent and the Cross*, 2:357.

121. C. Napier, *War in Syria*, 1:xxiv.

122. Napier was particularly keen on the last: see chapter 6, section "Napier or Wood, Smith or Elgin, Cairo or Constantinople?" For the idea that Britain could restore the commercial greatness of Tyre and Sidon, see Edward Smith's *Sailing Directions* and Smith, Sept. 18, 1846, FO 78/671.

123. Lindsay, *Letters on Egypt*, 2:313.

CHAPTER SIX

Constantinople, London, the Eastern Crisis, and the Middle East

IN THE SPRING OF 1839, Sultan Mahmud ordered an attack on Mehmet Ali's forces in Syria. The sultan's army was badly defeated at Nizip; his fleet defected; he died. The Ottoman regime seemed about to collapse. The following year, the European powers, apart from France, united to support the removal of Mehmet Ali from Syria; this was achieved by the end of 1840. This eighteen-month saga was a great European diplomatic crisis, and there is no need to revisit here its twists and turns, several of which concerned the continental balance of power. This chapter aims instead to consider what the crisis reveals about the British government's view of the Ottoman Empire and the Middle East. It examines the perspective of the Constantinople embassy and the Foreign Office, headed respectively by the Irish Whig peer Viscount Ponsonby and by Palmerston. It also considers the role of Charles Napier, the most important of the British navy officers involved in the Syrian operation. It argues that the embassy's support for strong Ottoman central government now became much more coherent and important than before, but that it was still not the only perspective that mattered in explaining British policy.

Some writers have always suggested that the British government had a free moral choice in this crisis, to support the sultan or Mehmet Ali, and that under Palmerston's influence it chose the sultan.[1] This makes Mehmet Ali more central to the story than he was. Though Palmerston personally disliked his governing philosophy, his rule in Egypt was not the issue. Nor was his vague talk of rejecting Ottoman sovereignty, which the powers had already made clear in 1838 that they would not tolerate. In any case, as Fahmy has

---

1. Temperley, *England and the Near East*, 93; Caquet, *Orient*, 4–6.

argued, it is doubtful whether he could conceive of full independence from the Islamic caliph. He sought the future security of his family as hereditary rulers of Egypt, its African hinterland, the Hijaz, and—he hoped—Syria as well. His assumption was that Constantinople would remain a weak centre and he could build another one within the Ottoman structure without alienating Europe. He is best seen as an over-mighty regional vested interest. His problem was the sultan's resentment of him, which was shared by a powerful anti-Mehmetist faction in Constantinople led by Hüsrev; they were determined to mobilise troops in Anatolia that could be used against him.[2] The resulting armed stand-off on the border with Syria had serious political and economic costs. Large-scale military expenditure on both sides destabilised the internal finances of the empire, and distorted the Egyptian and Syrian economies. Continued tension might easily escalate into a conflict that some of the powers would have to join, from fear that otherwise their interests would lose out in the subsequent partition of Ottoman territory.

Palmerston's main anxiety about Mehmet Ali's ambitions was that the weaker the Ottoman regime became, the more reliant it would be on the protection of Russia. Conversely, removing the armies from the contested border, and allowing taxes to be spent on developing local economies instead, would facilitate stability, commerce, and prosperity. More broadly, Palmerston's vision was for the Ottoman Empire to become a stronger fiscal-military regime, relying for security on a smaller, cheaper, but more efficient European-trained army.[3] Egypt, as a regional power within defined borders, was an essential part of this vision; there is no merit in viewing Britain as hostile to a strong Egyptian regime. Commercial reform was part of this British government agenda, but for broad strategic reasons more than for specific British economic gain. Since 1835, the embassy, and particularly Secretary of Embassy David Urquhart, had been pursuing this commercial agenda, hoping to strengthen Ottoman rule by removing monopolistic corruptions and reasserting core Islamic governing principles. The resulting commercial treaty of 1838 was also an encouraging sign that British embassy influence at Constantinople might be outstripping Russia's, and that Britain and the Ottomans had a shared vision of the empire's future as a strong, low-tax Islamic state.

Palmerston's hope of propping up the Ottoman Empire was hardly controversial in itself. In 1839, he expected the European powers to agree on a solution to the crisis caused by the battle of Nizip; they very nearly did. The ambassadors at the Porte gave a collective guarantee to resolve the crisis. Russia saw the benefits of abandoning the special military status that the treaty of 1833 had given it. All the powers were also willing to give Mehmet Ali's

---

2. Fahmy, *All the Pasha's Men*, chap. 7. See also Bulwer's shrewd assessment, June 28, 1838, FO 78/334 7; Wilkinson, *Three Letters*, 7–8.

3. Rodkey, "Rejuvenation of Turkey," 575–78.

family hereditary rule in Egypt. Europe fell out over France's insistence that the sultan should continue to allow Mehmet Ali some of the Syrian territory that he had allowed him before. France's insistence was not because it sought to overthrow the European order or wanted Mehmet Ali to be independent, but because removing Mehmet Ali from Syria by force was difficult to conceive, would have unknown consequences, especially for the region's Christians, and seemed inconsistent with the pledges given to him by France (and Britain) in 1833. But large swathes of the British press interpreted the rather confused policy of the French parliamentary regime in the same light as Napoleon's militarism after 1798. History also provided a reminder that there was nothing unusual or awkward about working with Russia to maintain a different policy—the familiar notion of Anglo-Russian spheres of influence within Ottoman territory. Palmerston's agreement with Russia and Austria that Britain could exercise military influence in Syria in 1840 was not a radical new departure in principle.

From the perspective of the Middle East, however, the degree of intervention required to remove Mehmet Ali from Syria involved major disruption. The obvious question to ask is whether Britain and the other powers had any understanding of the likely consequences. The standard assumption, founded on the Syrian history that British people knew, was that another semi-independent local ruler, or combination of rulers, would emerge, and that Amir Bashir in particular would continue to be a crucial player in Lebanon.

However, the Constantinople embassy thought differently, and fought, more determinedly than before, to assert Ottoman power in Syria. This was because of the sultan's declaration at Gülhane in November 1839, which opened the era of the Tanzimat reforms. Ponsonby and his assistant Richard Wood viewed the Edict of Gülhane as a promise by central authority to secure essential local fiscal and property rights, guaranteed by the force of law. It seemed to follow the logic of their former colleague Urquhart, that an Islamic regime could impose an effective and rational legal framework capable of rooting out corruption, cutting tax burdens, and winning over local factions by firm and fair rule. This policy triumphed, not because Britain had massive power over the regime, but because pursuing it was in the interests of Reshid and the dominant party in Constantinople politics, who were determined to use it to advance their agenda, and to destroy Mehmet Ali.

Nor were Ponsonby and Reshid the only players who mattered. Many European commentators interpreted the edict very differently (and wrongly): not as a valuable prop to an Islamic state, but as a concession to the traditional continental view that the empire should be judged by its amenability to Christian pressure. This interpretation was adopted by some British newspapers, and much more vigorously by Catholic public opinion on the continent; it paved the way for a sectarian policy of instructing the Porte that it must uphold Christian interests in Syria. Meanwhile, the embassy's defence of Ottoman rule in Syria led to a vehement clash with the British navy, led by Charles Napier, channelling the spirit of Sidney Smith against Ottoman governing morals, on behalf of the mountaineers and, in effect, Mehmet Ali. By the end of 1840, therefore, three conflicting Western visions for Syria had emerged: that of the embassy, that of local British navy and army officers, and that of predominantly continental and Catholic pressure groups. The resulting disagreements meant that neither stability nor European disengagement was likely there any time soon.

David Urquhart, Islam, and Free Commerce

Before 1835, the Constantinople embassy was not known for its commercial dynamism. Its long-serving consul-general, John Cartwright, the man in charge of British trade policy there, was a knowledgeable and popular figure, but a Levant Company veteran and no innovator. In September 1835, however, Palmerston appointed as the new secretary of embassy a brash and clever young Scot, David Urquhart, who had every intention of acquiring fame for himself and putting British policy in the East on a new and more successful course. Urquhart had already been in the East for several years, most recently sent by Palmerston in 1833 to make the commercial exploration of the whole region that Huskisson had urged in 1828—to tour Anatolia, Armenia, and Kurdistan in the hope of discovering the potential for profitable new local alliances against the Russians. However, except for one trip to the Black Sea region, he had not got further than Constantinople, where he saw the chance of creating a niche for himself. He had become Ambassador Ponsonby's aide, trusted by him to use press contacts to generate a public opinion in Britain to counter national complacency about the Russian threat.[4] He also came to see the value of commercial policy in limiting Russian influence. This realisation stemmed from his attempt to apply Bentham's prescriptions for the good government of Islamic peoples.

Urquhart had been introduced to Bentham through his mother, and had gone to work for the Greek cause in 1827–28. He decided to investigate the manners and customs of the Ottomans and the Greeks, hoping thereby to develop a reputation as a Benthamite expert on the region. He devoted three years to studying the financial details of local administration in European Turkey, after which he claimed to have discovered key principles of Ottoman government: decentralisation, municipal self-rule, and a reliance on direct taxation. Urquhart's argument was that these formed the basis of a defensible and viable economic policy. Conveniently, they were also in line with English values and preferences, making it easier for Britain to support them. He traced

4. Lamb, "Making of a Russophobe." For his intended itinerary, see the memo at FO 78/249 9.

their derivation from "the fundamental principles of Arabic legislation, . . . handed down as the constitutional and traditional doctrines of Islamism."[5]

In his view, Islam was not a false theology to be ridiculed—it taught no new dogmas, propounded no new revelation, and imposed no new priesthood. It was a coherent approach to government by Muhammad, based on cheap government, equal law, and free trade. Its central principle was attractive to a British liberal mind because it made "the executive authority subordinate to that of the law, based on religious sanction and on moral obligations." Islam combined "a faith, a code, and a constitution": it denounced monopolies and privileges, made men equal in the eye of the law, "consecrated the principles of self-government, and the local control of accounts." The morality of the Islamic home was also much sounder than most Europeans imagined. All this explained why it had spread so rapidly and powerfully under Muhammad.[6] The Wahhabi had recently revived the ancient Arabian rule of local assessment of wealth by municipal chiefs: half was kept by the municipality and half went to central government as tribute. Direct taxation of property on fair principles ensured that the rich would help the weak, while also checking extravagance by governors. The property tax fell on realised wealth, not the means of production. Nor did it increase the price of articles for the poor; that was why there was no pauperism in the empire. So Islamic governance, in theory, dispensed justice, mitigated oppression, and promoted patriotism by its appeal to ancient habits and traditions, while also boosting the value of land and property by encouraging the free exchange of commodities.[7]

Why had these principles been corrupted in so many parts of the empire? It was not because of any defects in Islam or in Ottoman legal principles, but because of abuses and corruption by self-aggrandising local pashas and bankers. A major cause was the system of auctioned tax farming (*iltizam*) introduced by the Ottomans, which had augmented duties and monopolies, mainly owing to the interference of non-Muslims: of Armenian, Greek, and Jewish middlemen financiers. They loaned money to pashas at high interest so that they could pay the Porte; they forced the peasants to borrow money as well, by demanding their taxes before the harvest. This placed ruinous burdens on producers, in defiance of the principle of low direct taxation, while pashas then resorted to monopolies, in an attempt to stop these middlemen taking all the profit. If extra duties and monopolies were outlawed by the municipality, and it confined itself to collecting a simple property tax, then the middlemen would be bypassed.[8]

5. Urquhart, *Turkey and Its Resources*, 15.

6. Urquhart, *Spirit of the East*, 1:xxvii–xxix. For his defence of the morality of Islamic marriage arrangements and the harem, see vol. 2, chaps. 25–26.

7. Urquhart, *Turkey and Its Resources*, 90–96.

8. Urquhart, 108–12, 188–90.

The original object of this analysis (matured between 1829 and 1831) was to solve the Greek question by proving that the Greek Christian rayas' demand for self-government and commercial freedom was compatible with Ottoman sovereignty. By 1833–34, with Greek independence conceded, Urquhart's main interest—and his career ticket—was to explain how rediscovering this Ottoman liberal dynamic could help Britain and the Porte to defeat the slow death-strangle of Russia. The empire needed to boost its commerce and its population, but its natural resources were so great, throughout the Balkans and Anatolia, that this could be done if the current crippling burdens were removed and the original commercial outlook was revitalised. Low duties, encouragement of international shipping, and opposition to prohibitions were historic Ottoman principles, not European impositions. Commerce was noble and sacred; its connection with religious pilgrimages was well known.[9] It was speculation and the corrupt activities of non-Muslim middlemen that had weakened Islamic power. Foreign merchants wishing to expand their trade with the East should rely on these beneficent principles rather than on setting up barriers and special protections through consular clout.

So Urquhart's aim was to highlight the efficient and attractive elements of historic Islamic political culture, and to warn against a European imperialism undermining "the conservative principles of the Turkish government and society . . . by a fatal imitation of Western manners, prejudices, and principles."[10] These Western enemies included those who abused Islam, but also foreign commercial pressure groups that sought exclusive advantages for themselves. This meant primarily the Russians, in Moldavia, Wallachia, and elsewhere around the Black Sea, since Urquhart's underlying concern was always to keep those fertile regions out of Russian hands. Russia's strategy was to cripple local exports that competed with its own goods. Lower duties throughout the Black Sea region would undermine Russian power there and stop it threatening the empire's independence. More optimistically, a system of mutually beneficial lower duties might eventually force Russia to liberalise its own economy.[11]

But Urquhart was also hostile to the complacent, arrogant Levant Company factories, which until recently had upheld protection systems, unwittingly aiding Russian power: they "resembled military establishments in a hostile country." Those merchants had no stake in the country, and traded exclusively through a network of Jewish, Armenian, and Greek vice-consuls; this was why Britain's name was not respected by Ottoman officials.[12] Like the Liberal Tories at home, Urquhart believed that the abolition of the Levant Company would bring Britain, and the Ottomans, great commercial benefits.

9. Urquhart, 134–36.
10. Urquhart, *Spirit of the East*, 1:xxxi.
11. Urquhart, *Turkey and Its Resources*, 169–70.
12. Urquhart, 185 (quotation), 211, 214.

New merchant operations in European Turkey and Anatolia, on the Danube and at Trebizond, would do more to strengthen Ottoman security and stability than expensive fleets or armies. Once tax farming and over-centralisation were abolished, mines to extract the great resources of Asia would proliferate.[13] If the Ottoman Empire could revert to the core principles of Islam, British liberal principles would win out over Russian Christian imperialism.

In Constantinople in late 1834, he proposed a commercial convention with the Ottomans, which would sweep away those corruptions and additions to the system, restore its basics, and confound all Russia's intentions. During the year he spent in Britain in 1835–36, before and after his appointment as secretary of embassy, he worked for such a convention, and promoted a media publicity campaign against Russia.[14] After the 1832 Reform Act, British public opinion seemed fixated on keeping taxes and defence spending at a minimum. The only way to persuade British taxpayers to take the Russian threat to the Ottoman Empire seriously was to stress the commercial dangers and advantages involved for Britain. In Urquhart's mind, therefore, the two projects— the creation of a Russophobic press and the pursuit of an Ottoman commercial convention—were intimately connected, and he regarded both as proper activities for a rising Constantinople diplomat. In February 1836, he submitted a draft commercial treaty to the Foreign Office.

His enthusiasm for a convention was by no means a solitary obsession; the time was ripe for it. Both sides sought to work within existing norms, though the British government's position was also shaped by its hostility to economic monopolies. The Foreign Office and the Board of Trade wanted to review the current Anglo-Ottoman terms of trade, but so did the Ottoman government. The capitulations of 1675 laid down a duty of 3 per cent on all goods imported into and exported from the empire by British merchants, but a tariff was also needed to specify the market value to apply to each category of produce. This needed regular revision; the one agreed in 1820 expired in 1834. By that time, currency depreciation meant that the Ottoman regime was collecting only between half and two-thirds of the 1820 equivalent. For this reason, from 1830 the Ottomans had been pressing for an increase of duty from 3 to 5 per cent, in order, they said, to fund their armies and maintain their independence. They also pointed out that Britain's tariffs on Ottoman goods were too high. They sent Nuri to England in 1835 as a special envoy to make their case.

13. Urquhart, 174, 176–77. By contrast, he paid little attention to the Middle East, probably not regarding it as of much commercial value, at least in the struggle against Russia. He viewed Mehmet Ali as a typical over-mighty and corrupt local governor who diverted revenues to building a power base through a standing army. He doubted that the Egyptians would get anywhere in Anatolia, on account of Turks' contempt for Arabs, or even in Syria where he was confident that Mehmet Ali's corruptions would antagonise the independent-minded inhabitants (233–36).

14. This is well covered by Lamb, "Writing Up the Eastern Question."

Meanwhile, British merchants had been complaining about the extra financial burdens, beyond the capitulations, that Ottoman provincial governors were imposing on them. These seemed increasingly vexatious for several reasons, and particularly so to merchants from outside the complacent Levant Company networks. Those merchants were instinctively critical of local governors' resort to monopolies—the licences that were sold to individuals allowing them to monopolise production and export of a particular product. Also, since 1827 the Ottoman government had changed its policy on taxing the purchase and sale of goods from the interior. The 1809 peace treaty applied the 3 per cent duty only to the exterior trade—to goods deriving from or to be exported to foreign countries. Foreign merchants who bought goods within the empire in order to sell them internally were instead taxed at the same rate as Ottoman ones (this was part of the attempt to undermine the protection racket in the consulates, by which so many native merchants sought the rights of European traders). This was not originally a great problem for British merchants, who took little part in the interior trade. However, from 1827 the government proposed to apply the standard local taxes to all goods bought by British merchants in the interior, even if they were ultimately for export. This imposed significant extra duties on British trade— often 15 per cent, and sometimes higher (33 per cent on olive oil, 24 per cent on silk). Merchants complained that this was a serious impediment to commerce. Moreover, the 1829 Treaty of Adrianople protected the Russians against these additional interior taxes; they were given liberty of commerce subject only to paying the standard customs duties.

The Board of Trade argued that in return for accepting the Ottoman case for a 5 per cent basic duty, Britain should ask for all the extra and uncertain local duties to be removed, and for the abolition of government monopolies wherever they applied. So there was an implicit consensus on the basics of a future arrangement. It offered Britain real benefits, though it seemed clear that Russia would not copy Britain's willingness to increase the basic duty on its trade to 5 per cent. In May 1835, a Foreign Office memorandum observed that the 5 per cent duty would strengthen Ottoman economic independence, which was not of benefit to Russia as it "is most deeply interested that Turkey should not be really independent."[15]

Though the shape of a settlement was widely agreed, neither government wanted to announce all its concessions in advance of talks, and many details needed to be settled in Constantinople. In late 1836 and early 1837, discussions there foundered in an atmosphere dominated by factionalism and conspiracy theories. Ponsonby and Urquhart were both vehemently anti-Russian, as well as status-obsessed and vulnerable to paranoia. Each quickly came to feel that

15. For these two paragraphs, see the Foreign Office memoranda of Apr. 29, 1835, FO 78/269 149, May 13, 1835, 78/268 60, and May 1836, 78/298 291.

the other was seeking to undermine him personally, as well as being overly reliant on connections whom the Russians could bribe. Urquhart in particular was convinced that Ponsonby's dragomans were untrustworthy.[16] The ultimate reason for this mutual suspicion was a broader irritation in the British embassy: it seemed unable to improve its standing with the Porte on any issue. Ponsonby and Urquhart both regarded the failure to settle the commercial arrangements as the main indicator that British influence at the Porte still lagged behind Russia's. The Ottoman ministers most hostile to British pressure to finalise the convention seemed openly sympathetic to Russia. Defending Russia's unique commercial bargain of 1829 was the corollary of defending its unique political bargain of 1833. Other figures at the Porte who were willing to press ahead with a convention hoped in return that Britain would make a greater commitment to their regime than Ponsonby was able to promise. Meanwhile, the European representatives at Constantinople, like the Porte itself, preferred to revise the tariff than to prioritise a new convention, which they felt would mainly benefit Britain. By 1837, Ponsonby was very frustrated at the lack of progress.[17]

Factional Gridlock at Constantinople

Being frustrated was not an unusual experience for Ponsonby. For most of the 1830s, Constantinople diplomatic life existed in a fevered stasis in which Britain's standing hardly changed, but there was a constant anxiety that it might, for good or ill. The Pera district, where the European embassies were situated, had a reputation for constant intrigues and endless partisan suspicion. In 1837, one visitor, Julia Pardoe, brandishing the weapon of womanly sense, noted that Pera was infested with the "plague . . . Politics." It was an "ant-hill; with its . . . ceaseless, restless struggling and striving to secure most inconsequent results."[18] Russian and British partisans attributed every setback to some plot of their rivals. Most declarations of the Porte seemed intentionally ambiguous. For example, it sent former grand vizier Reşid off to command an army in Kurdistan. Was this in order to strengthen the empire against attack from Mehmet Ali, or to create a new local power that might be unfriendly to Britain? The mutual suspicions of the European embassies permeated all discussions, intensified by the physical, linguistic, and cultural

16. Urquhart had also hoped for a more radical policy, lowering British import duties on Ottoman goods in order to make Russian raw-material exports less competitive. See Bolsover, "David Urquhart," 461–62.

17. See Ponsonby to Palmerston, Mar. 1 and May 9, 1837, FO 78/302 5, 78/303 65. On Urquhart's attacks on him, see Ponsonby's letters of Feb. 10 and March 15 and 29, 1837, FO 78/301 134, 78/302 61, 123.

18. Pardoe, *City of the Sultan*, 1:vii. For similar comments, see Bulwer, *Palmerston*, 2:256; Layard, *Autobiography*, 2:63.

obstacles to approaching the sultan, and uncertainty as to where power at court really lay at any one time. Since the ambassadors could not speak Turkish, they relied on embassy dragomen to make their communications for them. Urquhart was not the only man to suspect the loyalty of the Pisani family on which successive British ambassadors relied; another branch of it supplied the Russian dragoman.[19] For most of the 1830s, Ponsonby had no personal access to the sultan, unlike his Russian counterpart Butenev. He assumed that, owing to the Treaty of Hünkar İskelesi, the Russians could always get their way at court when necessary. His party Whiggism (he was brother-in-law of Prime Minister Grey) reinforced his tendency to see the Russians as the great enemies of progress, as did the small circle of liberal Polish exiles on whom he relied for information.

British neurosis was compounded because of an internal power battle between the sultan's palace, the Seraglio, and the bureaucratic offices, the Porte, and between factions in each place. A group emerged who wanted closer commercial and political relations with Britain and France: some of them had been ambassadors to Western capitals. In particular, they envied the status and security offered by the European diplomatic and civil services, compared with the Ottoman bureaucracy, which was still formally a scribal service of the sultan's slaves, dependent on his whim. In 1836, the two leading scribal officials were redesignated foreign and interior ministers. If this seemed to promise improved status and political stability, hopes were quickly dashed by an extraordinary palace crisis in 1836–37. This was partly triggered by the rash behaviour of Ponsonby, whose insecurity made him overreact to the punishment meted out to a British journalist, William Churchill, for injuring a boy while shooting. Ponsonby claimed that Churchill's treatment (being whipped and put in irons) was a humiliation designed by a pro-Russian court faction headed by Foreign Minister Akif. Shortly afterwards, Akif fell from power, not because of anything Ponsonby had demanded (his tirade had no supporters), but because his enemies ganged up on him. In reaction, Interior Minister Pertev, Ponsonby's ally, was also ousted, and strangled with a bowstring. The murder of Pertev, the leader of the Anglophile bureaucrats, shocked his followers into a determination to demand security of life for officeholders. Under the leadership of Pertev's protégé Reshid, this was widened in 1838–39 into a demand for an official code offering security of life and property to all Ottoman subjects, and for reductions in the sultan's arbitrary power in a number of areas (including over monopolies). Ottoman subjects and Western powers would then have more confidence in the consistency and equitableness of policymaking.[20]

19. Berridge, *British Diplomacy in Turkey*, chap. 3; Turner, *Journal of a Tour*, 1:62–63; Bolsover, "David Urquhart," 465.

20. For these changes, see Findley, *Ottoman Civil Officialdom*, 26–32, 72–79.

In early 1838, however, these changes were by no means likely to happen, and Akif, Halil, and other pro-Russian ministers regained their influence. Ponsonby's fundamental problem was that the sultan wanted one thing from Britain, which he could not give him: an alliance. In 1832, Namık was sent to Britain to ask for one against Mehmet Ali, but was refused by the cabinet, leading inexorably to the Russo-Ottoman treaty instead. This refusal was not because Britain was in an unusually isolationist or economical frame of mind after the 1832 Reform Act. It was because the Foreign Office had no interest in making an arrangement with the Ottomans outside the European Concert. Russia and France took the lead in trying to settle the 1833 crisis, just as they had done in the eighteenth century. Britain supported France in brokering the Convention of Kütahya, which legitimised Mehmet Ali's rule in Syria. This upset the sultan, who had hoped that Russia and Britain would unite to support him as in 1798. By giving Mehmet Ali control of Damascus and Jerusalem, and hence all the most venerated Islamic cities, it potentially threatened the sultan's legitimacy. However, the convention was only a verbal understanding, and had no force at law. In theory, the absolutist Mahmud had the power to change his provincial governors each year; he resented enormously the European assumption that Mehmet Ali should be supported permanently. In the summer of 1834, Mahmud was the first to argue that the Syrian revolts justified Mehmet Ali's removal from office. In September 1834, he asked Ponsonby whether Britain would support his deposition and removal by military means, in the event of further Syrian rebellions.[21]

Mahmud's obsession from 1834 to attack Mehmet Ali helped the British at Constantinople in one respect, because Russia did not encourage him either. Russia's reluctance demonstrated what wise commentators had been saying for some time: that Russia did not want a war over the spoils of the empire, just the continuation of the sultan's current dependent weakness. As Russia was offering Mahmud no more than Britain, Palmerston was relatively relaxed about the Syrian question. He did not want to take sides on it, but to use British naval power to dissuade both camps from aggressions. He made clear that, if Mehmet Ali attacked Anatolia, the British fleet would expect to protect Constantinople against him, and would get there before the Russians could. However, he was unwilling to give the sultan any promise of offensive military support; indeed in 1834 he ordered the British navy to prevent any move by the Ottoman fleet to attack Mehmet Ali.[22] Conflict must be avoided, because only a war would justify Russia seizing the straits, while peace allowed the British to build up influence with both sides.

21. See Ponsonby to Palmerston, July 25 and Sept. 15, 1834, FO 78/237 102, 78/238 124.

22. Bulwer, *Palmerston*, 2:182–83; Bailey, *British Policy*, 166.

For the same reason, Palmerston tried to manage anti-Russian sentiment in Britain. He encouraged Urquhart's initial attempts to use the press to publicise Russia's designs, agreeing with him that insular tax-cutting arguments were too dominant in British politics. Urquhart's campaign helped to persuade Parliament to accept naval spending increases in 1836. On the other hand, Palmerston sent Lord Durham to Russia as a special ambassador charged with smoothing tensions. When the sultan, buoyed by reports of Urquhart's journalistic successes, pushed for Britain to support a campaign against Mehmet Ali in 1836, he failed again.[23] When Urquhart created a crisis in the Black Sea area in 1836–37, in an attempt to generate a rising against Russia, Palmerston swiftly removed him from his post and from Constantinople—making a lifelong enemy in the process, but greatly relieving Ponsonby, who was now being attacked in the press by Urquhart's allies.[24]

So until 1838 little changed in British policy, despite swirling pressures, conspiracy theories, and factional squabbles. An uneasy equipoise continued, between Britain and Russia, between court factions, between the sultan and Mehmet Ali, and between progress and delay on commercial matters. Palmerston, a natural optimist, tended to assume that Russia's power would wane, as British influence at the Porte increased and the benefits of peace became apparent, along with the chance to reallocate resources from military spending to commercial development.[25] However, even he acknowledged that this would take a long time. Occasionally, he asked for permission to install British army advisers to boost Ottoman military effectiveness, but suspicion of Britain at the Porte always prevented these appointments; a few Prussians and Austrians were given those roles instead.[26] Those who were not natural optimists suspected that Britain and Russia were in fact squabbling over a dying regime.

Ending the Stalemate

This uneasy stasis was destroyed by one event in May 1838. Ostensibly, it posed a new problem; in reality, it offered the sultan and Britain convenient new opportunities. On May 25, 1838, Mehmet Ali told the British and French consuls-general in Egypt that the time had come to secure the gains that he had made for his family. Since the sultan refused to recognise them, he had decided that he would soon declare his independence from the Porte, and then resist the sultan's anticipated attack on him in Syria.[27] In talking about independence, he

23. Palmerston to Ponsonby, May 7 and Aug. 8, 1836, FO 78/271 67, 78/272 62. Ponsonby had sent a secret messenger to Britain to argue that Britain should force Mehmet Ali to obey the sultan: to Alexandre Blacque, Mar. 3, 1836, PPD, GRE/E/102, J3.

24. Webster, "Urquhart, Ponsonby, and Palmerston," 340–51.

25. Bailey, British Policy, 145, 149; Bulwer, Palmerston, 2:285, 287.

26. Rodkey, "Rejuvenation of Turkey," 575–86.

27. Campbell to Palmerston, May 25, 1838, FO 78/342 pt. 2, 119.

was flying a kite: it was a hypothetical inquiry designed to find out how much support he could expect from the British and French governments for a bid to secure his family's position as a hereditary regional power. He had probably been encouraged to make this inquiry by Britons with government connections: by Bowring, who was visiting him with semi-official status, and by Waghorn, now the East India Company's agent in Egypt in charge of the post.[28] After all, the Euphrates Expedition had failed, and Britain was developing the steamer route through Egypt, with Mehmet Ali's complete cooperation. He had consented to Campbell's request to abolish monopolies in Syria. Britain and France were in alliance against Russia in much of the world; would they really abandon him to a Russian-dominated sultan? Mahmud had been threatening aggression against him for four years, and no power had been willing to support his threats. The sultan had lost control of the Islamic Holy Cities, and his conceptual absolutism was being challenged at his own court by Pertev and his protégé Reshid. Mehmet Ali's inquiry was hypothetical; he could always resile from it. In fact, he did resile, quickly, by July, because he got no encouragement from any of the powers.

Mehmet Ali's kite was extremely useful to the sultan, to Ponsonby, and to the Foreign Office because it suited them all to claim that his ambition was now rebellion and expansion. The sultan could now press Europe again to support his removal from Syria, especially in view of the Druze rebellion in the Hawran, which seemed to leave the Egyptians newly vulnerable there. Talk of Mehmet Ali's "imperialism" justified Britain's forward policy in Arabia and the Persian Gulf—even though he was getting nowhere in the Yemen, while the Druze rebellion lessened the chance of him ever moving successfully against Baghdad. Now that he was the "tyrant of Syria," his dream of an Arab empire was dead.[29] The Foreign Office, the Constantinople embassy, and the Porte all now saw the benefits of agreeing the Commercial Convention. It was signed in August; the details were handled, on the British side, by Henry Lytton Bulwer, Urquhart's successor as secretary of embassy. It abolished monopolies and local interior supplementary taxes on goods for export, replacing the latter by a standard 9 per cent rate on top of the traditional 3 per cent duty. On imports, there would be a retailer's tax of 2 per cent in addition to the standard 3 per cent, thus securing the 5 per cent total duty for which the Ottomans had pressed. The most-favoured-nation clause would apply, so Britain would benefit from any lower rates that other countries, such as Russia, negotiated in future. France signed a similar treaty in November.

28. On Waghorn: Foreign Office to Campbell, June 9, 1838, FO 78/343 pt. 1, 4; Waghorn to Boghos, Apr. 6, 1838, FO 78/342 pt. 2, 14. On both, see Puryear, *International Economics and Diplomacy*, 75.

29. Bulwer, June 28, 1838, FO 78/334 7.

One reason why both Ponsonby and Palmerston were keen on the convention was that they expected it to weaken the revenue stream that Mehmet Ali got from monopolies in Syria and Egypt. In the latter, they supplied nearly 30 per cent of his total revenue, and over half of his army budget, and so seemed essential to his military strategy.[30] However, the convention prevented authorities from granting licences for monopolies on the sale of goods, whereas Mehmet Ali's Egyptian revenues came from his ownership of land as the sultan's representative. So he was able to implement the convention's provisions with little difficulty, as long as the sultan did not also refuse him the right to own land on his behalf. Though Ponsonby and Palmerston explicitly wanted Mahmud to do this, it was not practicable politics.[31] Bowring and Campbell hoped that the convention would make Mehmet Ali see the longer-term benefits of free trade for the Egyptian economy, and in February 1839, Ibrahim offered some of the wheat grown on his Egyptian lands for export free of any duty, in order to indicate that he was no protectionist. In Syria, meanwhile, the convention would have weakened Mehmet Ali's rule if he had been able to impose the monopolies that were his original intention. However, as noted in chapter 5, he had already been forced to abandon them, requiring him to resort to other unpopular taxes instead. Ironically, the convention itself actually increased Mehmet Ali's Syrian revenues, because the 2 per cent import retail tax applied even though there had been no equivalent interior duties in the past. This did not please British merchants.[32]

Nonetheless, the convention was politically significant in several ways. The regime and Britain had reached agreement on a major reform that indicated Ottoman support for British-style commercial development and freer trade. Ponsonby and Bulwer both fervently believed that the convention would strengthen the Ottoman economy, by cutting the cost of food, securing a more reliable income for the government, and checking the power of corrupt local governors. These were all essential if the regime was to arrest its decline in favour of the slow improvement for which Palmerston hoped. It would make it less dependent on Russia; it would indicate that Britain had the diplomatic upper hand at the Porte.[33] By so publicly insisting that the convention should apply to Mehmet Ali in Egypt and Syria, Britain, and the other countries that made similar treaty arrangements in future, were indicating support for the sultan's sovereignty over him.

30. Puryear, *International Economics and Diplomacy*, 73.

31. Ponsonby to Palmerston, Oct. 16, 1838, FO 78/332 321; Palmerston to Campbell, Oct. 12, 1839, FO 78/372 63.

32. See Campbell to Palmerston, Feb. 14, March 30, and Sept. 3, 1839, FO 78/343 49, 78/376 69, 249, and Bowring to Palmerston, Oct. 29, 1838, FO 78/345 143.

33. Bulwer, *Palmerston*, 2:287, 298–99; Ponsonby to Palmerston, May 10, 1838, FO 78/331 79; Bulwer, June 28, 1838, FO 78/334 7.

However, this raised the question of whether the sultan or the British had made the bigger commitment to the other. In February 1838, Palmerston had instructed Ponsonby to tell the Porte that it would gain "great moral and political support" from Britain if it concluded the convention. Ponsonby added that British "force and influence" would be used to ensure Mehmet Ali's compliance if necessary.[34] The sultan gained great pleasure and confidence from these pledges. Bulwer noted Sultan Mahmud's political astuteness in using the issue to drive a wedge between Europe and Mehmet Ali.[35] Palmerston wanted to get the European powers to agree that they would oppose any claim to independence by Mehmet Ali. In July, he told Campbell to tell Mehmet Ali that they all took that view. However, he could not get a formal agreement to that effect, since Mehmet Ali refused to make any fresh gestures of defiance to the sultan.[36]

Even so, Mahmud now proceeded as if the powers had taken that position, or that they would do if required. In January 1839, a new levy of eighty thousand Ottoman soldiers was raised for an attack on Syria. Encouraged by a Muslim insurrection in the Hawran in March against conscription and taxation, Ottoman troops eventually crossed the Euphrates in April 1839. Campbell believed that Russia had encouraged this belligerent position; others believed that Britain had.[37] But there was no reason to blame either. Not only Mahmud but also Hüsrev, Mehmet Ali's sworn enemy and the greatest influence on the Porte's Egyptian policy, were determined to attack him. Hüsrev had his own sources of information on discontent in Syria, plus great influence in military matters because of his long responsibility for army reform. The disastrous Ottoman army defeat at Nizip on June 24 then opened Anatolia to Ibrahim's forces, just as at the end of 1832. Sultan Mahmud died on July 1 and Constantinople politics descended into frenzied factionalism: Hüsrev declared himself grand vizier, and the kapudan pasha reacted by taking the fleet to Alexandria, claiming that the Russians would now be invited back, and that Mehmet Ali would protect it better.

Within a month, by the end of July 1839, the European ambassadors at Constantinople had agreed to take the future of the Ottoman Empire into their own hands. On July 27, they told the new sultan, Abdülmecid, to do nothing without consulting them. There seemed little alternative. But they were also aware that solutions were not impossible. Led by foreign minister Nesselrode, Russia soon acknowledged that the renewal of its privileged access

34. Palmerston to Ponsonby, Feb. 8, 1838, FO 78/328 10; Ponsonby to Pisani, Apr. 17, 1838, FO 78/330 236.

35. Bulwer, *Palmerston*, 2:263.

36. Palmerston to Campbell, July 7, 1838, FO 78/343 pt. 1, 8; Bailey, *British Policy*, 168–69.

37. Campbell to Palmerston, July 13, 1839, FO 78/374 167. See Temperley's balanced assessment of Ponsonby's role: *England and the Near East*, 99, 423–25.

to the straits, secured in 1833, would be unacceptable to Europe. A consensus quickly emerged in favour of an agreement that no foreign warships should be allowed to enter the straits in peacetime; this was formalised in 1840 among the four signatories to the Treaty of London and in 1841 among all five powers. By autumn 1839, the powers also agreed that Mehmet Ali was to be offered hereditary rule in Egypt. Great-power diplomacy seemed to be working well, and in September, Palmerston cheerily forecast to Bulwer that the powers should be able to protect the empire for the next ten years, while it pursued internal improvements, which he expected would result from international discussion and pressure.[38] In November, the British ambassador in Vienna boasted that there were no remaining questions between the powers, except about "the line of delimitation in Syria" separating Egyptian and Ottoman authority.[39] Unfortunately, this was to prove an insoluble problem.

Britain, France, and the Future of Syria

Palmerston, Ponsonby, and Bulwer all wanted Mehmet Ali to be removed completely from Syria, because the military stand-off between him and the sultan was doing immense damage to both sides, to the region itself, and to international relations. The need for two armed camps on the Syrian border forced both sides to prioritise conscription and military preparation, draining resources from productive enterprise and preventing rational financial and administrative reform. Palmerston was showing his disapproval of Mehmet Ali's style of government by now, though Bulwer was more sympathetic, acknowledging that the sultan's hatred was forcing Mehmet Ali to be an expansionist; if he showed any weakness, he would be attacked.[40] The issue was strategic: the only beneficiaries of this institutionalised tension would be those who thrived on Ottoman weakness. Palmerston was suspicious that Russia was willing for Mehmet Ali to be given "Diarbekir . . . the central key to the whole of Asia Minor"; it would make Constantinople much more vulnerable.[41] Dragoman Pisani and the embassy worried that, while Ibrahim could defeat the sultan's forces, he would still be immensely challenged dealing with the problems of Syria, which would allow a Russian army to move south and attack him. The ultimate fear was always of Russian expansion.[42] In a series of letters in July and August 1839, Campbell argued against the idea of

38. Bulwer, *Palmerston*, 2:298. For his idea that increased European public awareness of Ottoman governance defects would naturally generate pressure for reform, see Bulwer, 2:287.

39. Beauvale to Hodges, Nov. 16, 1839, FO 78/377 9.

40. Bulwer, *Palmerston*, 2:276–78, 283–84; Bulwer, June 28, 1838, FO 78/334 7. For Palmerston, see Rodkey, *Turco-Egyptian Question*, 92–94.

41. Temperley, *England and the Near East*, 93.

42. Alexander Pisani to Ponsonby, Nov. 23, 1840, PPD, GRE/E/477 59.

displacing Mehmet Ali from Syria, on the grounds that the Ottomans could not govern it well. As a result, he was removed as consul-general.[43]

By the start of 1840, the four European powers other than France were willing to agree that Mehmet Ali should be required to vacate Syria. This was despite the fact that Sultan Mahmud had himself proposed ceding part of Syria to Mehmet Ali in 1837.[44] At various times in 1840, a compromise partition of the area was proposed, in the hope of getting French support. The British government disliked the idea of giving Mehmet Ali southern Syria, fearing that it would entrench his power in the Hijaz and the Red Sea. Campbell and Thurburn could not see any benefit to Mehmet Ali either, as he would have to spend vast sums on defending the territory, while losing the revenues of Beirut.[45] Finally, in July 1840, the four powers signed a treaty agreeing to the sultan's request to help him maintain "the integrity and independence" of his empire. They committed to use force to remove Mehmet Ali from Syria, if he did not meet their two-stage ultimatum (though, in order to keep hopes of compromise alive, he could retain Acre and southern Syria as well as Egypt if he met the first deadline).[46] France's separation from the other powers derived from its adherence to the Convention of Kütahya in 1833, which had legitimised Mehmet Ali's rule in Syria. It seemed unfair now to deprive him of it, especially since it was not clear how he could be persuaded to leave, unless significant concessions were made to him. France also expected to have a particular say in the settlement of Syria, given its historic influence with the Maronites. Palmerston disliked France's logic, because it meant that the tensions between the Ottomans and Egypt would never be resolved.[47]

Once it was clear that Russia was willing to abandon its special rights to defend Constantinople, the basic reason for British and French cooperation, and the cause of their agreement over the Convention of Kütahya in 1833, disappeared. Naturally, Russia was delighted at the emergence of discord between them. Russia sought to play the game of 1806 against France again, encouraging Britain to police Egypt and Syria while it looked after the northern Ottoman territories.[48] Russia's position meant that it was impossibly risky for France to give its unequivocal support to Mehmet Ali. A number of French

43. Campbell to Palmerston, July 28 and Aug. 7, 1839, FO 78/375 64, 93.

44. Dodwell considered this to be an insincere bluff, done to please France: *Founder of Modern Egypt*, 167–68.

45. See Bulwer, *Palmerston*, 2:302, 330; Thurburn to Palmerston, Dec. 13, 1840, with Campbell enclosure, FO 78/426 98.

46. The proposal was not to give Mehmet Ali the whole pashalik of Sidon, but to separate off Beirut from it. The boundary would run between Cape Naqoura and the top of the Sea of Galilee, and then down the line of the Jordan and Dead Sea to Aqaba. See Hurewitz, *Diplomacy*, 117.

47. Pisani to Ponsonby, June 26, 1840, PPD, GRE/E/477 42.

48. Bulwer, *Palmerston*, 2:300.

politicians, especially Thiers, desperately wanted to be associated with a proud and assertive policy in the East. But Palmerston was always confident that France would not give Mehmet Ali military assistance, because of the naval balance in the Mediterranean and the fear of losing Algeria once the British cut its communication lines with its new colony. Though French ministers argued that Mehmet Ali was invincible, Palmerston thought this was a misjudgment: the withdrawal of troops from Arabia had already shown that his resources were limited.[49] Meanwhile, the outside risk that France might be willing to initiate the partition of the empire encouraged the other powers, and British domestic political opinion, to unite against it, summoning all the images that had been used against Napoleon in 1799. Palmerston told the cabinet that the choice was either to defend Ottoman sovereignty or to accept "the practical division of the Turkish Empire into two separate and independent states, whereof one will be the dependency of France, and the other a satellite of Russia; and in both of which our political influence will be annulled, and our commercial interests will be sacrificed." Despite strong Francophile instincts, it accepted his case.[50] The Tory opposition and most of the press also gave his policy general support.

France's options were further restricted because, as in 1798, the Russo-British argument was couched in terms of the defence of the sultan's territorial rights. Mehmet Ali was his rebellious vassal, and rebellion against *him* was an exercise in popular loyalty. Ponsonby was confident in a Syrian rebellion of ten thousand men; he could "answer for the inhabitants of Lebanon, the Emir Beshir and all, provided England will *act* and will support them."[51] Ibrahim was known to be planning to disarm the Maronites of the weapons that they had previously used against the Druze. As a result, a Maronite revolt began in late May, and news of this encouraged the powers to sign the Treaty of London in July. That they were Christians added to the consensus in favour of action. The pope supported the revolt, as, tellingly, did the French consul in Beirut, to the alarm of the Paris government.[52]

The main argument for the allied intervention in Syria was that a militarised Egyptian regime was oppressing the country and fomenting a damaging civil war within the empire. So it was easy to claim that its removal was bound to increase Syrian productivity and prosperity, helped by the implementation of the Commercial Convention; the tonnage of ships trading at Beirut doubled between 1835 and 1841.[53] However, there would clearly need to be a new

49. Bulwer, 2:308–9, 320–21, 349–54; Palmerston to Hodges, July 18, 1840, FO 78/403 43.

50. July 5, 1840, Bulwer, *Palmerston*, 2:359–60.

51. Ponsonby to Palmerston, Apr. 25, 1840, FO 78/393 138; Pisani to Ponsonby, June 26, 1840, PPD, GRE/E/477 42.

52. Farah, *Politics of Interventionism*, 36.

53. Bailey, *British Policy*, 102.

political settlement as well. Palmerston announced that the allied liberation of Syria would be accompanied by pressure on the sultan "to grant to his Syrian subjects such future arrangements as may make their condition happy and prosperous."[54] How did he plan to do that? In practice, he would expect local British officials to flesh out the answer in conjunction with the Porte. Could the diplomats and military men in the East agree what reforms would be necessary?

One clear aim was to restore the "liberties and privileges" of the Lebanese mountaineers.[55] They were familiar from 1799; their leader then, Bashir, had helped Sidney Smith to outwit Napoleon and Cezzar, and was still in place. He enjoyed a positive reputation in the West, partly because of memories of that struggle, but also because his power seemed to rest on an unusual degree of religious toleration. Visitors such as John Carne and Alphonse de Lamartine had celebrated his public respect for the diverse religious practices of the Christian, Druze, and Muslim communities of the mountain.[56] A balance of power between him and a local pasha seemed the best option. In 1838, Bulwer hoped that if Mehmet Ali could be persuaded to leave Syria, "another combination" of local interests could be restored under Anglo-French guarantee, on principles "less obnoxious" than those of previous Ottoman or Egyptian regimes.[57] Lebanese liberties and privileges were assumed to include Bashir's devolved government, the property rights of their landowning nobles, their freedom to bear arms, and their right to low taxation.

In June 1840, Ponsonby arranged with Reshid, now the Ottoman foreign minister, that a firman confirming these privileges should be taken to Lebanon by a confidential British emissary in order to get the mountaineers' support. This idea seems to have stemmed from Lord Alvanley, who had just been travelling in Syria.[58] The man whom Ponsonby selected for this mission was Richard Wood, who had become his most trusted assistant at the embassy. The thirty-four-year-old Wood was the son of an English Levant Company merchant at Constantinople who had become an embassy dragoman because of his abilities at translation. Wood, likewise, was linguistically talented—his mother seems to have been from a Mediterranean Catholic family—and succeeded his father in this role in 1834, having spent two years learning Arabic in Syria.[59] After Consul-General Farren had alerted Ponsonby to the unpopularity of

54. See his summary of allied objectives, to the Admiralty, July 16, 1840, FO 78/421 76.

55. This or similar phrases were often used by Wood (e.g., *Early Correspondence*, 145) and by Palmerston (e.g., 82 Parl. Deb. [3d ser.] [1845] col. 1525).

56. Parry, "Disraeli," 577–78. For Smith and Bashir in 1799, see chapter 1 above, p. 30.

57. Bulwer, *Palmerston*, 2:276–78.

58. Alvanley to Ponsonby, June 16, 1840, FO 78/394 180.

59. He was regarded by his detractors as an intriguing Levantine (see, e.g., Amir Bashir, quoted in Macfarlane, *Turkey and Its Destiny*, 2:65, and those quoted in R. Wood, *Early Correspondence*, 3).

Egyptian rule in Syria, Wood went back there in 1835–36 to discover the prospects for insurrection. He seemed the natural person to go again in 1840. But now he was no longer to travel just as Ponsonby's assistant. He represented an extraordinary, novel alliance between the British embassy and the Porte, which aimed to secure not just the traditional liberties of Lebanon, but also the imposition of Ottoman imperial power—and made the remarkable claim that they were compatible.

Reshid, Richard Wood, and the Edict of Gülhane

Though Ponsonby and Wood shared the general view that defending the historic privileges and liberties of Lebanon was necessary for peace in Syria, their emphasis was on the mechanics for getting these principles guaranteed. They quickly formed the view that the situation in Syria required decisive executive leaders capable of establishing and implementing defined rights at law, in order to win the people's confidence. Their faith in this strategy was boosted enormously by the proclamation of the Edict of Gülhane in the rose garden near the Topkapi Palace in Constantinople on November 3, 1839.[60] This proclamation in the name of the new sultan, Abdülmecid, was officially known as the Tanzimat Fermanı; in retrospect it was the opening salvo of the Ottoman Tanzimat reform programme, which stretched over the next four decades. It was clearly intended as the basis of the new Anglo-Ottoman strategy for Syria devised by Ponsonby and Reshid, who was the edict's reader and a significant influence on it. When Wood left for Syria in June 1840, he took two documents to aid the revolt: the firman upholding the mountaineers' privileges was accompanied by the edict. Reshid also gave Wood "the right to speak in the name of the Porte in his communications with the subjects of the Sultan" in Syria.[61]

Reshid was thirty-nine and had spent his career in the sultan's civil service. His politics were determined by his dealings with two senior Ottoman political figures: his major patron, Pertev, and the man he most detested, Mehmet Ali. The overarching principle of the edict was the extension of sultanic law to protect life, property, and other basic freedoms; its timing was made possible by the death of Mahmud in July. The edict was the culmination of the power struggle at court that Reshid and his allies had been fighting since the murder of Pertev, hoping to end arbitrary decision-making and to secure their own lives and positions. Its high-profile proclamation also owed much to Reshid's four years in Europe as ambassador to France and then to Britain between 1834 and 1838. Reshid was shocked by Mehmet Ali's

60. See, e.g., Ponsonby in R. Wood, *Early Correspondence*, 233.

61. Wood to Ponsonby, Aug. 23, 1840, FO 78/396 88; letters of Sept. 29, 1840, FO 78/397 86, 95.

skill in disseminating the notion that he was a uniquely civilised Eastern ruler. In Britain, and even more in France, Reshid constantly encountered admiration for his commitment to education, interest in technology, achievement of order, religious toleration, and apparent willingness to learn from French military and public health advisers. Implicitly and sometimes explicitly, contrasts were drawn with Ottoman barbarity.[62] Reshid saw that there was no hope of improving the standing of the empire in Europe without a dramatic change of image.

It is now widely understood that it is too simple to see the proponents of the Ottoman Tanzimat as a special breed of "reformers" dedicated to a "Westernising" programme.[63] Most Ottoman politicians wanted to make the state apparatus more efficient and to crack down on corruption, but they had divergent priorities: Hüsrev, for example, was a powerful opponent of Reshid's party, but was still very concerned to improve the state of the army. Hüsrev, and former allies of his like Halil and Akif, distrusted Reshid's apparent pandering to Western opinion, but also his attempts to build up new centres of bureaucratic power, bypassing traditional palace structures.[64] What is clear is that the challenge of Mehmet Ali forced Reshid and Hüsrev into an alliance. Then the death of Mahmud gave Reshid the political opportunity to argue for a theatrical declaration of principles at Gülhane. This would help to change Europeans' opinion of the Ottoman regime, and encourage them to see it as committed to the principles of defined laws and liberties and rational bureaucratic processes. But there was nothing "Western" in it, in the sense of hostility to Islam; nor was the West the main audience. The ultimate aim of the edict was to strengthen sultanic authority, and sultanic and shari'a law, against the tendency of provincial authorities and vested interests to disrespect and undermine them. The text was shaped by a Sunni Orthodox clerical school that had developed particular power at court and had trained young Abdülmecid.[65]

The edict promised a number of bureaucratic reforms to remove local abuses of power, including the abolition of monopolies, tax farming, and illegal taxes. Arbitrary levies for military service were to make way for a rational system proposed by a military council. Laws regulating security of life and property were to be formulated by the Council of Justice; a penal code was to be drawn up. No life could be ended, and no property confiscated, without public trial. The edict remarked—in passing—that these imperial concessions would extend to all subjects, to Muslims and to non-Muslim rayas, but made clear that this assumed their respect for "the sacred text of our law." The whole

62. Ozavci, *Dangerous Gifts*, chap. 7, esp. 184–88.
63. Bouquet, "Ottoman Modernisation." See also the interesting case of the Benthamite Hassuna D'Ghies of Tripoli, who had originally pursued the cause of independence for his country, but now became a "New Ottoman" bureaucrat: Coller, "Ottomans on the Move."
64. Shaw and Shaw, *Ottoman Empire and Modern Turkey*, 2:69, 73.
65. Abu-Manneh, "Islamic Roots."

thrust of the edict was to put "the sacred code of laws" on a more secure footing. The courts still upheld Islamic principles of justice: Christians accused
of crimes against a Muslim were judged in Islamic courts, and the edict confirmed that "the cause of every accused person shall be publicly judged in
accordance with our Divine Law."[66] As far as the major raya communities—
the Greek Orthodox, the Armenians, and the Jews—were concerned, the main
purpose of the edict was to indicate that they would retain the autonomy over
their internal justice arrangements that they had had for several hundred
years, in the *millet* system. Their leaders were at the Gülhane ceremony to
indicate their continuing official, if subordinate, place within the Ottoman
legal structure.

Ponsonby understood and approved all these points: the security of property and persons under the law, the promised fiscal and military improvements, but above all the attempt to strengthen the sultan's authority and
popular Muslim respect for him. He welcomed its aim of establishing more
harmony between sultanic and shari'a law: its declarations on religious
matters were "in perfect unison with the religion and interests and feelings
of the People."[67] There was another reason for his pleasure: the increased
accountability of the provincial pashas who exercised power in the sultan's
name, but who often abused it. As with the revised capitulations laid down in
the 1838 Commercial Convention, legal stipulations could now be cited whenever there was a breach of order affecting British interests or local peace. The
logic of the edict was that complaint to the central bureaucracy at Constantinople would expose and correct the corruptions of local authorities. Embassy
lobbying of the Porte would check the abuses of provincial pashas, and would
remind the sultan's ministers of the importance of upholding rule-based government. Strengthening the legal basis of sultanic rule in the empire increased
the power of the Constantinople embassy to challenge any abuses reported to
it by local British consuls.

The edict seemed particularly well shaped to address Syrians' grievances
of heavy and illegal taxation and brutal conscription. It promised to tackle the
abuses that had dominated Farren's dispatches as well as Urquhart's writings:
tax farming, monopolies, institutionalised peculation, and the failure to invest
in long-run agricultural improvement. Just before Wood left Constantinople,
Reshid had told him that the Porte would not tolerate abuse of power by its
governors in Syria. So when he arrived in Syria with the delegated powers, he
travelled wherever he could, reading the edict and promising that all illegal

66. For the text and quotations, see Bailey, *British Policy*, 277–79. For the background,
see Findley, "Tanzimat," 17–19; Anscombe, "Ottoman Reform," 183–85; Deringil, *Conversion and Apostasy*, 32–33.

67. Ponsonby to Palmerston, Mar. 23, 1840, FO 78/393 42; Nov. 5, 1839, FO 78/360
pt. 1, 14.

taxes and duties would be abolished under it.[68] Ottoman rule would revert to historic Islamic basics.

Throughout Wood's time of greatest influence in Syria, in 1840–41, he tried to get local Ottoman representatives to accept this pledge on taxation. He expected that, once all Mehmet Ali's extra taxes had been abolished, his self-aggrandising oppressiveness would be impossible for any pasha. Like Urquhart (and many nineteenth-century British liberals), Wood judged a polity's effectiveness on whether it could prevent ministers from imposing excessive burdens on the people—on whether it offered Bentham's "securities against misrule." He wanted to remove most of the expensive bureaucracy, and most of the powers, of the four separate *eyalet*s into which Syria had historically been divided, and to establish instead a small central government, a council, and a number of local councils, including in Lebanon.[69] Not surprisingly, this policy encountered resistance, especially from Izzet, the chief Ottoman representative in Syria, who disliked surrendering taxes.

Wood's other great anxiety was to rein in local chiefs who had got used to abusing their power. Their private interests must now be subordinated to the rule of law. This meant attacking their feudal arrogance even while upholding their legitimate property rights. Wood believed that the fundamental problem in Syria—in Nablus as much as in Lebanon—was that the people were "not oppressed by the Turkish Authorities but by their own Sheikhs." They must be made to see that a reformed Ottoman government would protect them better than the "old oppressive system" of "turbulent . . . Sheiks or feudal Lords" who bullied their poorer dependents into perpetuating a state of armed factionalism. These petty chiefs must abandon their feudal powers "in favour of an enlightened and general system of administration."[70] Amir Bashir was merely the most powerful of the many feudal relics whose greed and family disputes were preventing the establishment of a rule-based relationship between governors and governed. From an early stage in 1840, Wood convinced himself that Bashir's cousin Bashir Qasim would be a better bet in the task of suppressing "old family animosities and private feuds among the Emirs and Sheiks."[71]

So Wood was aiming at a new political structure that would discipline Ottoman officials and local chiefs alike. And though he disliked traditional Lebanese feudalism, he disliked sectarian partisanship more. He made various proposals for representative councils or divans, all of which deliberately made it impossible for either Christians or Druze to get a majority. His Syrian supreme council would have been composed of four representatives from Constantinople, four local Muslims and one non-Muslim, of different

68. R. Wood, *Early Correspondence*, 145, 174.
69. R. Wood, 225–29, 237–39.
70. R. Wood, 181, 215, 224.
71. R. Wood, 187, 197.

denominations, from each of the Syrian *eyalets*.[72] He saw religious parties, like feudalism, as potential obstacles to the idea of a united Syria loyal to the Porte, not least because of the opportunities that they might offer France and Russia to destabilise local politics for their own reasons. Wood's policy was for himself and Britain to referee local disputes until a viable Tanzimat-style constitution could be established securing a self-acting balance to check the three great problems of Syria: pasha rapacity, local feudal power, and sectarian rivalries. Strong government by fair-minded officials would regulate tensions between Christians and Muslims, and would defeat the sectarian mentality that thrived on allegations that the Islamic governing code was incapable of supplying communal justice.

Suspicion of Christian sectarianism was also the official British view of the Syrian intervention. Palmerston was clear that the intervention was to be conducted "in the name and in the support of the Sultan, that we may not be accused of acting on our own account, and may not excite any Mahometan fanaticism."[73] Meanwhile Ponsonby soon became alarmed by European commentators' desire to reframe the Tanzimat as a programme to secure Christian interests. He feared that Western pressure of this sort would reduce respect for the sultan's authority, and allow factions like the janissaries to appeal to Muslim popular sentiment against him. He came to feel that even Reshid deferred too much to European pluralist ideas, "the offsprings of frippery, French philosophy, and ignorant vanity," in ways that "alarmed religion and often offended manners."[74]

It was perhaps predictable that the Edict of Gülhane was so widely seen in Europe as giving a particular guarantee of good treatment to Christians. European opinion had become used to viewing Ottoman government through the prism of its handling of Christian interests. Press writers seized on the declaration that Christians and Jews as well as Muslims enjoyed rights under the law, and interpreted it to mean that those rights were equal in every respect. The revolt of Maronite Syrians was much discussed in French and Austrian newspapers, many of which assumed that their grievances stemmed from sectarian oppression and that the Edict of Gülhane had promised to abolish that. The Damascus affair popularised a contrast in European eyes, between Mehmet Ali's mistreatment of incarcerated Jews and the sultan's support for their liberation and decided opposition to anti-Semitic blood libels. So the new sultan's government was identified with declarations of fairness as between religions. Not surprisingly, many writers expressed scepticism that the Ottomans actually

---

72. R. Wood, 228.

73. Temperley, *England and the Near East*, 115.

74. Ponsonby to Palmerston, Sept. 30, 1839, FO 78/359 61; Mar. 16 and 23, 1840, FO 78/393 5, 42. The quoted remarks were to Jochmus, March 1842, cited in Bailey, *British Policy*, 208.

meant these declarations. Past critics of Turkish barbarity assumed that the promises that they thought had been made to Christians must be empty humbug.[75] The Austrian chancellor, Metternich, who like Ponsonby welcomed the edict primarily because it strengthened Islamic rule, was alarmed to note how many Austrian and German newspapers immediately highlighted the grievances of the Christian sects with which they sympathised. He saw that it set expectations for Ottoman governance impossibly high.[76]

European public anxiety to protect Ottoman Christians and Jews was to be very important in the future, but in 1840 Ponsonby and Wood's ideas for Syria encountered more immediate opposition from elsewhere—from another part of the British state. Ponsonby, anxious to encourage a Syrian uprising, asked for a small British squadron to be sent to Beirut.[77] Commodore Charles Napier arrived there on July 7, 1840. Napier was fifty-four, a Scot, and a veteran of the Napoleonic navy. His career had been launched by Dundas and the Dundasite naval officer Alexander Cochrane (the organiser of the landing at Abukir in 1801). He was also a sympathiser with popular causes: a campaigner for the abolition of flogging and other naval reforms, a failed Liberal parliamentary candidate, and a constitutionalist hero in the Portuguese Civil War. He was looking for naval excitement and a new patriotic political crusade. Once he got news of the Treaty of London, he had both, and more: he had the chance to be the new Sidney Smith.

Napier or Wood, Smith or Elgin, Cairo or Constantinople?

The Treaty of London gave Mehmet Ali ample time—twenty days from its presentation to him on August 16—to surrender, which he had no intention of doing. So it was not until early September that Napier was able to take significant steps against the Egyptian forces in Syria, which in the meantime had been boosted to at least seventy thousand, while the Maronite revolt had been put down in July. Napier's superior Sir Robert Stopford then arrived with a much larger British and Austrian fleet, charged with controlling the eastern Mediterranean, cutting the lines of communication from Egypt, and facilitating landings of Ottoman troops. Napier landed his allied force (5,300 Turks and 1,500 British marines) at Djouni; its main initial purpose was to encourage the mountaineers of Lebanon to come to collect muskets for their rebellion.[78] As Bashir remained loyal to Ibrahim, they were slow in arriving at first, but by mid-October, fifteen thousand muskets had been distributed

---

75. E.g., J. Reid, *Turkey and the Turks*, 64–65.

76. Šedivý, "Metternich's Judgement on Islam," 159–60.

77. Ponsonby to Palmerston, June 23, 1840, FO 78/394 201.

78. Britain's Syrian force also included also two hundred sappers and artillerymen.

(the Ottoman government had to pay the bill of £41,928). The allied forces captured Haifa, Tyre, and Sidon in late September. On October 11, the Egyptians evacuated Beirut, after Napier (who was briefly commanding the land troops) joined forces with Bashir's cousin Qasim to win an important land battle. Lebanon was now liberated from Ibrahim, who was forced inland to Damascus, while fifteen thousand more Ottoman troops landed in Syria. A period of stalemate ensued. Palmerston pressed for the fleet to attack the one remaining coastal challenge in Syria, the great fortress of Acre. Acre had resisted Napoleon and Ibrahim for months in 1799 and 1832, but fell in three hours of heavy bombardment on November 3. This was a major blow to the Egyptian cause. At the end of December, Ibrahim began his retreat from Damascus by the desert road, eventually arriving at Gaza in late January, from where he returned to Egypt. Despite much anger in France at the allied operation, it did not threaten to go to war, especially once the government of the assertive Thiers fell in late October.

On December 22, Russia's foreign minister Nesselrode boasted that "the Eastern question [is] settled."[79] Diplomatically, it could be regarded as a victory for Russia, or for Britain, or for both against France. Russia had found a different way of maintaining the interests that the 1833 treaty had secured: it had protected the sultan, while managing to avoid a permanent international guarantee of his independence, which would have reduced its power at Constantinople. The closure of the straits safeguarded its Black Sea fleet from attack by Britain or France. The Concert had been revived, at the expense of the liberal Anglo-French entente on European affairs, which seemed to have been destroyed.[80]

However, only in the narrowest diplomatic sense was the Eastern question "settled" by the end of 1840. The future of Syria was less clear at the end of 1840 than at the beginning, and Napier and Wood had fallen out about it. Wood had arrived with secret money. He made many trips to bribe and otherwise encourage potential rebels, since they were divided and badly armed.[81] In particular, he noted the lukewarmness of old Amir Bashir for the Ottoman intervention, but the much greater enthusiasm of his cousin Bashir Qasim. Once the allied forces had secured their position in the major ports in early October, he cut a figure of significance. He appeared with the Ottomans' representative in Syria, Izzet, and read the Edict of Gülhane to notables and chiefs. He used the firman from Constantinople to depose Bashir, who was exiled, and appoint his cousin amir of Lebanon in his place. He was also pleased at the departure of Izzet, who had resisted his emphasis on the edict

79. C. Napier, *War in Syria*, 2:56.

80. For Nesselrode's delight, see Rodkey, *Turco-Egyptian Question*, 230. For an account portraying Russia as the main beneficiary, see Schroeder's *Transformation* (736–56).

81. E. Napier, *Sir Charles Napier*, 1:419, 427.

and his promises of compensation to those whose property had been damaged in the conflict.[82]

Wood remained vexed by the small number of Ottoman officials who knew Syria, understood the principles of the Tanzimat, and were competent administrators. Nonetheless, he used his powers from the Porte to appoint "such governors of . . . Districts and Towns as I thought could be depended upon, . . . nominating also to the various offices under them my own people to act as a check upon them [and] to follow out my directions." As a result, "the country may be said to have been administered by us." However, the subtext of his messages to Ponsonby was that the Gülhane project would survive only if Reshid sent more able supporters of it to rule Syria.[83] In fact, Wood's low-tax principles could not be imposed on Syria in its current state. He himself estimated that, if the government restricted itself to levying taxes for which it had strict legal permission or any realistic chance of collecting, the revenues of Syria would fall to £330,000 from the £1.6 million that Ibrahim had managed to extract. So even he recognised that some recourse to unpopular extra taxes would be necessary. Meanwhile the Porte was unable to fulfil Wood's promises of compensation for property destroyed in 1840.[84]

Moreover, only the Egyptian military threat had kept Syrian internal conflicts in check. Once Ibrahim abandoned Damascus at the end of 1840, all the old local animosities revived and intensified. In February 1841, Wood sent Ponsonby a long catalogue of re-emerging conflicts—Muslim-Christian, Maronite-Druze, lord-peasant, Arab-townsman. He claimed that this was a natural consequence of the end of Egyptian repression, but also admitted that the various feudal lords and shaykhs did not yet respect the law, and that better government was urgently required before they would.[85] In particular, it became clearer and clearer throughout 1841 that the elderly Bashir Qasim could not rule Lebanon, and civil war there broke out in October, which led the Ottoman military to remove him from power and impose direct rule over it.

Though Napier had been complicit in the decision to depose Bashir's cousin in 1840, he assumed that the historic role of amir would continue. He expected the restoration of Lebanese self-government; he thought that Britain was in Syria to support a patriotic people fighting to be free. He fraternized, and drank wine, with the leading mountaineers, and found them practical men, just as Sidney Smith had done. The month of September 1840 at Djouni

82. R. Wood, *Early Correspondence*, 176, 192; Palmerston to Ponsonby, Nov. 9, 1840, FO 78/391 69.

83. R. Wood, *Early Correspondence*, 213; Wood memo, Dec. 14, 1840, FO 78/453 12.

84. R. Wood, *Early Correspondence*, 239–40. For the damage done by Wood's failure to deliver on his promises of money, see Rose to Palmerston, July 24, 1841, FO 78/456 85. For his "frequent and extensive promises" to support the Maronites, see Rose to Aberdeen, Jan. 5, 1842, FO 78/494.

85. R. Wood, *Early Correspondence*, 213–16; Wood memo, Dec. 14, 1840, FO 78/453 12.

was "one of the happiest of my life." The mountaineers seemed to like him in return: they called him the "Komodor el Keebeer," and the son of Sidney Smith, thinking that Commodore was their family name.[86] Napier repeatedly demanded that they should control not just Mount Lebanon but also the seaports of Sidon, Beirut, and Tripoli; "this would be most advantageous to them, and most beneficial to the interests of England. They would . . . have the sea open to the export of their produce without the vexatious exaction of the Turks." The Ottomans must not be allowed to return. They lacked the ability or inclination to govern the mountain; the attempt to do so would be morally repugnant, and, by fomenting sectarian division, would also bring on the hour of their own destruction. By 1842, incandescent at their reversion to direct rule, he was supporting a revolution in Lebanon to evict them.[87] Aware of British feeling in favour of the mountaineers, Palmerston raised for international discussion the idea of giving the amir of Lebanon some of the seaports. However, it was not acceptable in Europe: Metternich argued that to create another semi-independent entity in Syria would allow France the chance to agitate for a fully independent Lebanon under its naval protection.[88] In any case, the Ottomans had no intention of allowing the former Amir Bashir anywhere near Lebanon, exiling him to Malta and then Constantinople, while no other Shihab could govern it.

Napier fell out with Wood and the embassy even more over the question of Mehmet Ali's future. In November 1840, Napier reached the same conclusion that had driven Smith to make the Convention of al-Arish—that the enemy's troops were too deeply embedded to remove, especially given the low reputation of the Ottoman army. The British fleet could not safely stay off Syria through the winter, Ibrahim had sixty thousand men in the interior, and the mountaineers were vulnerable to attack from them, once they were no longer supported from the sea. The French might also be looking for a chance to benefit from proposing a compromise. On the other hand, that large army was a great drain on Mehmet Ali's resources, was in arrears of pay, in a hostile environment, and was liable to suffer defections. The Egyptians would lose in the end, and with the loss would go any chance of founding a dynasty. Napier had seen a letter from Palmerston, dated October 15, indicating that if Mehmet Ali submitted, Britain would still recommend hereditary rule in Egypt for his family. Taking that cue, Napier sailed to Alexandria and on November 27 got Mehmet Ali to submit to the sultan in return for hereditary tenure in Egypt and the safe withdrawal from Syria of his troops and equipment (which, after

86. C. Napier, *War in Syria*, 1:53; E. Napier, *Sir Charles Napier*, 2:55.

87. C. Napier, *War in Syria*, 1:119 (quotation), 2:280–81, 290–91, 296; E. Napier, *Sir Charles Napier*, 2:81, 391–93.

88. Palmerston to Ponsonby, Jan. 19, 1841, FO 78/427 10.

all, were legally the sultan's).[89] Once Mehmet Ali had agreed to sign the convention, Napier knew he had done the right thing but, like Smith in 1800, was very unsure how his dramatic démarche would play at home. He wrote to his wife: "I shall either be hung by the Government or made a Bishop."[90]

The Porte and the British embassy were both aghast at Napier's convention. In September, Reshid had led the imperial council to depose Mehmet Ali as governor of Egypt. Now, egging one another on, Ottoman ministers and Ponsonby tried everything in their power to secure his removal, and to frustrate Napier's settlement. They claimed that Mehmet Ali had not submitted; that the various conditions specified had not been met; that, if he were to be reinstated, he must not control Egypt's revenue in future; that there should be special qualifications added to the clauses about hereditary tenure. Ponsonby could not believe that the European powers would unite to recommend Napier's terms, but they did.[91] Palmerston tried to soften the blow by explaining that there was no way of getting Mehmet Ali out of Egypt without a major war, and there was no remote chance of international agreement on that.[92] Other diplomats were shocked at Ponsonby's attitude to a man of Mehmet Ali's stature and success. Metternich said his approach to Egypt was "the system of a bandit."[93]

Disquiet at the alliance between the British embassy and the Porte reached its height in January 1841, when an extraordinary tussle took place about Napier's pledge that Ibrahim's retreating army and equipment would be allowed safe passage back to Egypt. The Egyptian army was approaching Gaza, where it became clear that the Ottomans wished to destroy it, by a combination of military attack and expulsion into the desert to die. This policy was adopted with vigour by August von Jochmus, a young German officer who had arrived in the East looking for employment after an engagement with the British Legion in Spain, and had become a member of Ponsonby's entourage. Jochmus had been appointed to a senior position in the allied invasion force of Syria, and then, on Ponsonby's suggestion, had become commander of the Ottoman troops who made up most of that force.[94] Palmerston was content with Jochmus's appointment, as it underlined that this was an international operation. Nonetheless, he had also arranged for a dozen British army officers to go to Syria in November 1840 to provide discreet guidance on the campaign itself, and on Ottoman military reconstruction thereafter. This was the latest

89. C. Napier, *War in Syria*, 1:249–54, 282–83. See Napier to Boghos, Nov. 1840, FO 78/426 120.

90. E. Napier, *Sir Charles Napier*, 2:112.

91. See Ponsonby's many letters to Palmerston in FO 78/430, also Ponsonby to Reshid, Mar. 18, 1841, FO 78/432 263; Rodkey, *Turco-Egyptian Question*, 217–26.

92. Palmerston to Ponsonby, Jan. 29, 1841, FO 78/427.

93. Šedivý, *Metternich, the Great Powers*, 958.

94. See Jochmus, *Syrian War*, 1:1–11.

round in his battle to persuade the Ottomans to employ British officers to improve their military training.[95]

When Ibrahim's army approached Gaza, the stage was set for a confrontation between, on the one hand, Jochmus and his Ottoman force, strengthened by Wood and some Ottoman officials, and, on the other, the newly arrived British officer detachment (nominally subordinate to Jochmus) and the senior British naval officer at Jaffa (Houston Stewart), who was in close touch with Napier. Jochmus demanded an initial foray against some irregular Egyptian cavalry on January 15, which went badly. This added greatly to the British officers' doubts about his judgment; it also led to the death from fever of the British detachment's commander, Edward Michell. Jochmus had instructions from the Ottomans to destroy Ibrahim's army, and from Ponsonby not to suspend hostilities against the Egyptians until there was unanimous agreement on the terms of Mehmet Ali's submission. Wood backed these up, and demanded that Ibrahim be forced away from Gaza and to enter Egypt across the desert. Stewart pointed out that Palmerston, not Ponsonby, must be the judge of the submission arrangements, and insisted that Napier's agreement that the troops could retreat safely should be honoured. Jochmus retorted that he would "cut them to pieces" and "prevent a single Egyptian getting back to his country." Stewart declined naval support for Jochmus, instructed that no further hostilities should take place, and asked the British officers to ensure the maintenance of peace. The first contingent of Egyptians arrived at Gaza and pledged to accept the British officers' terms for orderly evacuation. The detachment's deputy commander Hugh Rose was sent into the desert to find the approaching Ibrahim, in order to extract the same agreement from him, while Stewart and Napier forbade the Ottomans to attack them. Ibrahim and his thirty thousand troops arrived at Gaza and were allowed to sail to Egypt. In the desert, they had had no water for three days, but Napier's reports suggested that they were still capable of beating the Turkish army. The following year, Napier published *The War in Syria*, a devastating indictment of the behaviour of Ponsonby, Wood, and Jochmus.[96] Even he did not know, however, that in the same month Ponsonby's journalist acolyte William Churchill was trying to arrange a loan to the Porte to be used to bribe Egyptian troops into submission, so that the Ottomans could recover Alexandria.[97]

95. Palmerston to Ponsonby, Dec. 11, 1840, FO 78/391 143, and Apr. 4, 1841, FO 78/427 92.

96. C. Napier, *War in Syria*, 2:93–94, 112–15, 121, 143, 157–68. The Jochmus remarks (as reported by Stewart) are at 114, and in Stewart to Stopford, Jan. 23, 1841, FO 78/465 251. See Stewart to Michell, Jan. 14, 1841, FO 78/465 242, for Palmerston's instructions overriding Ponsonby's. Jochmus's account glosses over most of the details, merely claiming that Napier exaggerated the strength of Ibrahim's army and that Stewart's argument that Ibrahim should be treated with "kindness" was "extraordinary": *Syrian War*, 1:lx–lxii, 107.

97. Churchill to Ponsonby, Jan. 11, 1841, PPD, GRE/E/134 59.

By the summer of 1841, when Palmerston decided that a consul-general should be reappointed in Syria, the parallels with the Egyptian tensions of 1800–1801 were uncanny. The appointment went to Hugh Rose, who since March had been the commander of the British military detachment. The army seemed to have the best chance of securing confidence across the spectrum of local interests. Wood was bitterly disappointed, believing that he was the most suitable candidate for the job, a belief that surely hardly anyone except Ponsonby shared.[98] As noted further in chapter 7, too many Syrian groups now saw Wood as an Ottoman partisan, while the upright Rose did not care for his bribery of individuals. Rose had a "superstitious horror of presents," feeling that a British officer needed to be seen to shun corrupt local customs.[99] Ponsonby was removed from Constantinople by the incoming Tory government. As in 1800–1801, the Ottomans in the field looked unreliable, untrustworthy, and bloodthirsty, and the Constantinople embassy lost moral weight through an excessive deference to their point of view.

When Napier went back to Alexandria to confirm the arrangements for Mehmet Ali's submission in January 1841, he wrote: "we must be sad blunderers if we do not see that our interest is identified with his." He was Britain's best support against Russia, and a great asset for traders and travellers. He should be independent in all but name, just paying tribute to the Porte.[100] The settlement that upheld his family's hereditary tenure in Egypt limited his army to eighteen thousand men, but this stipulation was designed to channel his revenues to productive purposes as much as to reassure the Ottomans. Dynastic pride, together with the 1838 commercial treaty, would encourage the Egyptian state to pursue economic development. Palmerston hoped that once Mehmet Ali abandoned his aspirations in Syria, he would abandon his oppression of his own subjects and see the mutual benefits, for them and him, of extensive land reclamation and investment.[101] In November 1839, the Foreign Office had arranged for its ambassador in Austria to send Mehmet Ali a coded message. It made clear that Britain was not his enemy except if he had ambitions for expansion in Asia. On the contrary, it was friendly to Egypt's "development and permanence and increase" as a hereditary power. It reassured him "that the order and security which he has established in Egypt, are more valuable to England by opening a short communication with India than to any other nation; that the commercial prosperity of Egypt reacts upon us; and that for these reasons the continuance of the system which Mehemet Ali has created in that country, is of high value and importance to us."[102]

98. Apart from A. B. Cunningham, whose introduction to Wood's *Early Correspondence* is highly romantic.

99. Rose to Canning, Dec. 11, 1843, FO 78/576.

100. E. Napier, *Sir Charles Napier*, 2:134 (quotation), 140–41.

101. Palmerston to Ponsonby, Dec. 17, 1840, FO 78/391 157.

102. Beauvale to Hodges, Nov. 16, 1839, FO 78/377 9.

Hereditary rule and quasi-independence for Egypt, under the umbrella of an Ottoman sovereignty that France would never dare to challenge, was in Britain's interest, just as it was Mehmet Ali's basic ambition.

By the middle of 1841, of the three Ottoman politicians contending for dominance within the empire, only Mehmet Ali was still in post. In 1840, Reshid had managed to get Hüsrev dismissed as grand vizier, convicted of bribery, and briefly exiled, but he had then been ousted from power himself in March 1841 and sent to Paris as ambassador. He was not to return to office until 1845; in the intervening years, the Porte fell into the hands of those who attacked the effects of the Gülhane Edict, not least because it had led to a loss of tax revenue. British influence at Constantinople was no greater than in the mid-1830s. Indeed, Ponsonby may have supported Reshid's attempt to cripple Mehmet Ali in early 1841 partly in the hope that success might save his declining reputation at court. Ponsonby's policy of an alliance between the British embassy and the Porte made sense only in particular and temporary circumstances. There were stronger and more permanent reasons for Britain to keep in with Mehmet Ali's Egypt, as long as he did not imperil the regime and the security of the Ottoman lands.

The question of how Syria would be governed was still the outstanding issue at the beginning of 1841. The intervention of 1840 brought the whole country to the attention of the European public. French newspapers in particular were keen to find evidence that British, Austrian, and Russian interference there had made matters worse. The intervening powers had assumed responsibility for Syria's future. How would they ensure popular rights and liberties? The Edict of Gülhane also increased expectations about the quality of future Ottoman rule. Behind all these concerns was one potentially enormous problem, now that the European public had started to think about the region. For millions of Christians all over Europe, Syria and especially Palestine were not just dry regions of limited productivity and prospects. They were the holiest lands on earth.

CHAPTER SEVEN

The Brief History of British Religious Sectarianism in Syria and Kurdistan

IN 1838, A middle-ranking British painter called David Roberts embarked on a drawing tour of Egypt and Palestine. He was known mainly for his Spanish lithographs, as well as his 1829 depiction of the Israelites leaving Egypt. On returning to Britain eleven months later, he still lacked a publisher willing to publish the fruits of his tour. Only in February 1840 did he sign a contract with F. G. Moon, who agreed to use high-quality lithographers for the volumes—as long as the great outlay involved was recouped by advance subscriptions. Over the next few months, Roberts and Moon succeeded beyond their dreams: they secured 393 pledges from wealthy patrons, many of the highest rank, including Queen Victoria and the crowned heads of the other four European powers. The subscriptions paid for the cost of production twice over. A series of magnificent volumes was published over seven years from 1842, *The Holy Land* and then *Egypt and Nubia*.[1] They established Roberts as a major artistic name. His timing had been perfect. In 1840, the elites of Europe very much wanted to demonstrate their enthusiasm for the Holy Land—and for the protection of Christianity there.

The continental powers already had significant links with the Christian Churches of Syria. France's criticism of the idea of restoring Ottoman rule there in 1840 had special political force because of its ties with local Maronite communities; they had been in some form of communion with the papacy since the twelfth century. Roman Catholic missionary activity had spread through Syria towards the Kurdish mountains. The Sacred Congregation for

---

1. See the pages on David Roberts's lithographs at Medina Arts, http://www.medinaarts .com/.

the Propagation of Faith was founded in Rome in 1622 to give a structure to this activity, and Jesuits and then Lazarists had made major efforts. There were also Capuchin and Carmelite missions in the Levant, while the Franciscan convent at Jerusalem had stewarded the Latin Holy Places since the Crusades. All the main Catholic establishments in the Middle East were protected by France, under its capitulations with the Ottoman Empire.[2] This Roman missionary effort continued the papacy's historic opposition to the Eastern Orthodox Churches. It had led to the emergence of significant numbers of Catholic converts from all five of the historic Churches of the East: the Greek Orthodox, Armenian, Syrian, Nestorian, and Coptic. These had formed their own communities. So, including the Maronites, there were eleven substantial Christian denominations spread across the region, six of them with Roman Catholic, or "Latin," links.

In addition, there were more than fifty thousand Druze in Syria, including powerful landowners on Mount Lebanon and in the Hawran, whose unorthodox and mysterious devotional practices, apparently based on a blend of the region's historic religions, made them of interest to Western travellers. Moreover, many European Jews, particularly from Russia and (Russian-ruled) Poland, sought to return to Palestine in their later years, complementing its native Jewish communities. Russia could legitimately claim to protect those immigrants. In reality, it showed more concern for the well-being of the numerous Greek Orthodox communities of the Levant. From 1840, therefore, European pressure ensured that the protection of all these sects—who made up nearly half the total population of Syria—would be a fundamental aspect of the debate over the future of those lands.[3] Was their security compatible with Ottoman rule? If not, what adjustments were needed? This was an urgent question for Britain as well as the continental powers.

The British, with no tradition of regional missionary activity, lacked a historic connection with any of these local sects. Moreover, British Protestants had great distaste for Roman Catholicism and Greek Orthodoxy, regarding both theological traditions as perverted by human agency—by popes and priests—whose real aim was power over their laity. Many British visitors to the region suggested that these priestly hierarchies were doing the underhand work of France and Russia, by indoctrinating congregations on political as well as religious matters. British Protestants asserted that such perverted theologies were singularly ill-suited for the conversion of Muslims to Christianity,

2. This excludes new Jesuit foundations after 1815. In 1844, Moore listed nine Carmelitan, Capuchin, and Lazarist convents and colleges in Beirut and Lebanon that were under French protection, plus four new Jesuit colleges that were not: to Rose, Dec. 4, 1844, FO 226/85.

3. See J. N. Colquhoun's figures, Apr. 2, 1842, FO 78/509. He gave the total population as 1.41 million. In 1836, Campbell gave it as 1.84 million, but with a rather similar sectarian breakdown: Aug. 23, 1836, FO 78/283 187.

and that this helped to explain the continuing survival of Islam. They naturally wanted to see true Christianity spread in the very lands where God had spoken to man. Palestine—the Holy Land—played an enormous part in the British religious imagination, just as it did for other Europeans.[4] Many British churchmen were also intrigued by the remaining independent Christian communities of the East, particularly the Nestorians, Syrians, and Copts who lived in parts of Kurdistan, Syria, and Egypt. These three Churches had shown admirable resistance over many centuries to papal, Greek Orthodox, and Muslim hostility. Missions to them might create useful new partnerships. Could they be regenerated and equipped to be a nucleus of a revived Asian or African Christianity? Some Anglican scholars of early Church theology wanted to extend this idea of partnership to the much larger Greek Orthodox Church, which they saw as a useful ally against Roman Catholicism. This, however, was a much less widely held enthusiasm, because of the political consequences of working with a body that was generally associated with Russia.

This chapter argues that Protestant religious agencies—Anglican and Dissenting—briefly had an impact on British policy to Syria and Kurdistan in the late 1830s and 1840s. They twisted it in sectarian directions, in an attempt to respond to the sectarianism being practised by the other powers. The idea of partnership with the ancient Eastern Churches was imagined in a variety of ways, the more perspicacious of which showed a degree of historical understanding and some willingness to compromise over non-essentials. Even so, this strategy made more sense in the comfortable libraries of Anglican clergymen than in the Middle East itself, because of a lack of detailed awareness of local circumstances, and a failure to appreciate the political and social power of Islam and of the more entrenched Christian denominations. These same shortcomings also afflicted, more profoundly, the other main Protestant activities in the East in these years, the more overtly proselytising American missions in Beirut and in Kurdistan, and the British, German, and American evangelical projects to help and convert Jews in Palestine. Most of these missionaries believed that the Bible alone could make the peoples of the East true Christians; many of them were suspicious of the episcopalian hierarchies of the ancient Churches, and, indeed, of the Church of England.

Between them, these Protestant agencies aimed to reach out to three communities in particular: the Jews in Palestine, the Druze in Lebanon, and the Nestorians in Kurdistan. There is good historical coverage of all three interactions, but, despite occurring simultaneously, they have been treated as separate processes, caused by isolated pressures. If we contextualise and compare them, we can appreciate better the reasons for their successes and failures, and their relationship with domestic and international politics. They exemplified a sectarian policy that was the result of political uncertainty and public

4. Bar-Yosef, *Holy Land in English Culture.*

pressure. The Eastern crisis of 1839–41 seemed to open the lands of the Middle East to Western religious and political intervention—because it was generally assumed in Europe that the Ottomans could not effectively rule them. The consequence of this Western competition was to show, by 1843, that Britain could not pursue a successful Christian policy in the Middle East. It would always be outmatched by French and Russian sectarian influence, and by practicalities on the ground. It was also clear, in both Lebanon and Kurdistan, that European sectarianism was having bad, even disastrous, consequences. Another solution was necessary.

Protestant Missions and Eastern Christians

It was not surprising that the leaders of the Church of England felt a responsibility to disseminate their faith across the world, since they were convinced that the Anglican Church had been the most reliable preserver of true Christian doctrine across time. Many Anglicans believed that Christianity had first arrived in England at a very early point. Augustine had then established the episcopal tradition, and generations of scholars had maintained the Church's soundness against error. At the Reformation, the nation had rebelled against the papacy's corruptions. Church traditions respected episcopal and historical authority, and professional learning, in balance with the right of the individual to interpret the Bible. Anglicans liked to assume the eventual reunification of Christianity, broadly on Anglican terms. This would necessarily require the defeat of the Roman Catholic alternative. As British global power grew in the eighteenth and nineteenth centuries, the international aspirations of the Church grew alongside it.

Church interest in the Levant and the Middle East, the birthplace of Christianity, was equally unsurprising. For at least two centuries, individual Anglican scholars had probed the history of Christianity there. Ottoman crises since 1760 spread the notion that Islam was on the wane, and that the battle to replace it was an open contest between the Christian Churches. As the region became more familiar and accessible, particular attention began to be paid to those Christian sects of great antiquity that had survived in pockets for fifteen hundred years despite the twin threats of Islam and papal proselytism. Their historical importance, virtue, and need for protection was stressed in Joseph Milner's seminal *History of the Church of Christ* (1794–1809). After the return of peace in 1815, history, anti-papalism and evangelicalism all suggested the benefits of closer engagement with Christian Churches in the eastern Mediterranean, the Levant, and north Africa. The bishop of London was responsible for overseas Anglican Church work, and this idea was taken up by William Howley, the bishop from 1813, and Charles Blomfield, who succeeded him in 1828 when he became archbishop of Canterbury. It was a concern of the Society for the Propagation of the Gospel, a long-standing Anglican outreach body, and of the more energetic new organisation that began missionary activity to Africa and the East in 1799, which soon became known as the Church Missionary Society. Britain's acquisition of Malta and the Ionian Islands seemed a providential boon in the task of making contacts in the eastern Mediterranean. William Jowett, a young Cambridge-educated Anglican clergyman, was sent to Malta in 1815 to establish the CMS's base for Christian work in these parts, and a printing press was set up there in 1825.

Yet to initiate Anglican activity in the eastern Mediterranean from scratch was a tall order, given the enormous local power of the Orthodox Church and the long history of Catholic missionary activity there. The latter was also boosted by the restoration of monarchies and Catholic power in Europe in 1814–15—extending to the re-establishment of the Jesuits. Moreover the ostensible object of the CMS, the conversion of local Muslims, was impossible throughout the Ottoman Empire; it was forbidden by law, and apostasy was punished by death. It was not possible until the overthrow of Islamic power (which, admittedly, many Christians expected to happen quite soon, because of its perceived decadence—and their own apocalypticism, unleashed by the French Revolution).

In practice, therefore, CMS activity from Malta proceeded with great caution. Jowett's main inspiration was Claudius Buchanan, who had developed a strategy for promoting Christianity in India at a time (before 1813) when direct missionary activity to non-Christians was politically impossible there. Buchanan's strategy had three parts: to improve the spiritual education of surviving Christian communities, such as the Syrians in Malabar, which might become a nucleus of true faith; to obtain from their libraries manuscript versions of the scriptures, in order to produce and circulate printed versions in vernacular languages to strengthen that education; and to lobby for the establishment of a formal Anglican episcopal structure aimed at improving the education of local Christians.[5] This third element led to the inauguration of the first bishop of Calcutta in 1814, but in the Middle East a similar idea was not practicable until 1841. In the meantime, Jowett tried to apply Buchanan's first two ideas to the Middle East. He claimed that the prerequisite for Muslim conversion was to persuade "the Ancient and Depressed Churches of the Levant . . . to join with us" in a strong Christian partnership.[6] They were the founding Churches of the world; surely their historic evangelising mission could be reborn.[7]

Jowett travelled around the eastern Mediterranean, including to Egypt, Syria, and Palestine, in order to investigate the condition of the various

5. Atkins, *Converting Britannia*, 227–29.

6. Jowett, *Christian Researches in the Mediterranean*, v–vi, 355 (quotation).

7. The Levant Company's chaplain at Smyrna, Francis Arundell, investigated the origins and remains of organised Christianity in Asia Minor in his book *A Visit to the Seven Churches of Asia.*

Christian Churches there. He lamented their "false doctrines, . . . vain and frivolous ceremonies, and [debased] standard of public morals and public opinion." Because of its numerical dominance in the Balkans and the Levant, most of his encounters were with the Greek Orthodox Church. He was appalled by the spiritual poverty of its laity and the superstitious ignorance of its clergy. But they were fellow Christians, and the aim must be to get them to exercise their private judgment and make their own account with God. This required improving their access to the Bible, which would teach sinfulness and personal responsibility for repentance, and would show up the wrong-headedness of their "reputed authorities and . . . metaphysical niceties." Jowett wanted to distribute Bibles in modern Greek and Arabic to Orthodox laymen.[8] In Syria, most of these laymen were Arabs who had poor relations with the Greek clergy. However, for those very reasons, the Greek clergy seemed hostile to Protestant missionary circulation of Bibles to them in languages that they could actually read, in case they developed intellectual independence. In most cases, they resisted Jowett's advances.

Jowett's other main interest was in the Copts in Egypt, and the Abyssinians to the south who were in communion with them. The Copts had survived as a separate sect because, like the Syrian and Armenian Churches, their pursuit of the Monophysite heresy in the fifth century had led them away from the mainstream conciliar tradition that later bifurcated into its Latin and Greek elements. Nineteenth-century Anglicans tended to see these heresies as regrettable, but appreciated that they arose from honest devotion to Christian scholarship; moreover, the priests seemed uninterested in defending them very vigorously. The Copts numbered at least 150,000 in Egypt alone. They could be a significant base for future Christian revival, if regenerated. Egypt had once been a Christian country for three centuries; it could become one again.[9] In 1819, Jowett travelled to Upper Egypt to give the Copts Arabic Bibles. He then urged a CMS mission to Egypt, which was established in 1826. It set up a school in Cairo in 1828, for Copts (and others), which prospered through the 1830s, followed by a teacher training seminary in 1833. The CMS missionaries developed an excellent relationship with the Coptic patriarch and hierarchy, who seemed to appreciate receiving the Bibles. One missionary, John Lieder, was pleased to note that at first the patriarch greeted him, "O my son"; a few years later, "O my brother"; and now, out of respect, "O my father." Lieder eventually became so strongly associated with the Coptic

8. Jowett, *Christian Researches in the Mediterranean*, 3–4, 87–88, 293–95 (quotations at 4, 295). For the Arabs, see also Turner, *Journal of a Tour*, 1:478–79, and Hopwood, *Russian Presence in Syria*, 27.

9. Jowett, *Christian Researches in the Mediterranean*, 93; [Platt], *Journal of a Tour*, 1:137–38, 2:1–3. See also the prospectus for the "Association for the Furtherance of Christianity in Egypt," bound together with *Christianity in Egypt*, in 4765.bbb.19, British Library.

Church, and so reluctant to attempt any proselytism, that in 1860 the CMS had to ask him to leave.[10] For Jowett, the greater prize was the estimated two million Christians living in Abyssinia, whose leader was appointed by the Coptic patriarch in Alexandria. Jowett hoped that if Abyssinian Christianity could be regenerated, it could convert most of Africa. His confidence about prospects there was greatly boosted by the information that Consul Salt in Egypt gave him, and his chance meeting with Nathaniel Pearce when the latter came to Egypt in 1819.[11] In 1829, the CMS sent two missionaries to Abyssinia, including Samuel Gobat.

CMS activity in the Middle East therefore came to centre mostly on the second of Buchanan's objectives: the hunt for authentic versions of vernacular scriptures, the older the better, which could then be printed and recirculated, in the hope that this would improve the spiritual understanding of local Christian communities and make possible closer future ties with the Anglican Church. This continued a previous history of Anglican collection of manuscripts from the East: in the seventeenth century, Archbishop Laud had built up a large library in Oxford to facilitate oriental scholarship in the university, including important Arabic texts. Edward Pococke, chaplain to the Levant Company in the 1630s, pursued studies in Hebrew, Syriac, and Ethiopic. In the 1650s, Isaac Basire travelled to the Levant with the aim of reaching out to Eastern Churches and translating the prayer book catechism into local vernaculars.[12]

In the monasteries of the Middle East, much more than in India, there lay a treasure trove of original Coptic, Syriac, and Ethiopic manuscripts, many from nearer the time of Christ than the versions commonly used in Europe. Buchanan had located a Syriac version of the New Testament in India, which Samuel Lee, a talented young Cambridge scholar, finished transcribing and editing after his death in 1815. Lee also obtained and brought to publication an Ethiopic version of the Old Testament. At Aswan in Upper Egypt in 1819, Jowett began to study Ethiopic and Amharic, and later found an Amharic scriptural manuscript that he hoped would be the key to regenerating Christianity in Abyssinia—like "the lighting of a Pharos on the inhospitable shores of the Red Sea!" In 1823, he bought the whole of the Ethiopic New Testament from the Abyssinian convent in Jerusalem.[13] From 1828, a Buckinghamshire clergyman, Henry Tattam, made several trips to Egypt looking for Arabic and Coptic lexicons and scriptural commentaries, to be taken home, edited, and printed. In the 1830s, he produced a copy of the four gospels side

10. Sedra, *From Mission to Modernity*, 52–57, 100–102. For the quotation, see Salibi and Khoury, *Ottoman Syria*, 3:214. See also Atkins, *Converting Britannia*, 227.

11. Jowett, *Christian Researches in the Mediterranean*, 126, 171–74, 219–20. The priest who led the Church from 1841, Abuna Salama III, had been a star pupil of the CMS seminary in Egypt.

12. Bulman, *Anglican Enlightenment*, 44–45, 63–64.

13. Jowett, *Christian Researches in the Mediterranean*, 143–44, 203 (quotation).

by side in Arabic and Coptic for Copts' use, and a Coptic edition of the twelve minor prophets. The old Coptic Bible had once made their Church powerful; a new one would advance the day "when the Christians of Egypt shall return to their former purity as a Church." These texts would allow Anglicans and newly re-spiritualised Copts to cooperate, on the basis of a shared liturgy and episcopalian structure.[14] In 1839 and 1842, Tattam bought Coptic, Sahidic, and Syriac manuscripts (of Greek classical as well as Christian texts) from Egyptian monasteries, especially from Suriani in the Nitrian Desert. He had government subsidies, of £300 and then of £1,000, to buy them for the British Museum.[15] It seemed a national priority to collect and protect these manuscripts—not least because the French were sniffing after them. Tattam felt that proper translations of early Christian manuscripts would weaken the theological arguments of the papacy.[16]

This policy could be justified for its longer-term benefits. But it did not disguise the short-term failure of the CMS station to win many friends on the ground. After twenty years of activity, it was clear that it had made significant local inroads only in Egypt, where its schools depended on Mehmet Ali's toleration policy. In 1839, there were 96 boys in Lieder's day school and 144 in a newly opened girls' school run by Alice Holliday (who soon became Mrs. Lieder). The schools encouraged the reading of the Arabic New Testament and the Coptic catechism. Attendees included 12 Muslim boys and 9 girls: Mehmet Ali allowed Muslims to participate, and asked Holliday to teach in his own harem. He also facilitated Tattam's 1839 monastery visits.[17] Yet, Holliday aside, the English were reluctant to become missionaries in the Middle East, even in Egypt. Jowett's books failed in their aim of persuading zealous young men to join the CMS, and the four missionaries who arrived in Cairo in 1826 were Swiss-German artisans from the Basel Protestant seminary.[18]

The CMS faced many obstacles in persuading local Christian groups to build partnerships.[19] Latin and Greek religious leaders had strong motives to work with Ottoman officials to block any Protestant attempts to establish a local presence.

14. B. [Harrison], *Christianity in Egypt*, 1–22, 31–36; [Platt], *Journal of a Tour*, 1:194–95 (quotation).

15. Some were held back; in 1847, the government paid an intermediary £3,500 for them. See B. [Harrison], *Christianity in Egypt*, 77–78, 83–86, 95; Curzon, *Visits to Monasteries*, appendix (369–73).

16. B. [Harrison], *Christianity in Egypt*, 15–20. See Tattam, *Defence of the Church*.

17. [Platt], *Journal of a Tour*, 1:92–93, 133, 2:11–14; Salibi and Khoury, *Ottoman Syria*, 3:138–39, 214.

18. Sedra, *From Mission to Modernity*, 41–42.

19. A parallel failure had been the Palestine Association. In 1805, William Hamilton and others had set it up to explore Palestine's geography and biblical archaeology, but it funded no activities of note and held no meetings after 1808: it was wound up in 1834. See Kark and Goren, "Pioneering British Exploration."

The clearest case of this was the struggle faced by the much more assertive Protestant mission that the American Board of Commissioners for Foreign Missions sent to Syria in the late 1810s. In Massachusetts, the timing appeared propitious for such an undertaking: "prophesy, history and the present state of the world seem to unite in declaring that the great pillars of the Papal and Mahometan impostures are now tottering to their fall."[20] The British preacher Henry Martyn, who had done pioneering work for the Christian message in India and Persia, had already achieved great posthumous fame in missionary circles for his holiness of character, devotion to the cause, and self-sacrificing death in Anatolia in 1812.[21] Arriving in the Mediterranean in 1819–20, the first American missionary, Pliny Fisk, talked to Jowett in Malta, learned oriental languages at Smyrna, and eventually established a precarious base in Beirut in late 1823, after three more young men joined him in 1822. Unfortunately, his original companion, Levi Parsons, was permitted "only a hasty view of the land of promise [before] he was called to the higher and holier employments of the New Jerusalem," the first of several mission members to die in the cause.[22]

The Americans experienced two abortive visits to Jerusalem. They also encountered controversy after they gathered with Jowett and Joseph Wolff at a house in Aintoura in Lebanon in 1823, which Lewis Way, a wealthy English clergyman, planned to turn into a missionary centre. The Maronites and the papal authorities complained that this meeting was an affront to the Lazarist mission that had been based there. In order to keep the peace, Amir Bashir ordered the Protestants to abandon the house. A third attempt on Jerusalem by two of the Americans in early 1824 ended with their arrest for distributing tracts to Christians and Jews. Rome protested again. The result was an Ottoman firman stressing that the distribution of Bibles and psalters from Europe was forbidden in the empire. In addition, the dean of the Sacred Congregation forbade Catholics from using Bibles printed by Protestant agencies; the Maronite patriarch enforced this rule throughout Lebanon. A papal bull condemned Protestant biblical translations. The Ottomans and Roman Catholics seemed to be in league against the missionaries.[23]

Such interventions by Ottoman authorities aimed to prevent sectarian disorder; they also recognised the local power of the Maronites and the Catholic ecclesiastical establishments. Individual Protestant missionaries who lacked supporters and were likely to foment religious dissension could not expect the same favours. Effective missionary work among Jews or Orthodox Arabs was also certain to annoy the local leaders of these raya communities, who

20. Tibawi, *American Interests in Syria*, 11.
21. Brian Stanley, "Ardour of Devotion."
22. Salibi and Khoury, *Ottoman Syria*, 3:122.
23. Tibawi, *American Interests in Syria*, 27–29.

could use the *millet* system to maintain communal loyalty in several ways. An individual who underwent religious conversion would probably lose his social and cultural support networks, and possibly his job and home. Missionaries looked culturally alien: there was little tradition of Bible reading, and Protestant services lacked eye-catching ceremonial, enthusiasm, and visible identity. Because of the lack of Protestant churches and processions, Catholic and Orthodox priests often gibed that the British had no religion: they called them freemasons or atheists. Anglican activists felt that Muslims held them in contempt because of this perception.[24] For all these reasons, the Americans in Syria had achieved nothing by 1828, when they had to leave Beirut for two years on the outbreak of the Russo-Ottoman war. In the 1830s, even once Egyptian rule there began, they fared hardly any better: there was a Greek Orthodox protest against their mission in 1836.[25] Reflecting on the structural problems facing Protestant activists, and the inbuilt advantages of the Catholic mission structure, F. W. Newman expected that "all the Christians of Turkey will become Romanist."[26]

Jerusalem, City of Sin

The American missionaries had incurred the greatest wrath of the Ottomans and the other Christian bodies when they attempted to reach Jerusalem. Jerusalem was a holy city for Muslims as well as for Christians, and the Ottomans knew that social peace there could be preserved only by enforcing a wary compromise between the existing sects. The CMS warned the Americans in 1820 that Jerusalem was completely inappropriate for a new Protestant missionary station.[27] Many British visitors there discerned an unspoken bargain between Catholicism, Greek Orthodoxy, and Islam. At this time, Western travellers almost always had to stay in one of the Latin or Greek convents. They had to share the streets with masses of Christian pilgrims, mostly Greek Orthodox. When they visited the Holy Places, especially the Church of the Holy Sepulchre, they were confronted with the competing superstitions of Roman and Orthodox monks, the blind faith of their adherents, and the superintendence of the whole scene by lazy Ottoman officials wheedling fees out of ignorant pilgrims.

Every aspect of this experience seemed to be the antithesis of true faith. Jerusalem was a reminder of the evils of religions run by priests, who prevented the ignorant from accessing the word of God, and claimed that sins were to be absolved by obeying their orders. Jowett thought that the power of these

24. See, e.g., Turner, *Journal of a Tour*, 2:72–73; Salibi and Khoury, *Ottoman Syria*, 3:153; Addison, *Damascus and Palmyra*, 2:157–59; Layard, *Nineveh and Its Remains*, 1:163; G. H. Rose to Aberdeen, Mar. 16, 1843, FO 78/548.

25. Tibawi, *American Interests in Syria*, 79.

26. F. Newman, *Personal Narrative*, 93.

27. Tibawi, *American Interests in Syria*, 19.

people in Jerusalem was a sign of its abandonment by God.[28] The convents of the various denominations seemed monuments to worldliness and spiritual decay. Their members were indolent, did not read, and overindulged in alcohol. At the Greek convent, "strong, rosy, greasy, lazy lay-brothers, dawdling in the sun" bore "every sign of easy conscience and good living." These places were funded by the contributions of pilgrims and of pious Europeans. Greedy Turks saw the money cascading in and taxed them heavily.[29] The pilgrimages were money-spinners for all, but were painful to behold. They depended on ignorance. Poor, uneducated pilgrims endured great inconvenience and cost, so that priests could make a corrupt living. Jowett and William Turner noted that pilgrimages had fallen out of favour with the Latins, because they were a financial drain on the convents, but the Greek priests still persuaded their flock to undertake them and pay accordingly. Gobat observed that pilgrims paid on average £20 to rich monasteries; this was ten or twenty years' earnings. They were badly looked after: one fell over a precipice. Every year, some drowned because they thronged into the muddy Jordan unable to swim.[30]

The priests persuaded their followers to "fall down prostrate, and embrace with rapture, the very spot measured to an inch . . . at which some event of Scripture-History is said to have taken place."[31] The worst infatuation was the ceremony of Holy Fire at the Church of the Holy Sepulchre, which never ceased to amaze and appal British travellers after Henry Maundrell wrote about it in 1703, and which, accordingly, they were determined to witness.[32] On Good Friday, the priests extinguished the candles guarding Christ's supposed tomb. The following day, the pilgrims assembled with tapers, and prayed for heaven to send new fire. The patriarch passed the secretly lit fire through an aperture; a pilgrim received it, having paid a particularly large sum for the privilege, in return for a promise of eternal salvation. The ecstatic pilgrims then spread it through the church; many deliberately burned their faces, hoping to absolve their sins. The "frantic dances half-naked" of the pilgrims in the overcrowded church led to accidents most years; Frederick Henniker claimed that "the orgies that take place upon the occasion, are worse than Bacchanalian."[33] In 1834, hundreds suffocated to death failing to get through a locked door. The

28. Jowett, *Christian Researches in Syria*, 243.

29. Jowett, 123, 245–46; Buckingham, *Travels in Palestine*, 233–36, 252–54; E. Clarke, *Travels in Various Countries*, 1:531; Thackeray, *Notes of a Journey*, 200 (quotation).

30. Jowett, *Christian Researches in Syria*, 244; Turner, *Journal of a Tour*, 2:212; Gobat, *Life and Work*, 80; Salibi and Khoury, *Ottoman Syria*, 3:372; Martineau, *Eastern Life*, 3:151.

31. Jowett, *Christian Researches in Syria*, 221–22.

32. Maundrell, *Journey from Aleppo to Jerusalem*, 93–96.

33. Henniker, *Notes*, 278. See Turner, *Journal of a Tour*, 2:200; Connor in Jowett, *Christian Researches in the Mediterranean*, 437; Gobat, *Life and Work*, 80 ("frantic dances").

gruesome scene was witnessed by Robert Curzon, and by Ibrahim, making his first visit to Jerusalem since his conquest of Syria. His soldiers killed several pilgrims in order to get him out.[34]

Almost every British traveller was shocked by the perversion of religion in a place designed to commemorate Christ's atonement for the sins of man. James Silk Buckingham thought the Church of the Holy Sepulchre "a temple combining the most surprising mixture of credulity and imposition, devotion and wickedness, that has ever issued from any one source since the world began."[35] To Miss Platt, its "heartless semblance of the Religion of Christ, disguised by outward pomp and vain display" was an outrage in the very city where that religion's founder had lived and died for man's salvation. Henniker found the "small, unworthy building" a "scene of hypocrisy, brutalization, and contention." The American missionary William Thomson regarded it as a fraud for "paganized Christians": one might as well perform one's "devotions in a pagoda."[36] British visitors observed that the church was run as a source of wealth for the Ottomans. The Greeks had bought the handsomest parts of the building by paying the most money, for repairs and to bribe the governor, and the Latins were left with a "dim and gloomy Chapel." If the Christian sects ever asserted their position strongly enough to rouse local Muslim animosity against them, the Ottomans would just charge more money for their security. As it was, they levied a poll tax upon pilgrims at the door; the Muslim attendants stood around smoking.[37]

Visiting Jerusalem was nonetheless essential for the Christian. It allowed William Thackeray to demonstrate his gratitude—but also his "shame and humility"—in contemplating the place where "the great yearning heart of the Saviour interceded for all our race." Seeing the city from afar for the first time, Robert Curzon wanted to walk barefoot to the gate in acknowledgment of Christ's sacrifice for him, though was too embarrassed to do so. But he, like many devout travellers, also assumed that after that "Great Murder," God had "poured out the vials of his wrath upon the once chosen city."[38] His visit convinced Turner that "the prophecies which predicted the abomination of

34. Curzon, *Visits to Monasteries*, chap. 16.

35. Buckingham, *Travels in Palestine*, 252.

36. [Platt], *Journal of a Tour*, 2:315; Henniker, *Notes*, 278; Thomson in Salibi and Khoury, *Ottoman Syria*, 3:368–69. See also E. Napier, *Reminiscences of Syria*, 2:146–47.

37. Jowett, *Christian Researches in Syria*, 250–51 (quotation); Henniker, *Notes*, 278; Turner, *Journal of a Tour*, 2:165–69.

38. Thackeray, *Notes of a Journey*, 204, 212 (first three quotations, including "Great Murder"); Curzon, *Visits to Monasteries*, 158–59, 206 (last quotation). It should be said that not all these sentiments need be taken at face value, given that some were written for a large audience: hence "demonstrate." One reason that Caroline Fox liked Kinglake's *Eothen* was that he wrote about Jerusalem as he felt, not as he "ought to feel": Fox, *Memories of Old Friends*, 2:47.

the holy places" had been accomplished. Miss Platt could think of nothing in the annals of nations comparable to "the heart-thrilling calamities" that God had inflicted on the city; famines, bloodshed, and sieges had left it "desolate." Thomas Skinner could have "wept with disappointment" on arriving and discovering it "dressed in mourning," given over to Muslims, its monuments crumbling—"the most sombre picture that can be fancied." Elers Napier also found a city of the dead, with narrow, dark, filthy streets, as prophecy foretold. Henniker could detect "not one symptom of either commerce, comfort or happiness." Jowett in 1823 saw "meanness, and filth and misery, not exceeded, if equalled, by any thing which I had before seen": "I have not spent one happy day in Jerusalem."[39]

The afflictions of modern Palestine showed that it was "not *now* a favoured land. It is not now nearer to God than England, nor is Jerusalem than London."[40] Travel accounts since the mid-eighteenth century had stressed its barrenness and desolation.[41] But there was still a lot of spiritual refreshment to be had by experiencing the Holy Land in the right imaginative spirit. For a start, there was the view of Jerusalem from outside the city, from where the meanness of its Arab reality could be ignored. As Jowett remarked, "the distant view is all." "The rest," he added, "must be supplied by a spiritual sense of an ever-present Saviour."[42] Gazing on the Mount of Olives, and the road to Bethany, was a highlight of any visit, because they were the very places where Christ had walked, taught, and shown his "inexpressible Love and Benevolence."[43]

For the British voyager, the Holy Land was a holy landscape—a place where natural scenery helped the imagination to reach a better understanding of the history of God's relationship with man. Britons travelled with their Bibles and aimed to bring the biblical messages alive. Some sought exact proofs of those prophecies that indicated God's wrath towards the Holy Land's depraved ancient inhabitants. It was salutary to view the drying nets of the fishermen at Tyre, the great trading hub that Ezekiel had foretold would be reduced to a bare rock for those very nets.[44] But there was also much scepticism about the

39. Turner, *Journal of a Tour*, 2:204, and [Jolliffe], *Letters from Palestine*, 102, for a similar comment; [Platt], *Journal of a Tour*, 2:310–11; Skinner, *Adventures*, 1:198; E. Napier, *Reminiscences of Syria*, 2:139–40 (Lamentations 1:1); Henniker, *Notes*, 274; Jowett, *Christian Researches in Syria*, 208, 242.

40. John Kitto, *The Land of Promise* (1851), quoted in Bar-Yosef, *Holy Land in English Culture*, 125.

41. Talbot, "Divine Imperialism."

42. Jowett, *Christian Researches in Syria*, 208, 222.

43. Thackeray, *Notes of a Journey*, 204.

44. On Tyre, see W. M. Thomson in Salibi and Khoury, *Ottoman Syria*, 3:115; Keith, *Evidence of the Truth*, 195, 496; Bruce, *Travels and Adventures*, 16–17. For other examples, see, e.g., Jowett, *Christian Researches in Syria*, 253–54. There was a thriving market in Britain for compilations of drawings by recent travellers displaying the ruination of

"innumerable sites which the Romish Church has pretended to identify with the scenes of Holy Writ."[45] It was awe-inspiring to trek to austere, elemental Sinai and to sense the thunderous force with which God had spoken to Moses there—even though the precise location of this encounter seemed much less certain than the monastery authorities claimed.[46] Arrival at the Sea of Galilee brought back childhood Sunday School memories of Christ preaching to fishermen: they could still be seen in their boats on the lake, plying the same trade and dealing with the same winds.[47] The lake's "beautiful . . . transparency" was irresistible. Bathing in its "crystal waters" also washed off the fleas of Tiberias, in Jolliffe's case, or shut out unpleasant memories of the Arab women's bath, in Harriet Martineau's.[48] She bathed in the Jordan as well—"a narrow river; but it is truly majestic from its force and loveliness." Young men playfully tested their strength across its fifty-foot width, showing their manly superiority to clumsy Eastern pilgrims by swimming it with one arm, like Kinglake, or timing themselves, like Turner.[49] For Protestants, the Jerusalem that mattered was a spiritual state, not an unprepossessing Arab town. As William Blake and countless others had said, it could be built anywhere, in this life or the next, through faith and discipline.

The Appeal to Jews and Its Limits

One additional complexity of Jerusalem was that between five and seven thousand Jews lived there. Many had travelled from Russia or Poland to die in Palestine, either in Jerusalem or in other favoured settlements such as Safed or Tiberias. The presence of Jews was a major part of Jerusalem's appeal to missionaries. In 1809, a separate society had been founded for Protestant mission work among the Jews, the London Society for Promoting Christianity among the Jews, usually known as the London Jews' Society. It relied on the enthusiasm of former Jews, mostly from northern continental Europe, who had converted to Christianity and wished to persuade others to accept the New Testament and the divinity of Jesus; eleven of the first fifteen LJS missionaries

---

Middle Eastern locations that had been the subject of biblical prophecy: this was the aim of Horne's *Landscape Illustrations of the Bible*.

45. [Platt], *Journal of a Tour*, 2:306. For this reason, there was much support for the New York theologian Edward Robinson, whose *Biblical Researches in Palestine* (co-authored with Eli Smith) suggested that most of the Jerusalem shrines were inauthentic: see Shepherd, *Zealous Intruders*, 80–83.

46. [Platt], *Journal of a Tour*, 2:167–70; Martineau, *Eastern Life*, 2:256–60.

47. Jowett, *Christian Researches in Syria*, 174–76; Thomson in Salibi and Khoury, *Ottoman Syria*, 3:110; Bowring in Fox, *Memories of Old Friends*, 1:91.

48. [Jolliffe], *Letters from Palestine*, 34–35; Otter, *Edward Daniel Clarke*, 2:119; Martineau, *Eastern Life*, 3:246–49.

49. Martineau, *Eastern Life*, 3:151–52; Turner, *Journal of a Tour*, 2:224–26; Kinglake, *Eothen*, 120.

were Germans.[50] In the 1820s, the movement's profile was helped by the publicity generated by the former Jewish (and former Catholic) Anglican missionary Joseph Wolff, another German. He travelled extensively, flamboyantly, and foolhardily in the Middle East and Asia, keen to argue theologically with anyone who rose to his bait. Wolff was an eclectic eccentric who was drawn to the Middle East for many reasons: to prove the accuracy of the Bible, to find the scattered tribes of Abraham, to challenge the grip of the papacy and the mosques, and to encourage local Christians to commune with the Anglican Church. He sent back long reports emphasising his providential survival in the face of obstacles. What he actually achieved was another matter: Bowring thought that he had "retarded the progress of Christianity in the East by about a century and a half," by his attacks on Muhammad, instead of stressing the common ground between Christianity and Islam.[51] Subsequent missionaries to the Jews in Baghdad likewise tended to create offence by their indiscriminate enthusiasm for distributing tracts.[52]

In the 1820s, the LJS benefited from financial support from a few very wealthy Englishmen, such as Henry Drummond, Sir Thomas Baring, and Lewis Way. Such men read biblical prophecy literally, as forecasting the return of the children of Israel to their homeland, leading the way for the Second Coming of Christ. Their influence focused LJS activities on Jerusalem—rather than, say, Damascus, where there were at least as many Jews.[53] Biblical literalism was on the rise in the early nineteenth century, and expectations of Ottoman collapse after 1821 fed apocalyptic hopes for the sudden, dramatic fall of Islam in the Holy Land.[54] Nonetheless, their hopes for the return of the Jews to Palestine and their conversion to Christianity were always a minority enthusiasm in Britain—the biblical references to Jews returning to their homeland were more generally assumed to be allegorical allusions to Christians. Most of those who toyed with such hopes did not emphasise them much in public, appreciating that they appeared far-fetched and were easily satirised.[55]

In practice, LJS activity was distinguished mainly by its concern for the spiritual and material plight of the Jews that it encountered in Palestine, and its indignation at their oppression by the papacy and Islam. The high point of

50. Lewis, *Origins of Christian Zionism*, 58.

51. Bowring in Fox, *Memories of Old Friends*, 1:66. On Wolff, see Hopkins, *Sublime Vagabond*.

52. The British resident in Baghdad had problems with them in 1835 and again in 1846: see Taylor, Oct. 2, 1835, FO 195/113 pt. 1B 20, and Rawlinson, Nov. 23, 1846, FO 78/237 692.

53. There were probably over five thousand: see Frankel, *Damascus Affair*, 32. William Holt Yates claimed that there were sixty thousand: Jan. 2, 1841, FO 78/464 6.

54. See Bebbington, *Evangelicalism in Modern Britain*, chap. 3; Vereté, *From Palmerston to Balfour*, 92, 104; Lewis, *Origins of Christian Zionism*, chaps. 3–4.

55. Lewis, *Origins of Christian Zionism*, 331; Bar-Yosef, *Holy Land in English Culture*, 185–87, 193.

Lewis Way's influence was the protocol on the improvement of the legal and social condition of European Jews that he persuaded the powers to agree at the Congress of Aix-la-Chapelle in 1818. When Jowett left Jerusalem in 1823, he tearfully interpreted its sorry state as the relentless continuation of the treading down of Jerusalem by the gentiles, that had begun with the Roman attack on the city in 70 CE.[56] Many LJS activists regarded Britain as an elect nation because of its pure apostolic Christianity; it was a modern Israel charged with the protection of humanity, not least the Jews, from the reviving power of Romanism.[57] The Bible showed that the Jews had a fundamental role in human history, receiving the word of God, keeping it alive, and ensuring its success and transmission. They were suffering enough because of their separation from God; it was not for Protestants to oppress them further.[58] So the LJS men who went to Syria in the 1820s and 1830s cooperated extensively with the CMS and American missions, regarding them all as fighting the same foes.

Hans Nicolajsen, a Danish Anglican usually known as John Nicolayson, took advantage of Egyptian rule in Jerusalem to set up as the LJS's missionary there in 1833 (after a previous failed residence in 1826–28). George and Matilda Whiting of the American Board joined him in 1834. They sent converted Jews into Jewish communities and distributed charity and medical aid. However, they faced the same problems as the Protestant missions elsewhere in the region: opposition from the Greek and Latin ecclesiastical operations, and an inability to offer converts enough institutional protection to compensate for the economic, emotional, and cultural losses of leaving their community. European Jews who travelled to Palestine to die were particularly inappropriate missionary targets, as they actively sought to embrace Jewish traditions.

Yet it was the LJS's very triviality that made it significant. It was a standing reminder of the problems facing British religious activity in the Middle East compared with other sects: the lack of established religious institutions, of a building to show off Protestant services, and of great-power protection. Nicolayson was concerned with all these issues, not just with the Jews. He began as a privately funded missionary, but he quickly saw, as did many Anglicans at home, that the established Church needed an institutional presence in Jerusalem if it were to be taken seriously. Increasing numbers of Englishmen were visiting Jerusalem and did not want to stay in the convents. They wondered why Christianity in its pure apostolic form was not represented there as well as Romanism and Orthodoxy. Mehmet Ali seemed set to continue administering Syria; he prided himself on his tolerance, and was anxious for British

56. Jowett, *Christian Researches in Syria*, 270–71. See Price and Price, *Road to Apocalypse*, 64–68.

57. Lewis, *Origins of Christian Zionism*, 166.

58. Jowett, *Christian Researches in Syria*, 449–51.

friendship. Nicolayson travelled to Britain, was ordained an Anglican priest in early 1837 by the bishop of London, and returned to Jerusalem with the bishop's sanction, explicitly to build a church. He bought two plots of land for the purpose in 1838. Such a project would require political support: the Ottomans would normally refuse to sanction a new Christian church in a Muslim Holy City. In March 1837, Palmerston got Campbell to ask Mehmet Ali for permission for a church.[59] Sir Thomas Baring of the LJS, the father of a member of the cabinet, pressed for it. So did Anglicans with links with Egypt, such as Tattam, Edward Bickersteth, and W. R. Fremantle, and the American missionaries.[60] But the case for the church got bogged down in the same politics that had stimulated it. Mehmet Ali saw that a Protestant church in a Muslim Holy City was much more contentious than one in Alexandria, so he referred the decision to the sultan.[61] Neither wanted to offend the ulema, or France.

So it was that British power first appeared at Jerusalem in a different guise—in the shape of William Young, who was appointed the first European consul to the city in 1838, and arrived in March 1839. The decision to appoint a consul had been taken by Palmerston in October 1836 and was unconnected with the LJS mission; Young became a member of the society only after being appointed. Farren had first suggested the idea of a consul in Jerusalem in 1834, subordinate to him. This reflected his empire-building tendencies, but was mainly because of the rapid growth of British travel to the city, and the need to get British travellers protected and respected by the local administration. When he suggested it again in 1836, in the light of Russian and French political activity in Jerusalem, Palmerston agreed.[62] The choice of Young was in effect left to Nicolayson and Niven Moore in Beirut, who both recommended him; Young was a business partner of Moore. Campbell in Egypt accepted the case for a consul because he assumed that Mehmet Ali would allow a Protestant chapel, which would need official protection.[63] One of Young's priorities on arriving at Jerusalem was to continue to lobby for the building.

The arrival of a British consul in Jerusalem and the movement for a church were driven by general concerns about British influence, much more than by the specific interests of the LJS. This is often not understood, because of Palmerston's ambiguous letter of appointment to Young, of January 31, 1839, which stated that "it will be part of your duty . . . to afford protection to the Jews generally."[64] Around this sentence a large historiography has arisen,

59. Lewis, *Origins of Christian Zionism*, 253–55.

60. B. [Harrison], *Christianity in Egypt*, 23–24; Salibi and Khoury, *Ottoman Syria*, 2:441.

61. Lewis, *Origins of Christian Zionism*, 258–60.

62. Farren to Palmerston, Nov. 20, 1834, and Sept. 18, 1836, FO 78/243 223, 78/292 84; Foreign Office memo, Nov. 2, 1836, FO 78/260 190.

63. Eliav, *Britain and the Holy Land*, 24, 113–15.

64. Hyamson, *British Consulate in Jerusalem*, 1:1–2.

which reads it as suggesting that Britain wanted to create a sectarian Jewish interest, and to encourage Jews to settle in a homeland in Palestine. If there was such a policy, the natural explanation for it would be that Palmerston's son-in-law was Lord Ashley, one of the most active political evangelicals. Ashley was delighted with Young's appointment for showing that Britain was "the first of the Gentile nations that has ceased 'to tread down Jerusalem'!" At this point, however, it is unlikely that even Ashley thought a Jewish homeland could be a practical political endeavour.[65]

In fact, the declaration of January 1839 was not as momentous as it seems. The wording was Palmerston's only in the sense that he scribbled approval on a dispatch of Campbell's that had already proposed that Britain should give "protection to the Jewish Nation in general." By this phrase, Campbell did not mean that Britain should make a special bid to win Jewish support; on the contrary, the idea arose from his discussions with the other European consuls in Egypt. They asked him if Young, as the only Western consul, would represent their European citizens in Palestine for them and channel their complaints, which was normal practice in places in which most powers did not have a consul.[66] Nearly all of the European subjects in Palestine were Ashkenazi Jews, who had immigrated from Russia and Austria (or from the parts of Poland that those powers governed). So Campbell and Palmerston were indicating that Young was to represent the interests of those Russian and Austrian Jews, on behalf of the consular body. Campbell assumed that this would mainly involve protecting property rights. In 1834, Muslims had attacked the property of Russian, Austrian, and British Jews at Safed, and Campbell and his colleagues had arranged its restitution.[67] Most Jews in Jerusalem were Sephardic Jews who were Ottoman subjects. They were not under European protection, and the Foreign Office instruction cannot have intended to include them formally, because of their *millet* status within the Ottoman Empire. However, Campbell's use of the word "nation" may suggest a hope that the *millet* leaders might want to use Young as a conduit for any grievances that they wished to bring to Mehmet Ali's attention.

Palmerston and Young both saw benefits for Britain in befriending Palestine's returning Jews and earning their gratitude. Young wanted to make a difference in Jerusalem, wanted to project British humanitarian power, and had also read his Bible. He was flattered that the chief rabbis came out to meet him on his arrival, and that Britain had been "the first among the nations to shew herself the friend of the children of Israel, by sending to the City of David

65. [Ashley], "Lord Lindsay's Travels," 190; Hodder, *Shaftesbury*, 1:233.

66. Campbell to Palmerston, Dec. 10, 1838, FO 78/344 212, and Palmerston's note for John Bidwell, Jan. 26, 1839, FO 78/344 215. Campbell's dispatch is reprinted in Eliav, *Britain and the Holy Land*, 120–21. The dispatch of January 31 was written by Bidwell (head of the Foreign Office consular department).

67. Campbell to Palmerston, Oct. 4, 1837, FO 78/320 116.

a representative." He collected much evidence of Jewish poverty, neglect, and oppression by the authorities, helped by the reports of LJS workers.[68] Tattam and Miss Platt arrived in Jerusalem a week after Young and noted that the Jewish leaders "regard him at once as the defender of their rights and the redresser of their grievances."[69] Unfortunately, his activities quickly came to annoy Russia. Within a few months, the Russian consulate of Syria and Palestine (in Beirut) decided to assert its own responsibility for its Palestinian Jews, even though the Russian consul in Egypt had previously taken a different view. This owed much to the individual who was appointed Syrian consul in 1838, Konstantin Bazili. It also, doubtless, owed much to the increasing temperature of the Eastern crisis over the summer of 1839, and the powers' anxiety to assert their existing rights in Ottoman territory, in case it collapsed. In the summer, Bazili visited Jerusalem and appointed Isaiah Bardaki (known as Rabbi Yeshaiah) as *wakil* to represent the Russian Jews officially. Austria agreed that he should represent its Jews too. So Bardaki's local influence made him the acknowledged protector of European Jews, a position that the Ottomans accepted. In December 1839, the Foreign Office told Young to appoint a separate *wakil* for British Jews in Jerusalem, but the numbers were so small that this was impracticable.[70]

The War of Institutional Christianity over Syria

Until 1839, the salient feature of British religious activity in Syria was its failure to secure a foothold, and the Foreign Office's lack of concern about that. However, Russia's burgeoning interest in its Palestinian Jews was one sign that Syria was going to be both a political and a religious battleground. Its history, and its crucial geographical position in any conflict between Christianity and Islam, made this inevitable once the Eastern crisis developed. In 1840, Church of Scotland author J. G. Macvicar described it as "the keystone which unites Europe with Asia, the telegraph station between East and West," and therefore the means of realising Isaiah's prophecy to enlighten "Gentiles . . . to the ends of the earth."[71] The Damascus affair of spring 1840, discussed in chapter 5, could be seen as an indictment of Ottoman/Egyptian rule for inciting tensions between Catholics and Jews, but also as a shocking exposé of French Catholic ambitions. The affair mobilised Jews, but also others, to scrutinise both aspects. In July, non-sectarian meetings in London, Manchester, and Portsmouth petitioned the Foreign Office against the persecution of Jews

---

68. Hyamson, *British Consulate in Jerusalem*, 1:7–8 (quotation), 10–11.

69. [Platt], *Journal of a Tour*, 2:336–37.

70. Hyamson, *British Consulate in Jerusalem*, 1:25–29; Eliav, *Britain and the Holy Land*, 126–29.

71. [Macvicar], *Catholic Spirit of True Religion*, 168 (Isaiah 49:6).

in the Middle East.[72] The archbishop of Canterbury and the Church of Scotland formally asked the government to secure toleration for both Jews and Christians in the Ottoman Empire.[73] The assumption that France was trying to promote Catholicism in Syria was a major cause of British public interest in the East. The decision by the other powers to remove Mehmet Ali created a debate across Europe about what should replace him in these religious heartlands. One pamphlet sent to the Foreign Office in 1840 insisted that it was "for the redemption of Canaan that God is now contending."[74]

If the Ottomans, the Egyptians, and the Catholics were all unsuitable rulers of Syria, might there be a benefit in encouraging the return of the Jews, under British or European protection? In late July 1840, nine days after the Treaty of London foreshadowed a power vacuum in Syria, Ashley considered that a scheme for Jewish restoration to Palestine might be practicable. In 1839, the Jewish philanthropist Moses Montefiore had floated the idea of acquiring land in Palestine and establishing a company to invest in Jewish agricultural settlement. This had led to (unfounded) press rumours that such a project was already under way. By August 17, there was enough momentum behind the idea for *The Times* to publish documents and an editorial on the idea of restoration, explicitly not on "scriptural grounds" but as "a new element of the Eastern question."[75] Ashley had in fact just raised the issue with Palmerston, who had written to Ponsonby suggesting that the Porte should provide incentives to wealthy Jews to settle there, since this would boost Syrian revenues and stability.[76]

The idea of strengthening the Jewish presence in Palestine was now canvassed in two very different forms. Palmerston clearly envisaged some modest settlement under reformed Ottoman rule, initiated and funded by benevolent Western capitalists like Montefiore to help with Syrian economic development. However, many religious-minded people had the much more radical idea of a Jewish buffer state, in order to separate the sultan and Mehmet Ali. Several wrote to urge this on the Foreign Office. Two of them told Palmerston that, by re-establishing the state of Judea, he would "call . . . a nation into existence" and throw "a halo of glory" around his foreign policy. One correspondent

72. FO 78/421, 44, 125, 159. For the meeting in the City of London on July 3, see also Frankel, *Damascus Affair*, 222–24.

73. Nov. 21 and Dec. 4, 1840, FO 78/425 141, 259.

74. FO 78/421 237.

75. Montefiore, *Diaries*, 1:167; A. Green, *Moses Montefiore*, 130; *Times*, Aug. 17, 1840, 4.

76. Hodder, *Shaftesbury*, 1:310–11; Palmerston to Ponsonby, Aug. 11, 1840, cited in Hyamson, *British Consulate in Jerusalem*, 1:33–34. At the beginning of December 1840, Lady Palmerston, who had clearly been exposed to the evangelical enthusiasms of her son-in-law, patriotically wondered if the rapid fall of Acre portended something miraculous: perhaps the British had been providentially chosen to fulfil biblical prophecies about Jewish restoration: E. Temple, *Letters of Lady Palmerston*, 243.

pointed out that, assuming the Bible was true, Jewish restoration must happen one day. Another observed that Providence would frustrate any diplomatic
solution to the Eastern question that ignored Scripture.[77] Interest in the idea
of a Judean buffer state is not too surprising, since most British children were
more familiar with the geography of Old Testament Palestine and the twelve
tribes than with that of modern England. In 1847, the government inspector
noted that in some schoolrooms it was the only map available. In 1856, when
the British civil service initiated competitive examinations for entry, candi-
dates for junior clerkships in the education division were required to draw
a map of Palestine's territorial divisions at the time of Christ's birth.[78] While
Palmerston and Montefiore saw Jewish colonies through the prism of capital
investment and liberal modernity, Ashley and Lindsay imagined the recreation of an Old Testament idyll. "Vestiges of the ancient cultivation" already
abounded, so if the Jews became "once more the husbandmen of Judaea and
Galilee," the land would "burst . . . into universal luxuriance—all that she ever
was in the days of Solomon."[79]

In fact, hopes for Jewish settlement did not monopolise public discussions
about how to keep the Ottomans, Mehmet Ali, and the French out of Syria. Sir
William Hillary campaigned for southern Syria to be a sovereign state under a
new chivalric body that he was actively publicising, the Order of Saint John of
Jerusalem. The order, he claimed, was the heir to the Crusader tradition of the
Knights Hospitaller. Frederick Bevan proposed an independent Palestine with
the Church of England as its established Church. Nicholas Crommelin urged
"a free state, similar to Hamburgh," open to commercially minded inhabitants
of all nations.[80]

The Foreign Office batted away all these ideas. Palestine's population was
85 per cent Muslim; it contained a Muslim Holy City. There was no Jewish
political movement capable of governing a state. Even Montefiore's investment plans remained undeveloped. The only justification for the intervention of 1840 was the restoration of Ottoman sovereignty. Any buffer state
would require European policing. The European powers would squabble for
dominance in it. The new French prime minister Guizot was rumoured to
be preparing a plan for the internationalisation of Jerusalem, together with
European guarantees for the Christians of Syria. This might restore French
predominance in Syria and please French Catholic voters. Palmerston and

77. See FO 78/388 198, 78/421 235, 78/422 4, 131. In 1843, Alexander Keith anticipated
that Judea would be given to the Jews on the impending collapse of the Ottoman Empire:
Land of Israel, 477.

78. Foliard, *Dislocating the Orient*, 87–90; Bar-Yosef, *Holy Land in English Culture*,
127–28.

79. [Ashley], "Lord Lindsay's Travels," 189; see the footnote added to the third edition
of Lindsay, *Letters on Egypt* (London: Henry Colburn, 1843), 2:71.

80. See FO 78/466 261, 78/425 235, 78/464 4.

Metternich were intensely suspicious: "religious protections pave the way for political dismemberments." However, Metternich himself, like the other European leaders, was being bombarded with suggestions from the public for a Christian or Jewish kingdom in Palestine. He pressed the Porte to increase the autonomy of the Ottoman governor of Jerusalem; as a result, the governor was given special responsibility for the protection of his Christians.[81]

Prussia was particularly keen to stop any plans for Jerusalem that gave the Catholic and Orthodox Churches special rights in Syria. It wanted to work with Britain in demanding recognition for Protestantism as well. Its initial proposal was that Syrian Christians should be protected by three European residents, acting on behalf of Catholics, Orthodox, and Protestants respectively. Protestants would have joint Anglo-Prussian protection and a place of worship within the Church of the Holy Sepulchre.[82] This plan was almost as unrealistic as the idea of a buffer state, but it indicated the Protestant seriousness of the new Prussian king, Friedrich Wilhelm IV. He saw his calling as the promotion of Christian unity and regeneration, facilitated by Ottoman decline. He loathed the papacy, as did his leading advisor Christian Bunsen, who had been removed from his role as Prussian envoy to the Vatican in 1838 by papal pressure. Both men wanted a collaboration with Britain to promote the Protestant religion in the Middle East as the only viable basis for the eventual global reunification of the Church.

By June 1841, Friedrich Wilhelm's aspirations had coalesced into a new and more plausible plan: a joint Anglican-Lutheran bishopric of Jerusalem. This would symbolise the fellowship between the two Protestant churches, would give them crucial political weight and institutional presence at Jerusalem, and would allow them to take the fight to papal missionary activity in the East, and eventually to Islam. It would provide Middle Eastern Protestantism with a recognised episcopal head who could reach out to other Churches, would give weight to the Anglo-German LJS mission, and would encourage German Lutherans to appreciate the merits of episcopalianism. The as yet unbuilt Anglican church in Jerusalem would be a purified temple for a "national and universal Christian foundation."[83] Friedrich Wilhelm IV sent Bunsen to Britain that month to persuade the archbishop of Canterbury of the idea.[84]

He needed no persuasion. Archbishop Howley, and Bishop Blomfield of London, had already been thinking hard about a bishop for the Middle East. This was part of their concern to build the Church's global role, which was

---

81. For Guizot, see Vereté, *From Palmerston to Balfour*, chap. 5 (quotation at 145). For Metternich, see Caquet's *Orient* (182–86), which shows that Guizot's ideas were never as coherent as his rivals, or Vereté, thought. The Ottomans combined Jerusalem with Jaffa and Gaza to create an enlarged *sancak* with special powers of self-government.

82. Greaves, "Jerusalem Bishopric," 336.

83. Bunsen, *Baron Bunsen*, 1:599–600.

84. For his instructions, see Hechler, *Jerusalem Bishopric*, 2:2–18.

threatened both by the papacy and by internal challenges. At home, it was under pressure from Dissent and from the Liberal government's preference for loosening the Church-state partnership after the pluralist constitutional reforms of 1828–32. In the 1830s, legislation was introduced making some of the historic revenues of the Church of England in Ireland and in Canada available for the needs of the non-Anglican majorities there. So the Church was now very conscious of the need to rely on its own resources to raise its global profile. The episcopal structure was weak in the colonies, and Howley and Blomfield did not trust voluntary missionary activity to spread sound religious doctrine there. In the course of the 1830s, the diocesan structure in Canada, India, and Australasia was extended, but this was known to be just the first step needed in a strategy of stronger local organisation throughout the empire, headed by bishops. Howley and Blomfield began a major campaign for colonial bishoprics, building on the public mood in Britain in favour of Church defence, which was reviving the fortunes of the Conservative party. Ashley, Lindsay, and the young William Gladstone were among the Tories active in it. This led to the founding of new bishoprics in New Zealand, Tasmania, Guiana, and Antigua in 1841–42.[85] An indication of the growth of Anglican enthusiasm for global evangelising activities at this time is shown by the increase in the annual voluntary income of the Society for the Propagation of the Gospel, which had been £1,459 in 1821 and £7,402 in 1831, but rose to £44,318 in 1841 and £84,909 in 1851. The income of the CMS, which had benefited much more from the enthusiasm of the 1810s and 1820s, rose from £39,814 in 1832 to £90,305 in 1842. Average yearly LJS income was £12,687 in the 1820s and £30,020 in the 1840s.[86]

Blomfield definitely intended this global mission to include the original Christian heartlands of the Middle East, where Anglican activity lagged so far behind that of Roman Catholics. His appeal of April 1840 for new bishoprics envisaged the day when the Church of England would "be recognised, by all the nations of the earth, as the stronghold of pure religion, and the legitimate dispenser of its means of grace: and will be a chosen instrument in the hands of God for purifying and restoring the other branches of Christ's Holy Catholic Church."[87] In October 1838, Ashley had already floated the idea of a bishopric at Jerusalem, linked to Malta and the existing Anglican chaplaincies around the Mediterranean.[88]

In July 1840, just after the signing of the Treaty of London, Howley and Blomfield sent George Tomlinson on a mission to the Levant. He was Howley's

---

85. See Strong, *Anglicanism and the British Empire*, chap. 4.

86. Tennant, *Corporate Holiness*, 190, 214; A. Green, "British Empire and the Jews," 187–88.

87. Strong, *Anglicanism and the British Empire*, 200.

88. Hodder, *Shaftesbury*, 1:235.

former chaplain, and secretary of the Church's senior outreach society, the Society for Promoting Christian Knowledge (SPCK). The three men hoped to build on increased public interest in the Ottoman Empire, and to create connections with the historic Churches of the East. After Tomlinson returned, they proposed that an Anglican bishop, based in Malta, should coordinate this activity around the Mediterranean, and in April 1841 Blomfield connected this idea with the colonial bishopric campaign. In December 1840, Howley pressed the government to secure toleration for Christians as well as Jews in the Ottoman Empire, particularly so that the ancient Churches of the East could maintain their independence from aggressive Roman missions. One of the particular objects of Tomlinson's journey was to make contact with the bishops of the Greek Orthodox Church and to urge more cooperation in the circulation of printed Bibles in Greek, Arabic, Turkish, and Armenian throughout the region. This would be facilitated by the current political understanding between Britain and Russia. Tomlinson argued that, as Anglicans could not beat the Greek Church's local strength among Orthodox laymen, they should work with it: "the only rational—and, as it appears to me, the most Christian—way of improving their spiritual condition, is to support and improve their own institutions."[89]

So when Bunsen arrived in London in late June, he found that the Church hierarchy was very keen on his idea of a Protestant bishopric of Jerusalem. The Germanophile Queen Victoria shared this view, and terms were settled. Nomination to the post would alternate between Britain and Prussia, but the archbishop would be able to veto the Prussian nominee. A Lutheran candidate would have to receive Anglican ordination. The government passed the legislation necessary to allow a bishop of the Church to minister in a foreign country and to be a foreign subject. The king of Prussia gave half the endowment necessary to pay the bishop's stipend; the British portion was raised by voluntary means, superintended by four lay trustees.[90]

The territorial remit of the Bishopric of Jerusalem was agreed to be the heartlands of Christianity in 500 CE: Palestine, the rest of Syria, Chaldea, Egypt, and Abyssinia. So it complemented a Malta-based Mediterranean bishopric, which was created in 1842. The latter had to be called the Bishopric of Gibraltar, since the British government had already acknowledged a Roman Catholic bishopric of Malta, but its Malta base signified that its jurisdiction would reach through the eastern Mediterranean, as far as the British embassy in Constantinople and the consular chapel in Smyrna. It therefore fell to the bishop of Gibraltar to liaise with the Greek Church around the shores of the Aegean, in the way that Tomlinson had foreshadowed in his 1840 report.

---

89. Tomlinson, *Report of a Journey*, 22, 69–83, 118–20 (quotation at 72); Howley to Foreign Office, Dec. 4, 1840, FO 78/425 259, 261.

90. Greaves, "Jerusalem Bishopric," 340–48.

Unsurprisingly, Tomlinson was appointed to the Gibraltar see in 1842, by Peel, whose children he had tutored.

The Jerusalem episcopate was founded on the principle of cooperation with the Syrian, Nestorian, and Coptic Churches—rather than challenging the authority of their patriarchs, which the Latin patriarch of Jerusalem did. The bishop was also told to be on good terms with the Greek Church, and Howley appointed George Williams as the bishop's chaplain in that particular hope. Howley's official "Statement of Proceedings" described the bishopric's object as to secure "relations of amity [with] the ancient Churches of the East, strengthening them against the encroachments of the see of Rome, and preparing the way for their purification." By setting forth pure Christianity in Jerusalem for the first time, it also promised to help the "desultory efforts" so far made for the conversion of Jews. "The hand of Providence" could be seen in the recent events in the Ottoman Empire that had allowed Britain and Prussia to open a door for "the advancement of the Saviour's kingdom, and for the restoration of God's ancient people to their spiritual birthright."[91]

In other words, the Jerusalem bishopric represented both main facets of Protestant religious interest—most immediately, to reach out to the Churches of the East, but also to promote the welfare of Jews in whatever ways might become practicable. In Jerusalem itself, however, its creation strengthened the impression that the aim of Britain and Prussia was to play the game of sectarian Christian rivalry. The Spanish minister assumed they would press for a separate *millet* for Protestants. The French consul in Beirut feared that Britain would attempt a protectorate over the Maronites.[92] When the first bishop, Michael Solomon Alexander, a converted Prussian Jew who was professor of Hebrew at King's College London, arrived in early 1842, he faced so much antagonism from the existing denominations that Hugh Rose, the consul-general in Syria, had to get the Ottoman government to guarantee his protection. "All are more or less, I regret to say, against him."[93] Aberdeen, the new Tory foreign secretary, was conscious of the need to pacify the other powers and the Ottomans over his appointment. In May 1842, he reminded Alexander, who was known to have a particular interest in the conversion of Jews, that he was forbidden to proselytise. His jurisdiction was merely spiritual, so he could not offer British protection to any Ottoman subject whom he might convert. In any case, Alexander could not reach out to the European Jews, since Russia, through Bardaki and Bazili, continued to protect them— and Bazili was upgraded to be consul-general in Syria in 1843. In the autumn of 1842, three Russian Jews who were being tried by Bardaki for an offence wanted to escape his jurisdiction. They took refuge with the LJS missionary Ewald, claiming to be interested in Protestantism. Bazili demanded that they

91. For Williams, see Greaves, 348. For the statement, [J. Neale], *Documents*, 6–7.
92. Farah, "Protestantism and British Diplomacy," 338–39.
93. Rose to Aberdeen, Jan. 26, 1842, FO 78/494.

be handed back; Young supported his request. Alexander refused to do so, but eventually had to give in. Relations between Young and Alexander never recovered, and Rose had to make clear to the latter that to give asylum to Jews who were subject to Russian authority violated international law.[94]

In January 1844, Young lashed out at religious people in Britain who imagined that his role as consul in Jerusalem was "to shape a course in order to meet the views of a popular reading of Prophecy" about Jewish restoration. They needed to "regard the actual condition of these Countries" and understand "the real position and wants of their present inhabitants," or else they would damage Britain's cause, and the Jews, by stirring up hostility from Latins and Greeks. When Alexander died suddenly in November 1845, the LJS mission in Jerusalem had only made thirty-one converts.[95] There was now a clear gulf between its aspirations and the priorities of the British government. When Thomas Tully Crybbace travelled from Stirling to London to advocate the return of the Jewish nation to Palestine, he was drily told by the head of the Foreign Office that this matter did not come "under [our] cognizance."[96]

The British government continued to try to uphold Jewish rights in more practical ways. In April 1841, at Ponsonby's suggestion, Palmerston issued a circular to British consuls in the empire that they should watch for cases of oppression or injustice to Jews and report them to local authorities and to Constantinople. He reminded them that in the Edict of Gülhane the Porte had pledged to protect the legal rights of all its subjects; moreover, the sultan had issued a special firman guaranteeing Jewish civil rights after his meeting with Montefiore in November 1840. Palmerston had also wanted to get special assurances from the Porte for European Jews settling in Palestine, because he thought that they would not otherwise risk their capital. However, Ottoman ministers (and Ponsonby) had argued that that there was no evidence that this was required, and that it would create awkward precedents and tensions. In fact, there was hardly any sign of European capital investment.[97]

Bishop Alexander's clash with the Russians also further delayed the attempt to build the Protestant church in Jerusalem. Despite the lack of permission for construction, a foundation stone had been laid, but then local complaints prevented further digging. In February and August 1841, Palmerston got Ponsonby to press the matter at the Porte, finding it difficult to understand how, "at a moment when the whole of Syria has so lately been restored to the Sultan by the powerful interposition of Great Britain, so small a favour as this could be refused to the British Government upon grounds of

94. Hyamson, *British Consulate in Jerusalem*, 1:46–48, 57–60; Rose to Aberdeen, Feb. 6 and 15, 1843, FO 78/535.

95. Young to Canning, Jan. 8, 1844, FO 195/210 137. For figures, see Tibawi, *British Interests in Palestine*, 75.

96. Addington to Crybbace, Mar. 8, 1844, FO 78/588.

97. Lewis, *Origins of Christian Zionism*, 241; Hyamson, *British Consulate in Jerusalem*, 1:35–40; A. Green, *Moses Montefiore*, 205–8.

a pedantic adherence to Mahomedan doctrines."[98] Construction began again, but permission was still unforthcoming. After the affair of the Russian Jews, the local governor pointedly stopped the work in January 1843.[99]

As sectarianism increased, the Ottomans were becoming more adept at playing the powers off against one another. Other European powers felt the need to set up consulates in Jerusalem: Prussia in 1842, France and Sardinia in 1843. Moreover, in 1842, the Greek Orthodox patriarch of Antioch sent a delegation to Russia to seek material and moral support against intensified Catholic and Protestant missionary activity in the region. As a result, an archimandrite, Uspenski, was sent on a tour of Syria and Palestine in 1843–44 to find ways of strengthening the Orthodox position. In 1845, one visitor to Jerusalem observed that "in a paltry, inland, eastern town, without trade or importance of any kind, sit the five consuls of the great European powers, looking at each other, it is difficult to say why or wherefore."[100]

Bishop Alexander's personal history gave him a particular concern with the Jews of Palestine. However, for many churchmen at home, the primary anxiety about the East continued to be the threat from Roman Catholicism. This led to Britain becoming entangled with both the Druze and the Nestorians. In each case, the original cause was the zeal of local American Protestant missionaries.

The Druze and the Perils of Sectarianism in Syria

Until the late 1830s, British interest in the Druze was limited and primarily political. They came to British attention during the struggle with France for Syria in 1799, when there was a widespread assumption that the people of Mount Lebanon were mostly Druze and that Bashir was "Prince of the Druze." There was concern that the French were wooing them, apparently claiming that they were "Dreux," descendants of European Crusaders who had taken refuge in the mountains. Their resistance to France in 1799 won them much respect, and established their identity as independent, military-minded defenders of mountain freedoms, hating all potential subjugators, Frankish or Islamic. Lebanon developed a reputation as "for ages the refuge of the oppressed, and the seat of liberty and independence," which was why there was such emphasis in 1839–40 on the need to defend their historic privileges.[101] Edward Clarke, who encountered some Druze near Galilee in 1801, and

98. Aug. 23, 1841, FO 78/429 149.

99. Lewis, *Origins of Christian Zionism*, 264–65.

100. Herschell, *Visit to my Father-Land*, 190–91. The Russians did not yet have a consul, but worked through the local convents. For the Uspenski mission, see Hopwood, *Russian Presence in Syria*, 33–38.

101. W. Kelly, *Syria and the Holy Land*, 151–52; Burckhardt, *Travels in Syria*, 203–4; E. Napier, *Reminiscences of Syria*, 1:165–66 (quotation).

Burckhardt, who spent time with them a few years later, stressed their manly integrity and probity.

Observers believed that, in order to maintain their independence, they had adopted the external religious forms of whichever dominant powers sought to oppress them. They professed Islam to satisfy the Ottomans, but this was a subterfuge. Their genuine beliefs were unknowable by outsiders; they were kept secret by the Druze religious elite, the *akil* class. For prudential or syncretic reasons, they appeared to have adopted forms from all the faiths they had encountered—Islam, Christianity, and the old pagan traditions. Clarke got the impression that sometimes they worshipped a golden calf symbolising animal desire, after which the men were allowed to sleep with any woman of their choice. This made him speculate that they were descended from the pagan Israelites of the Old Testament. Subsequent travellers found this story fanciful; most, in fact, stressed their relatively elevated treatment of women, and lack of interest in polygamy. Though the Druze remained mysterious, the consensus was that they were shaped less by religious belief than by their communal pride, resistance to tyranny, and determination to defend their independence by arms—raising a militia of up to forty thousand if necessary. It was assumed that, the *akil*s apart, they were worldly people who drank wine and believed little.[102]

That they would resist French missionaries and Islamic domination did not mean they were reliable friends. The Levant Company agent John Barker pointed out in 1803 that they were too numerically insignificant to be the basis of a Syrian nation, even if one were desirable, which it was not.[103] It became clear that they were too faction ridden even to govern Mount Lebanon. Bashir, who was soon realised not to be a Druze himself, was the superior force because he knew how to keep a balance between them and the Maronites. However, for missionaries, the idea of a people as yet unawakened by religion, but hostile to the enemies of Protestantism, was irresistible. Clarke's book made Jowett interested in them, while in 1820 one CMS missionary thought that it might be possible to reach them, once their Maronite neighbours started reading the Bible.[104]

The American missionaries in Beirut found them particularly tantalising. They had failed in all their previous operations, having alienated Latin and Greek priests, Jewish rabbis, and weary Ottoman governors. There was pressure back in America to wind the mission up. The great attraction of the Druze was that, unlike other sects, they were not "subject to ignorant and bigoted

102. E. Clarke, *Travels in Various Countries*, 1:458–59; Burckhardt, *Travels in Syria*, 200–204; Jowett, *Christian Researches in Syria*, 11, 38–39, 48, 62; W. Kelly, *Syria and the Holy Land*, 145–46; Salibi and Khoury, *Ottoman Syria*, 3:147.

103. Barker, *Syria and Egypt*, 1:71.

104. Tibawi, *American Interests in Syria*, 78n; Connor in Jowett, *Christian Researches in the Mediterranean*, 445–46.

priests, who can excommunicate them for hearing the truth or reading the Bible . . . they are free as their mountain air."[105] Under the Ottomans, they had no protected *millet* status; in fact, they professed to be Muslims in order to avoid the historic oppressions imposed on non-Muslim sects. The arrival of Egyptian government in Syria improved the position of the Christians and worsened theirs; in spring 1835, Ibrahim disarmed and began to conscript them, treating them as Muslims. They now emphasised their special religious status and need for foreign protection. They welcomed the missionaries' proposal to establish schools in their villages, and some applied to be preachers and teachers there. Several of their political leaders began to bid for British support, though the missionaries hoped they were looking to convert to Protestantism. Four new missionaries were sent to their districts in 1838.[106] By February 1840, Ambassador Ponsonby was alarmed by the degree of Druze friendliness to the British and Americans, and told Richard Wood that he must not promise them any special freedoms or rights: all they could expect was the preservation of the mountaineers' general privileges under the rule of the sultan.[107]

The Americans observed that if there had been a Protestant *millet* available for them in 1839, the Druze would have converted to Protestantism in order to get British protection.[108] This would have turned their mission from a twenty-year failure into a glorious success. That was the very reason why a Protestant *millet* was out of the question. Mehmet Ali and Bashir were united on the extreme undesirability of allowing the Druze to invoke European protection, and insisted that they must be treated as Muslims. The Greek priests were also hostile to the Americans, and campaigned to stop their schools in Lebanon in 1836.[109] One American missionary claimed that the Orthodox hierarchy did so little to support their communities that nine-tenths of the Greeks would become Protestant in a moment if they could get British or American protection. In contrast, because French power in Syria was so well established, the Latin missions had been able to woo Greeks in Hasbaya with "a single leg of mutton." The missionary William Thomson feared that the Druze, likewise, were being "left to fall into the withering embrace of the Roman harlot."[110]

In 1840–41, as French policy to Syria diverged from Britain's, many feared that France would seek to create its own political interest in the fastnesses of Lebanon—as the poet and philosopher Lamartine had advocated after his visit of 1832. That was one reason why Napier and Wood were so keen to cultivate

105. Salibi and Khoury, *Ottoman Syria*, 3:209.

106. Salibi and Khoury, 3:186–87, 193–99.

107. Ponsonby to Wood, Feb. 12, 1840, FO 78/392 215.

108. Robinson and Smith, *Biblical Researches in Palestine*, 3:464.

109. Tibawi, *American Interests in Syria*, 77–78; Salibi and Khoury, *Ottoman Syria*, 3:82, 97–99.

110. Salibi and Khoury, *Ottoman Syria*, 3:41, 100 (quotation 1), 203 (quotation 2).

the Maronites throughout the 1840 revolt. In early 1841, with France looking to rebuild its local influence, the fear was bound to revive. In March, it was reported that the French had distributed £5,000 among them.[111] In reaction, the Druze became of concern to the Church of England as well as the missionaries. William R. Fremantle, an evangelical Buckinghamshire clergyman and friend of Tattam, had visited Syria in early 1839. He lobbied to establish a channel for the Druze to convert to Protestantism, and suggested sending a CMS missionary to them. He emphasised their dislike of Romanism and Islam. He also wondered if their founding ancestors were perhaps English Crusaders who had fled to the Lebanese mountains. Alternatively, they might have connections with the druids.[112] In Malta, a serious young man with CMS connections, George Percy Badger, proposed himself for the mission, having collected information about the Druze from the American missionaries in Beirut, with whom his sister worked.[113] In the summer of 1841, the CMS's Samuel Gobat, having returned from Abyssinia, spent a month with them to ascertain the practicability of a mission. He found the same as his predecessors: the *akils* were polite and were good family men; they wanted Druze children to receive a good secular education; they had no objection to the teaching of the Bible. In fact, they were quite curious about it, as long as it was not forced on them.[114]

In this new situation, the American missionaries made one more attempt to get the British to protect the Druze. Thomson and Eli Smith went to live among them, tried to set up schools for them, and urged them to seek British protection. In May 1841, Thomson approached Hugh Rose, the commander of the British forces in Syria, to try to forge a connection. Rose was interested, particularly in view of the money that the French (and later also the Austrian) public were sending to the Maronite communities and convents, to repair the war damage of 1840. So he urged Palmerston to support the Druze request for British help with their schools (but not for protection), and Palmerston committed the government to do so. Rose wrote warmly of the sincerity and humanity of the Druze leader Numan Jumblatt, and Numan sent his younger brother Ismail to England for education as a symbol of his friendship with Britain.[115]

It is not surprising that Farah, and several other historians over the years, have taken this incident as evidence of British sectarian support for the Druze, in the hope of countering French influence with the Maronites. It was bound to appear in that light, even though Rose and Palmerston saw it differently. They believed they were warning France not to encourage the Maronites to

111. Farah, "Protestantism and British Diplomacy," 339; Bridgeman, Mar. 24, 1841, FO 78/453 196.

112. Fremantle, *Eastern Churches*, 40–41.

113. Allen and McClure, *Two Hundred Years*, 306.

114. Gobat, *Life and Work*, 193–97.

115. For Numan's agency in this episode, see Ozavci, *Dangerous Gifts*, 252.

press for independence. Neither Palmerston nor Rose believed that France or the Maronites wished to uphold sultanic authority in Lebanon, whereas their own assistance to the Druze was explicitly conditional on them pledging loyalty to the Ottoman regime. They hoped to persuade the Druze to work with the new status quo. Palmerston held the traditional belief that Mount Lebanon was a Druze stronghold that could not be governed without their cooperation. So he had no difficulty convincing himself that British "influence" with the Druze would be "serviceable to the Porte."[116]

Moreover, Rose agreed with Numan Jumblatt and other Druze leaders in criticising Wood's plan for a Syrian council, because it threatened the mountaineers' freedoms that the war had been fought to preserve. Jumblatt complained that Wood had not given them enough places on the proposed divan. He also claimed that this was the result of Wood's own Roman Catholicism. Palmerston later used this charge to explain why he had made Rose and not Wood consul-general of Syria. How far this supposed fact, on its own, swayed the choice is difficult to say. What is certain is that Wood was seen to be a partisan figure who had exacerbated the tensions in Lebanon, and that a new start was needed. If the British were to reprise their traditional policy of holding the ring between local interest groups, Rose was by far the better bet.[117]

Britain's Druze initiative had three consequences. The first was the final stage in the falling-out between the Foreign Office and army on the one hand, and the Constantinople embassy and Wood on the other, discussed in chapter 6. Rose complained that Wood refused to address local anger at his Porte-inspired plan. Wood's strategy for limiting Druze opposition was to arrest a dozen Druze leaders and send them to Constantinople. Once this was discovered, the Druze leaders declined even to come to meet him, without guarantees of protection from Rose. Ponsonby was furious at the initiative and at the appointment of Rose as consul-general over Wood. In response, he encouraged the Porte to press for the removal of the British military force still stationed in Syria. Rose claimed that Ponsonby and Wood were puppets of the Ottomans, whose concern was to prevent British exposure of their misgovernment in Syria. By the time the Ottoman request about the troops reached London, Palmerston was out of office, and his Tory successor Aberdeen was keen to smooth relations

116. Palmerston to Ponsonby, Aug. 17, 1841, FO 78/429 131. See Farah, "Protestantism and British Diplomacy," especially 326 and 329 for the Americans' role. For a typical assumption about British support for the Druze, see Shaw and Shaw, *Ottoman Empire and Modern Turkey*, 2:134. Cunningham's strange account alleges that Rose and Palmerston's argument that their Druze initiative would assist the Porte was a ruse, "to console the Queen": R. Wood, *Early Correspondence*, 30.

117. For these three paragraphs: Rose to Palmerston, June 6 and 22, 1841, FO 78/455 157, 173; Palmerston to Rose, July 15, 1841, FO 78/454 15. Cunningham accepted the general view that Wood was a Catholic, but see Ozavci's *Dangerous Gifts* (246) for a belated claim by his supporters that he was raised as a Protestant.

with France and Russia and to cut defence costs. He approved the withdrawal of the detachment, which was completed at the end of 1841. However, he left Rose in office as consul-general (for the next decade), and approved his actions when the Porte criticised them.[118]

Second, the British government delegated the task of Druze schooling to the Church of England. This led to a rift with the American missionaries who had promoted the idea. Palmerston arranged for Nicolayson to go from Jerusalem to make the initial arrangements for the schools, knowing that the Jerusalem bishopric was about to be set up and that Nicolayson, and hence the school initiative, would be under the bishop's authority. When Nicolayson arrived in Lebanon in October, he alienated the missionaries with his talk of "the Church" and "the bishop." The American Board was very suspicious of the philosophy of episcopacy and of the Anglo-Prussian plan to affiliate with the degenerate Churches of the East, for which it had never had any time. So the missionaries felt that Britain had betrayed their plans for the Druze, and their wider purpose in Syria.[119]

The irritation was mutual: Rose felt that the missionaries had antagonised the Maronite patriarch by starting their own schools among the Druze in the spring, forcing the Ottoman government to stop their proceedings. Rose insisted that the only way to get schools functioning was with the approval of the Ottoman authorities. Rose was also annoyed with the missionary Gobat, who in the summer had distributed tracts on Mount Lebanon urging the Druze to convert, in defiance of the British government's desire to dissociate itself from any conversion efforts. Rose demanded that any future CMS activity must be subject to his control, and that British agencies should decline to proselytise among people of other faiths (just as the British did in India or Malta). He also stipulated that British schools on Mount Lebanon should be established only where sanctioned by Ottoman and Druze leaders, in Druze districts, and should not teach religion. In other words, Rose was quickly learning the disadvantages of sectarianism for Anglo-Ottoman relations and for practical British influence.[120] He was also determined to remain on good terms with the Maronite leaders and to dissuade them from rebellion. In private, Rose was a serious Christian and an advocate of Anglo-Orthodox unity (his father was one of the Jerusalem bishopric trustees).[121]

118. Rose to Palmerston, Aug. 28, 1841, FO 78/456 203; Rose to Wood, Feb. 18, 1842, FO 226/32 43. For Ponsonby's role, see R. Wood, *Early Correspondence*, 31. See Aberdeen's support for Rose: to Canning, Jan. 22, 1842, FO 78/473 33.

119. On the missionaries, see Tibawi, *American Interests in Syria*, 96–100; Farah, "Protestantism and British Diplomacy," 331.

120. Rose to Palmerston, Sept. 7 and 16, 1841, FO 78/456 263, 274; to Aberdeen, Oct. 7, 1841, FO 78/457 63.

121. On his hopes for Anglo-Orthodox unity, see Rose to Aberdeen, Jan. 4, 1845, FO 78/618 3.

Third, the council plan was rejected by the Lebanese leaders, on several grounds. Mutual suspicion between Druze leaders and the Maronite patriarch then led to a brief civil war in October. Rose blamed the Maronite patriarch for inciting tenant revolts against heavy feudal taxation, and the weak Ottoman government for encouraging the Druze to retaliate. The result of the war was that the patriarch was put in his place and feudal rights were upheld. However, the Druze aggression was embarrassing for Rose, because any attacks on Christian interests risked alienating public opinion in France and elsewhere.[122] After the war, France and Austria demanded a Christian governor in Lebanon. To start with, so did Britain. The Druze chiefs realised that the British would not protect them. Instead, they appealed to the sultan to save them as Muslims from the humiliation of submitting to a Christian governor. They blamed the American missionaries for originally undermining their allegiance.[123] By 1842, Numan Jumblatt was finding the role of Druze leader too stressful, in view of the number of Ottoman, Maronite, and Druze opponents that he had acquired. He declared his retirement to a religious life, while in 1843 Ismail had a mental breakdown in England and had to be repatriated.[124] No other Druze figure was to be as congenial to British officials.

All these events showed the unattractiveness of a sectarian policy. The Ottomans would not tolerate American missionary proselytism, which risked introducing new Western interests into Lebanon when they were trying to secure their own direct rule. The Druze were unlikely to give Britain reliable influence anyway. Rose repeatedly made clear that Britain aimed to uphold the legitimate interests of all sects under the Tanzimat, irrespective of religion. Once the military detachment left in late 1841, it was obvious that Britain would have influence only by working with all the sects and with the other powers. Rose was annoyed by the bishop of Jerusalem's naive hostility to Islam and failure to keep on terms with the powerful Orthodox Church.[125] Though the SPCK voted money for a mission to the Druze, it never took place,

122. Rose to Aberdeen, Oct. 28 and Nov. 8, 1841, FO 78/457 157, 78/458 4.

123. Farah, "Protestantism and British Diplomacy," 341–42. For the wider Lebanese political situation, see Makdisi, *Culture of Sectarianism*, 63–65, W. Harris, *Lebanon*, 139–43.

124. Ismail was staying at Woolwich, looked after by Captain Lethbridge, a Royal Artillery officer, and Assaad Kayat, a well-connected Syrian in London. In 1842, enemies of the Jumblatts had spread the rumour that he wished to return, when he did not. In February 1843, he became sick, agitated, fanciful, and occasionally violent; this appears to have been connected with the controversies in Syria about his and his family's property. Numan claimed to have had a similar malady in his youth. Aberdeen sent him back to Syria, where he arrived in May, to the relief of Numan and Rose. See Aberdeen to Rose, Apr. 3, 1843, FO 78/534; Rose to Foreign Office, Mar. 5, 1843, FO 78/535, Apr. 6 and May 4, 1843, FO 78/536; Lethbridge to Foreign Office, Feb. 16, 1843, FO 78/547; Foreign Office memo, Mar. 30, 1843, FO 78/548.

125. Rose to Aberdeen, Mar. 3, 1842, FO 226/29, and Mar. 27, 1842, FO 78/494.

because of the civil war and government discouragement. Even in the CMS, the traditional view re-emerged that the Druze were religiously unreliable and unknowable, and not likely to be worth much attention.[126]

However, the Church of England had not lost its appetite for exploratory partnerships with Middle Eastern sects. Just as the door was closing in Syria, so it was opening in Kurdistan among the Nestorians, and George Percy Badger, foiled in his dream of a Druze mission, was selected to reach out to them instead.

The Nestorians of Kurdistan

The Christians inhabiting the mountains north of Mosul have been of intermittent interest to outsiders for so many centuries that they have acquired many different names. As a people, they are frequently now called Assyrians. In the early Christian era, their language, and then they, became known as Chaldean. In the eighteenth and nineteenth centuries, they split into two groups under pressure from Roman Catholic missionary activity, which complicates matters further. Here, for convenience, I shall use the term "Nestorians" to describe members of this Church who had rejected conversion to Roman Catholicism, and "Chaldean" or "Chaldean Catholic" for those who had converted. This is a formula often used at the time, though there was a great deal of variation; some people called the Nestorians Nazarenes instead. Their Church is now usually called the Church of the East.

Before the late 1830s, there was little British enthusiasm for the Nestorians. The few Britons who explored the area seeking local allies were much more interested in the Kurds. Claudius and Mary Rich travelled in the Mosul area in late 1820 after their heady stay in Sulaimaniya, but did not go to the Nestorians' stronghold of Hakkari—though they heard reports of their ferocity. Rich visited one village, Teliskof, just north of Mosul, and noted its "extreme dirtiness, which, with the smell of liquor, is, I am sorry to say, the characteristic of a Christian village in these countries."[127] His primary interest was in the ancient Christian convents of the area, because of their Syriac and Arabic manuscripts, some of which he acquired, helping to promote his reputation as a man of learning. The publication of Rich's *Narrative* in 1836 drew attention to the antiquarian riches of these remote places.[128] In 1834, James Baillie Fraser inspected Kurdistan during his tour of Persia and Mesopotamia on behalf of the Foreign Office. Fraser's response was the same as Rich's: the Nestorians had historic treasures and were fierce fighters who could easily defend themselves from invasion, but they were "barbarians, . . . rude and

126. Farah, "Protestantism and British Diplomacy," 341; Bowen, *Memorials*, 301.
127. Rich, *Narrative of a Residence*, 1:277, 2:101.
128. Rich, 2:77–78, 92–93, 104, 119, 306–11.

suspicious" who distrusted everyone and were worthless as allies. Fraser, him-self a Scot like Mary Rich, had more time for the Kurds, whose customs, sim-plicity, and pride he compared to the old Highland clans. Even so, he observed that Kurdistan—"rocky Assyria"—could never have been the powerhouse of the ancient Assyrian Empire. Its evident poverty had bred hardy soldiers whose talent had led them to "overrun and possess themselves of the more fertile plains and provinces adjoining them." (There were interesting parallels here for a Highland Scot.) The wealth of ancient Assyria came from its Asian acquisitions, not the "black and howling wilderness" of Kurdistan itself.[129]

However, religious scholars knew that these Christians had been empire builders themselves, coming out of the mountains hundreds of years ago to spread their religion in India, Persia, and China. Claudius Buchanan's dis-covery of Syriac biblical manuscripts in Malabar suggested to Jowett that the Nestorians who had planted the faith "from Aleppo to Travancore" must have been formidable missionaries. Jowett hoped that the resulting publication of Samuel Lee's Syriac New and Old Testaments in 1816 and 1823 would help Westerners to reach out to this "immense body of Christians" in their Middle Eastern strongholds.[130] Robert Walsh, the Levant Company chaplain at Con-stantinople, met a Nestorian bishop in 1822, and then used the religious press to publicise the Nestorians' independence, their venerable history, and their missionary activities in India; he also greatly exaggerated their numbers, at half a million.[131] In 1830, the American missionaries Eli Smith and H.G.O. Dwight began a three-year investigation of Asia Minor and Persia. This led to the establishment of a mission base at Urmia in north-west Persia, in order to reach the Nestorians nearby and those over the border to the west in Ottoman Hakkari. They too felt that, once revivified, the Nestorians could "exert a com-manding influence in the spiritual regeneration of Asia." Urmia was attractive also because Abbas Mirza, the crown prince of Persia based in the north-west of the country, seemed to be encouraging Western settlement as a bulwark against Russia (though he promptly died). The American mission at Urmia was begun in 1835, by Justin Perkins and Asahel Grant. It operated thirteen schools with 340 pupils by 1839, and a printing press from late 1840.[132]

Joseph Wolff had met some Persian Nestorians in 1825 and called them "in sentiment complete Protestants."[133] Eli Smith also hoped for common theological ground with them, on account of their toleration, their rejection of auricular confession, and their dislike of image worship and the cult of

129. Fraser, *Travels in Koordistan*, 1:59 (quotation 1), 116–17, 182 (other quotations).

130. Jowett, *Christian Researches in Syria*, 14. For awareness of the missionary activi-ties in China and Persia, see Salibi and Khoury, *Northern Iraq*, 1:1–2.

131. Robert Walsh, *Residence at Constantinople*, 2:406–13; for his articles, see O'Flynn, *Western Christian Presence*, 601.

132. Salibi and Khoury, *Northern Iraq*, 1:1–2, 52, 65–66, 242.

133. Wolff, *Missionary Journal*, 152.

Mary.[134] The name "Nestorian" referred back to the doctrines of the heretical fifth-century theologian Nestorius, but sympathisers claimed that their supposed veneration of him was a Catholic slur. In any case, the disputes about the nature of Christ between Nestorius and his contemporaries were semantic and no longer properly understood.[135] The important point was that these people had introduced Christianity to the region, perhaps as early as the first century, and had remained uncontaminated by superstitions and unscriptural doctrines since, through being cut off in the mountains.[136] Roman Catholic missionaries had worked among them in the sixteenth century, and more continuously since 1750. In 1778, they had converted the bishop of Mosul and founded a Chaldean Catholic Church, promising to protect local Christians from Muslim oppression. Those missionaries had also created Catholic converts from the ancient Syrian Christian community, usually called Jacobites, which had bases in Aleppo, Mardin, and Mosul, and who were Monophysites, like the Copts, Abyssinians, and Armenians. This successful Catholic activity made the resistance of the "free Syrians" and Nestorians in the mountains all the more impressive. Layard later called the Nestorians "the Protestants of Asia."[137]

One young Chaldean from Mosul played a large part in awakening British religious interest in Kurdistan. This was Christian Rassam, the eldest son of a powerful local family that for a century had been an arbiter of the religious loyalties of Mosul Christians. His eighteenth-century ancestors had helped to negotiate the conversion of the town's Nestorians to Rome, on account of the protection that it offered against Kurds and Muslims. However, he claimed that the Rassams had also fought to preserve local communal customs and rituals against Lazarist pressure for the adoption of various Romish practices, such as the rosary and the use of holy water. Recently, this pressure had widened an existing split among the Chaldeans, and created two factions. Rassam—and the American missionaries—argued that this split could be used to protect Mosul Chaldeans from French influence, and to restore harmony between them and the Nestorians of Hakkari. Rassam himself had left Mosul in the late 1820s, originally intending to train for the Church in Rome, but had fallen in with the CMS mission in Cairo while staying there with an uncle. Swayed by the missionaries' admiration for the history of the Eastern Orthodox Churches, he went to work at the CMS station in Malta,

134. Salibi and Khoury, *Northern Iraq*, 1:1.

135. Hormuzd Rassam argued this at length in J. Newman's *Thrones and Palaces* (383–91). So did Layard, in *Nineveh and Its Remains* (1:260–69). See also Badger, *Nestorians and Their Rituals*, 2:353–57, and Southgate, *Syrian (Jacobite) Church*, 146.

136. Rassam in J. Newman, *Thrones and Palaces*, 371; Ainsworth, *Christian Aborigines*, 12–14.

137. Layard, *Nineveh and Its Remains*, 1:269. For "free Syrians," see F. Newman, *Personal Narrative*, 34.

translating religious works into Arabic and Syriac. While there, in early 1835, he was appointed interpreter to the Euphrates Expedition. Rassam then persuaded other expedition members that a reunited Christian community, hostile to Rome, could be created in Mosul and Kurdistan.[138] This would of course require guidance and mediation by those with local influence. Rassam quickly grasped that this might involve a job for him.

After the expedition broke up in 1836, its leaders, Chesney and Lynch, proposed further exploration of the Tigris-Euphrates region, to be undertaken by the new riverboats for which they pressed. Both men assumed, incorrectly, that their new steamers would be able to ascend the Tigris as far as Mosul. So Mosul could become a key British base, commercially and strategically, checking Russian incursions into Kurdistan (the Russians had occupied Urmia in the war of 1828). Two members of the expedition proposed themselves for this reconnaissance: Rassam, drawing on his local knowledge, and William Ainsworth. Ainsworth was a young geologist and surgeon enthusiastic about exploration—he was known as "Young Strabo" on the expedition because he was apt to quote classical writings on local geography—who hoped to find coal, copper, and silver in Kurdistan and launch its commercial development. Chesney envisaged that the Nestorians' fighting prowess, plus their coal deposits, would create "a defensive nucleus against all aggressive designs." Ainsworth later wrote a pamphlet portraying them as the Christian "aborigines" of the East, preceding Islamic usurpers. Britain should protect them from this brutal imperialism, just as the Church of England should aspire to help the natives of Australasia. The steamer would be the key to the reinvigoration of Christianity; its "noisy paddles" were "moving like a vision of future glory through the very heart of the land of biblical history."[139]

There was also the chance of a government post. In August 1837, Lynch and Ambassador Ponsonby discussed increasing the British presence at Mosul. In these years, the Foreign Office was planning new consulships in the Ottoman borderlands with Russia—including at Erzurum on Kurdistan's northern edge, where James Brant was sent in 1836. Rassam himself may well have come up with the idea of a consul at Mosul—with the right to trade, for his ultimate aim was to set up as a powerful local merchant with British support. Ponsonby hoped that a post there would help his embassy to strengthen Ottoman influence over the Kurds. Lynch flattered the ambassador by telling him, extremely implausibly, that Ince Bairaktar, the new pasha of Mosul (the first one to be appointed direct from Constantinople rather than from the Jalili clan), was

138. On Rassam, see Roper, "Christian Rassam," esp. 187, and the memoir in WPLP, MS 2817, esp. 41–42. For his claims, see the memoir and Salibi and Khoury, *Ottoman Syria*, 3:114–15. For others saying similar things, see Southgate, *Syrian (Jacobite) Church*, 139–45, and Salibi and Khoury, *Northern Iraq*, 1:17, 29, 167.

139. Chesney to Ponsonby, Dec. 6, 1837, PPD, GRE/E/131, B65; Ainsworth, *Christian Aborigines*, 50–51.

"in Your Lordship's hands."[140] The idea was approved in 1839, and Ponsonby successfully nominated Rassam for it. Ainsworth, who had expected it himself, was distraught when he finally found out, which was not until March 1840.[141]

The mixture of political and religious hopes driving the Ainsworth-Rassam expedition was shown by its funding. In January 1838, the Royal Geographical Society and the SPCK (guided by the archbishop of Canterbury) each agreed to provide half the cost, £500. The Royal Geographical Society was closely connected with government, having been founded in 1830 by John Barrow, the civil servant at the head of the Admiralty. Its *Journal* published several articles about Kurdistan and Mesopotamia in 1839; Chesney sat on its council.[142] Rassam had come to Britain in late 1837 to help to secure this funding, and generated a lot of interest, as a traveller from "Abraham's country." He seemed to embody the customs and doctrines of a Church that predated the Romanising perversions of the Middle Ages. He talked knowledgeably about Church unity, and implied that his people would accept the leadership of the Church of England. He offered to send six young Mosul Christians to Oxford University, which gratefully agreed to teach them for free.[143] He promised to report on the condition and educational needs of the Nestorian and Jacobite churches, explore their manuscripts, and inaugurate discussions with the patriarch at Mosul. Archbishop Howley hoped for "many and great advantages to the interests of our holy Religion, if the Mission should succeed."[144]

In fact, it failed in every respect. Ainsworth insisted that his scientific expertise was central to it, so he spent months in Britain and France training in astronomy and geology. As a result, they could not reach the Anatolian mountains until the winter of 1838–39, just when the weather made progress difficult. As Ponsonby hoped that the mission would benefit Ottoman authority, they went to the camp of the Ottoman commander Hafiz Pasha—just in time for his disastrous defeat by Ibrahim at Nizip. This defeat badly damaged the Ottomans' reputation among the Kurds, making the whole area almost ungovernable. Wisely, Ainsworth and Rassam went back to Constantinople. They returned to Kurdistan in 1840 in line with their backers' expectations, but little was achieved: Ainsworth's young wife died in Erzurum, they ran out of money, and Rassam was anxious to take up his post at Mosul.[145]

140. Lynch to Ponsonby, Aug. 1837, FO 78/306 119; Rassam to SPCK, Aug. 6, 1839, WPLP, MS 2821 183.

141. Ainsworth to Washington, Mar. 23, 1840, Ainsworth Papers, RGS/CB2.

142. See the articles by Ainsworth, Forbes, H. Lynch, and J. Ross in the *Journal of the Royal Geographical Society* 9 (1839).

143. See memoir, WPLP, MS 2817; Chesney to Ponsonby, Dec. 6, 1837, PPD, GRE/E/131, B65.

144. Coakley, *Church of the East*, 25.

145. Ainsworth's lengthy reports on the expedition are in Ainsworth Papers, RGS/CB2.

This setback counted for little, because in 1840–41, the Eastern crisis increased the stakes and the opportunities for the European powers all over the Ottoman Empire, and Kurdistan was no exception. Religious minds hoped that Britain's successful defence of the empire against Catholic France would lead to increased access to its ancient Christian communities. Ainsworth met Mar Shimun, the Nestorian leader, and then George Tomlinson, during the latter's visit to Constantinople, and pressed the latter to work for the regeneration of the Nestorians. Tomlinson reported home that "never since the Reformation" had the Anglicans had such an opportunity to reach out to the Churches of the East. These bodies still contained "the PRINCIPLE of vitality"; the "flame of purity and zeal" could easily be rekindled in them.[146]

Alarming reports were coming in (from the Americans, and Taylor in Baghdad) of increased and well-funded French missionary activity among these communities. Eugène Boré had started a school in Mosul in 1839. In November 1840, Rassam claimed that "great numbers of Jesuits" were spreading over the East opening schools and seminaries. In April 1841, he asserted that the French were offering to protect the Nestorians from increased Kurdish pressure, if they would convert.[147] But perhaps the Church of England could strike back: the split in the local Chaldean Church had widened, and many Mosul Chaldeans were apparently ready to break away from the Roman Church, with the right encouragement. Horatio Southgate, an American Episcopalian, was becoming an expert on the Chaldean and Jacobite struggles with Rome, and met Tomlinson in Constantinople to discuss their situation.[148] On the other hand, the activities of the American missionaries in Urmia were themselves alarming. Asahel Grant had decided to make a pitch to reach the Nestorians of Hakkari. In October 1839 he made what was to be the first of four visits to them in the next three years. He, likewise, was excited to contemplate the probable impact of "their dauntless and untiring zeal" on the peoples of Asia, when harnessed to "the power of the press and all the increasing means of modern times."[149] But the Anglicans felt that the American missionaries would corrupt, divide, or alienate the Nestorians, owing to their lack of sympathy with episcopalian traditions.

So Tomlinson urged the SPCK to send a mission to the Nestorians. This would benefit from the local presence of Rassam, who was now in residence in Mosul. The cross of England flew proudly from his house, "showing far and wide the badge of the faith in which we worshipped."[150] The establishment

146. Ainsworth to Washington, Oct. 16, 1840, Ainsworth Papers; Tomlinson, *Report of a Journey*, 75–6, 78 (quotations).

147. Salibi and Khoury, *Northern Iraq*, 1:108, 226–27, 421, 427–28; Taylor to Hobhouse, Aug. 31, 1840, Broughton, F213 10; Rassam to Palmer, Nov. 4, 1840, WPLP, MS 2819; Coakley, *Church of the East*, 34.

148. See Southgate, *Narrative of a Tour*, 237–38, and *Syrian (Jacobite) Church*.

149. Salibi and Khoury, *Northern Iraq*, 1:219, 231–34.

150. Southgate's words, in his *Syrian (Jacobite) Church*, 135–36.

of the Jerusalem bishopric in late 1841 promised even more support for the episcopalian cause. When the Lebanese civil war made an SPCK mission to the Druze impossible, the society diverted it to Kurdistan instead, voting £500 for it.[151] The mission had two objectives. One was to encourage Mar Elia of Alkosh, the anti-Roman claimant to the patriarchate of the Chaldean Church, in his apparent wish to enter into "amicable relations with the Church of England." The other was to initiate a relationship of goodwill with the Nestorian leader Mar Shimun, to help him with the spiritual education of his people, to give him Bibles if he wanted them, and to collect manuscripts that would make possible more suitable versions in future.[152]

The twenty-six-year-old George Percy Badger was appointed to lead the mission. The son of a British army schoolmaster stationed in Malta, he had connections with the CMS station there. Moreover, his sister had married Rassam in 1835, suggesting that the two men could easily work together. When Badger came to England for ordination in 1841, Rassam told him to visit William Palmer, an Oxford University enthusiast for communion between the Church of England and the Orthodox Churches, who had taken up Rassam in 1837. Badger imbibed, much more rigorously and uncompromisingly than Rassam ever did, Palmer's high church vision of the catholicity of the Church, and his hope of unification on the basis of early Church theology. Badger wanted to convince the Nestorians, the Jacobites, and the secessionists to Rome that their heresies and rejections of early Church Council rulings were of little spiritual value and should be given up for the sake of fellowship in "the one, holy, catholic, and apostolic Church."[153] He strongly disapproved of the theological basis of both the French and American missions. When Rose had dealings with him on his way to the East in 1842, he concluded that "Mr Badger is one of the last persons I should wish to see employed as he states. There is a good deal of religious excitement at Mosul and Mr Badger who if he is not a little mad is very strange will I fear increase it."[154]

When Badger reached Mosul, he found more obstacles to the triumph of episcopal Anglicanism than he can have imagined. After the humiliation of Nizip, the strongly Muslim Kurds were dominant locally, and politics focused on appeasing and managing them. This meant, among other things, that there was no prospect of the implementation of the Tanzimat. The pasha, Bairaktar, disliked the presence of a Western consul who could report on his doings; he arrested and tortured Rassam's groom on a trumped-up charge. Local Muslims protested at the appearance of the British flag.[155] French religious power

151. Allen and McClure, *Two Hundred Years*, 307. See Ainsworth, *Christian Aborigines*, 46–48.

152. Badger, *Nestorians and Their Rituals*, 1:xiv–xv.

153. Badger, 2:359.

154. Rose to Aberdeen, July 30, 1842, FO 226/24 66.

155. Rassam to Taylor, Mar. 22 and Dec. 19, 1842, FO 195/204 66, 124; Southgate, *Syrian (Jacobite) Church*, 136.

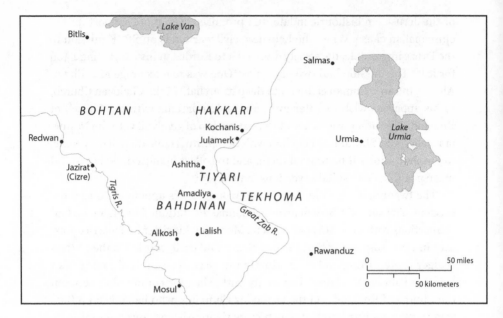

MAP 6. Nestorian Kurdistan

was strongly entrenched, and the first French consul arrived in May 1842 to strengthen it. Badger's assistant James Fletcher was impressed and alarmed by the organisation and the political influence of the Romanists. Compared with all the other Christians, they were "better dressed, they have more intelligence, their churches and their houses are cleaner, and more elegant. . . . The sovereignty of Rome in the East, seems indeed inevitable." The influence of the French, together with the wrong-headed Americans, would mean "the annihilation of Oriental Christianity as a system."[156]

When Badger set off to parley with Mar Shimun at his base in Kochanis, his only weapons were his gifts, which included two pairs of red boots, a canister of snuff, some ginger, twenty pounds of coffee, twenty pounds of incense, and two large scarlet cloaks. When he arrived, he discovered that the Americans had Mar Shimun's ear, because of Grant's four missions and the medical, educational, and financial help that he could offer. Badger had no money and no schoolbooks. He wrote home that the mountaineers "appear to be an over-reaching and gift-loving people" and that the only way to compete with American power was to set up a permanent educational operation funded by an annual grant for books.[157] This was not part of the SPCK's plan.

Mar Shimun's bigger problem was with the local Kurds. He had fallen out with his local amir in Hakkari, Nurallah Bey, and refused to pay taxes to him.

156. Fletcher, *Notes from Nineveh*, 1:140–41, 363.
157. Badger, *Nestorians and Their Rituals*, 1:197, 247–51 (quotation at 249).

Nurallah noted that this insubordination began after Grant's first visit. The Kurds were alarmed by the schoolhouse that Grant's American mission was building at Ashitha, which resembled a fort and occupied a strategic position on a low hill above the valley: "a better defensive and offensive position could not have been chosen."[158] They assumed that foreign Christians were encouraging a Nestorian rebellion. More generally, they were irritated that the Nestorian districts of Tiyari and Hakkari hindered their resistance to Pasha Bairaktar's attempts to subordinate them. He had already neutered the influence of Ismail, the hereditary Kurdish governor of Bahdinan, with the assistance of Mar Shimun, whose territories bordered Bahdinan.

Mar Shimun probably hoped that with Western protection he could defeat Kurdish pressure and become the sole local ruler of Hakkari, subject only to the sultan. In late 1842, the Kurdish chiefs formed a united federation under Bedir Khan Beg, the amir of Bohtan, to assert their power against the Ottomans. Bedir Khan Beg encouraged small-scale Kurdish actions against the Nestorians, who retaliated, creating more tension.[159] When the Kurds decided to attack the Nestorian villages, Bairaktar turned a blind eye. He thought that Kurd-Nestorian conflict would make both sides easier to manage. He was as irritated by the Western religious missions as the Kurds were, and plainly disliked the monitoring of him by the British and French consulates. In July 1843, the Kurds burnt Nestorian villages and churches, destroyed their crops, and left thousands dead (three and a half thousand, including thirty priests and sixty deacons, but initial estimates were ten thousand). Women were taken as slaves and forced to convert to Islam. Most of the patriarch's family were murdered. The defining story of the massacre was when a Kurd took hold of Mar Shimun's aged mother, tossed her in the air, cut her body in half with his sword, and floated the halves down the river Zab as a message to the patriarch. Grant's schoolhouse was stormed and used by Kurds as a garrison; when Nestorians tried to recover it, they were defeated, and three bags of human ears from Ashitha were sent to Bedir Khan Beg.[160]

Henry Ross, a British observer, attributed Mar Shimun's refusal to cooperate with Nurallah to "European counsels." He meant Badger. There was considerable speculation about what Badger had promised Mar Shimun in their meeting in early 1843, which was interrupted by a message from Nurallah summoning Mar Shimun to meet him, which he ignored. Badger denied that he had promised anything, and this is probably true, as he had nothing to promise.[161] Nonetheless, it was clear that the sectarian competition between

158. H. Ross, *Letters from the East*, 65–66.

159. Aboona's *Assyrians, Kurds, and Ottomans* provides the best modern account of these conflicts.

160. Rassam to Canning, July 29 and Oct. 31, 1843, FO 195/228 13, 42.

161. Ross, *Letters from the East*, 65. In *Nestorians and Their Rituals* (1:190–91), the oversensitive Badger criticised an insinuation by Ainsworth that his visit to Mar Shimun

the British, the French, and the Americans had played a crucial part in the Kurdish and Ottoman decision to remove the Nestorian threat to their own political plans. A particularly brutal anonymous article in the *Morning Chronicle* assaulted the three religious missions, but mainly the "Puseyite" Badger and the "papist" French for their intrigues against the Americans, who were first in the field and were trying to do good. These two sectarian intrigues had perpetrated "a great crime against humanity," destroying "one of the most ancient and most interesting sects in the world."[162] Badger wanted to stay in Mosul, but was recalled in December 1843. The SPCK was clear that it had no appetite for a permanent mission in Kurdistan.[163]

The *Morning Chronicle*'s article was one of a number by the same correspondent, based in Constantinople. His name was Henry Layard, and he was being employed by the new ambassador, Stratford Canning, to improve the embassy's media profile. His articles reflected the view of the embassy there, that religious meddling on sectarian principles was doing great damage to British policy, and to the East. Over the next few years, Canning and Layard were influential in formulating an alternative strategy for Kurdistan, and for the Ottoman Empire generally. It was the policy that the Constantinople embassy had always wanted to pursue, of close collaboration with the Ottoman government in order to impose better local administration. Despite all the objections to it, it now seemed the only remaining option. The next two chapters trace its impact, the first in Kurdistan and the second at Constantinople. It was in pursuit of a new policy for Kurdistan that Layard himself went to Mosul in 1845—and, as a result, found himself internationally famous.

----

had contributed to the massacre: Ainsworth, *Travels and Researches*, 2:253–55. In fact, Ainsworth's criticism was almost entirely of the Americans' cultivation of the Nestorians, which he attributed to their jealousy of his own earlier expedition. In any case, Ainsworth's text must essentially have been written (and was formally published) before the massacre. Badger's real animus was surely against Henry Layard, who condemned his "Puseyite" meddling in Kurdistan both in private and anonymously in public; Ross was a friend of Layard. Layard to Canning, Dec. 9, 1842, LPBL, 38975 104; "The Levant Mail," *Morning Chronicle*, Sept. 5, 1843.

162. "Levant Mail."

163. Blomfield to Badger, Feb. 3, 1844, Blomfield Papers, FP 40 4.

CHAPTER EIGHT

Confining the
Sectarian Problem

SYRIA, KURDISTAN, FRANCE,
AND THE PORTE

THE MASSACRE OF Nestorian Christians in Kurdistan in July 1843, in the face of the negligence of the local Ottoman pasha, invited European public outrage. The Earl of Aberdeen, foreign secretary in Sir Robert Peel's Tory government, observed that "nothing indeed could be more calculated to indispose the feeling of European nations" towards the maintenance of the Ottoman Empire.[1] Here was another opportunity for French moral grandstanding in particular. It increased the risk that France would advocate a denominational, pro-Maronite strategy for Lebanon, the biggest unresolved problem in the Middle East. Both Kurdistan and Lebanon fell to Aberdeen and the Tory government of 1841–46 to tackle. The difficulty for Britain in both cases was to restrain French sectarianism on the one hand and Ottoman governing instincts on the other. This was a delicate balance. French pressure to protect local Christians derived its potency from the shortcomings of Ottoman government. These shortcomings also alienated the powerful local groups who needed to be involved in any solution. Britain, therefore, could not simply uphold the policy of the Porte in either region.

The British government and its Syrian consul-general Hugh Rose were aware that the Lebanese mountaineers were deeply suspicious of Ottoman central power and that they expected Britain to honour its past commitments to them. So the Foreign Office and Rose distanced themselves from the heavy-handed pro-Ottoman policy that the British embassy had tried to impose on

---

1. Aberdeen to Canning, Nov. 4, 1843, FO 78/2698.

Syria in 1840–41. It was they, much more than the embassy—now headed by Stratford Canning—who shaped British strategy in Lebanon. They helped to define the local compromise settlement that was agreed in 1846, but equally crucial here was the more emollient approach of Reshid, who returned as Ottoman foreign minister in October 1845. Ingrained suspicion of the Porte was also a great theme of politics in Kurdistan, where British influence was very limited. But then a second Nestorian massacre in 1846 put the Kurds beyond the pale, and made it both possible and necessary to help the Porte to try to check Kurdish disobedience. This was the policy of Canning and his local agent Henry Layard. It involved a marked change from the era of Claudius Rich; it also brought new problems.

What united British policy in both regions was a decisive repudiation of the sectarian approach that some Anglican figures at home had been urging in 1840–41. The temptation to build up a party among a particular religious community was to be avoided at all costs. Canning sent Layard to Kurdistan partly because he distrusted the religious bias of Britain's Chaldean consul in Mosul, Christian Rassam. The Foreign Office and Canning hoped to persuade France to dilute its sectarianism in Syria and Kurdistan in favour of a policy of cooperation. British officials continued to support the grievances of various oppressed religious minorities, but they were now careful to operate through Constantinople rather than against it, and to use the Tanzimat as the rationale for protecting civil rights throughout the empire.

Another example of British cooperation with the Porte was the achievement of protected *millet* status for the empire's Protestants, which was gained in two stages, in 1847 and 1850. In fact, the British embassy exaggerated its role in securing this outcome; it was part of a process by which the Porte extended *millet* status to nearly all Christian groups in the 1840s, including the Catholic communities of Syria and Mesopotamia. The extension of *millet*s had bureaucratic benefits for the regime. It also helped newly protected religious groups to safeguard their property and freedoms from assault by proselytisers—thus restricting the activities of Protestant as well as Catholic missionaries. As a result, Protestantism made few inroads; it remained confined to a very small number of scattered raya communities. Moreover, for various reasons, very little could be done for the Nestorians. So Roman Catholic interests remained strong in both Syria and Kurdistan, while the groups who looked to the British to take up their rights at Constantinople were non-Christian ones. These included the Druze and the Yazidi, and Palestinian Jews from Europe—a special case because in 1849 the Russians chose to hand them over to British protection. The upshot of all these changes was that the hopes nurtured by domestic religious opinion came to nothing: Britain was no more of a Christian power in the Middle East in 1850 than it had been in 1830.

Finding a Balance in Lebanon

It is often said that politics in Lebanon became divided on sectarian lines between Christians and Druze in the 1840s, and largely because of European power involvement.[2] Ozavci has argued, instead, that sectarianism was already apparent there and was exploited by local political actors.[3] The discussion of this issue is complicated by the fact that historians use the term "sectarianism" to mean subtly different things. However, the main aim of British policy was to check its operation in politically its most dangerous form; that is, the demand of some Maronite politicians and their French and Austrian supporters to turn Lebanon into a self-governing territory dominated by Christians. This preventative policy was successful, mainly because the Ottomans at Constantinople would not accept the French demand either. Even so, it took several years to achieve. The British applied sectarianism in a more limited sense, of discussing solutions for Lebanon primarily in terms of securing the safety of the various religious sects, but so did everyone else, in what was now a complex situation. This sectarianism was limited, among other things, by the continuing pressure to protect other objectives as well, especially the feudal powers of the social elites, which the intervention of 1840 had promised to guarantee. A general protection of sects' rights at law had two wider merits. It allowed the French to retreat gracefully from the untenable idea of Christian self-government, and it was compatible with the principles of the Tanzimat.

Britain's fear was that French public opinion would demand Christian-dominated self-government in Lebanon, in order to protect the Maronite Christians and to avenge France's humiliation in 1840. Austrians also had links with the Maronites and might join in. If Catholic Europe agitated for this outcome, Britain could rely on only Russian and Ottoman opposition to it. The Nestorian massacres (and the apostasy issue discussed in chapter 9) gave France and Austria more cause to make a public defence of Maronite and Catholic interests in Syria. In 1844 Nicolas Murad, archbishop of Laodicea, toured Europe to get support for the Maronite struggle.[4] In January 1845, and again in December 1845 and January 1846, Guizot, the French prime minister, and Metternich, for Austria, explicitly demanded the return of the Shihab

2. Farah, "Protestantism and British Diplomacy," and the subtler reading of Makdisi, *Culture of Sectarianism*, chap. 5. The latter account offers an impressive analysis of local politics, but its use of British evidence is selective, it is only occasionally interested in differentiating British and French motives (see p. 71), and the final stage of its argument requires it to focus on the activities of American missionaries rather than British agents. On page 62, it labels Wood's plan as sectarian—yet Wood was a fervent anti-sectarian.

3. Ozavci, *Dangerous Gifts*, chaps. 9–10, esp. 244.

4. See Hakim, *Lebanese National Idea*, 53–62.

family to provide a Christian amir over Lebanon.[5] Aberdeen removed British troops from Syria in late 1841 in the hope of preventing France from justifying a similar level of military involvement. As it was, the French sent warships to lie off Beirut in September 1842 and October 1845, giving the impression that they might intervene to protect the Maronites.

Britain's policy was shaped by what it thought the intervention of 1840 had been designed to restore: the traditional rights of the mountaineers. These were generally assumed to include deliverance from oppression and heavy taxation, the maintenance of landed property rights, and the right of tribes to bear arms. It was essential that Mount Lebanon should be governed "directly by rulers selected from among themselves, and not by Mahometan officers."[6] However, the Ottomans demanded the latter, not least in order to avoid French and Austrian interference (as well as British protection of the Druze, though that risk was diminishing). The mountaineers made clear that they would not tolerate direct Ottoman rule. The Porte had also failed to provide the compensation promised (by Wood) to various parties for damage done in the war, which led to embarrassing questions in the House of Commons about Britain's responsibility to those in need.[7]

Lebanese politics were fraught not just because of the risk of French and Austrian interference, but because Cairo and Constantinople had a tradition of exploiting local animosities. Mount Lebanon was no haven of peace before Western intervention. Amir Bashir Shihab had entrenched his dominance by killing a number of rivals and confiscating their property, some of which he had given to the Maronite Church to build up its power base. The removal of several rivals had left the Jumblatts as the dominant Druze family; Bashir Jumblatt had then challenged Amir Bashir, and fomented distrust of his increasingly overt Christianity. Jumblatt lost the struggle and was executed in 1825.[8] Bashir Shihab's position was further strengthened by Mehmet Ali's backing for him as a way into Syria. After the Egyptians took the country and confirmed Shihab rule on the mountain, the Jumblatt family leaders went into exile. When Bashir was removed in 1840, the Ottomans restored the family's lands, re-establishing them as major political players. This made tension between them and their largely Maronite tenants highly likely.[9] By 1841, most of the leading Druze families trusted neither the Shihabs nor the Maronite Church.

When the Ottomans removed the Shihabi Amir Bashir Qasim in January 1842 and imposed direct rule over the mountain, European opinion was

5. Canning to Aberdeen, Dec. 10, 1845, and Feb. 4, 1846, FO 78/603, 78/637.

6. Aberdeen to Canning, Oct. 24, 1842, FO 78/474.

7. Palmerston to Cowley, Dec. 7, 1846, FO 78/636.

8. Traboulsi, *History of Modern Lebanon*, 9–12.

9. Ozavci, *Dangerous Gifts*, 245–47.

appalled at this betrayal of the promises of 1840. There were many demands for another Shihab family representative to be appointed amir instead, to recognise the principle of Lebanese self-government. Napier, together with other naval officers, joined this campaign, adducing Turkish "fanaticism" against Christians. So did Canning on arriving at Constantinople, in conjunction with the other ambassadors.[10] By July 1842, however, Aberdeen and the British government had abandoned the Shihabs. It was clear, given the extent of Ottoman and Druze hostility to them, that none of them had the authority to unite and pacify Lebanon.[11]

Aberdeen instead supported a new plan, which had first emerged in the spring. This proposed self-government through power-sharing between Christians and Druze under nominal Ottoman sovereignty. The region would be divided into two geographical districts, the northern one governed by a Christian *kaymakam* and the southern one by a Druze. The European powers rallied around this proposal, and the Porte agreed to implement it in November, on condition that the Shihabs were ruled out as *kaymakam*s. The plan was attributed to many different authors; it was usually identified with Metternich, though in 1844 he turned against it for betraying Christian interests.[12] Wood, who disliked it on different grounds, as too sectarian, thought it was a plot of the current Russian-influenced anti-Tanzimat Ottoman government: it would allow the French and the Russians to meddle, leading to instability, but also thereby give the Ottomans an excuse to divide and rule.[13]

Consul-General Rose disagreed with Wood's view of it, arguing instead that it was sectarian only to the degree that was now necessary, as the Christians and Druze were already fundamentally opposed to each other. His claim was that the plan limited the degree of sectarianism, in particular by dividing the region geographically rather than by sect, so that many Maronite tenants in southern Lebanon would continue to be governed by Druze lords.[14] It thus helped the other objective of 1840, which was to secure elite landowner rights. For Rose, "the whole of Syria, particularly Lebanon, is feudal from Gaza to the Euphrates," and upholding those rights was essential in preventing both Ottoman interference and bloody conflict. From now on, Aberdeen, Rose, and Canning all urged a compromise along these lines, until it was adopted with modifications in May 1846. They agreed that the core priorities were to stop direct Ottoman rule, to give both Christians and Druze confidence that their

10. Canning to Aberdeen, Mar. 16 and June 9, 1842, FO 78/476, 78/478.

11. Aberdeen to Canning, July 21, 1842, FO 78/474.

12. Aberdeen to Canning, July 21, 1842, FO 78/474; Canning to Aberdeen, May 31, 1844, FO 78/557.

13. Wood to Canning, May 4, 1842, FO 78/498; to Aberdeen, Oct. 26, 1842, FO 78/499. For Wood's belief that Ottoman direct rule would benefit Russia, see also Wood to Rose, Aug. 25, 1845, FO 226/92.

14. Rose to Aberdeen, Nov. 4, 1842, FO 78/496.

rights were secure, and to protect the feudal rights of Druze lords over the southern Christians.[15]

As these principles were extremely difficult to reconcile, there was enormous scope for dissension. Until 1843, the Ottomans were very reluctant to abandon the idea of direct Muslim rule over at least part of Lebanon. The problem then became how to safeguard rights for Christians in the districts of mixed population. In 1843 a special, more sectarian, arrangement was agreed to secure Christian rights in the mixed town of Dayr al-Qamar. The Druze family that ruled over most Christians were the Jumblatts, so much of the discussion about the role of Druze elites in Christian areas revolved around the family's new leader, Numan's younger brother Said, whose status and reputation Maronites and Ottomans attacked. The Maronites increased their lobbying in 1844, and by 1845 Guizot was pressing for the Dayr al-Qamar arrangement to be extended to other mixed districts, at the expense of feudal principles.[16] Maronite disaffection led to another brief civil war in April–May 1845. This strengthened Guizot's hand to demand more rights for the Christians, and if possible the return of the Shihabs. The Ottomans used the same disorder to argue the case for more direct rule. They responded to the civil war by trying to disarm the mountain, leading to widespread accusations of their bad faith and underhand determination to take back control.[17] As late as February 1846, Guizot and Metternich were demanding the return of the Shihabs, and the Ottomans were vehemently refusing to consider it.

The final plan, proposed by Şekib, the commissioner sent to the area by the Porte, was agreed in stages in 1845–46. It preserved a geographical rather than sectarian partition into two regions, and the maintenance of notable feudal responsibility for law and order and revenues locally. In the southern division, representatives of the leading Druze landed families were put in charge of each of the five administrative districts. However, the sectarian principle was recognised by the appointment of a Christian *wakil* beneath them, charged with judicial and tax-collecting functions among his own people; he would also have a role in the determination of mixed judicial cases. If the two officials clashed, they could appeal to the *kaymakam*. There would also be an administrative council, which included a judge and an advisor for each of the Maronite, Druze, Sunni, Greek Orthodox, and Greek Catholic sects. This system certainly did not remove all tensions, but those that remained tended to

15. Rose to Aberdeen, Feb. 8, 1845, FO 78/618 81. For Wood's concern to secure the "wealth, influence and power" of the Druze elites, see Wood to Rose, Aug. 25, 1845, FO 226/92.

16. Rose to Aberdeen, Feb. 8, 1845, FO 78/618 81. For Rose's defence of Said Jumblatt, see Rose to Aberdeen, May 17, 1845, FO 78/618 285; to Canning, June 11 and July 30, 1845, FO 78/619.

17. Canning to Aberdeen, Nov. 5, 1845, FO 78/602.

be social or personal rather than sectarian, thus crucially limiting the scope for French and Austrian interference.[18]

Through these years, Britain and Russia had cooperated to oppose French and Austrian pressures for Shihabi restoration. One of the main benefits of the controversial Russian state visit to Britain in summer 1844 was that Aberdeen and Nesselrode agreed that Guizot and Metternich would not get their way over the Shihabs. This understanding continued into 1846.[19] Another key development was Reshid's return to power in Constantinople in December 1845. Reshid saw the need for a compromise between the Porte and the various European consuls, and smoothed the way for the acceptance of Şekib's blueprint.

So there was significant British tension with France over Syria in 1844–46 (paralleled by disputes in several other parts of the world, including Morocco and Greece, as Aberdeen's attempt at a French entente broke down). However, this disagreement was always kept within bounds. Britain's argument was that the settlement of 1845–46 gave France what it *should* want, because it offered the soundest approach to Maronite protection. Britain was trying to force France to adopt its own vision of joint pressure by the five powers to force the Ottomans to respect the principles of good government for all interest groups. When French consul Bourée complained to Rose that Maronites were being abandoned to Druze rule in southern Lebanon, he responded that, on the contrary, they were the best protected Christians anywhere in the Ottoman Empire, because they had *wakil*s locally to watch over their interests, plus five consuls in Beirut all on the lookout for any persecution of Christians, plus an Ottoman governor and garrison that could be pressed to intervene if necessary. Rose rejected French claims that the Amir Bashir had been a model Christian ruler: he had been "the Nero of the Levant," blinding people by torture with a hot iron.[20] He felt that the local strength of the Maronites gave France considerable influence, but that the Şekib plan ensured that the interests of the Ottoman pasha, the Druze, and the Maronites would all be held in a balance. Rose asserted that self-government by *kaymakam*s left the Ottomans with more authority than an attempt to impose a direct rule that they could not sustain.[21] Perhaps Reshid thought much the same.

18. See Traboulsi, *History of Modern Lebanon*, chap. 2. In 1852, Moore claimed that sectarian quarrels persisted in Dayr al-Qamar because the *wakil*s had not yet been appointed: Rose to Pisani, Aug. 28, 1852, FO 78/894.

19. See Aberdeen to Rose, July 8, 1844, FO 78/575; Aberdeen to Canning, Sept. 13, 1844, FO 78/553; Canning to Aberdeen, Apr. 4, 1846, FO 78/639. On April 3, 1847, Palmerston claimed that France was still trying to frustrate British policy in Syria: to Wellesley, FO 78/674. In February 1848, however, Cowley believed that France wanted to let the Syrian question "sink into oblivion" but that Rose was always keen to report French intrigues in order to show that he could defeat them: to Palmerston, Feb. 6, 1848, FO 78/727.

20. Rose to Aberdeen, Mar. 7, and to Canning, Mar. 25, 1844, FO 78/576.

21. Palmerston agreed with Rose on this last point: to Cowley, July 7, 1847, FO 78/675.

The settlement of 1846 was a complex compromise that gave something to all the contending forces. It was neither a surrender to, nor a victory over, sectarianism, which most of the participants claimed to want to limit.[22] Rose and Aberdeen, two oversensitive men, tussled over the credit for it.[23] The British were pleased at the securities that the Ottomans had been willing to grant to the various interests—for example, the principle that the evidence of Christian rayas would be recognised in criminal cases, unlike in most of the empire.[24] As a devout Christian himself, Rose was proud that he had the trust of Maronites, as well as Druze leaders and local Ottoman officials. He also knew that Britain had to stand well with those local Muslims who disliked central Ottoman rule.[25] He wanted to be a local powerbroker between all the parties, as the British army had tried to be in 1840–41. Practical self-government in Lebanon also gave him influence against Stratford Canning in Constantinople, a situation he exploited in 1849 when he was on leave in England and got Palmerston to tweak policy without even consulting Canning, to the latter's anger.[26]

After 1846, Syrian politics, as far as the European powers were concerned, mainly involved identifying and stopping attempts by the Porte to extend its direct powers.[27] At the 1847 election in Britain, Palmerston boasted how quiet Syria was, and that the intervention of 1840 had worked. In 1850, the post of consul-general was abolished as no longer necessary, and the Foreign Office moved Rose to be deputy to the Constantinople ambassador—again without consulting Canning.[28] To say that Canning was not pleased would be an understatement.

22. The British government's argument that Shihabi restoration was a front for French and Austrian sectarianism was not the only light in which the restoration plan could be viewed. In his novel *Tancred* (1847), Disraeli proposed Shihabi restoration and the maintenance of the French entente, on the ground that the Shihabs could best uphold the traditional feudal principles that were the only way of pacifying Mount Lebanon. He claimed that Peel, Aberdeen, and Rose had surrendered to sectarianism in accepting the new policy of 1842—as part of his wider attack on the anti-conservative nature of Peelite Conservatism. See Parry, "Disraeli," 578–80.

23. Aberdeen was so fearful that the settlement would not be agreed until after the Tories lost office that he upbraided Rose for not cooperating adequately with other powers, in a characteristically carping letter that crossed with Rose's triumphal announcement of his achievement in establishing it. On returning as foreign secretary, Palmerston delighted in reassuring the touchy Rose that his achievement was appreciated and that he should continue to stand up boldly for British interests. Aberdeen to Rose, Apr. 24, 1846, FO 78/657; Rose to Palmerston, Aug. 8, 1846, FO 78/659; Palmerston to Rose, Sept. 28, 1846, FO 78/657.

24. Tibawi, *Modern History of Syria*, 115.

25. Rose to Aberdeen, June 8, 1844, FO 78/577; to Canning, May 7, 1845, FO 78/598.

26. Lane-Poole, *Stratford Canning*, 2:129.

27. Canning, Apr. 20, 1850, and Apr. 19, 1852, FO 78/819, 78/891; Rose, Oct. 30, 1852, FO 78/894.

28. H. Temple, *Speech of Lord Viscount Palmerston*, 27. The consul-generalship was restored on the outbreak of the Crimean War, because of fears of renewed religious tension.

Persecution, Protestantism, and the Tanzimat

In late 1845, the Porte finally gave permission for the building of the Protestant church at Jerusalem that had been repeatedly obstructed since 1839. Construction was completed in 1849. This permission came after much pressure at home: a petition signed by Archbishop Howley, Bishop Blomfield, fourteen hundred clergy, and fifteen thousand laity was presented to the government by Ashley, now Lord Shaftesbury, in March 1845.[29] It is unlikely that this had any influence on the decision, which was almost certainly a reward for British support for Şekib's new Lebanon policy, which was being unveiled at the same time. In other words, it was a quid pro quo for consistent British opposition to French sectarianism (and, as noted below, to American missionary activity in Hasbaya). Likewise, in 1846, Consul Rawlinson in Baghdad worked with the Ottoman authorities to rein in London Jews' Society (LJS) activism there.[30]

Aberdeen led the way in abandoning the half-hearted British sectarian policy discussed in chapter 7, in favour of an alternative way of responding to requests from Christian raya communities for British assistance. Some of these groups expressed an interest in becoming Protestants, in return for British protection. On other occasions, Eastern Christians—Syrian Jacobites in particular—who were trying to preserve their religious independence asked for British support against Catholic missionary pressure to convert to Romanism. What should Britain do in such cases? Protestant missionaries naturally wanted to help the former, developing the policy that had briefly been tried out on the Druze in 1841. Aberdeen was opposed, feeling that to do so would embroil Britain deeply in local contentions and would annoy the other powers. Most of those who sought to convert to Protestantism were Orthodox Christians, so their defection might well anger Russia. Equally, befriending sects that claimed to be experiencing Catholic aggression ran the risk of upsetting France. Aberdeen was determined to try to smooth over relations between the five powers on this and everything else. However, he did not want to abandon these groups, on humanitarian grounds. He argued that Britain's task was to encourage the Porte to determine their fate itself, equitably.

Aberdeen first set out this position in early 1842 in response to petitions from the ancient Syrian Jacobite, or Monophysite, Church centred on Mardin and Mosul. As a result of Catholic missionary activity, a breakaway sect of Syrian Catholics had been formed in the late eighteenth century, based in Aleppo. It was now under French protection. In 1837, the French ambassador at Constantinople secured a firman authorising the Syrian Catholic Church to take possession of the four Syrian Jacobite churches in Mosul and physically divide them down the middle. This aggressive act was blamed on local

29. Lewis, *Origins of Christian Zionism*, 267.
30. Rawlinson to Wellesley, Nov. 23, 1846, FO 78/237 692, 698.

Catholic missionaries in Mosul trying to exploit Jacobite anxiety during the disorder in Kurdistan, by offering French protection to converts. Apparently, some of the Syrians were forced to accept the Catholic creed. The Porte issued a series of contradictory firmans about the churches. The idea of petitioning the British embassy came from Horatio Southgate, the American Episcopalian missionary who was keen to protect the ancient Syrian Church. In response, Aberdeen laid down firm instructions that Britain must not create an "English party" of Christians in this way; it would simply encourage other powers to defend their own denominational rights more intensively, and "the entire fabric of the Empire" would collapse. The Constantinople embassy should instead tell the Porte that if the empire wished to survive, it must treat "all its Christian subjects without distinction, with justice and moderation, and thereby endeavouring to attach to the rule of the Sultan that most valuable class of the population of the Empire." It must judge disputes between Christians impartially and humanely, and prevent the unsuccessful party in such disputes from being "exposed to imprisonment, banishment or confiscation of their property." Canning passed this message to Ottoman ministers several times, and told them not to be intimidated by foreign pressure.[31]

However, the message had limited effect, because—in Canning's eyes—the Porte continued to be willing to be bullied by both French and Russian pressure. In October 1843, he reported that though he had stopped the Catholics from getting the whole building, the Syrian churches in Damascus and Mosul remained partitioned, and that he did not have any weapons to match French influence over local Ottoman officials, which often took the form of bribes. This was doubly galling, since at this time the Porte was still refusing to allow the construction of the Protestant church at Jerusalem.[32]

In late 1843, a substantial portion of the Greek Orthodox community in Hasbaya, in the south of Lebanon, refused to pay the tax arrears demanded by the pasha of Damascus and his *mütesellim*. In early 1844, their leaders approached the Anglican bishop of Jerusalem and the American missionaries in Beirut to inquire if they would receive them as Protestants in return for paying these arrears. This request was refused by both, but the Americans wanted to use the opportunity to re-establish village schools, which they had operated there in the 1830s. In May 1844, Eli Smith claimed that one-third of the Greeks in Hasbaya genuinely sought conversion to Protestantism, on account of the spiritual neglect and oppression of their clergy. They had even abandoned swearing and drinking, showing their good faith. In July 1844, Orthodox priests applied force to try to compel the seceders to return. They were supported by the local Ottoman authorities, who were not keen for a new

31. Aberdeen to Canning, Jan. 22, 1842, FO 78/473 11; to Rose, Sept. 23, 1842, FO 78/493.

32. Canning to Aberdeen, Oct. 31, 1843, FO 78/522.

religious sect to emerge, and by Bazili, the Russian consul-general in Beirut, who claimed that Russia protected them.[33] Neither Rose nor Aberdeen was willing to encourage the Greeks to convert. During the Russian state visit to Britain in the summer of 1844, Aberdeen confirmed to Nesselrode that Britain would not support the "injudicious zeal" of the missionaries. For Aberdeen, this was a trade-off for Anglo-Russian cooperation in Lebanon against the French and Austrians. Aberdeen was also determined to prevent the Russians from escalating the crisis by claiming to protect all Greek Orthodox rayas in the empire.[34]

The difficulty came once the Hasbaya Protestants began to be attacked by their opponents. Gangs of young men assaulted them, and they were deprived of their jobs and driven out of their villages. For Rose, this was now a matter of civil rights: the British would intervene on behalf of any Syrian in a similar situation.[35] Wood, now consul in Damascus (under Rose), told his pasha, in whose territory Hasbaya was, to uphold the sultan's pledge under the Tanzimat that no Christians would be persecuted, and in July he did so. His local subordinates did not take the same view, or were unable to act on it. Wood therefore got the pasha to remove the local governor. The converts were allowed back to their homes, but the unrest continued, and in December they were stoned. The Hasbaya was unstable for other reasons: local Druze families as well as the Greeks raised issues about the composition and behaviour of the local authorities, and factionalism and mutual distrust became rife on all sides. Bazili continued to encourage the Greeks to stand firm, and hinted that British support for the Protestants might lead to the withdrawal of Russia's support over Lebanon.[36] The affair was getting completely out of hand. Moreover, Wood could not resist unleashing his arrogance of 1840 all over again: this was his chance to assert, as he had consistently done since being appointed to Damascus, that the Ottomans had made a commitment to Tanzimat-style government, but were turning a blind eye to local corruptions instead, encouraged by Russian influence.[37] Rose, now fearing that Wood was endangering the "great policy" of Lebanon settlement, tried to rein him in, and concentrated on persuading the Ottomans to agree that they had a

33. For this crisis, see Farah, "Protestantism and Politics," 325–32. For Eli Smith, see Rose to Aberdeen, June 10, 1844, and the enclosure, FO 78/577.

34. Aberdeen to Rose, Sept. 19 and Nov. 16, 1844, FO 78/575. Rose agreed, and had already voiced the same alarm about stirring up Russian sectarianism on behalf of the Orthodox: to Aberdeen, May 29, 1842, FO 78/495.

35. Rose to Canning, July 25, 1844, FO 78/577.

36. See Wood letters, Aug. 3 and Dec. 16 and 19, 1844, FO 78/579 168, 291, 289.

37. Wood to Aberdeen, Sept. 11, 1844, FO 78/579 234. Hence his periodic complaints against pashas of Damascus who continued the tax farming and corruption that he had hoped the Tanzimat would stamp out: see Wood to Aberdeen, Nov. 6, 1843, FO 78/538 252; Dec. 29, 1845, 78/622 236.

responsibility to prevent further oppression. He helped secure a settlement in February 1845 that restored peace on condition that the Protestants did not hold public meetings. Aberdeen reprimanded Wood by forwarding him Russian complaints that his support for the Protestants was excessive and was encouraging them to convert.[38] But he also arranged for the Russians to warn Bazili against too zealous a partisanship for the local Greeks. Aberdeen hoped that British and Russian consular agents would work together to press the Ottoman authorities to secure local order.[39] The Lebanese civil war then came to Hasbaya in April 1845, the missionaries abandoned it, and when Şekib arrived in 1846 he told them not to go back.

Meanwhile another crisis had arisen. In 1845 and early 1846, tensions grew up in Armenian communities in Constantinople, Trebizond, and Erzurum, stemming from the success of American Protestant missionaries in all three places in introducing Armenian laymen to closer Bible study. They reached the conclusion that elements of Armenian ritual were idolatrous. Though the missionaries insisted that they wanted their students to remain in the Armenian Church, the local priests excommunicated them. The latter also imposed civil penalties, including—according to reports—preventing the dissidents from conducting a trade, driving them from their homes, and mild torture. On one estimate, there were about a thousand of them (four hundred in Constantinople), but many thousands of other Armenians were secret adherents of Protestantism.[40] Canning saw the Armenian patriarch, and believed that he had persuaded him to stop the persecutions, though local reports persisted to the contrary. The patriarch declared anathema against the seceders. They declared themselves a separate Church, with the support of the American missionaries Dwight and Schauffler.[41]

The Armenian affair exposed the broader problem that most Christian raya sects in the empire were organised in their own *millet*s that gave their leaders—the patriarch in this case—great powers over potential dissidents in their "nation." They could imprison, fine, or exile individuals without the chance to seek redress from the Ottoman authorities. Individuals needed the permission of their sectarian corporations in order to engage in a trade.[42] There was

38. Rose to Wood, Nov. 30, 1844, FO 226/37; Aberdeen to Wood, Dec. 20, 1844, FO 78/579 55, and Feb. 20, 1845, 78/622 1.

39. Aberdeen to Canning, Dec. 20, 1844, FO 78/553; Aberdeen to Buchanan, Dec. 31, 1844, FO 65/297.

40. These are Alison's figures: he said there were 110,000 Armenians in Constantinople altogether: memo, Oct. 1846, FO 78/644. See also Layard to his mother, Sept. 17, 1845, LPBL, 58149 192.

41. For the affair, see Canning to Foreign Office, Mar. 18, May 17, and July 20, 1846, FO 78/638, 78/639, 78/641; Wellesley to Foreign Office, Oct. 10 and 19, 1846, plus missionary letter of Aug. 22, 1846, FO 78/644; *Missionary Herald* 42 (1846): 298–99.

42. See the preliminary note on *millet*s, p. xvi.

little incentive for any of these Christians to abandon their birth communities. Moreover, the Ottoman authorities had no interest in encouraging dissidents outside the *millet*s, as the Hasbaya affair had shown. So the British embassy decided to ask for the recognition of the Armenian Protestants as an independent community with its own spiritual head and an agent recognised at the Porte. This was on humanitarian grounds, though clearly there was a political benefit too: "the preponderating influence over the Christians now enjoyed by France and Russia . . . would thus be balanced and a check be given to the former's too active and widely organised schemes of proselytism and education."[43] In 1846 Ali Efendi, the Anglophile foreign minister at the Porte, agreed to the proposal that the Protestants should enjoy the same status as the Latins, with all their business with the Porte transacted through an appropriate official, who would also hear their grievances. Behind the scenes, however, Ali encountered resistance from other ministers and from wealthy Armenians, and got cold feet. He urged local pashas to safeguard Protestant communities suffering persecution, explicitly in order to avoid the need for a separate *millet*. In March 1847, Palmerston and Christian Bunsen, the Prussian ambassador to Britain, who had demanded a *millet* for Protestants in 1841, joined forces again to demand their official recognition as a sect with protected rights.[44]

In November, this was finally agreed, and the announcement letter was circulated to those provinces where small Protestant communities were known to exist. Wood used it to get official protection for the Protestants of Hasbaya, who now apparently numbered fifty, and who were still suffering persecution. Their case did not go well at first. The Muslim governor of Hasbaya told the three community leaders who asked for his intervention that he would cut their heads off if they did not return to the Orthodox religion. Wood had to get a second order from the pasha of Damascus. An evangelical Church was established locally, and the missionaries returned to preach. However, celebrations were premature, since it was soon discovered that the vizierial letter of protection applied only during the tenure of the governors who received it. By accident or design, the Protestants themselves had not been granted any chartered rights, so they had no body to liaise with their appointed Ottoman bureaucrat. Individual Armenian Protestants were still persecuted at Constantinople and Damascus, and the police seemed disinclined to intervene. These issues needed to be put right by a firman in 1850, which formally constituted the Protestants as a *millet*.[45]

43. Wellesley to Palmerston, Oct. 10, 1846, FO 78/644. Canning agreed: to Aberdeen, Mar. 18, 1846, FO 78/638.

44. Wellesley to Palmerston, Nov. 2, 1846, FO 78/645; Palmerston to Wellesley, Mar. 22, Apr. 3, and July 7, 1847, FO 78/673, 78/674, 78/675.

45. The papers are in "Correspondence Respecting the Condition of Protestants in Turkey," 89–90, 94–100. See Farah, "Protestantism and Politics," 333–34, though he assumes that the edict of 1847 was dictated by British pressure over Hasbaya.

Institutionalising Protestant Weakness

The establishment of a Protestant *millet* gave the American missionaries a small number of congregations throughout the empire, and a chance to preach without obstruction. However, it also underlined that any future conversions would be strictly voluntary. Each *millet* was able to complain if its members were subjected to aggressive proselytism, and the Orthodox and Latin ones were all very capable of protecting themselves. So there were few converts from those communities, and Protestantism made little headway in practice in the years before the Crimean War.

The strategic problems of the Church of England in the East were shown by the very limited success of the Jerusalem bishopric. For a start, the bishop was given no powers in the Protestant *millet*, which was structured as a lay body—as the embassy, the Americans, and the Porte all demanded. A new bishop, Samuel Gobat, was appointed in 1845, and quickly engendered renewed suspicion among the other Christian sects. As a Church Missionary Society (CMS) missionary with a twenty-year-long interest in proselytising among indigenous Christians, Gobat turned the bishopric in that direction, and away from the LJS's focus on the Jews. He argued that the social conditions for large-scale Jewish immigration were lacking, set his face against creating dependent pauper converts, and suggested that God would pursue restoration in his own time.

This produced a major rift with the new British consul in Jerusalem, James Finn, and his wife Elizabeth, who were prominent members of the LJS. The row between them continued for over a decade and was fought out in the sectarian British evangelical press, damaging them both. The small British community in Jerusalem became riven by "mutual most childish jealousies," as Holman Hunt put it.[46] But though this weakened Gobat's base, he was as unrestrained in his enthusiasm for making conversions among the Greek Orthodox rayas as Bishop Alexander had been among the Jews. He claimed that the restrictions on such activity were only Aberdeen's personal interpretation of the foundation agreement, and no reflection of the king of Prussia's vision.[47] He wanted to exploit local lay Greek Orthodox dissatisfaction with their priests, and started a school for one such seceding community at Nablus. Naturally, the Orthodox leaders protested; they got the school broken up in 1851, while a Roman Catholic crowd attacked another one at Nazareth in early 1852. Then local Greeks stormed the mission house at Nablus in November 1853 and drove out the Protestant converts. This indicated the local power of the Orthodox and Catholic

---

46. Jack, "No Heavenly Jerusalem," 192 (quotation); Gobat, *Life and Work*, 241–43. The final crisis after the war is covered well in "No Heavenly Jerusalem" (198–201), and in Eliav's *Britain and the Holy Land* (77–81).

47. Jack, "No Heavenly Jerusalem," 188.

communities. In 1853, by contrast, the congregation of the Protestant church at Jerusalem numbered thirty-four English adults, twenty-one Prussians, thirty-two converted Jews, and twenty Arab communicants.[48]

While Gobat pushed without much success in one direction, Finn took British policy in Palestine in a different one, back towards protecting the Jewish immigrants from eastern Europe. Russia had insisted on claiming them in 1839, largely because of suspicion at the creation of a British consulate at Jerusalem. However, they were never a priority; from 1847, Russia started to identify much more vigorously with Orthodox Church activity at Jerusalem instead. The Ashkenazi Jews who came to Palestine from Russian territory usually had only a twelve-month pilgrim's passport, which their government was reluctant to renew. Those who disobeyed pressure to return were in danger of being declared stateless, but as they were not rayas they could not expect protection by the local (Sephardi) *millet*. In 1848, Bazili willingly took up Finn's suggestion that Russian Jews in this situation could be placed under British protection if they refused to return to Russia. This outcome was agreed by the two governments, on condition that the British would accept only those who had a letter of dismissal from the Jewish rabbi Bardaki, the Russian *wakil*. By November 1849, three hundred families had come over, so that the British were protecting a considerable proportion of the population in Safed and Tiberias. The discussions did not go smoothly, because some in Bardaki's party regarded the arrangement as a plot by the Finns to facilitate Jewish conversions. Palmerston had to warn Finn not to use his position to sway their religious opinions, but he also attributed these complaints to a desire by Bardaki's followers to continue the "arbitrary and oppressive authority" that he had exercised over the Jews while under Russian protection.[49] With Britain's assistance, a long-standing dispute over tax demands on the Russian Jews at Safed whose houses had been destroyed in the 1837 earthquake was settled in their favour. Finn intervened in Hebron in 1852 to try to defend the protected Jews from oppressive taxation by the local Arab leader.[50] He and his associate John Meshullam, himself a converted Jew, both employed Jewish paupers on agricultural projects; this led to more allegations by the rabbis in 1853 that he was trying to bribe them to convert.[51] After the Crimean War, Finn came to regard his struggle to moderate the power of the rabbis' tribunals over protected Jews as a personal crusade, leading to a very strong rebuke from the Foreign Office in 1861.[52]

48. Tibawi, *British Interests in Palestine*, 109, 129, 131.

49. The extensive correspondence on this affair is in Hyamson, *British Consulate in Jerusalem*, 1:123–59. Palmerston's quotation is at 130–31.

50. Hyamson, *British Consulate in Jerusalem*, 1:148–49; J. Finn, *Stirring Times*, 1:248–60, 270.

51. Tibawi, *British Interests in Palestine*, 128–29.

52. J. Finn, *View from Jerusalem*, 313–15. For a balanced view of the struggle, see Eliav, *Britain and the Holy Land*, 76–77.

Gobat's behaviour, meanwhile, was condemned by a group of Anglo-Catholic clergymen in Britain who were trying to promote dialogue and eventual union between Anglicanism and Orthodoxy—a cause which they felt he was ruining. Led by John Mason Neale, who had published a two-volume history of the patriarchate of Alexandria in 1847, they complained to the archbishop of Canterbury twice, in 1850 and in 1853. By 1853, they were also clearly trying to dampen rampant press Russophobia. The Church hierarchy defended Gobat, somewhat half-heartedly, but the question of relations with other Churches—Lutheran or Orthodox—had clearly become very contentious within Anglicanism, mainly owing to the divisive impact of the Oxford Movement.[53]

Gobat blamed the British government for failing to support the interests of Protestantism in the region. In 1847, he complained to Rose that Britain's error "has been to consider the inhabitants of Syria as a *nation*, whilst there is no nationality, but only *sects*. This the French and Russians understand very well, and they both have their parties or sects."[54] The anti-British rhetoric of Gobat—who was, after all, a Swiss with close cultural ties to Prussia—made for an ever-more glacial relationship with the patriotic Finn, especially during the Crimean War.[55]

Gobat was of course right that Britain was not behaving like France and Russia: Palestine was witnessing increasing rivalry between Catholic and Orthodox religious missions. As early as 1844, Consul Young had noted that France and Russia had decided to assume "the Characters of Protectors of the Native Churches," and that Britain needed to keep out of this battle.[56] The Orthodox patriarch of Jerusalem had previously been based at Constantinople, but in 1845, Cyril II was elected by the monks of Jerusalem and moved there. He developed a strategy to reinvigorate the local Greek clergy and improve their spiritual effectiveness among their Arab coreligionists. Two years later, the papacy appointed Giuseppe Valerga Latin patriarch of Jerusalem, and he became the first resident Catholic bishop there since the Crusades. This escalation of local sectarian zeal was alarming on several grounds—not least to those who had followed the recent activities of Valerga in Kurdistan.

The Problem of Order in Kurdistan

The Nestorian massacre of 1843 revealed British local impotence. Stratford Canning lamented Kurdistan's remoteness from "any British settlement, or place accessible to British power."[57] Ottoman central authority over the mili-

---

53. Tibawi, *British Interests in Palestine*, 103–4; Gobat, *Life and Work*, 294–96; [Neale], *Documents*.

54. Gobat, *Life and Work*, 236–39 (quotation at 238).

55. Tibawi, *British Interests in Palestine*, 133–34.

56. Young to Canning, Jan. 8, 1844, FO 195/210 137.

57. Canning to Rassam, Sept. 28, 1843, FO 78/2698 74.

tant Kurdish tribes was notoriously weak, the pasha of Mosul had to cooperate with at least some of them in order to discipline others, and any hope of introducing the Tanzimat was a dream. All Canning could do was to ask the Porte to send an official commissioner to the region to ensure that the Nestorian prisoner-slaves were liberated, that the Kurds evacuated Nestorian country, that assistance was given to rebuild destroyed houses, and that the Nestorians were given legal protection. Kemal was selected for this mission. Canning sent his own commissioner to accompany him and keep him "steady." This was Richard White Stevens, since 1840 Britain's first vice-consul at Samsun on the Black Sea coast. Canning told Stevens that he must get the Ottomans to protect Mar Shimun and his people, but not offer British protection himself. In February 1844, Stevens reported that the value of property destroyed was 2.7 million Ottoman piastres and that three hundred women and children had been enslaved.[58] Bearing in mind the proximity of the Nestorians to the Persian border, and the need to reassure Persia, Stevens was also joined for a time by Francis Farrant, formerly a respected officer on the British military mission in Persia, and now a member of the Ottoman-Persian boundary commission.

Stevens and Farrant formed a noticeable British presence in Mosul. But one reason why this was necessary was that Christian Rassam, the existing consul there, was a Christian raya rather than a British subject. In 1839, it might have looked shrewd to appoint a Chaldean to the post, but his clear identification with the suffering Nestorians (he was still organising shelter and support for two hundred of them in early 1844) and his sometimes intemperate outbursts on the subject, weakened Ottoman and Kurdish respect for him. His financial affairs added to the difficulty: in order to operate as a merchant in Mosul, he had developed complex mutual funding arrangements with the pasha, Ince Bairaktar. After the latter's death in January 1844, his heirs relentlessly pursued the remaining debts. This became a messy saga that the Porte was able to use for years to compromise Rassam's independence of action. As a raya, he was also pursued by the authorities for various excess tax demands, which had the same result.[59] Farrant, moreover, was not above using racist language about Rassam. Canning later regarded Rassam's case as a "vicious example" of why rayas should not be British consuls.[60]

58. Canning to Aberdeen, Dec. 31, 1843, and to Stevens, Dec. 21, 1843, FO 78/2698; Stevens report, Feb. 24, 1844, FO 195/228 209.

59. For the early stages, see Rassam to Canning, Sept. 25, 1845, and Mar. 2, 1846, FO 195/228 535, 590. See Layard to Ross, Aug. 25, 1849, May 13, 1850, Mar. 18 and Apr. 28, 1851, LPBL, 38941, 38, 42, 50, 52.

60. For Farrant, see Botta to Layard, Feb. 12, 1849, LPBL, 58161 59. For Rawlinson's coolness to Rassam, see H. Ross, Letters from the East, 39. See Canning to Palmerston, Mar. 26, 1850, FO 78/818. The 1809 Anglo-Ottoman peace treaty had ruled out the appointment of Ottoman subjects as British consuls.

Rassam's status and religious fervour were not the only issues: the local pasha and Kurdish chiefs naturally resented a British commissioner's presence. If anything, it weakened Ottoman legitimacy; the Kurds used it as a reason not to cooperate, and in April they murdered the Jacobite Syrian patriarch at Jebel Tor as well. Stevens had arrived hoping that he could support Kemal in imposing order on the Kurds, but by June he realised that Bedir Khan Beg was the key local player. He went to interview him in the mountains, treated him with great respect, and extracted a promise not to molest more Christians.[61] In the autumn, brigandage was rife, and the Kurds retook the Amadiya fortress from the Ottomans. Once most of the slaves were liberated, and after Bedir Khan Beg made more promises of good behaviour, the Ottomans withdrew Kemal's mission at the end of 1844—without securing reparations for the Nestorians' property, let alone any formal protection. Stevens naturally had to withdraw with him. The Porte had accepted the reality of Kurd power, and the unpopularity of continuing Anglo-French meddling.[62] Kurdish self-government offered lower taxes and better order than the pasha of Mosul could do. The new pasha, Kiritli, sent in early 1845, did not improve matters: he announced his arrival by "strangling the three principal men of the town." He evaded consuls' visits, made Bedir Khan Beg lavish presents, oppressed farmers with tax demands, and seemed to be "an improved edition of Nero," with one eye and one ear.[63]

Another problem was French local behaviour. Canning was convinced that French complaints to the Porte about Stevens's mission had contributed to its termination.[64] The French seemed to regard Kurdistan as their rightful province, because of the strength of the Chaldean and Syrian Catholic Churches; they had intervened to liberate Syrian Jacobites enslaved by Kurds during a military battle over Rawanduz in the mid-1830s.[65] They could offer the Nestorians sectarian protection, as they were doing with the Maronites in Lebanon in 1844. The price seemed certain to be conversion to Catholicism. The charitable aid that the French consul Paul-Émile Botta was sending was coming through the Chaldean Catholic Church.[66] In June 1844, Giuseppe Valerga, a delegate from the Propaganda Fide and assistant to the Catholic bishop of

61. Stevens to Canning, Mar. 8, 1844, FO 195/228 215; Rassam to Canning, Apr. 6, 1844, FO 195/228 116; Stevens report on Bedir Khan Beg, July 10, 1844, FO 78/2698.

62. Stevens to Canning, Nov. 17, 1844, and Feb. 25, 1845, FO 195/228 343, 370; Canning to Aberdeen, Jan. 30, 1845, FO 78/2699.

63. The comments are Layard's: to his mother, Nov. 3, 1845, LPBL, 58149 199; to his aunt, Nov. 13, 1845, LPBL, 58154 139. See also Stevens to Canning, Mar. 8, 1845, FO 195/228 372. On Kurdish government effectiveness, see Shields, *Mosul before Iraq*, 53.

64. Canning to Aberdeen, Dec. 3, 1844, FO 78/564, and Jan. 30, 1845, FO 78/2699.

65. Rassam to Canning, Aug. 27, 1843, FO 195/228 28.

66. Rassam to Canning, Dec. 18, 1843, and July 26, 1844, FO 195/228 66, 152; Layard to his mother, Feb. 17, 1844, LPBL, 58149 139.

Baghdad, arrived at Mosul. His purpose was to open an extension to the Italian Dominican mission that had been stationed there for a century: an extra house had been bought by the dragoman of the French consulate for the purpose.

The populace created a storm of protest, as rumours circulated that the house was not only a forbidden church but also contained weapons with which the Muslims would be subjugated. As with Grant's schoolhouse at Ashitha, the assumption was that Franks were coming to take over. The townspeople tore down the house to chants of "Allah Akbar" and stoned Botta and Valerga in the street; Valerga was also attacked with a knife. The incident led to recrimination between the French—who blamed Kemal for inadequate military support and the ulema for inciting the people—and the Ottomans, who criticised Botta and Valerga for inflammatory behaviour.[67] The French ambassador at Constantinople demanded recompense: he insisted that the qadi and ulema should be brought for trial at Constantinople. His behaviour reminded Canning of the counterproductive "overbearing spirit" that the French were showing in Syria.[68] (The French ambassador had also behaved in the same way in defending the rash act of his consul in Jerusalem, de Lantivy, in insisting on flying the tricolour there, even though a protesting crowd tore it down.) However, Valerga was not the only incendiary religious figure in Mosul. Just before the incident, the Society for Promoting Christian Knowledge (SPCK) missionary George Percy Badger was still there, staying with Rassam. He was inciting him to take a stand for Christianity—for example, over a Nestorian slave girl who had converted to Islam, despite the fact that Britain had no rights of protection over the girl. Stevens, sure that Badger's "religious party feeling" was damaging Britain's standing, got him to go home.[69]

In June 1844, Canning told Rassam that this "sectarian rivalry" and "spiritual warfare" between the British and French must stop. Instead, both countries' agents should pursue "a system of mutual forbearance, [and] direct their entire efforts to the encouragement of a good understanding and loyal confidence between the various classes of the Sultan's subjects and their common government."[70] As in Syria, the only way that Britain could do any good was by avoiding sectarianism and trying to work with France to force the Ottomans to impose better government for all. However, once Stevens had withdrawn, it was not clear how Britain could get enough local influence to do this. The answer emerged serendipitously.

Henry Layard was twenty-five when he arrived in Constantinople in 1842 after nearly three years of adventurous wandering around the Ottoman and

67. See the accounts of Rassam, to Canning, June 30, 1844, FO 195/228 145, and of H. Ross, *Letters from the East*, 23–25 (misdated).

68. Canning to Aberdeen, Aug. 1, 1844, FO 78/560.

69. Stevens to Canning, May 5, 1844, FO 195/228 244.

70. Canning to Rassam, June 20, 1844, FO 78/2698.

Persian Middle East, much of it spent with the Bakhtiari tribe in Khuzistan, in south-west Persia. Desperate to avoid returning to life as a trainee lawyer in London, he stayed there and made himself useful to Canning, who quickly came to value his enterprise, his intelligence, and his willingness to share his own conspiracy theories about Britain's many enemies in and beyond the city. He undertook undercover missions for Canning, and publicised the embassy line in several newspapers, which also gave him an income. He wanted a diplomatic job: "the East offers an ambitious man a vast field."[71] Yet he lacked connections; vacancies always seemed to be filled by young men of political or social rank. In 1844 and 1845, Canning made various attempts to persuade the Foreign Office to make him an attaché. While the last of these was being considered, Canning decided to send Layard to Mosul for a few months, supported by himself.

This was not just to kill time, but also because the attaché role could be justified for Layard only in relation to the work of the Ottoman-Persian boundary commission, which would shortly begin in earnest, if the two sides could be persuaded to sign a treaty (see chapter 10). Canning hoped that Layard would improve his credentials by gathering more local information about Kurdistan. Layard had had the idea of digging into the enormous mounds just to the east and south of Mosul that were widely believed to contain what was left of the ancient Assyrian city of Nineveh. He had seen them on two visits to Mosul in 1840 and 1842. On the second, he had met Botta, who had just arrived as French consul, despite the lack of French commerce there. The French had justified his posting by arranging for him to excavate a similar mound at Khorsabad just north of the town. Layard got on well with Botta, who sent him impressive information about his discoveries, which Layard publicised in the *Malta Times* in early 1845.[72] So Layard's excavation project was designed to achieve several objects, including the subtle increase of Western presence locally and the promotion of Anglo-French cooperation. But it would last only a few months: Canning told him to cultivate goodwill with the local pasha, to keep clear of contentious questions, and to disguise his connections with the embassy.[73]

This short-term arrangement succeeded better, and had more consequences, than either Canning or Layard could have expected. This was despite the fact that the Foreign Office declined to make Layard an attaché; his previous connections with the Bakhtiari made it too risky to have him negotiate with the Persians.[74] Within a few weeks of starting to dig, Layard made major

71. Layard to Mitford, Aug. 12, 1842, LPBL, 58159 6.
72. See the articles of Jan. 21 and Feb. 11, 1845, in LPBL, 58174 (scrapbook).
73. Canning to Layard, Oct. 9, 1845, LPBL, 38976 231.
74. Aberdeen to Canning, Oct. 7, 1845, FO 78/593.

archaeological discoveries, soon outstripping anything that Botta had found. By March 1846, he had unearthed the remnants of several palace walls containing spectacular bas-reliefs depicting battle scenes from ancient Assyria, and some pairs of enormous winged bulls and lions standing guard at the entrance to state rooms. So there seemed every incentive for him to stay in Mosul in the longer term. Canning, his funder, became excited to think of the antiquarian fame that his assistant would bring him. Another of his protégés, Charles Alison, was in Bodrum supervising the acquisition for Britain of reliefs from the Temple of Halicarnassus, one of the wonders of the ancient world. In 1846, Canning expected that, when they arrived at the British Museum, they would throw the great political crisis of the day, the repeal of the corn laws, "into the shade."[75] With the Assyrian sculptures as well, Canning's fame would surely eclipse that of his predecessor, Lord Elgin.

Meanwhile Layard's presence in Mosul seemed to be helping to pacify the situation. Through the two winters of 1845 and 1846, he kept large numbers of Nestorians from destitution by employing them on the excavations; they were organised by his indefatigable helper, Rassam's young brother Hormuzd. As the weather improved and they went back to work their fields, he relied more on the local Arab tribes.[76] He also continued his intellectual cooperation with Botta. Their rivalry can easily be exaggerated, since in 1846 Canning and Layard needed to get vizierial permission to excavate, which involved demolishing France's claim that its excavation rights extended to all the local mounds. Then they had to secure official funding from the British Museum for the continuation of the project to the summer of 1847, which required them to exploit national embarrassment that Botta's state funding was so much more lavish. Botta had a similar friendly ambivalence: a friend of both men remarked that his occasional jibes about "la perfide Albion . . . entirely depend on how much opium he has taken."[77]

In 1846, the prospects for effective political activity in Kurdistan also improved. After Reshid's return to power at Constantinople in late 1845, Canning became confident that he could get the Porte to impose a better solution locally. Kiritli was immediately dismissed: his greedy tax demands had damaged Mosul's agricultural productivity. Rassam and Layard hoped for the return of all the refugees to their valleys, the abolition of tax farming, a tax holiday from Constantinople, and the implementation of the Tanzimat.[78] Tayyar, an old friend of Reshid's, arrived as pasha in May 1846, promised equitable

75. Lane-Poole, *Stratford Canning*, 2:148.

76. Layard, *Nineveh and Its Remains*, 1:331–33.

77. H. Ross, *Letters from the East*, 23. The best account of their friendship is in Larsen's *Conquest of Assyria*.

78. Rassam to Canning, Aug. 10 and Nov. 20, 1846, FO 195/228 661, 699. Layard to Canning, Mar. 8, 1846, LPBL, 58159 55.

taxation, and talked the right language about agricultural improvement and Christian-Kurd cooperation. The local Muslim religious leaders had managed to stop Layard's excavations three times, but Tayyar supported him against them—even when one of them called him a "dog" and Layard hit him with his stick. "With one blow I cut thro' his enormous turban and laid his head open"—but Layard still came to no harm. Canning's young agent also met Suffuq, the leader of the great Shammar tribe of Arabs, and proposed that he be allowed to levy a fixed tax per head in return for guaranteeing the safety of all travellers through his territories.[79] Added to the astonishing scale of his discoveries on site, everything seemed to be going very well.

The major problem remained the tensions between the Nestorians and the Kurds. It was no secret that Bedir Khan Beg was preparing another attack on the Christians in the Tekhoma, having taken over the neighbouring district. He talked the language of jihad and was rumoured to have become a dervish.[80] In September 1846, Tayyar made a trip to the Nestorian areas and invited Layard to accompany him. Layard never subsequently explained why he was invited, but he seems to have intended a fact-finding mission to a region that had long interested him, a check on the progress of resettlement, and a signal that Britain supported the attempts that Tayyar was making to smooth tensions. He saw signs of intermittent prosperity, but was appalled by continuing destitution in valleys subject to Kurdish oppression, where the sultan's order to exempt them from taxation was being ignored. Nonetheless, he hoped that Tayyar's visit and his support had done some good—and might save the Nestorians from "the impending danger."[81]

This was not the case. Bedir Khan Beg attacked the Tekhoma a few days later. Over five hundred Nestorians were killed; menacing tax demands forced many others to leave for Persia. One reason for the death toll was that Bedir Khan Beg said that he did not want to take slaves again, because it gave European consuls and Turks the chance to interfere.[82] Tayyar had failed. A few weeks later, he was on another expedition with his soldiers when they twice disobeyed his guidance and plundered rich Arab tribes, one of which was outside his jurisdiction. He fell ill in camp and bled to death when his bandages mysteriously fell off in the night. It seemed that the Ottoman troops had had enough of his peace-mongering. His detractors did not mourn for the "infidel."[83]

79. Layard to his uncle, June 1, 1846, LPBL, 58154 155; to Canning, Apr. 6, 1846, LPBL, 58159 62.

80. Rassam to Wellesley, Sept. 19, 1846, FO 195/228 671.

81. Layard to his mother and his aunt, both Oct. 5, 1846, LPBL, 58150 25, 58154 167.

82. Rassam to Wellesley, Sept 19 and Nov. 16, 1846, FO 78/2699; Badger, *Nestorians and Their Rituals*, 1:370–71.

83. Rassam to Rawlinson, Dec. 3, 1846, FO 195/228 706; to Wellesley, Dec. 26, 1846, FO 195/228 714.

Britain, France, and Religious
Protection in the New Kurdistan

The second Nestorian massacre brought matters to a head. Palmerston, now foreign secretary again, bluntly told the Porte that "a general feeling of disgust and indignation will extend from one end of Europe to the other," against the government that allowed its Christians to be attacked in this way with impunity.[84] The ambassadors at Constantinople all made it clear that the Kurds would have to be subjugated. Even so, it took time for the Porte to assemble the necessary expedition, and by the time it set off most Nestorians had abandoned the mountains for Persia or Mosul. Bedir Khan Beg refused demands to surrender, and in June 1847 decided on war with the Ottomans, but most of his allies melted away and made their own arrangements with the regime. He capitulated in July, was exiled in some comfort to Crete, received an official salary, continued to collect revenue from his lands, and lived for twenty more years. Among his ninety-nine reputed children were Ottoman officials and several of the leading Kurdish nationalists of the early twentieth century.[85]

The British embassy advocated bringing Kurdistan under Ottoman control. Layard wrote a long memorandum to that effect, from which Reshid claimed to have profited. It argued for a new local authority in the Kurdish mountains, with military powers and two regiments at its disposal, until it made the area loyal to the sultan. It should have the authority to punish flagrant crimes immediately; it should build roads to open up the mountains; it should investigate its mines and other resources; it should introduce the Tanzimat. No Kurdish chief should retain any local power: they were all inveterately hostile to Ottoman authority, and fanatically hostile to the Nestorians, as the second massacre had shown.[86] In December, the Porte did indeed create a major new *eyalet* covering Kurdistan, with substantial powers, under Esad Pasha. The Mosul pashalik was reduced in size and transferred to its superintendence, away from Baghdad. The Tanzimat was to be introduced into the whole region, and the powers of local Kurdish chiefs greatly reduced. Kurdistan survived as a separate *eyalet* until 1867.[87]

Unfortunately, it was not long before British observers became critical of the gap between aspiration and reality. Rawlinson in Baghdad thought Esad "a mere old woman." By August, Rassam was pointing to the Ottomans' failure

84. Palmerston to Wellesley, Jan. 6, 1847, FO 78/2699.

85. Ateş, *Ottoman-Iranian Borderlands*, 83.

86. Layard memo, n.d., and Cowley to Palmerston, Oct. 17, 1847, FO 78/2699. For Reshid's praise, see Cowley to Palmerston, Dec. 2, 1847, FO 78/689. Layard plainly disliked Kurdish arrogance and greed: see *Nineveh and Its Remains*, 1:73–77, 206–9.

87. It is worth noting that a document in the Ottoman archives had already proposed the establishment of a Kurdistan *eyalet* in 1846, if the dating is correct: see Özoğlu, *Kurdish Notables*, 60–61.

to redress several examples of oppression of Jacobites and other Christians. "What can be expected when the Porte bestows such a vast extent of country on a man whose mental and bodily faculties are so impaired by age as to render him fit for nothing . . . but to sit in his study composing poetry . . . , leaving the administration of his Pashalic in the hands of his Greek slaves." The new pasha of Mosul, Vecihi, who had won popularity by abolishing monopolies and implementing the tithe system for agriculture, was annoyed that the restructuring deprived him of the Kurdish centre of Jazirat (Cizre), which he felt he could have governed better than Esad.[88] But Vecihi's reduced taxation annoyed his *defterdar*, and he was quickly replaced by Ashkar Ali, who increased it. Rassam, never charitable in his judgments, considered Ashkar Ali stupid, lazy, and "more fit for a Dervish"; nor, he suggested, could he control the Kurds. In turn, Ashkar Ali and his *defterdar* were quickly removed, in the summer of 1849.[89] The pattern—unpredictable taxation policy by officials, complaints about their greed by European consuls, a frequent turnover, but no fundamental change—seemed all too familiar. By 1850, it was difficult to detect improvement, certainly around Mosul where Layard, now on his second digging expedition, was infuriated by the many obstacles to transport and security. He also noted that Turkish misgovernment in the mountains was so bad that most locals would now prefer Kurdish rule.[90] The Kurds were in rebellion against tax demands, while in 1854 there was major unrest in the town, caused by taxes and factional instability. The only remedy that occurred to Britain was to set up a new consulate at Diyarbekir in the new *eyalet*, to monitor the pasha of Kurdistan, to develop its commercial potential, and to secure the rights of its Armenian Protestant community. This was done in 1852.[91]

By 1850, British observers were uncomfortably aware that the authority protecting the Christians of Kurdistan was not a strong Ottoman administration upholding the Tanzimat, but France and the Catholic Church. The Catholics had greatly extended their influence in Kurdistan, mainly through their own missionary efforts, but assisted by the prolonged insecurity of the Nestorians. The papacy had been reaching out to the twenty thousand or so Chaldean Catholics since 1830, when their leader Yohannan Hormizd had been raised to the status of patriarch so that his Church could enjoy full communion with Rome. The major step forward came in 1837 when Laurent Trioche, already familiar with local circumstances as diocesan administrator,

88. Rawlinson to Layard, Jan. 28, 1848, LPBL, 38978 23; Rassam to Canning, Aug. 6 and 21 and Oct. 16, 1848, FO 195/301 307, 312, 321.

89. Rassam to Canning, Dec. 23, 1848, Jan. 22, May 28, and June 25, 1849, FO 195/301 333, 343 (quotation), 382, 384.

90. Layard to Ross, Sept. 2, 1850, LPBL, 38941 44.

91. Rawlinson to Canning, Apr. 25, 1849, and Dec. 29, 1851, FO 78/775, 78/890. W. R. Holmes was appointed there. On the rebellion of 1854, see Shields, *Mosul before Iraq*, 86–87.

was appointed bishop of Baghdad and apostolic delegate to the Chaldeans, and toured the Mosul region to make overtures to them. Trioche supported Mar Zeya's side in the split in the Chaldean Church that followed Yohannan's death. This was partly in order to end the principle of selection through particular families, but also because he seemed the best hope of implementing Westernising liturgical changes. By 1844, Trioche and Mar Zeya had seen off the threat from Yohannan's nephew Mar Elia (the alternative candidate, who enjoyed Badger's support). However, once this had happened, Zeya declined to support Westernising the liturgy. A group of Chaldean bishops and monks, who had always been opposed to him, united with Trioche to drive him out as patriarch in 1846. Trioche supported the election of one of them as his successor, but throughout 1846 and 1847 this was bitterly opposed by many Chaldeans in Mosul and Diyarbekir. The Porte claimed to support their opposition, demanding that the Church should elect a patriarch more acceptable to local congregations. Ottoman ministers at the Porte told the British embassy several times that they would not tolerate this French assertiveness. In January 1848, Trioche left for Rome. He appeared to have been defeated.

However, by the end of the year he was back, promoted to archbishop of Baghdad; moreover the pope confirmed the election of his candidate as Chaldean patriarch, as Joseph VI Audo, and the Porte made no further objection. All this indicated how much the Catholic Church benefited from French diplomatic support. Rassam complained that the local pashas were too weak in the face of French power at Mosul (which he thought depended on abuse of the protection system—he counted sixty-three locals in receipt of it). Trioche's main concern was to integrate the Chaldean Church into the global Catholic community and to encourage doctrinal uniformity. This was no easy matter, however. During his long reign, Joseph VI Audo himself was to become an increasingly keen defender of Chaldean religious traditions against Westernising pressures.[92]

The main reason why the Chaldean Church was able to strengthen its appeal to Nestorian refugees was because in 1844 it secured *millet* status at Constantinople—owing, it appears, to work by Botta, Trioche, and Mar Zeya. The Porte recognised its right to manage its administrative affairs and to protect its members against persecution and oppression. It also recognised Mar Zeya as patriarch, a great blow to Mar Elia. The Porte gave the same status to the converts from the Syrian Church.[93] This was a notable victory for the French—the more so given that the Porte was still resisting the idea

92. For these two paragraphs, see Filoni, *Church in Iraq*, 68–73; Badger, *Nestorians and Their Rituals*, 1:161–72. There are many letters from Rassam to Canning on this dispute: see, e.g., Apr. 17, 1848, FO 195/301 274, on Esad's timidity in face of the French, and Jan. 22, 1849, FO 195/301 343, on the protégés. Cowley and Canning also wrote frequently about it to Palmerston: e.g., on Ali Efendi's commitment, see Sept. 3, 1847, FO 78/686.

93. Filoni, *Church in Iraq*, 68.

of a Protestant *millet*. The status was given in response to Kurdish attacks on all the local Christians, but it was a major defeat for the Nestorians—and for Badger and Rassam, who had argued that the Nestorians were the historic religious grouping and the Chaldeans mere seceders from it.[94] The Chaldeans' new status made it much more attractive for Nestorians fleeing to Mosul to change their allegiance. Those who emigrated to Persia also encountered active French missionaries. Two Lazarists built a chapel in Urmia in spring 1843, and then Giuseppe Valerga, Trioche's assistant, settled near Salmas. The missionaries opened a seminary for the education of future Chaldean priests, which offered apostolic teaching reassuring Nestorians of the doctrinal soundness of the Chaldean Church.[95] Valerga's missionary work in the Middle East must have impressed the right people at Rome; his appointment as patriarch at Jerusalem followed swiftly.

In contrast, the British could not make headway with the Nestorians. Mar Shimun was naturally frustrated by the inability of any foreigners to provide practical help to his people. Rassam tried to keep him in Mosul, but he escaped twice, apparently fearing that Britain would send him to Constantinople. His refusal to trust the Ottomans made the latter unwilling to recognise his patriarchal status. Between 1847 and 1849 he was in Urmia, but he fell out with the American missionaries there who converted some of his aides; he felt they were undermining his authority. Rassam and Badger both continued to hope for another Anglican mission, and Rassam wrote home to encourage this in January 1848. The CMS sent John Bowen to the region on an investigation, but it was decided not to interfere with the Americans in Urmia, under whose aegis an independent Protestant Nestorian Church was formed in the 1850s. Even the Americans decided against another mission to the mountain districts, while, in search of religious allies, Mar Shimun's right-hand man now reached out to the Russians. During his visit to Hakkari in 1850, Layard sorrowfully recorded the continuing privations of Nestorian farmers betrayed by Ottoman promises of tax relief, but concluded that nothing could be done for them.[96]

Other visitors took the view that this rump of warmongering mountaineers had limited appeal. Henry Ross felt their aggressive behaviour had brought their troubles on their own heads; Felix Jones found them more abrasive and unwelcoming than local Muslims. Justin Sheil, Britain's minister in Persia, had never liked them, thinking them untrustworthy, mercenary, and intolerant; Mar Shimun was a "downright pope."[97] Western fantasies about the

---

94. Rassam to Canning, Dec. 18, 1843, FO 195/228 66.

95. O'Flynn, *Western Christian Presence*, 724–25, 734, 737, 755.

96. O'Flynn, 628–30, 637–38; Layard, *Discoveries in the Ruins*, 378–79, 406–7, 424–30; Guest, *Survival among the Kurds*, 112.

97. H. Ross, *Letters from the East*, 82; J. Jones, *Memoirs*, 469–70 (he might equally have meant the Chaldeans); Sheil, *Glimpses of Life and Manners*, 348–56.

Nestorians' evangelising potential had been exploded. Nor could they be refashioned into an advance guard for global Church reunification, as Badger's mentor, the Oxford don William Palmer, had hoped. Hormuzd Rassam visited Oxford in 1848 with Layard, and Palmer tried to inculcate in him the same patristic enthusiasms that he had tried on his brother a decade earlier. Hormuzd took his instruction in early church doctrines seriously, but Layard was relieved to see that, once back in Mosul, he had jettisoned his concordance and was flirting with the Arab girls.[98] The policy of British religious sectarianism was truly dead. The British came tacitly to accept that the Christian world in Kurdistan was an area of French dominance, American missionary pockets, and British near-irrelevance—but that this hardly mattered. Layard, for example, had a generalised concern for the peoples of northern Iraq, and a lifelong friendship with Hormuzd Rassam, but seems instinctively to have preferred dealing with Arabs over Nestorians. In 1847, he was employing as excavators two hundred Arab families from tractable local tribes, who gave him a "Cadi's power" to settle their disputes. He revelled in the opportunity to act as a better protector of their women than the local Ottoman rulers could: he claimed to have stopped domestic beatings, arranged amicable divorces, and prevented abduction by eager young men (by raising the market rate to twenty sheep). It might seem "curious," he observed, that they appealed to a Christian, but "they find it cheaper, as they have neither to give a bribe or pay fees." In the evening, they all danced to the pipe and drum.[99]

The greatest British success in Kurdistan came not with a Christian sect, but with the Yazidi. As a heterodox religious minority, judged not to be a people of the book, the Yazidi had no protection at all from the Kurds or the Ottoman authorities, and had been attacked several times. In 1842, the Mosul pasha Bairaktar had raided their territory after demanding exorbitant sums from them, and "the head of the Chief with sixty pair of human ears were brought to Mosul and suspended at the River Gate for a whole day."[100] Their reputation as devil-worshippers attracted Western curiosity.[101] In 1846, Layard became the first foreigner invited to witness the religious highlight of the Yazidi year, the seven-day Feast of the Assembly at Lalish, because Christian Rassam had freed the Yazidi chief's deputy from imprisonment at Mosul for communal

---

98. Layard to Ross, May 19, 1848, LPBL, 38978 87 (on Palmer as "one of those queer chaps who ought long ago to have been pitched into the Propaganda at Rome"), and to his mother, Nov. 24, 1849, LPBL, 58150 115.

99. See Layard, *Nineveh and Its Remains*, 1:121, 354–65, 2:146–49; Layard to his aunt, July 27, 1846, LPBL, 58154 159 (for the quotations), and to Cecilia Berkeley, June 14, 1847, LPBL, 58165 40. Oddly, Shawn Malley claims that Layard's plan for Arab agricultural settlement was "frankly brutal": *From Archaeology to Spectacle*, 40.

100. Rassam to Taylor, Dec. 19, 1842, FO 195/204 124.

101. Fletcher, *Notes from Nineveh*, 226, 242–43; Grant in Guest, *Survival among the Kurds*, 88.

non-payment of tax. Whereas they were reputed by Muslims and missionaries to enjoy debauchery, Layard found them moral, quiet, inoffensive, and hospitable. In fact, he thought that by sitting with the Yazidi around their camp fires and hearing their traditional stories, the traveller would get a better understanding of "Holy Writ." He contrasted them with the dogmatic qadi who was responsible for a new attack on them, which he saw as a deliberate strategy to excite sectarian animosities. Layard hoped that the imposition of the Porte's direct authority in Kurdistan would remove these reactionary influences.[102]

Instead, the first consequence was to threaten them with military service, because the authorities argued that they were liable for conscription into the Ottoman army. Several aspects of military service clashed with their religious observances—such as the requirement to take a weekly bath with Muslims, to wear blue, and to eat the standard food rations. Local governors had also continued to oppress them with heavy tax demands and, apparently, by taking children as slaves. With Rassam's support, the Yazidi chief sent representatives to Constantinople to complain about these oppressions. When Layard returned there from England, he persuaded Canning to take up the Yazidi cause. In mid-1849, the government issued a firman acknowledging their legal status, with distinct civil rights under the Tanzimat. Illegal taxation and child slavery were prohibited, and assurances were given about their treatment if they were required for the army. Layard also procured an order for the restitution of the alms lost during the tensions of 1846–47. He then travelled to Mosul with the Yazidi negotiators. South of Bitlis, at the village of Koshana, the whole population turned out to meet them, dressed in white with leaves and flowers in their turbans. By the time they reached Redwan, they had acquired a cavalcade of followers: men on horseback with firearms, musicians with drums and pipes, priests and children. As Layard descended from his horse, two sheep were slain in front of him. Raki circulated freely and dancing continued all night. Then he was privileged to view and sketch the *sanjak*, the emblem of the Yazidi religion, the peacock angel that had fuelled the notion that they were devil-worshippers.[103]

By 1850, Britain—unlike France—had in effect abandoned any claim to be a Christian power in the Middle East. On the other hand, it had achieved something for the Jews and the Yazidi, and had played an important role in securing the uneasy accord between Maronites and Druze in Lebanon. Yet its abandonment of an explicit Christian identity would not have been apparent to most religious observers at home. A great proportion of the British public discussion of the Ottoman Empire continued to be organised around the

---

102. Layard, *Nineveh and Its Remains*, 1:271–72, 287, 293–94, 306–7, 317–21; Layard, *Discoveries in the Ruins*, 40–41.

103. Layard, *Discoveries in the Ruins*, 4, 42–48; Guest, *Survival among the Kurds*, 104–5.

prospects for Christianity in the lands of its origin. But the stage was shifting: British religious concern was coming to focus not on Middle Eastern localities, but on the future character of Ottoman rule itself. The main question now was whether the Porte could learn how to treat all its religious minorities, and particularly its Christians, with due respect and sympathy. Britain's claim was that the progress of Christianity in Ottoman lands would depend on the direction of government policy at Constantinople, so that was where national attention should be directed. The achievement of the Protestant *millet* could be presented as an early step in an uplifting journey towards full toleration for pure religion. This argument was pushed strongly by Stratford Canning at Constantinople. It fitted with his personal need to fight a great crusade, and it won him admiration in religious circles at home. It also fitted with Britain's wider political objectives after 1846. Whether it fitted with the reality of Ottoman governing practice was another matter entirely.

CHAPTER NINE

Stratford Canning and the Politics of Christianity and Islam

STRATFORD CANNING was British ambassador to the Ottoman Empire for almost sixteen years from January 1842, and was intimately involved with the issues discussed in the rest of this book. He was determined to promote British interests at the Porte, and became more influential than any previous ambassador, though not as influential as he wished to be. Canning's instincts were to work through the central Ottoman government to secure civil rights for all minorities—to use British influence at Constantinople to force local officials to behave appropriately. This meant supporting the Porte in its desire for more power over its provinces. Such a strategy would also strengthen Canning's own power, at the Porte itself and over his consuls—whose numbers were expanding along with the growth of British political and economic interests.[1]

This meant that Canning engaged with religious issues in a different way from the consuls in Syria and Kurdistan. Whereas their major concern was about France, his was about Russia. When Aberdeen and the Tories returned to power in 1841, they pursued a traditional policy of working with Russia to defeat French Catholic sectarianism and stabilise the East. The Lebanese policy of Aberdeen and Rose should be seen in that light. Aberdeen continued to believe what Tories had generally believed before 1830: that Ottoman sovereignty was artificial; that Russia and Austria had legitimate interests in the Balkan interior, whereas Britain did not; and that it was essential to maintain European unity and hence continental stability. He wanted all policy at Constantinople to be agreed between the five powers, and with Russia in

---

1. From fourteen to twenty-five between 1836 and 1842: Greaves, "Jerusalem Bishopric," 329.

particular. Canning, however, continued Ponsonby's conspiratorial view of Russian trickery at Constantinople. He was convinced that Russia wanted to keep the Porte dependent on its protection. He concluded that Russia liked Ottoman mistreatment of Christians, because it justified its intervention in the Balkans. Canning discerned a powerful alliance between Islamic tradition-alists and Russian ministers at Constantinople, against him. He became con-vinced that the empire was being misgoverned by Islamic illiberalism, which was a political more than a theological system.

As a result, Canning became an increasingly zealous advocate for Chris-tian rights throughout the empire. When Palmerston returned to the Foreign Office in Russell's Liberal government of 1846, he and Canning began a cam-paign for civil equality between Muslims and non-Muslims, without which they argued that the empire would fall. Its main plank was a demand for Christian evidence to be accepted in trials involving both Muslims and Chris-tians. Canning pressed this repeatedly on the Porte. The underlying purpose was political rather than religious: to defeat Russia and Islamic reaction, and reorient the Ottoman Empire in a liberal direction. It was also part of Palm-erston's wider European strategy after 1848, in which Russia was clearly the major threat. Local French sectarianism might be a continuing nuisance in parts of the Middle East, but it was not a major obstacle to a wider Anglo-French cooperation. After Canning's assistant Henry Layard made his name by his excavation of Nineveh, he represented ancient Assyria as a suggestive precursor to modern Russian illiberalism.

By 1850, Canning, Palmerston, and most Liberals had decided that Brit-ain needed to defend Ottoman government power while trying to correct its behaviour. They took the embassy's traditional support of the Porte, and rephrased it in liberal ideological terms. Canning and Palmerston justified the continued existence of the Ottoman Empire by tying it to a very liberal inter-pretation of the Tanzimat, which they said Russia was trying to frustrate. They defended the empire not as it was, but as it might become if British influence were allowed proper sway. The problem with this strategy was that to insist on the principle of Christian civil equality risked inflaming Muslim-Christian tensions, and asked too much of Ottoman ministers. Their friendship, there-fore, was grudging at best.

Canning, Russia, and Islam

Stratford Canning's return to the Ottoman capital in 1842 was his fourth posting there. He had been Adair's assistant between 1808 and 1812, ambas-sador briefly in the mid-1820s, and a special commissioner in 1831–32. He now intended to make his mark properly. He brought to the task a forceful, driven personality, an evangelical sense of duty, and a fantasising classicist's thirst for fame. Many people commented on his aloofness, perseverance and indomitable will. Yet, though he boasted endlessly of his minor victories over recalcitrant Ottomans, foreign rivals, and unnamed shadowy forces, the recurring theme of his career was disappointment. This was the case throughout his time in Constantinople, but it also explained why he was stuck there at all.

Canning owed his career to his older cousin George, the coming man in British Tory politics for twenty years after Pitt's death in 1806, who arranged for his various diplomatic postings and gave him a political creed before his untimely demise shortly after becoming prime minister in 1827. George projected an assured optimism about post-Napoleonic Britain's global mission, and dominated the House of Commons with thrilling rhetoric. Stratford aspired to a similar command of British foreign policy, but was a painful failure as a public speaker, lacking charisma, popularity, or a light touch. Whereas George successfully courted the media as Member of Parliament for Liverpool, Stratford got a parliamentary seat by marrying the daughter of the owner of the most notorious of rotten boroughs, Old Sarum. After the 1832 Reform Act, he slowly realised that he would never reach high office domestically. He would settle for being governor-general of India—but others, less inflexible, peremptory, and oversensitive, were always preferred. When the Tories returned to government in 1841, and Peel and Aberdeen were looking for a replacement for Ponsonby at Constantinople, Canning was an obvious choice. Though he had moved with the Huskissonites towards Reform, he had moved back with the Stanleyites towards Peel in the mid-1830s, reflecting his bureaucrat's dislike of partisan, populist politics. Yet he always regarded the post as a stepping stone to something higher. He returned to Britain for two extended leaves, in 1846–48 and 1852–53, on each occasion plainly in search of a better role from new ministers—which they never offered. He was, therefore, hardly overjoyed to be chained to his embassy desk. As a young man, he called Constantinople a "vile hole," and moaned about the heat, the work, the plague, and the bodies floating through the Bosporus.[2] His mission was to change it.

Canning remained closer to his old Liberal Tory associate Palmerston than to Aberdeen, because of their respective views of Russia. For him, Russia was now Britain's great enemy, in the East and globally—which explains why Palmerston kept him in post after 1846. He fell out with Aberdeen in 1843, criticising him for advising the Ottomans to bow to Russian pressure over Serbia. Aberdeen's magisterial rebuke reminded him that Ottoman independence was "very imperfect," that Britain herself had broached it in 1840 for good reasons, and that the empire would survive only by prudent behaviour, not by intriguing against legitimate Russian treaty rights in Serbia where Britain had no special interests.[3] Canning's anxiety about Russia was intensified by his

2. Lane-Poole, *Stratford Canning*, 1:111, 433; for his dislike of partisan politics, see Lane-Poole, 1:123–24, 190–91.

3. Aberdeen to Canning, May 20 and June 9, 1843, FO 78/513. For one Canning outburst against Aberdeen, see Layard, *Autobiography*, 2:70–71.

suspicious mindset and his taste for conspiracy theories. His main suspicion was the standard British one that Russia sought to keep the empire weak and dependent. It wanted to prevent the reform of Ottoman public finances and the removal of corrupt practices, because this would make the empire more vigorous and prosperous. If the Ottomans continued to oppress and mistreat Orthodox Christians, Russia would claim to protect them and would gain political influence by doing so. Russia's allies were the Orthodox clergy who exercised such repressive power over their laity. Canning had access to complaints from several British consuls in the Balkans that the Orthodox bishops there were depraved, licentious, and politically active on Russia's behalf. His predecessor Ponsonby had managed to get the sultan to depose the Greek patriarch of Constantinople in 1840, after he had strengthened his doctrinal and political grip over his priests, and had ordered his clergy in the Ionian Islands not to cooperate with the British administration.[4]

In 1842–43, evidence seemed to be piling up that the Ottoman regime favoured a reactionary and intolerant Islamic policy—in Lebanon, in encouraging the religious massacres in Kurdistan and at Karbala, and in failing to challenge Muslim "fanaticism" at Mecca and Mocha. Canning became convinced that Ottoman ministers who acquiesced in Muslim attacks on Christians, and failed to stand up to the ulema, were doing Russia's work. Religious conflict suited Islamic clerics, but also Orthodox ones; it strengthened the hold of both over their followers. For Canning's first three years at Constantinople, the government was dominated by men like Riza Pasha, a palace survivor from Mahmud's era, and Rifat, who openly regretted the declarations at Gülhane in 1839. To Canning this was an "old tory peculating suspicious deceitful junto." In some cases they might be Russia's conscious agents, but most of them simply calculated that it was easier politically, and more lucrative for them personally, to continue to govern in the old ways, relying for support on a combination of popular Muslim fervour and behind-the-scenes Russian acquiescence.[5]

All Canning's suspicions about the regime seemed confirmed in late August 1843. An Armenian shoemaker called Avakim, who had been brought up as a Christian, was executed in Constantinople for apostatising from Islam. According to the British embassy account, he had only briefly converted to the faith after disturbing the peace when drunk and fearing heavy punishment by the courts. Becoming ashamed of his new Muslim identity, he had fled to the Aegean for some months, but eventually returned to Constantinople and assumed his former existence, only to be denounced to the authorities and asked to assert his belief in Islam, which he refused to do. Apparently, the policeman charged with the execution needed so much alcohol beforehand

4. Fairey, *Great Powers and Orthodox Christendom*, 58–86, 97–99.

5. Canning to Aberdeen, Dec. 1 and 13, 1843, FO 78/523; Lane-Poole, *Stratford Canning*, 2:144 (quotation).

that he made four drunken efforts to sever the head, before giving up and cutting his throat. Avakim's head was placed between his thighs, and his body paraded through the streets to popular jeers; his hat, the symbol of his rejection of Islam, was put on his back.[6] The event was very widely reported in Europe, simultaneously with the accounts from Kurdistan of the Nestorian massacres. Britain and France both felt that European governments now had a responsibility to force the Ottomans to change policy, or it would be impossible to justify their rule over Christians any longer. Later in the year, news arrived of a second, similar execution, of a Greek at Bursa. In March 1844, after much debate between the powers and Ottoman ministers, in Constantinople and in European capitals, the Ottoman government pledged "to prevent henceforth the execution and putting to death of the Christian who is an apostate," and the sultan gave Canning his personal assurances on the subject.[7]

Canning was sure that the execution stemmed from a reactionary political stance at the Porte. He ascertained that "neither the Mufti nor the Ulema, but Hafiz Pasha, president of the Council, was the chief obstacle to mercy. He is a bigot, and a bad man." The death penalty for apostasy was spelled out not in the Qur'an but in the Sunna, the corpus of Islamic legal customs—but the practical issue was the same, whether the regime would impose the customary laws or not.[8] The grand mufti himself had declined to pronounce on the issue, urging instead that the Porte should consider it by reference to the needs of state. Sultan Mahmud had let these laws remain dormant; the decision to revive them was a political strategy "to revive religious prejudice as a basis of political regeneration." In January 1845, Canning told his brother that this was a "deadly struggle with corruption." If the regime was to survive, it must promote tolerance and equity between Christians and Muslims, as in India. At the audience when the sultan gave Canning his pledge not to implement the death penalty for apostasy, he apparently thanked Canning for the Indian government's fairness as between the religions.[9]

Canning made sure that everyone appreciated his heroic achievement in securing the Ottoman commitment. He immediately wrote to all his consuls emphasising his role in the victory. His official biographer took the same approach in his lengthy and hagiographical account.[10] It boosted his popularity with Christian opinion at home, as did gaining permission for the Jerusalem church, and the establishment of the Protestant *millet*. In reality, however, the affair had been managed by the combined pressure of the five powers,

6. Canning to Aberdeen, Aug. 27, 1843, FO 78/521. For three other accounts, which differ from one another on important details, see Subaşı, "Apostasy Question," 5–8.

7. Subaşı, "Apostasy Question," 10–15, 24 (quotation).

8. Canning to Aberdeen, Aug. 27, 1843, FO 78/521; Subaşı, "Apostasy Question," 2–3.

9. Canning to Aberdeen, Jan. 16, 1844, FO 78/554; Lane-Poole, *Stratford Canning*, 2:98, 135.

10. Lane-Poole, *Stratford Canning*, 2:89–100.

and by Ottoman ambiguity. The initial running was made by Bourqueney, the French ambassador, who demanded a written guarantee not to carry out any more executions for apostasy, at a time when Canning feared that this might create counterproductive tensions between Ottoman ministers, and that it was better to ask for private assurances.[11] After the news of the second execution, Aberdeen realised the need to coordinate an informal response with Russia and Austria. Both of those powers disliked the grandstanding of Bourqueney and Canning. They wanted to draw a clearer distinction between the corpus of Islamic law, which European powers had no business to challenge, and the practice of government. Metternich criticised even Aberdeen for muddying the two in some of his dispatches, and insisted that they be separated. The compromise Ottoman declaration was agreed in March 1844, after Nesselrode instructed his ambassador at Constantinople to pass on Russia's friendly advice that executions for apostasy should cease.[12]

There was no change to the law, nor was any new policy announced in the provinces; official language just mentioned "postponement" of sentences.[13] Aberdeen could not resist pointing out to Canning that he had not supplied any details about the difference that his interventions had actually made. He also reminded him of the importance of not becoming the "avowed protector" of Ottoman Christians, and not interfering in the internal arrangements of the empire; this would risk a damaging Muslim backlash.[14]

Palmerston, Canning, and the Liberal Project

Unabashed, Canning told his brother in January 1845 that his victory over the Islamic hardliners on apostasy was "the first dagger thrust into the side of the false prophet and his creed. Such wounds may widen, but they never close."[15] Canning's battle against his Russian and Ottoman enemies was turning him into a Christian knight. This is perhaps not surprising in a Liberal Tory evangelical, but it marked a change of direction from the Whiggish Ponsonby, whose concern about the Tanzimat had been that it might jeopardise popular Islamic respect for the sultan's regime. Canning's aroused fervour might not

11. Canning to Aberdeen, Nov. 17 and Dec. 1, 1843, FO 78/523; Subaşı, "Apostasy Question," 15.

12. Subaşı, "Apostasy Question," 13, 16–17, 25. Nesselrode shared Metternich's view that the European powers should not demand an alteration of the fundamental laws of Islam, and Aberdeen agreed that subtle pressure on the sultan by each of the five powers would be better than a formal collective demand: see Aberdeen to Stuart de Rothesay, Jan. 16, 1844, FO 65/297, and Stuart's reply, Feb. 6, 1844, FO 65/298.

13. Deringil, *Conversion and Apostasy*, 39, 69–75.

14. Aberdeen to Canning, Apr. 19, 1844 (both dispatches), FO 78/552, and Canning's obfuscating reply, May 17, 1844, 78/557.

15. Lane-Poole, *Stratford Canning*, 2:135.

have mattered. In 1846, the Tories fell from power in Britain, and Palmerston returned to the Foreign Office. Canning went home, leaving Henry Wellesley (Lord Cowley from 1847) in temporary charge at Constantinople. He expected to get another post, and never to return. The other post did not materialise. Instead, Palmerston convinced him that there was a major task to be done at Constantinople, and that he would support him in it. In October 1847, in London, the two men thrashed out a future British policy towards the empire.

This policy centred on the removal of legal distinctions between Muslims and rayas, so that Christians would now receive equal treatment. Palmerston's great principle from now on was that it "is impossible for Turkey to take her proper and natural place among the powers of Europe until the Rayah subjects of the Sultan are treated with exactly the same degree of justice and favour as His Mussulman subjects, nor until all civil and political distinctions between the different sects . . . are entirely swept away."[16] Canning saw this as a battle to root out illiberalism in the regime, and to educate Reshid and the reformers into their duty. When he returned to Constantinople in early 1848, he saw himself, in a fine evangelical phrase, as the "chosen instrument" of a regeneration project. This policy would undercut Russia's ability to exploit Christian grievances in the Balkans and Anatolia, and France's ability to do the same in Syria. The immediate programme had three specific elements. Christians would be allowed to serve in the army, with their own officers. They would no longer pay the special sectarian tax, the haraç (once a poll tax, now a military exemption tax). Above all, the courts must accept the evidence of Christians on the same basis as Muslims.[17] The hope was that the acceptance of Christian evidence in mixed courts would increase the confidence of Greek Orthodox laymen in judicial processes, and reduce their dependence on Russia and their clerics.[18]

Generally, in the Ottoman realms, criminal cases involving an Ottoman subject as either plaintiff or defendant could be tried only in Islamic courts, with judgments and sentences passed by Islamic judges. Evidence from non-Muslims was not admissible, and the evidence of two Muslims was required to prove guilt. British communities in the empire had accepted these terms. The capitulations governing their status laid down that special mixed sittings would be used for criminal cases involving a British subject and an Otto-man subject. In such cases, a dragoman or other representative of the British embassy could attend and debate the evidence, but the court would still oper-ate on Islamic law principles. (Christian evidence was, however, accepted at

16. Palmerston to Cowley, Sept. 13, 1847, FO 78/675.

17. For the details, see Canning's memo, early Oct. 1847 (which contains the "chosen instrument" remark), and Palmerston's (urging "the equalization of the two races" and the need to "counteract . . . foreign influences . . . in the very heart" of the empire), Oct. 30, 1847, both in FO 78/691. See also Lane-Poole, *Stratford Canning*, 2:160–62.

18. Rose to Clarendon, Apr. 2, 1853, FO 78/931; Tibawi, *Modern History of Syria*, 115.

the Constantinople commercial court—a reminder that the main benefit of the capitulations for the European powers was to protect their trading rights and property.) As late as 1844, Aberdeen was content with this state of affairs. However, the growth of British travel around the empire increased the risk of miscarriages of justice, because of the courts' unwillingness to accept Christian testimony. In 1845, Sir Lawrence Jones was murdered at Macri (Fethiye) on the Anatolian coast, and it took a long time to get the brigands arrested and lightly punished. Palmerston remained very exercised by the Jones case.[19] Moreover, there were two other reasons why he and Canning hoped for progress on the issue of Christian evidence.

The first, paradoxically, was that increasing numbers of British subjects were committing major crimes, including murder, a situation that was alarming the Ottoman authorities as well as creating problems for the embassy. This was because of the number of Maltese and Ionian British subjects living in the Ottoman Empire, quite a few of whom had histories of misbehaviour in their own country. A Maltese committed a murder at Smyrna in 1842, and three more serious cases followed in 1842–44. If its subjects could not be brought to justice, Britain's reputation at the Porte would be severely damaged.[20] The capitulations had always allowed foreign powers to administer their own justice in cases on Ottoman soil that did not involve Ottoman subjects, but this idea had thrown up a number of legal difficulties. In 1843–44 the British government solved these by new regulations legalising consular jurisdiction of criminal cases between British subjects throughout the Ottoman Empire. The Foreign Jurisdiction Act of 1843 and Order of Council in June 1844 established that consuls could exercise the same judicial powers as the Crown did in its own realms, as long as these were consistent with the capitulations. This entrenched the principle that British consuls in the empire had extraterritorial judicial functions in relation to their own subjects. As was often remarked, this was necessary only because the Ottoman judicial system operated on Islamic rather than Christian legal foundations: in Christian states, extraterritoriality for British subjects was not necessary. Palmerston made the point that it would be much better if the British could be confident that Ottoman justice applied equally to all religions. In 1846, Wellesley also thought this state of affairs regrettable and contrary to the spirit of Gülhane. He declared that the British government would hail the day with joy when the Crown "could conscientiously give over the lives and property of her subjects to the sole protection

19. Aberdeen to Canning, Aug. 7, 1844, FO 78/553; Palmerston to Wellesley, Aug. 20, 1846, FO 78/636. For the case, see Macfarlane, *Turkey and Its Destiny*, 1:28–30.

20. There were 2,208 British subjects in Constantinople in 1846, of whom 1,963 were Maltese or Ionian; 104 were charged with offences that year. This was over ten times the number of arrests of French and Russian subjects: Palmerston memo, Mar. 19, 1847, FO 78/673; Wellesley to Palmerston, Feb. 3, 1847, FO 78/678. See White, *Three Years in Constantinople*, 1:154–59.

of the Ottoman Porte"; then, "Turkey would have been recognised as within the pale of civilized nations."[21]

In 1846, therefore, the embassy pushed for the admission of Christian evidence in the Islamic court process, in the hope of protecting British subjects in cases against Ottoman subjects, and of improving the reputation of Ottoman justice. However, in September 1846, Reshid told Wellesley that it was impossible for the Ottoman government to budge on this matter: "every Mussulman would be against it."[22] As long as this state of affairs continued, there was a risk of inflammatory outcomes in serious British-Ottoman cases. Some consuls tried to deal with this by publicising informally the evidence of Christians where it seemed appropriate, in the hope of influencing the Islamic courts.[23] In 1849, Canning made other attempts to press the matter on the Porte, with no more success.

The second possible lever for change was the Porte's anxiety about its authority in Egypt. The untried Abbas replaced Mehmet Ali as viceroy in 1848; this was the moment, if ever, for the Ottomans to challenge Egypt's drift towards practical independence. The Tanzimat facilitated this challenge because it put the sultan's powers on a firmer legal basis. Canning's support for the Tanzimat heightened the Porte's chances of entrenching the sultan's legal authority in Egypt. In early 1850, Abbas's opponents, led by Mehmet Ali's former prime minister, Artin (an Armenian Christian), congregated in Constantinople to organise a movement against him, and alighted on the policy of using sultanic authority to force Egyptian justice arrangements into line with those in Constantinople. They proposed the introduction of mixed courts to try cases between Europeans and Ottoman subjects. Independently, Palmerston had been urging this for Egypt since 1848. The Egyptian criminal justice system was basic and harsh, involving much use of the bastinado, and as a result the European consuls had secured the right to try nearly all mixed cases themselves.[24] Naturally, therefore, the consular community in Egypt disliked the idea of mixed courts, and would be likely to accept them only if Christian evidence was accepted. In April 1850, a firman was published in Constantinople establishing mixed courts in Egypt, and provisions for the

21. Palmerston to Murray, Feb. 9, 1848, FO 78/756; Wellesley to Palmerston, Sept. 4, 1846, FO 78/643.

22. Wellesley to Palmerston, Sept. 4, 1846.

23. See Ozil, *Orthodox Christians*, 93.

24. In 1877, McCoan, in *Egypt as It Is* (284), claimed that consular abuse of these powers had expanded greatly since the death of Mehmet Ali, pointing to the existence of courts in seventeen foreign consulates. In 1833, however, Campbell presented the system as of deeper root, saying that the Egyptian government habitually relied on the consulates to try all non-capital cases between its subjects and Egyptians, and that the British consulate had inherited these powers from the Levant Company: to Palmerston, May 15, 1833, FO 78/231 185.

hearing of evidence in them. Christian as well as Muslim evidence was to be collected, and in the great majority of cases the consul or deputy attending the trial would participate in the judgment and sentencing.[25] In other words, in the hope of subordinating Egypt, Ottoman ministers had agreed to accept the admission of Christian evidence, but only in Egyptian courts. In fact, the Egyptian reforms were delayed by the Ottoman-Egyptian crisis of 1850–52 and then by the European consuls' unwillingness to abandon their powers. Canning, however, was pleased to have established his principle. He wanted to believe Reshid's promises that these provisions for Christian evidence would soon be imposed in the rest of the empire.[26]

In practice, however, nothing was done, despite Canning's frequent protestations: "it is altogether painful to observe with what unreasonable tenacity the professors of Islamism still adhere to their misapplication of religious principles." In June 1853, with Russia about to invade Moldavia and Wallachia in order to protect its Christians, the Foreign Office pressed again for the removal of this "erroneous religious" principle. It was only the war crisis of 1853–54 that made the Porte so desperate for European friends that it produced a firman in February 1854 decreeing that tribunals judging criminal cases involving both Ottoman and foreign subjects would hear evidence impartially from all.[27]

Similarly, the *haraç* was not abolished until 1855. Nor were Christians allowed to serve as regular soldiers before the war. The most that Canning achieved was to agitate about the rights of Christians who had converted to Islam but regretted it, which he and Palmerston made a question of British diplomatic dignity.[28] Another irritation to him was that the slave market continued in private at Constantinople, despite the abolition of public sales in 1847. In 1851, Canning complained at endless official "shuffling" in response to his pressure to end the Ottoman slave traffic.[29]

It seemed no easier to impose the secular elements of the Tanzimat: to root out tax farming, money lending, corruption, and uncertain official tenures. In 1850, Canning noted with exasperation that tax farming was being extended

25. Special arrangements were needed for crimes carrying the death penalty, since only the sultan could order a death sentence. The Porte insisted on referring Egyptian death sentences to the sultan. This created prolonged tension between the Porte and Abbas, as Artin doubtless intended: see chapter 11. For the various views, see Murray to Palmerston, Apr. 30, 1847, FO 78/707; Palmerston to Murray, Feb. 9, 1848, FO 78/756; Canning to Murray, Apr. 19, 1850, FO 78/819.

26. McCoan, *Egypt as It Is*, 284; Canning to Palmerston, May 5, 1850, FO 78/820.

27. For the Foreign Office, see Clarendon to Canning, June 24, 1853, FO 78/925. "Erroneous religious" replaced "fanatic" in the draft. For Canning's quotation, and the firman, see *PP* (1854), 4–7. For changes in the 1850s, see Ozil, *Orthodox Christians*, 93.

28. See, e.g., Palmerston to Canning, May 23, 1848, and July 3, 1850, FO 78/731, 78/815, and the related correspondence in each case.

29. Wellesley to Palmerston, Jan. 18, 1847, FO 78/677; Lane-Poole, *Stratford Canning*, 2:212–13.

more widely in the provinces, and that many ministers personally benefited from it. Both Wellesley and Canning continued to pepper their dispatches with despairing references to the "cancer" of corruption rife throughout the administration.[30] When the Porte finally succumbed to twenty years of pressure to introduce British officers to improve Ottoman military training, Admiral Slade reported that "each ship is a castle of indolence."[31]

In 1850, the problems with the Tanzimat project came into full view. After a Christian insurrection in Bulgaria, local Muslim gangs went on a revenge killing spree: Palmerston feared European public outrage and a response from Russia, which was still occupying nearby Moldavia and Wallachia.[32] Ottoman authority had plainly collapsed in Baghdad and Mosul. The most alarming shock came in October 1850, with forty-eight hours of attacks by local Muslims on Christians in wealthy, apparently stable Aleppo. Some were killed, much property was destroyed, Greek girls were raped, Syrian churches were burnt, and the Syrian patriarch later died. Debate continues on the causes of the events, which were complex. However, most British observers assumed that the key was Muslim resentment at the increasing prosperity and power of Christians who benefited from European trade.[33] One suggested that such outbursts of Muslim savagery were instinctive angry responses to any improvement of status for local Christians. "Every Moslem heart in Arabistan beat high to be allowed to seize their prey, their own lawful prey; which the Franks had so long withheld from them."[34]

The Constantinople embassy managed to persuade *The Times* that the Aleppo riots were the work of "retrograde" forces and that the repression of them showed the sultan's commitment to "toleration and civil equality." In reality, however, neither Palmerston nor Canning had any solutions to offer, beyond continuing to support Reshid's faction at the Porte while constantly admonishing it for its weakness. Palmerston warned the regime that unless there was "rapidly progressive improvement in the whole system of Turkish government," Western support for the Ottoman Empire would be withdrawn—but as far as Britain was concerned, these were empty words, as everyone knew.[35] Canning could see that something more was needed to convince min-

---

30. Canning to Palmerston, May 4, 1850, FO 78/819; Cowley to Palmerston, Mar. 21, 1848, FO 78/728.

31. Enclosed in Canning to Palmerston, July 6, 1850, FO 78/821.

32. Canning to Palmerston, Aug. 19, 1850, FO 78/821; Palmerston to Canning, Oct. 25, 1850, FO 78/816.

33. For Baghdad, see chapter 10 below, and Canning to Palmerston, Nov. 5, 1850, FO 78/824 (forwarding local letters, on the same day as he wrote about Aleppo). Masters, "1850 Events in Aleppo," 3–20; F. Neale, *Eight years in Syria*, 2:117–34.

34. F. Walpole, *Ansayrii*, 3:219.

35. "The Massacre at Aleppo," *Times*, Dec. 5, 1850, 5; Palmerston to Canning, Dec. 16, 1850, FO 78/816.

isters to support his proposed reforms, but his two ideas, the offer of a unilateral alliance, in late 1849, and of a loan of £5-6 million, in 1850-51, were shot down by Palmerston: both were politically impossible, while the loan would make Ottoman finances worse. So Canning was forced back on what he did best: haranguing ministers about their unwillingness to confront "corruption, peculation, insurrection, massacres, pillages and financial disorder."[36]

Layard later lamented Canning's "constant bullying" of Ottoman ministers, and his determination to make them subservient to him. He felt that he never gave them credit for their courage and their internal difficulties, and that his expectations of them were so unrealistic that they had to lie to him, which made him angrier still. Naturally, they preferred the softer touch of the Russians. Canning's egotism and conspiratorial nature made him an immensely difficult colleague.[37] In 1855, Grenville Murray, while still one of his attachés, published an infamous anonymous attack on him—rechristening him Sir Hector Stubble—in Dickens's *Household Words*. "He was haughty and stiff-necked beyond any man I have ever seen. He trampled on other men's feelings as deliberately and unflinchingly as if they were wooden puppets made to work his will."[38] Canning had spectacularly bad relations with his three Middle Eastern satraps, in Baghdad, Egypt, and Syria, all of whom were more relaxed than he was about the realities of Eastern politics and the nature of Islamic society. He got Taylor—who had never believed that the Tanzimat could be brought in at Baghdad—sacked, but Rawlinson, his replacement, was just as "Indian" in his mentality.[39] His conviction that Charles Murray in Egypt was promoting Abbas's independence from Constantinople made for a poisonous relationship (see chapter 11). Rose in Syria seemed too wedded to the army tradition of pragmatic even-handedness between the Ottomans and local groups. Yet Murray and Rose achieved more for Christians in Egypt and Lebanon than Canning ever did.

When the Foreign Office imposed Rose on Canning as his secretary of embassy, there was a remarkable falling-out. Rose arrived at Constantinople in 1851 with seven horses, a cow, a calf, a Maltese washerwoman, and a black Coptic groom (whom she accused of trying to rape her), and expected, as was traditional, that they would live in Canning's embassy house. Canning's idea of his status and that of his grand new embassy in the European quarter of Constantinople definitely did not involve a prominent role for such a menagerie. By the autumn, he and Rose were not on speaking terms, and the Foreign

36. Palmerston to Canning, Jan. 7, 1851, FO 78/848; Canning's quotation is to Layard, Nov. 30, 1850: see Lane-Poole, *Stratford Canning*, 2:213–14.

37. Layard, *Autobiography*, 2:58–59, 84–85, 139–41; to Ross, June 26, 1856, LPBL, 38941 74. Hornby recorded Canning's trenchant views on how to treat Ottomans: Hornby, *Autobiography*, 73–74.

38. Reprinted as [Murray], *Roving Englishman in Turkey*, 12–14 (quotation at 12).

39. Taylor to Hobhouse, Jan. 31, 1840, Broughton, F213 10.

Office had to intervene.[40] But Rose became acting ambassador when the frustrated Canning left for England in 1852, and, as a long-serving Tory soldier, was more phlegmatic about the Ottomans' survival prospects; he rather admired their shrewd management of sectarian divisions. He believed that the empire was slowly evolving, that Muslim power was gradually declining, and that it was no more misgoverned than Italy, Spain, or South America. The Porte did not need a loan, which powers like France would use to get more influence. Commerce was growing, capital was coming in, and Islamic rule would become more liberal.[41] Other experienced consuls similarly took the view that Aleppo-style "fanaticism" was an unusual event that occurred only when the basic principles of equitable government were betrayed by greedy factions.[42] "Unturking" the Turk would benefit just France and Russia.[43] Even Layard thought that Canning's civil equality policy was "monstrous" and likely to have counterproductive effects on Muslim opinion.[44]

When Canning left Constantinople in 1852—as he assumed, for the last time—he knew his project had not worked.[45] He had not secured significant rights for Christians, and he had not stopped Russia from using Christian grievances to lean on the Porte. Russian bullying remained defter than his own. If the Canning-Palmerston strategy for Christian civil equality does not look a complete failure, it is only because it was achieved through the war that it was devised to prevent.

Henry Layard and the Lessons of Nineveh

Henry Layard shared the declining optimism at Ottoman prospects in the early 1850s. During 1850, which he spent on his second excavation of the ancient Assyrian mounds near Mosul, he encountered a series of obstacles to progress, including major local disorder. This second expedition was funded by the British state, and in March 1849 Palmerston arranged for Layard to have a paid attachéship at Constantinople to accompany his appointment on it.[46] This was the diplomatic post that he had been trying to secure since 1842. However, in 1851 he gave up diplomacy and returned to Britain. This second expedition concentrated on a mound very near Mosul, where he opened the South-West Palace of Sennacherib and the massive cuneiform library of

---

40. The extensive correspondence on this matter, Sept.–Dec. 1851, is in FO 78/858, 78/859, and 78/879.

41. Rose to Foreign Office, July 26 and Oct. 26, 1852, Jan. 20 and March 10 and 17, 1853, FO 78/893, 78/894, 78/928, 78/930.

42. Barker, *Syria and Egypt*, 1:42–49.

43. White to Layard, Apr. 26, 1844, LPBL, 38976 7.

44. Layard to Murray, May 29, 1856, Murray Papers, NLS 40678 66.

45. Lane-Poole, *Stratford Canning*, 2:215.

46. Palmerston to Canning, Mar. 20, 1849, FO 78/768.

Ashurbanipal. In the process he proved beyond doubt that this was the real Nineveh, the capital of the Assyrian Empire at his height, and that the mound of his first excavation was its earlier capital Nimrud, twenty miles to the south. He had become an international celebrity; he aspired to better openings at home than the unpromising arena of the Ottoman Empire could provide at this point. Within a few months of returning, Layard had become a Liberal Member of Parliament and a government minister.

The reason for this celebrity—and the reason for the state funding for him and his further expedition—was the great success of Layard's account of his first expedition, *Nineveh and Its Remains*, which was published in February 1849. The cult of Layard and Nineveh, and the lifelong association of his name with it, can be explained on three levels. One was simply the drama of the discovery, the novelty of uncovering a whole civilisation that was hardly known to exist before, and the technological skill involved in doing so and in bringing the exhibits back to London for the public to see. Among the highlights of the book were the drawings of the many bas-reliefs that had lined the walls of the palace, showing men fighting, besieging cities, hunting lions, and swimming on skins, which brought the humanity of the Assyrians to life. Above all, there were the half-dozen pairs of lamassu that Layard found, mostly perfectly preserved, showing how men nearly three thousand years ago conceived of "the wisdom, power, and ubiquity of a Supreme Being"—with the head of a man, the body of a lion, and the wings of a bird.[47] The excavations of the lamassu by local Arabs under his direction were captured in drawings that became famous, and the *Illustrated London News* enthusiastically charted the voyage of one of them to its final resting place in the British Museum. Gold lapel studs with embossed winged bulls became a craze.

The arrival of the Assyrian statues and bas-reliefs at the museum prompted a reconfiguration of its layout to showcase the material brought back from the Ottoman Empire since the days of Elgin. The whole west side of the ground floor was given over—as it more or less still is—to the Elgin Marbles, the Rosetta Stone, Layard's findings at Nimrud and Nineveh, and the monuments recovered from Halicarnassus and from Charles Fellows's expedition to Xanthos. Public interest in the artefacts broke down the old notion of the museum as primarily for a knowledgeable gentlemanly elite. A vigorous debate ensued about the relative artistic merits of the various ancient civilisations now displayed there, and the process by which taste was developed and transmitted between them.[48] Public thirst to visualise and celebrate different historical cultures was reflected in the Great Exhibition in Hyde Park in 1851, and again when the massive glasshouse of 1851 was reconstructed in Sydenham in 1854

47. Layard, *Nineveh and Its Remains*, 1:70.

48. Bohrer, *Orientalism and Visual Culture*, chap. 4; Moser, *Wondrous Curiosities*, 200–215.

as the Crystal Palace. Layard was given £5,000 to design the Nineveh Court for the new Crystal Palace, one of a series of historical "Fine Arts Courts" that were the brainchild of his friend Owen Jones, including ones on Egypt, Greece, and Rome. Jones, an enthusiast for Islamic art, used the opportunity to introduce the Victorians to it, particularly in his Alhambra Court. Layard's pictorial reconstructions of the excavated palaces were also used to great effect in panoramas and stage designs in London theatres, as promoters sought to bring ancient Assyria to life for the public.[49]

Part of what was being celebrated here was British ingenuity, and the second reason for the popularity of *Nineveh and Its Remains* was the depiction of Layard's own character and achievement. His narrative brought out the initiative and perseverance required to manage single-handedly a complex excavation, defeating the obstacles to success thrown up by uncomfortable circumstances and by hostile Ottoman officials and religious leaders. Layard himself wanted to emphasise his ability to mix with Arabs and Nestorians. However, it was striking how many reviewers read his volumes in terms of the superior qualities of British leadership, celebrating the "justice and courage" needed to turn "wild groups of gesticulating and screaming Arabs and Chaldeans . . . to the most patient and persevering workmen." The treasures he sought "were only to be obtained by the co-operation and assistance of idle and unruly Arabs and Asiatics, debased by Turkish habits and customs." "Books such as this may help to keep us proud of the name of Englishmen." *The Times* noted that his self-command and courage gave him "the faculty of ruling others as well as of controlling himself."[50]

Layard himself was more concerned to stress his lack of privilege, suggesting that his familiarity with local life derived from years of travelling in the East, "careless of comfort and unmindful of danger . . . unembarrassed by needless luxuries." With "no patron and with small means," his aim had been not to ally with "the great and affluent of other nations," but to "sojourn among the people, that I might be . . . improved by their council."[51] Layard's determination to portray himself as a democratic man of action, rather than as an aristocratic Grand Tourist, established his political character. He became one of the first heroes of the more classless political culture that was Britain's sedate version of the continental revolutions of 1848, and this explained his rapid political rise. At the beginning of 1852, only a few months after he returned from his second dig at Nineveh, he was appointed to the role of under-secretary in the Foreign Office, a significant office just outside the

49. Layard, *Nineveh Court*; Ziter, *Orient on the Victorian Stage*, 150–60.

50. *Examiner*, Jan. 6, 1849 (quotations 1, 2, and 4); Mayor of Leeds, *Leeds Mercury*, Jan. 29, 1853 (quotation 3); review of Layard's *Discoveries*, *Times*, May 17, 1853. The articles cited in the footnotes in this section are nearly all in LPBL, 58174 (scrapbook).

51. Layard, *Nineveh and Its Remains*, 1:1; "Layard at Aylesbury," *Buckinghamshire Advertiser*, June 19, 1852.

cabinet, by the Liberal prime minister Lord John Russell and the foreign secretary Lord Granville. The radical *Daily News* hailed him as "a man of the
people," whose appointment strengthened Russell's government, which had
been badly damaged by Palmerston's sacking in December 1851. Palmerston's
foreign policy had played to the liberal press and had angered Prince Albert
and the court, who were accordingly blamed for his dismissal. Layard was
appointed to counter the perception that the government was now an aristocracy: Granville, Palmerston's successor, was viewed as a court stooge, and
nicknamed "my lady's lapdog." To the *Daily News*, Layard's appointment "sets
at naught exclusion and caste pretensions; it is a search in the proper direction for real merit; . . . it indicates a desire to employ the true workers of life."
There was a desire in the 1850s to have more plain-spoken, vigorous, straightforward political speakers—open, clear, and genuine rather than aristocratic
and effete or dissembling or trite. Layard came across as "manly and vigorous,
not rhetorical."[52]

One consequence of the public admiration for Layard's enterprise was that
he got all the credit and fame of the Nineveh excavations. No one remembered
that Canning had got the permission for them and made the initial payments.
When Canning left Constantinople in 1846, he expected to be remembered
mainly for his antiquarian patronage. The new galleries in the British Museum
that housed the Temple of Halicarnassus and the Assyrian marbles stood right
next to the gallery displaying the Elgin Marbles—but they never bore Canning's name. It was a subject that made both Layard and Canning extremely
sensitive; their relationship never fully recovered. Canning's assumption that
Layard was merely an artisan whose labours demonstrated his own benefi-
cence and taste was one of the many casualties of the change in British political culture after 1848.

The third reason for the popularity of Layard's *Nineveh* was its implication for religion and religious politics. When he was awarded the Freedom of
the City of London in 1853, it was for demonstrating "the accuracy of Sacred
History."[53] It was often said that he had proved the Bible true. This was not
because he had discovered any proofs of particular biblical events, though
he did find tablets that mentioned over fifty names from the Old Testament.
Because of the difficulties of deciphering cuneiform, it was very difficult to
establish any detail about Assyria at this point. Nineveh featured in the popular imagination primarily through the Old Testament passages describing or
prophesying the destruction of Assyria's mighty and proud imperial rule. This

52. *Daily News* editorial, Feb. 14, 1852; Layard himself recognised this in his nomination speech as Member of Parliament for Aylesbury: *Buckinghamshire Advertiser*, July 10,
1852. See *Newcastle Chronicle*, June 9, 1855. For the context, see Parry, *Politics of Patriotism*, 203.

53. For the full encomium, see Malley, *From Archaeology to Spectacle*, 1.

was a time of great discussion about the utility and accuracy of biblical prophecies. Very many commentators regarded the discovery of the city's physical
remains as a rebuttal of advanced religious thinkers who had cast doubt on the
veracity of the Old Testament. Layard described himself musing on Zepha-
niah's prophecy that God would make Nineveh "a desolation and dry like a
wilderness," with flocks lying down in its midst. Whereas the monuments of
ancient Egypt had always survived to show its former power, Nineveh's had
been buried in mounds; his destiny was to reveal them.[54] For many commentators, the actual appearance of a destroyed city was a fresh reminder
of that prophecy, perhaps even a demonstration by God of his handiwork.
The prophecy had stated that Nineveh was to be forgotten in the records of
men; "the discovery of its entombed greatness is the fulfilment." To religious
writers, each of Layard's discoveries declared that the voice that rang through
Nineveh's streets predicting her desolation was "the voice of God."[55]

At a time of considerable challenge to religion and the Bible from infidel-
ity and atheism, Layard did not demur from the view that his discoveries were
a providential event "to confound the sceptic and to strengthen our faith in
God's holy word."[56] There is no reason to think that he cynically manipulated
the fame in religious circles that his discoveries gave him, though his icono-
clastic friend Charles Alison told him that he should.[57] Layard was from a
Huguenot Protestant family, and the Bible was important to him. However,
he was also intellectually curious, socially liberal and easy-going, and a scholar
with a genuine interest in a variety of religious faiths. As a teenager, he lived
with his uncle and aunt in Bloomsbury, right next to the British Museum, and
prided himself on his network of Enlightenment-minded friends. His world
view had little in common with that of apocalyptic evangelicals who anticipated with relish the imminent fall of the Islamic usurpers in these regions.
Evangelicals had always had a taste for imagining the destruction of Nineveh
and the divine power that it demonstrated. In 1853, Charles Kean took advantage of Layard's discoveries to recreate that cataclysm on the London stage,
using the designs that he had uncovered.[58] In the Old Testament, Nahum had
interpreted the fall of Nineveh as God's punishment of human arrogance.
"With an overflowing flood he will make a complete end of the adversar-
ies." Layard's mother teased him on his new status as a "God-send . . . to the
Saints and such like" who believed such things; he had previously enjoyed

54. Layard, *Nineveh and Its Remains*, 1:70–71.

55. *Buckinghamshire Advertiser*, Apr. 17, 1852; *Telegraph and Courier*, May 7, 1853.
The evangelical publisher Thomas Nelson exploited this enhanced interest in archaeologi-
cal evidence of prophecy with his digest *Ruins of Sacred and Historic Lands* (1850): see
Pemble, *Mediterranean Passion*, 192.

56. *London's Roll of fame*, 204.

57. Alison to Layard, June 17, 1846, LPBL, 38976 389.

58. In *Sardanapalus*: Ziter, *Orient on the Victorian Stage*, 159–60.

ridiculing the claims of biblical literalists like Alexander Keith.[59] It should also be noted that, even to a devout Bible reader like James Fletcher, the lessons from Nineveh were not as overpowering as those from Babylon, whose destruction seemed to stem directly from the sins of its rulers in enslaving the Jews and ignoring God's warnings. The downfall of Nineveh taught a much more conventional lesson about ambition, human vanity, and the evanescence of power.[60]

Layard, at any rate, interpreted the fall of Nineveh as a story of human corruption, not divine wrath. Its fate indicated how not to run a society. Between 1851 and 1853, he gave a series of speeches to popular audiences, often Mechanics' Institutes or other assemblies of working men. He stressed that Nineveh's problem was its social disharmony. In Nineveh there were:

> but two classes in society, the governing, consisting of the few who monopolised knowledge, and consequently power; and the governed, the many who had no knowledge and power. They were bound together by no tie. . . . Such is the history of eastern nations to this day. [Christianity, however, teaches us] that all classes of society should be bound together by one common tie: that knowledge is the common property of us all, and that power—not the power of oppressing our fellow-creatures, but the power of adding to their happiness, and contributing to their welfare—is available to every member of the community.[61]

Moreover, the "high priests and pontiffs of their days, the bishops and clergy, made a trade and a mystery of religion. Consequently, there was no bond of union or sympathy between the ministers of religion and the worshippers." The rulers of Nineveh "had no rational faith nor true liberty; their religion was a gross and demoralising superstition, their political condition the mere arbitrary will of one man or of one class." The winged bulls they worshipped were symbols of their idolatry. Their mistake was in not seeing that nations "must be communities of progress, and representatives of the people should be the reflex of the people's mind." History taught that nations that did not draw their strength from their people always fell.[62]

There were three connected messages for the present in all this. One was the need for politicians always to promote collaboration and understanding between classes at home. He told the Peterborough Mechanics' Institute that, had there been a similar body devoted to popular education in Nineveh, it

59. Layard's mother to Layard, Jan. 20, 1850, LPBL, 58150 120; Layard to Louisa Linton, Mar. 2, 1844, LPBL, 58153 88; Layard to Murray, Mar. 20, 1849, Murray Papers, NLS 40677 26.

60. Fletcher, *Notes from Nineveh*, 1:207.

61. Layard at Peterborough Mechanics' Institute, *Lincolnshire Chronicle*, Feb. 6, 1852.

62. Layard at Aylesbury, *Buckinghamshire Advertiser*, July 10, 1852 (quotations 1 and 3), and at the Guildhall, *London's Roll of Fame*, 204–5 (quotation 2).

would not now be "a heap of earth."[63] The second was that religious leaders must also act as tolerant guides of the whole nation, rather than a separate and arrogant priesthood with superior pretensions to theological truth. This was an attack on high church Anglicans and Roman Catholics, and their (mostly Tory) followers; Layard was instinctively a liberal anti-clerical. The idolatry of Catholicism or Greek Orthodoxy was the modern equivalent of Nineveh's winged bulls. This connected to the third message, on foreign policy. Britain believed in ethical values, and wished to extend them in the East. Russia, however, was an autocracy, which was instinctively sympathetic to Ottoman misgovernment. The Ottomans should govern their countries less like the ancient Assyrians and more like the British (should) in India.[64] That was the only basis on which their empire would survive and Russian ambitions to succeed it be frustrated.

In other words, Nineveh for Layard represented the same combination of political and religious illiberalism against which Canning crusaded at Constantinople. In his interpretation, Nineveh symbolised the present-day battle in the East between Enlightenment values and intolerant autocracy. His great good fortune politically was that this message further boosted his fame in 1853, when the threat from Russia became the main talking point in politics. He became one of the earliest and most persistent critics of Russian policy, and of the appeasement of Russia by Aberdeen, who was now prime minister. His maiden speech of August 1853 attacked Aberdeen for his peace-mongering at the expense of national interests, and invoked his weak behaviour over Serbia in 1843 (when Layard had been Canning's secret agent there). When the Crimean War broke out in March 1854, Layard bitterly attacked Aberdeen's failure to prepare effectively for war.[65]

In the spring of 1853, Layard hoped to burnish his credentials as a foreign policy expert further, by returning to Constantinople to resolve the disputes between Russia and France over the Holy Places. He travelled out with Canning, on the latter's final return there as ambassador. The trip was a disaster. Canning could not disguise his dislike of Layard's enhanced status, and refused to treat him as an equal: the journey was "intolerable," and once at Constantinople Canning resumed his "reign of terror" over his staff. Layard quickly returned, feeling that he was given nothing serious to do, while Canning boasted that he had solved the diplomatic tensions.[66] Time was to show otherwise.

63. *Lincolnshire Chronicle*, Feb. 6, 1852.

64. Layard was a critic of the bureaucratic arrogance of British rule as currently practised in India, in 1853 and especially after the 1857 uprising.

65. 132 Parl. Deb. (3d ser.) (1854) cols. 217–43.

66. Layard to his aunt, Apr. 25, 1853, LPBL, 58156 145.

Canning faced the same obstacles as ever in making headway at the Porte. Ottoman ministers knew by now what to expect from him. He had been haranguing them about legal principles and political reforms for long enough. Unfortunately, his struggle with them over the Tanzimat was only the half of it. All the way through the 1840s and 1850s, he was also upbraiding them on another set of issues. Britain said repeatedly that it was committed to upholding the "integrity" of the Ottoman Empire. Yet when it came to defining Ottoman territorial rights, especially along the whole southern and eastern fringe of the empire where the British also had interests, it turned out that British ideas of that "integrity" were very different from Ottoman ones, and, curiously, much less generous.

CHAPTER TEN

The Ring of Steam, the Lands of Islam, and the Search for Order

IN THE 1840S, steam power consolidated Britain's hold over the routes to India, the mouth of the Red Sea, and the Persian Gulf. Monthly steam travel between Suez and India became routine, with Aden as a stop en route. The change wrought by steam was not always smooth, because the technology encountered periodic setbacks.[1] Moreover, budgetary pressures continued to limit investment in new ships. However, these were minor qualifications to an undoubted success story. The major reason for the limited spending was that British naval superiority in the region was assured. It was not even necessary to use steamships in the Gulf in order to secure paramountcy, which was confirmed by the permanent agreement of 1853 with the Trucial chiefs.

This chapter discusses Britain's strategies for promoting order along the southern and eastern borders of the Ottoman Empire where it had naval authority. Disorder and instability would be bad and expensive in themselves, and the only means by which other powers might upset the status quo. The most continuously challenging problem was the border between the Ottoman and Persian Empires, which Britain attempted to stabilise in conjunction with Russia, in order to defuse the entrenched hostility between these two political and religious foes. This was an example of Aberdeen's Tory strategy of working with Russia to secure global peace.

It was also an example of the tensions that frequently arose between Britain and the Ottoman Empire during these years. These derived partly from different conceptions of territorial sovereignty. The Ottoman regime

---

1. Marsden and Smith, *Engineering Empires*, chap. 3. See also Lynn, "'Imperialism of Free Trade,'" 28.

instinctively saw its function as being to protect the lands of Islam, the *dar al-Islam,* from the foreigner, and so had an expansive definition of its reach that went well beyond its practical ability to exercise local control. Its assertiveness on this score became more pronounced during the 1840s, in the Gulf and in the Red Sea as well as on the Persian border. The Porte insisted that the Saudi ruler Faysal, the sharif of Mecca, and the sharif of Abu Arish in the Yemen were acting on behalf of the sultan, whether they recognised it or not. It also continued to claim authority over Abyssinia. It pushed these arguments not just from principle, but also from concern at the evident increase in British power, in the Gulf and in Aden and its hinterland. In these areas, Britain's need to secure order as cheaply as possible, and ideally to develop local economies, was directly at odds with the Ottomans' vision, both for the lands and for their own spiritual authority. British influence seemed to be encroaching nearer and nearer to the Muslim Holy Cities in the Hijaz. In the Middle East, the European country that most consistently challenged Ottoman territorial assumptions was Britain.

By the 1850s, Britain found Ottoman behaviour in this region much more of a challenge than Russian or French activity—not least because it might require an increased naval commitment. In the Gulf and around Aden, the Ottoman claims were defeated, though in the middle of the Red Sea, at Massawa, they were not. In asserting British power, and trying to limit Ottoman rights, policymakers sometimes relied on arguments founded on treaties and therefore on the language of international law, but only where it seemed helpful. To an outsider, Britain's behaviour on the Middle Eastern waterways cannot have seemed any less assertive than Russia's behaviour in its Balkan sphere of influence.

Ottoman Sovereignty and the Persian Border

In the summer of 1842, foreign ministers Aberdeen and Nesselrode agreed that Britain and Russia would work together to settle the border disputes between the Ottoman and Persian Empires. This was a logical consequence of Anglo-Russian cooperation in the crisis of 1839–41. It also reflected the Tory view that Britain's Afghan war had been a humiliating and expensive failure that need not be repeated if Britain and Russia worked together to resolve Asian tensions. There were few areas where tensions were more institutionalised than along the ancient border between the great Sunni and Shi'i empires. Each was used to exploiting problems caused by the incursions and depredations of marauding border tribes. There were two particular zones where such behaviour threatened to lead to war: the Kurdish border province of Sulaimaniya, and the lands settled by the Ka'b Arabs where the Karun river flowed into the Shatt al-Arab and the Gulf. The idea of a joint commission to settle the border disguised continuing mutual suspicion between Britain and Russia. Indeed, Britain agreed to the commission partly from fear that otherwise Russia would mediate on its own, as it now had influence over both empires. Britain was no longer on good terms with Persia: it had no minister there between 1838 and 1842. Britain's naval presence in the Gulf necessarily gave it some weight in affairs in the south of the country, but its continuing occupation of Persia's Gulf island of Kharaq created severe tensions with the regime (until Aberdeen ordered its evacuation in late 1842). From 1841, meanwhile, the new government in Constantinople was in British eyes alarmingly receptive to Russian pressure.

As a result, if Britain wanted to influence the border resolution process, it would have to rely mostly on its understanding with the pasha of Baghdad— Necip between 1842 and 1849. The fundamental reason why Britain was so concerned to work in harmony with Necip throughout the 1840s was the need to promote peace on the border, and to resolve various potential tensions within the pashalik that might damage peace prospects. Powerful Kurdish, Arab, and Shi'i groups needed to be carefully managed. The other reason why Necip mattered was because Britain, and indeed Russia, wanted to exclude the French from building up influence in this sensitive border region. Despite its lack of trade, France was now hoping to develop Baghdad as a regional base, on the strength of the Catholic missionary activity in the region noted in chapter 8. It sent a warship from Réunion into the Gulf in 1842. The new French consul-general at Baghdad, Loève-Veimars, claimed ceremonial precedence over the British consul, on the strength of the ancient French capitulations. Fortunately, whatever other problems the British had with the pasha, "we have old Nejib in our hands" when it came to checking France's attempt to insert another European presence into the region. The threat mostly disappeared.[2]

The boundary mediation was an attempt to steer two regimes, which traditionally had expansive and clashing views of their historical and religious function, to accept a precisely territorial, "European" definition of sovereignty. Since the sixteenth century, Ottoman sultans had claimed to guard the lands of Islam from theological subversion as well as foreign invasion, and proclaimed fatwas against the heretical Safavid shahs of Persia. Shi'i ideas of jihad, meanwhile, involved punishment for Muslims who failed to obey its imams. Until the nineteenth century, the Ottomans and Persians represented their wars largely in confessional terms.[3] The 1823 peace treaty signed at Erzurum was the first in which the Ottomans accepted Persia as a legitimate Muslim state rather than as a territory to be won for the caliph and the Sunni religion. Sultan Mahmud consciously chose to treat Persia as a Muslim friend and a foreign power to

2. Rawlinson to Layard, May 26, 1847, LPBL, 38977 291. The Porte rejected the French claim by adopting the international rules of diplomatic precedence and ceremonial equality agreed at Vienna in 1815: Wellesley to Palmerston, Apr. 1, 1847, FO 78/680.

3. Ateş, *Ottoman-Iranian Borderlands*, 10–12.

which his government could grant specific rights.[4] Here he was reverting to an older, more syncretic notion of Ottoman religious identity. The 1823 treaty also tried to settle territorial claims along the border, not for the first time.

So there was nothing inherently offensive about what Britain and Russia were now asking the Ottomans and Persia to do, especially since both were anxious to keep in the background, and to recognise the independence and dignity of the contending powers. The British ambassador Stratford Canning instructed Fenwick Williams, the British commissioner, in those terms. It was agreed that a commission would assemble at Erzurum. It would define the frontier, on the basis of treaty documents where possible, and otherwise by examining customary tribute arrangements. It would fix the terms of compensation for recent border attacks, allocate the tribute due from the wandering border tribes, and make a commercial agreement along the lines of the Anglo-Ottoman treaty of 1838.[5] Nonetheless, no one underestimated the challenges. In 1845, Henry Rawlinson, the British consul at Baghdad, feared that "no treaty however concluded and by whatever party guaranteed, can possibly lead to any real or permanent tranquillity. [W]here, as is the case between the courts of Tehran and Constantinople, a predisposition exists to take offence," border conflicts "will ever afford convenient grounds of national quarrel."[6]

These tensions meant that the commission had not finished its work by 1854, when this book ends. At the outset, Nesselrode set out a compromise solution: free Persian access to the Gulf port of Muhammara, in return for accepting Ottoman sovereignty over Sulaimaniya.[7] Unfortunately, on each side someone could always be guaranteed to make a fiery speech against concession. On the whole, the British felt that the Ottoman side was the most unreasonable. In July 1845, Canning detected "no abatement of the arrogant and contemptuous feelings with which [the Porte] presumes to treat every question connected with Persian interests." In November, Williams unwisely believed that a settlement was imminent and that "we can escape from this purgatory." The Treaty of Erzurum, which did indeed confirm Sulaimaniya as Ottoman and Muhammara as Persian, was not signed until 1847, though the Ottomans then delayed ratification until 1848. Discussion now moved to the more precise and vexed issue of boundary delimitation, another "hopeless errand," which led to the commissioners tramping long sections of border territory.[8]

4. Masters, "Treaties of Erzurum," 10–12.

5. Canning to Williams, Jan. 13, 1843, FO 78/515.

6. Rawlinson to India House, Mar. 26, 1845, IOR L/P&S/9/14 50.

7. There was also a third disputed area, the mountain region of Zohab south of Sulaimaniya, where there was no natural boundary: see Ateş, *Ottoman-Iranian Borderlands*, 100–104.

8. Canning to Aberdeen, July 3, 1845, FO 78/599; Williams to Layard, Nov. 15, 1845, LPBL, 38976 243; Alison to Layard, June 2, 1848, LPBL, 38978 94.

There was crisis at the outset. Williams and his assistant Robert Curzon reached Erzurum in February 1843 to hear that an estimated five thousand Shi'a had just been killed in their holy city of Karbala within the Baghdad pashalik, just south of the capital. When Necip was appointed to Baghdad in 1842, he had particular orders to tranquillise Karbala, which for some years had refused to pay tribute to Ottoman pashas and was in the hands of a dozen different gangs who in his eyes were refugees and outlaws.[9] Necip besieged the town and, after warnings, attacked it in January 1843. Hundreds were killed having sought sanctuary at the shrine of Abbas; the British surgeon who inspected the site reported that "the cloth of gold covering the defunct Gent's bones is now red with blood."[10] Naturally it took months to pacify the angry Persian delegation. It was agreed that Necip must repair the shrines and ensure safe conduct of pilgrims to and from Karbala.

The Karbala crisis made British officials focus on a policy of pressing Necip to ensure that religious peace was maintained between Sunni and Shi'a in the pashalik. Francis Farrant, a British officer who had helped to train Persian troops and had then been attached to the boundary commission, was sent to Baghdad to accompany the official Ottoman investigation of the massacre, and to reassure the Persians that it was sufficiently fair. The long-standing British political agent at Baghdad, Robert Taylor, was removed, because it appeared to Canning and to Lord Ellenborough, the Tory governor-general of India, that he had endangered the negotiations by not doing more to restrain Necip. Taylor had been informed of Necip's plans two months before the attack, but had tried to deal with him on his own. Ellenborough replaced him with Henry Rawlinson, who, like Farrant, had spent years training Persian soldiers, and therefore seemed well placed to win Persian trust. Ellenborough gave Rawlinson extra powers over British officers in the Gulf, if this was necessary to resolve any border tensions. It was also agreed that the political agent (who had carried the additional title of Foreign Office consul since 1841) should henceforth report mainly to Constantinople and the Foreign Office, because Baghdad affairs impacted so much on European diplomacy.[11] There was a suggestive coda to these events in 1849, on the death of two widows of the nawab of the Indian state of Awadh. This resulted in a bequest of at least £10,000 per year to the shrines of Karbala and Najaf for religious and charitable purposes. The question immediately arose how this was to be administered, since the fear was that the Shi'a would now get enough revenue to foment serious "political excitement" or indeed avaricious Ottoman retaliation. By 1852, despite much hesitation, the inevitable conclusion was reached that the only fair and safe way to dispense this annual award was for the British consul at

9. See Litvak, "Karbala."
10. Ross to Taylor, Jan. 22, 1843, FO 195/204.
11. For this incident, see Parry, "Steam Power," 168–70.

Baghdad himself to process and monitor it, and so the consul became involved in the judicious management of the revenues of the Karbala shrine.[12]

The other major difficulty exposed by the boundary talks was the management of the border Kurds, especially in the province of Sulaimaniya that had so concerned Claudius Rich. The Persians had frequently taken advantage of Ottoman weakness to force the Baban chiefs there to direct their tribute to them instead. Davut had tried to challenge Persian dominance in Sulaimaniya throughout the 1820s, but had failed. The plague and the fall of Davut in 1831 paved the way for an agreement in 1832, which accepted that Sulaimaniya belonged to the sultan, but legitimised the tribute to Persia. When Fraser visited Sulaimaniya in 1834, he found it a wreck, owing to Persian spoliation, the large tribute, and the plague. In 1844, Felix Jones reported that the town was half its size in Rich's time.[13] However, there were limits to Persian influence there, not least because the Babans were Sunnis. Through the 1820s and 1830s, there was a persistent struggle for incumbency between the two surviving sons of Abdurrahman—Mahmud, who had impressed Rich in 1820, and his younger brother Sulayman—as they took up Baghdad and Persia in turn against the other. Taylor formed the view that this superficial hostility to each other was in fact an informally coordinated dance to avoid complete subordination to either side.[14] In 1838, Persia's civil war gave the Ottomans hope of a breakthrough: they persuaded the new Baban pasha, Sulayman's son Ahmed, to adopt the Turkish costume and pledge his soldiers to the sultan. After Sulayman's death in 1839 there was a three-way battle for control in Sulaimaniya between Ahmed, Mahmud, and Mahmud's son Ali (who had converted to Shi'ism and lived in Persia). The Baghdad regime chose Mahmud, who was old, tired, and religious; in March 1840, the Persians challenged him and installed Ali by force. When this attempt at a Shi'i takeover met local resistance, the Persians turned to Ahmed instead, who took power, but by 1841 he had switched to the Ottoman side, leading the Persians to open talks with Mahmud.[15]

These interminable power plays manifestly weakened all those involved. The Baghdad pashalik was particularly suspicious of young Ahmed's aspirations for independence. On at least three occasions between 1839 and 1843, the Ottomans supported his claims to the chieftainship, only to find that he was unwilling to accept their demands in practice. By 1843, Ahmed was attacking tribes across the Persian border, a provocative move now that the boundary commission was assembling. Mahmud had taken refuge in Tehran, and so there was a risk that Persia would take up his cause again. However, Ahmed

12. Rose to Malmesbury, July 18, 1852, FO 78/893. See Litvak, "Money, Religion, and Politics."

13. Fraser, *Travels in Koordistan*, 1:147–55; J. Jones, *Memoirs*, 207.

14. July 16, 1832, IOR L/P&S/9/95 206.

15. This paragraph summarises Taylor's extensive reports to India House on Sulaimaniya after 1830 in IOR L/P&S/9.

disliked the size of the tribute demanded by Necip, and might easily court the Persians himself. In 1843, Necip decided to discipline Ahmed by promoting the cause of his younger brother Abdullah. Fearing yet more family factionalism, and desperate to avoid Ottoman-Persian conflict, Rawlinson and Farrant tried to mediate between Necip and Ahmed, promising the latter safe conduct if he came to Baghdad. Necip was determined to settle the matter locally, and also had orders from the Porte to avoid "European interference" in Sulaimaniya's affairs. In 1845, he deposed Ahmed. Abdullah was made Necip's governor, but could offer only "imbecile and unproductive rule." After trying to raise troops against him, Ahmed was exiled to Constantinople. Abdullah was soon moved on, and the Babans lost their hereditary rights in Sulaimaniya.[16] Both brothers were absorbed into the Ottoman bureaucracy as governors elsewhere.[17]

When the Treaty of Erzurum in 1847 confirmed that Sulaimaniya was Ottoman territory, Necip's strongman policy seemed vindicated. The end of Baban rule coincided with the defeat of Bedir Khan Beg, and followed the demise of the mir of Rawanduz as well. The quasi-independent Kurdish amirates were at an end. However, in practice the Babans and other Kurdish clans continued to exercise a lot of local influence.[18] The borderlands still belonged to them. Rawlinson, like Fraser before him, saw them as fine, independent, and courageous warriors who would be the best defenders of the frontier in a future war against Russia or Persia.[19] The European powers had pressed Persia not to interfere in Ottoman territory, but this understanding depended on the maintenance of Anglo-Russian concord. When it collapsed, in 1853, the Persians reverted to threatening military movements near the border.[20] Even so, Sulaimaniya was not the commission's greatest problem. That came when it tried to get the Ottomans to accept the quid pro quo—a limitation on their sovereignty in the Gulf.

Conflicts with Ottomanism: Muhammara and the Gulf

Disagreement centred on Muhammara (now Khorramshahr), a port on the east bank of the Shatt al-Arab at its junction with the Haffar canal. The Haffar canal had been built to connect the Shatt al-Arab to the Karun River, the gateway into Persian Khuzistan, and the canal now provided the best access

16. For the quotations, Rawlinson to Canning, Sept. 2, 1845, and to Sheil, June 22, 1846, FO 195/237 350, 584. Rawlinson's many reports are well summarised in Ateş, *Ottoman-Iranian Borderlands*, 71–75.

17. For Ahmed's later career, see Atmaca, "Resistance to Centralisation," 529.

18. Ateş, *Ottoman-Iranian Borderlands*, 75; McDowell, *Modern History of the Kurds*, 4.

19. Rawlinson to Bidwell, Jan. 6, 1847, FO 195/272 10, and to Layard, Sept. 30, 1846, LPBL, 38977 54.

20. Canning to Clarendon, Dec. 17, 1853, FO 78/941A.

to the Gulf from the Karun River for Persian trade, though there was an inferior, natural exit from the Karun slightly further east. So Muhammara had an attractive position. Built in 1812, it was controlled by Kaʿb Arabs who were already an independent trading power and who used it to build themselves up. Muhammara and the surrounding Kaʿb territory, like everything on the banks of the Tigris and Euphrates, was assumed by the Ottomans to be theirs by right of conquest in the sixteenth century.

However, no historic treaty shed much light on the sovereignty of the eastern side of the Shatt al-Arab. As they had spread so much into Persian territory, the Kaʿb paid tribute to Persia, and had converted to Shiʿism in the eighteenth century, but they also paid land rent at Muhammara to the Basra government, recognising that the Ottomans had once possessed it. Like the Baban Kurds, they were used to playing each side off against the other in order to remain largely independent of both. Under the local governor, Jabir al-Mirdaw, and the tribal shaykh Thamir, Muhammara developed commercially as a threat to Basra on the other side of the Shatt al-Arab, depriving the pashalik of vital customs revenues. This goaded Baghdad pasha Ali Rida to attack Muhammara, claim it for the Ottomans, and plunder its warehouses in 1837. The Kaʿb now split: Thamir accepted Ottoman sovereignty claims, while Jabir refused to do so and sought Persian protection. In 1841, the governor of Persian Khuzistan attacked Thamir and deposed him as tribal leader, in favour of his nephew Faris. The Persians now claimed the eastern bank of the Shatt al-Arab up to Qurna, and demanded that the Ottomans bear the cost of rebuilding Muhammara, or else they would destroy Basra. The Ottomans responded by threatening war against Persia. It was this threat that had led to the establishment of the Boundary Commission.[21]

Canning, helped by Layard's local knowledge, argued for Ottoman control of the east bank, on the grounds that it would stop the risk of Persian and thus Russian influence in the Gulf. He was furious, as was the Porte, to find that Aberdeen rejected his opinion in search of consensus with Russia.[22] In 1845, a draft treaty proposed giving the town and adjoining lands to Persia, with free navigation of the rivers. In fact, Persia was still occupying Muhammara and refusing to leave. The Ottomans encouraged the Kaʿb not to submit to Persian revenue demands, which they were declining to do anyway. For two years, the Ottomans refused to concede, and stationed a guardship at the mouth of the Haffar canal to assert their rights over the bank. Rawlinson reported that this prolonged crisis was encouraging local Arabs to plunder trading vessels.[23] The

21. Ateş, *Ottoman-Iranian Borderlands*,113–17. For its commercial status, see Fattah, *Politics of Regional Trade*, 197–99; Floor, "Rise and Fall," 291–93.

22. Layard, *Early Adventures*, 2:437–38.

23. Rawlinson to Canning, Aug. 5, 1846, FO 195/237 630, to Wellesley, Mar. 3, 1847, FO 195/272 66.

treaty was signed in 1847, confirming that the town of Muhammara was Persian, and guaranteeing free passage of the Shatt al-Arab to both Persian and Turkish ships. However, the Ottomans now demanded that Britain and Russia should agree to the principle of Ottoman sovereignty over the Shatt al-Arab itself, in an explanatory note. So when the commissioners moved on to a detailed topographical survey of the contested boundary areas, all the old clashing positions were adopted again. In May 1850, the commission decided to adjourn altogether, rather than endure a hot summer debating such matters in the Gulf: the British went on an archaeological dig instead. In 1851, tensions increased; three Ottoman warships anchored opposite Muhammara. Eventually a compromise proposed by Williams gained acceptance: it gave the Ottomans all the navigable parts of the Shatt al-Arab, aiming to safeguard Basra's commerce, while confirming that the Haffar canal and the town of Muhammara were Persian. The Ka'b confirmed that they would accept Persian sovereignty; Thamir never returned to the chiefship. Jabir, however, remained more or less independent in Muhammara, while making his own fixed payment to the Persians. In 1857, Jabir supported the Persians during their war with Britain, while Shaykh Faris and the Ka'b encouraged the British.[24]

In short, the commission had pursued a studied neutrality on the question of Muhammara, rather than the defence of Ottoman sovereignty claims that Canning expected. On the British side, this was not just because Aberdeen sought consensus with Russia, nor because the Persians were occupying the town. It also reflected three underlying considerations, all of which ultimately stemmed from British power in the Gulf. First, the British had no objection to two viable ports at the entrance to the Gulf, held by different powers, rather than one. They could be played off each against the other, while British naval and commercial power would force them both to respect British interests, just as the value of Indian trade in Basra had always given Britain influence at Baghdad. If the British wanted more influence in Persia, the ability to interfere with trade with Muhammara was a good tactic for getting it. This was illustrated most effectively in the Anglo-Persian war of 1856–57, when British forces actually occupied Muhammara, an even better way of forcing the Persians to negotiate than taking Kharaq had been in 1838.

Secondly, for the same reason, British influence in southern Persia, already significant along the coast, was bound to grow, negating the risk that the Russians, whose power was all in northern Persia, could ever benefit by Persian access to the Gulf. On the contrary, the country might even split. At the beginning of the Crimean War in 1854, the British sent five frigates in succession up the Shatt al-Arab over a period of four months to make it quite clear to the Persians, and the Russians, that this was a zone of British influence.[25] Thirdly,

24. See Ateş, *Ottoman-Iranian Borderlands*, 120–21, 134–36, 154–61; Floor, "Rise and Fall," 294–95.

25. *PGP*, 6:245–46.

considerations of sovereignty mattered only infrequently: the reality in peacetime was that Jabir and his tribesmen controlled Muhammara, which was an attractive free trading port. For the British, dealing with a natural trader like Jabir was as easy as dealing with the various other Arab tribes around the coast of the Gulf.

While the outcome pleased Britain, it did not satisfy the Ottomans. Losing a potentially significant Gulf port in return for an intractably difficult Kurdish border province was not obviously a great bargain. As a result, from the signing of the Treaty of Erzurum onwards, the Ottomans made difficulties for Britain in the Gulf. The Porte and Necip tried to assert the Ottomans' own sovereign claims there. The Porte now gave the province of Basra an increased status and indicated that its reach included Hasa in eastern Arabia, and Qatar. Necip announced plans for an Ottoman naval arsenal. In 1849, Ottoman ministers told Canning that they aimed to place steamers in the Euphrates and in the Gulf, and hinted that they would make a claim on Bahrain. The British saw this as a challenge to their own "supreme authority in the Gulf." In 1850, Samuel Hennell, the British resident in the Gulf, expressed alarm that the chief of Bahrain, or any of the Trucial shaykhdoms, might seek Ottoman protection in order to resist the authority of Britain; this must be prevented. The Bombay government and Palmerston agreed that Ottoman claims over Bahrain were unacceptable and that its independence must be upheld. Three cruisers were sent to make the point.[26] The immediate fear was not of Ottoman steamers, which did not exist, but that the Ottomans might do a deal with Faysal, who since 1843 had been consolidating his position as Saudi ruler, and who had threatened Bahrain in 1847 during the tensions over the Treaty of Erzurum. The Ottomans could claim that he was acting on their behalf, since he was invested as lieutenant in Central Arabia by the sharif of Mecca. Indeed, in 1852 the pasha of Baghdad argued that Faysal was claiming Bahrain on their behalf.[27] The British had no problem with Faysal as such—his operations on the Gulf shore could be managed, and in 1852 a warship was sent to Muscat to encourage peace between him and its ruler—but a move on Bahrain was another matter, because of its wealth and the importance of its neutrality to the stability of the Gulf.

The other danger posed by the threat of an Ottoman navy in the Gulf was that, by casting doubts on British paramountcy, it might revive Arab piracy. Poor Arab traders would be tempted to return to plunder, if they thought they could play British and Ottoman authorities against each other.[28] This would be a retrograde step, since British ambitions to secure order in the Gulf were increasing significantly in the mid-1840s. In 1846, Hennell agreed informally

26. J. Kelly, *Britain and the Persian Gulf*, 399–402; the quotation is in Bombay to India House, Aug. 6, 1847, FO 78/723.

27. Rawlinson to Rose, Aug. 23, 1852, FO 195/367.

28. Rawlinson and Kemball to Cowley, May 26 and July 6, 1847, FO 195/272 212, 336.

with the Persian governor of Fars that British ships would police the Persian shore looking for pirates, though this agreement was not made public. In 1845, Muscat bowed to British pressure and agreed to confine its slave trading to the African coast rather than the Gulf. In 1847, the Porte agreed to forbid Ottoman vessels and subjects from engaging in the slave trade, giving British warships limited rights of search and seizure over them. Meanwhile, Hennell persuaded the Trucial shaykhs to ban the slave trade in 1847. Britain's assault on the slave trade, as on piracy, was part of its aim of creating an ordered space for free commerce.[29]

Hennell assumed that Necip would also allow British cruisers to behave in Ottoman waters as they did in the Gulf, and seize Arab and Persian pirate vessels. In other words, he hoped to take advantage of Britain's new local power, and the Ottoman-Persian negotiations, to broker a consolidated peace on piracy, in which both empires would accept British supremacy. However, Necip quickly made clear informally that he would refuse this, as a breach of Ottoman rights under international law. There followed a revealing debate among British diplomats as to whether to uphold Hennell's request. Rawlinson and Palmerston both agreed that it was unwise to press Necip on the matter, and that it should be dropped. This was not simply because it was a breach of international law, but for two more specific reasons. First, it would set a precedent allowing other powers—such as the Russians in the Caspian Sea—to violate the neutrality of Ottoman ships and harbours. Second, it would allow the Porte to reject a formal British application and to declare its own rights and naval ambitions in the Gulf very forcefully, with awkward long-term consequences. Since piracy around Basra was not a major problem, it would be better to proceed through informal pressure, if a specific outrage occurred that needed rectifying.[30]

The Baghdad pashas continued to irritate the British, especially once the London government's concern over the slave trade increased in the late 1840s.[31] As early as February 1845, Rawlinson noted that Necip seemed "to exhibit day by day a more determined resistance to measures of European intervention." In May 1848, he described him as "daily more bigoted, more avaricious, more faithless and more foolish."[32] In 1852, Necip's successor Namık declared that the orders of 1847 to stop the slave trade, sent to Baghdad by the Porte under British pressure, were not as far-reaching as the British claimed,

29. J. Kelly, *Britain and the Persian Gulf*, 377, 587–89. See Crouzet, "Slave Trade Jurisdiction."

30. See Palmerston: note, Feb. 7, 1847, FO 78/718, and to Cowley, Nov. 6, 1847, FO 78/676; J. Kelly, *Britain and the Persian Gulf*, 378–79.

31. This became an important tension in Anglo-Ottoman relations from now on: see Toledano, *Ottoman Slave Trade*, chap. 3.

32. Rawlinson to Bombay, Feb. 22, 1845, IOR L/P&S/9/14 45, and to Layard, May 10, 1848, LPBL, 38978 77.

and had lapsed. Slavery, he said, was "one of the most cherished domestic and religious institutions of Turkey"; in November sixteen slave boys were openly for sale at Baghdad.[33] This was a striking gesture of resistance to Western pressure—all the more so given that, nineteen years earlier, Namık had appeared in London as a new model Ottoman ambassador seeking a British alliance, and had impressed everyone with his civility, education, and grace. Not for the first, or last, time in the Middle East, British local officials grasped that in practice they had to lower the pressure coming from London for a vigorous assault on slave trading.[34]

Ottoman assertiveness, however, merely encouraged the British to secure their own position in the Gulf to head off any challenge. When the maritime truce in the Gulf expired after ten years, it was replaced by a permanent truce in 1853, guaranteed by the British resident and negotiated by Hennell's successor Kemball. It offered the shaykhs permanent protection and "peace in perpetuity." All the Trucial rulers agreed to prevent hostilities between them, and to rely on the British authorities to obtain reparations for any act of aggression on them. The Ottoman navy in the Gulf remained a phantom for some decades. Meanwhile, in 1861, the British met continuing threats to Bahrain, from the Saudis and others, with the first of several treaties guaranteeing its independence. The local British representatives rejected Ottoman claims to sovereignty, either in the Gulf or over Faysal, and insisted that Gulf security was a British responsibility.[35]

So naval power guaranteed British authority on the coast. Whether it could also improve the economic condition of the pashalik of Baghdad was a greater challenge.

Steam Power, Economic Improvement, and Regional Security in Baghdad

In March 1840, Ali Rida, Necip's predecessor as pasha of Baghdad, wrote a paper for the Porte on how to restore the "ancient prosperity" of the pashalik. It requested that instead of asking Baghdad for tribute, central government should give him fifteen thousand soldiers, six warships, and twenty gunboats. With this force, he promised to confine the marauding Arab tribes to their pasture grounds, regain control of lands that they had appropriated, discipline the tribes on the border with Persia, and secure peace. These changes would increase revenues so much that the government could soon levy a higher

33. Rawlinson to Rose, Aug. 24 (quotation) and Nov. 17, 1852, FO 195/367.

34. The reduction in the Indian Navy's presence in the Gulf in 1853 because of the Burmese War revived the trade further: Otte, "Course of Unceasing Remonstrance," 100.

35. J. Kelly, *Britain and the Persian Gulf*, 407, 513–14, 526–29. For the treaties of 1861 and 1853, see Aitchison, *Treaties*, 12:159–60, 180–81.

tribute. Leaving aside the request for troops rather than tribute (which was presumably his main objective), the idea of improving the management of Mesopotamia's fertile lands would have been familiar to most British observers. In 1845, Rawlinson followed his predecessor Taylor in calling for irrigation schemes and for incentives to settle the Arabs as farmers. Henry Blosse Lynch, the commander of the four British steamers on the Mesopotamian rivers, had also been advocating such measures, and argued for them when passing through Constantinople in 1840 during his emergency trip to London.[36]

In 1839–40, Lynch and his father-in-law Taylor hoped to work with Ali Rida to revive Taylor's plan of 1830 to improve authority and prosperity in the pashalik. The immediate circumstances—the threat from Mehmet Ali in the south, and Persia and the Kurds in the east—added some urgency, but the core strategy was the one that Taylor had worked out with Davut: to use steam power to impose order and develop the local economy. Conveniently, it would also make money for enterprising Britons from his own family. Lynch's trip home was to lobby for a permanent steamer flotilla under his command, but also to urge his two younger brothers, Tom and Stephen, to come out to Baghdad to found a trading company to benefit from increased British interest in the region. They arrived in 1841 and established Lynch Brothers. Lynch hoped to become the Samuel Briggs of Baghdad, using political links with the ruling pasha to build up a favoured import-export business. This would be all the more lucrative since in 1840 Lynch expected that Britain and Mehmet Ali would become long-term enemies, so that the Euphrates rather than the Nile would henceforth be the main conduit for Anglo-Indian communications.

Things did not go to plan for Henry Lynch. While he was away, his deputy, Dugald Campbell, felt obliged to make a trip up to Beles in 1841, but ran his steamer aground. By 1842, Lynch had to admit that the Syrian reaches of the Euphrates, above Hit, were not navigable, a great blow to the whole enterprise. The steamers had to carry so much fuel, food, and weaponry that they were too heavy for the ascent.[37] His accounts, moreover, were in complete disarray, infuriating Bombay.

Worst of all, the replacement in 1841 of the Palmerston-Hobhouse axis by the Tory combination of Aberdeen in London and Ellenborough as Indian governor-general punctured the vision of steam-powered expansion in Mesopotamia, while the new ministers were also keen to repair British relations with Egypt. Three of the four steamers were recalled to India at various times in 1842, as was Lynch, and the dromedary post was axed (though it

36. Rawlinson to Canning, Jan. 8, 1845, FO 195/237 211; Taylor to India House, Mar. 31, 1840, IOR L/P&S/9/114 25.

37. Campbell to Hobhouse, Aug. 14, 1841, IOR L/P&S/9/119 699; Lynch to Ellenborough, Aug. 14, 1842, FO 195/113 pt. 3, 85; Lynch to Fitzgerald, June 25, 1842, IOR L/P&S/9/13.

was reinstated in 1844). Lynch made one last bid to challenge this order and stay in Baghdad, by relying on the ambition of the new pasha, the decisive and energetic Necip. Taylor and Lynch worked with Necip on a plan that the pasha should take over the operation of the remaining steamer, the *Nitocris*, or buy a replacement, and that Lynch should command it with a British crew and twenty thousand shells imported from India. Taylor urged this idea on the astonished Indian government, which regarded it as unthinkable.[38] It would have meant surrendering Britain's control over the steamer, and the special rights given to it by the firman, while Lynch, commanding the steamer in Necip's name, would have lost the British the reputation they sought for even-handedness as between Ottomans and Arabs. Necip would have gained more practical independence as against Constantinople, and the only British beneficiaries would have been the Taylor-Lynch family.

The plan also reckoned without Alexander Hector, the leading rival merchant to the Lynches in Baghdad, who decided to strike a blow at the family economic interest that Taylor had built up at the residency. Hector had had to surrender the administration of the dromedary post to Lynch; he also claimed that the Lynches (but not he) were allowed to evade river duties by transporting goods in residency boats under the British flag. For years he had also suspected the dealings of the residency dragoman Catchick, an Armenian merchant and long-standing connection of Taylor's from Basra days, who had made large sums out of other merchants through his control of the Baghdad exchange, and allegedly exploited his residency position to take bribes from locals. Hector wondered how in nine years he had amassed £30,000. Hector complained to India and London, and threatened to leave Baghdad. This complaint about the Taylor-Lynch financial network arrived in both places at almost the same time as Canning's protest about Taylor's handling of the Karbala affair. In fact, Hector claimed that the lead, powder, and shot used in the Karbala massacre had been brought upstream by the *Nitocris*, adding fuel to his claim that it was becoming a personal military vessel for Necip.[39] The conjunction of these two allegations ensured Taylor's dismissal, and Lynch's removal to India.

Might this drama open the way for a different model of British economic relationships at Baghdad? Hector was able to pursue his attack because Henry Layard, whom he had befriended when at Baghdad, was now at Constantinople as Canning's unofficial assistant. Layard shared his indignation at Taylor's vested interest network, and argued that Hector represented a much more dynamic capitalist economic vision. Hector had offered to invest capital in irrigation schemes near Baghdad and a cotton press at Muhammara,

---

38. [Malet], *Précis*, 136; Taylor to Bombay, Mar. 7, 1843, IOR L/P&S/9/13; Stark to Addington, Oct. 30, 1843, IOR L/P&S/3/15.

39. Parry, "Steam Power," 167–69.

but residency hostility had apparently poisoned Necip against him. Layard and Hector argued that Britain should abandon Lynch's fixation with the upper Euphrates, and should focus on the rivers that were clearly navigable by steam—the Tigris, and in particular the lower reaches of the Karun into Persia.[40] The potential navigability of the Karun had interested Chesney, who suggested an expedition there in 1836, inspired by the fact that Alexander's henchman Nearchus had reached Susa in 324 BCE. Layard had spent months living with the Bakhtiari in Khuzistan in 1840, and had become convinced that they would be excellent trading partners (and political allies) for the British. When he reached Baghdad in 1842, he persuaded one of the flotilla's officers, William Selby, to take a steamer, and himself, up the Karun. They navigated to Ahvaz and Shuster, where they grounded, using this as an opportunity to cultivate the tribes. Hector proposed himself as consul at Muhammara, at the same time growing produce along the banks of the Karun.[41]

However, this idea was plainly unrealistic, since by 1844 Muhammara was effectively a war zone, occupied by Persia. So in 1844–45, Hector and Layard turned their search for commercial partners to Sulaimaniya instead, and to the young Ahmed Pasha. Layard was presumably influenced in this choice by Rich's praise for the abundance and liberality of Sulaimaniya, just as he had been inspired by Rich's account of the mounds of Nineveh. Hector's economic hopes for Sulaimaniya coincided neatly with Rawlinson's aspirations to mediate between Necip and Ahmed in order to remove the threat that Ahmed posed to the boundary commission. Therefore both men went to Sulaimaniya in late summer 1844, accompanied by Felix Jones, who had succeeded Lynch as commander of the steamer operation. They were duly impressed. Despite an appearance "not prepossessing; and an impediment in his speech," Ahmed projected something that Jones found alluring: "he devotes most part of the night to financial and political correspondence" and the day to military and agricultural improvements. Rawlinson fell in love with the fertile uplands of Sulaimaniya, just as Rich had done: "it was as though we had suddenly emerged from barbarism to civilization." He regarded Ahmed as "the most enlightened, humane, and energetic Prince that it has ever been my lot to meet with, among the tribes of Kurdistan."[42] Bearing the fate of Rich in mind, they should have been more cautious. Their journey angered Necip, who claimed that Rawlinson had no right to interfere on the frontier. Moreover, Hector

40. Stirling to Aberdeen, June 5, 1843, IOR L/P&S/3/14; Hector to Layard, Oct. 8, 1842, Mar. 11 and 24, and Apr. 5, 1843, LPBL, 38975, 73, 187, 196, 204; Layard to Mitford, Aug. 12, 1842, LPBL, 58159 6, and to Canning, Dec. 9, 1842, LPBL, 38975 104.

41. Chesney, *Expedition for the Survey*, 2:698, 701; Selby, "Account of the Ascent," 231, 242; Layard to his mother, May 26, 1842, LPBL, 58149 71; Hector to Layard, Oct. 8, 1842, LPBL, 38975 73.

42. J. Jones, *Memoirs*, 208–9; Rawlinson to Canning, Oct. 30, 1844, and Aug. 6, 1845, FO 195/237 186, 325.

played into Necip's hands by foolishly agreeing to Ahmed's request to buy two thousand English muskets for him, in contravention of the twenty-third article of the capitulations. Hector's avarice probably made little difference to Ahmed's fate, but it put British meddling in Sulaimaniya in a very bad light, summoning up memories of Rich's defiance of Baghdad in 1820.[43] The consequence was not only the abolition of Baban rule in Sulaimaniya, but also the ending of hopes for British-led economic development there.

By 1850, it was clear to everyone that there was no chance of rapid economic progress anywhere in the pashalik, either working with Necip or separately. The basic problem was the Baghdad government's inability to secure order, which seemed to be growing. The Euphrates was less navigable in 1850 than in 1840, owing to the failure to repair embankments that controlled the spring floods. Necip's increasingly heavy taxation pushed many tribes away from cultivation to brigandage, and then to revolt.[44] There was a particular problem in controlling the two powerful Arab tribes in the north of the pashalik, the Anaza and the Shammar, especially after Suffuq, the long-time Shammar leader, lost his authority and his tribe fell prey to bitter factionalism. He was murdered in 1847, not in the traditional Arab blood feud, but by an Ottoman soldier—the consequences seemed "very black for the Turks."[45] Necip was removed in 1849, after complaints at his "corruption, rapacity, injustice and tyranny," from Rawlinson and Canning, but more importantly from rival Ottoman officials.[46] His fall from power was a reminder that the Porte's overriding concern in a distant province like Baghdad was to prevent the emergence of another strongman so entrenched that he might aspire to match the independence of Mehmet Ali.

One of Necip's critics, Abdi, succeeded, but found himself at the mercy of Shammar Arabs who plundered the grain supplies. By 1850, none of the main roads was safe: the major Arab tribes were uncontrollable, the Khezail and Zubaid were at war, protection for traders had collapsed, plundered goods were sold in the bazaars, and revenues remained uncollected. Layard thought the Baghdadi merchants faced ruin.[47] Abdi had no troops, because their

43. When the first thousand arrived, Ahmed had to make Necip a present of them, but, once removed from government, he could not pay Hector's bill. Eventually Canning leant on the Porte to get Necip to pay for them, though was embarrassed by the mercenary Hector's high interest charges.

44. J. Jones, *Memoirs*, 363–65; Rawlinson to Canning, May 13, 1846, FO 195/237, and May 23, 1849, FO 78/776.

45. Rawlinson to Layard, Oct. 27, 1847, LPBL, 38977 347.

46. Rawlinson to Canning, May 23, 1849; Canning to Palmerston, June 18, 1849; both FO 78/776. Palmerston to Canning, June 7, 1849, FO 78/769; Loftus, *Travels and Researches*, 9–12.

47. Canning to Palmerston, Nov. 5 and Dec. 4 and 18, 1850, FO 78/824, 78/825, with forwarded enclosures from Rassam, Layard, Kemball, and Jones.

commander Namık had taken them to Sulaimaniya, where the Kurds were still causing trouble. Nomad chiefs had superseded the Baban aristocracy, had neglected the fields, and had seized goods for themselves. By 1853, the authorities in Baghdad were forced to rely for order in Sulaimaniya on the Babans once more.[48] Namık succeeded as pasha, but alienated the Arabs so badly that they confederated against him. In 1852, Rawlinson concluded that the Ottomans had nowhere near enough troops to be able to impose their authority on the Arabs, and no chance of collecting the revenue needed to run the state. The ultimate problem, he felt, was that the Ottomans were an alien occupying power. In a place "where in fact there is no amalgamation whatever between the governing party and the mass of the inhabitants, disorder spreads with the rapidity of contagion. A single instance of successful opposition to authority creates a thousand rebels."[49] In 1848 and 1849, Felix Jones traced the bed of the ancient Persians' Nahrawan canal north of Kut and east of Baghdad, admired their engineering and their dams, and lamented the many failings of Turks and Arabs that had produced the present wilderness and left it to the jackals. Yet he still hoped that his explorations would inspire "European capitalists" to import machinery to fertilise those "rich plains."[50]

If we view the British vision for Baghdad as one of improved order, prosperity, and commercial prospects, they failed to realise it before the Crimean War. In this regard, the contrast between Baghdad and Egypt became more and more glaring throughout the 1840s. New British merchants willing to risk their capital did not appear; Hector retired to England in 1857. The limited field was left to the deeply embedded European firms like Svoboda and Lynch Brothers who could rely on local financial networks (mostly Armenian, like that of Lynch and Taylor). Layard abandoned the East in 1851, fed up with the anarchy. Even the men of the Boundary Commission increasingly devoted their time to archaeology. In 1849, Layard had suggested excavating the mounds of ancient Susa in the Karun region, in the hope of unlocking the secrets of the great Achaemenid Empire, which had ruled so much of the world from there. The expedition, he pointed out, could take advantage of the intimidating effects of the Boundary Commission's presence on the local marauding tribes. It had an immense retinue of "eighty horse loads (half of beer and wine)."[51] Rawlinson, W. K. Loftus, and J. G. Taylor all made important archaeological discoveries there.

48. Rawlinson to Canning, May 17 and Dec. 28, 1853, FO 195/367, and Aug. 10, 1853, FO 78/957.

49. Rawlinson to Canning, June 10, 1845 (quotation), and Apr. 21, 1852, FO 78/599, 78/892; to India House, Feb. 2, 1852, IOR L/P&S/9/14 139.

50. J. Jones, *Memoirs*, 93–94, 97–98, 107–10, 128, 133–34 (quotations).

51. Layard to Hawkins, Feb. 5, 1849, FO 78/811, and to his aunt (quotation), Jan. 5, 1849, LPBL, 58155 76; Loftus, *Travels and Researches*, chaps. 27–31. J. G. Taylor, Robert Taylor's younger son, was appointed British vice-consul at Basra in 1852.

However, though economic development might have been desirable, there were more fundamental aims: the maintenance of British local power against any likely rivals. These were France and Russia, but also, increasingly, the Ottoman Empire itself. The British did not succeed in working with Necip to transform the pashalik's economy, but the result was that the pashalik did not become strong enough to challenge Britain's basic military and naval paramountcy on the waterways.

In fact, British policymakers increasingly saw the Gulf and the Mesopotamian rivers as one connected strategic region. One symbol of this was the remaining steamer that the Indian government kept afloat on the rivers, the *Nitocris*, which was succeeded by the *Comet* in 1852. The *Nitocris*'s presence was saved by the forceful arguments made by Rawlinson between 1844 and 1846, together with the return to their old cabinet posts in 1846 of Hobhouse and Palmerston, who demanded that it be kept, though the Bombay government wanted to recall it.[52]

Rawlinson's case was that Britain derived many benefits from the fact that "our flag is at present supreme" in Mesopotamia. The steamer "strengthens the hands of the British Agent in the most effectual, and . . . least ostentatious, manner possible." It underlined British superiority to France. It forced Necip to acknowledge British power. Not least, in Rawlinson's eyes, it allowed him and Necip to maintain a robust semi-independent relationship, without either of them having to kowtow to their nominal superiors at Constantinople. It also gained the respect of the Arabs, therefore minimising plunder and harassment on the rivers (even if not on the roads).[53] When the British merchants in Baghdad petitioned for the steamer's retention in 1846, they argued that it engendered in the Arabs a "wholesome dread of the power of the British Government."[54] Felix Jones spent most of his time as steamer commander in cultivating good relations with the Arabs on all the rivers, just like his Indian Navy predecessors. In 1854, he produced a detailed analysis for government of the 155 tribes "which I am best acquainted with in Irak." He made occasional trips to Mosul, or as near as the steamer could get to it, in order to promote British interests with the pasha of Mosul as well as the Obeid, Anaza, and Shammar tribes.[55] When a British seaman on the *Nitocris* killed an Arab in a brawl at Maqil in 1845, the Muntafiq chief agreed to waive the blood expiation only because the man was English, "for the sake of our long friendship."[56]

52. Hobhouse note on Rawlinson to London, May 28, 1846, IOR L/P&S/9/14; Palmerston memo, Dec. 16, 1846, FO 78/656.

53. *PGP*, 6:173–75; Rawlinson to Bombay, Feb. 22, 1845, IOR L/P&S/9/14.

54. Petition to Rawlinson, Oct. 27, 1846, IOR L/P&S/9/14.

55. J. Jones, *Memoirs*, 369–86 (quotation at 386); Rawlinson to Jones, Mar. 31, 1846, FO 195/237 511.

56. Rawlinson had to pay £60: to Aberdeen, June 26, 1846, FO 78/656; see Jones to Rawlinson, Dec. 18, 1845, FO 195/237.

In theory, another argument for retaining the steamer was that it might facilitate commercial development; Palmerston himself, characteristically, supported the retention of the *Nitocris* on those grounds.[57] In 1846 Canning got the Porte to force Necip to give permission for British commercial boats to navigate the Tigris under their own flag, in the hope that merchants might invest in commercial steamers themselves.[58] In practice, however, this did not happen until after the war. Moreover, Rawlinson always prioritised the pursuit of order and good relations with the river Arabs over commercial interests. Rawlinson and Jones criticised Hector and the Lynch brothers for being too grasping and unreasonable; they complained about Arab obstruction, but they encountered it only when they tried to evade long-established river payments.[59] Rawlinson had humiliated the Lynch brothers in 1847 when he felt they had lied to him about a diamond transaction with Jewish merchants. He declined to support them in the local commercial court, and criticised in front of the residency servants their "impertinent and familiar" manner to him.[60]

When he broke his collarbone hunting boar and finally had to retire in 1855, Rawlinson was succeeded by Arnold Kemball, who had been in the Gulf since 1842 and had followed Hennell as resident there; Kemball was himself succeeded in that post by Felix Jones. There was now clearly one common approach to defining British interests in the Baghdad-Gulf region. Throughout it, British authority rested on naval power—in reserve. After 1844, the British needed only three cruisers to maintain their authority in the Gulf. In Mesopotamia, the impact of the steamer was necessarily limited, and it periodically had to be sent to Bombay for repair.[61] But the 1853 treaty secured British rights and predominance in the Gulf, while the British never forgot the need to insist on their permanent rights under the firman of 1834 to run steamers on the rivers. In 1861, the firman was used to justify the introduction by Lynch Brothers of commercial steamships between Baghdad and Basra. A regular steam service from Basra to Bombay began the following year, with which the Ottomans never managed to compete.

In 1848, when a global war with Russia once again seemed a risk, the Indian government developed a new professionalism in its strategic thinking on the region. Jones, who had already produced some detailed maps, was

57. Palmerston memo, Dec. 16, 1846, FO 78/656.

58. Parry, "Steam Power," 164–65.

59. *PGP*, 6:52–54, 58–59; J. Jones, *Memoirs*, 363–65. See Rawlinson's correspondence, including the approval of the governor-general for his rejection of their complaints, sent by Canning to the Foreign Office, May 28, 1853, FO 78/932.

60. Rawlinson to Palmerston, Mar. 31, 1847, and to Cowley, June 28, 1847 (quotation), FO 195/272; Rawlinson to London, Feb. 27, 1845, IOR L/P&S/9/14. See Parry, "Steam Power," 170.

61. J. Kelly, *Britain and the Persian Gulf*, 370; *PGP*, 6:54; J. Jones, *Memoirs*, 363–65.

appointed surveyor in Mesopotamia and increased his operations. Attention began to turn seriously to its defence. Rawlinson talked of moving a couple of brigades into Baghdad to protect it from Russia. In 1850, Kemball thought that with "two well-equipped river steamers" and five to eight thousand soldiers, Britain could exercise "a most perfect control . . . over all the tribes of the pashalic." The Arabs were "naturally unwarlike," the economic resources great, the potential for river transport excellent.[62] In 1853, Jones and his assistant William Collingwood drew up a detailed map of Baghdad, to be used in the event of war. Most of the notes for it were scribbled on Collingwood's shirt cuffs in secret explorations of the town.[63] Confidence in the Arabs' instinctive preference for Indian rule over Ottoman was intoxicating, and occasionally there was talk of a British occupation, on the assumption that the Ottoman Empire could not survive.[64] But, most of the time, the British accepted that upsetting the status quo was undesirable. All that was needed was to encourage the Arabs to respect order. That this was nominally Ottoman order was an unnecessarily abstract way of thinking. The five warships that the British stationed in the Shatt al-Arab in the first few months of 1854 were there mainly to warn the Arabs against taking advantage of the war to rebel.[65] British power was now more visible than Ottoman sovereignty. The overwhelming assumption of officials in these years was that, though the future was unknowable, the Tigris, the lower Euphrates, and the Karun, and the Gulf into which they flowed, were crucial parts of the British imperial defence system.

Aden: A New Centre of Stability

In the fifteen years after 1839, Britain kept hold of Aden, its new acquisition at the bottom of the Red Sea, and developed it into the hub of a small regional empire. This development was halting and cautious, which was hardly surprising given that this was a new area of British imperial activity and had no obvious support, other than passing ships, within a thousand miles. Indeed, for some years there was opposition to the acquisition from a Tory school, headed by Indian governor-general Ellenborough, which arose from distrust of Palmerstonian bombast, an anxiety to make economies, a fear of being sucked into expensive local conflicts, and a desire not to antagonise other powers.[66]

---

62. Rawlinson to Layard, May 10, 1848, LPBL, 38978 77; Kemball to Canning, Nov. 6, 1850, FO 78/825; Rawlinson to Malmesbury, July 21, 1852, FO 78/907.

63. Markham, *Indian Surveys*, 29; J. Jones, *Memoirs*, xxix.

64. See Rawlinson memo for Foreign Office, June 14, 1853, FO 78/957.

65. *PGP*, 6:245–46, which notes that they had the "tacit consent" of the Porte.

66. Marston, *Red Sea*, 107–10; see [Holme], "Occupation of Aden."

This opposition diminished only when it became clear that the defence of Aden was less of a headache than was originally feared. Until 1843, most local shaykhs were avowedly hostile. The sultan of Lahej continued to dispute Stafford Haines's interpretation of their original agreement. He called the British kafir invaders, and in 1840 organised several night-time attacks and a blockade. Some officials in India proposed a campaign to overthrow him, but the Indian government rejected this, since it did not want to become responsible for the whole territory of Lahej—citing, as ever, the Bani Bu affair. India eventually sanctioned a brief military attack on the sultan in October 1841, which brought him to peace talks. From the end of 1843, the hinterland accepted British rule in Aden, subject to the payment of annual compensation to the various tribes affected (£230 per annum). In twelve years, £175,000 was spent on forts and walls to secure the boundaries. After the death of Sultan Muhsin in 1847, a strong alliance between Haines and his successors became the norm.[67] A consensus emerged that the British were not going to vacate Aden, but nor did they wish to take further territory, though Haines had originally hoped to do so, in order to revive the regional economy.

Aden remained a very unusual place. It was a convenient naval base—a garrison town with a coaling station, where ships could be refitted. There were no birds, animals, or trees—"not the smallest particle of vegetation."[68] The first stone houses were not built until the mid-1840s. It quickly became a reliable stopping place for steamers, with which Anglo-Indian passengers and naval officers became very familiar. From 1845, the monthly P&O service from Hong Kong and Calcutta docked there, as well as the Bombay one. By 1850, there was a hotel for the steamer passengers, run by Parsees of Bombay who served "fried fish—a luxury even to the sumptuously regaled guest of the steamer."[69] Visitors were offered camels and horses for rides around the territory. Already in 1843, the population was twenty thousand. In 1844, Cornwallis Harris envisaged that it would become "queen of the adjacent seas," under "mild but firm government." Eager merchants would settle and rescue it from "ruin and degradation . . . tyranny and misrule"; it could then eclipse "even its ancient opulence and renown."[70] This was somewhat fanciful. However, Haines ruled Aden by treating it as a cosmopolitan port city of business. He recognised that because so many ships came and went, the population was shifting rather than stable. This made it different from most settlements in Arabia: religious communities were weak, and there was a strong commercial ethos. Haines relied on an intelligence service led by local Jewish and Persian traders, his "cronies." His philosophy was to show the Arabs "that you

67. Waterfield, *Sultans of Aden*, 177; Gavin, *Aden*, 50, 74–78.
68. Griffith and Griffith, *Journey across the Desert*, 1:17.
69. *Route of the Overland Mail*, 59.
70. W. Harris, *Highlands of Aethiopia*, 1:29.

perceive their intentions before they are prepared to carry them out, and . . . that you are their superior in tact, intellect, judgement and activity of purpose, that their secret thoughts are known to you, that your information is sure, secret, and correct." Once they grasped this, an Englishman would gain "moral power" over them, and could rule by "goodwill, kindness and respect."[71]

The major economic question for Haines was how far Aden could be made into a coffee trading port, and what this meant for Mocha further to the north. Could both be friendly to British interests, or would Aden need to be developed as a rival outlet? The East India Company (EIC) retained a local agent at Mocha, and continued to regard it as independent of the Ottomans, pointing out that the 1821 treaty with Mocha offered the British better trading terms than the Ottoman trade treaty of 1838. However, the Ottomans treated Mocha as theirs, on the basis that Mehmet Ali had managed to control it. Moreover, most coffee from Mocha and Hudayda still went northwards to Egypt and the Middle East. The Ottomans hated British control of Aden, often known as the "eye of the Yemen," and were determined to frustrate it.

When Egypt withdrew from Mocha, Hudayda, and the Yemeni lowlands in early 1840, it left them in the possession of the most powerful local leader, Sharif Husayn of Abu Arish, in return for tribute. Husayn quickly indicated his hostility to Britain, and discussed possible collaboration with other shaykhs against Aden. When the Indian Navy officer Robert Moresby arrived at Mocha later that year, he repeatedly hoisted the Union Jack over the house of the departed Indian agent. Each time, Husayn had it hauled down, eventually sawing off the mast, claiming that the Ottomans had not given permission for Britain to have a consulate there. Husayn also seized property from the agent and other Indian merchants, some of whom were imprisoned or forced to make large illegal payments. Haines argued that these acts must be avenged, that Mocha was independent, and that the 1821 treaty should be enforced. In 1843, the Foreign Office reached the same conclusion, citing earlier history and the fact that Husayn himself had rejected the Porte's own demands to hand the sea towns over, during the Ottoman-Egyptian conflict.[72]

In 1842, Canning arranged with the Porte that it would send a commissioner to Mocha to investigate the compensation due to British merchants. The commissioner, Ashraf, appeared there in 1842 and again in 1843, but finally upheld Husayn's rule. Canning interpreted this as the consequence of Husayn's local strength and the Porte's weakness in the Yemen, but in fact the Porte agreed with Husayn that Haines's demands over Mocha, and the treaty of 1821, were unacceptable, because they disregarded Ottoman sovereignty. The Ottoman regime was alarmed that Britain might ally with the imam of

71. Jacob, *Kings of Arabia*, 253–54. See Gavin, *Aden*, 44–46.
72. See the Foreign Office memo, Jan. 14, 1843, FO 78/551; Bombay report, Feb. 17, 1843, FO 78/549.

Sanaa to expand northwards along the coast and even threaten the Hijaz. In 1843, the Ottoman pasha of the Hijaz upheld Husayn's local authority, asserted Ottoman sovereignty in the Yemen and Asir, and announced that Britain must accept this if it wished to fly the flag at Mocha. To Canning, this was one more example of the Porte's "perverse" and "deceitful" policy to Britain in 1843.[73] On six different occasions in 1840–42, the imam of Sanaa had offered Haines an alliance to drive Husayn out of the Yemeni ports, but the cautious governments in London and Bombay declined to support this move, fearing that it would escalate local tensions and give an incentive for the French to interfere. It was better to remain neutral between the imam and his many enemies.[74]

In 1844, the British government's legal advisor declared that Britain should accept the Ottoman claim to control Mocha (but nowhere else in the Yemen), as the Porte had now persuaded Husayn to pay tribute to it. Husayn then insisted on imposing duties on Indian merchants in excess of the 1838 treaty, and no one seemed able to do anything about it. The Indian government now declined to appoint a new agent at Mocha. This was in part an acceptance that it was now in the European diplomatic sphere. However, it was also significant that Mocha was no longer needed as a steamer stop, because Aden, with its excellent harbour, was secure.[75]

Predictably, within a few years, Husayn fell out with the Porte after failing to pay enough tribute. The Ottomans now tried to impose a more reliable regime at Mocha, a move that backfired badly. Their initial incursion created disturbance that encouraged the imam of Sanaa to attack the lowlands, successfully at first. This forced a retaliatory Ottoman troop intervention in 1849, commanded by Tevfik, which resulted in heavy Ottoman levies on the sea towns and much discontent, plus high duties on the Mocha trade as before. Haines estimated that the total demand made by the Ottomans on their Yemeni possessions in 1849 was 417,000 German crowns, which was completely unsustainable given the shrivelling of commerce.[76] An attempt at peace broke down, and most of Tevfik's troops were killed by local Yemeni forces. Tevfik himself died in 1850, and the Ottomans were defeated in 1851 by Asiri tribesmen, while Sanaa was convulsed by factionalism. So most of the Yemen collapsed into chaotic civil war, which took years to resolve.[77]

73. Canning to Aberdeen, Mar. 31 and Dec. 13, 1843, FO 78/517, 78/523; Farah, "Anglo-Ottoman Confrontation," 141–42.

74. Farah, "Anglo-Ottoman Confrontation," 139; Gavin, *Aden*, 73.

75. Farah, "Anglo-Ottoman Confrontation," 144–45; India Board to Foreign Office, Jan. 11, 1844, FO 78/588.

76. Haines to Bombay, June 13, 1849, FO 1/4 360.

77. Farah, "Anglo-Ottoman Confrontation"; Marston, *Red Sea*, 151–52. For the lengthy Ottoman attempt to recover imperial rule in the Yemen after that, see Kühn, *Empire*.

The effect of all this was to damage Mocha profoundly as a base for the coffee trade. Meanwhile, Aden was made a free port in 1850 on the Singapore model; all customs duties by land or sea were abolished. The Ottoman governor of Hudayda naturally complained that this was "injurious to the Sublime Porte." Most Indian, American, Banyan, and French traders moved their custom to Aden, in order to avoid the 5 per cent and 12 per cent duties levied by the Ottomans, and to benefit from the political stability. The amount of coffee passing through Aden rose fourfold in two years. The value of the trade at Aden was £600,000 in the early 1850s.[78] As a coup de grace, the British continued to acknowledge Ottoman sovereignty at Mocha itself, so that Canning was able to assert the rights of those coffee merchants who still traded there. Continuing instability meant that Mocha was almost abandoned by the late 1860s.

Mocha was also relevant to the British because it had traditionally exercised authority over Zayla, on the African side of the Gulf of Aden, which was the only town with permanent trading facilities on the Somali coast. In 1840, Britain was hoping to buy an island off Zayla, so as to prevent any risk of the French securing a foothold on that part of the coast, which they might use as an entry point to Abyssinia. Moresby's misunderstanding with Husayn about the residency flag at Mocha had come about when he sailed over to ask Husayn for permission to purchase this island. The purchase went ahead, but it was overruled by India because Husayn had meanwhile written to Bombay indicating that he would agree to it only if Britain withdrew from Aden, which was plainly not a good bargain. The Indian government under Ellenborough continued to be suspicious of Haines's expansionist instincts, so in 1843 it rejected a proposition from a local chief who had since captured Zayla from Mocha. This chief, Hajj Shermarki, wanted it to become an African colony of Aden's, with attractively low customs duties.[79] As there was little Indian trade to Zayla, this seemed to Ellenborough an unnecessary extension of local activity, which might be more trouble than it was worth.

However, the proposal was interesting because it revealed Shermarki's consistent interest in a beneficial commercial arrangement with Britain. He was a major merchant and political figure further along the Somali coast at Berbera. He was already known in Indian circles because in 1825, as an athletic young man, he had saved the lives of most of the crew of a British ship, the *Mary Ann*, when it was plundered by locals at Berbera.[80] There was no permanent town there, but an important trade fair ran for six months of the year. This attracted merchants from the African interior, especially from

78. Kour, *History of Aden*, 71; Marston, *Red Sea*, 159–62; Gavin, *Aden*, 54; Waterfield, *Sultans of Aden*, 200.

79. Marston, *Red Sea*, 108–9.

80. Burton, *First Footsteps in East Africa*, 1:12–15.

Harar (whose "forbidden city" status contributed to the British myth of massive untapped African wealth). The fair sold live sheep (castrated to prevent any risk of future competition), gums, coffee, ivory, and clarified butter—and, not least, slaves, to merchants with less punctilious governments than those of Aden. Banyan merchants had long brought African produce from Berbera to Arabia, but Shermarki saw that the trade would benefit greatly from the emergence of Aden as a secure entrepot. He erected two towers at Berbera in 1844, to form a makeshift garrison. Aden merchants started to provide credit to Somali caravan leaders to go inland and return with purchases the next year. By 1848, four-fifths of Aden's revenue came from duties charged on products imported from Berbera. In 1847, Haines noted that two-thirds of coffee sent to England as "Mocha coffee" in fact now came from Berbera, escaping the high duties charged at Mocha. When, in 1847, Mehmet Ali, in an expansionist flourish, claimed for Egypt the whole eastern coast of Africa right round to Cape Guardafui, Shermarki and the British had a common interest in protesting and defeating its application to the Somali coast.[81] The only problem with Shermarki was that the pursuit of good relations with him required naval officers to tread softly in their operations against the slave trade: he had eight in his own house.[82]

So, by the 1850s, Aden had acquired its own hinterland—in the Yemen, whose coffee was increasingly exported through Aden rather than Mocha, and along the Somali coast each side of Berbera, where, in the Indian Navy tradition, Haines's assistant Charles Cruttenden visited every part of it and established good relations with the various tribes. The local chiefs around Aden had become reconciled to the British presence. Ottoman sovereignty over the Yemen had been effectively challenged, and limited to the town of Mocha, just as it was becoming an increasingly unattractive prize. Finally, in 1855, the Aden and Bombay governments developed the idea of occupying the island of Perim at the mouth of the Red Sea, and it was secured in 1857. Though the ostensible reason for possession was to build a lighthouse, there was also a fear that, were the Ottoman Empire to collapse, France might take the island, so this should be pre-empted. The British claim to Perim was justified on the simple basis that the last people to live there had been British forces in 1799 and 1801. As no one had occupied it since, it was deemed unnecessary to ask anyone's permission, and certainly not that of the Ottomans. Perim, like Aden, remained British until 1967.[83]

81. Abir, *Ethiopia*, 18–19, 132–33; Gavin, *Aden*, 52–53; Bruce Stanley, "Berbera," 89–91; Haines to Bombay, July 29, 1847, FO 1/4 81.

82. F. W. Grey of HMS *Endymion*, Jan. 4, 1842, FO 78/508.

83. See Vernon Smith in 146 Parl. Deb. (3d ser.) (1857) cols. 141–42. A lighthouse was indeed built between 1857 and 1863. There is a lot of excellent content on Perim on the website of Peter Pickering and Ingleby Jefferson, Perim Island, https://peterpickering .wixsite.com/perim.

The French, the Ottomans, and the
Western Red Sea Harbours

As the cases of Aden and Perim showed, the British and Indian governments quickly accepted the need to control the mouth of the Red Sea against all rivals. To start with, this meant mainly the French. After the British took Aden, France seemed likely to want a base on the African shore of the Red Sea. This was a particular concern in 1840, when the French were tempted to support Mehmet Ali's bid to retain Syria. Later in the 1840s, France increased its interest in Abyssinia, on the same basis as it did in Kurdistan, in support of Catholic missionaries wishing to reach out to the ancient local Christian Church, which had survived, apparently providentially, amid Muslim hostility. But the French were increasingly not the main problem. Mehmet Ali periodically argued that Ottoman Egypt's hinterland rightfully included Abyssinia. Moreover, there was a battle for influence in the Red Sea between the Ottoman and Egyptian regimes in the late 1840s, part of their more general struggle (which is considered in chapter 11).

For Britain, therefore, there were three potential rivals that needed to be kept in check along the western Red Sea shore in the 1840s. The two most important harbours along the coast were around Tajoura (Djibouti) immediately opposite Aden, and at Massawa further north. They were significant in themselves, but they were also the main entrances to the southern and northern Abyssinian uplands. So the story of these two harbours is partly about British and French missions to reach inland Abyssinia. However, there are already excellent accounts of those almost entirely unsuccessful attempts to win friends inland among the various Abyssinian rulers.[84] Here the focus will be on these two ports themselves. The story they tell is that Britain was able to deal fairly easily with the French threat, but not so easily with the Ottomans and the Egyptians, who claimed dominance at Massawa as a commercial extension of the Hijaz region and its Holy Cities. The episode of Massawa shows that Ottomans and Egyptians had common interests in working together against Britain, and many advantages over it in the middle of the Red Sea. Here, finally, the British discovered the limits of their reach.

{◄◄◄◄◄)(►►►►►}

Britain's seizure of Aden was a major blow to whatever lingering ambitions France had in the Arabian Sea area. A French admiral acknowledged that it was "the Gibraltar of the Red Sea, but with a better harbour."[85] Nonetheless,

---

84. Especially Rubenson's *Survival of Ethiopian Independence*, but there is also useful analysis in Abir's *Ethiopia* and Ram's *Barren Relationship*.

85. Waterfield, *Sultans of Aden*, 157.

the Eastern crisis of July 1840 made Palmerston and Hobhouse think that France was bound to pursue some compensatory acquisition on the Red Sea coast, and that this must be stopped. The India Board noted with concern the activities of the French ship *L'Ancobar*, sailed by Edmond Combes and Maurice Tamisier, who had previously travelled in Abyssinia. It was heading for the bay of Tajoura, presumably with the intention of proceeding inland to the most powerful figure in southern Abyssinia, the ruler of Shewa, Sahle Selassie (whose palace was at Ankobar). Combes was acting for a company formed in 1839 under French government protection, to buy somewhere (preferably Zayla) and establish it as a French port in response to Britain's acquisition of Aden. Hobhouse told the Indian government to instruct Haines at Aden to pre-empt this move by securing land at Tajoura for Britain.[86] Moresby therefore bought Moucha Island from the local sultan of Tajoura, ostensibly for thirty-two bags of rice (since the sultan did not want jealous rivals to rob him) but secretly also for 1,100 German crowns.[87]

Not content with this modest acquisition, the Indian authorities decided on an expensive mission to bestow presents on Sahle Selassie, who was generally known as negus, or king, of Shewa. Their anxiety about Shewa was stimulated by Johann Ludwig Krapf, the Church Missionary Society (CMS) missionary to Abyssinia. Since the days of William Jowett, Abyssinia, with its two million Christians, had been a major CMS priority, in the hope of making connections with the local priests and recovering ancient biblical manuscripts for republication in Amharic to help future missionary activity throughout eastern Africa. In the 1830s, Samuel Gobat and Carl Wilhelm Isenberg headed the CMS's Abyssinian missions. Krapf, who had joined the Basel evangelical seminary from a Lutheran farming family in south-west Germany, then replaced Gobat. Shortly after arriving in Tigre in northern Abyssinia in 1838, Isenberg and Krapf were expelled. They blamed this on collusion between Abyssinian priests and a French party that was trying to promote Catholicism. Krapf went to Shewa instead, where he had been invited by Sahle Selassie, probably on the assumption that he could help in constructing stone church buildings, like a previous missionary, Aichinger.

In Shewa, Krapf encountered another French adventurer, Charles-Xavier Rochet d'Hericourt. Rochet had been on an exploration of the African interior, but was now returning to France on what he claimed was a mission from the king. He suggested that Sahle Selassie was asking for French help to expand his territory, reunite the old Abyssinian Empire, and forge a trading channel all the way across Africa to the river Niger. In retrospect, it is obvious that Rochet had taken liberties in claiming that Sahle Selassie was asking for these things, in the same way that Salt and Coffin had done when they were trying

86. Rubenson, *Survival of Ethiopian Independence*, 83; Marston, *Red Sea*, 121; Hobhouse to Auckland, July 4, 1840, Broughton, F213 7.

87. Waterfield, *Sultans of Aden*, 139–40.

to build friendships with the rulers in Tigre after 1805.[88] Nonetheless, the credulous Krapf returned to Aden and reported to Haines and Campbell that Rochet's plan was to establish "a French Abyssinia . . . in opposition to British India"—but that he could be outwitted if the British got to Sahle Selassie first, with guns and medicines. Krapf urged that a British expedition to the king would have three great benefits. It would protect Abyssinian Christianity from Romanist pressure; it would encourage the king to suppress Shewa's slave trade (which involved three to four thousand slaves per year); it would "open the channel of discoveries, commerce, and civilization to the centre of Africa."[89] Also in Aden was Charles Beke, a self-proclaimed Abyssinian expert whose two great aims—which both failed—were to attack the slave trade and secure a consulship for himself.[90] Both men persuaded Haines that the sultan of Tajoura, with whom Britain had just signed a treaty, had enough authority inland to make an expedition to Shewa safe.

At this time, the Indian government still retained a taste for displaying its military and economic power, and dazzling local potentates, by high-profile missions conveying expensive presents. So it approved the idea of such an expedition, because of the French threat and the slave trade, but also because it was attracted by the myth of the great untapped wealth of the interior, and the merits of African scientific exploration. Hobhouse disliked these ostentatious tactics, but was too late to stop them.[91] The gifts chosen for the king numbered five thousand articles in all, including five hundred stand of arms, one hundred pistols, shawls, silks, tobacco, a model steam engine, a hand-organ, two small chandeliers, and a field-officer's tent containing a portrait of the queen.[92] The presents were accompanied by a European military escort of thirty, and six hundred porters. The Indian army officer Cornwallis Harris was chosen to lead the venture, following the success of his book about his pioneering game hunt in the Cape in 1836–37. This had become a bestseller, on account of his lively style, enthusiasm for open spaces, drawings of unusual animals, and zeal for shooting them, which the Indian government must have regarded as an attractive skill set to an Abyssinian chief.[93]

If the aim of the expedition to Shewa was to win any local influence, it was an absurd failure. Krapf had given no indication of the difficulty of the terrain. Harris had understood that Shewa was seven days' march from Tajoura,

88. Marston, *Red Sea*, 127–28; Rubenson, *Survival of Ethiopian Independence*, 147–51.

89. Rubenson, *Survival of Ethiopian Independence*, 151; Krapf to Campbell, July 3, 1840, FO 1/3 53.

90. For Palmerston's "indifferent opinion" of Beke, see July 24, 1839, FO 78/387 118; Dec. 11, 1846, FO 1/4 5.

91. Marston, *Red Sea*, 130–31, 135; Hobhouse to Palmerston, Dec. 14, 1840, FO 1/3 67.

92. However, some money was saved by including the gifts that the government had sent out in 1832 for the ras of Tigre (see below, p. 328), which were in packing cases in a Bombay warehouse: Waterfield, *Sultans of Aden*, 147–48.

93. W. Harris, *Wild Sports*.

but the journey took forty-seven, including a long section across arid salt plains, during which the dogs, cattle, and some horses died from thirst. Two of the British officers were murdered by robbers. The sultan of Tajoura had no authority away from the coast. When Harris arrived at Shewa, he found the king much less impressed than he had expected, and possibly disconcerted by the escort's march in full uniform into the centre of the hall, where they "performed the manual and platoon exercises amidst the ornamental clocks and musical boxes, jewelry, gay shawls and silver cloths which strewed the floor." The movements of Harris and the men were carefully restricted, and they were in effect prisoners until released in early 1843. Krapf and the other missionaries were not allowed to return.[94] Moreover the sultan of Tajoura also seemed unfaithful to Britain, and too loyal to the sharif of Abu Arish; he allowed three servants of Britain's local agent there to be murdered.[95]

In private, Harris now advocated concentrating on northern Abyssinia instead. The British public, however, received a different impression. "The celebrated African Nimrod" received a highly flattering welcome when he returned home. He was given a knighthood for opening the land of Prester John to slave-free commerce, though in fact the treaty he signed led to nothing. The king of Shewa was portrayed as a powerful Christian descendent of Solomon and the queen of Sheba. The press recounted Queen Victoria's gratification at his presents, which included a rare "blood mule from the royal stud" for the infant Prince of Wales.[96]

The only benefit of the £22,000 spent on the mission was to indicate to the French how determined the British were to secure local predominance.[97] Rochet returned in 1842 with Louis Philippe's presents for the king, but achieved nothing except another meaningless "treaty." Moucha Island remained nominally British until 1887, when it was given to France so that it could establish itself in Djibouti, in return for French acceptance of British rule in Zayla as well as Berbera and thus the whole of British Somaliland. Since no British officers had ever bothered to occupy Moucha, this was not a bad bargain. The French had to buy their steamer coal in Aden until a coal depot in Djibouti was agreed for them in 1862 as part of the smoothing of Anglo-French relations after the Crimean War.

{⟨⟩}

94. Rubenson, *Survival of Ethiopian Independence*, 155–67; Harris to Bombay, June 25, July 19, and Aug. 24 (quotation), 1841, FO 78/470, 78/471, 78/508.

95. Haines to Bombay, Oct. 8, 1841, FO 78/471 15.

96. Marston, *Red Sea*, 172; *Illustrated London News*, Sept. 2, 1843, 160; Bombay to India House, May 20, 1843, FO 78/550.

97. Foreign Office to India Board, Sept. 9, 1851, FO 78/885.

Notwithstanding the brief flurry of excitement in London at Harris's mission, Shewa was not what the British usually meant when they talked of Abyssinia. Most British interest focused on the northern highlands, the provinces of Tigre and Gondar. These were the territories that Valentia and Salt had targeted, and where Pearce and Coffin had lived. In the 1840s, there were fresh attempts to make worthwhile political and economic connections with the northern Abyssinian princes. As before, these focused on gaining access from the major Red Sea port of Massawa, or the nearby bay of Amphila, which might provide an alternative outlet for trade. The vision of Valentia and Salt survived: to forge a link between this coast and the remote highlands that would increase Abyssinians' interactions with the wider world. As several historians have shown, these attempts to open up Abyssinia had no real success before the 1860s. This was partly because of tension between the various princes, culminating in 1853–55 when Ras Ali and Wibe were both overthrown by Kassa, who proclaimed himself Emperor Tewodros II. Moreover, Britain lacked local power, and there was no reason for inland chiefs to fear the British name.[98]

There has been much less interest in considering what Britain's policy to Tigre and Gondar reveals about its attitudes to Ottoman influence and sovereignty on the coast. Massawa had been conquered by the Ottomans in 1557, and was an established part of the Red Sea economy, with close ties to Jeddah. The port was on a small island that was relatively easy to defend even if the mainland was insecure. However, the Ottomans could not control the coastal mainland, let alone the trading routes inland to Tigre, and this destroyed any chance of commercial development. By the 1800s, Ottoman authority had been delegated to the sharif of Mecca (four hundred miles away) and the local ruler, the naib of Arkiko, who levied tribute on the Ottomans for the right to charge duties at the port of Massawa. In the 1810s, Salt had urged the expulsion of the sharif, and his Ottoman overlords, as a necessary precursor to the increase of British and Indian trade, and wanted the ras of Tigre to drive them out so that Massawa could be under British protection. It was not a priority for any ras to do this, as he was already the strongest local influence on the coast, and could usually control the naib in practice.[99] Undeterred, Salt continued to signal his dislike of Ottoman power claims, whether from Constantinople, Egypt, or Jeddah. If instead the only local powers were petty Arab

98. Rubenson, *Survival of Ethiopian Independence*; Abir, *Ethiopia*; Ram, *Barren Relationship*. See Plowden's gloomy memo, Mar. 23, 1853, FO 1/7 192. It should be noted that the consuls' vision was much more political than religious. Salt naturally did not want to discourage Jowett's dreams of missionary progress in Abyssinia, but there was no love lost between either Coffin or Plowden and the missionaries. On missionary suspicion of Coffin's unorthodox views, see Rée, *Paire of Intelopers*, 282, 291. For Plowden: Rubenson, *Survival of Ethiopian independence*, 180.

99. Rubenson, *Survival of Ethiopian independence*, 50; Abir, *Ethiopia*, 5. For Salt's plans, see chapter 2, pp. 77–78.

chiefs, the British would have more chance to dominate, in alliance with the inland Abyssinians.

As British consul-general in Egypt after 1815, Salt consistently warned Mehmet Ali against any attempt to strengthen his power, either in Abyssinia or on its coast.[100] Salt was acting entirely on his own initiative, and was mildly reprimanded by the Foreign Office for getting involved in Red Sea affairs. The main feeling in London in the 1820s was complete indifference towards Abyssinia. This was shown most strikingly in July 1828, when William Coffin, Viscount Valentia's servant whom Salt had left in Tigre, appeared at the door of the Foreign Office with a letter to George IV from its dominant prince, Sebagadis. Sebagadis's letter asked for a renewal of Salt's expedition of 1810, to include gifts for his churches, plus the loan of a hundred cavalrymen for a year or two. Coffin had come on from Alexandria, where he had probably doctored the letter at the suggestion of the dying Salt, to add the request for the hundred cavalrymen and for the British to take a Red Sea port (Amphila or Massawa).[101] He had the misfortune to arrive in London during the unadventurous tenure of the Duke of Wellington's government. The Foreign Office disclaimed any interest in Abyssinia, passing the letter to the Colonial Office, which it regarded as responsible for all of non-Ottoman Africa. The senior civil servant at the Colonial Office, R. W. Hay, refused to accept this burden, and a passive-aggressive interchange of letters between the two departments occurred over the next year, before the Foreign Office agreed to take on responsibility for this obscure country. It then took another year to persuade Aberdeen to do anything about the request of Sebagadis or the now destitute Coffin, to which he eventually responded in 1830 only because steam communication in the Red Sea was becoming a live question. Even so, it was not until Palmerston arrived at the Foreign Office in November 1830 that a real effort was made to return an answer, after Valentia (now Lord Mountnorris) urged him, as a fellow admirer of their "lamented friend Mr Canning," to send to Tigre "a few thousand matchlocks" no longer wanted by the EIC. Four years after setting foot in Britain, Coffin was allowed to return to Abyssinia with an answer to the prince, together with the matchlocks from India, to which the British government added some dentists' instruments, pliers, and saws. By the time he arrived at Massawa, Sebagadis had been beheaded in an uprising.[102]

In the 1830s, Patrick Campbell, Britain's new consul-general in Egypt, legitimised the idea that Abyssinia was a British interest. In 1833–34, Mehmet Ali reoccupied Massawa for Egypt after the rebel Turkçe Bilmez had snatched it, and sought to integrate it into his system for governing the Hijaz. A few

100. Halls, *Henry Salt*, 2:177, 181, 205–6.

101. Rubenson, *Survival of Ethiopian Independence*, 59–64.

102. This correspondence, entertaining for those who appreciate dysfunctional bureaucracy, takes up the whole of FO 1/2.

years later, the effects of his conquest of Khartoum and Sennar (most of modern Sudan) in 1820–24 became apparent, as many Sudanese Muslims pushed into the borderlands with Abyssinia. In 1836–37, his troops started significant operations on the Sudanese-Abyssinian borderlands, trying to hunt down rebel leaders (one of whom had killed his son Ismail at Shendi in 1822) and to secure new revenues and potentially gold. When these operations did not go well, reinforcements were sent from Cairo; soon there were twenty thousand troops in the region.[103] On both occasions, Campbell warned Mehmet Ali that Britain took an interest in preserving the independence of Abyssinia, and received assurances that he would not attack it. For good measure, in order to show Britain's commitment, Campbell described Coffin as the British agent in Abyssinia, which was true only in that he was the only British subject there.[104] In 1839, when the Foreign Office decided to inform Mehmet Ali that Britain was "friendly" to the increase of his power in Africa, Palmerston qualified the message by excepting any increase of territory "at the expence of the Abyssinians whom HM's Govt. would be sorry to see subjected to Mahometan conquerors."[105] The 1841 firman that defined the future extent of Mehmet Ali's African territory excluded Abyssinia. The Tories' return to power then lowered the temperature. When the Foreign Office received through Coffin another friendly letter from Wibe, the new power in Tigre, Aberdeen deliberately chose not to reply to it.[106]

However, when Palmerston returned to the Foreign Office in 1846, he decided to increase Britain's presence in the Red Sea. In June 1847, a young British Nile explorer, Walter Plowden, arrived in Egypt from Abyssinia, having been shipwrecked in the Red Sea. He claimed to be carrying yet more presents to the queen, this time from Ras Ali of Gondar, Wibe's rival and nominal overlord, who seemed interested in English protection. Plowden travelled to London, where he wrote a memorandum arguing for the promotion of trade with the ras. On reading it, in August 1847, Palmerston decided to send a consul to Abyssinia. This was presumably what Plowden had planned all along. Once the Foreign Office discovered from his uncle that he was a "high spirited and enterprising youth," whose four years as a clerk in India had shown his lack of "steadiness for a mercantile life," Palmerston concluded that he was the obvious choice—especially since the importunate Beke was the only other plausible candidate. His salary was fixed at £500 a year.[107]

In establishing the Abyssinian consulate, Palmerston may genuinely have hoped to open up Tigre and Gondar to British commerce. He was always

103. Abir, *Ethiopia*, 99–108; Rubenson, *Survival of Ethiopian Independence*, 69.
104. Campbell to Palmerston, Oct. 20, 1833, and Oct. 3 and Dec. 14, 1837, FO 1/3, 5, 7, 23.
105. Palmerston to Hodges, Nov. 28, 1839, FO 78/377 7.
106. Rée, *Paire of Intelopers*, 311–13.
107. See the memos and notes in FO 1/4, 54, 61, 63.

interested in long-term commercial opportunities, and the formal aim of the consul was "the protection of British trade with Abyssinia and the countries adjoining thereto."[108] However, it is unlikely that this was his main aim, since the highlands were clearly remote and unstable, and he had ample experience of the puzzling ambiguity of Abyssinian princely requests. There were Banyan Indian traders operating at Massawa, but no more than in the past. They had always had their own local protection networks; besides, Haines regarded himself as defending their interests through the Indian Navy. In 1852, only £28,000 of Indian goods, mostly cotton cloth, was imported at Massawa; no British ship had ever called there to trade.[109]

The more immediate and urgent problem for Britain was Egyptian activity on the Red Sea coast itself around Massawa, and the risk that France might exploit it. In 1846, the Ottomans had agreed to Mehmet Ali's request to transfer to his authority Massawa and Suakin, which the powers had forced him to return to the Porte, with the Hijaz, in 1841. Mehmet Ali wanted these African ports so that Egypt could control more effectively the Muslim tribes in Sudan. There had already been a brief Egyptian army foray to Habab in 1844, within three to four days' march of Massawa. In other words, Mehmet Ali was seeking a rapprochement with the Ottomans in order to unpick the restrictions imposed on him by the European powers in 1841. Massawa was a costly base for the Hijaz authorities to maintain, and Mehmet Ali offered a generous tribute for it. To Palmerston, whose suspicions of Mehmet Ali were reviving in 1847, this was sinister enough, but correspondents were also telling him that the French might make a bargain with the Egyptians to promote their own interests on the coast. There had been a French consul at Massawa, Alexandre Degoutin, since 1841, appointed when the Egyptians previously controlled it. The French had bought some land at Edd further down the coast, and in 1845 they floated a scheme to establish a port at Arkiko.[110] Degoutin was used to negotiating with the local authorities, and also protected a Lazarist mission sent to Abyssinia in 1839 under Giustino De Jacobis.

The existence of a French consul at Massawa explains why Palmerston established a rival to him, but also exposes the incoherence of British thinking about the area. Degoutin had been appointed because he recognised Egyptian-Ottoman authority over Massawa, but Palmerston took the opposite view, instructing that Plowden's purpose was to uphold "the independence of the native ruler," by which he meant the naib of Arkiko, supported by Wibe. Palmerston was responding to the logic of Plowden's memoranda, which were all

108. This is argued by Ram, *Barren Relationship*, 39–41. Palmerston, Jan. 3, 1848, FO 1/5.

109. Ram, *Barren Relationship*, 61. Haines, Aug. 25, 1847, in FO 1/4.

110. Rubenson, *Survival of Ethiopian Independence*, 108, 112–13; Abir, *Ethiopia*, 123. See Charles Johnston to Palmerston, Nov. 13, 1847, FO 1/4 121.

about the need for Britain to befriend the naib as the local power and establish a safe harbour for the trade from Tigre to the Red Sea. Plowden—rephrasing Salt—proposed that the British should purchase either Massawa Island or some land around Arkiko bay—though in fact Palmerston opposed this as it would infringe the "independence" of the naib. Plowden's local experience was entirely African, and so he ignored the Ottomans' existence, assuming that British money could establish a local presence. The Foreign Office confirmed that Plowden would be consul to independent Abyssinia, and expressed the hope that he would live outside Ottoman territory, even though stationed at Massawa.[111]

However, it was conceptually impossible for Plowden to be based outside Ottoman territory, because the Ottomans/Egyptians claimed the whole coast. The Porte proclaimed its sovereignty over Abyssinia, or Habesha, as an extension of the pashalik of the Hijaz. When the Egyptian governor, Ismail Haqqi, arrived at Massawa in 1847, he asserted his right to the eastern coast of Africa round to Cape Guardafui. Moreover, by the time Plowden arrived, the Egyptians had crushed the naib's practical independence. Egyptian troops burned Arkiko to the ground in June 1847, and installed an Egyptian garrison. They went further, abolishing the tribute that the Ottomans had paid the naib in return for the possession of Massawa Island and the right to collect duty there.[112] Earlier in the year, news filtered through that the Egyptians had seized the valuable salt mines of Adigrat and would impose a salt monopoly. This prompted fears of a "vast African empire" headed by Mehmet Ali.[113] Plowden from the beginning found himself in an extremely awkward position. Though formally his job was to promote trade with independent Abyssinia, he now had to contest unacceptable Ottoman territorial claims on the coast and inland, while based at a port that the Egyptians controlled in practice as well as theory, and where he lacked any official authorisation from them.

As it happened, the specific threat from Egypt was quickly dispelled, because Wibe disliked the attempt to overthrow the naib and to remove the annual tribute that he received for Massawa, since this weakened the security of his merchant traders there. He sent troops in to burn Arkiko and Minkullu in early 1849, and made it clear that he would not allow any Ottoman-Egyptian base on the coastal mainland. In 1849, Egypt, which had only ever had one battalion on Massawa Island, pulled out, and returned it to the Ottomans.[114] This followed a campaign by Charles Murray, the British consul-general in

111. Plowden memos, Aug. 20 and 28, 1847; Palmerston note, Aug. 22, 1847; and Foreign Office memo, Nov. 1847; all FO 1/4 61, 72, 65, 130; Palmerston to Plowden, Jan. 3, 1848, FO 1/5.

112. Rubenson, *Survival of Ethiopian Independence*, 30, 117–18; Miran, *Red Sea Citizens*, 59–60.

113. Plowden memo, Nov. 17, 1847, FO 1/4 124.

114. Rubenson, *Survival of Ethiopian Independence*, 108, 119; Abir, *Ethiopia*, 134.

Egypt, to prevent Egypt from imposing a government monopoly on the export of goods from Sennar, through their new ports of Massawa and Suakin, which would be in violation of the 1838 treaty. He got the monopoly overturned with help from Constantinople, and regarded Mehmet Ali's bid for Massawa as a last dying vanity.[115] Moreover, for separate reasons, Wibe expelled De Jacobis's Lazarist mission in 1848, which proved that the French had no more purchase in Abyssinia than the British.

However, whether Massawa was in Egyptian or Ottoman hands, the fundamental problem remained the same. The Ottomans claimed, and exercised, sovereignty at Massawa, from their base at Jeddah. There, as at Mocha, they were very hostile to Britain's ambitions—indeed, more so than the Egyptians had been during their brief efficient tenure of the port. The Jeddah regime refused Plowden permission to rebuild his hut after the burnings, so in 1850 he was living in a tent, which he felt demeaned Britain's name among visiting Abyssinians. The Porte refused to grant Plowden consular rights at Massawa, unless Britain acknowledged that Abyssinia was an integral part of Ottoman dominions. Canning concluded that, as over Muhammara and the Yemen, "the Sultan's mind appears to have been infected with exaggerated notions of right." Palmerston was similarly unyielding.[116] The issue of sovereignty remained stalemated. The dispute turned into a more practical one about the duties to be levied on goods imported by Indian merchants through Massawa, as the Ottomans insisted that internal duties of 12 per cent applied, rather than import tariffs of 5 per cent. The council at Constantinople proved more responsive to British pressure on this point, agreeing a temporary proposal that Massawa should be declared a free port with no duties at all due, until an agreement could be reached. However, this was never implemented by the Ottoman local authorities, which continued to demand a 12 per cent duty on transiting goods, with no prospect of redress. Moreover, they carried on the lucrative slave trade, and forced the naib to pay them tribute.[117] In 1854, Plowden complained that the governor of Massawa, who had been removed for insulting him, had been promoted to be governor in Jeddah itself.[118] His position remained as fraught and impotent as ever.

The Ottomans had several advantages over the British in the battle for influence within the Red Sea. The proximity to Mecca and Medina meant that many local Muslims could easily be convinced to treat Britain as an

115. Murray to Palmerston, July 3 and Nov. 4, 1848, FO 78/757.

116. Plowden to Palmerston, Apr. 14, 1850, FO 1/6 112; Canning to Palmerston, Aug. 5, 1850, FO 78/821; Palmerston to Canning, Aug. 26, 1850, FO 78/816. In 1853, the Foreign Office thought the Porte would still refuse to budge: Sept. 29, 1853, FO 1/7 247.

117. Canning to Palmerston, Mar. 1 and 26, 1851, FO 78/853; Plowden to Canning, Sept. 27, 1853, FO 1/7 301; Bruce to Clarendon, Nov. 24, 1854, FO 1/8 373. For the tribute, see Miran, *Red Sea Citizens*, 61.

118. Plowden to Clarendon, Mar. 17, 1854, FO 1/8 59.

unsympathetic and alien power. It mattered greatly to Ottoman political and spiritual authority to protect the Holy Cities from European interference. In 1778, when the sultan had rejected the EIC's requests to sail up the Red Sea, he had warned the Egyptian government that "to suffer Franks' ships to navigate therein . . . is betraying your Sovereign, your religion, and every Mahometan."[119] Davut—the former pasha of Baghdad now in honourable retirement as the guardian of the Prophet's Tomb at Medina—was horrified to see British and French consular flags flying at Jeddah.[120] Archibald Ogilvie, installed in 1838 as the first European and British vice-consul at Jeddah, as part of Waghorn's plan for a Red Sea mail service, had never been able to impose himself on local politics. From about 1840, the increasingly powerful Red Sea steamers found it neither necessary nor attractive to call there. His authority waned; he became a drunkard; he was shot at on his terrace; in 1849 he was insulted in the bazaar and could get no redress; in 1851 Plowden found him slumped insensible at his desk after a mental breakdown.[121] He was removed, but one of his successors was murdered along with the French consul in an anti-European protest in 1858. In 1855, Richard Burton, presumably for personal career reasons, made a case for a senior British consul at Jeddah, on the basis that there were fifteen hundred Indians there and at Mecca. This, however, was a dubious argument. Indian Muslim traders had flourished long before Ogilvie, dominating the Hijazi trade since the eleventh century.[122]

In this region more than anywhere, the fundamental tensions between Ottoman and British political needs and priorities were exposed, and Britain had no way of resolving them. However, the interior of the Red Sea mattered a great deal more to the Ottomans than to the British, unlike the southern end or the Gulf, which were both essential for imperial power. There, Britain had been able to see off Ottoman threats. Once it controlled Aden, and once British steamers could sail from Suez to Aden without stopping, the sea's internal politics became much less of a concern. The Indian Navy worried less about Jeddah, Massawa, or Mocha in 1850 than it had in 1800. The steam passage was secure because the British controlled the southern end of the Red Sea—and because they were equally confident about their predominance at the northern end, where it mattered most of all.

119. Kimche, "Opening of the Red Sea," 71.
120. Farah, "Anglo-Ottoman Confrontation," 163.
121. On these incidents: Marston, *Red Sea*, 158; Cumming, *Gentleman Savage*, 35–36; Freitag, "Helpless Representatives," 370–71; Burton, *Personal Narrative*, 1:195.
122. Burton, *Personal Narrative*, 3:256–57. His other argument was that a consul would regulate and protect the Indian hajj pilgrims.

CHAPTER ELEVEN

The British Corridor in Egypt

IN JUNE 1855, Foreign Secretary Clarendon set out British policy to Egypt with admirable clarity. The British, he wrote, "want no ascendancy, no territorial acquisition; they only want a thoroughfare; but a thoroughfare they must have, free and unmolested."[1] By 1855, no one could dispute that they had constructed such a thoroughfare. British passengers expected comfortable travel across the country, docking from a European steamer at Alexandria and boarding an Indian one from Suez. They entrusted goods, mail, and gold of enormous value to this route, without qualms about its security. They were building the first railway in the Middle East across Egypt, in order to quicken and assist this transit. Egypt was a valuable trading partner of Britain. Traveller familiarity with it gave Egyptian culture a significant presence in London lecture halls and at the Crystal Palace.

Britain naturally denied that it wanted ascendancy; it claimed that the thoroughfare it sought was equally available to people of any country.[2] In practice, it imposed great pressure in defence of its interests, several times. It had to fight French and Ottoman opposition before it could build the railway. In the pursuit of order, it had to battle with Constantinople in defence of the draconian punishment system of Mehmet Ali and his successors. France was Britain's historic enemy in Egypt, and for most of this period most people assumed a continuation of that rivalry. Yet Britain's tenacity in defending its interests, and its massive reserve power in the Mediterranean and in India, made it clearer and clearer that this was not an equal battle. By the early 1850s, even Napoleon III was ready to accept France's junior status in Egypt, and to work with Britain to promote European interests and security there. The greatest threat to those interests now seemed to lie elsewhere: in the Ottoman Empire itself, and its ability to appeal to the Muslim identity and practical

1. June 18, 1855, cited in Harcourt, "High Road to India," 20.
2. Paget to Malmesbury, Jan. 2, 1853, FO 78/966.

insecurities of the Egyptian regime after Mehmet Ali's death. The Ottomans, and the Russians, wanted to keep old Anglo-French rivalries alive. In 1844, Tsar Nicholas advised the British government to carry on working with Russia against the French threat in Egypt.[3] By the 1850s, France was keen to expose the baselessness of that scare.

England in Egypt, Egypt in England

A traveller to Alexandria in the years after 1841 might have been forgiven for wondering if the dispute between Mehmet Ali and the British government over Syria had ever taken place. In 1843, Britain imported and exported a quarter of the goods passing through the port, £548,000 of a total sum of £2.33 million. British shipping was twice the size of any other country's. Two years later, the value of the exported goods, mostly cotton and wheat, had doubled. The increasing reliability of steam transport also meant that, by 1845, six times as much of the town's export business went directly to Britain as in the 1830s (rather than via Malta).[4] Over 4,000 British-born people passed through Alexandria in 1842, rising to 6,000 in 1846. In 1842, 1,390 of these were visitors and crew on British merchant vessels, reflecting the fact that steamers had greatly cut the time for passengers to reach Egypt from Britain— from forty to fourteen days between 1834 and 1844. Another 1,570 were on the British warships that frequently visited the harbour, and 800 were travellers on the integrated service between Britain and India. The number of passengers on the Indian transit via Suez nearly tripled in the next three years, reaching 2,300 by 1845-46.[5] The increase in British visitors to the town, on top of the growth of British commercial houses, led to a fundraising drive to complete the Protestant church for which Mehmet Ali had given land. In 1844, there was only one foundation stone, "on which the Arabs copulate, and a trench in which they perform a dirtier process."[6] Work began properly in 1845 and was finished in 1854. Named after Saint Mark, the founder of African Christianity, its design combined early Christian and Islamic forms with the Star of David. It aimed to symbolise the common heritage that Protestantism shared with local Coptic, Muslim, and Jewish traditions.[7]

3. See Figes, *Crimea*, 69.

4. The figures are Consul Stoddart's: Mar. 23, 1844, and May 29, 1846, FO 78/584, 78/663.

5. Stoddart, Feb. 21, 1843, FO 78/542; Consul Walne's report in Murray to Palmerston, June 6, 1847, FO 78/707.

6. Barnett to Bidwell, Mar. 22, 1844, FO 78/583.

7. Crinson, *Empire Building*, 120. For the Star of David, see "Church Photography by Alexandria Muslims," Jayson Casper (website), Sept. 9, 2012, https://jaysoncasper.com /2012/09/09/muslim-church-photography-in-alexandria/.

The boom in steam travel to Egypt, and beyond to India, owed a lot to the involvement of a private company, the Peninsular Steam Navigation Company, which, on merging with another enterprise in 1840, became known to the world as P&O. Travellers had often complained about the shortcomings of the Admiralty steamers in the Mediterranean, built for war rather than consumer comfort, and the Indian Navy ones south of Suez, with their deck piles of coal, public washing arrangements, and cockroaches. In 1840, the government issued a contract for a monthly commercial steamer service from Southampton to Alexandria, for passengers, cargoes, and the government mail, with a reducing subsidy over five years. P&O won the contract, and secured a royal charter on condition of also running a subsidised contract mail service from Suez to India. For the latter, it built new flagships, the *Hindostan* and *Bentinck*, to cope with the monsoons, and began a Calcutta–Suez run in 1843. The *Bentinck* was launched amid much publicity and as a showpiece for luxurious travel; each cabin had a marble-covered basin stand, mirrors, drawers, writing apparatus, and venetian blinds. The focus on Calcutta was essential in order to make money: in 1845, when the Suez–Calcutta service became monthly, two thousand travellers used it. The Indian Navy continued to run the Suez–Bombay service until P&O took it over in 1852.[8]

Anxious to fend off competition from French steamers in its Mediterranean operations, P&O gave the novelist William Thackeray a free berth in 1844, in return for publicising his trip to Egypt, Palestine, and Constantinople.[9] He produced illustrated pieces for *Punch*, and a book under his nom de plume Michel Angelo Titmarsh in 1846. Thackeray was the first person to write about Egypt as a self-consciously modern tourist. He made the country seem familiar and easily accessible. His book was published only two years after Alexander Kinglake's idiosyncratic travelogue *Eothen*, but deliberately rejected that book's bravura individualism. Because of its target audience, it played up to some populist *Arabian Nights* fantasy stereotypes of the East that Kinglake had been self-consciously trying to escape. But its main point was that, for the modern traveller, creature comforts rightly came first. Kinglake's romantic presentation of the desert was misleading. Now that the locals took Morison's pills, "Byronism becomes absurd instead of sublime, and is only a foolish expression of cockney wonder." English materialism was everywhere: Pompey's Pillar was covered in English graffiti, including an advertisement for Warren's shoe blacking. On the Nile boat to Cairo, the first pyramids came into view: "several of us tried to be impressed; but breakfast supervening, a rush was made at the coffee and cold pies."[10] The popularity of such

8. Harcourt, *Flagships of Imperialism*, 57, 69, 81–86; Hoskins, *British Routes to India*, 224, 252.

9. Ray, *Thackeray*, 297–301.

10. Thackeray, *Notes of a Journey*, 93 (quotation 1), 245, 252–53 (quotation 2), 282.

journeys led to a publishing boom: Robert Curzon in 1849 noted the flood of "little volumes about palm-trees and camels, and reflections on the Pyramids." Gardner Wilkinson shrewdly converted one of his earlier works into Murray's *Handbook on Egypt*, first published in 1847. Already in 1843, Cornwallis Harris had observed "several grotesque parties, in straw hats, plodding steadily towards Mount Sinai, on the back of the dromedary." At Luxor in February 1850, Consul-General Charles Murray found sixty English travellers, in twenty separate parties, who had paid to be taken up there by Nile boats.[11]

In Cairo, Thackeray stayed at the Hotel d'Orient, a new French establishment with sixty rooms, built for the England–India transit: "as large and comfortable as most of the best Inns of the South of France." Dinner was at 6 p.m., involving thirty Indian officers in mustachoes and jackets, ten civilians in spectacles, and ten pale-faced ladies with ringlets drinking pale ale. This was "England in Egypt . . . with her pluck, enterprise, manliness, bitter ale and Harvey sauce." The passengers from Suez had arrived on a track *"jonché* with soda-water corks" that signposted the route across the desert. Thackeray's book praised Thomas Waghorn's skill in developing the transit: he had brought the pyramids a month nearer to England.[12] Waghorn had been pioneering passenger links across Egypt since 1835, and had organised the mail service across Egypt for the East India Company (EIC) from 1837. In 1841, he merged his operation with a competing outfit run by two British engineers, Hill and Raven. They were agents for the Bombay Steam Committee, for which they built seven way stations along the ninety-mile Cairo–Suez land route. Raymond Wellsted had earlier pointed out how easy it would be to develop this track, "as level as any Macadamised road in England . . . I should recommend an omnibus."[13] After 1841, Waghorn, Hill, and Raven had the resources to invest in the whole transit route, and bought a steamboat for the Nile section of the Alexandria–Cairo leg. Hill and Raven ran a "British Hotel" in Cairo, with the assistance of a former pastry cook from Northamptonshire called Samuel Shepheard, who had gone to sea but been sacked for insubordination at Suez while employed on a P&O mail boat. In 1849, Shepheard, now the owner of the hotel, acquired a larger site near the Hotel d'Orient; this was a grant from Viceroy Abbas, who had bonded with him while gazelle hunting. Shepheard's Hotel soon became a central attraction of European Cairo, and was "more English than England itself" to the visiting Anthony Trollope.[14]

One tourist to Constantinople and Egypt in 1849 was the fledgling London impresario Albert Smith. In May 1850, he turned the experience into

11. Curzon, *Visits to Monasteries*, v; Harris in St. John, *Egypt and Nubia*, 261; Murray to Palmerston, Apr. 2, 1850, FO 78/841.

12. Thackeray, *Notes of a Journey*, 255–59, 290 (quotations at 255, 258, 290).

13. Wellsted, *Travels in Arabia*, 2:295–96.

14. Trollope, *Bertrams*, 467. For Shepheard and Abbas, see Bird, *Samuel Shepheard of Cairo*, 46–47.

The Overland Mail, a one-man comical, pictorial, and musical entertainment at Willis's Rooms. His script took Thackeray's approach further, by presenting Egypt through the eyes of a stereotypical uncultured English traveller who was never impressed by anything he saw. Smith deliberately ridiculed "the absurdly false and over-coloured medium" of previous romanticised accounts. "I preferred being the commonplace Cockney ignoramus that I am, to seeming the imaginative scholar, which I am not." He added anecdotes and songs about the idiosyncrasies of the travelling party, and three-dimensional dioramas of Eastern scenes painted by William Beverley.[15] Smith's show opened a few weeks after a very popular diorama, *The Route of the Overland Mail to India*, in Regent Street. This was part of P&O's publicity machine, and was the work of four commissioned painters. Accompanied by lectures and music, it ran for three seasons, and drew a large and fashionable audience, including the royal family. In its first season, there were nine hundred showings and 200,000 admissions.[16]

Albert Smith's show opened three days after the appearance in London of the most celebrated Egyptian arrival of the 1850s. Obaysch was a hippopotamus, named after the Nile island where he was captured, and was to spend the rest of his life at London Zoo. Despite a marked tendency to immobility, not surprising in a nocturnal animal forced to be on daytime display, Obaysch proved to be very popular, and attracted up to ten thousand visitors to the zoo daily: visitor numbers doubled for the year 1850.[17] Obaysch was a gift from Viceroy Abbas, organised by Consul-General Murray, in a deliberate attempt to strengthen Anglo-Egyptian relations. He also has a wider symbolism, signifying the substantial profile that his country enjoyed in England in the 1850s. The organisers of the 1851 Great Exhibition invited Egypt to send exhibits of local manufactures and natural resources directly, rather than through Constantinople. They were displayed separately, and were awarded a Council Prize.[18] The Porte was furious. The twenty-six-year-old civil servant Nubar, Abbas's chief translator, an Armenian nephew of Boghos, and later Egyptian prime minister, made his name while in London for the skill he displayed as the viceroy's diplomatic representative and delegate to the exhibition.

When the Crystal Palace was relocated to Sydenham in 1854, Egypt was again given a prominent place, which was suggestive in a different way. The Egyptian Court was chosen by Owen Jones to be one of the historical fine arts

15. A. Smith, *Hand-Book*; Fitzsimons, *Baron of Piccadilly*, 88–96 (quotations at 96, 94).

16. Stocqueler, *Memoirs of a Journalist*, 184–86; Altick, *Shows of London*, 207–9. The pictures are reproduced in the *Route of the Overland Mail*, and the thirty-one watercolours are held in the P&O Heritage Collection.

17. Root, "Victorian England's Hippomania"; Simons, *Obaysch*.

18. Murray to Palmerston, Apr. 17, 1851, FO 78/875; Palmerston, Dec. 1, 1851, FO 78/876.

courts that would demonstrate the phases of human artistic achievement.[19] Designed by Jones and Joseph Bonomi, the court offered elaborate reconstructions of Egyptian temples, tombs, and sculptures, including the statue of Ramses from Abu Simbel, and a number of friezes showing military and processional scenes. The aim was to stress the variety and richness of its pharaonic culture, rather than its bulk (almost all the exhibits were small-scale models). It mirrored the simultaneous representation of ancient Assyrian culture in Layard's nearby Nineveh Court. The new Crystal Palace was designed to present for popular consumption human cultural endeavour over a longer historical time frame than had been displayed in one place before. The representation of works of art from so long ago encouraged an increasingly nuanced debate about how human artistic prowess had developed, and how civilisational excellence in taste should be defined. Jones asserted that the pinnacle of Egyptian civilisation was reached in very early times—perhaps its finest achievements had not yet been unearthed—and that in Egypt the Romans were merely unoriginal copyists. Conventional views about the crudeness, brutality, or sheer oddity of Egyptian taste still held the field, but there was now an avant-garde interest, stimulated mainly by German scholarship, in exploring in detail the beliefs and customs of pre-Roman Egypt, and their influence on later cultures.[20]

Most importantly, there was a growing willingness to see pharaonic Egypt as a foundational civilisation in which man had first worked out the ideas about divinity, the future state, and human ethics that had profoundly shaped the Judeo-Christian inheritance. Florence Nightingale and Harriet Martineau were two of the intellectually curious travellers who explored Egypt in the late 1840s with the aim of seeking early signs of those ideas. Nightingale spent hours and days in tombs observing the attributes of ancient Egyptian civilisation, concluding that they were a "race of giants" whose brilliance had "overflowed and fertilised" the rest of the world.[21] Martineau's *Eastern Life* argued that Egyptian priests had invented the monotheism out of which Judaism and then Christianity had developed, and, in Osiris, had created the

19. Jones had also argued for Cleopatra's Needle to be brought over and made one of the building's focal points, though this plan foundered on the anxiety of some shareholders that it was in bad repair and not likely to justify the cost of transport. Samuel Briggs, and Joseph Hume in Parliament, had been pushing for its homecoming since 1851. See Briggs to Palmerston, Nov. 12, 1851, FO 78/2116 188; Piggott, *Palace of the People*, 48.

20. See O. Jones and Bonomi, *Description of the Egyptian Court*, 4–5. Samuel Sharpe argued in the same pamphlet (57–60) that of all the pupils of Egyptian style, only the Greeks improved on it. For the balance of opinion about antiquities, see Moser's *Wondrous Curiosities* (203–12). For the lack of fundamental change in attitudes to Egypt, but the countercultural significance of work by British Unitarians like Sharpe and the German Christian Bunsen, see Gange's *Dialogues with the Dead* (38–45, 108–19). For background, see Moser, *Designing Antiquity*.

21. F. Nightingale, *Letters from Egypt*, 73–74, 139, 152–53, 160–61, 187–88 (quotations).

notion of a Messiah. She claimed that Moses imbibed his religion from them, and that when his Hebrew followers refused to follow his spiritual lead without ritual, he had given them an Egyptian ritual too, which Jesus purged for a purer spiritual ideal. Such arguments were not original in themselves. For well over a century, there had been interest among theologians and freethinkers in speculating about ancient Egypt's contribution to later civilisations. However, improved access to the region, together with intense mid-century public questioning of biblical chronology, ensured much more publicity for these ideas. Even so, Martineau had to find another publisher, after John Murray rejected the book as "a conspiracy against Moses."[22]

In short, in the 1850s the British public could visualise and imagine Egypt in a greater variety of ways. The evangelical idea of the land of slavery was no longer so prominent (though Nightingale in fact still applied it to modern Egypt, in contrast to its glorious past).[23] The sense that economic development was transforming the country was part of the appeal of Selim Aga, the Sudanese slave boy bought and freed by Briggs's partner Robert Thurburn and educated in Britain, who became a high-profile advocate of a pan-African railway as a way to end the slave trade.[24] A lot of this familiarity was the result of greater access, through steam travel, the boom in book and newspaper coverage, and the Great Exhibition. There was a tendency to assume British ownership, at some level, over the Egypt that they witnessed and engaged with. Harriet Martineau ridiculed the sole British tourist she encountered at Thebes who was convinced that Arabs were about to fleece him. She wondered how he could have failed to notice that everyone else was absolutely confident in the security afforded by the combination of Egyptian law and order, Britain's reputation, and Arab cheery kindness.[25]

There was a curious paradox here. The total acreage of this "England in Egypt" was minute, no more than the narrowest of corridors across the country. As Trollope noted, British culture held sway only within five hundred yards of Shepheard's Hotel. Beyond that, Cairo was "absolutely oriental."[26] And even in that small corridor of materialism, the security of all these wealthy Britons, their goods, and their mail, was entirely dependent on the septuagenarian Mehmet Ali and his strongman rule up to 1848, and the fortunes of his precarious dynasty after his death.

22. See Roberts, *Woman and the Hour*, chap. 6. For Murray, see Martineau, *Autobiography*, 2:295. For the role of Egyptian archaeology in broader disputes about biblical chronology in the 1860s, see Gold's "Ancient Egypt" (218–21).

23. She was appalled by the relentless government oppression of the Egyptians, their "animal submission," and their "debased life": F. Nightingale, *On Mysticism and Eastern Religions*, 214, 246.

24. [Selim Aga], *Africa Considered*; McCarthy, *Selim Aga*.

25. Martineau, *Eastern Life*, 1:287–88.

26. Trollope, *Bertrams*, 474–75.

Mehmet Ali and the Transit

On April 24, 1843, Sir Robert Peel, the British prime minister, rose in the House of Commons to make a "public acknowledgement." It had nothing to do with the matter under discussion (consular estimates) and was clearly a move planned with his questioner, the Liberal Member of Parliament and arch-Mehmetist John Bowring. Peel wished to

> bear this public testimony to the liberal and enlightened conduct of the Pacha of Egypt, with respect to the transmission of the Indian letters during the late operations on the coast of Syria. . . . It is impossible, but that the proceedings of England must have appeared to him unjust, and excited his dissatisfaction; and it was a great proof of a generous and enlightened mind, that these proceedings never induced him to throw the slightest difficulty in the way of the communications with India. Other countries may boast of more enlightenment than the Pacha of Egypt, but I much doubt if, under similar circumstances, any other power would exhibit so great a degree of liberality.[27]

Peel's statement was a declaration of friendship to Mehmet Ali (and to Bowring). More such declarations followed: in 1845, the government gave him Queen Victoria's portrait set in diamonds, as thanks for his continued help with the mails. This approach was also reassuring to merchants, who took the same view. In September 1841, the Bengal Chamber of Commerce sent Mehmet Ali their appreciation for his goodwill towards the transit, and commented with some sharpness on the "dignified and impressive example which your Highness has afforded to the nations of Christendom."[28]

Peel's remarks, which Mehmet Ali quoted at many convenient opportunities in the years to come, were a significant contribution to a long discussion about the transit between the two governments in the mid-1840s. Unknown to the travellers, for whom the experience was essentially seamless, this was a very tense discussion on both sides.

Despite P&O's domination of the steamer service on both sides of Egypt, its charter did not allow it to control the land transit. The EIC and government had a monopoly over the transmission of the Indian mails, which was managed first by Waghorn and then by John Lyons, under the nominal superintendence of the British consul-general. Naturally, P&O was very concerned about the reliability and rapidity of the transit, and about the duties payable on the goods that it was transporting across Egypt en route between England and India. The firm sought allies with connections to the Egyptian government who could smooth its way. No British company was better connected to

27. 68 Parl. Deb. (3d ser.) (1843) col. 884.
28. July 2, 1841, at FO 78/451 184.

the regime than the venerable Briggs & Co., and so P&O made Samuel Briggs its agent at Alexandria, while his partner Robert Thurburn became a P&O board member. In 1841, with their help, Arthur Anderson of P&O negotiated with the Egyptian government a low transit duty of 0.5 per cent on goods that it conducted through Egypt. In return, Mehmet Ali agreed to protect the communication lines by military police. To carry the goods, Anderson invested in two steamers for the Nile, and carriages and vans for the desert route. However, he could not establish a company to manage the transit, because it was contrary not only to the terms of the royal charter, but also to Mehmet Ali's monopolistic instincts. Mehmet Ali was careful to stress that the unusually low transit duty was experimental, and that there must be strict limits to Anderson's investments in transit infrastructure: a third P&O steamer on the Nile and a hotel at Suez were vetoed. In view of its very large investments in ocean steamers, P&O naturally disliked the short-term nature of these arrangements. In 1843, the nervy Anderson made an ill-judged foray into the political sphere, arguing that what was really needed was a canal between the Mediterranean and the Red Sea. In the same year, London merchants were also pressing for a permanent agreement with the Egyptian government about the transit arrangements.[29]

These expressions of anxiety, together with Peel's parliamentary encomium in April, were responses to the formation in early 1843 of the Egyptian Transit Company. The new company greatly expanded the number of horses and camels available for the land route, and secured (from the Bombay Steam Committee) a lease on the desert way stations until 1848. Though this appeared to be a step forward, it did not disguise the precarity of the transit arrangements. The company was formed in the name of Thurburn, Hill, and partners, with P&O's blessing. P&O's view was that a self-standing private company of this sort was unlikely to last for the long term; it hoped to take it over, with the British government allowing it to run the mail contract. Thurburn funded the company with £20,000 and an extra £16,000 to buy out the various assets owned by Hill's company (Hill had died). Briggs & Co. had run into financial difficulties on account of bad Indian loans in the economic crisis of 1842, and Thurburn hoped that this new venture would restore his fortune. However, the devil was in the detail: the capital that Thurburn invested in the new Egyptian Transit Company had been borrowed from Mehmet Ali.

As soon as the company was formed, it was clear that Mehmet Ali was in fact its "principal," as the *Bombay Times* put it, and that he was aiming at government control of the transit, with no private British or Indian

29. See Harcourt, "High Road to India," 29–33; Stoddart to Bidwell, Sept. 23, 1841, FO 78/452 218; merchant memorials, Sept. 1843, FO 78/550; A. Anderson, *Communications with India, China.*

competition.[30] It was no real surprise when, in 1845, he told Thurburn that he wished his government to take over the company. Thurburn was in no position to oppose, as he was still in debt, had other financial obligations to the viceroy, and wanted to retire to Scotland.[31] P&O agreed to sell to the new nationalised Egyptian Transit Administration (ETA) its two Nile boats, for which it no longer had a use, and in 1848 the Bombay Steam Committee waived its right to extend the leases on the way stations.

By the late 1840s, almost all travellers felt that this nationalised arrangement worked very well. Though the ETA was formally an arm of the government, with Egyptian names on the board, most of the practical power rested with trusted British operators: Richard Lee Green in Alexandria and Charles Betts in Suez. Green, in fact, was a member of an old Levant Company family, and yet another family connection of Samuel Briggs. The first act of the new transit service in March 1846 was to reduce passenger fares from £15 to £12 and cargo costs to £8 per ton.[32] Connections improved: in 1847 the ETA committed to a maximum time of eighty-five hours for the whole journey, ship to ship, which was reduced to seventy-five hours in 1852. After 1848, Viceroy Abbas invested in new steamers, track boats, wharves, jetties, warehouses, sheds, and hotels. Letters were never lost. The tariff stayed at 0.5 per cent, until it was reduced to 0.25 per cent in 1854. The volume of cargo tripled between 1852 and 1856, made possible by more steamers and investment in camels, so the low tariff was still very profitable for the government. In 1854, £6.4 million of gold, silver, and specie was transmitted as well, in perfect safety. The number of passengers doubled between 1852 and 1856.[33] Between Cairo and Suez, they took a six-person van drawn by four horses. More desert way stations were built and they became much cleaner. At the central station, the passengers dined on roast fowls, pigeon, mutton, pale ale, and wine, though one inexperienced officer on his way to India complained that the champagne was un-iced. In the early 1840s, many travellers had found the journey bone-shaking, exhausting, and unpunctual. Ten years later, the complaints about high charges and chaotic disorganisation had all but disappeared, though the experience remained a vivid one for writers.[34]

However, great effort had been necessary in order to reach this happy position. Between 1844 and 1847, there were long disputes about the way forward,

30. *Bombay Times*, May 31, 1843, in *Narrative of a Journey from Southampton*, appendix, 33. In 1845, Mehmet Ali told Consul Barnett that the loan had always been intended as a precursor to a takeover: to Aberdeen, June 5, 1845, FO 78/623.

31. Thurburn to Palmerston, Nov. 12, 1847, FO 78/724.

32. All the details are in Barnett to Aberdeen, Mar. 15 and June 8, 1846, FO 78/661B.

33. Harcourt, "High Road to India," 37–49.

34. See, for example, Griffith and Griffith, *Journey across the Desert*, vol. 1, chap. 4 (Lucinda Darby Griffith in 1843); Bevan, *Sand and Canvas*, 56–57 (1842). By comparison, the 1858 account of Russell, *My Diary in India* (1:34–41), is much tamer.

because many people were reluctant to abandon the idea of British control of the transit, while there was also an ideological distrust of Mehmet Ali's monopolistic instincts. Moreover, Constantinople objected to direct talks between Britain and Mehmet Ali, which implied his independence. In 1844, Bowring persuaded Foreign Secretary Aberdeen to take advantage of the passage through Egypt of the new governor-general of India, Henry Hardinge: Hardinge should meet Mehmet Ali and make a treaty to grant British agents permission to organise the mail passage in perpetuity, for a fixed payment of £10,000 per annum. This idea of a high-level discussion, acknowledging the dignity of Mehmet Ali's position, underlines—like Peel's statement—the Tories' instinct that the sovereignty of the Porte was a "fiction" and that Egypt was a British interest that enjoyed "virtual independence."[35] Hardinge and Mehmet Ali had an amicable conversation, and a treaty seemed likely, until Constantinople pointed out that Mehmet Ali was not able to make a treaty with the governor-general of India, or anyone else. The Foreign Office now had to pretend that what was proposed was merely a commercial arrangement with the British Post Office, and sent a Post Office employee, Henry Bourne, to sign the treaty instead. Since Henry Bourne lacked the status of the governor-general, Mehmet Ali took offence.[36]

In December 1844, he signified that he would sign the treaty, but only on condition of taking over the Egyptian Transit Company and of Britain accepting his monopoly over passenger transit arrangements.[37] That, in fact, was why it was nationalised in 1845. But the British government refused to accept the proposed monopoly over the transit, since some departments naively hoped that free-market operators might set up in opposition to it. This view came from Charles Trevelyan and the British Treasury, and from India. The unfortunate Consul-General Barnett felt that he had to press the argument about competition, but slowly became aware that Bowring was telling Mehmet Ali that he need take no notice of it. Barnett resigned. Bowring was right—Trevelyan's laissez-faire principles were irrelevant. The Egyptian government already had a monopoly on the Nile steamers, while Mehmet Ali declined to guarantee that any Arabs who let their animals for private hire to Englishmen on the land route would not be punished.[38] Moreover, he pointed out that whereas the Transit Administration would respect the low tariff of 0.5 per cent on goods passing through Egypt, goods conveyed by other operators would

35. Aberdeen's words, to Murray, May 22, 1846, Aberdeen Papers, BL Add. MSS 43246 114. For the need to treat Mehmet Ali with dignity, see Aberdeen to Barnett, Aug. 13, 1844, FO 78/582.

36. Barnett to Aberdeen, Nov. 6, 1844, FO 78/582.

37. Barnett to Aberdeen, Dec. 14, 1844, FO 78/582.

38. See the Treasury printed summary, Apr. 1, 1845, in FO 78/632, and Trevelyan, Feb. 19, 1846, FO 78/669. On Barnett, see Barnett to Bidwell, Nov. 19, 1844, and Feb. 17, 1846, FO 78/583, 78/663, and to Aberdeen, Jan. 29, 1845, FO 78/623.

be subject to the 3 per cent duty that they should pay under the 1838 Anglo-Ottoman Treaty.[39] The British eventually accepted the Egyptian government monopoly—and in doing so they won themselves advantages much greater than were available from Ottoman policy.

Mehmet Ali had another aim in these negotiations. This was to stir up rivalry between the European powers at his court, so as to stop them ganging up on him, as most of them had done in 1840. The European consuls in Egypt noted his increasing intransigence during the 1840s. Some of this may have been due to age and incipient mental instability, but mostly it was a calculated policy of keeping the Europeans, and especially the British and French, at odds with each other.[40] He encouraged John Alexander Galloway, brother of the now-dead Galloway Bey, to revive the latter's plan of 1834 for a British-built railway, in the hope that this would encourage Britain to accept his terms over the transit. At the same time, he exploited French public anger about the railway idea, by encouraging France to put forward plans for a canal. He probably had no intention—and certainly had no financial means—of proceeding with either.[41] In 1847, he finally ruled out both schemes. By now, he was feigning ostentatious loyalty to the Ottoman sultan, especially on religious issues. He had provocatively suggested that Britain and France were wasting their time in agitating the apostasy question in 1844. In early 1845, a Copt was beaten to death by Muslims at Damietta, a religious killing that was normally unheard of in Egypt.[42] In 1846, Mehmet Ali visited Constantinople, spent an estimated £250,000 in presents to important figures at court, and portrayed himself as a faithful Muslim. He wanted to reassure the Porte that his family would remain loyal to the Ottoman regime after his death. When he returned, he received the acting British consul not in his normal simple costume, but in the Turkish full dress of his rank, a blue frock coat overcharged with gold embroidery and several large jewels.[43]

After Mehmet Ali's first mental crisis in the summer of 1844, the European consuls became very concerned about the future of Egypt after his death, particularly because his designated successor Ibrahim was also far from well, and in fact predeceased him. Could the regime sustain itself, or had the whole project been due to the genius of one individual? Barnett was pessimistic about the maintenance of order and security in Egypt in future. Would it revert to Ottoman control, at just the time that most of Europe regarded the empire as death-bound? In July 1848, Consul-General Murray thought that British or French

39. Murray to Palmerston, June 6, 1847, and attached report from Consul Walne, FO 78/707.

40. Barnett to Bidwell, Apr. 19, 1843, FO 78/542; Lyons to Owen, July 27, 1844, FO 78/590; Murray to Palmerston, Feb. 9, 1847, FO 78/710.

41. Barnett to Aberdeen, Nov. 1, 1845, FO 78/623; Hallberg, *Suez Canal*, chaps. 6–8.

42. Barnett to Aberdeen, Mar. 20, 1844, and Mar. 31, 1845, FO 78/582, 78/623.

43. Stoddart to Palmerston, July 30 and Aug. 29, 1846, FO 78/661B.

occupation was the only alternative to re-annexation by the Porte, because the successors within Mehmet Ali's family were "all equally odious and incapable."[44] In 1846, on returning to office, Foreign Secretary Palmerston made clear to Constantinople ambassador Canning that Britain would not support any Ottoman plan to diminish Egypt's current degree of self-government.[45]

Anxiety about the future of Egypt and its likely retreat into Ottomanism prompted a thought that would previously have been heretical. If the Egyptian government sought to emphasise its friendship with Constantinople and its contempt for Europe, should the Western powers try to cooperate in defence of their common interests? This notion did not have much traction in 1844–46 because of the breakdown of the Anglo-French entente globally, but there was some collaboration over plans for Ibrahim's visit to Britain and France in the summer of 1846. While Mehmet Ali lived, these two ideas—concern to resist the reabsorption of Egypt into a declining Ottoman Empire, and a willingness to work with France to achieve that—remained embryonic. In 1848, Mehmet Ali was declared "imbecile," Ibrahim succeeded and died within months, and Abbas became viceroy in November. Those same ideas now came to dominate British policy.

Abbas and the Railway Project

On October 17, 1851, Lord Edward Russell appeared off Alexandria in command of two warships, HMS *Vengeance* and HMS *Encounter*. He was there because Palmerston had ordered these ships to Egypt to "give encouragement and moral support" to Abbas.[46] Lord Edward, who, as it happens, was the half-brother of the then British prime minister, Lord John Russell, stayed for nearly a month and had a very pleasant time, visiting Abbas and other dignitaries. His purpose was to await the arrival of a letter from Constantinople. The letter was the expected surrender by the Porte to the repeated British demand that Abbas should be allowed to build a railway from Alexandria to Cairo, that ultimately would continue to Suez. If the Porte did not agree to the demand, Murray instructed Russell to keep his warships there, so that Britain's "moral support and countenance" could continue while the defiant construction of the railway began.[47] Lord Edward's guns, in other words, were to give British backing to Abbas against the Ottoman sultan.

How had this happened? A railway from Alexandria to Suez was the first British demand to the new viceroy, in December 1848. At first, Abbas

---

44. Stoddart to Aberdeen, Aug. 6, 1844, FO 78/582; Barnett to Aberdeen, Apr. 16, 1845, FO 78/623; Murray to Palmerston, July 6, 1848, FO 78/757.

45. Palmerston to Canning, Aug. 1, 1846, FO 78/635.

46. Palmerston to Admiralty, Aug. 4, 1851, FO 78/885.

47. Murray to Russell, Oct. 19, 1851, FO 78/886.

did not seem at all keen, though in 1850 he became more ambivalent.[48] In March 1851, he signalled that he would support it; in July, his government committed to build the line between Alexandria and Cairo. Murray expected that this would reduce the journey, which currently took more than a day, to six or seven hours. One reason why Abbas sent Nubar to London for the Great Exhibition was to make the contracts for rails and carriages, under the guidance of Robert Stephenson, the leading railway engineer, whose plan it was. Nubar's visit was therefore doubly offensive to the Porte, because it implied that Britain was actively encouraging the development of Egypt into an independent thoroughfare to India, raising the question of how far it would still need Constantinople.

In London, Palmerston told the Ottoman ambassador, Musurus, that the settlement of 1841 left Mehmet Ali's family in hereditary possession of an Egyptian government that was entitled to collect and spend its own revenues, as long as it paid the agreed tribute to the sultan. The railway was a purely commercial enterprise, which would benefit Egypt's prosperity. The Porte, however, insisted that Abbas had no right to build a railway without the sultan's permission. Canning raised the temperature by telling Murray that Abbas would be deposed unless he asked for it. Palmerston suggested that Abbas should apply for permission, but also that his application would be supported by the public opinion of Europe, by which he meant the power of the British government.[49] The Porte's demand for Abbas to seek its permission created a minor sensation when reported in the British press at the end of September, and major Chambers of Commerce protested to the Foreign Office about Ottoman interference. At a meeting at the London Tavern, two hundred City men, including Briggs and Anderson, urged the immediate building of the railway, censured the Constantinople government, and praised "that great and wonderful man" Mehmet Ali for developing the transit.[50]

Palmerston left the Porte in no doubt that it had to approve the building of the railway, and the immediate crisis was averted. The Porte's letter to Abbas granting permission for the construction arrived in early November, allowing Lord Edward Russell to leave. In December, Arthur Anderson of P&O came to Egypt with a declaration of support for Abbas from the London Tavern meeting. He told him that "the British nation would never passively submit to the sacrifice of the important interests it now has in Egypt, which would be

48. Palmerston to Murray, Dec. 21, 1848, FO 78/756; Murray to Palmerston, Apr. 19, 1849, FO 78/804 135. See Hoskins, British Routes to India, 294–97.

49. Murray to Palmerston, June 27, July 17, and Sept. 4, 1851; Murray to Canning, July 23, 1851; and Palmerston to Murray, Aug. 23 and Sept. 19, 1851; all FO 78/875, 78/876. Canning to Palmerston, May 17 and June 4, 1851, FO 78/855, 78/856.

50. The Chambers of Commerce of Southampton, Manchester, and Glasgow petitioned the Foreign Office: FO 78/886, 78/887. For the London Tavern meeting, see Daily News, Oct. 15, 1851.

caused by the government falling again into the hands of the Divan of Constantinople." Abbas was generally feted by the British press, which praised his love of horseracing; a perplexed Frenchman claimed that he must have bought *The Times*.[51] The railway was finished in 1856, and the second leg, to Suez, in 1858. The first director of the Egyptian railways was an Englishman who had converted to Islam, Henry Selby Rickards (Abdallah Bey). By 1873, the journey between Alexandria and Cairo took just four and a half hours. After the 1857 Indian Rebellion, over five thousand troops were sent from Britain to India by the railway; a rate of £10 was paid for each officer and £5 for privates.[52]

One by-product of the building of the first railway in the Middle East was that some individuals mooted plans to use British construction expertise in other parts of the region. This was not surprising: some years earlier, Cornwallis Harris had imagined pilgrims soon whirling to Mecca on a locomotive.[53] Now a lobby arose for a Euphrates railway from Antioch to Basra. This was headed by James Bowen Thompson, a medical philanthropist in Damascus, and supported by other evangelicals with Syrian connections, such as Holt Yates and George Gawler, and some former members of the Euphrates Expedition, including Ainsworth. Here was a demonstration of the continuing rivalry between proponents of investment in the two different routes across Ottoman territory—the Euphrates versus the Red Sea. Evangelicals preferred the Syrian option, arguing that railways might improve the local economy, and hence the prospects for Christianity. The idea was pursued for a few months in 1852. Though Rose in Constantinople was willing to argue that a railway would help to pacify the region, he recognised that the Ottomans did not really want more of a European economic presence there, and were motivated mainly by jealousy of Egypt.[54] In 1853, another project was aired: John Wright, an Irish railway entrepreneur, urged a railway from Gaza to the Euphrates, to be built jointly by Britain and France, in order to promote a scheme of settlement in Palestine. This, he explained, would validate his interpretation of Isaiah 49, that Ireland had been chosen to accomplish the return of the Jews to Jerusalem. Unfortunately, the Foreign Office was unable to help him.[55]

51. Anderson to Wilcox, Dec. 18, 1851, FO 78/922. On Abbas and the British press, see Toledano, *State and Society*, 117–19, 127; Senior, *Conversations and Journals*, 1:241.

52. D. Reid, *Whose Pharaohs?*, 68; H.J.L.B., review of *L'Egypte*, 452.

53. St. John, *Egypt and Nubia*, 261.

54. See the various papers, March 1852, in FO 78/922. The Foreign Office, Canning, and Rose took the idea seriously, but see Rose to Malmesbury, July 4, 1852, FO 78/893. Nothing happened. In 1853, Bowen Thompson was still pressing for action, but his main hope was now for a consular position in charge of postal communication: to Russell, Feb. 16, 1853, FO 78/972.

55. See John Wright to Clarendon, Oct. 29, 1853, and Foreign Office reply, Nov. 8, 1853, FO 78/975. He enclosed his pamphlet, *Ireland the Restorer of Israel under the Protection of France and England*, a reworking of a similar tract that he had urged on Napoleon III.

A Rage for Order

Abbas had not come round to the British request to build an Egyptian railway because he shared John Wright's enthusiasm for technology. Rather, he was desperate for friends in order to defeat a campaign at the Porte to remove him and to install someone more subservient to the Ottomans. In September 1850, he told the British consul in Cairo that he would ignore French opposition to the railway and support it, but that he wished at the same time to apply for British protection.[56] The campaign against him was funded by members of his family in exile at Constantinople, and coordinated by Artin, Mehmet Ali's last prime minister, who had (reportedly) run off there with 2.5 million French francs that he had gained from selling government wheat and cotton at public auction while minister of commerce.[57]

Reshid worked with Artin, presenting the move against Abbas in terms of the application of the Tanzimat. For Reshid, the great principle of the Tanzimat was the establishment of central government authority over the provinces, through the implementation of defined laws that secured basic liberties for the subject. He insisted that Abbas's legal code (almost entirely inherited from Mehmet Ali) should be submitted for approval at Constantinople. One of the attractions of this strategy for Reshid was that Canning, and he assumed the British government, was bound to support his position. As a Foreign Office memorandum put it in May 1851: "the Tanzimat is humane, just, and moral: the Abbas code Draconic and brutal; oppressive towards the fellahs and unjust; in fact it is a code devised for the pleasure of the Prince and the slavery of the lower classes."[58]

Reshid had reckoned without Charles Murray, the British consul-general in Egypt. Murray did not just oppose the application of the Tanzimat to Egypt and its Sudanese dependency, he ridiculed the idea. He argued that Mehmet Ali's firm code was necessary to secure order. Three million Arabs were kept in line only by the fear of rapid and severe punishment. Within six months of the Tanzimat's introduction, English tourists to the cataracts of Upper Egypt would be robbed, and the Indian mail would need guards. Why should Egypt be reduced to the state of Baghdad, Kurdistan, and the Hijaz, "theatres of constant robbery and pillage," where armed guards and blackmail to robbers were required for safety? The Ottoman Empire had repeatedly shown its incapacity to create an ordered and prosperous society, which depended on economic improvements that it had failed to make. As a result, the Tanzimat could not be applied in large parts of it, and where it had been applied, it had "suddenly

56. Walne to Murray, Sept. 20, 1850, FO 78/841.

57. Hunter, *Egypt under the Khedives*, 112; Murray to Palmerston, Feb. 6, 1851, and to Canning, Feb. 14, 1851, FO 78/875.

58. Addington memo, May 9, 1851, FO 78/883.

removed the restraints of fear from populations who scarcely acknowledge any other control." Egypt was so important for Britain, commercially, strategically, and in terms of lives and property, that the experiment must not be made there. It was an obvious attempt by the Porte to humiliate Abbas, perhaps to produce internal instability, and to seize direct control over the enormous revenues of Egypt.[59] Canning admitted that the Porte was jealous of Abbas's good relations with Britain. Murray rejected complaints from Constantinople that the size of the Egyptian army exceeded the eighteen thousand to which Mehmet Ali had pledged to limit it in 1841. Though lower than previously, it was thirty thousand because such a force was necessary to secure order. He pointed out that in 1849 the sultan had acquiesced in that policy, hoping to draw on it in case he had to fight Russia and Austria.[60]

If the Tanzimat were to be fully imposed on Egypt, various administrative changes would be necessary, but one immediate question predominated. This was whether sentences of capital punishment would need to be remitted to Constantinople for the sultan to approve or commute. The Edict of Gülhane curtailed the discretionary power of provincial courts to pass death sentences, which they were used to doing in the sultan's name. The object was to prevent the abuse of power by local authorities, and to provide a bureaucratic check at the centre that regular legal process had been followed. The *qisas*, the power to impose the death penalty in cases of murder, belonged to the heirs of the murdered man where these could be found, but otherwise only to the sultan. The sultan had delegated this power to Mehmet Ali, and it was the foundation of the Egyptian punishment system. In July 1851, George Le Mesurier, an Indian army officer who had surveyed Egyptian military defences, thought that the planned railway could be built and maintained only if the *qisas* remained in Abbas's hands. Otherwise, desert tribes would make the transit and trips to the cataracts impossible within a year, and Egypt would become like the Hijaz or Tripoli. P&O, which had commissioned six new steamers on hearing of the railway contract, also wrote to urge upholding Abbas's right of *qisas*. The Foreign Office agreed. In the same memo in which he described the draconian Abbas code, Henry Addington, the permanent under-secretary, continued: "there is no question however that . . . the Tanzimat could not be properly carried out in Egypt, especially in that humane part in which it is required that reference shall be made to Turkey before death can be inflicted."[61]

59. Murray to Palmerston, Feb. 6 and 17, June 27, 1851 (quotation 1), and Murray to Canning, Feb. 14, 1851, FO 78/875; Murray to Palmerston, Oct. 5 (quotation 2), and Nov. 26, 1851, FO 78/876. The Oct. 5 letter also referred to the recent riots at Aleppo.

60. Canning to Palmerston, Nov. 21, 1851, FO 78/860; Murray to Palmerston, Mar. 27, 1851, FO 78/875.

61. Le Mesurier to Foreign Office, July 17, 1851, FO 78/884; Howell to Palmerston, Sept. 10, 1851, FO 78/885; memo, May 9, 1851, FO 78/883.

Palmerston supported Abbas against "foreign and domestic intriguers" opposed to him at the Porte. However, he was not prepared to deny that the sultan had sovereign rights over life and death. So he advised accepting the principle and hoping that the Ottomans would respond to British pressure to compromise on the practice.[62] In July 1851, Murray persuaded Abbas to acknowledge the sultan's rights, and asked Canning to get the latter to grant the *qisas* for life to each succeeding Egyptian viceroy. For a long time, the Porte would not yield. Reshid thought that he could bargain with Egypt and with Britain about the *qisas* in return for accepting the building of the railway.[63] In January 1852, 117 British merchants and residents at Alexandria and Cairo complained to the Foreign Office about the Ottoman stance.[64] Granville, Palmerston's replacement as foreign secretary, forwarded the complaint, and strongly urged the Porte to give way, given the importance of the threat of the death penalty for the maintenance of tranquillity and security of life and property in Egypt. He warned that failure to comply might well lead to "very disastrous consequences to the Turkish Empire." The British government agreed to send two more warships to Alexandria in case the Ottomans threatened to attack it.[65]

Finally, the matter was settled. The Porte sent an ambassador to Cairo to offer the *qisas* for two years, which was extended in discussions to six and then seven, and eventually for Abbas's lifetime. Tellingly, in return, Abbas agreed to write off the debt of £250,000 that he was owed by Constantinople, and to make advance payments of future tribute.[66] This helped to resolve the Porte's immediate financial problems, which were troubling Canning. However, it required Abbas to arrange an English loan in the City, through the agency of P&O. It was ironic that Constantinople was able for the time being to avoid the eventually ruinous post-war policy of reliance on international loans, only because its behaviour forced the more creditworthy Egyptian government down the same road.

62. Palmerston to Canning, Apr. 7 and July 24, 1851, FO 78/849, 78/850; to Murray, Jan. 1, 1852, FO 78/915.

63. Murray to Canning, July 23, 1851, FO 78/875; Canning to Palmerston, July 4, 1851, FO 78/856. For the central government's determination to impose the principle on Baghdad later in the 1850s, see Aykut's "Judicial Reforms, Sharia Law" (12).

64. Murray to Granville, Jan. 24, 1852, FO 78/916. Anderson had told the London Tavern meeting that there was no need for the imposition of the "Tanzemaat" in Egypt because only three Egyptians had suffered capital punishment in five years: *Daily News*, Oct. 15, 1851. Murray thought the figure was twenty-five in three: to Palmerston, Sept. 5, 1851, FO 78/876.

65. Granville to Canning, Jan. 19 and Feb. 6, 1852, FO 78/888; Malmesbury to Murray, Apr. 22, 1852, FO 78/915.

66. Rose, Murray, Paget, to Malmesbury, Apr. 14 and 16, and Dec. 7, 1852, FO 78/916; Murray to Canning, Apr. 24, 1852, FO 78/916.

This affair showed that the gulf between the Constantinople embassy and British officials in Egypt was as wide as in 1801 or 1840. In September 1851, Canning told Palmerston confidently that the sultan would remove Abbas if he did not come into line, because he held all the cards: the influence of his name, the power of the anti-Abbas faction in Constantinople, and the increase of Ottoman power in the Hijaz.[67] Canning suggested that Murray was an empire builder, and that the Ottomans were rightly suspicious of this new "foreign influence . . . of a consular description."[68] The Ottomans may or may not have disliked Murray's behaviour, but Canning clearly loathed it. At an embassy dinner in January 1852, Canning's long-time colleague, his oriental secretary Charles Alison, declared that Murray was in receipt of a payment of £1,000 a year from Abbas, which had been disguised as support of his infant son (Murray's wife had died shortly after giving birth). This was overheard by a naval officer and reported to Murray. In fact, Abbas's mother had just given the baby a diamond ring in sympathy. Murray complained: Alison had suggested that he was in contempt of Foreign Office regulations. Canning tried to brush off the complaint by settling for a small correction in a Constantinople newspaper. The Foreign Office insisted on a public apology, and supplied the words.[69]

After he left Egypt, Murray claimed three achievements there. One was the railway, against French and Ottoman opposition. A second was Egypt's preservation from the Tanzimat—"legalised anarchy"—despite Canning's obstruction. The third was the gift of Obaysch to the queen and London Zoo. Obaysch was a fitting symbol of Abbas's search for British protection against his many enemies, and Murray achieved a fame, of sorts, as "Hippopotamus Murray."[70] He also got his way over the size of Abbas's army. By 1853, it was at fifty thousand, with the acquiescence of the Porte.[71]

Yet this was a telling fact. If Constantinople was to thrive in war, it needed military assistance from Egypt, as in the 1820s. If it was to survive financially, it also needed Egypt's tribute. There was no reason for it to doubt that it would get both. Even Mehmet Ali had never conceived of himself as fully independent of the sultan. The indolent Abbas was temperamentally much less likely

67. Canning to Palmerston, Sept. 4, 1851, FO 78/858. The Hijaz was an important battleground between the Ottomans and Egyptians, because Abbas had been born there in 1812 to Mehmet Ali's son Tusun, who was trying to subdue the Wahhabi. It remained an important power base to him as a devout Muslim, even though in 1841 control of the Hijaz had reverted to Constantinople. The Porte removed the sharif of Mecca in 1851 as part of that battle. Presumably this helps to explain increased Ottoman hostility to British activity at Jeddah and Massawa, discussed in chapter 10. Murray blamed Canning for weakening Britain's influence in the Red Sea: Mar. 27, 1852, FO 78/916.

68. To Palmerston, Sept. 17, 1851, FO 78/858.

69. Murray to Malmesbury, Apr. 14, 1852, FO 78/916; Malmesbury to Canning, May 5, 1852, FO 78/888; Addington to Alison, July 23, 1852, FO 78/919.

70. Maxwell, *Sir Charles Murray*, 244–45.

71. Canning to Clarendon, June 17, 1853, FO 78/933.

to oppose his sovereign. His desire for British protection had been aimed at defeating a factional struggle against him, not at asserting his independence. Once those struggles were over, there was every reason to expect him to be a loyal servant of Muslim Ottoman interests. Ideologically, Abbas, educated in the harem "amid a herd of slaves," posed no threat to the sultan's values. Nor was he an easy ally for Britain, because of his conspicuous consumption on palaces and processions, and reliance on favourites. Murray's successor Frederick Bruce lamented in 1854 that Abbas instinctively clung to "monopoly" and "arbitrary government," and relied on "incapable and inexperienced" administrators.[72] Despite his service over the railway, was he someone on whom Britain could depend? Might it be better to think about the balance of interests in Egypt in a different way?

The French and the Sultan

The spring of 1852 was one of the lowest points in Anglo-French relations in the nineteenth century, owing to Louis Napoleon's coup in late 1851 and the subsequent suspicion of him in Britain. It is all the more striking, therefore, that the powers of Europe quickly cooperated to confirm the Ottoman-Egyptian agreement on the *qisas*, which required amending the settlement of 1841.[73] In essence, France agreed not to make difficulties over it. At the time, the significance could easily be missed. By now, the assumption that Britain and France were in permanent rivalry in Egypt had been ingrained for over fifty years. Palmerston himself tended to see French influence behind every manoeuvre against Britain's Egyptian interests. Travellers like W. H. Russell continued to fret about the apparent predominance of French, not British, "moral influence" on the streets of Cairo. In 1854, Bruce rued the tendency for there to be a British and a French party on most questions.[74] While Abbas appeared to be pursuing a British policy as viceroy, it was widely assumed that his heir Said was in league with the French—and when Abbas was murdered in a palace intrigue in 1854, the usual conspiracy theories had a brief outing. In fact, Bruce acted quickly to ensure that Said succeeded to power in accordance with the rules laid down in 1841. He continued ostentatiously to support him.[75]

Those who still interpreted Egyptian politics in terms of European rivalry had not learned the lesson from Mehmet Ali's last years. He had not responded to defeat by the four European powers by taking up the fifth. What authority

72. Bruce (who as it happens was Elgin's son) to Clarendon, Mar. 16 and Aug. 13, 1854, FO 78/1035, 78/1036.

73. Canning to Malmesbury, May 12, 1852, FO 78/892.

74. Russell, *My Diary in India*, 1:32–33; Bruce to Clarendon, Mar. 16, 1854, FO 78/1035.

75. Bruce to Clarendon, July 17, 1854, FO 78/1036; Senior, *Conversations and Journals*, 2:18–21.

or authenticity would that have given a Muslim ruler? He fell back increasingly on the support of Islam. Abbas, similarly, had antagonised Westernising Egyptian reformers; for example, by withdrawing support for Mehmet Ali's linguistic and technical schools.[76]

In 1854, Bruce observed that whenever Abbas flattered him, it was because he was trying to sow "disunion between the agents of France and England who have really but one interest, namely, the security of foreign commerce, and the introduction of a better system of administration. By playing us off in this way against each other, the Pasha hopes that he will be able to carry out his retrograde views without any serious consequences to himself."[77] The Porte's strategy often seemed similar: to divide the Western powers, in order to undermine Egyptian freedom of action and to strengthen its own claims over Egyptian government and revenues.[78] So Bruce encouraged Said to act confidently in pursuit of Egypt's own interests as a growing power, and semi-independently of "more ignorant, more stupid, more corrupt" Constantinople.[79] The revenues deriving from British and French commerce, and the number of Egyptians whom it enriched, were ultimately the best security for the Egyptian government's freedom of action. As Joseph Bonomi had observed ten years earlier, "English gold, English influence is silently taking possession of Egypt. It is an immense thoroughfare that cannot now be shut."[80] Egyptian cotton exports had averaged about 200,000 hundredweight for most of the 1840s, but reached a plateau of 500,000 in the mid-1850s. British capitalists' excitement about the railway reflected their sense of the country's enormous potential.[81]

To emphasise the importance of commerce also underlined Britain's practical ascendancy in Egypt. In 1851, Murray was confident that "our important and increasing interests here must ensure a corresponding increase of legitimate influence."[82] In 1847, his consul at Alexandria, John Stoddart, insisted that British interests far outweighed France's, and that Britain must expect to occupy Egypt in any crisis. He wrote the Foreign Office a historical essay on the country's importance as the great link between West and East, a link that Britain could easily reforge. One important way to knit "firmly together . . . the disjointed portions of our territorial greatness" was by strengthening British "authority among Mahometan populations, whose pilgrimage [we] will

76. Hekekyan in Senior, *Conversations and Journals*, 2:214–16. For Abbas's changes, see Toledano, *State and Society*, 43–51.

77. Bruce to Clarendon, Mar. 16, 1854, FO 78/1035.

78. Hekekyan in Senior, *Conversations and Journals*, 1:207–8, 2:64, 67, 107–8.

79. Bruce in Senior, *Conversations and Journals*, 2:36.

80. Joseph Bonomi to Birch, Sept. 1844, Bonomi Papers, CUL Add. MS 9389/2/B.

81. Landes, *Bankers and Pashas*, 331. See Layard to Ross, Sept. 23, 1851, LPBL, 38941 53.

82. Murray to Canning, Nov. 12, 1851, FO 78/876.

protect and favour."[83] In 1849 and 1850, two Indian army officers openly conducted far-reaching surveys of Egyptian fortifications and army resources, in order to make clear Britain's military priorities in a likely European war.[84]

In 1848, French consul-general Barrot agreed with Stoddart: "the possession of Egypt is a necessity for the existence of England. . . . If England finds herself engaged in war . . . her first endeavour will be to occupy Egypt." Crucially, Napoleon III recognised British primacy in 1852, dropped French opposition to the Egyptian railway, and instructed his new consul-general, Sabatier, accordingly. Throughout 1853, Sabatier underlined France's view that the British rightly expected to exercise a predominant interest there.[85] The Anglo-French wartime alliance then underpinned the joint efforts of Bruce and Sabatier to encourage first Abbas, and then Said, to undertake "general measures of improvement and good administration."[86]

The Crimean War, therefore, strengthened the emerging agreement between Britain and France on the need to improve Egyptian government and to bolster its practical independence from Constantinople's pressure.[87] Of course, it would have better if a war had not been necessary. Unfortunately, if Napoleon III was willing to play second fiddle to Britain in Egypt, this was not the case everywhere.

83. Stoddart to Palmerston, Feb. 9, 1847, FO 78/710.

84. James Outram and George Le Mesurier: Bombay to India House, July 25, 1850, and Apr. 3, 1851, FO 78/883.

85. Hallberg, *Suez Canal*, 105, 113; Paget to Malmesbury, Jan. 3, 1853, FO 78/966.

86. Bruce to Clarendon, Mar. 16, 1854, FO 78/1035.

87. For French, and Anglo-French, informal imperialism in Egypt over the next twenty years, see chapter 5 of Todd's *Velvet Empire*.

CHAPTER TWELVE

Jerusalem and the Crimean War

IN THE LAST FEW CHAPTERS, we have journeyed with the British around the Middle East of the 1840s and 1850s—from Lebanon across Syria into Kurdistan, down the Ottoman-Persian border, past Baghdad and Basra into the Persian Gulf, around the Arabian coast to Aden, and up the Red Sea to Egypt. Now our journey reaches its end, for, like so many millions of pilgrims over the centuries, we are arriving at Jerusalem. But the Jerusalem we are visiting, the Jerusalem of 1853, was no exemplary city on a hill. It remained, in almost every respect, stony and depressing ground for the British visitor. This was less because of its overwhelmingly Arab ambience—though this was a shock to many—than because of the excessive influence of traditional European politics. It was the Middle Eastern town most given over to rival French and Russian sectarianisms. Each party, under the guise of religious demands, competed to dominate Ottoman officials locally, and by extension in Constantinople. Jerusalem was the town that demonstrated the limits to the British strategy of trying to weaken the political potency of French denominationalism and Russian protection claims.

Unholy Places

One British visitor, in May 1853, was the liberal Anglican clergyman and intellectual Arthur Penrhyn Stanley. Stanley was on a tour of the Holy Land, which resulted in one of the classics of Victorian historical geography, his book *Sinai and Palestine*. Stanley used his very developed poetic imagination and his scholarly learning to reach plausible insights into the life and circumstances of Christ and the Jewish people before him, hoping thereby to make the New and Old Testaments convincing to a modern audience. He was establishing himself as the most sympathetic and popular liberal theologian of his age, and an irritant to dogged biblical literalists, such as the Scot Alexander Keith.[1] On the Sunday before Ascension Day 1853, Stanley preached in the extremely new and small Protestant church in Jerusalem. His theme was the blessing of Christ's presence in the daily lives of his disciples, but the much greater blessing to humanity that resulted from his removal from that mundane sphere. The modern traveller should relish being able to walk where Christ had walked, but should remember that "questions of sacred topography, scenes of sacred events, however solemn, however interesting, however edifying, are not, and never can be, religion itself. . . . We are Christians, not because He dwelt in Palestine, not because He died at Jerusalem, not because His body was laid in the sepulchre," but because by his ascension he opened the kingdom of Heaven to all believers. "Whatever superstitions may have overclouded the place of His birth, His burial, His resurrection, His ascension" explained nothing about Christ's example and love, because these were available everywhere, irrespective of "those earthly barriers which divide nation from nation, church from church."[2] With these words, Stanley was taking aim at foes rather more threatening than Alexander Keith—at the Catholic and Orthodox monks of the Jerusalem and Bethlehem religious establishments, and the two European powers which at that moment were lined up angrily behind them.

France aimed to recover from the embarrassment of the 1840 Eastern crisis by exploiting the connections that the Catholic Church was making with Maronites, Chaldeans, and Syrians. European Catholics expected that Jerusalem would be the coordinating centre of their Church's increased activity in the Middle East, and Giuseppe Valerga arrived there in January 1848 as the first resident Latin patriarch since the Crusades. However, there was no reason in principle why France should gain politically by this. As Valerga had been appointed by the new pope, Pius IX, neither the British nor the Ottoman government regarded it as sinister. Pius IX was regarded in Britain as a liberal on Italian politics, critical of France and Austria. Britain and the Porte both encouraged the Vatican's pursuit of diplomatic ties with Constantinople in 1847–48, in the hope that this would, in Palmerston's words, "get rid of much of the interference of France and Austria" on behalf of the Catholic rayas.[3] An informal agreement on Vatican representation was reached in April 1848. By 1849, however, Pius IX had been forced out of Rome by revolution, and then reinstalled as ruler of his central Italian territories by French troops. His liberalism and his capacity to stand up to France were thereafter much diminished. By 1850, the new French leader, Louis Napoleon, was keen to play the Catholic card in order to entrench his domestic support. From now on, the

1. Keith, *Scripture versus Stanley*; Pemble, *Mediterranean Passion*, 188–91.

2. Stanley, *Sermons*, 359–60.

3. Palmerston to Cowley, Apr. 3, 1847, FO 78/674. See Brennan, *Pope Pius the Ninth*, 122–24.

policies of the papacy and of the French government towards Jerusalem were very similar, expressed in the alliance between Valerga and the local French consul Botta. With Egypt and Lebanon quiet, Jerusalem would once more be France's cause in the East.

On the floor of the grotto in the Church of the Nativity in Bethlehem, the Catholic monks had set a silver star with a Latin inscription to mark Christ's birthplace. In October 1847, it disappeared after a sectarian scuffle. This was plainly the work of their Orthodox rivals, who had primacy over most of the site. The Latins had to enter their own chapel by a side door, because they lacked keys to the main door of the church. The French authorities complained, but it was not until 1850 that the Paris government asked its ambassador at Constantinople, Jacques Aupick, to take up this issue. He pointed to the capitulations attached to the Franco-Ottoman treaty of 1740—made at the high point of the Ottomans' dependence on French support, during their conflicts with Russia and Persia. In this formal treaty was a recognition of French rights of protection over the clergy of the Latin rite anywhere in the empire, and their freedom to worship in all churches in their possession. The French claimed that this must include the Church of the Nativity, the tomb of the Virgin in Gethsemane, and the Church of the Holy Sepulchre in Jerusalem, which was shared with Greeks, who had for some time been behaving arrogantly, damaging Crusader tombs in 1808 and in 1842 getting the sultan's permission to decorate the cupola with Orthodox iconography. The French claim was validated by Eugène Boré's investigations of national rights over these "Holy Places," begun during his visit of 1847–48 and published in 1850. He said that the Orthodox counterclaims relied on forged documents.[4]

The real significance of France's step lay in the wider context of the Eastern question in 1850: the ongoing international tension stemming from the 1848 revolutions, which revealed a destabilising power vacuum across large parts of central and eastern Europe. After the revolution in Bucharest in June 1848, the Russians occupied the Ottoman Balkan provinces of Moldavia and Wallachia. They had the treaty right to occupy the provinces temporarily, when necessary to restore stability and with the acquiescence of the Porte. Palmerston regarded that as an "exceptional and vicious" concession to Russia caused by past Ottoman weakness: the aim must be to stop any more similar concessions.[5] But they continued to occupy the region while they helped the Austrians in their brutal suppression of the Hungarian and Transylvanian revolutions in 1849. This in turn reflected both powers' extreme anxiety to prevent the spread of revolutionary principles. Moreover, Russia was supporting Austria in demanding that the Ottomans should surrender several thousand Hungarian refugees who had fled into Ottoman territory, including

4. Fairey, *Great Powers and Orthodox Christendom*, 123–24.
5. To Canning, Feb. 26, 1849, FO 78/768.

the Hungarian leader Kossuth. The sultan had given them his hospitality, supported by Britain and France. All three governments insisted that the refugees were protected under "the principles of international law," as long as they did not plot against the tranquillity of other states.[6] Yet Russian and Austrian pressure on the Porte continued, in the hope of achieving "the Porte's habitual submission to the superior fortunes and calculating energies of a neighbour."[7] In late 1849, the crisis was very acute. Both Britain and France moved their navies towards the entrance of the Dardanelles to indicate their willingness to protect the empire if necessary; the British one, which arrived first, at one stage advanced almost to Constantinople, until Russia protested. Palmerston was pleased by the rapidity and unanimity with which the cabinet had acted. This was exactly the sort of issue on which liberal and radical opinion in Britain and France was most easily inflamed. Many protest meetings were held on the subject in 1849–50, and Russian and Austrian behaviour was widely compared to that of the old Holy Alliance, which in the 1820s had similarly formed an international cartel against liberal refugees.[8]

France's claim to the Holy Places deliberately connected the legal guarantees given by the sultan to France in 1740 with that to the refugees. In each case, Russia was attempting to use its bullying powers to ride roughshod over the protections provided by international law. This was a neat political strategy, not only because of the light in which it placed Russia, but also because it aimed to make the Ottomans uphold the principles of 1740, in order to show their respect for international law, and to make the British take France's side. Louis Napoleon, Bonaparte's nephew, had been elected French president in late 1848; he boasted that he wished to revise the 1815 treaty settlement that constrained France's global ambitions. Many British people were getting extremely anxious about his restlessness. But it was difficult to object in instances where his policy rested on respecting a treaty: the "safest of all foundations, those of justice and international right."[9]

Nonetheless, Britain was still very embarrassed by France's assertiveness over the Holy Places, and the heated Russian and Greek Orthodox response to it as the issue spiralled out of control over the next three years. This was partly because of the inherent ludicrousness of two of the most powerful countries in the world squabbling over stars, door keys, and cupola decorations in pursuit of a sectarian triumph. At Constantinople, it seemed to acting ambassador Hugh Rose that they were using the very places of Christ's birth and death to sacrifice the essential message of Christianity in favour of the "puerilities and

6. See, e.g., Ali's draft note, in Canning to Palmerston, Sept. 3, 1849, FO 78/779; Palmerston to Canning, Nov. 30, 1849, FO 78/771.

7. The phrase is Canning's, to Palmerston, Nov. 26, 1849, FO 78/782.

8. Lane-Poole, *Stratford Canning*, 2:199–202; Sinha, *Asylum and International Law*, 21, 42–43.

9. Rose to Malmesbury, Nov. 23, 1852, FO 78/895.

passions with which man has disfigured it."[10] But it was mainly because it was so deliberately offensive, unwise, and counterproductive. It was plainly unrealistic to try to deny all Greek Orthodox pilgrims as well as clergy access to the holiest sites of their religion. The Russian case rested on the sheer number of Greek Orthodox subjects in the empire: at least ten million in all, including a third of a million in Syria. Nesselrode's remark that many Orthodox would take offence at any change to the current compromise over access to the holy sites was a threat to condone future unrest. Moreover, Tsar Nicholas saw himself as the protector of his religion. Britain recognised that he would regard any serious diminution of Orthodox rights as an unacceptable loss of "moral influence."[11] Britain stayed strictly neutral and repeatedly counselled moderation to both sides.

The Balkan tensions were eventually settled for the moment in 1851 with the release of the refugees to safety. The "Holy Places" dispute was resolved only in May 1853, after a disastrous ratcheting up of mutual Franco-Russian resentment and suspicion. The Porte set up commissions examining the historical claims of each side. In May 1851, Napoleon sent a new ambassador, Lavalette, who was a clerical partisan and behaved accordingly. In September, the Russians threatened to end their amity with the Ottomans if long-standing Greek rights were not recognised. Early in 1852, a settlement appeared to have been reached, on the basis that the 1740 treaty implicitly recognised Greek claims to the sites exercised before then. Hopes that this was an end to the matter foundered, because the formal Ottoman declarations to each side proved inconsistent, and France accused Russia of applying undue pressure to twist the Porte's arms. Having been recalled to France, Lavalette returned to Constantinople on a warship (in violation of the straits settlement of 1841), claiming that he and his country had both been humiliated. By late 1852, the battle seemed no less intense, though now reduced to the question of control of the two doors needed to get to the Latin chapel at Bethlehem. Rose despaired that the peace of Europe seemed to depend on the keys to "a great door and a little door."[12] By spring 1853, the passion was burnt out, Napoleon said that he would no longer press the matter, and a complex settlement was reached in May about conditions of access.

The problem was that the issue "in reality is a vital struggle between France and Russia for political influence, at the Porte's cost, in her dominions."[13] Both were desperate to improve their standing in Constantinople—not just against the other but also against Britain, of so much more weight than during their eighteenth-century rivalries. Britain could not rely on either side seeing

10. Rose to Russell, Feb. 22, 1853, FO 78/929.
11. Clarendon to Canning, Feb. 25, 1853, FO 78/924; Goldfrank, *Crimean War*, 80–81.
12. Rose to Malmesbury, Oct. 1, 1852, FO 78/894.
13. Rose to Malmesbury, Nov. 20, 1852, FO 78/895.

reason. Nor was it practicable or desirable for it to guarantee the empire alone. At the height of the refugee crisis in late 1849, the Porte asked Britain for a defensive alliance, and was refused. British ministers continued to complain about the Ottomans' inability to deliver the Palmerston-Canning programme on Christian civil rights, an inability that they thought encouraged Russia's activities in the Balkans. They feared that to pledge British military support would give the Porte less incentive to reform.[14] This was an impossible balancing act, especially as suspicion of Napoleon's domestic ambitions and international revisionism was immense. His coup d'état of November 1851 was followed by his proclamation as Emperor Napoleon III a year later; these events prompted an invasion panic in Britain. In March 1853, the Russians, feeling that France was deliberately seeking to destroy respect for them among the Orthodox population of the empire, dispatched Prince Menshikov to Constantinople to try to win concessions. Rose immediately wanted to send the fleet to the Dardanelles to strengthen the Porte's backbone, but the cabinet overruled him because it thought that Napoleon was still the main cause of the tension in the East, and that to send in the navy would play into his hands.[15]

Unfortunately, Menshikov's visit signalled an intensification of Russian pressure on the Porte, expressed in the secret treaty that he wanted it to sign. Menshikov's proposed treaty aimed to establish Russia's right to make representations to the sultan on behalf of the Greek Orthodox population of the East. Russia had for some time been advancing such claims, based on a creative interpretation of the 1774 Treaty of Küçük Kaynarca (which in fact had given Russia this right only for the Orthodox in Moldavia and Wallachia, and for one Russian church in Constantinople).[16] Menshikov demanded that Russia should have the formal written right to interpose at the Porte on behalf of any Orthodox community, on the grounds that after the tortuous Holy Places discussions, the Porte could not be relied on to uphold informal agreements. These terms were unacceptable to Britain and France, because they would restore the idea of special Russian rights at Constantinople, as in 1829–39. Stratford Canning thought it vicious sectarianism, like France demanding the right to complain about Britain's government of Irish Catholics.[17] Russia's demand was driven partly by anxiety over the loss of influence at Constantinople, especially if Britain and France worked together, and partly by concern about the growth of liberal sentiments in the Balkans and eastern Europe—for example, in a developing crisis in Montenegro (which Austria also encouraged). For Russia, and for Britain and France, the issue was

14. Clarendon to Canning, Feb. 25, 1853, FO 78/924.

15. A. Taylor, *Struggle for Mastery*, 52–53. For Russian and Orthodox insecurity, see Fairey, *Great Powers and Orthodox Christendom*, 126–28.

16. See Davison, "Russian Skill."

17. Canning to Clarendon, Apr. 9 and May 22, 1853, FO 78/931, 78/932. For the Russian claim, see Jelavich, *Russia's Balkan Entanglements*, 120–24.

now about the European balance of power. Russia also worried that its rivals wanted more commercial influence in the Black Sea and Danube. Menshikov had some Ottoman ministers removed, but failed to force the Porte to accept his terms. On May 21, he broke off negotiations and left Constantinople. Within six weeks, Russian forces had occupied Moldavia and Wallachia.[18]

There are many accounts of the intense European diplomacy of the next eight months, but the core fact was that the five-power diplomatic system that had claimed to preserve peace since 1815 could not cope with the mutual ideological suspicions prompted by the 1848 revolutions, and the restless insecurities of France and Russia. It was not possible for the powers to agree on a settlement between Russia and the Ottomans, because Britain and France felt that none of the proposals from Russia and Austria respected the sovereign authority of the sultan, while Russia and Austria felt that Britain and France were agitating the Porte to make difficulties. Russia completely distrusted France because of Napoleon's swagger, yet expected Britain to restrain his activities. This was because of Russian respect for Aberdeen, who was now prime minister—but in the exquisitely unfortunate position of heading a coalition government including Palmerston and Lord John Russell. Aberdeen, as always, would have liked to put more trust in the five-power system and in its centre, Vienna. He still believed that any lasting settlement of the Eastern question had to respect Russia's legitimate concerns about Christian rights and European stability. However, Palmerston, Russell, and most cabinet Liberals (and most of the press) felt that Russian demands must be opposed vigorously. They also believed that, in the circumstances, cooperation with Napoleon III was the only way of managing him. Moreover, from early autumn the Ottoman government was willing to declare war on Russia, if necessary, because it was confident that it could count on British and French support. This was a rare chance to secure the empire's future. Some Ottoman ministers saw war against Russia not as an age-old jihad but as a chance for spiritually charged national rejuvenation. In September 1853, Canning reported them hoping that Muslim enthusiasm for the cause would defeat the reactionaries at court who "have hitherto obstructed the introduction of useful measures, particularly in respect of foreign capital and industry."[19] In the end, war was inevitable.

Whose War?

What the Crimean War was about depended on one's vantage point. For most of British public opinion, the issue was Russian aggression and the need to resist it vigorously. National honour was at stake if the British navy in the eastern Mediterranean did not do this. Russia was a threat to liberalism and

---

18. Lane-Poole, *Stratford Canning*, 2:269–72; A. Taylor, *Struggle for Mastery*, 53.
19. Canning to Clarendon, Sept. 1, 1853, FO 78/938.

constitutionalism over most of Europe: if Britain did not act, Europe would "go by default," swallowed in Russia's "universal empire."[20] Russia had shown a bullying disregard for Ottoman sovereign rights. If its permanent occupation of Moldavia and Wallachia was permitted, "international law ceases to exist, and the mutual obligations upon which society depends are grossly violated."[21] Europe must be persuaded of the need to uphold those principles. The politics of the war showed who was willing to do so and who was not. Queen Victoria lectured the king of Prussia on his failure to join the alliance to "protect international law in civilised Europe."[22]

For the British embassy in Constantinople, one component of the criticism of Russia was its alliance with the Greek Orthodox clergy, and the political, mental, and spiritual oppression that the latter seemed to exercise over Orthodox laymen. Canning and Rose hoped that a Russian defeat in the war might give the Greek layman civil and religious freedom from the corruption and mistreatment of the Greek hierarchy. Layard argued that "in fighting for the Turks we are fighting for the Christians"—and not for "Islamism."[23] Some of the animosity was directed at Greek Levantine merchants who traded under the Russian flag in the Levant. By doing so, they got the benefits of the 1838 treaty, the terms of which had subsequently been extended to Russia. These traders, together with Armenians, seemed increasingly adept at importing British manufactures, which might explain why Britain had not gained the expected advantages from the abolition of the Levant Company. In 1856, the Alexandria correspondent of *The Times* feared that Greek merchants were so well organised that they would soon control the whole trade there. Layard condemned the "roguery, the duplicity, and the meanness" of the Greek traders.[24]

Since the war of 1854 was overwhelmingly seen as a war against Russian oppression, illiberalism, and imperialism, the question of whether the Ottoman Empire was worth fighting for was much less prominent. The British public did not enter the war in order to defend the empire as it existed in 1853. In the years before the war, newspapers and journals remained as critical of Ottoman morals as ever. In writing up his holiday of 1844 for a popular audience, William Thackeray brought out all the old stereotypes about Constantinople: a young sultan prematurely aged by debauchery; the murder of infants who might rival him; the stifling, fattening decadence of harem life; a government "as rotten, as wrinkled, and as feeble as the old eunuch" whom he

20. Parry, *Politics of Patriotism*, 213–18.

21. Draft Foreign Office dispatch, June 25, 1853, FO 78/925.

22. Victoria, *Further Letters*, 52–54.

23. Rose to Malmesbury, Jan. 1, 1853, FO 78/928; Rose to Clarendon, Mar. 28, 1853, FO 78/930; Canning to Clarendon, May 22, 1853, FO 78/932; [Layard], "Turks and the Greeks," 537–38, 557–58 (quotations). See also Kingsley, *Alexandria and Her Schools*, xviii.

24. See Landes, *Bankers and Pashas*, 26n3; Macfarlane, *Turkey and Its Destiny*, 1:25; Layard, "Turks and the Greeks," 555–56.

spotted crawling around its entrance.[25] Charles Macfarlane, a Tory journalist, toured the empire in 1847 and 1848 looking for signs of improvement in governance since his previous visit of 1827; he concluded that such talk was a con. Christian testimony was ignored; the Tanzimat could not be implemented in Asia; the Armenian moneylenders remained all-powerful; the British naval officer Baldwin Walker had to resign at the arsenal after he tried to challenge their commission system. Ali Efendi, the most prominent Anglophile at the Porte after Reshid, was a fraudulent courtier who cultivated Europeans on public occasions, but longed to retreat to the harem, wear traditional clothes, and cross his legs. He and Reshid had been corrupted by office and employed vast retinues of flatterers, to whom the British embassy had to pay bakshish on each visit. These retinues had morals so vicious that Macfarlane had to leave his young son at home for safety. The Tanzimat had accelerated the decline of Islamic morals, thereby increasing crime and sapping Ottoman military vigour with Voltairian unbelief.[26] Macfarlane exposed these failings at length in *Turkey and Its Destiny* in 1850, and produced a popular version in 1853, *Kismet*. In 1855, the missionary Samuel Farman reprised his view that the abolition of the janissaries and the other Westernising reforms had just produced institutional weakness, a loss of faith, and alcoholism.[27]

For these reasons, the traditional Tory view that a pragmatic understanding with Russia was the only sensible policy in the East still had supporters in 1853. Significant numbers of Church of England clergymen sympathised with the principle of partnership with the Greek Orthodox Church. In 1853–54, their intellectual leader John Mason Neale wrote a novel, *Theodora Phranza*, in order to humanise the devoutly Christian Byzantines who had martyred themselves defending Constantinople in 1453 from the infidel. The prominent radical Richard Cobden had also long argued that Russia was much more likely than the Turks to spread commerce and civilisation throughout the Levant.[28] In fact, many of those who wanted an understanding with Russia were now toying with some sort of partition of Ottoman territory between the powers. Moreover, so was the tsar himself in early 1853: he raised with the British ambassador the idea of a new settlement of the East (hinting that Britain might take Egypt), though his vague suggestions were amiably rebuffed. *The Times* also broached the idea of partition, unsurprisingly causing horror at the Porte.[29] Macfarlane supported

25. Thackeray, *Notes of a Journey*, 112–34 (quotation at 134).

26. Macfarlane, *Turkey and Its Destiny*, 1:72, 184, 2:137–51, 177–82, 237–38, 347–48. This was Mehmet Emin Ali Pasha (1815–71), who was foreign minister or grand vizier almost continuously from 1846 to his death.

27. Farman, *Constantinople*, 15–22. For Farman, the war was necessary, but on anti-Russian grounds.

28. [Cobden], *Russia*, esp. 138–42.

29. Rose to Clarendon, Mar. 17, 1853, FO 78/930. For the tsar's remarks, see *PP 1853*, 9–12, and Figes, *Crimea*, 105–7.

it, and thought it should be handled by a "congress of *all* Christendom." He recognised that Russia had played a useful role checking continental revolution; it was learning the benefits of commerce and the value of the protection of property and the rule of law, like Britain in India. The queen's cousin, the Duke of Cambridge, might be given Egypt and Syria to rule.[30]

Meanwhile, the liberal and radical press were reluctant to mount a full-hearted defence of the Turks, but by late 1853 they were practically united in opposition to appeasement of aggressive, barbaric Russia. Over the next couple of years, their hostility was given extra weight by religious writers and preachers who argued that the Crimean War was just, because it was a struggle for freedom and law in Europe.[31] *Hypatia*, Charles Kingsley's novelistic critique of early Christian monkish obscurantism, massively outsold J. M. Neale. For Kingsley, the battle was between law and "the northern Anarch," whose victory would return the world to "a second Byzantine age of stereotyped effeminacy and imbecility." The Ottoman Empire was comparatively irrelevant, since in any case it was collapsing, fatally deprived of its original political strength and moral purpose. However, Alexandria might regain the status it had had in Ptolemaic times, as a hub for the exchange of Eastern and Western trade and ideas.[32]

The drift to war generated great speculation in religious circles that the East, so long a place of stasis, was moving to a new, more promising phase. The Turkish proverb that Muslims would rule in Constantinople for four hundred years (that is, until 1853) was excitedly pressed into service. If biblical prophecy pointed to the fall of Islam, the war would surely bring it forward. The same might be true of the return of the Jews.[33] Most of this writing implied that by winning the war, Britain would be able to do God's work and shape the region's future. Western intervention, together with missionary activity and the manifest decline of Islamic vigour, would implant "the vivifying impulses of social and political regeneration," and deliver the region "from the bonds of death unto life."[34] Islam was a "dark cloak of ignorance and superstition" that the swords of "our brave soldiers and sailors" would rip to shreds, so that

30. Macfarlane, *Kismet*, 374–75, 395 (quotation)–403.

31. M. Taylor, *Decline of British Radicalism*, 223–32; O. Anderson, "Reactions of Church and Dissent," 211.

32. Kingsley, *Alexandria and Her Schools*, xi (quotation 2), xviii (quotation 1), 169.

33. The Earl of Carlisle expected the East "very shortly, to become the theatre of completed Scripture Prophecy": *Diary*, 2. John Aiton anticipated the advent of British rule in Egypt and probably Syria and Mesopotamia: *Drying up of the Euphrates*, 70–71, 75. See also Faber, *Predicted Downfall*. For a contemporary intellectual attack on the "crazy infatuation about the prophecies," see Mackay's *Rise and Progress of Christianity* (vi). For the proverb, Macfarlane, *Kismet*, 146–47.

34. Churchill, *Mount Lebanon*, 1:vii. For the evangelicals' view that Isaiah 18:2 meant to specify Britain's role in the process of Jewish restoration, see Kochav's "'Beginning at Jerusalem'" (92–93).

Turkey and the Holy Land could be clothed in the brighter garb of "education, religion, and commerce."[35] If Russia's army ever arrived in "Canaan," its fate was prefigured in the Bible: "she goes to inherit, not the land, but the doom denounced against Gog and Magog—to whiten with the bones of her slain the hills and valleys of Judah."[36]

The Crimean War did not fulfil these apocalyptic expectations. Nor, except in Italy, did it realise radical hopes for an immediate liberation of central and eastern Europe from the oppression of Russia and Austria. What it did deliver was the core policy on which Britain and France fought the war. In late 1853, the Porte requested, and Russia refused, its "formal admission into the circle of Europe's international law and system of mutual respect for each other's rights."[37] Under Article VII of the Paris peace treaty of 1856, the powers declared that the empire could "participate in the advantages of the public law and system (concert) of Europe." Each pledged to respect, and to guarantee, its independence and territorial integrity. Article VIII established a process of mediation for any disputes between the Porte and the powers.

What did this language of international and public law actually mean?[38] There had been previous treaties between the Porte and European powers. In the sixteenth and seventeenth centuries, the French had negotiated several alliances with the Ottoman Empire, justifying these not only by reasons of state (against the Habsburgs) but also on the grounds that Muslims as well as Christians could be trusted to respect "the law of nations," and to keep their word.[39] The Porte had used the language of international law to protest about infringements of its borders since at least 1798. It had had permanent resident diplomats in London, Berlin, Vienna, and Paris since the early 1830s (but not Russia until 1857), and it had had a dedicated foreign ministry since 1836.[40] On the other hand, the concept of the "public law of Europe" was nowhere near as developed as it was by the time a Permanent Court of Arbitration was established at the Hague in 1899, underpinned by a body of writing from jurists who, from the 1870s, were increasingly regarded as authorities in the field of international law.[41] The suggestion by one scholar that, long before 1850, "treatises of international law were on every diplomat's reference shelf"

35. F. Neale, *Islamism*, 2:315.

36. Farman, *Constantinople*, 43.

37. Canning to Clarendon, Dec. 31, 1853, FO 78/941B.

38. There is now a substantial literature on the relation of the Ottoman Empire to the international legal system in this period. See especially Pitts, *Boundaries of the International*, chap. 2; Fitzmaurice, "Equality of Non-European States"; Palabiyik, "Emergence of the Idea"; and the other works cited below.

39. Malcolm, *Useful Enemies*, chap. 5.

40. Naff, "Ottoman Empire," 159; Yurdusev, *Ottoman Diplomacy*, 137.

41. For a good introduction to their work between 1835 and 1870, see Sylvest's "Foundations of Victorian International Law."

would have surprised Henry Stanley, who was appointed attaché at Constantinople in 1852, and complained at the lack of any such reference collection there. There was no atlas, no good history of the empire, and none of the standard works, by Vattel, Grotius, or Wheaton, among others. The Foreign Office, he discovered, was not in the habit of supplying such literature to any embassy, beyond a copy of Hertslet's *Treaties* and the *State Papers*.[42]

So when politicians and diplomats talked of "international law," they did not mean an authoritative body of academic writing, but primarily the stipulations in existing treaties that supplied frameworks and precedents for managing disputes, especially by respecting existing borders. If the "public law of Europe" meant anything beyond that, it was a commitment to follow civilised norms of diplomatic behaviour.[43] To complain that "international law" was being ignored in a dispute meant that a strong power was using force or the threat of it to bully a weak one into compromising its sovereignty, rather than treating it as an equal. This was an offence against morality.

Therefore the primary purpose of the declaration of 1856 was to force Russia to pledge to treat the Ottoman Empire with proper respect. Russia must give up the notion that international norms should be determined by its own interpretation of Christian priorities. The Ottomans had an instinctive distrust of the way that the European congress system had developed after 1815. In 1821, a high-ranking official at Constantinople told the British ambassador that "the great object of alarm to the Porte was the Holy Alliance," which they interpreted as "a secret league against the Mahomedan Empire." They feared that the tsar's rhetoric would mobilise the Christian states to expel it from Europe.[44]

Many British radicals were similarly sceptical of Russian and Austrian religious rhetoric, and the tendency to prioritise Christian rights over those of other religions. One petition of 1853 against Russian aggression expressed

42. Stanley to Spencer Ponsonby, Oct. 22 and 29, 1853, and Hammond to Ponsonby, Oct. 29, 1853, FO 78/970. The suggestion is in Horowitz, "International Law," 448. When, in 1852, Edward Scovell, a young army captain, was struggling with the commission from Palmerston to educate a few promising Egyptian youths who were in London to train for the diplomatic profession, he encountered the same problem, owing to "a deficiency in our diplomatic literature, or rather . . . our utter destitution in this respect, which has compelled us to have recourse to a foreign country and language for our most necessary and ordinary text-books on the various branches of diplomatic science": to Addington, June 9, 1852, FO 78/923. Scovell had presumably been told this by the young Travers Twiss, whom he had engaged to teach them this subject, and whose writings subsequently did a great deal to rectify that deficiency. Palmerston had—interestingly, in view of Egypt's formal status as an Ottoman province—laid down that their programme of instruction should include international law in 1847: to Sami, July 9, 1847, FO 78/722. The students were sent to England that year by Mehmet Ali, but were recalled by Abbas in 1852.

43. Orakhelashvili, "European International Law," 337.

44. Strangford to Londonderry, Sept. 25, 1821, FO 78/101 160.

horror at "the doctrine that faith is not to be kept with heretics and that Mahommedans are not to be recognised in the community of nations . . . every nation is under the same obligation to uphold international law that every individual is to uphold the law of his own land."[45] In 1857, Layard condemned Palmerston's policy to Persia and China on the same grounds, lamenting that it did not seem "bound by the same Laws of right and wrong that govern the relations of Christian States."[46] However, as this very example indicates, there was no consensus on whether international law applied outside a European context; jurists continued to disagree on that subject for decades.[47] Many non-European rulers did not see sovereignty in Western territorial terms in any case. Layard was chiding Palmerston for not upholding the morality and fairness that he expected of an Englishman, not for breaking a binding legal contract. The reason for admitting the Ottoman Empire to the European concert in 1856 was not because everyone accepted that a universalist Enlightenment view of international law had replaced a Christian conception of it. It was because Britain and France insisted that this particular country had been maltreated under the Vienna system for Russia's benefit, and had rights that needed to be respected if the European balance was to be maintained in the Balkans.

Article IX of the Treaty of Paris made a formal connection between the empire's admittance into the system of European public law and the sultan's *hatt-ı hümayun*, or Imperial Reform Order, of February 1856. This pledged that Ottoman subjects' freedom of worship, treatment at law, and admission to public and military service would be "without distinction of Religion or of Race." Britain and France were clear that these two declarations were inseparable; the empire was entitled to the protection of international law to the extent that its own legal processes secured the rights of all its own subjects.[48] This *hatt-ı hümayun* established religious equality as a general principle: civil and military schools were opened to all, and mixed tribunals were established for cases involving both Muslim and non-Muslim subjects.[49] It was the work

45. From Chester, forwarded by Dudley Coutts Stuart, Aug. 25, 1853, FO 78/974.

46. *Bucks Herald*, Mar. 14, 1857; report in scrapbook, LPBL, 58174 249.

47. See Fitzmaurice, "Equality of Non-European States." For a bracing critique of scholars who have tried to argue that international law derived from a specifically European tradition, see Orakhelashvili's "European International Law."

48. E.g., Canning to Clarendon, discussing the conditions of Britain's support for the empire, Dec. 31, 1853, FO 78/941B.

49. The *haraç* tax on non-Muslims, originally a land tax on produce, then a poll tax, now in effect a military exemption tax, was abolished in 1855, but was replaced by a more explicit military exemption tax, the *bedel*. Muslims were liable to this charge as well, but only if a conscription was imposed that they wished to escape. The *hatt-ı hümayun* allowed Christians to serve as regular soldiers, in principle but not in practice. Many Christians in Syria now refused to pay the *bedel*, claiming willingness to serve. One cause of the 1860 Damascus riots was Muslim resentment at this refusal. See Ma'oz, *Ottoman Reform*, 202–5.

of a new generation of Ottoman ministers, led by Ali and Fuad, who were willing to abandon the language of Gülhane and shari'a law. The war was not fought to defend a successful Ottoman liberalism; rather, its tragic death toll made the powers of Europe agree to press the Porte to govern on these terms in future.

The fundamental question, however, was whether the *hatt-ı hümayun* could be applied so as to satisfy Christian rayas, yet also mollify Muslims distrustful of Western influence. By the 1870s, it was clear that it did not reassure the Christian rayas of the Balkans, and therefore the continental powers. Almost immediately after 1856, it also began to feed Muslim ill feeling in parts of the Middle East.

Britain and France responded by trying to promote order in the region as well as their separate interests. Napoleon III regarded France as the war's main victor. The humbling of Russia in the East was a great long-term French interest. Napoleon now expected a freer rein to defend Catholic interests there, and got his chance when disorder erupted in Lebanon in 1860. Deep tensions between peasants and feudal lords, exacerbated by strong feelings against the *hatt-ı hümayun*, led to massacres of Christians on Mount Lebanon.[50] Then in July, Muslims in Damascus attacked the prosperous Christian quarter and killed three thousand people, after tensions largely caused by Christians' new expectations of fiscal equality. Whatever the complex reality, these two crises created consensus in the West that hostility between Muslims and Christians in Syria was deeply ingrained, and that the war left Britain and France with a duty to moderate it.[51] France emphasised its special claims to local influence in Syria, and sent troops to secure order there. However, the Ottomans acted quickly to punish the ringleaders, to remove negligent local office holders, and to address the immediate needs of displaced Christians. This made French intervention practically superfluous.[52] The regimes then worked together in setting terms for a new quasi-constitutional settlement for an autonomous Mount Lebanon.[53]

Western anxieties about order in the East were heightened because of the Indian Rebellion of 1857. Then, in 1858, the British and French consuls in Jeddah, and a dozen other people under European protection, were murdered by a crowd hostile to what they saw as the growth of British influence there. This followed a dispute about the status of a merchant ship from India. The local authorities determined that it should fly the Ottoman flag, but the British consul interpreted this as seizure of the ship. He ordered the flag's replacement by the British one, leaving the Ottoman banner trampled underfoot. After the

50. Fawaz, *Occasion for War*.
51. Rogan, "Sectarianism and Social Conflict."
52. Rogan, *Arabs*, 121–22.
53. Ozavci, *Dangerous Gifts*, chap. 13.

ensuing killings, the British officers on the spot demanded immediate executions, but the authorities explained that the *qisas* stipulated the need for the sultan's consent first. Interpreting this as obstruction, a British ship bombarded Jeddah for two days. The London government supported the naval officers in insisting on public executions for the murderers "without tedious references to Constantinople."[54] Even before these events, the British government had, along with the other powers, indicated its lack of faith in current Ottoman legal arrangements. At Paris in 1856, they had all agreed that it would be premature to abolish their extraterritorial jurisdiction over their own subjects. A year after the *hatt-ı hümayun*, Britain strengthened extraterritoriality by establishing a professionally run Supreme Court in Constantinople, which took over most of the consular jurisdiction. Its first judge, Edmund Hornby, regarded the court as a prototype for the other embassies. It also tackled a great backlog of complex property disputes involving Britain's Maltese and Ionian subjects.[55]

Napoleon's France asserted itself in several parts of the world in the late 1850s, and increased spending on defence, prompting another invasion scare in Britain in 1859. So it is not surprising that the British government had concerns about French behaviour in the Middle East. But those concerns quickly gave way to a spirit of Anglo-French cooperation, driven by awareness of the need to work together in order to maximise influence and security in their Middle Eastern spheres of interest, and indeed across Asia. Napoleon made no attempt to cause difficulties over the Indian Rebellion, and Britain and France sent joint expeditionary forces to China in 1857 and 1859 in order to prise open its markets and diplomatic channels.

The greatest example of this ambivalent cooperation was the Suez Canal. To commercial opinion, it was a self-evidently beneficial idea. It was the natural next step after the completion of the railway line from Cairo to Suez in 1858. A dozen mercantile towns held meetings that year in its support.[56] However, the British government was much less keen. In the 1840s, the canal had been seen as a "French" project in competition with the "English" railroad. Its main projector was Ferdinand de Lesseps; the (Egyptian) company that was set up to fund it in 1858 was based in Paris; the majority of its shares were held by Frenchmen. Palmerston instinctively saw it in traditional terms as a piece of French assertiveness, and Palmerston was now prime minister. Seventy-two in 1856, he looked back—past the crisis of 1840, all the way to the struggle with Napoleon over Egypt, in his teenage years. A great deal of his adult life had been spent looking out for French or Russian conspiracies, and taking

54. Seymour Fitzgerald, for the government, July 22, 1858: 151 Parl. Deb. (3d ser.) (1858) cols. 1932–33. See Ochsenwald, "Jidda Massacre of 1858."

55. Hornby, *Autobiography*, 93–100, 144. See Kayaoğlu, *Legal Imperialism*, 113, 121–24.

56. See Milner Gibson in 150 Parl. Deb. (3d ser.) (1858) cols. 1378–79.

pleasure in defeating them. So he went on record several times opposing the construction of the canal, which he claimed would make Egypt more valuable to a European power hostile to British India, and thus endanger the integrity of the Ottoman Empire.[57]

However, after the 1859 invasion scare died away, to be replaced by a major Anglo-French free-trade treaty in 1860, so did any attempt by the government to challenge the building of the canal. Most people agreed with the radical Member of Parliament J. A. Roebuck, who in 1858 had argued that it would bring India, and indeed China, Australia, and East Africa, "many thousands of miles nearer England," and consolidate the empire after the 1857 uprising in India. Gladstone, the coming man of Liberal politics, thought the scaremongers were ridiculous: with Aden and Perim, Britain controlled the southern end of the canal, while its maritime supremacy in the Mediterranean secured the northern end.[58]

In the 1860s, it became obvious that it would be a commercial boon to the world's greatest economic power. Bulwer, now Britain's ambassador in Constantinople, went to inspect the works in 1862 and became an astonished convert to its benefits, not only for commerce but for British "mastery" in Egypt. After its opening in 1869, it was the buckle that joined the British and Asian economies together, the greatest example of the corridor of modernity that Britain had been building across Egypt for fifty years. Three-quarters of its shipping was British in 1870.[59] A major reason why successive governments had opposed the scheme in the 1850s was Ottoman alarm about it. So it was telling how many Members of Parliament (including Gladstone) regarded that alarm as of little relevance when they discussed the matter. Palmerston was quite right that the canal drove a wedge between the Egyptian viceroy and the Porte, by increasing the risk that a Western power would separate Egypt from the sultan in order to secure the passage to India.[60] He just chose not to take this argument to its obvious conclusion. The canal made it even more imperative than it already was for Britain to be that power.

Across most of the empire, the peace of 1856 seemed to provide stability. This produced a cascade of Western capital, seeking to fund infrastructure projects in the empire at attractive interest rates. It was now, much more than

57. 146 Parl. Deb. (3d ser.) (1857) cols. 1044–45; 150 Parl. Deb. (3d ser.) (1858) cols. 1379–84.

58. 150 Parl. Deb. (3d ser.) (1858) cols. 1363–65 (Roebuck), 1391 (Gladstone).

59. Harcourt, "High Road to India," 61; Hallberg, *Suez Canal*, 199–208; Searight, *Steaming East*, 126.

60. 146 Parl. Deb. (3d ser.) (1857) col. 1044. For the opposition of the 1858 Conservative government on the same grounds, see Seymour Fitzgerald in 150 Parl. Deb. (3d ser.) (1858) col. 1374. Gladstone criticised Palmerston's implication that Egypt should be kept subordinate to the Porte at the expense of its own commercial development, which the canal would clearly benefit: 150 Parl. Deb. (3d ser.) (1858) cols. 1388–89.

after 1838, that Britain reaped the benefits of increased commerce with the Middle East. Its spheres of influence in Egypt, Baghdad, and the Gulf were all greatly consolidated. Unfortunately, Western loans built a pyramid of debt that the governments in Constantinople and Egypt were increasingly unable to service. The bankruptcy of both in 1875–76 created a new Eastern crisis—a crisis that showed the Ottomans just how much continental Europe cared about their interests in the search for stability in the Balkans, and just how much the British government cared about them in the search for it in Egypt.

Conclusion

FROM THE 1780S, India was Britain's most important imperial possession. From 1798, it seemed very vulnerable to attack by European rivals. The protection of the lands and waterways of the Middle East from those rivals became a major British project in the first half of the nineteenth century. That project raises four broad questions: How was naval power used to secure Britain's position and build up influence with local chiefs, and Arab leaders in particular? What sort of political arrangements did British officials think might be possible there, and what did these ideas owe to the region's history and religious heritage? What was the relationship between British attitudes to the Middle East and to the Ottoman Empire? And how far do these themes help to explain British engagement with the region in subsequent periods—in the second half of the century, and then after the First World War?

❧

British strategy was to build a strong sphere of influence by means of naval power. This power was used to mediate between factions and to make local pashas and chiefs respect Britain as the most reliable source of order. In Syria in 1799, Sidney Smith aimed to impose British authority on all the local rulers and to prevent them from defecting to Napoleon. He also established connections with Egyptian Mamluks and Arabs. In Egypt, between 1801 and 1803, the British army of occupation followed the same policy. Supported by the British government, it tried to secure a peace among Ottomans, Mamluks, Arabs, and Copts, in order to prevent instability that a returning French expedition might exploit. Claudius Rich aimed to be the indispensable ringmaster among Ottomans, Arabs, and Kurds in the Baghdad pashalik. He reached as far inland as the Kurdish mountains, still relying on British naval and commercial power at Basra to give him weight. He alienated Bombay officials by meddling in the interior, and by lavish expenditure to accompany it. They preferred to stick to Basra and the coast, where Britain could assert itself more cheaply and effectively. The Saudis' strength in Arabia meant that the Bombay Marine developed a wary respect for their activities in the Persian Gulf. Naval officers sought a balance between Saudi and Omani power even before the beginnings of the Trucial system in the 1820s. By the 1850s, that system had made the Gulf a British lake. After 1815, control of the Cape and Mauritius as well as India ensured Britain's dominance in the Indian Ocean. Properly exercised, British naval power was too great for the Ottoman pashas of Egypt and Baghdad to ignore; both of them also wanted revenues from Indian trade. In Egypt, Mehmet Ali became more powerful than any predecessor, but continued to see the overriding benefits of working with Britain. The pasha of Baghdad aspired to the same degree of autonomy.

In all these areas, Britain was careful to acknowledge respect for Ottoman sovereignty and to deprecate European aggression against it. It had no ambition to undermine the sultan's territorial claims and to rule directly. On the contrary, this would have three bad effects. It would remove the comparison that made Ottoman representatives look unpredictable and biased, a comparison that might encourage locals to seek British protection and mediation. It would require a more invasive policy: more penetration inland, forced taking of sides, and alienation of powerful local groups, which would eat up resources and goodwill. And it would play into the hands of European rivals: they would demand compensating gains elsewhere, while Britain could no longer criticise their imperialist agenda. But where the Porte had local influence, it was just one more faction to involve in the mediation process. British officers believed that it was only through British agency that Ottoman ministers had been able to recover a significant stake in Egypt in 1801 (or in Syria in 1840). This made them more conscious of some responsibility for local stability. The army persuaded the London government to try to check Ottoman ambitions in Egypt after 1801 (to the distaste of the Constantinople embassy).

Very quickly after 1798, most local British officials formed the view that the Ottoman authorities were incapable of providing good government, because of institutionalised corruption and a short-termist approach to land management. The Islamic caliphate was a husk of its former self, its old military fervour softened by decadence, its stolid fatalism unsuited to modern economic opportunities. It lacked popular confidence; it could not secure order across vast swathes of its territory. Many Britons also instinctively assumed that the Porte remained more hostile to Britain than to France or Russia; hence Rich's extraordinary animosity against its influence at Baghdad. Once British paramountcy was secured in the Gulf and around Aden, by the 1840s, naval officers were also anxious to counter the Ottomans' revival of claims to sovereignty in places to which they had no practical title. Those claims would allow local chiefs to acknowledge a rival source of power, which would undermine British authority, or at least make it much more expensive to reassert.

So British agents tended to see the Ottomans as imperialists, and themselves as helping to secure local justice. They wanted to offer protection where necessary to the Arabs, to the Lebanese and Kurdish mountaineers, and to the Jews of Palestine. They saw present-day overtaxing pashas as the latest in a series of invaders who had destroyed the region's potential. Hugh Rose lamented the misgovernment of Baghdad, which had "made a desert of a garden, and excited revolt, where conciliation and prudence might have made of the benighted Arabs of the Irak, grateful adherents of the Sultan and useful servants of the state." The Turk had blighted the garden of the Old World with a poisonous upas tree.[1] A major reason why Harford Jones, Viscount Valentia, and Thomas Perronet Thompson respected the Wahhabi (and why Jones and Valentia at times feared them) was the contrast that they offered to Turkish indolence, materialism, and brutality. Wahhabi puritanism seemed authentic and elemental; it also illustrated that Arabs were less corrupted by money than their Ottoman overlords. Jones ridiculed Mehmet Ali's assumption that they could be permanently destroyed "by his gold, rather than the valour of his troops"; they were bound to rise again. For the same reason, John Lewis Burckhardt assumed that the Ottomans would eventually be driven out of the Hijaz. Perronet Thompson thought Wahhabism a "great struggle for freedom" against "Turkish domination." Arabs also seemed much more reliable fighters than the Turks, and much more willing to cooperate with British commanders against common enemies.[2] Observing them at Mocha and Hudayda, Katharine Elwood appreciated their "wild independence and . . . manly frankness . . . , which is very different from the obsequiousness and servility of other Oriental nations." Relative to the Turks, their "vivaciousness, astuteness, and curiosity [were] quite European."[3]

This inextinguishable temperamental independence suggested that the Arabs would not easily be subordinated by the Ottomans, France, or Russia.[4] So British agents realised the benefits of cultivating that independence. During the campaigns of 1798–1801, they used money and military power to win Arab cooperation, paying promptly and regularly for their services. They prided themselves on their reputation for honouring financial obligations.[5] In

1. Rose to Pisani, Aug. 21, 1852, FO 78/893; Kingsley, *Alexandria and Her Schools*, xv–xvi.

2. Jones Brydges, *Account*, 2:114; Burckhardt, *Travels in Arabia*, 52; Thompson, "Arabs and Persians," 225–26; Kennedy memo, May 24, 1833, FO 78/223 68.

3. Elwood, *Narrative of a Journey*, 1: 351, 328. This did not prevent her from also writing of Arab dirtiness and "simplicity": 1:291.

4. Or, of course, the Persians: Wellsted contrasted Bedouin patriotism and independence with Persians' lives as "polished slave[s]" (*Travels in Arabia*, 1:368).

5. See chapter 1, p. 43, and, for later examples: F. Newman, *Personal Narrative*, 91; Wellsted, *City of the Caliphs*, 2:269–71. Buckingham noted that at Tiberias the English were praised because they "always paid twice as much as the people of any other nation for

the 1820s and 1830s, the Indian Navy officers spent years surveying the seas around Arabia, communicating with the tribes, and enjoying the local food.[6] They identified an Arab avarice that could be usefully harnessed, and a basic humanity that, if they reciprocated it, could be nurtured. British respect for Arabs had strict limits.[7] Had a coherent Arab empire-state been possible, it would have created strategic problems for Britain. There was brief concern that Mehmet Ali might manage to found one: it might incite Islamists to destabilise British India, or provide the only means for France or Russia to buy its way into the region, by bribing the Egyptian viceroy. But Mehmet Ali was no Arab himself, and by 1840 the raggedness of his attempts to control Arabia was apparent; the threat disappeared.

From the 1830s, steam power, especially in Mesopotamia, was a valuable aid in intimidating the Arabs into appreciating British might. It also promised to strengthen the authority of the pasha of Baghdad, which plague had weakened, if he was willing to accept judicious British assistance. This would boost order and stability in the pashalik against external threats. Ostensibly, these threats came from Mehmet Ali. In reality, the main concern was Russia, and to an extent Persia, which seemed so vulnerable to Russian pressure. Baghdad and the Gulf became stages on which Britain would display its might, modernity, and confidence in order to defeat Russian ambitions, and to remind Russians that their influence at Constantinople itself was of little local consequence. In 1838–40, Britain pursued the same forward policy in Aden and the Gulf as in Afghanistan.

In strengthening its own power in the Middle East in the 1830s against potential enemies, Britain could claim to be propping up Ottoman sovereign authority there. Yet, at the same time, the Middle Eastern part of the Ottoman Empire was being shaped into an outwork of Indian defence. In India too, steam power on the rivers was used to move troops about, and to impress locals and enemies; the first railway followed in 1849. The ministers of the Liberal governments of the 1830s and 1846–52 saw the struggle with Russia as a global one. Palmerston inherited through Huskisson the Dundasite principle that a coherent strategy was needed, spanning Europe and Asia,

---

any service rendered to them": *Travels in Palestine*, 460. Kinglake had a different take on the subject, noting that Arabs instinctively expected to be forced to surrender their goods to passing travellers, and were not used to providing goods for payment, but that well-bred Englishmen nonetheless paid them liberally as they left, in order to salve their own consciences: *Eothen*, 240–41.

6. For Wellsted's enthusiasm for the "kabobs" and meatballs of Basra, see *City of the Caliphs*, 1:148.

7. I have (almost always) avoided the word "Arabophilia," as too sweeping. Nearly all British observers regarded Arabs as "primitive" in some sense or other, and were tempted to criticise aspects of their character or culture. The same applied to T. E. Lawrence: see Meyers, "Lawrence and the Character of the Arabs."

to combat the challenges of European rivals. The Grant brothers (his fellow Huskissonites) and Hobhouse (his India secretary) shared that vision. Steam and commercial power could give Britain more strength across Eurasia than Dundas ever imagined possible. These men were not seriously alarmed that Russia could penetrate Indian borders; the main concern was always to assert Britain's regional power in order to subjugate potential rebels within India itself. In 1830, the East India Company admitted that its fear was "not so much actual invasion by Russia as the moral effect which would be produced among our own subjects in India . . . by the continued apprehension of that event."[8]

This idea of strengthening India through technology can perhaps be seen as a liberal governing strategy. Scholars of imperial political thought have valiantly tried to define a "Liberalism" that can be applied to India in this period, but this can be done only by adopting an oddly narrow definition of Liberalism, based merely on the writings of a few idealistic thinkers, rather than on the study of what Liberal governments did and said.[9] The founding myth of British Liberalism as a political movement, after the 1832 Reform Act, was that it could provide good government because it understood how to retain popular confidence. It could integrate the British nation as an effective and politically active community; it could also give Catholics proper political representation, and therefore pursue a union of consent with Ireland. Then, by harnessing national energies, a Liberal British state would lead the world against a Russia that after 1828 was aggressive as well as repressive. Strong government by popular consent would always defeat blustering autocracy.[10] It followed that Liberalism in that sense—political Liberalism, the creed of British Liberal governments—could not be applied to India, because its core principle was effective political representation, whereas India remained a garrison state.

Nonetheless, the Palmerston-Hobhouse strategy involved standing up to Russia, and to internal Indian critics, by expressing the strength of the British state in India—in terms of financial power, technological mastery, administrative competence, and good order, translated into military efficiency. The expectation was that a feeble, antiquated regime would quail in the face of applied modernity. So the Indian army was mobilised boldly and proactively

8. Ingram, *Beginning of the Great Game*, 11–15, 55 (quotation).

9. Mehta, *Liberalism and Empire*; Pitts, *Turn to Empire*; Mantena, "Crisis of Liberal Imperialism." This is not to deny that Macaulay and the Mills, the three men always held up as archetypal "Liberals," had some influence on the government of India, but the earliest and best discussion of Liberalism and empire also recognised its limits in practice: Metcalf, *Ideologies of the Raj*, chap. 2, esp. 36–38. Moreover, all three were choice representatives of the irresponsible Anglo-Indian bureaucracy against which the Liberal reformers of the 1850s campaigned.

10. For Palmerston's speeches of 1828–30 on this, see p. 116 above. See, more broadly, Parry's *Politics of Patriotism* and *Rise and Fall*.

on the North-West Frontier. The result was the Afghan War, which was a disaster in several ways. Even so, it demonstrated British intent unmistake-ably, both to Afghan rulers and to Russia, and it provided the justification for the conquest and pacification of Sind and the Punjab in the 1840s. This strategy was criticised then, as it can be now, but its proponents continued to believe that it consolidated Indian security on its western flank.[11]

⟨⌁⟩

In the Middle East, as in India, an additional hope for steam was that it might develop commerce on the coasts and rivers, increasing revenue and strength-ening popular loyalty. These visions melded British capitalist confidence with romantic recollections of the region's ancient prosperity. The imaginations of Popham and Wellsted in the Red Sea, Lynch and Jones in Baghdad, and travellers to Palestine like Ashley and Lindsay far outstripped the reality. One reason why hopes of economic prospects were frustrated was the nature of Ottoman rule, except in Mehmet Ali's Egypt. The steamships on the Euphrates were, as Ainsworth wrote, "like a vision of future glory," rather than effective weapons of transformation—they were too few and the obstacles of gover-nance too great. The same applied to most talk of economic development, such as Jewish settlement schemes in Palestine. Moses Montefiore seems to have considered them premature, and Palmerston became less optimistic about getting the Ottomans to facilitate them. Capitalists needed more secu-rity for landholding than the Porte would grant, while most emigrants were too elderly and spiritually inclined to become agricultural entrepreneurs.[12] Officials could only hope that British influence over local rulers might gradu-ally strengthen order and offer security for investment.[13]

11. Ingram, *Empire-Building*, chap. 9.

12. Ainsworth, *Christian Aborigines*, 51. Gawler was the main advocate of Jewish settlement schemes: see his report of Nov. 10, 1849, to the Foreign Office, FO 78/813, and his later lecture *Syria and Its Near Prospects*. Palmerston responded to the report by urg-ing the Porte to permit European Jews to own land in Palestine: to Canning, Jan. 28 and Mar. 23, 1850, FO 78/814. See Palmerston's attempts to press the Ottomans to liberalise their approach to land holding (pp. 225, 231, above), but also, by 1851, his doubts about "the expediency of encouraging British subjects to invest capital" there, given his failure to date: Mar. 2, 1851, note, FO 78/882. Abigail Green shows how non-committal Moses Montefiore was towards these schemes: *Moses Montefiore*, 254–56, 324–26, 396–97.

13. Though this book has discussed economic visions of the future, it has not consid-ered economic realities except at specific points, as their impact on regional policy was limited. The embassy at Constantinople cared a good deal about safeguarding British trade within the empire as a whole, and tariff discussions occupied a lot of the time of the consul-general there. Moreover, Canning was a Liberal Tory who felt that attracting new capital from Britain would be essential in improving its prosperity and stability (see, e.g., Canning to Aberdeen, Oct. 30, 1845, FO 78/602). However, throughout this period most

Though hardly any British officers in, or visitors to, the Middle East had any immediate aspiration to govern it, they could not help thinking about the prospect of doing so, because, at least before 1840, the collapse of the Ottoman Empire was almost universally expected. Such thoughts were naturally affected by the experience of British rule in India. In the British imagination, India was becoming a land of law against age-old oriental despotism. The Permanent Settlement of 1793 claimed to defend property rights against arbitrary power. In 1813, Robert Smith asserted that "the meanest rights of the meanest native stand on the solid base of law and justice." The reality was a legal jumble that owed a lot to local customs. The flaws in Indian justice arrangements legitimised resistance in some respects, yet allowed uncontrollable lower courts to condone acts of white violence.[14] However, the effectiveness of the myth was often noted by British officials in the Middle East, who reported local Arabs contrasting Ottoman misrule with Britain's reputation for legal fairness in India.[15]

In one important respect, the Middle East seemed more likely to be receptive to the principles of good government than India had been. It had produced Christianity and had been governed by Roman law, whereas India had always been regarded in Britain as culturally alien. India was not directly ruled by government and Parliament before 1858—largely because so many British people insisted that their politicians would be corrupted by the increased patronage and financial powers that direct responsibility for managing India's poisoned wealth would give them. It could be brought under direct British government only after the 1857 rebellion, once anger at the mistakes of its arrogant and irresponsible bureaucracy outweighed declining fears about "old corruption."[16] In 1801, the British soldiers in Egypt observed with astonishment the wasteful stately luxury of their Indian army counterparts: they jeered that they were "the army of Darius."[17] Bombay civil servants bullied Rich, Stafford Haines, and Felix Jones with the callous cruelty of the desk-bound autocrat.

By contrast, the Middle East excited imaginations because of the familiarity of its history. It goes without saying that that familiarity was misconceived

---

British trade with the empire continued to be, as in the days of the Levant Company, with the Aegean and Anatolian coasts, the Danube, and the Black Sea area, rather than with the Arab lands. In the Middle East, most of the trade under British protection was conducted by Indian merchants who had their own long-standing support networks. As noted in chapter 10 (for Baghdad), there was sometimes tension between consuls, who prioritised good relations with local regimes and tribal chiefs, and the handful of British merchants who cut corners when trying to make their way in places like Beirut and Baghdad.

14. Metcalf, *Ideologies of the Raj*, 7–8, 13; Marshall, *Problems of Empire*, 68–69, 184 (quotation); Kolsky, *Colonial Justice*; Benton, *Law and Colonial Cultures*, 129–40.

15. Parry, "Steam Power," 167.

16. Alborn, *Conceiving Companies*, chap. 2; Dickinson, *India*.

17. Mackesy, *British Victory in Egypt*, 225.

and romanticised; that is not the point. Visions of improvement gave officials some sense of purpose and identity in what were otherwise discouraging and discomforting conditions. The British army in Egypt had to endure ophthalmia, sand lice, and fleas. Lax quarantine procedures and inadequate medicine alarmed all travellers. The plague of 1831 ravaged Baghdad as if it were a modern Babylon. In a delirium caused by fever, Raymond Wellsted shot himself in the mouth in Muscat and never recovered physically or mentally. One naval officer, in the intolerable heat of the Gulf summer, saw his men "die in the utmost agony and raving mad, from exposure to the sun, after a few hours' illness." Yet that same officer charted every stop of his expedition by reference to the record left by Alexander's naval commander Nearchus 2,150 years before, and was pleased to note the continuing accuracy of his account of fishing practices.[18]

When Mackintosh, Rich, and Chesney thought about Baghdad, they thought about Alexander the Great using his courage and judgment to humiliate the decadent Orientals farther east. Baghdad was still threatened by the Persians and by the Russians; could it be saved for civilisation? In 1801, William Hamilton hoped to bring Egypt back into the greater Europe that the Romans had mapped out. Could the British help to supply it with tax reductions and peace—the policies for which Ptolemy V was thanked in the address preserved on the Rosetta Stone that Hamilton secured for the British Museum? In 1849, Layard claimed that the ancient civilisation that he had unearthed at Nineveh showed "the debt which the West owes to the East," but also implied that the West should now repay the debt by a civilising mission to the modern inhabitants of those countries. In 1854, Charles Kingsley argued that the Romans had established the only acceptable type of empire, governing "with tolerable justice" Syrians and Egyptians who could not govern themselves, and making them "better and more prosperous people, by compelling them to submit to law."[19] Was it visionary to think that law might be re-established throughout these lands, by the Romans' successors, uniting West and East as they had done?

The Indian Navy's interest in developing steam power and commerce on the rivers of Mesopotamia was based on its unrivalled fertility and prosperity 2,500 years earlier. In the same way, the appeal of Aden to Haines and his fellow officers owed much to their study of the trading power of ancient Hadramaut and the Queen of Sheba. All that was needed to restore this prosperity was irrigation and commerce. Basic technology would turn deserts back into the gardens they had been—the Hanging Gardens of Babylon, or even the Garden of Eden, associated with Qurna near Basra. Here, according to Wellsted,

18. Kempthorne, "Notes Made on a Survey," 278 (quotation), 273.

19. Layard, *Nineveh and Its Remains*, 2:85–86; Kingsley, *Alexandria and Her Schools*, xv.

"man in the image of God was first created and here in his most perfect form is he yet found."[20] Water was the region's key life-giving ingredient, and not just in the phials that tourists brought home from the River Jordan. British travellers imagined Christ preaching to thousands of happy, hard-working families around the fertile shores and well-stocked waters of the Sea of Galilee, in contrast to the rotting carcasses of the Dead Sea. Irrigation and steam power would remove the universal blight of depopulation and declining agricultural revenues. Perhaps they could also empower effective communities that would value their property and would respect orderly government.

Some British visitors and commentators therefore assumed that marauding Arab tribes could be persuaded to settle on riverbanks to tend crops and livestock peacefully and productively. As they had never been slaves, they would naturally take to being industrious free farmers. Other observers saw the Arabs less as participants in a potential orderly commercial future than as reminders of a primeval, divinely ordered past. They noted their established laws and customs, and their patriarchalism, infused with a healthy respect for wisdom and for tribal opinion.[21] For Kinglake and Disraeli, they offered a window into "the Elder World."[22] There was some admiration for the resistance of primitive desert tribes to morally corrupting urban values, though also some fear that Ottoman misgovernment and the arrival of wealthy Europeans had tempted them into a predatory cupidity.[23] Ainsworth asserted that the "mental privileges of the Arabs," the "descendants from the most noble stocks of the human race," had not declined, but they had been "overwhelmed by moral despotism and political insecurity."[24] Consciousness of their biblical ancestry was ever-present in the background. In his *History of the Jews* in 1830, Henry Milman used modern accounts of the Arabs to interpret the biblical material about Abraham's marriage arrangements. George Rose attributed the Arabs' tradition of circumcision to the Abrahamic divine covenant and its theme of purification.[25]

20. Wellsted, *City of the Caliphs*, 1:146.

21. See, e.g., Layard, *Nineveh and Its Remains*, 1:95–96; Wellsted, *Travels in Arabia*, 1:259.

22. Kinglake, *Eothen*, 5; Disraeli, *Tancred*, 2:205.

23. Fraser, *Travels in Koordistan*, 1:357–58; J. Jones, *Memoirs*, 110, 133, 223–24. Here I am talking about relative experts, not casual tourists to the area, who often had instinctive prejudices against the Arabs, either because they arrived with expectations shaped by the Bible, or simply because they found them culturally unfamiliar and threatening.

24. Chesney, *Expedition for the Survey*, 2:698. In *Tancred*, Disraeli expressed a similar admiration, pointing out that the Arabs, like the Jews, never mixed their blood by marrying out: Parry, "Disraeli," 595–96. Thomas Hope had said the same in *Anastasius*.

25. Rose, *Early Spread of Circumcision*, 9–11. In 1844, John Jebb described the history of Arabia as "indissolubly connected . . . with the birth, the growth, and the maturity of man," in a way that Egypt's was not: [Jebb], "Forster on Arabia," 326–28.

The deserts of the Middle East were where God had given laws to his people to make them a society. British travellers climbed what the guides claimed was Mount Sinai—even though their biblical knowledge told them that the topography was not quite right—so that they could imagine how it must have felt to receive divine guidance so immediately. In the Arabian desert, Muhammad thought that he too had heard God's injunctions, which inspired him to devote his life to waging war on the sins and errors of mankind. Reading Gibbon in Baghdad in 1809 taught Mary Rich to admire "Mahomet and the first Arabian heroes."[26] Gibbon, like a number of eighteenth-century writers, took pleasure in rebelling against conventional Christian abuse of Islam. He presented Muhammad as a crusader for a simple, inspiring, charitable monotheism, which had quickly taken root in much of the world. His emphases on the social benefits and proven permanence of Islam were taken up by several others, including by Thomas Carlyle in 1840, in one of his most famous and influential lectures. "These Arabs believe their religion, and try to live by it! . . . —believing it wholly, fronting Time with it, and Eternity with it . . . Belief is great, life-giving. The history of a Nation becomes fruitful, soul-elevating, great, so soon as it believes." Carlyle had also been influenced by Edward Lane's *Manners and Customs of the Modern Egyptians*, which showed him how deeply Islamic assumptions were embedded in Egyptian daily life.[27] In the Middle East, as in India, some British intellectuals became orientalist scholars, keen to understand better the history of local cultures.[28]

Of course, many Victorians continued to hold a more conventionally dismissive view of Islam, and two opposing answers were always given to the question of how far it was compatible with good government. Many who visited the East only briefly, such as Richard Cobden, had already decided to blame Ottoman regime failings on their "brutalising religion" that "disdain[ed] all improvement and labour." The "impostor of Mecca" defended slavery and polygamy, and taught Turks to govern by savagery and the sword, spreading devastation and pestilence over their realms. Likewise, Addison's journey confirmed his view that a code of law based on the precepts of the Qur'an could not be a proper legal code. Claudius Rich, who saw his years in Baghdad as training for a high-level post in imperial India, continued to look down on Islam as incompatible with improvement because it rejected all modern developments in "science, art, history, manners."[29] Many visitors were pleased

---

26. To Maitland Erskine, Oct. 1, 1809, RPBL, 80751 111.

27. Carlyle, "Hero as Prophet," 70. See Ahmed, *Edward W. Lane*, 119. For emphasis on how early Islam was adapted to the needs of its hearers, owed much to Muhammad's character, and depended little on the sword, see [W. Taylor], "Mohammed and Mohammedanism."

28. See, e.g., Irwin, *For Lust of Knowing*; Franklin, *Orientalist Jones*.

29. [Cobden], *Russia*, 130–31, 209; Addison, *Damascus and Palmyra*, 1:391–94; Rich, *Narrative of a Residence*, 1:310. See also J. Reid, *Turkey and the Turks*, 64.

to note that it seemed to be losing strength in Ottoman realms, though this claim was usually based not on Middle Eastern experience but on the growing relative influence and prosperity of Christians in the Balkans and the Levant.

Other observers, however, were very clear that Islam should and must be the basis of any reform of governance in the East. Ambassador Ponsonby welcomed the 1839 Edict of Gülhane for several reasons, but fundamentally because it would strengthen the sultan's authority as Islamic caliph, by increasing Muslim popular confidence in him. An influential body of thinkers searched for a legal code to which Muslims could relate, that would supply this confidence and so give the regime the strength necessary to defeat French or Russian threats. When secretary to the Constantinople embassy in the 1830s, David Urquhart argued that the Ottoman Empire should strip its corruptions away to reveal its original foundation on Arab governance principles of decentralisation, free trade, and direct taxation. His central argument was that Arab culture placed governments in subordination to a comprehensible and simple Islamic legal code that would restore Muslim confidence and revivify the empire. The Arabophile Thomas Perronet Thompson devised the 1820 Gulf treaty, the foundation of the Trucial system, on the assumption that the British and the Gulf shaykhs could form an alliance based on a mutual respect for law. Both men were followers of Jeremy Bentham, who was concerned to secure the independence, viability, and vigour of Islamic regimes. An indigenous patriotism, founded on a clear, morally acceptable legal philosophy, would defend them against collapse and Russian imperialism. The difficulty in assessing Mehmet Ali was whether he respected law and civilisation or not. British travellers witnessed first-hand the security he brought to the small section of the country that they visited, and they admired his gestures towards European civilisation. Yet in other ways he was a tyrannical pharaoh. The Benthamite Bowring admitted that he was a despot, but argued that his strong, vigorous rule offered the best of both worlds, giving Muslims patriotic confidence and Christians tolerance.

In practice, if law and order were to be imposed in a morally acceptable way, British officials usually assumed that they would have to be involved. Britain tended to act as a non-sectarian power, believing that it could hold the ring between religious groups while respecting Islamic culture. By contrast, hardly any British consuls in the Middle East regarded the promotion of Christianity as a priority. They imagined that it might well revive in the wake of eventual economic development, but that would take a long time. There was a lot of British Christian interest in the Middle East, but it was generated overwhelmingly by domestic opinion. Bishops and missionaries alike were brought up on the idea that early Christianity had spread like wildfire across Asia and Africa from its original colonies in Syria and Kurdistan. They hoped against hope that this could happen again. The Church of England proposed missions to the Nestorians in Kurdistan. Evangelicals also advocated the restoration of the Jews to Palestine in the hope of facilitating Christ's Second Coming. Palmerston nodded to this sectarian pressure briefly in 1840–41, fearing that other powers would successfully use their own denominational strategy to win local predominance. The consequences were counterproductive tensions between British, French, and American religious missions, which severely exacerbated local conflicts in Lebanon and Kurdistan. This was not in British interests. The crisis of 1841–43 made clear that, unlike France, Austria, or Russia, Britain had no significant Christian denominational interests to defend in the East. Protestantism remained a lightweight political force: there were two Anglican churches in the whole Middle East in 1854. Britain seemed better off using its influence to press the Ottomans to protect the interests of all oppressed religious minorities—mostly non-Christian ones.

So there was a significant amount of British respect for Islam in a Middle Eastern context, and significant abstract interest in improving the situation of the Arabs. However, such sentiments need to be distinguished sharply from British views about Ottoman rule. There has always been a tendency to assume that British diplomatic support for the Ottoman Empire can be explained by a generalised admiration for Islam or Eastern culture—that there was such a thing as "Turcophilism."[30] This is not a helpful way of thinking. There was almost no admiration for the Turks as such, because there was very little study of them except as a governing class, in which light they were nearly always seen as a corrupt, self-serving, duplicitous failure. Very few observers imagined that Muslims could rule Balkan Christians well. If Foreign Office backing for the Ottoman Empire had to rest on an intellectual defence of Turkish governing morals, it would not have survived for a year.

Fortunately, it did not. This fact has been obscured, because historians have assumed both that British governments were unusually keen defenders of Ottoman rule and that they did so by referencing the Tanzimat and the prospects of state reform. This is to take a particular argument, advanced mainly in the late 1840s and 1850s, and apply it universally. It is also to exaggerate the clout of British ambassadors at Constantinople. They usually wanted to promote central Ottoman power, but they lacked the leverage to do so until Reshid emerged as a plausible embodiment of it, and they rarely had control over Britain's Middle Eastern policy, because of countervailing pressures from officials and interest groups in Egypt and in India.

30. One recent statement of this view is in Gürpinar's "Rise and Fall of Turcophilism," though he uncovers almost no unqualified Turcophilism, apart from David Urquhart's. But it is held, instinctively, by many others. I held it myself until I researched this book.

We need instead to put centre stage the Tory approach to European affairs that dominated British politics until 1830 and that remained important thereafter. Until the 1860s, foreign policy was in the hands of men who were influential during the Napoleonic Wars, or were shaped politically by them. The basic priorities established during the war survived—to check French and Russian global pretensions, to defend India and naval supremacy, and to rely on European caution and common sense to prevent a partition of Ottoman lands that would endanger the other objectives. The Ottoman Empire was to endure, not by moral justifications, but by the mutual self-interest and cooperation of the powers.

The European settlement of 1814–15 was substantially shaped by British foreign secretary Castlereagh. For him, the "concert of Europe" was a structure devised to overcome the failings of the successive short-lived wartime coalitions of 1793–1809. It was a mechanism to force four great powers to subordinate their selfish differences of opinion to the task of checking the aggression of France—or of any other power that threatened continental peace. It emphasised the maintenance of existing territorial boundaries against an aggressor, but for most British politicians this territorial conservatism had no ideological or dynastic implications. It was embarrassing for them that Metternich and Tsar Alexander claimed that the concert should uphold an ideological conservatism as well, and repress outbreaks of liberal and nationalist sentiment all over the continent, acting as a "Holy Alliance." Russia, Austria, and Prussia had gained a lot from successive revisions of European borders since the 1770s, seizing the territories of Poles, Italians, and others. Where might their "holy" autocratic appetites take them next? In the 1820s and 1830s, in reaction to these claims, George Canning and Palmerston pursued a policy of trying to limit and localise the operation of the concert, so that Britain and France acquired more influence over the affairs of Belgium, Portugal, and Spain than Austria or Russia did, and were able to settle them pragmatically.

The peculiarity of the "Eastern question" was that the full concert had to be involved, because Britain, France, Austria, and Russia all had vital direct interests in the future of the Ottoman Empire. All British foreign secretaries recognised that any potential aggression against, or undermining of, the Ottoman Empire must be resolved by international agreement. However, this raised the question of whether this agreement was to be achieved flexibly, by realpolitik, or whether ideology—in the shape of religion—would intrude. How far should the future of this Muslim empire be determined by explicitly Christian aspirations?

In the 1820s, George Canning tried for a pragmatic understanding with Russia, cooperating over Greece and sacrificing the commitments that Britain had made in 1809–14 to defend Persia against aggression.[31] Russia presided

31. Ingram, *Britain's Persian Connection*, chaps. 10–11.

over a strong sphere of influence within the Ottoman Empire, in the Balkans and the Black Sea area, which it regarded as necessary for its security and which it wanted to consolidate. From 1805, it offered to recognise Egypt as a similar British sphere of interest. After 1810, there was no need for Britain to express a view on that subject one way or the other, but the offer was never forgotten. Moreover, many Tories, preoccupied with the defence of institutional religion in domestic politics, instinctively sympathised with Russia's view that the Eastern question should involve the protection of Christianity and its promotion over declining Ottomanism. When the Tory Party split in the late 1820s, and Canning's followers Palmerston and Huskisson separated from Wellington and Aberdeen, it was because they increasingly disagreed with the latter's alarmed anxiety to uphold institutional Christianity, in Britain, Ireland, and abroad. They were willing instead to abandon the Tories and to harness and guide the popular pressures that conservative Christians regarded so negatively. For Palmerston, Russian assertiveness, like domestic radical agitation and Irish Catholic organisations, should be dealt with boldly and imaginatively rather than by fear or appeasement—by vigorous British government policy based on popular confidence.[32]

Despite this important difference of opinion, the general assumption that Ottoman affairs must be settled by European concert continued to shape British policy. Indeed, Britain lacked the power to do anything else: it ceased only slowly to be the weakest of the three great powers at Constantinople. France and Russia had historically tussled for supremacy there by applying various sorts of pressure; Napoleon's invasion of Egypt had been one more form of it. In return, their local protégés received special commercial benefits. In contrast, no British ambassador before Stratford Canning was dominant at the Porte for any length of time, and Canning had much less power than he wished, or than the monstrous egotism of his dispatches implied.[33] Britain never volunteered to defend the Ottoman Empire on its own, and lacked the resources to do so. From the early 1800s, the British government also set its face against the other powers' enthusiastic use—and abuse—of the protection system in order to win favours with the regime. The Foreign Office preferred to bow to the domestic campaign against "old corruption" in the public service, and to root out traditional Levant Company cronyism. This was not always easy, because London and Constantinople had little power over local consuls and their established networks. Moreover, in the parts of the Middle East that were influenced by Indian governing practice, the culture of mutual present giving continued, as was shown by Rich's behaviour in Baghdad and Harris's expedition to Shewa. By the 1840s, however, the norm was coming to be Rose's

32. Parry, *Politics of Patriotism*, 146–51.

33. Ozan Ozavci shows in "Priceless Grace" how Robert Liston was well regarded by one party at the Porte at the time of the Congress of Vienna, because of intense Ottoman disquiet about Russia, but was still far from fully trusted.

"superstitious horror of presents." He felt they were "almost invariably meant to be the first steps of corruption."[34]

Despite lots of tensions at Constantinople, Britain aimed to work with Russia and Austria, as well as France, at least until the mid-1840s. Austria under Metternich usually adopted a pragmatic conservative approach to Eastern problems, while Palmerston convinced himself that if Britain asserted itself confidently enough, it could make Russia come to terms. This cooperation was most striking in 1839–40. Russia and Austria agreed with Britain to remove Mehmet Ali from Syria in order to avoid the empire's imminent collapse. Historians from Temperley to Caquet have written as if Britain was here exercising a free choice between "Turkey" and "Egypt," like choosing between two sides in an election.[35] It was no such thing. The European powers were upholding the sovereignty and legitimacy of a historic empire, which even Mehmet Ali acknowledged, and which France was expected to support. Britain had a profound interest in a prosperous and vigorous Egyptian regime, but granting independence to its self-made septuagenarian pasha offered Europe no long-term stability. France could not realistically challenge a European consensus on the subject—unless it had still been run by a force of nature like Napoleon Bonaparte rather than by parties of squabbling parliamentarians. Moreover, the other powers united around the reassuringly historical policy of hostility to French restlessness, so that in 1840 there were many parallels with 1798–99. Russia and Austria maintained their fundamental objective, which was to stabilise the empire as a weak regime whose future would be determined by the interests of the Christian powers. The 1841–46 Tory government, in which Aberdeen was foreign secretary, chose to work with Russia, to acknowledge Ottoman sovereignty while strengthening Britain's Egyptian sphere of interest, and to check French denominationalism. This involved accepting Ottoman influence in Lebanon, using pressure at Constantinople to mitigate its shortcomings, and disappointing liberals who had expected independence for the mountaineers. Some Tories even supported the idea of partnership with the Greek Orthodox Church, in opposition to Roman Catholic missionary activity in the East.

In parallel with this policy, many Tories—and other British observers—were comfortable with using the language of fixed racial difference between Europeans and Orientals, Christians and Turks. Milman and Macfarlane believed that Turkish national character was "to a certain degree, inborn." Aberdeen told the editor of *The Times* that the Turks were "crapulous barbarians."[36] Likewise, the radical Richard Cobden regarded them as "destructive savages"

34. Rose to Canning, Dec. 11, 1843, FO 78/576. Though the commercial protection networks were slowly eroded, the judicial framework for British subjects became stronger: see the discussion of extraterritoriality below. The two are too often run together.

35. See p. 174, above.

36. [Milman], "Turkish Empire," cited approvingly in Macfarlane, *Kismet*, 12; Laughton, *Henry Reeve*, 1:288.

defined by swords, slippers, and sexual excess, the three enemies of his ideal of orderly capitalist development. In the 1830s, Cobden waged a pamphlet war with David Urquhart about the future of the Ottoman Empire, which derived from their different perspectives on Levantine history. Urquhart sought to reform Ottoman government on venerable Arabic lines, but Cobden was a Christian moralist who regarded Russian rule at Constantinople as far preferable, historically, morally, and economically, to that of Muslims. He looked forward to Russia replacing "the lasciviousness of the harem," "the voice of the eunuch and the slave," and the "huts which now constitute the capital of Turkey," with an "assemblage of high-souled and beautiful women," "the voices of men of learning," and "a splendid and substantial European city."[37] Gladstone, an admirer of both Cobden and Aberdeen, continued to draw on this heritage in various ways. He thought that Russia's government was approved by its own people and was an appropriate defender of Eastern Orthodoxy, a purer Christianity than Roman Catholicism. Though he did not want to see Russian rule at Constantinople, he hoped to see a Greek empire restored there and Muslim power removed from Europe, as Aberdeen had also wanted in 1829.[38]

However, the issue of Russia became more politically contentious throughout the 1830s and 1840s. At home, most liberals and radicals became intensely suspicious of global Russian objectives. Struggles over liberalism and nationalism in various parts of Europe created international ideological tensions, over which Britain and France usually took one view and Russia and Austria the opposite one. The five-power system functioned less and less well, even before 1848. At Constantinople, the British embassy took up trade talks in order to challenge Russian power. Despite apparently winning this battle and securing a new Anglo-Ottoman commercial treaty in 1838, the embassy still seemed less influential than its Russian counterpart in the early 1840s, because the Ottomans did not feel strong enough to throw off the latter's protection.

Then came the three shocks of 1843—the massacres at Karbala and in Kurdistan, and the apostasy execution—which implied that Ottoman ministers acquiesced in barbaric acts committed in the name of Islam. European newspapers talked of Islamic "fanaticism." Stratford Canning now identified an alliance between Russian and Islamic conservatives. He thought that illiberal Muslim rulers deliberately fanned sectarian antagonism by exciting popular anger at the idea of concessions to Christians. Mutual Muslim-Orthodox hostility was assisted by the Greek Church hierarchy, which kept its lay worshippers loyal by keeping them ignorant. Russia only pretended to care for

37. [Cobden], *Russia*, 141 (quotations), 208–9. Cobden's polemic (1836) drew substantially on the just-published memoir of the Levant Company chaplain Robert Walsh, *Residence at Constantinople*: see 1:260–62.

38. See particularly [Gladstone], "War and the Peace,", esp. 155; Matthew, "Gladstone," esp. 425–27.

Balkan grievances; in fact, it thrived on Orthodox resentment. In the 1820s and 1830s, political Islam had seemed in decline, sapped of its old military ferocity and confused about how far to follow European example. If it seemed stronger now, the implication was that it had gained strength from outside, from Russian support.

From 1847, Canning and Palmerston, foreign secretary in Russell's Liberal government, turned to a new policy. They pressed the Porte to establish full civil equality between Muslims and non-Muslims, focusing particularly on the legal system, where Christian evidence was not accepted in trials between Christians and Muslims. The empire must become a land of law, like India, in order to tackle the grievances of Balkan Orthodox Christians and strengthen the regime against the Russian threat. Although based on an interpretation of the Edict of Gülhane, this was Victorian liberal interventionism: Britain was taking responsibility, single-handedly, for the introduction of stronger legal guarantees for Ottoman minorities. It had concluded that this was the only basis on which the empire could, or deserved to, survive, and the only basis on which British protection could be justified.

This approach was a liberal policy in two wider senses. First, it had a European dimension. It implied not only that Russian illiberalism was the real enemy of Ottoman independence and dignity, but that all truly liberal powers should follow the British agenda. It was part of an attempt to establish an agenda for international affairs that could unite Britain and a liberal France. In 1847, France was courting Austria and Russia, particularly over Poland, rather than Britain. Palmerston wanted France instead to work with Britain, on Britain's terms. He wanted to make Britain and France pre-eminent at Constantinople, but also to recast the European concert, tilting the balance away from the conservative powers. With luck, the tsar would then balk at challenging the phalanx of Western military, economic, and political might. The 1848 revolutions divided Europe into ideological camps, and Palmerston intensified his concern to maintain good relations with France. The dispute about the Hungarian refugees who fled to the Ottoman Empire allowed Britain and France to present the Porte as a humanitarian regime struggling for independence against bullying Russian thuggery.

Second, the policy fitted with a fundamental principle of domestic Liberalism—that entitlement to political citizenship should rest on non-sectarian grounds. The Liberal Party was founded on opposition to what it portrayed as a dominant and intolerant Church-state alliance, and on a claim that good government involved reconciling sectarian differences instead. After 1829, Catholic Emancipation forced Liberal politicians to build a coalition with Irish Catholic Members of Parliament if they wanted to be in office. The sine qua non of good government in Ireland—and in the most problematic British colony, Canada—became religious pluralism, the sacrifice of the institutional privileges of the Anglican Church to the extent necessary to retain the confidence of the Catholic population. In the pursuit of constitutional inclusiveness, Liberals had to accommodate the political claims not only of non-Protestants, but also of non-Christians, once Jewish emancipation became an issue in 1847. In December 1847, one Liberal cabinet minister argued that Jews should be allowed to become Members of Parliament because it involved the same principle of civil equality that the government now asked the Ottoman sultan to adopt.[39]

The Canning-Palmerston plan was therefore an aspirational liberal vision. However, the Edict of Gülhane was shaped by several influences at the Ottoman court, not just by Anglophiles, and the legal system that it upheld was based on Islamic law. Richard Wood had assumed that this was not an obstacle to liberal governance: efficient, zealous local pashas should be able to find a way of smoothing tensions between religious groups by firm, fair rule, making sure that Christian evidence was recognised in mixed trials without undermining the sultan's legal authority. But there were nowhere near enough governors of that calibre to satisfy Canning or Wood. That was why Canning had decided to ask the Porte to make legal equality a *principle*. This was unrealistic, not least because to be seen to give in to Western Christian pressure on the matter would itself damage sultanic authority enormously.

The gap between the aspiration and reality in most parts of the Ottoman Empire can be seen in the determination of the Foreign Office to consolidate the principle of extraterritoriality in the 1840s and extend it in the 1850s. The British government gave the embassy and its consuls judicial power over British, Maltese, and Ionian subjects throughout the empire. This was despite claiming that it would like nothing better than to be able to entrust their fate to Ottoman legal processes, as soon as Christian evidence was accepted in mixed tribunals. For the Foreign Office, instituting secure extraterritoriality in this part of the world was a great step forward. One important illustration of this was the Don Pacifico controversy of 1850. It is usually seen as an example of British gunboat diplomacy towards the Greeks, but it is more telling to see Palmerston's goal as being to secure the same degree of legal protection for British subjects in independent but turbulent Greece that the new consular jurisdiction arrangements gave their counterparts in neighbouring Ottoman lands.[40]

In the early 1850s, Russia and Napoleon III's France became increasingly reckless and revisionist in their foreign policies, and tension between them led to a major war in 1854. At one level this was a traditional struggle for dominance at Constantinople. Most British people chose to regard it instead as a war to protect the European balance of power from sinister Russian aggression.

39. Viscount Morpeth: 95 Parl. Deb. (3d ser.) cols. 1375–76.
40. For the Ionian problem that prompted the controversy, see Benton and Ford, *Rage for Order*, 114–15.

This resulted in Britain going to war to resist the Russian influence at Constantinople that Tories had accepted for the last fifty years. French and British victory in the Crimean War made it look as if both powers were more devoted to the existing Ottoman regime than they were. The war was fought to change it—to force the sultan to accept new protectors and new values. The values that it was required to accept were spelt out in the *hatt-ı hümayun* of 1856, in which the Porte promulgated civil equality for its Christian subjects. The edict that Palmerston and Canning had tried to force on the Ottomans in order to avoid a war was now obtained from them as the price of victory in it.

However, the declaration of the *hatt-ı hümayun* did little to mollify continental public opinion. In fact, by contributing to sectarian disturbances within the empire, it entrenched European doubts—in France as well as Austria and Russia—about the capacity of the Ottomans to rule Balkan and Lebanese Christians. In 1866, the European powers united to support the local movement that demanded that Prince Carol be made hereditary ruler of the Danubian Principalities (generally known as Rumania from now on). Britain followed the lead of France in working for this outcome. The settlement assumed continuing nominal Ottoman suzerainty, but this was henceforth ignored by most Rumanian politicians. The scene was set for the Eastern crisis of 1875–78, which ended with independence for those Balkan regions that already had self-government (Rumania, Serbia, and Montenegro), and self-government for most of the rest—the Bulgarian lands.

This was the overwhelming demand of European public opinion, including in Britain, where, after another Reform Act in 1867, the political power of Christian protest reached a new height in the Bulgarian agitation of 1876. That agitation was a popular acknowledgment of Britain's responsibility to safeguard Balkan Christians if mistreated by the Ottoman regime that British soldiers and sailors had conditionally saved in 1854–56.[41] Significantly, the most famous of the agitators was Gladstone, Aberdeen's heir and an enthusiastic advocate of a Christian European concert. He followed the lead of the eighty-three-year-old Earl Russell, who demanded a reversion to George Canning's policy of 1827, of working with Russia to protect the Greeks. The ninety-year-old Stratford Canning put on his armour one more time and supported it as well.[42] At the heart of the agitation were Anglican high churchmen like H. P. Liddon and Malcolm MacColl, who wanted the Orthodox Church to be restored at Constantinople; historians sympathetic to them such as E. A. Freeman, who demanded that aggressive and barbarian Muslims be expelled from Christian Europe; and Protestant Dissenters, mobilised by the newspaper

---

41. Parry, *Politics of Patriotism*, 326–27.

42. For Russell, see Shannon, *Gladstone*, 95–96. Gladstone's famous phrase calling for the Turkish governing class to clear "bag and baggage" out of Bulgaria had been used by Stratford Canning in 1821, in relation to Greece: Lane-Poole, *Stratford Canning*, 1:307.

editor W. T. Stead, who concluded the same in the face of more evidence associating Islam with the sword, rape, and slavery in the Balkans.[43] Tory Anglican churchmen in Disraeli's Conservative cabinet, like Salisbury and Carnarvon, sympathised with this Christian agenda. As a result, Disraeli, who was trying to focus on other aspects of the Eastern crisis—especially the Russian threat to India—had less room for manoeuvre than he wanted.

The events of 1875–78 showed that Christian Europe did not believe that the Ottoman Empire could govern on liberal Enlightenment principles. Many people in Britain had probably always shared that view; the vigorous expression of it in 1876 was an unprecedentedly populist intervention in foreign policy. Already in 1866, Lord Clarendon, now foreign secretary again, felt that British opinion knew too much about "the united ignorance and stupidity of the Mahomedans" to accept their continued occupation of the Balkans.[44] This anti-Ottoman feeling may also have been intensified by a shift away from liberal and universalist assumptions among European elites, as their states began to prioritise imperial conquest, and as racial categories and distinctions became more commonly used by politicians and intellectuals. In the 1870s and 1880s, boasts about the innate civilisational superiority of the West became more vociferous, accompanying competitive military advances by the European powers in Africa and by Britain and Russia in Asia. In turn, these boasts naturally prompted a lot of insecurity in the threatened regions, and a search to organise local politics around alternative principles. Muslim intellectuals promoted the idea of a distinctive Muslim world. Moreover, from the time of the Russo-Ottoman war of 1877, Ottoman leaders had less compunction about presenting Islam as the basis of the regime's political identity— helped by the loss of Christian territory in 1878. It was suggestive that, after the experience of the *hatt-ı hümayun*, the Constantinople regime learned to avoid further reforms that looked like a surrender to European pressure to infringe Islamic law.[45]

By 1880, therefore, the consensus of British political opinion was clearly hostile to Ottoman governing values. If one aspect of this was a more racialised political discourse in an age of Darwinian science, there were also strong elements of continuity with past Tory support for the idea of a Christian European concert against anti-Christian enemies, and with an equally long-standing radical-Dissenting Christian humanitarianism. Moreover, most British approval of Islam had always come from a radical-Benthamite tradition

43. Shannon, *Gladstone*, esp. 30, 33, 103, 190. On Freeman, see Morrisroe, "Eastern History with Western Eyes."

44. Mosse, *Crimean System*, 3.

45. For the hardening of British racial attitudes, see Hyam, *Britain's Imperial Century*, 155–66. For the impact on Christian-Muslim relations, see Aydin, *Idea of the Muslim World*, 61–62. For changes in the Ottoman regime's handling of the slavery issue, see Rogan, *Arabs*, 122.

that was much more pro-Arab than it had ever been pro-Turk. Palmerston had made various attempts at a distinctive strategy for Ottoman defence, but the main benefit in doing so was domestic: to mobilise British public opinion behind an interventionist military policy in 1840 and in 1854. On each occasion, support for intervention was driven mainly by a sense of indignation—at French and then at Russian unscrupulousness. This achievement was striking, given Britain's isolationist tendencies, but Palmerston's strategy was much less successful in terms of answering the Eastern question itself. His series of policy gambits never created a special relationship between Britain and the Ottoman Empire, or convinced the other powers to accept Britain's lead for any length of time. For far too long, it has been assumed that what Mosse called "the time-honoured principle of the integrity of the Ottoman Empire, the 'Palmerstonian system,'" was a core element of British policy.[46] This book has shown instead that this "system" was operative only for a couple of decades, during which it embodied shifting assumptions and objectives. This was not surprising, since Britain was never willing to defend the Ottoman Empire on its own, so its strategy for doing so was always reliant on the views and conditions laid down by other powers. Palmerston himself took the candid view that the peace of 1856 would not last for more than ten years, and that new ways would need to be found by the next political generation to restrain renewed Russian aggression.[47]

⬦

Yet there is an apparent paradox here. Though British sympathy for Ottoman rule in Europe was limited, fragile, and declining, upholding Ottoman sovereignty in the Middle East remained of great benefit to Britain. It provided a cheap and effective way to maintain British influence in that region, while ensuring that France and Russia were kept out of it. The history of British engagement with the Middle East after 1854 shows that it was much easier to consolidate its position on that basis before 1914 than to be the imperialist itself, as Britain became after the First World War.

By the 1850s, Britain's commercial and political influence in Egypt was undeniable. Growing British support for the Egyptian regime throughout the 1800–1850 period was driven primarily by the economic interests of the main merchant networks, and the needs of the passengers and operators of the transit. Their priorities were always unsentimental—order and stability—but they also appreciated Mehmet Ali's apparent respect for British, European, and Christian culture. Few of them shared the enthusiasm of the Constantinople embassy for the Tanzimat, which from the perspective of Cairo and

46. Mosse, *Crimean System*, 155.
47. Mosse, 1–3.

Alexandria looked like sultanic bluster—more audacious, but no more appropriate, than previous attempts by the Porte to interfere in Egyptian affairs. Christians in Egypt already enjoyed protection, while the benefits of extraterritoriality meant that Europeans there had little need to worry about the viceroy's draconian punishments.

Britain also clearly had naval superiority all around Arabia, and this seemed slowly to be strengthening British influence across the region. The perception that it was a supporter of the Ottoman Empire may even have helped British authority in India, to the extent that Indian Muslims believed that Britain was helping to defend the independence of their caliph.[48] From now on, British India took an increasing interest in organising the "steamship hajj" for its Muslims, with significant cultural and political consequences for the Mecca region.[49] British diplomatic pressure during the Crimean War contributed to the sultan's firman of 1857 that suppressed the African slave trade in Egypt and Baghdad (but not the Hijaz), and to subsequent attempts to enforce it. What is more striking, however, is the consistent general appreciation shown by Britain's consuls in Egypt, the Red Sea, and the Gulf that domestic slavery was an entrenched Islamic custom underwritten by shari'a law, and that sensitivity, patience, and compromise were needed in dealing with it.[50]

After the Crimean War, as before, the core British interest in the Middle East remained the defence of the two routes across it that had been identified since 1798. From the beginning, considerable effort had gone into securing both. However, there was also always an element of rivalry between the promoters of each. In the 1830s, the development of powerful steamships had swung the balance decisively in favour of the Red Sea option. Even so, interest in the alternative route, from Syria down the Mesopotamian rivers to Baghdad and the Gulf, survived the failure of the Euphrates Expedition. In 1840, Henry Blosse Lynch journeyed to Europe to get more resources for his Mesopotamian steam flotilla, because he assumed that the Eastern crisis would make London a permanent enemy of Mehmet Ali's Egypt. In fact, he was wrong, because Egypt was simply too valuable to Britain to make into an enemy. Still, the idea of steamers in Mesopotamia was raised again in 1847 when there were briefly doubts about the goodwill of the Egyptian regime. In 1852, a Euphrates railway project was mooted because of the crisis over the Egyptian railway plan, and it was revived in 1857 because of post-war concern that the French might try to use the idea of a Suez Canal to gain predominance

48. Yapp hints at such thinking: "Great Mass of Unmixed Mahomedanism," 8–9.
49. M. Low, *Imperial Mecca*.
50. For the firman and its effects, see Toledano, *Ottoman Slave Trade*, 126–36. For consuls' comments and policy in the 1850s and 1860s, see Otte, "Course of Unceasing Remonstrance," 96–104. This is why British diplomatic pressure against the slave trade, noticeable in so many parts of the world at this time, has not played a larger part in this book.

in Egypt. It resurfaced in 1878–79 as well.[51] By then, Lynch Brothers, now clearly the leading British company in Mesopotamia and southern Persia, was running a commercial steamer operation between Baghdad and Basra that made Baghdad "well nigh as vulgarised by the inroad of excursionists as the Rhine or Venice."[52]

Occasional anxiety about Egyptian reliability aside, the main reason for continuing interest in Mesopotamia, before and after 1854, was geopolitics. If Russia was Britain's real enemy in the East, it was reasonable to doubt that British predominance down in Egypt would adequately counter Russian aggression towards India. After all, Russia had been offering Alexandria to Britain since 1805. The Russian government and Bismarck both indicated at several points during the 1870s Eastern crisis that they would be willing for Britain to be given Egypt in a scheme of Ottoman partition.[53] Disraeli's government was understandably wary of this gift so generously proffered by the German chancellor. The Eastern crisis seemed to Disraeli to be largely about Russian assertiveness in the Balkans and at Constantinople. One way or another, Russia now appeared likely to acquire naval access to the Mediterranean.[54]

What could be done to mitigate this threat? The old island acquisition strategy (originally John Malcolm's) to protect the Euphrates route to India had focused on the sweltering Gulf. Now it re-emerged nearer to home. In 1878, the Ottomans agreed to Britain's request to administer Cyprus and build a base there, in return for a guarantee of defensive military assistance in Anatolia. Disraeli told the queen that Cyprus was "the key to western Asia." It was also a demonstration that Britain had not emerged empty-handed in the latest reduction of Ottoman power.[55] One incidental consequence was that in the

---

51. See the letters of E. F. Charlwood and R. Montgomery Martin about Euphrates steamers in August 1847, FO 78/722. For the railway plan of 1852, see p. 348, above. In 1857, there was a lot of discussion about a Euphrates railway, led by the Indian railway promoter William Patrick Andrew. See his *Letter to Viscount Palmerston*, with contributions from Chesney, McNeill, Sheil, Ainsworth, and Tom Lynch. In 1879, Andrew was chairman of the Stafford House Committee for promoting the construction of a railway from the Gulf to the Mediterranean. Lynch was also active: see T. Lynch, *Across Mesopotamia to India*. In 1855, the naval officer William Allen proposed a canal from the Mediterranean to the Dead Sea and the Gulf of Aqaba, also as an alternative to the Suez Canal.

52. This was through the Euphrates and Tigris Steam Navigation Company. For the quotation: C. Low, *Indian Navy*, 1:xii. For the broader effects, see C. Cole, "Controversial Investments."

53. Blowitz, *My Memoirs*, 165; Busch, *Our Chancellor*, 2:92–93. For Bismarck's concern to use the Eastern question to make Britain and Russia eventual rivals in the region, see Stone, "Bismarck and the Great Game," 157.

54. Disraeli's view was that the Russo-German offer of Egypt would divide Britain and France but not stop Russian aggression. Only an acquisition in Asia Minor would do the latter: Seton-Watson, *Disraeli*, 109, 172, 225–26.

55. Seton-Watson, 422–26 (quotation at 423).

1880s Cyprus was chosen by British evangelicals as the location for a short-lived settlement for Jews returning to the East, in the face of official hostility to the idea in Syria.[56] Meanwhile, biblical archaeology, also funded largely by domestic evangelicals, developed apace in both Palestine and Egypt in the same decade.[57]

The Eastern crisis of the 1870s underlined the indisputable importance of Egypt to Britain. (Indeed, some observers argued that controlling Egypt would also secure Syria and so would protect the Euphrates route from Russian attack.)[58] The India secretary, Lord Salisbury, would have been willing for Britain to occupy Egypt in 1877 if necessary, even if it brought on a wider partition.[59] The Egyptian regime went bankrupt in 1876, as a consequence of the flood of Western capital into it since 1856. Britain and France—the source of most of that capital—quickly moved in to impose financial rigour. This rigour helped to bring about a popular revolt. In 1882, Britain, citing disorder and likely financial chaos, invaded Egypt and occupied Alexandria, for the third time in the nineteenth century.

Gladstone, now prime minister, portrayed the intervention of 1882 as a necessary action on behalf of the civilised world against military violence. He ordered cannon fire in the London parks to celebrate the great victory of Tell el Kebir.[60] He was thinking back to the old Concert view that Egypt was a legitimate sphere of British interest within the Ottoman Empire. Britain was as justified to intervene temporarily in pursuit of "order" there as Russia had been in Moldavia and Wallachia. For Gladstone, therefore, this was a very traditional response that did not challenge Ottoman sovereignty. In the late nineteenth century, an abstract question was sometimes mooted: What mattered more to Britain, Cairo or Constantinople? There was only one answer, geopolitically—the same answer that had already been given in 1801, 1807, 1833, 1841, and 1851. Egypt was essential; Constantinople was contingent. But the British did not want the question to be posed, and tried for many years after 1882 to avoid posing it.[61] They continued to claim that nothing much had changed, and that their occupation secured Egypt within the Ottoman domain.

Britain did not—could not—leave Egypt, for a variety of reasons. The Scramble for Africa in the mid-1880s turned into a European competition for African territory. Acquisitions became a matter of prestige and press celebration; they were also assumed to offer economic benefit through the

56. I owe this information to Professor Simon Dixon, whose research is forthcoming. There is some detail in Ben-Artzi, "Jewish Rural Settlement."

57. See, e.g., Moscrop, *Measuring Jerusalem*; Gange, *Dialogues with the Dead*, chap. 3; Gange and Ledger-Lomas, *Cities of God*.

58. See Dicey "Our Route to India," 683. I owe this reference to Roland McKay.

59. Seton-Watson, *Disraeli*, 219.

60. Parry, *Politics of Patriotism*, 351–52.

61. K. Wilson, "Constantinople or Cairo."

exploitation of the mysterious African interior. Western rule in Egypt desta-bilised existing power structures and heightened the anxiety that withdrawal would risk order. British intervention in Egypt had been justified in 1882 by a whole host of arguments less cautious than Gladstone's. There was, as ever, anxiety about French motives, particularly given their keenness to negotiate with the revolt's leader, Urabi. The War Office worried about losing control of the Suez Canal to any enemy. The bondholders wanted to secure their repay-ments. Dissenting moralists feared that an Arab regime would revive slavery. Joseph Chamberlain and other radicals speciously claimed that Britain must save the Egyptian constitutional movement from Urabi's militarism.[62] Alexan-dria became Britain's best harbour in the eastern Mediterranean.

For most of the military and Anglo-Indian world, British control of Egypt was a natural and overdue development. Indian soldiers and civil servants were used to travelling through it, and assumed that it would benefit from Indian-style government. An increasingly imperially minded press took the same view. Direct rule after 1858 normalised British governing practice in India and removed such domestic controversy as there had been about it in the 1840s and 1850s. From 1883, Consul-General Evelyn Baring's plan was to impose on Egypt the principles of budgetary prudence, military retrench-ment, and agricultural investment that he had observed his cousin, Lord Northbrook, pursue as viceroy of India in the 1870s. His assumption was that low taxes would quell discontent and create a more prosperous peasant small-holder class. His policies created a financial boom, and his self-publicity put his rule in a favourable light back home, even though his overbearing repres-sion, hostility to protection for industry, and distrust of middle-class educa-tion made him deeply unpopular in Egypt.[63] In the 1890s, the Gladstonian Liberals who had tried to minimise the significance of their original occu-pation slowly lost the initiative within the Liberal party to a group of "Lib-eral imperialists" led by Lord Rosebery and Edward Grey (another cousin of Northbrook). Grey insisted that Egypt, Sudan, and some other parts of East Africa were non-negotiable elements of Britain's security zone for the defence of India. In 1906, now foreign secretary, he admitted that Britain's position in Egypt was "what we all know, but never say"—its ruler.[64]

Once other powers grasped this non-negotiable British stake in Egypt, they reacted accordingly. Egypt drew Britain inexorably into European rivalries. It had to defend Egypt against France and Russia, which had never previously been able to unite against Britain. The occupation led directly to the Naval

---

62. Parry, *Politics of Patriotism*, 347–53. See the analysis by William Mulligan in "Deci-sions for Empire." For Chamberlain's and Dilke's uncertainty about their own claims, see Chamberlain, "Sir Charles Dilke," 240–42.

63. See Owen, *Lord Cromer*, and the stimulating recent treatment by Aaron Jakes, *Egypt's Occupation*.

64. Otte, *Statesman of Europe*, 304.

Defence Act of 1889, which pledged to keep the British navy as strong as the next two world navies combined.[65] That in turn prompted the Franco-Russian alliance of 1894 and the naval arms race that brought about the First World War. In 1884, William Harcourt warned that occupying Egypt would bring "all the evils of becoming a Continental state." That is to say, it would make defence strategy so much more complicated than when Britain could behave just as an island power.[66]

Britain eventually had to abandon serene aloofness and become entangled in continental alliances. In 1904, an entente with France secured British predominance in Egypt. The corollary was the emergence of an understanding about Mediterranean defence that soon made France the main power there while Britain defended the Atlantic and Channel against Germany. In 1914, Britain chose to ally with France and Russia against Germany, not just because of the German threat in the North Sea (which could be defeated on its own) but because abandoning France and Russia would mean that their victory in the war would probably hand the Mediterranean to them and jeopardise both Egypt and India. By 1887, when Bismarck was already exploiting French and Ottoman anger at Britain to try to trap it in his diplomatic web, Lord Salisbury "heartily wish[ed] we had never gone into Egypt. Had we not done so, we could snap our fingers at all the world."[67] William Hamilton had got his wish. Britain had brought Egypt back into a greater Europe. In the same way, Russia, Austria, and Germany had rescued the Balkans. Unfortunately, the Europeans were even less able to agree peaceably on how to govern their expanded world than the Romans had been.

⁂

The First World War eventually destroyed the Ottoman Empire, which had sought German and Austrian protection against the historically terrifying combination of Britain, France, and Russia that confronted it. But before that, this venerable entity displayed a vigour that alarmed the British on several fronts: its declaration of jihad against British rule in the East, its repulsion

---

65. The two-power standard had not been formal policy for decades, though in the 1820s and 1830s a three-power standard had been a general aim, when it was much easier because of the exhaustion of most continental navies after the French wars. In August 1848, Prime Minister Russell had denied that a two-power standard was necessary: 100 Parl. Deb. (3d ser.) col. 1303. While this view partly reflected great pressure for defence cuts from radical Members of Parliament, it was also a benefit of the foreign policy that he and Palmerston were pursuing, of keeping France and Russia as far apart as possible, especially in the Mediterranean, and of localising disputes in various parts of the world in order to minimise the global threat to Britain.

66. Parry, *Politics of Patriotism*, 354.

67. Cecil, *Robert Marquis of Salisbury*, 4:41–42.

of repeated Anglo-French assaults on Constantinople, and its willingness to encourage German interest in Mesopotamia's rivers and oil. In November 1914, Indian troops seized Basra from the Ottomans, and protected the newly built Anglo-Persian oil pipeline on the Gulf coast. Many British strategists, channelling the traditional Bombay mindset, thought these pre-emptive actions quite enough. Former Indian viceroy Curzon was one of those who warned that an expedition into inland Mesopotamia would incur too much risk and responsibility and create too many vulnerabilities.[68] However, a panic about the German threat, plus anxiety to impress the Arabs, meant that these warnings were downplayed. The Mesopotamia campaign proved very draining and hit disaster at Kut in 1916.

Those who knew their history would be aware that the natural way for Britain to counter the Ottoman call to jihad was to mobilise Arab loyalties. It was obvious to the British representatives in Egypt, McMahon and Storrs, that the Hashemite sharif of Mecca, Husayn, should be built up as a superior rallying point for Arab Muslim sentiment. Husayn was encouraged to think that the British would support an Arab revolt against the Turks, leading to postwar Arab rule (with British assistance) across the region, excepting a small and undefined French interest in Lebanon and northern coastal Syria. Here was another revival of a theme of this book—the gap between the consular perspective on the spot and the Eurocentric one in London, where maintaining the French wartime alliance was absolutely paramount. The result of the latter was the Sykes-Picot agreement, which assumed Anglo-French spheres of interest throughout the region, and which reflected the French Catholic influence across Lebanon, Syria, and Kurdistan that had been entrenched in the 1840s. The two perspectives were bound to clash horribly, once Husayn's son Faysal led an Arab revolt that left him installed at Damascus by the end of 1918. Faysal was abetted by the young military intelligence officer T. E. Lawrence, who thought the French were every bit as unsuited to govern Arabs as his swashbuckling predecessors had in 1801. For Faysal, Syria and the Hijaz were one entity. In making the post-war settlement, however, Britain felt the need to support French claims to Damascus, naturally angering Husayn and his son. The French mandate in the new Syria and Lebanon lasted until independence in 1943–46, despite several rebellions by Druze and others.

The final blow to a Hashemite empire came from Arab disunity, but here too British traditions played their part. Ibn Saud had restored the old Wahhabi power base at Riyadh in 1902; he then took the eastern Arabian province of Hasa from the Ottomans in 1913. In 1915, the former resident in the Persian Gulf, Percy Cox, made an agreement with him, drawing him into the British Gulf protectorate that had begun in the Trucial States and had then been extended to Bahrain, Kuwait, and eventually Qatar. This was a mutual defence

68. Gilmour, *Curzon*, 477.

network: it protected the Gulf coast from the Saudis' expansionist tendencies, but it also brought them into a regional alliance against the Ottoman-German threat. However, it left Ibn Saud free to roam westwards, and his eyes were naturally on Mecca and the Hijaz. After initial clashes with the Hashemites on the border in 1919, Britain presided over a short-term peace between the two sides, but the embittered Husayn rejected a permanent understanding. In 1924–25, the Saudis drove him and his son Ali out of the Arabian Holy Cities and the rest of the province. Within a few years, Ibn Saud had proclaimed the kingdom of Saudi Arabia.[69]

The post-war settlement established an uneasy compromise between Anglo-French imperial defence concerns and the newly dominant international language of national self-determination. Egyptians who had resented Cromer's rule and fought against the Turk in the war would not tolerate the perpetuation of a British protectorate after it, and the Egyptian khedives became monarchs of an independent Egyptian state in 1922. Britain, however, retained control over Egyptian defence, imperial communications, and the safeguarding of the rights of minorities; this naturally created a nationalist grievance. Meanwhile, British mandates were established in Iraq, Transjordan, and Palestine. Article 22 of the Covenant of the League of Nations described the duty of guiding these territories towards independence as a "sacred trust of civilisation." They would become lands of law in the fullest sense, with functioning constitutions and legal and administrative systems. Husayn's sons were installed as Britain's rulers: Abdullah in Transjordan and Faysal in Iraq.

Iraq reconstituted in a new form the three Ottoman pashaliks that Britain had monitored after 1798 and that the pasha of Baghdad had always tried to draw into his orbit. Although the Sykes-Picot agreement had allocated the Mosul area to France, it was added to Baghdad and Basra because the British army occupied it in 1918, having taken Baghdad the year before. The seizure of Mosul was partly because of its oil potential, but also because one school of thought in India regarded the whole of Iraq as an important outpost of imperial defence. This drew on a historical British vision of the territory as a strategic entity whose stability required a judicious balance to be held between Sunni, Shi'a, Kurd, Christian, and Yazidi. Indeed, in 1920 Britain also aimed to establish an autonomous Kurdistan in the mountains north of Mosul, which were not ceded to Iraq. This followed the proposal of a Kurdish state at Versailles in 1919 by Şerif, grandson of Baban Pasha Ahmed's deputy during his rule in Sulaimaniya in the 1840s.[70] Accordingly, Kurdish autonomy was laid down in the Treaty of Sèvres in August 1920, along with provision for an

69. See Rogan, *Arabs*, 222–28, and more generally, for this and the following paragraphs. For the railway from the Mediterranean to the Gulf, mentioned on p. 401, 188.

70. I owe this information about Şerif's family to Metin Atmaca.

independence plebiscite (which might also be extended to the Kurdish areas in the Mosul province of Iraq) and special protection for the Chaldean Christian minorities. However, as with most provisions of the Treaty of Sèvres, these plans foundered on successful Turkish military resistance to what Turks saw as the dismemberment of their own country.

In Iraq, meanwhile, Faysal tried to aim at balancing sects, and a functioning constitution was established, with substantial Kurdish autonomy, but Britain continued to find the cost of securing order high. In 1932, it accepted Iraqi independence, while retaining substantial powers over defence and communications, as in Egypt. Whether Faysal would have succeeded in fashioning an independent Iraqi monarchy is a moot point; his original goal, after all, had been a westward-facing Arab empire. The regime's authority waned after his sudden death in 1933; British military control had to be reimposed after a pro-German government emerged during the Second World War; large-scale nationalist opposition was triggered by the larger regional strains of the 1950s; the monarchy was overthrown in 1958.

Finally and, as ever, most problematically, there was Palestine. When General Allenby's army wrested it from the Ottomans in late 1917, Britain inherited the responsibility of settling its future. Most leading British politicians distrusted the idea of internationalising it, arguing that, if France was to have Syria, Britain should control the territory to its south. This would secure the eastern approach to the Suez Canal. It would also allow the realisation of a repeated hope during the war—a railway between the Mediterranean and the Gulf, finally making Britain and India one strategic unit. The Balfour Declaration of November 1917 stated the cabinet's desire to secure a home for the Jewish people in Palestine—subject to not prejudicing the civil and religious rights of non-Jewish communities there. The declaration can be seen as offering a humanitarian spin on Britain's territorial objective—a spin that seemed necessary especially in view of the likely importance of America in shaping the post-war settlement. It reflected the power of evangelical philo-Semitism across the Atlantic. It also reflected Balfour's own romantic classical-biblical vision of the civilisational benefits of a cultured Jewish homeland, and his sense that the similarly romantic Germans would offer Zionists much the same if Britain did not. Curzon, who knew the Middle East and its Arabs much better than Balfour did, thought a Jewish Palestine fundamentally misconceived and divisive. Yet his Asian experience counted for little in London discussions, in the face of a typical British insouciance about the ease with which a liberal military power could mediate sectarian differences on the ground, and defuse them.[71] Allenby had entered Jerusalem modestly, on foot; he promised to

---

71. Gilmour, *Curzon*, 480–83. Philip Alexander's "Why Did Lord Balfour" (207–12) emphasises Balfour's childhood grounding in Scottish Old Testament teaching, and his resulting sense of Christians' debt and moral duty to the Jews.

protect the sacred buildings and spaces of all three great religions. Perhaps he would play the role that Stuart had played in 1802 and Rose in 1841, using the threat of British guns to force restless locals to compromise with one another.

There is no need here to rehearse the many crises of the British mandate in Palestine as it grappled with Zionism, increased Jewish immigration in the 1930s, and Arab suspicions and factionalism. Before 1918, whenever Arabs or Jews regarded Britain as a relatively fair power broker, this was in comparison with the Ottomans, and perhaps with other powers. Once Britain was the responsible imperial authority, it was much less easy for it to avoid perceptions of bias, double-dealing, and occasional brutality. Nor did Britain gain much benefit from what had seemed likely immediately after 1918: Anglo-French diplomatic and military cooperation in Syria-Palestine. Whenever the two powers were able to collaborate effectively, the resulting show of force threatened to stoke nationalist resentment. Yet the establishment of spheres of influence for each power also led to the institutionalised rivalry that Britain had tried to avoid in the nineteenth century. There was some low-level British support for the Druze rebellion in French Syria, and for the independence movements in Syria and Lebanon in World War Two. Some Frenchmen, meanwhile, gave help to Jewish terrorists in Palestine. Men on the spot were led to indulge in such spats because of ingrained suspicions, together with a tendency to exaggerate their own importance and promote their own careers. The combined effect of all this activity soured relations badly.[72]

By the 1950s, it was easy to forget that British involvement in the Middle East had begun with the aim of protecting an Indian subcontinent that had become independent in 1947. When the last British troops left Egypt, on December 23, 1956, they did so in the aftermath of a failed campaign fought with France and Israel against an Egyptian government that had nationalised the Suez Canal and sought to create an Arab revolt against European imperialism. Ironically, the Americans played a role that would have been familiar to nineteenth-century Britons—the role of the intimidating mediator who could impose peace on warring factions, demonstrating moral and military superiority in the process. Britain could act that part as a foil to Ottoman rule before 1918, but not thereafter. Yet the Americans in turn would soon discover the difficulty of sustaining an uncompromised ascendancy in such complex circumstances.

⟨ ⟩

Although there were important elements of continuity in twentieth-century British (and French) Middle Eastern imperialism, it was naturally different from what had gone before—in extent, in execution, in economic objectives.

---

72. For this Anglo-French tension, see Barr, *Line in the Sand.*

Britain's military presence in Egypt ended, as it began, as an imperial project, but in the beginning the imperial project was just the defence of India. In the years before 1854, British territorial and strategic ambitions in the region grew, but remained limited; this may help to explain why they were mostly successful. Each of the three great European wars that took place between 1793 and 1918 ratcheted up British commitments. In each case, Britain originally reacted to what it saw as French, Russian, or German imperial ambitions. However, its response took on a life of its own, driven partly by short-termist pre-emptive anxieties, and partly by longer-term hopes for improvement, which were often unrealistic or self-deceiving.

This book has been written in the belief that the early British encounter with the Middle East is interesting in its own right, rather than for whatever help it may give in understanding later events. It is interesting because it illuminates how British officials and commentators approached the defence of national interests in an important part of the world, and the variety of perspectives that made up that response. Engagement with the region was driven by many factors, ranging from geopolitics to history and religion, and took many forms, which defy reduction to simple caricature or retrospective attitudinising. Opinions about the Middle East and what it might become were shaped by familiarity with, and curiosity about, its past civilisations, which had supplied the modern world with its legal and spiritual foundations. But there was also significant, albeit racialised, awareness of the people who now lived there, their cultures and their tribulations. Many Britons appreciated the need to tread carefully in lands that remained mysterious in many respects and that resisted easy conquest by anyone. Many, meanwhile, were always preoccupied with more immediate concerns and self-interested ambitions. Nor can British behaviour be understood unless it is placed alongside the gambits of other European powers, of the Ottoman regime, and of local political leaders who never thought of themselves as the passive victims of omnipotent Westerners. All this meant that Britain approached the Middle East with a mixture of caution and occasional paranoia about rivals' ambitions. There were dreams of what the region might become, if the doings of God and man ever permitted it. However, in general, it was possible to believe that that transformation would happen any time soon only if one prioritised apocalypticism over realism.

In 1842, Viscount Castlereagh, a British nobleman in his thirties and nephew of the former foreign secretary, followed the fashion of the day and made a tour of Egypt and Sinai. When in Cairo, he commissioned the painter John Frederick Lewis, who resided there, to capture his trip on canvas. Lewis's resulting painting, *A Frank Encampment in the Desert of Mount Sinai, 1842*, appears, superficially, to be a statement of British power.[73] Castlereagh lies

---

73. As argued by Nicholas Tromans in "Orient in Perspective" (107–8).

in an open tent, shaded from the fierce sun. A dead gazelle indicates that he has been hunting; his dog is by his side. He sprawls complacently in Eastern clothes. The comforts of Britain have accompanied him: newspapers, teacups, a bottle of Harvey's sherry. A respectful and respectable Arab shaykh has arrived with his retinue, to guide him across the desert. Yet Castlereagh appears to us an absurd figure: fat, lazy, pale, as out of place as his teacups. The shaykh who attends him is dignified, clean, upright, independent. He is much more truly at ease, for these are his lands. There is a narrow but unbridgeable gulf between these two dominant figures.

And what of the location? Castlereagh has spread his British possessions at the bottom of Mount Sinai. The gazelle and the sherry seem significant. Are they the modern equivalent of the calf and the dancing in the tents of the Israelites, which infuriated Moses as he descended from the mountain? Moses carried the two tablets of the Law in his hands, but was so annoyed at the ungodliness and unworthiness of his people that he smashed them. The Israelites, suitably chastened, moved on. Soon, Viscount Castlereagh would also move on, like other arrogant Europeans who could not fit in (but unlike Lewis himself, he implied). The Arabs would endure. So would the austere elemental purity of the desert wilderness. So would the rubble of broken tablets that had pointed the way to the rule of law and to the social benefits that that might bring. The promised land seemed likely to remain tantalisingly out of reach.

ACKNOWLEDGMENTS

IN RETROSPECT, I seem to have been working on this book for a decade, but for at least half that time I had very little idea of how it would end up. For several years, I collected material because it seemed interesting, and because no one else seemed to be doing the same. As I have improved my understanding, I have inevitably discovered a good deal of existing work on aspects of the topic, and my original and superficial views on it have fortunately been washed away. I have filled in gaping holes in my knowledge, while uneasily aware of how many probably remain. More positively, I hope that others may now be persuaded to explore aspects of this topic in more depth.

Many years ago, I considered starting a project on nineteenth-century British attitudes to the Ottoman Empire, inspired by reading I had done on the religious politics of the Eastern question in Britain, and by two great books that it would have tried to straddle: Frank Turner's *The Greek Heritage in Victorian Britain*, and John Pemble's *The Mediterranean Passion*. I abandoned it for other things, but in due course I conceived of writing a biography of Henry Layard, with the aim of picking up some of those threads. It was while researching the Layard Papers in the British Library that I realised that there was probably less new to say about his excavation of Nineveh, and the reaction to it, than there was about British policy in Baghdad in the 1840s, which no one seemed to know about, so I produced an article on that. In 2012, casting around for a theme for a new undergraduate course, I decided to offer something on British political, cultural, religious, and economic engagement with Ottoman lands between the 1830s and the 1870s. I thought that students might find all these different strands interesting, and that we could explore whether they could be connected up in ways that books had not yet done, though I had only the sketchiest of ideas about how to make these connections. At first, the focus was on Baghdad, Syria, and Palestine, because I assumed that Egypt was a French preserve. I was also very busy administering the Isaac Newton Trust, on top of my normal workload. Fortunately, this helped to persuade the Leverhulme Trust to award me a Major Research Fellowship for three years from 2015, to try to produce something coherent out of these ideas.

I am enormously grateful to the Leverhulme Trust for this opportunity, and I can only hope that this book is a worthy reflection of its faith in the project. I decamped to London and took up residence in the British Library, where I found a stimulating peace in the silent camaraderie of the Rare Books Room in particular. Its staff have been wonderfully helpful. I went nearly as often to the National Archives at Kew, to immerse myself in volumes of official correspondence, which there was no risk of anyone else ordering; my only worries were the survival rates of the cygnets, ducklings, and goslings in the lake in the grounds. Slowly, I grasped a number of points that I really should have seen earlier: that the story turned on two routes, that something called "geopolitics" might be relevant, that Egypt was fundamental, and, most important of all, that everything made much more sense by starting in 1798 and tracing the many continuities from there. I began to ponder how to write about the cacophony of different perspectives that I encountered, which for a long time seemed unmanageable, though richer and more interesting than conventional talk of "Orientalism" suggested. It was only at a late stage that I properly connected up the various Indian Navy writings on the Arabs, or, in fact, the Benthamites' views of Islam.

When the fellowship came to an end, I realised that I had to restructure my undergraduate special subject completely. Over the six years that the course has run in total, teaching it has been a tremendous pleasure as well as an invaluable discipline. Seminar discussions with bright and engaged students have helped me to all sorts of new insights and angles; this book would have made much less sense without them. I have also benefited greatly—more than they probably realise—from conversations with graduate students, particularly with Graham Earles on international law and Roland McKay on geopolitics.

By March 2020, I was well into the process of revising draft chapters, but still a long way from the finishing line, when the coronavirus pandemic struck, and everyone was locked down. For the last ten months, this typescript has been a demanding companion, furiously dividing itself into more and more chapters, frequently driving me mad with its challenges, yet more frequently keeping me sane by offering crucial focus. Without the amazing resource that is www.archive.org, I could never have begun to tackle the remaining few hundred queries and absences, let alone to produce respectable footnotes. The digital support offered by the Cambridge University Library has also been invaluable. All the references have been checked except my notes from manuscript collections, where it is quite possible that poor typing has occasionally produced inexact dates and folio references.

Throughout, I owe a tremendous debt to the master and fellows of Pembroke College for their companionship and support (and for some financial aid with the maps), to many members of the Cambridge History Faculty for the same, and in particular to Andrew Arsan, Assef Ashraf, Arthur Asseraf, Duncan Bell, Paul Cavill, Joya Chatterji, Chris Clark, Saul Dubow, Renaud Gagné, Ben Griffin, Tim Harper, Boyd Hilton, Shruti Kapila, Peter Mandler, Charles Melville, Renaud Morieux, James Raven, Sujit Sivasundaram, Geraint Thomas, Roger Tomkys, Chika Tonooka, and Paul Warde for assistance and inspiration in various ways. Help from outside over the years that this project has been gestating has come from John Bew, David Cannadine, Pierre Caquet, Tom Crewe, David Gange, Holger Hoock, Joseph la Hausse de Lalouvière, Charles Lockwood, Bill Lubenow, Alex Middleton, Paul Read-man, and Kathryn Rix. I've enjoyed conversations with Guillemette Crouzet on the Gulf, David Feldman on Disraeli and race, Munro Price on Lewis Way, John Curtis and Andrew George on Layard, Stefania Ermidoro on Layard and on J. G. Taylor, Patrick Peebles on Layard and Ceylon, Jacqueline Reiter on Home Popham, Margot Finn on the Riches, Amir Theilhaber on Friedrich Rosen, Andrew Fitzmaurice on Egyptian students, Georgios Varouxakis on West and East, Jonathan Morris on coffee, and Metin Atmaca on the Babans. I am particularly grateful for the rich information about the Lynch family that His Honour Christopher Young gave me at several points. Michael Axwor-thy and I enjoyed several chats on Persia before his untimely death. Michael Ledger-Lomas provided a running series of stimulating thoughts on a number of themes of the book, latterly from halfway around the world.

Simon Dixon contributed dozens of illuminating conversations, on Anglo-Russian topics and many others, not least in the National Archives cafete-ria; he also kindly read the typescript at a late stage. Ozan Ozavci gave me an invaluable close reading of parts of it, and an advance copy of his own important book. Gareth Atkins commented on chapter 7 at a crucial point in its evolution. I have been greatly helped by the encouragement of the two anonymous readers for Princeton University Press, and by the care and atten-tion shown by Ben Tate, Josh Drake, Dimitri Karetnikov, Jenny Wolkowicki, and Maia Vaswani at the Press. Susan Pennybacker kindly arranged for me to speak at the University of North Carolina at Chapel Hill, where I benefited a lot from talking with her and with Cemil Aydin, Sarah Shields, and Penny Sinanoglou. Andrew Preston and the late Chris Bayly helped greatly with my article, "Steam Power and British Influence in Baghdad, 1820–1860," which appeared in the *Historical Journal* in 2013, and which shaped chapters 4 and 9. Mark Curthoys commissioned me to write entries on Samuel Briggs and Robert Taylor for the online *Oxford Dictionary of National Biography*, and some of the material in my entry on Briggs is reproduced here by kind permis-sion of Oxford University Press. My thanks are due to the owners of manu-script collections cited in the bibliography, and to the archivists concerned, for permission to use their collections.

I remain immensely grateful for the support and friendship of Judith Ayling, Richard Brent, Adrian Clark, Hazel Clark, Matthew Cragoe, Rich-ard and Jo Fisher, Julian Hoppit, Joanna Lewis, John Lotherington, Phillips O'Brien, and Alison Turton. And I owe more than I can say to Miri Rubin and Gareth Stedman Jones for their unceasing companionship and hospitality over many years—as well as for stimulating comments that persuaded me to rewrite both the introduction and conclusion.

I have done as much as I can to present this project as a neat and coherent piece of finished research. In reality, though, I still think of it as a dish not yet set, a story capable even now of being reshaped by some middle-of-the-night illumination. When, as a young lecturer at King's College London, I expressed some dissatisfaction with work that I had published earlier, Peter Marshall reassured me, pointing out that historians just had to accept the challenge of revisiting and revising their own assumptions, as their perspectives, and those of others, inevitably changed. In 2019, at the age of eighty-six, he produced a new magnum opus on Edmund Burke and the British West Indies, a model to us all. Nothing better sums up why the writing of history is such a challenging, infuriating, addictive experience.

THIS BIBLIOGRAPHY IS ORGANISED in three sections. The last two list the books and articles that I have found most useful for the project, which I have divided between primary and secondary works. These works appear in the footnotes only in short form. The footnotes also refer to newspapers, which are not listed here. Unless indicated in the relevant footnote, they can all be found in the standard electronic newspaper databases. Some standard reference works, such as the *Oxford Dictionary of National Biography*, are not listed below or in the footnotes, though I have used them a lot.

The first section lists the manuscript collections that I have consulted, plus some printed collections of official papers. For the collections cited most frequently in the footnotes, I have used abbreviations there. These abbreviations are indicated below. All abbreviations in footnotes relate to this category of material.

Manuscripts and Official Collections

NATIONAL ARCHIVES, KEW (FO [FOREIGN OFFICE] OR WO [WAR OFFICE])

FO 1	Abyssinia
FO 24	Egypt
FO 65	Russia
FO 78	Ottoman Empire
FO 195	Constantinople embassy
FO 226	Beirut
WO 1	Egypt and Malta

BRITISH LIBRARY (BL)

Aberdeen Papers, BL Add. MS.
Broughton Papers, Mss Eur. Cited as Broughton.
Hekekyan Papers, BL Add. MS.
Huskisson Papers, BL Add. MS.
India Office Records. Cited as IOR.
Layard Papers, BL Add. MS. Cited as LPBL.
Liverpool Papers, BL Add. MS.
Mackintosh Papers, BL Add. MS. Cited as MPBL.
Peel Papers, BL Add. MS.
Rich Papers, BL Add. MS. Cited as RPBL.
Thomas Perronet Thompson Papers (microform from Hull University Archives; Papers relating to the Persian Gulf and India [DTH/2]). Cited as TPTP.
Valentia Papers, BL Add. MS. Cited as VPBL.
Wellesley Papers. Cited as WP.

OTHER ARCHIVAL COLLECTIONS

Ainsworth Papers, Royal Geographical Society.

Blomfield Papers, Lambeth Palace Library.

Bonomi Papers, Cambridge University Library.

Castlereagh Papers, Public Record Office of Northern Ireland.

Donoughmore Papers, Public Record Office of Northern Ireland.

Dundas Papers, National Records of Scotland. Cited as DPNS.

Murray Papers, National Library of Scotland.

Ponsonby Papers, University of Durham. Cited as PPD.

Rawlinson Papers, Royal Geographical Society.

William Palmer Papers, Lambeth Palace Library. Cited as WPLP.

PRINTED OFFICIAL COLLECTIONS

Aitchison, C. U., ed. *A Collection of Treaties, Engagements, and Sanads Relating to India and Neighbouring Countries.* 13 vols. Calcutta: Government of India, 1909.

Appendix to the Report from the Select Committee of the House of Commons on the Affairs of the East-India Company, 16th August 1832. London: Court of Directors, 1833.

Bowring, John. "Report on Egypt and Candia." *Parliamentary Papers* (1840), vol. 21.

"Communications Respecting Turkey Made to Her Majesty's Government by the Emperor of Russia, with the Answers Returned to Them, January to April 1853." *Parliamentary Papers* (1854), vol. 71. Cited as *PP 1853*.

"Correspondence Respecting the Condition of Protestants in Turkey." *Parliamentary Papers* (1854), vol. 72. Cited as *PP* (1854).

"Correspondence Respecting the Condition of Protestants in Turkey." *Parliamentary Papers* (1851), vol. 57. Cited as *PP* (1851).

Douin, G., and E. C. Fawtier-Jones, eds. *L'Angleterre et l'Égypte: La politique mameluke.* 2 vols. Cairo: Société royale de géographie d'Égypte, 1929. Cited as *LPM*.

Historical Manuscripts Commission. *Report on the Manuscripts of J. B. Fortescue, Preserved at Dropmore.* 10 vols. London: HMSO, 1892–1927.

Hurewitz, J. C. *Diplomacy in the Near and Middle East: A Documentary Record: 1535–1914.* Princeton, NJ: D. Van Nostrand, 1956.

[Malet, A.]. *Précis Containing Information in Regard to the First Connection of the Hon'ble East India Company with Turkish Arabia.* Calcutta, 1874. British Library, IOR V/27/270/14.

The Persian Gulf Précis. 8 vols. Gerrards Cross, UK: Archive Editions, 1986. Cited as *PGP*.

"Report from the Select Committee on Steam Communication with India." *Parliamentary Papers* (1837), vol. 6. Cited as *PP* (1837).

"Report from the Select Committee on Steam Navigation to India." *Parliamentary Papers* (1834), vol. 14. Cited as *PP* (1834).

Other Primary Sources

Adair, Sir Robert. *The Negotiations for the Peace of the Dardanelles in 1808–9.* 2 vols. London: Longman, 1845.

Addison, Charles G. *Damascus and Palmyra: A Journey to the East.* 2 vols. London: Richard Bentley, 1838.

Ainsworth, William Francis. *The Claims of the Christian Aborigines of the Turkish or Osmanli Empire upon Civilized Nations.* London: Cunningham and Mortimer, 1843.

——. "Notes on a Journey from Constantinople, by Heraclea, to Angora, in the Autumn of 1838." *Journal of the Royal Geographical Society of London* 9 (1839): 216–76.

——. *A Personal Narrative of the Euphrates Expedition.* 2 vols. London: Kegan, Paul, Trench, 1888.

——. "The Termination of the Transport." *Ainsworth's Magazine* 6 (1844): 233–46.

——. *Travels and Researches in Asia Minor, Mesopotamia, Chaldea, and Armenia.* 2 vols. London: J. W. Parker, 1842.

Aiton, John. *The Drying up of the Euphrates, or, The Downfall of Turkey, Prophetically Considered.* London: Arthur Hall, 1853.

Alexander, James Edward. *Cleopatra's Needle, the Obelisk of Alexandria: Its Acquisition and Removal to England Described.* London: Chatto and Windus, 1879.

Anderson, Arthur. *Communications with India, China etc: Observations on the Practicability and Utility of Opening a Communication between the Red Sea and the Mediterranean.* London: Smith, Elder, 1843.

Andrew, William Patrick. *Letter to Viscount Palmerston on the Political Importance of the Euphrates Valley Railway.* London: Wm. H. Allen, 1857.

"Antiquity." In *Janus; or, The Edinburgh Literary Almanack,* 307–15. Edinburgh: Oliver and Boyd, 1826.

Arundell, Francis. *A Visit to the Seven Churches of Asia.* London: John Rodwell, 1828.

[Ashley, Lord]. "Lord Lindsay's Travels—State and Prospects of the Jews." *Quarterly Review* 63 (1839): 166–92.

Badger, George Percy. *The Nestorians and their Rituals: With the Narrative of a Mission to Mesopotamia and Coordistan in 1842–1844.* 2 vols. London: Joseph Masters, 1852.

Barker, Edward B. B. *Syria and Egypt under the Last Five Sultans of Turkey: Being Experiences, during Fifty Years, of Mr Consul-General Barker.* 2 vols. London: Samuel Tinsley, 1876.

Belzoni, Giovanni. *Narrative of the Operations and Recent Discoveries within the Pyramids, Temples, Tombs, and Excavations, in Egypt and Nubia.* London: John Murray, 1820.

Bentham, Jeremy. *The Correspondence of Jeremy Bentham.* Vol. 12, *July 1824 to June 1828.* Edited by Luke O'Sullivan and Catherine Fuller. Oxford: Clarendon, 2006.

——. "Essay on the Influence of Time and Place in Matters of Legislation." In *The Works of Jeremy Bentham,* 11 vols., edited by John Bowring, 1:169–94. Edinburgh: William Tait, 1838.

——. *Jeremy Bentham's Economic Writings.* Critical Edition. Edited by W. Stark. 3 vols. London: Allen and Unwin, 1952–54.

——. "Securities against Misrule." In *The Works of Jeremy Bentham,* 11 vols., edited by John Bowring, 8:555–600. Edinburgh: William Tait, 1843.

Bevan, Samuel. *Sand and Canvas: A Narrative of Adventures in Egypt, with a Sojourn among the Artists in Rome.* London: Charles Gilpin, 1849.

Blowitz, Henri Stephan de. *My Memoirs.* London: Edward Arnold, 1903.

Bonaparte, Napoleon. *Proclamations, Speeches and Letters of Napoleon Buonaparte during His Campaign of Egypt.* Translated by Trent Dailey-Chwalibog and Brittany Gignac. De Paul University, 2009. https://via.library.depaul.edu/cgi/viewcontent.cgi?article=1005&context=napoleon.

Bowen, John. *Memorials of John Bowen . . . Compiled from His Letters and Journals by His Sister.* London: J. Nisbet, 1862.

Bowring, John. "Anglo-Turkish War: Egypt and Syria." *Westminster Review* 35 (1841): 187–224.

——. *Autobiographical Recollections of Sir John Bowring.* Edited by L. B. Bowring. London: H. S. King, 1877.

Brougham, Henry. *Brougham and His Early Friends: Letters to James Loch 1798–1809.* Edited by R.H.M. Buddle Atkinson and G. A. Jackson. 3 vols. London, 1908.

———. *An Inquiry into the Colonial Policy of the European Powers.* 2 vols. Edinburgh: E. Balfour, 1803.

Bruce, James. *Bruce's Travels and Adventures in Abyssinia.* Edited by J. M. Clingan. Edinburgh: A. and C. Black, 1860.

Buckingham, James Silk. *Autobiography of James Silk Buckingham: Including His Voyages, Travels, Adventures, Speculations, Successes and Failures.* 2 vols. London: Longman, 1855.

———. *Travels in Mesopotamia.* 2 vols. London: Henry Colburn, 1827.

———. *Travels in Palestine, through the Countries of Bashan and Gilead, East of the River Jordan.* London: Longman, 1821.

Buckingham and Chandos, Duke of. *Memoirs of the Court and Cabinets of George III.* 4 vols. London: Hurst and Blackett, 1853–55.

Bunbury, Sir Henry. *Narratives of Some Passages in the Great War with France from 1799 to 1810.* London: Richard Bentley, 1854.

Burckhardt, John Lewis. *Travels in Arabia, Comprehending an Account of Those Territories in Hedjaz which the Mohammedans Regard as Sacred.* London: Henry Colburn, 1829.

———. *Travels in Syria and the Holy Land.* London: John Murray, 1822.

[Burgess, Thomas]. *Motives to the Study of Hebrew.* London: T. Lunn, 1814.

Burton, Richard F. *First Footsteps in East Africa, or, An Exploration of Harar.* London: Tylston and Edwards, 1894.

———. *Personal Narrative of a Pilgrimage to El-Medinah and Meccah.* 3 vols. London: Longman, 1855–56.

Carlisle, Earl of. *Diary in Turkish and Greek Waters.* London: Longman, 1854.

Carlyle, Thomas. "Lecture II: The Hero as Prophet." In *On Heroes, Hero-Worship and the Heroic in History*, 39–71. London: Chapman and Hall, 1840.

Carne, John. *Letters from the East.* London: Henry Colburn, 1826.

Castlereagh, Viscount. *Correspondence, Despatches, and Other Papers of Viscount Castlereagh.* Vol. 5. Edited by Marquess of Londonderry. London: William Shoberl, 1851.

Chesney, Francis Rawdon. *The Expedition for the Survey of the Rivers Euphrates and Tigris, Carried on by Order of the British Government, in the Years 1835, 1836, and 1837.* 2 vols. London: Longman, 1850.

———. *The Russo-Ottoman Campaigns of 1828 and 1829.* 3rd ed. London: Smith, Elder, 1854.

———. "A Special Meeting of the Society, held on Monday, the 14th of May, 1838." Speech given at the Special Meeting. *Journal of the Royal Geographical Society of London* 8 (1838): xiii–xv.

Churchill, C. H. *Mount Lebanon: A Ten Years' Residence from 1842 to 1852.* 3rd ed. 3 vols. London: Saunders and Otley, 1853.

Clarke, Edward Daniel. *Travels in Various Countries of Europe, Asia and Africa: Part the Second: Greece, Egypt and the Holy Land.* 3 vols. London: Cadell and Davies, 1812–16.

[Cobden, Richard]. *Russia.* Reprinted in *The Political Writings of Richard Cobden*, 2 vols., 1:122–272. London: T. Fisher Unwin, 1903.

Curzon, Robert. *Visits to Monasteries in the Levant.* 6th ed. London: John Murray, 1881.

[Dawson-Damer, George Lionel]. *Thoughts on the Question of the East, Suggested by a Tour in Turkey, Syria, and Egypt.* London: W. Clowes, 1840.

Description of a View of the Bombardment of St. Jean d'Acre, with the City and Surrounding Country, Now Exhibiting at the Panorama, Leicester Sq. Painted by Robert Burford. London: Geo. Nichols, 1841.

Dicey, Edward. "Our Route to India." *Nineteenth Century* 1 (June 1877): 665–85.

Dickinson, John. *India: Its Government under a Bureaucracy.* London: Saunders and Stanford, 1853.

Disraeli, Benjamin. *Tancred; or, The New Crusade.* 3 vols. London: Henry Colburn, 1847.

Elgin, Lady. *The Letters of Mary Nisbet of Dirleton Countess of Elgin.* Edited by Nisbet Hamilton Grant. London: John Murray, 1926.

Ellenborough, Lord. *A Political Diary 1828–1830.* Edited by Lord Colchester. 2 vols. London: Richard Bentley, 1881.

Elwood, Anne Katharine. *Narrative of a Journey Overland from England, by the Continent of Europe, Egypt, and the Red Sea, to India.* 2 vols. London: Henry Colburn and Richard Bentley, 1830.

Evans, George de Lacy. *On the Designs of Russia.* London: John Murray, 1828.

Faber, G. S. *The Predicted Downfall of the Turkish Power: The Preparation for the Return of the Ten Tribes.* London: Thomas Bosworth, 1853.

Farman, Samuel. *Constantinople in Connexion with the Present War.* London: Wertheim and Macintosh, 1855.

Finn, James. *Stirring Times, or Records from Jerusalem Consular Chronicles of 1853 to 1856.* 2 vols. London: C. Kegan Paul, 1878.

———. *A View from Jerusalem 1849–1858: The Consular Diary of James and Elizabeth Anne Finn.* Edited by Arnold Blumberg. Rutherford, NJ: Fairleigh Dickinson University Press, 1980.

Fitzclarence, George. *Journal of a Route across India, through Egypt, to England in the Latter End of the Year 1817, and the Beginning of 1818.* London: John Murray, 1819.

Fletcher, James P. *Notes from Nineveh, and Travels in Mesopotamia, Assyria, and Syria.* 2 vols. London: Henry Colburn, 1850.

Forbes, Frederick. "A Visit to the Sinjár Hills in 1838, with Some Account of the Sect of Yezídís, &c." *Journal of the Royal Geographical Society of London* 9 (1839): 409–30.

Fox, Caroline. *Memories of Old Friends: Being Extracts from the Journals and Letters of Caroline Fox . . . from 1835 to 1871.* 2nd ed. Edited by Horace N. Pym. 2 vols. London: Smith, Elder, 1882.

Fraser, James Baillie. "Memorandum on the Present Condition of the Pachalic of Bagdad and the Means It Possesses of Renovation and Improvement." November 12, 1834. Appendix E of [Malet], *Précis,* xxxviii–xlix.

———. *Travels in Koordistan, Mesopotamia, etc.* 2 vols. London: Richard Bentley, 1840.

Fremantle, William R. *The Eastern Churches: An Address to the Lord Bishop of Lincoln.* London: James Nisbet, 1840.

Gawler, George. *Syria and Its Near Prospects.* London: Hamilton, Adams, 1853.

[Gladstone, W. E.]. "The War and the Peace." *Gentleman's Magazine* 1 (1856): 140–55.

Griffith, George, and Lucinda Darby Griffith. *A Journey across the Desert from Ceylon to Marseilles.* 2 vols. London: Henry Colburn, 1845.

Groves, Anthony N. *Journal of a Residence at Bagdad, during the Years 1830 and 1831.* London: James Nesbit, 1832.

Haines, Stafford B. "Memoir of the South and East Coasts of Arabia." Parts 1 and 2. *Journal of the Royal Geographical Society of London* 9 (1839): 125–57, and 15 (1845): 104–59.

Hamilton, William. *Remarks on Several Parts of Turkey.* Part 1, *Aegyptiaca: An Account of the Antient and Modern State of Egypt, as Obtained in the Years 1801, 1802.* London: T. Payne, 1809.

Harris, W. Cornwallis. *The Highlands of Aethiopia.* 3 vols. London: Longman, 1844.

———. *The Wild Sports of Southern Africa.* London: John Murray, 1839.

[Harrison], B., ed. *Christianity in Egypt: Letters and Papers Concerning the Coptic Church, in Relation to the Church of England during the Primacy of Archbishop Howley, 1836–1848.* London: Association for the Furtherance of Christianity in Egypt, 1883.

Head, C. F. *Eastern and Egyptian Scenery, Ruins etc.* London: Smith, Elder, 1833.

Hechler, William H., ed. *The Jerusalem Bishopric: Documents*. 2 vols. London: W. H. Trübner, 1883.

Henniker, Frederick. *Notes, during a Visit to Egypt, Nubia, the Oasis, Mount Sinai, and Jerusalem*. London: John Murray, 1823.

Herschell, Ridley H. *A Visit to My Father-Land, Being Notes of a Journey to Syria and Palestine in 1843*. 5th ed. London: J. Unwin, 1845.

[Holme, Frederick]. "Occupation of Aden." *Blackwood's Magazine* 53 (1843): 484–95.

Hope, Thomas. *Anastasius: or, Memoirs of a Greek: Written at the Close of the Eighteenth Century*. 3 vols. Long Riders' Guild Press, 2008. First published 1819 by John Murray (London).

Hornby, Edmund. *An Autobiography*. London: Constable, 1929.

Horne, Thomas Hartwell. *Landscape Illustrations of the Bible*. 2 vols. London: John Murray, 1836.

Hughes Thomas, R., ed. *Arabian Gulf Intelligence: Selections from the Records of the Bombay Government, New Series, No. XXIV, 1856, Concerning Arabia, Bahrain, Kuwait, Muscat and Oman, Qatar, United Arab Emirates and the Islands of the Gulf*. Cambridge, UK: Oleander, 1985.

Hulton, Jessop. *South Arabia: The "Palinurus" Journals*. Edited by W. A. Hulton. Cambridge, UK: Oleander, 2003.

Huskisson, William. *Substance of Two Speeches, Delivered in the House of Commons, on the 21st and 25th of March 1825 . . . Respecting the Colonial Policy and Foreign Commerce of the Country*. 2nd ed. London: J. Hatchard, 1825.

Hutton, James. *Selections from the Letters and Correspondence of Sir James Bland Burges*. London: John Murray, 1885.

Hyamson, Albert M., ed. *The British Consulate in Jerusalem in Relation to the Jews of Palestine, 1838–1914*. 2 vols. London: Jewish Historical Society, 1939–41.

Irby, Charles Leonard, and James Mangles. *Travels in Egypt and Nubia, Syria, and the Holy Land*. London: John Murray, 1845.

[Jebb, John]. "Forster on Arabia." *Quarterly Review* 74 (1844): 325–58.

Jochmus, Augustus von. *The Syrian War and the Decline of the Ottoman Empire, 1840–1848*. Berlin: Albert Cohn, 1883.

[Jolliffe, Thomas Robert]. *Letters from Palestine, Descriptive of a Tour through Galilee and Judaea, to Which are Added, Letters from Egypt*. 2nd ed. London: James Black, 1820.

Jones, James Felix. *Memoirs of Baghdad, Kurdistan and Turkish Arabia*. Cambridge, UK: Cambridge Archive Editions, 1998.

Jones, Owen, and Joseph Bonomi. *Description of the Egyptian Court Erected in the Crystal Palace*. London: Bradbury and Evans, 1854.

Jones Brydges, Harford. *An Account of the Transactions of His Majesty's Mission to the Court of Persia in the Years 1807–1811, to Which is Appended a Brief History of the Wahauby*. 2 vols. London: James Bohn, 1834.

Jowett, William. *Christian Researches in Syria and the Holy Land, in 1823 and 1824, in Furtherance of the Objects of the Church Missionary Society*. London: Church Missionary Society, 1825.

——. *Christian Researches in the Mediterranean, from 1815 to 1820*. London: Church Missionary Society, 1822.

Kayat, Assaad. *A Voice from Lebanon, with the Life and Travels of Assaad Y. Kayat*. London: Madden, 1847.

Keith, Alexander. *Evidence of the Truth of the Christian Religion, Derived from the Literal Fulfilment of Prophecy*. 36th ed. Edinburgh: William Whyte, 1848.

——. *The Land of Israel According to the Covenant with Abraham, with Isaac, and with Jacob*. Edinburgh: William Whyte, 1843.

——. *Scripture versus Stanley: or, A Refutation of the Rev. A. P. Stanley's Principle of the Poetical Interpretation of Scripture*. London: T. Nelson, 1861.

Kelly, Walter Keating. *Syria and the Holy Land, Their Scenery and Their People*. London: Chapman and Hall, 1844.

Kempthorne, G. B. "Notes Made on a Survey along the Eastern Shores of the Persian Gulf in 1828." *Journal of the Royal Geographical Society of London* 5 (1835): 263–85.

Kinglake, Alexander. *Eothen, or Traces of Travel Brought Home from the East*. Oxford: Oxford University Press, 1982. First published 1844 by John Ollivier (London).

Kingsley, Charles. *Alexandria and Her Schools: Four Lectures*. Cambridge, UK: Macmillan, 1854.

Lane, Edward William. *An Account of the Manners and Customs of the Modern Egyptians*. 2 vols. London: Charles Knight, 1836.

Laughton, J. K. *Memoirs of the Life and Correspondence of Henry Reeve*. 2 vols. London: Longman, 1898.

Layard, Austen Henry. *Autobiography and Letters from His Childhood to His Appointment as HM Ambassador at Madrid*. Edited by W. N. Bruce. 2 vols. London: John Murray, 1903.

——. *Discoveries in the Ruins of Nineveh and Babylon*. London: John Murray, 1853.

——. *Early Adventures in Persia, Susiana, and Babylonia*. 2 vols. London: John Murray, 1887.

——. *Nineveh and Its Remains*. 2 vols. London: John Murray, 1849.

——. *The Nineveh Court at the Crystal Palace*. London: Bradbury and Evans, 1854.

[——]. "The Turks and the Greeks." *Quarterly Review* 94 (1854): 509–58.

Leech, Harry Harewood. *Letters of a Sentimental Idler*. New York: D. Appleton, 1869.

Leibniz, Gottfried Wilhelm von. *A Summary Account of Leibnitz's Memoir, Addressed to Lewis the Fourteenth, Recommending to that Monarch, the Conquest of Egypt, as Conducive to the Establishing a Supreme Authority over the Governments of Europe*. London: Hatchard, 1803.

Lindsay, Lord. *Letters on Egypt, Edom and the Holy Land*. 2 vols. London: Henry Colburn, 1838.

Loftus, William Kennett. *Travels and Researches in Chaldea and Susiana . . . in 1849–52*. London: James Nisbet, 1857.

London's Roll of Fame: Being Complimentary Votes and Addresses from the City of London. London: Cassell, 1884.

Lynch, H. Blosse. "Note Accompanying a Survey of the Tigris, between Ctesiphon and Mósul." *Journal of the Royal Geographical Society of London* 9 (1839): 441–42.

——. "Note on a Part of the River Tigris, between Baghdád and Sámarrah." *Journal of the Royal Geographical Society of London* 9 (1839): 471–76.

Lynch, Thomas Kerr. *Across Mesopotamia to India by the Euphrates Valley*. London: Waterlow, 1879.

Macfarlane, Charles. *Kismet; or, The Doom of Turkey*. London: Thomas Bosworth, 1853.

——. *Turkey and Its Destiny: The Result of Journeys Made in 1847 and 1848 to Examine into the State of That Country*. 2 vols. London: John Murray, 1850.

Mackay, Robert William. *A Sketch of the Rise and Progress of Christianity*. London: John Chapman, 1854.

Mackinnon, W. A. *History of Civilisation*. 2 vols. London: Longman, 1846.

Mackintosh, Robert James. *Memoirs of the Life of Sir James Mackintosh*. 2 vols. London: Edward Moxon, 1835.

[Macvicar, J. G.]. *The Catholic Spirit of True Religion*. London: Scott, Webster, and Geary, 1840.

Madden, Richard R. *Egypt and Mohammed Ali, Illustrative of the Condition of His Slaves and Subjects*. London: Hamilton, Adams, 1841.

Markham, Clements R. *A Memoir on the Indian Surveys*. London: Allen, 1871.

Martineau, Harriet. *Eastern Life: Present and Past*. 3 vols. London: Edward Moxon, 1848.

———. *Harriet Martineau's Autobiography*. 3 vols. London: Smith, Elder, 1877.

Maundrell, Henry. *A Journey from Aleppo to Jerusalem, at Easter A.D. 1697*. Oxford, 1703.

McCoan, J. C. *Egypt as It Is*. London: Cassell, Petter and Galpin, 1877.

[McNeill, John]. "Invasion of India." *Blackwood's Magazine* 22 (1827): 267–80.

Mignan, Robert. *Travels in Chaldaea, Including a Journey from Bussorah to Bagdad, Hillah, and Babylon*. London: Henry Colburn, 1829.

[Milman, H. H.]. "The Turkish Empire." *Quarterly Review* 49 (1833): 283–322.

Mirza Abu Taleb. *Westward Bound: Travels of Mirza Abu Taleb*. Edited by Mushirul Hasan. Oxford: Oxford University Press, 2005.

Montefiore, Moses. *Diaries of Sir Moses and Lady Montefiore*. Edited by L. Loewe. 2 vols. London: Griffith, Farran, 1890.

Morier, John Philip. *Memoir of a Campaign with the Ottoman Army in Egypt, from February to July 1800*. London, 1801.

[Murray, Grenville]. *The Roving Englishman in Turkey: Sketches from Life*. London: G. Routledge, 1855.

Napier, Sir Charles. *The War in Syria*. 2 vols. London: John W. Parker, 1842.

Napier, Elers. *Reminiscences of Syria, and Fragments of a Journal and Letters from the Holy Land*. 2 vols. London: T. C. Newby, 1843.

Narrative of a Journey from Southampton to Bombay . . . Performed between the 12th October and the 13th December 1842. Madras: B. Lacey, 1843.

Neale, F. A. *Eight Years in Syria, Palestine and Asia Minor from 1842 to 1850*. 2 vols. London: Colburn, 1851.

———. *Islamism: Its Rise and Its Progress*. 2 vols. London: James Madden, 1854.

[Neale, John Mason]. *Documents Connected with the Foundation of the Anglican Bishopric in Jerusalem: And with the Protest against Bishop Gobat's Proselytism*. London: Joseph Masters, 1853.

Newman, Francis William. *Personal Narrative, in Letters, Principally from Turkey, in the Years 1830–3*. London: Holyoake, 1856.

Newman, John P. *The Thrones and Palaces of Babylon and Nineveh*. New York: Harper and Brothers, 1876.

Nightingale, Florence. *Collected Works of Florence Nightingale: On Mysticism and Eastern Religions*. Edited by Gérard Vallée. Waterloo, ON: Wilfrid Laurier University Press, 2003.

———. *Letters from Egypt: A Journey on the Nile 1849–1850*. Edited by Anthony Sattin. London: Barrie and Jenkins, 1987.

Pardoe, Julia. *The City of the Sultan, and Domestic Manners of the Turks in 1836*. 2 vols. London: Henry Colburn, 1837.

[Peacock, Thomas Love]. "On Steam Navigation to India." *Edinburgh Review* 60 (1835): 445–82.

[Platt, Miss]. *Journal of a Tour through Egypt, the Peninsula of Sinai, and the Holy Land, in 1838, 1839*. 2 vols. London, 1841.

Playfair, R. L. *A History of Arabia Felix or Yemen, from the Commencement of the Christian Era to the Present Time; Including an Account of the British Settlement of Aden*. Bombay: Education Society's Press, 1859.

"Pompey's Pillar." *Naval Chronicle* 27 (1812): 111.

Popham, Home Riggs. *Concise Statement Relative to the Treatment of Sir Home Popham since His Return from the Red Sea*. London: John Stockdale, 1805.

Reid, John. *Turkey and the Turks: Being the Present State of the Ottoman Empire*. London: Robert Tyas, 1840.

"Report of a Committee of the House of Commons, to Whom the Petition of the Trustees of the British Museum, Relative to Mr. Rich's Collection of Manuscripts, Antiquities, and Coins, Was Referred." *Gentleman's Magazine* 95 (1825): 326–28.

Rich, Claudius James. *Narrative of a Residence in Koordistan, and on the Site of Ancient Nineveh.* Edited by Mary Rich. 2 vols. London: James Duncan, 1836.

Rivaz, F. F. *A Proposal, by Which Two Essential Objects Would Be Simultaneously Attained: Firstly, the Complete Security of the British Territories in India, Whatever Possessors Egypt and Malta Might Eventually Have; Secondly, a New, Extensive, and Profitable, Channel of Commerce Opened, without Infringing on the Effective Trade, but by a Simple Modification in the East-India Company's Charter.* London: J. Asperne, 1813.

Robinson, Edward, and Eli Smith. *Biblical Researches in Palestine, Mount Sinai, and Arabia Petræa: A Journal of Travels in the Year 1838.* 3 vols. London: John Murray, 1841.

Rose, Sir George Henry. *The Early Spread of Circumcision.* London: J. Hatchard, 1846.

Ross, Henry James. *Letters from the East 1837–1857.* Edited by Janet Ross. London: Dent, 1902.

Ross, John. "Notes on Two Journeys from Baghdád to the Ruins of Al-Hadhr, in Mesopotamia, in 1836 and 1837." *Journal of the Royal Geographical Society of London* 9 (1839): 443–70.

The Route of the Overland Mail to India, from Southampton to Calcutta. London, 1852.

Russell, William Howard. *My Diary in India, in the Year 1858-9.* 2 vols. London: Routledge, 1860.

Salibi, Kamal, and Yusuf K. Khoury, eds. *The Missionary Herald: Reports from Northern Iraq 1833–1870.* 3 vols. Amman: Royal Institute for Inter-Faith Studies, 1997.

——, eds. *The Missionary Herald: Reports from Ottoman Syria 1819–1870.* 5 vols. Amman: Royal Institute for Inter-Faith Studies, 1995.

Salt, Henry. *A Voyage to Abyssinia, and Travels into the Interior of that Country, Executed under the Orders of the British Government, in the Years 1809 and 1810.* London: F. C. and J. Rivington, 1814.

Selby, W. B. "Account of the Ascent of the Kárún and Dizful Rivers, and the Ab-í-Gargar Canal, to Shuster." *Journal of the Royal Geographical Society* 14 (1844): 219–46.

[Selim Aga]. *Africa Considered in Its Social and Political Condition with a Plan for the Amelioration of Its Inhabitants.* London, 1853.

Senior, Nassau William. *Conversations and Journals in Egypt and Malta.* Edited by M.C.M. Simpson. 2 vols. London: Sampson Low, 1882.

Seton, David. *The Journals of David Seton in the Gulf, 1800–1809.* Edited by Sultan Muhammad al-Qasimi. Exeter, UK: University of Exeter Press, 1995.

Sheil, Lady. *Glimpses of Life and Manners in Persia.* London: John Murray, 1856.

"Sir Home Popham's Embassy to the States of Arabia, and to the Pacha of Egypt." *Literary Journal* 2 (July–December 1803): 125–28, 249–53, 443–46.

Skinner, Thomas. *Adventures during a Journey Overland to India, by Way of Egypt, Syria and the Holy Land.* 2 vols. London: Richard Bentley, 1836.

Slade, Adolphus. *The Sultan and Mehemet Ali, or, The Present Crisis in Turkey.* London: Saunders and Otley, 1839.

Smith, Albert. *A Hand-Book to Mr. Albert Smith's Entertainment, Entitled the "Overland Mail."* London, 1850.

Smith, Edward. *Sailing Directions for the Coast of Syria from Ancient Joppa to the Gulf of Iskanderoon.* London: W. Eden, 1840.

Society for Promoting Female Education in China, India, and the East. *History of the Society for Promoting Female Education in the East, etc.* London: Edward Suter, 1847.

Southey, Robert [Don Manuel Alvarez Espriella, pseud.]. *Letters from England.* 2nd ed. 3 vols. London: Longman, 1808.

Southgate, Horatio. *Narrative of a Tour through Armenia, Kurdistan, Persia and Mesopotamia.* 2 vols. New York: D. Appleton, 1840.

———. *Narrative of a Visit to the Syrian (Jacobite) Church of Mesopotamia.* New York: D. Appleton, 1844.

Spencer, Earl. *Private Papers of George, Second Earl Spencer, First Lord of the Admiralty 1794–1801.* Edited by H. W. Richmond. 4 vols. London: Navy Records Society, 1913–24.

Spilsbury, Francis B. *Picturesque Scenery in the Holy Land and Syria, Delineated during the Campaigns of 1799 and 1800.* London: G. S. Tregear, 1823.

Stanley, Arthur Penrhyn. *Sermons Preached Mostly in Canterbury Cathedral.* London: John Murray, 1860.

St. John, James Augustus. *Egypt, and Mohammed Ali; or, Travels in the Valley of the Nile.* 2 vols. London: Longman, 1834.

———. *Egypt and Nubia: Their Scenery and Their People.* London: Chapman and Hall, 1845.

[———]. "The Surveys of the Indian Navy." *Foreign Quarterly Review* 35 (1845): 454–88.

Stocqueler, J. H. *Fifteen Months' Pilgrimage through Untrodden Tracts of Khuzistan and Persia in a Journey from India to England . . . in the Years 1831 to 1832.* 2 vols. London: Saunders and Otley, 1832.

———. *The Memoirs of a Journalist.* Bombay: *Times of India,* 1873.

Tattam, Henry. *A Defence of the Church of England against the Attacks of a Roman-Catholic Priest.* London: Hatchard and Son, 1843.

[Taylor, William Cooke]. "Mohammed and Mohammedanism." *Foreign Quarterly Review* 12 (1833): 192–208.

Temple, Emily Mary, Viscountess Palmerston. *The Letters of Lady Palmerston.* Edited by Tresham Lever. London: John Murray, 1957.

Temple, Henry John, Viscount Palmerston. *Speech of Lord Viscount Palmerston to the Electors of Tiverton, on the 31st July, 1847.* London; Smith, Elder, 1847.

Thackeray, William M. *Notes of a Journey from Cornhill to Grand Cairo, by Mr. M. A. Titmarsh.* London: Chapman and Hall, 1846.

Thompson, Thomas Perronet. "Arabs and Persians." *Westminster Review* 5 (1826): 202–48.

Tomlinson, George. *Report of a Journey to the Levant, Addressed to His Grace the Archbishop of Canterbury.* London: Gilbert and Rivington, 1841.

Trollope, Anthony. *The Bertrams.* Oxford: Oxford University Press, 1991.

Turner, William. *Journal of a Tour in the Levant.* 3 vols. London: John Murray, 1820.

Urquhart, David. *The Spirit of the East, Illustrated in a Journal of Travels through Roumeli during an Eventful Period.* 2 vols. London: Henry Colburn, 1838.

———. *Turkey and Its Resources: Its Municipal Organization and Free Trade.* London: Saunders and Otley, 1833.

Valentia, George, Viscount. *Voyages and Travels to India, Ceylon, the Red Sea, Abyssinia, and Egypt, in the Years 1802, 1803, 1804, 1805, and 1806.* 4 vols. London: William Miller, 1809–11.

Victoria, Queen of Great Britain. *Further Letters of Queen Victoria, from the Archives of the House of Brandenburg-Prussia.* Edited by Hector Bolitho. London: Thornton Butterworth, 1938.

Vincent, William, ed. *The Periplus of the Erythrean Sea: Containing an Account of the Navigation of the Ancients, from the Sea of Suez to the Coast of Zanguebar.* 2 vols. London: Cadell and Davies, 1800–5.

Waghorn, Thomas. *Egypt as It Is in 1837.* London: Smith, Elder, 1837.

Walpole, Frederick. *The Ansayrii (or Assassins) with Travels in the Further East, in 1850–51.* 3 vols. London: Richard Bentley, 1851.

Walpole, Robert, ed. *Memoirs Relating to European and Asiatic Turkey: Edited from Manuscript Journals.* London: Longman, 1817.

Walsh, Robert. *A Residence at Constantinople during a Period Including the Commencement, Progress and Termination of the Greek and Turkish Revolutions.* 2 vols. London: Frederick Westley and A. H. Davis, 1836.

Walsh, Thomas. *Journal of the Late Campaign in Egypt.* London: Cadell and Davies, 1803.

Warburton, Eliot. *The Crescent and the Cross; or, Romance and Realities of Eastern Travel.* 3rd ed. 2 vols. London: Henry Colburn, 1845.

Wellsted, J. Raymond. "Memoir on the Island of Socotra." *Journal of the Royal Geographical Society of London* 5 (1835): 129–229.

——. "Narrative of a Journey from the Tower of Ba-l-haff, on the Southern Coast of Arabia to the Ruins of Nakab el Hajar, in April 1835." *Journal of the Royal Geographical Society of London* 7 (1837): 20–34.

——. "Observations on the Coast of Arabia between Ras Mohammed and Jiddah." *Journal of the Royal Geographical Society of London* 6 (1836): 51–96.

——. *Travels in Arabia.* 2 vols. London: John Murray, 1838.

——. *Travels to the City of the Caliphs, along the Shores of the Persian Gulf and the Mediterranean.* 2 vols. London: Henry Colburn, 1840.

White, Charles. *Three Years in Constantinople; or, Domestic Manners of the Turks in 1844.* 3 vols. London: Henry Colburn, 1845.

Whitelock, H. H. "Descriptive Sketch of the Islands and Coast Situated at the Entrance of the Persian Gulf." *Journal of the Royal Geographical Society of London* 8 (1838): 170–84.

Wilkinson, J. Gardner. *Manners and Customs of the Ancient Egyptians.* 3 vols. London: John Murray, 1837.

[——]. *Three Letters on the Policy of England towards the Porte and Mohammed Ali.* London: John Murray, 1840.

——. *Topography of Thebes, and General View of Egypt.* London: John Murray, 1835.

Wilson, Daniel. *Bishop Wilson's Journal Letters, Addressed to his Family during the First Nine Years of his Indian Episcopate.* Edited by Daniel Wilson. London: J. Nisbet, 1863.

Wilson, Erasmus. *Cleopatra's Needle: With Brief Notes on Egypt and Egyptian Obelisks.* London: Brain, 1877.

Wilson, Robert Thomas. *History of the British Expedition to Egypt: To Which Is Subjoined a Sketch of the Present State of that Country and Its Means of Defence.* 2nd ed. London: T. Egerton, 1803.

Wittman, William. *Travels in Turkey, Asia Minor, Syria, and across the Desert into Egypt during the Years 1799, 1800, and 1801.* London: Richard Phillips, 1803.

Wolff, Joseph. *Missionary Journal of the Rev. Joseph Wolff, Missionary to the Jews.* Vol. 3. London: James Duncan, 1829.

Wood, Richard. *The Early Correspondence of Richard Wood 1831–1841.* Edited by A. B. Cunningham. London: Royal Historical Society, 1966.

Biographies and Secondary Works

Abir, Mordechai. "The 'Arab Rebellion' of Amir Ghalib of Mecca, 1788–1813." *Middle Eastern Studies* 7 (1971): 185–200.

——. *Ethiopia: The Era of the Princes; The Challenge of Islam and the Reunification of the Christian Empire 1769–1855.* London: Longman, 1968.

——. "Modernisation, Reaction and Muhammad Ali's 'Empire.'" *Middle Eastern Studies* 13 (1977): 295–313.

Aboona, Hirmis. *Assyrians, Kurds, and Ottomans: Intercommunal Relations on the Periphery of the Ottoman Empire.* Amherst, NY: Cambria, 2008.

Abu-Manneh, Butrus. "The Islamic Roots of the Gülhane Rescript." *Die Welt des Islams* 34 (1994): 173–203.

Ahmed, Leila. *Edward W. Lane: A Study of His Life and Works and of British Ideas of the Middle East in the Nineteenth Century*. London: Longman, 1978.

Aksan, Virginia H. *Ottoman Wars, 1700–1870: An Empire Besieged*. Harlow, UK: Longman, 2007.

Alborn, Timothy L. *Conceiving Companies: Joint-Stock Politics in Victorian England*. London: Routledge, 1998.

Alexander, Constance M. *Baghdad in Bygone Days, from the Journals and Correspondence of Claudius Rich, Traveller, Artist, Linguist, Antiquary, and British Resident at Baghdad, 1808–1821*. London: John Murray, 1928.

Alexander, Philip. "Why Did Lord Balfour back the Balfour Declaration?" *Jewish Historical Studies* 49 (2017): 188–214.

Allen, W.O.B., and Edmund McClure. *Two Hundred Years: The History of the Society for Promoting Christian Knowledge 1698–1898*. London: SPCK, 1898.

Altick, Richard D. *The Shows of London*. Cambridge, MA: Belknapp, 1978.

Anderson, M. S. *The Eastern Question, 1774–1923*. London: Macmillan, 1966.

Anderson, Olive. "The Reactions of Church and Dissent towards the Crimean War." *Journal of Ecclesiastical History* 16 (1965): 209–20.

Anscombe, Frederick F. "Islam and the Age of Ottoman Reform." *Past & Present* 208 (2010): 159–89.

——. *State, Faith, and Nation in Ottoman and Post-Ottoman Lands*. Cambridge: Cambridge University Press, 2014.

Arsan, Andrew. "'There Is, in the Heart of Asia, . . . an Entirely French Population': France, Mount Lebanon, and the Workings of Affective Empire in the Mediterranean, 1830–1920." In *French Mediterraneans: Transnational and Imperial Histories*, edited by Patricia M. E. Lorcin and Todd Shepard, 76–100. Lincoln: University of Nebraska Press, 2016.

Ateş, Sabri. *The Ottoman-Iranian Borderlands: Making a Boundary, 1843–1914*. Cambridge: Cambridge University Press, 2013.

Atkins, Gareth. *Converting Britannia: Evangelicals and British Public Life, 1770–1840*. Woodbridge, UK: Boydell, 2019.

Atmaca, Metin. "Negotiating Political Power in the Early Modern Middle East: Kurdish Emirates between the Ottoman Empire and Iranian Dynasties (Sixteenth to Nineteenth Centuries)." In *The Cambridge History of the Kurds*, edited by Hamit Bozarslan, Cengiz Gunes, and Veli Yadirgi, 45–72. Cambridge: Cambridge University Press, 2021.

——. "Resistance to Centralisation in the Ottoman Periphery: The Kurdish Baban and Bohtan Emirates." *Middle Eastern Studies* 5 (2019): 519–39.

Aydin, Cemil. *The Idea of the Muslim World: A Global Intellectual History*. Cambridge, MA: Harvard University Press, 2017.

——. *The Politics of Anti-Westernism in Asia*. New York: Columbia University Press, 2007.

Aykut, Ebru. "Judicial Reforms, Sharia Law, and the Death Penalty in the Late Ottoman Empire." *Journal of the Ottoman and Turkish Studies Association* 4 (2017): 7–29.

Bailey, Frank Edgar. *British Policy and the Turkish Reform Movement: A Study in Anglo-Turkish Relations 1826–1853*. Cambridge, MA: Harvard University Press, 1942.

Baldry, John. "The Yamani Island of Kamaran during the Napoleonic Wars." *Middle Eastern Studies* 16 (1980): 246–66.

Barkey, Karen. "Aspects of Legal Pluralism in the Ottoman Empire." In *Legal Pluralism and Empires, 1500–1850*, edited by Lauren Benton and Richard Ross, 83–107. New York: New York University Press, 2013.

Barr, James. *A Line in the Sand: Britain, France and the Struggle that Shaped the Middle East*. London; Simon and Schuster, 2012.

Barrow, John. *The Life and Correspondence of Admiral Sir William Sidney Smith*. 2 vols. London: Richard Bentley, 1848.

Bartle, G. F. "Bowring and the Near Eastern Crisis of 1838–1840." *English Historical Review* 79 (1964): 761–74.

Baruzi, J. *Leibniz et l'Organisation religieuse de la terre*. Paris: Félix Alcan, 1907.

Bar-Yosef, Eitan. *The Holy Land in English Culture 1799–1917: Palestine and the Question of Orientalism*. Oxford: Clarendon, 2005.

Bebbington, David W. *Evangelicalism in Modern Britain: A History from the 1730s to the 1980s*. London: Unwin Hyman, 1989.

Ben-Artzi, Yossi. "Jewish Rural Settlement in Cyprus 1882–1935: A 'Springboard' or a Destiny?" *Jewish History* 21 (2007): 361–83.

Benton, Lauren. *Law and Colonial Cultures: Legal Regimes in World History, 1400–1900*. Cambridge: Cambridge University Press, 2002.

———. *Search for Sovereignty: Law and Geography in European Empires, 1400–1900*. Cambridge: Cambridge University Press, 2010.

Benton, Lauren, and Lisa Ford. *Rage for Order: The British Empire and the Origins of International Law, 1800–1850*. Cambridge, MA: Harvard University Press, 2016.

Berridge, G. R. *British Diplomacy in Turkey, 1583 to the Present*. Boston, MA: Martinus Nijhoff, 2009.

Bhacker, M. Reda. *Trade and Empire in Muscat and Zanzibar: Roots of British Domination*. London: Routledge, 1992.

Bierman, Irene A., ed. *Napoleon in Egypt*. Reading, UK: Ithaca, 2003.

Bird, Michael. *Samuel Shepheard of Cairo: A Portrait*. London; Michael Joseph, 1957.

Bohrer, Frederick N. *Orientalism and Visual Culture: Imagining Mesopotamia in Nineteenth-Century Europe*. Cambridge: Cambridge University Press, 2003.

Bolsover, G. H. "David Urquhart and the Eastern Question, 1833–37: A Study in Publicity and Diplomacy." *Journal of Modern History* 8 (1936): 444–67.

Bonacina, Giovanni. *The Wahhabis Seen through European Eyes (1772–1830): Deists and Puritans of Islam*. Leiden: Brill, 2015.

Bouquet, Olivier. "Is It Time to Stop Speaking about Ottoman Modernisation?" In *Order and Compromise: Government Practices in Turkey from the Late Ottoman Empire to the Early 21st Century*, edited by Marc Aymes, Benjamin Gourisse, and Élise Massicard, 45–67. Leiden: Brill, 2015.

Bourne, Kenneth. *Palmerston: The Early Years, 1784–1841*. London: Allen Lane, 1982.

Brady, Alexander. *William Huskisson and Liberal Reform*. 2nd ed. London: Frank Cass, 1967.

Brennan, Richard. *A Popular Life of Our Holy Father Pope Pius the Ninth*. New York: Benziger Brothers, 1877.

Bulman, William J. *Anglican Enlightenment: Orientalism, Religion and Politics in England and Its Empire, 1648–1715*. Cambridge: Cambridge University Press, 2015.

Bulwer, Henry Lytton. *The Life of Henry John Temple, Viscount Palmerston*. 2 vols. London: Richard Bentley, 1870.

Bunsen, Frances Baroness. *A Memoir of Baron Bunsen*. 2 vols. London: Longman, 1868.

Burns, Ross. *Damascus: A History*. London: Routledge, 2007.

Busch, Moritz. *Our Chancellor: Sketches for a Historical Picture*. 2 vols. London: Macmillan, 1884.

Buzan, Barry, and George Lawson. *The Global Transformation: History, Modernity and the Making of International Relations*. Cambridge: Cambridge University Press, 2015.

Caquet, P. E. *The Orient, the Liberal Movement, and the Eastern Crisis of 1839–41*. London: Palgrave Macmillan, 2016.

Carrott, Richard G. *The Egyptian Revival: Its Sources, Monuments, and Meaning.* Berkeley: University of California Press, 1978.

Carruthers, Douglas, ed. *The Desert Route to India: Being the Journals of Four Travellers by the Great Desert Caravan Route between Aleppo and Basra, 1745-1751.* London: Hakluyt Society, 1929.

Cecil, Gwendolen. *Life of Robert Marquis of Salisbury.* 4 vols. London: Hodder and Stoughton, 1921-32.

Chamberlain, M. E. "Sir Charles Dilke and the British Intervention in Egypt, 1882: Decision Making in a Nineteenth-Century Cabinet." *British Journal of International Studies* 2 (1976): 231-45.

Charmley, John. "Britain and the Ottoman Empire, 1830-1880." In *Religion and Diplomacy: Religion and British Foreign Policy, 1815 to 1941*, edited by Keith Robbins and John Fisher, 61-83. Dordrecht: Republic of Letters, 2010.

Clark, E. M. "Milton's Abyssinian Paradise." *University of Texas Studies in English* 29 (1950): 129-50.

Clarke, John. *British Diplomacy and Foreign Policy: 1782-1865: The National Interest.* London: Allen and Unwin, 1989.

Coakley, J. F. *The Church of the East and the Church of England: A History of the Archbishop of Canterbury's Assyrian Mission.* Oxford: Clarendon, 1992.

Cole, Camille. "Controversial Investments: Trade and Infrastructure in Ottoman–British Relations in Iraq, 1861-1918." *Middle Eastern Studies* 54 (2018): 744-68.

Cole, Juan. *Napoleon's Egypt: Invading the Middle East.* New York: Palgrave Macmillan, 2007.

———. *Sacred Space and Holy War: The Politics, Culture and History of Shi'ite Islam.* New York: I. B. Tauris, 2002.

Coller, Ian. "Ottomans on the Move: Hassuna D'Ghies and the 'New Ottomanism' of the 1830s." In Isabella and Zanou, *Mediterranean Diasporas*, 97-116.

Coltrin, Chris. "Picturing Political Deliverance: Three Paintings of the Exodus by John Martin, Francis Danby, and David Roberts." *Nineteenth-Century Art Worldwide* 10 (2011). http://19thc-artworldwide.org/pdf/python/article_PDFs/NCAW_402.pdf.

Cooke, Neil. "The Forgotten Egyptologist: James Burton." In *Travellers in Egypt*, edited by Paul and Janet Starkey, 85-94. London: I. B. Tauris, 1998.

Crinson, Mark. *Empire Building: Orientalism and Victorian Architecture.* London: Routledge, 1996.

Crouzet, Guillemette. *Inventing the Middle East: Britain and the Persian Gulf in the Age of Global Imperialism.* McGill-Queen's University Press, forthcoming.

———. "'A Slave Trade Jurisdiction': Attempts against the Slave Trade and the Making of a Space of Law (Arabo-Persian Gulf, Indian Ocean, Red Sea, circa 1820-1900)." In *Legal Histories of the British Empire: Laws, Engagements and Legacies*, edited by Shaunnagh Dorsett and John McLaren, 234-48. Abingdon, UK: Routledge, 2014.

Cumming, Sir Duncan. *The Gentleman Savage: The Life of Mansfield Parkyns 1823-1894.* London: Century, 1987.

Cunningham, Allan. *Anglo-Ottoman Encounters in the Age of Revolution: Collected Essays.* Edited by Edward Ingram. London: Frank Cass, 1993.

Curl, James Stevens. *Egyptomania: The Egyptian Revival; A Recurring Theme in the History of Taste.* Manchester: Manchester University Press, 1994.

Davies, Charles E. *The Blood-Red Arab Flag: An Investigation into Qasimi Piracy, 1797-1820.* Exeter, UK: University of Exeter Press, 1997.

Davison, Roderic H. "'Russian Skill and Turkish Imbecility': The Treaty of Kuchuk Kainardji Reconsidered." *Slavic Review* 35 (1976): 463-83.

Deringil, Selim. *Conversion and Apostasy in the Late Ottoman Empire.* Cambridge: Cambridge University Press, 2012.

Dodwell, Henry. *The Founder of Modern Egypt: A Study of Muhammad 'Ali.* Cambridge: Cambridge University Press, 1967.

Douwes, Dick. *The Ottomans in Syria: A History of Justice and Oppression.* London: I. B. Tauris, 2000.

Downs, Jonathan. *Discovery at Rosetta.* London: Constable, 2008.

Eliav, Mordechai, ed. *Britain and the Holy Land 1838–1914: Selected Documents from the British Consulate in Jerusalem.* Jerusalem: Yad Izhak Ben-Zvi, 1997.

Eppel, Michael. "The Demise of the Kurdish Emirates: The Impact of Ottoman Reforms and International Relations on Kurdistan during the First Half of the Nineteenth Century." *Middle Eastern Studies* 44 (2008): 237–58.

Fahmy, Khaled. *All the Pasha's Men: Mehmed Ali, His Army and the Making of Modern Egypt.* Cairo: American University in Cairo Press, 2002.

Fairey, Jack. *The Great Powers and Orthodox Christendom: The Crisis over the Eastern Church in the Era of the Crimean War.* Basingstoke, UK: Palgrave Macmillan, 2015.

Farah, Caesar E. "Anglo-Ottoman Confrontation in the Yemen, 1840–9." In *Arabian Studies*, edited by R. B. Serjeant and R. L. Bidwell, 137–69. Cambridge: Cambridge University Press, 1990.

———. *The Politics of Interventionism in Ottoman Lebanon, 1830–1861.* London: Centre for Lebanese Studies, 2000.

———. "Protestantism and British Diplomacy in Syria." *International Journal of Middle East Studies* 7 (1976): 321–44.

———. "Protestantism and Politics: The 19th Century Dimension in Syria." In *Palestine in the Late Ottoman Period: Political, Social and Economic Transformation*, edited by David Kushner, 320–40. Jerusalem: Yad Izhak Ben-Zvi, 1986.

Fattah, Hala Mundhir. *The Politics of Regional Trade in Iraq, Arabia, and the Gulf, 1745–1900.* Albany: State University of New York Press, 1997.

Fawaz, Leila Tarazai. *An Occasion for War: Civil Conflict in Lebanon and Damascus in 1860.* London: Centre for Lebanese Studies, 1994.

Feldman, David. "The Damascus Affair and the Debate on Ritual Murder in Early Victorian Britain." In *Judaism, Christianity, and Islam: Collaboration and Conflict in the Age of Diaspora*, edited by Sander L. Gilman, 131–52. Hong Kong: Hong Kong University Press, 2014.

Figes, Orlando. *Crimea: The Last Crusade.* London: Allen Lane, 2010.

Filoni, Fernando. *The Church in Iraq.* Washington, DC: Catholic University of America Press, 2017.

Findley, Carter Vaughn. *Ottoman Civil Officialdom: A Social History.* Princeton, NJ: Princeton University Press, 1989.

———. "The Tanzimat." In *The Cambridge History of Turkey*, vol. 4, *Turkey in the Modern World*, edited by Reşat Kasaba, 9–37. Cambridge: Cambridge University Press, 2008.

Finn, Margot C. "Material Turns in British History, III: Collecting; Colonial Bombay, Basra, Baghdad and the Enlightenment Museum." *Transactions of the Royal Historical Society* 30 (2020): 1–28.

Fitzmaurice, Andrew. "The Equality of Non-European States in International Law." In *International Law in the Long Nineteenth Century*, edited by Randall Lesaffer and Inge van Hulle, 75–104. Brill: Leiden, 2018.

———. "Liberalism and Empire in Nineteenth-Century International Law." *American Historical Review* 117 (2012): 122–40.

Fitzsimons, Raymund. *The Baron of Piccadilly: The Travels and Entertainments of Albert Smith, 1816–1860.* London: Geoffrey Bles, 1967.

Floor, Willem. "The Rise and Fall of the Banū Ka'b: A Borderer State in Southern Khuzestan." *Iran* 44 (2006): 277–315.

Foliard, Daniel. *Dislocating the Orient: British Maps and the Making of the Middle East, 1854–1921*. Chicago: University of Chicago Press, 2017.

Fortescue, J. W. *A History of the British Army*. Vol. 4, *1789–1801*. London: Macmillan, 1906.

———. *A History of the British Army*. Vol. 6, *1807–1809*. London: Macmillan, 1910.

Frankel, Jonathan. *The Damascus Affair: "Ritual Murder," Politics, and the Jews in 1840*. Cambridge: Cambridge University Press, 1997.

Franklin, Michael J. *Orientalist Jones: Sir William Jones, Poet, Lawyer, and Linguist, 1746–1794*. Oxford: Oxford University Press, 2011.

Frary, Lucien J., and Mara Kozelsky, eds. *Russian-Ottoman Borderlands: The Eastern Question Reconsidered*. Madison: University of Wisconsin Press, 2014.

Freitag, Ulrike. "Helpless Representatives of the Great Powers? Western Consuls in Jeddah, 1830s to 1914." *Journal of Imperial and Commonwealth History* 40 (2012): 357–81.

Fry, Michael. *The Dundas Despotism*. Edinburgh: Edinburgh University Press, 1992.

Gange, David. *Dialogues with the Dead: Egyptology in British Culture and Religion 1822–1922*. Oxford: Oxford University Press, 2013.

Gange, David, and Michael Ledger-Lomas, eds. *Cities of God: The Bible and Archaeology in Nineteenth-Century Britain*. Cambridge: Cambridge University Press, 2013.

Gavin, R. J. *Aden under British Rule, 1839–1967*. London: Hurst, 1975.

Ghorbal, Shafik. *The Beginnings of the Egyptian Question and the Rise of Mehemet Ali*. London: Routledge, 1928.

Gilmour, David. *Curzon*. London: John Murray, 1994.

Gobat, Samuel. *Samuel Gobat, Bishop of Jerusalem, His Life and Work: A Biographical Sketch, Drawn Chiefly from His Own Journals*. London: James Nisbet, 1884.

Gold, Meira. "Ancient Egypt and the Geological Antiquity of Man, 1847–1863." *History of Science* 57 (2019): 194–230.

Goldfrank, David M. *The Origins of the Crimean War*. London: Longman, 1994.

Gordon, Sir Arthur. *The Earl of Aberdeen*. London: Sampson Low, 1893.

Grant, James. *The Scottish Soldiers of Fortune: Their Adventures and Achievements in the Armies of Europe*. London: George Routledge, 1889.

Greaves, R. W. "The Jerusalem Bishopric, 1841." *English Historical Review* 64 (1949): 328–52.

Green, Abigail. "The British Empire and the Jews: An Imperialism of Human Rights?" *Past & Present* 199 (2008): 175–205.

———. *Moses Montefiore: Jewish Liberator, Imperial Hero*. Cambridge, MA: Harvard University Press, 2010.

Green, Nile. *The Love of Strangers: What Six Muslim Students Learned in Jane Austen's London*. Princeton, NJ: Princeton University Press, 2016.

Guest, J. S. *The Euphrates Expedition*. London: Kegan Paul International, 1992.

———. *Survival among the Kurds: A History of the Yezidis*. London: Kegan Paul International, 1993.

Gürpinar, Dogan. "The Rise and Fall of Turcophilism in Nineteenth-Century British Discourses: Visions of the Turk, 'Young' and 'Old.'" *British Journal of Middle Eastern Studies* 39 (2012): 347–72.

Gust, Onni. "Remembering and Forgetting the Scottish Highlands: Sir James Mackintosh and the Forging of a British Imperial Identity." *Journal of British Studies* 52 (2013): 615–37.

Hakim, Carol. *The Origins of the Lebanese National Idea, 1840–1920*. Berkeley: University of California Press, 2013.

Hallberg, Charles. *The Suez Canal: Its History and Diplomatic Importance*. New York: Columbia University Press, 1931.

Halls, J. J. *The Life and Correspondence of Henry Salt*. 2 vols. London: Richard Bentley, 1834.

Harcourt, Freda. *Flagships of Imperialism: The P&O Company and the Politics of Empire from Its Origins to 1867*. Manchester: Manchester University Press, 2006.

———. "The High Road to India: The P&O Company and the Suez Canal, 1840–1874." *International Journal of Maritime History* 22 (2010): 19–72.

Harding, James. *Babylon and the Brethren: The Use and Influence of the Whore of Babylon Motif in the Christian Brethren Movement, 1829–1900*. Eugene, OR: Wipf and Stock, 2015.

Harris, William. *Lebanon: A History, 600–2011*. Oxford: Oxford University Press, 2012.

Harrison, Robert T. *Britain in the Middle East, 1619–1971*. London: Bloomsbury Academic, 2016.

Hawley, Donald. *The Trucial States*. London: Allen and Unwin, 1970.

Hayes, Paul. *The Nineteenth Century, 1814–80*. Modern British Foreign Policy. London: Adam and Charles Black, 1975.

Headrick, Daniel. *The Tools of Empire: Technology and European Imperialism in the Nineteenth Century*. Oxford: Oxford University Press, 1981.

H.J.L.B. Review of *L'Egypte et ses chemins de fer* by Lionel Wiener. *Geographical Journal* 81 (1933): 451–52.

Hodder, Edwin. *The Life and Work of the Seventh Earl of Shaftesbury*. 3 vols. London: Cassell, 1886.

Hoock, Holger. *Empires of the Imagination: Politics, War, and the Arts in the British World*. London: Profile, 2010.

[Hook, Theodore Edward]. *The Life of General Sir David Baird*. 2 vols. London: Richard Bentley, 1832.

Hopkins, Hugh Evan. *Sublime Vagabond: The Life of Joseph Wolff, Missionary Extraordinary*. Worthing, UK: Churchman, 1984.

Hopwood, Derek. *The Russian Presence in Syria and Palestine 1843–1914: Church and Politics in the Near East*. Oxford: Clarendon, 1969.

Horowitz, Richard S. "International Law and State Transformation in China, Siam, and the Ottoman Empire during the Nineteenth Century." *Journal of World History* 15 (2004): 445–86.

Hoskins, H. L. *British Routes to India*. London: Cass, 1966.

[Howard, Edward]. *Memoirs of Admiral Sir Sidney Smith*. 2 vols. London: R. Bentley, 1839.

Hunter, F. Robert. *Egypt under the Khedives 1805–1879: From Household Government to Modern Bureaucracy*. Pittsburgh: University of Pittsburgh Press, 1984.

Hyam, Ronald. *Britain's Imperial Century, 1815–1914: A Study of Empire and Expansion*. Basingstoke, UK: Palgrave Macmillan, 2002.

Ingram, Edward. *The Beginning of the Great Game in Asia, 1828–1834*. Oxford: Clarendon, 1979.

———. *Britain's Persian Connection 1798–1828: Prelude to the Great Game in Asia*. Oxford: Clarendon, 1992.

———. *The British Empire as a World Power*. London: Frank Cass, 2001.

———. *Commitment to Empire: Prophecies of the Great Game in Asia, 1797–1800*. Oxford: Clarendon, 1981.

———. *Empire-Building and Empire-Builders: Twelve Studies*. London: Frank Cass, 1995.

———. "From Trade to Empire in the Near East, III: The Uses of the Residency at Baghdad, 1794–1804." *Middle Eastern Studies* 14 (1978): 278–306.

———. *In Defence of British India: Great Britain in the Middle East, 1775–1842*. London: Frank Cass, 1984.

Irwin, Robert. *For Lust of Knowing: The Orientalists and Their Enemies*. London: Allen Lane, 2006.

Isabella, Maurizio, and Konstantina Zanou, eds. *Mediterranean Diasporas: Politics and Ideas in the Long 19th Century*. London: Bloomsbury Academic, 2016.

Ito, Takashi. *London Zoo and the Victorians, 1828–1859*. Woodbridge, UK: Royal Historical Society, 2014.

Jack, Sybil M. "No Heavenly Jerusalem: The Anglican Bishopric, 1841–83." *Journal of Religious History* 19 (1995): 181–203.

Jacob, Harold F. *Kings of Arabia: The Rise and Set of the Turkish Sovranty in the Arabian Peninsula*. London: Mills and Boon, 1923.

Jakes, Aaron. *Egypt's Occupation: Colonial Economism and the Crises of Capitalism*. Stanford, CA: Stanford University Press, 2020.

———. "The World the Suez Canal Made." Public Seminar, April 2, 2021. https://publicseminar .org/essays/the-world-the-suez-canal-made/.

Jasanoff, Maya. *Edge of Empire: Conquest and Collecting in the East, 1750–1850*. London: Fourth Estate, 2005.

Jelavich, Barbara. *Russia's Balkan Entanglements, 1806–1914*. Cambridge: Cambridge University Press, 1991.

Johnson, L. G. *General T. Perronet Thompson, 1783–1869: His Military, Literary and Political Campaigns*. London: George Allen and Unwin, 1957.

Kark, Ruth, and Haim Goren. "Pioneering British Exploration and Scriptural Geography: The Syrian Society/The Palestine Association." *Geographical Journal* 17 (2011): 264–74.

Katz, David S. *The Shaping of Turkey in the British Imagination, 1776–1923*. N.p.: Palgrave Macmillan, 2016.

Kayaoğlu, Turan. *Legal Imperialism: Sovereignty and Extraterritoriality in Japan, the Ottoman Empire and China*. Cambridge: Cambridge University Press, 2010.

Kelly, J. B. *Britain and the Persian Gulf, 1795–1880*. Oxford: Clarendon, 1968.

Khan, M.G.I. "British Policy in Iraq, 1828–43." *Journal of the Asiatic Society of Bangladesh* 18 (1973): 173–94.

Kimche, David. "The Opening of the Red Sea to European Ships in the Late Eighteenth Century." *Middle Eastern Studies* 8 (1972): 63–71.

King, Elspeth. *The People's Palace and Glasgow Green*. Glasgow: Drew, 1985.

Kochav, Sarah. "'Beginning at Jerusalem': The Mission to the Jews and English Evangelical Eschatology." In *Jerusalem in the Mind of the Western World, 1800–1948*, edited by Yehoshua Ben-Arieh and Moshe Davis, 91–107. Westport, CT: Praeger, 1997.

Kolsky, Elizabeth. *Colonial Justice in British India*. Cambridge: Cambridge University Press, 2010.

Koppes, Clayton R. "Captain Mahan, General Gordon, and the Origins of the Term 'Middle East.'" *Middle Eastern Studies* 12 (1976): 95–98.

Kour, Z. H. *The History of Aden, 1839–1872*. London: Frank Cass, 1981.

Kühn, Thomas. *Empire, Islam, and Politics of Difference: Ottoman Rule in Yemen, 1849–1919*. Leiden: Brill, 2011.

Laidlaw, Christine. *The British in the Levant: Trade and Perceptions of the Ottoman Empire in the Eighteenth Century*. London: I. B. Tauris, 2010.

Laisram, Pallavi Pandit. *Viewing the Islamic Orient: British Travel Writers of the Nineteenth Century*. London: Routledge, 2006.

Lamb, Margaret. "The Making of a Russophobe: David Urquhart—the Formative Years, 1825–1835." *International History Review* 3 (1981): 330–57.

———. "Writing Up the Eastern Question in 1835–6." *International History Review* 15 (1993): 239–68.

Lambert, Andrew. "The Tory World View: Sea Power, Strategy and Party Politics, 1815–1914." In *The Tory World: Deep History and the Tory Theme in British Foreign Policy, 1679–2014*, edited by Jeremy Black, 121–48. Farnham: Ashgate, 2015.

Landes, David S. *Bankers and Pashas: International Finance and Economic Imperialism in Egypt*. New York: Harper and Row, 1969.

Lane-Poole, Stanley. *The Life of Stratford Canning, Viscount Stratford de Redcliffe*. 2 vols. London: Longman, 1888.

Larsen, Mogens Trolle. *The Conquest of Assyria: Excavations in an Antique Land 1840–1860*. London: Routledge, 1994.

Leask, Nigel. *Curiosity and the Aesthetics of Travel Writing, 1770–1840: "From an Antique Land."* Oxford: Oxford University Press, 2002.

Lewis, Donald M. *The Origins of Christian Zionism: Lord Shaftesbury and Evangelical Support for a Jewish Homeland*. Cambridge: Cambridge University Press, 2010.

Litvak, Meir. "Karbala." In *Encyclopaedia Iranica*, online edition, originally published December 15, 2010, last updated April 24, 2012. https://iranicaonline.org/articles/karbala.

———. "Money, Religion, and Politics: The Oudh Bequest in Najaf and Karbala, 1850–1903." *International Journal of Middle East Studies* 33 (2001): 1–21.

Lockman, Zachary. *Contending Visions of the Middle East: The History and Politics of Orientalism*. Cambridge: Cambridge University Press, 2004.

Low, Charles Rathbone. *History of the Indian Navy: 1613–1863*. 2 vols. London: Richard Bentley, 1877.

Low, Michael Christopher. *Imperial Mecca: Ottoman Arabia and the Indian Ocean Hajj*. New York: Columbia University Press, 2020.

Lynn, M. "The 'Imperialism of Free Trade' and the Case of West Africa, c.1830–c.1870." *Journal of Imperial and Commonwealth History* 15 (1986–87): 22–40.

Macbride, Mackenzie, ed. *With Napoleon at Waterloo and Other Unpublished Documents of the Waterloo and Peninsular Campaigns*. London: Francis Griffiths, 1911.

Mackesy, Piers. *British Victory in Egypt, 1801: The End of Napoleon's Conquest*. London: Tauris Parke Paperbacks, 2010.

Majer, Michele. "*La Mode à la Girafe*: Fashion, Culture, and Politics in Bourbon Restoration France." *Studies in Decorative Arts* 17 (2009–10): 123–61.

Makdisi, Ussama. *The Culture of Sectarianism: Community, History, and Violence in Nineteenth-Century Ottoman Lebanon*. Berkeley: University of California Press, 2000.

Malcolm, Noel. *Useful Enemies: Islam and the Ottoman Empire in Western Political Thought, 1450–1750*. Oxford: Oxford University Press, 2019.

Malley, Shawn. *From Archaeology to Spectacle in Victorian Britain: The Case of Assyria, 1845–1854*. Farnham, UK: Ashgate, 2012.

Manley, Deborah, and Peta Rée. *Henry Salt: Artist, Traveller, Diplomat, Egyptologist*. London: Libri, 2001.

Mansel, Philip. *Levant: Splendor and Catastrophe on the Mediterranean*. New Haven, CT: Yale University Press, 2011.

Mantena, Karuna. "The Crisis of Liberal Imperialism." In *Victorian Visions of Global Order: Empire and International Relations in Nineteenth-Century Political Thought*, edited by Duncan Bell, 113–35. Cambridge: Cambridge University Press, 2007.

Ma'oz, Moshe. *Ottoman Reform in Syria and Palestine, 1840–1861*. Oxford: Clarendon, 1968.

Marlowe, John. *Anglo-Egyptian Relations, 1800–1956*. London: Frank Cass, 1965.

Marsden, B., and C. Smith. *Engineering Empires: A Cultural History of Technology in Nineteenth-Century Britain*. Basingstoke, UK: Palgrave Macmillan, 2005.

Marshall, P. J. *Problems of Empire: Britain and India, 1757–1813*. London: George Allen and Unwin, 1968.

Marsot, Afaf Lutfi al-Sayyid. *Egypt in the Reign of Muhammad Ali*. Cambridge: Cambridge University Press, 1984.

Marston, Thomas E. *Britain's Imperial Role in the Red Sea Area 1800–1878*. Hamden, CT: Shoestring, 1961.

Masters, Bruce. "The 1850 Events in Aleppo: An Aftershock of Syria's Incorporation in the Capitalist World System." *International Journal of Middle East Studies* 22 (1990): 3–20.

———. "Levant Company." In *Encyclopedia of the Ottoman Empire*, edited by Gabor Ágoston and Bruce Masters, 333. New York: Facts on File, 2009.

———. "The Treaties of Erzurum (1823 and 1848) and the Changing Status of Iranians in the Ottoman Empire." *Iranian Studies* 24 (1991): 3–15.

Matthew, H.C.G. "Gladstone, Vaticanism, and the Question of the East." *Studies in Church History* 15 (1978): 417–42.

Maxwell, Herbert. *Sir Charles Murray: A Memoir*. Edinburgh: William Blackwood, 1898.

Mayes, Stanley. *The Great Belzoni*. London: Putnam, 1959.

Mazower, Mark. *Governing the World: The History of an Idea, 1815 to the Present*. London: Penguin, 2012.

McCarthy, James. *Selim Aga: A Slave's Odyssey*. Edinburgh: Luath, 2006.

McDougall, James. "Sovereignty, Governance, and Political Community in the Ottoman Empire and North Africa." In *Reimagining Democracy in the Mediterranean, 1780–1860*, edited by Joanna Innes and Mark Philp, 127–52. Oxford: Oxford University Press, 2018.

McDowell, David. *A Modern History of the Kurds*. London: I. B. Tauris, 1996.

Mehta, Uday Singh. *Liberalism and Empire: A Study in Nineteenth-Century British Liberal Thought*. Chicago: University of Chicago Press, 1999.

Melman, Billie. *Women's Orients: English Women and the Middle East, 1718–1918*. London: Macmillan, 1992.

Metcalf, Thomas R. *Ideologies of the Raj*. The New Cambridge History of India III.4. Cambridge: Cambridge University Press, 1994.

Meyers, Jeffrey. "T. E. Lawrence and the Character of the Arabs." *Virginia Quarterly Review* 80 (2004): 135–52.

Mikaberidze, Alexander. *The Napoleonic Wars: A Global History*. Oxford: Oxford University Press, 2020.

Miller, Christopher. "Orientalism, Colonialism." In *A New History of French Literature*, edited by Denis Hollier, 698–705. Cambridge, MA: Harvard University Press, 1994.

Miran, Jonathan. *Red Sea Citizens: Cosmopolitan Society and Cultural Change in Massawa*. Bloomington: Indiana University Press, 2009.

Mitsein, Rebekah. "What the Abyssinian Liar Can Tell Us about True Stories: Knowledge, Skepticism, and James Bruce's *Travels to Discover the Source of the Nile*." The 18th-Century Common, March 16, 2015. https://www.18thcenturycommon.org/james-bruce/.

Moore, J. C. *The Life of Lieutenant-General Sir John Moore*. 2 vols. London: John Murray, 1834.

Morrisroe, Vicky. "'Eastern History with Western Eyes': E. A. Freeman, Islam and Orientalism." *Journal of Victorian Culture* 16 (2011): 25–45.

Moscrop, J. J. *Measuring Jerusalem: The Palestine Exploration Fund and British Interests in the Holy Land*. London: Leicester University Press, 1999.

Moser, Stephanie. *Designing Antiquity: Owen Jones, Ancient Egypt and the Crystal Palace*. New Haven, CT: Yale University Press, 2012.

———. *Wondrous Curiosities: Ancient Egypt at the British Museum*. Chicago: University of Chicago Press, 2006.

Moshenska, Gabriel. "Unrolling Egyptian Mummies in Nineteenth-Century Britain." *British Journal for the History of Science* 47 (2014): 451–77.

Mosse, W. E. *The Rise and Fall of the Crimean System, 1855–71: The Story of a Peace Settlement*. London: Macmillan, 1963.

Müge-Göçek, Fatma, and Murat Ozyüksel. "The Ottoman Empire's Negotiation of Western Liberal Imperialism." In *Liberal Imperialism in Europe*, edited by Matthew P. Fitzpatrick, 193–217. Basingstoke, UK: Palgrave Macmillan, 2012.

Mulligan, William. "Decisions for Empire: Revisiting the 1882 Occupation of Egypt." *English Historical Review* 135 (2020): 94–126.

Naff, Thomas. "The Ottoman Empire and the European States System." In *The Expansion of International Society*, edited by Hedley Bull and Adam Watson, 143–69. Oxford: Clarendon, 1984.

Napier, Elers. *The Life and Correspondence of Admiral Sir Charles Napier.* 2 vols. London: Hurst and Blackett, 1862.

Nicolini, Beatrice. *Makran, Oman, and Zanzibar: Three-Terminal Cultural Corridor in the Western Indian Ocean, 1799–1856.* Leiden: Brill, 2004.

Nieuwenhuis, Tom. *Politics and Society in Early Modern Iraq: Mamluk Pashas, Tribal Shayks and Local Rule between 1802 and 1831.* The Hague: Martinus Nijhoff, 1982.

Nightingale, J. *Memoirs of Her Late Majesty Queen Caroline, Consort of King George the Fourth.* Vol. 1. London: J. Robins, 1821.

Ochsenwald, W. L. "The Jidda Massacre of 1858." *Middle Eastern Studies* 13 (1977): 314–26.

O'Flynn, Thomas S. R. *The Western Christian Presence in the Russias and Qajar Persia, c.1760–c.1870.* Leiden: Brill, 2016.

Oliver, Andrew. *American Travelers on the Nile: Early U.S. Visitors to Egypt, 1774–1839.* Cairo: The American University in Cairo Press, 2014.

Onley, James. *The Arabian Frontier of the British Raj: Merchants, Rulers and the British in the Nineteenth-Century Gulf.* Oxford: Oxford University Press, 2007.

———. "The Politics of Protection in the Gulf: The Arab Rulers and the British Resident in the Nineteenth Century." *New Arabian Studies* 6 (2004): 30–92.

Orakhelashvili, Alexander. "The Idea of European International Law." *European Journal of International Law* 17 (2006): 315–47.

Otte, T. G. "'A Course of Unceasing Remonstrance': British Diplomacy and the Suppression of the Slave Trade in the East, 1852–1898." In *Slavery, Diplomacy and Empire: Britain and the Suppression of the Slave Trade, 1807–1975*, edited by Keith Hamilton and Patrick Salmon, 93–124. Brighton: Sussex Academic Press, 2012.

———. *Statesman of Europe: A Life of Sir Edward Grey.* London: Allen Lane, 2020.

Otter, William. *The Life and Remains of Edward Daniel Clarke.* 2 vols. London: George Cowie, 1825.

Owen, Roger. *Cotton and the Egyptian Economy, 1820–1914: A Study in Trade and Development.* Oxford: Clarendon, 1969.

———. *Lord Cromer: Victorian Imperialist, Edwardian Proconsul.* Oxford: Oxford University Press, 2004.

———. *The Middle East in the World Economy, 1800–1914.* London: Methuen, 1981.

Ozavci, Ozan. *Dangerous Gifts: Imperialism, Security, and Civil Wars in the Levant, 1798–1864.* Oxford: Oxford University Press, 2021.

———. "A Priceless Grace? The Congress of Vienna of 1815, the Ottoman Empire and Historicising the Eastern Question." *English Historical Review* (forthcoming).

Ozil, Ayşe. *Orthodox Christians in the Late Ottoman Empire: A Study of Communal Relations in Anatolia.* London: Routledge, 2013.

Özoğlu, Hakan. *Kurdish Notables and the Ottoman State: Evolving Identities, Competing Loyalties, and Shifting Boundaries.* Albany: State University of New York, 2004.

Özsu, Umut. "Ottoman Empire." Chap. 18 in *The Oxford Handbook of the History of International Law*, edited by Bardo Fassbender and Anne Peters. Oxford: Oxford University Press, 2012.

Palabiyik, Mustafa Serdar. "The Emergence of the Idea of 'International Law' in the Ottoman Empire before the Treaty of Paris (1856)." *Middle Eastern Studies* 50 (2014): 233–51.

Parkinson, C. Northcote. *War in the Eastern Seas, 1793–1815.* London: George Allen and Unwin, 1954.

Parry, Jonathan P. "Disraeli, the East and Religion: *Tancred* in Context." *English Historical Review* 132 (2017): 570–604.

——. *The Politics of Patriotism: English Liberalism, National Identity and Europe, 1830–1886*. Cambridge: Cambridge University Press, 2006.

——. *The Rise and Fall of Liberal Government in Victorian Britain*. New Haven, CT: Yale University Press, 1993.

——. "Steam Power and British Influence in Baghdad, 1820–1860." *Historical Journal* 56 (2013): 145–73.

Pemble, John. *The Mediterranean Passion: Victorians and Edwardians in the South*. Oxford: Clarendon, 1987.

Philipp, Thomas. *Acre: The Rise and Fall of a Palestinian City, 1730–1831*. New York: Columbia University Press, 2001.

Piggott, Jan. *Palace of the People: The Crystal Palace at Sydenham, 1854–1936*. London: C. Hurst, 2004.

Pitts, Jennifer. *Boundaries of the International: Law and Empire*. Cambridge, MA: Harvard University Press, 2018.

——. "Legislator of the World? A Rereading of Bentham on Colonies." *Political Theory* 31 (2003): 200–234.

——. *A Turn to Empire: The Rise of Imperial Liberalism in Britain and France*. Princeton, NJ: Princeton University Press, 2005.

Porterfield, Todd B. *The Allure of Empire: Art in the Service of French Imperialism, 1798–1836*. Princeton, NJ: Princeton University Press, 1998.

Price, Munro. "'Our Aim is the Rhine Frontier': The Emergence of a French Forward Policy, 1815–1830." *French History* 33 (2019): 65–87.

Price, Munro, and Stanley Price. *The Road to Apocalypse: The Extraordinary Journey of Lewis Way*. London: Notting Hill, 2011.

Puryear, Vernon John. *International Economics and Diplomacy in the Near East: A Study of British Commercial Policy in the Levant, 1834–1853*. Stanford, CA: Stanford University Press, 1935.

Quinn, Simon. "British Military Orientalism: Cross-Cultural Contact with the Mamluks during the Egyptian Campaign, 1801." *War in History* (2019): https://doi.org/10.1177/0968344519837303.

Ram, K. V. *The Barren Relationship: Britain and Ethiopia, 1805 to 1868; A Study of British Policy*. New Delhi: Concept, 1985.

Rawlinson, George. *A Memoir of Sir Henry Creswicke Rawlinson*. London: Longman, 1898.

Ray, Gordon N. *Thackeray: The Uses of Adversity, 1811–1846*. London: Oxford University Press, 1955.

Rée, Peta. *A Paire of Intelopers: The English Abyssinian Warriors*. Petergate, UK: Quacks, 2011.

Reese, Scott S. *Imperial Muslims: Islam, Community and Authority in the Indian Ocean, 1839–1937*. Edinburgh: Edinburgh University Press, 2017.

Reid, Donald M. *Whose Pharaohs? Archaeology, Museums, and Egyptian National Identity from Napoleon to World War I*. Berkeley: University of California Press, 2003.

Ridley, Ronald T. *Napoleon's Proconsul in Egypt: The Life and Times of Bernardino Drovetti*. London: Rubicon, 1998.

Risso, Patricia. "Competition for Bahrain during the Early Decades of al-Khalifa Rule, Especially in the Years 1799–1803." In *Bahrain through the Ages: The History*, edited by Shaykh Abdullah bin Khalid al-Khalifa and Michael Rice, 458–66. London: Kegan Paul International, 1993.

Roberts, Caroline. *The Woman and the Hour: Harriet Martineau and Victorian Ideologies.* Toronto: University of Toronto Press, 2002.

Rodkey, Frederick Stanley. "The Attempts of Briggs and Company to Guide British Policy in the Levant in the Interest of Mehemet Ali Pasha, 1821–41." *Journal of Modern History* 5 (1933): 324–51.

———. "Colonel Campbell's Report on Egypt in 1840, with Lord Palmerston's Comments." *Cambridge Historical Journal* 3 (1929): 102–14.

———. "Lord Palmerston and the Rejuvenation of Turkey, 1830–41: Part I, 1830–39." *Journal of Modern History* 1 (1929): 570–93.

———. *The Turco-Egyptian Question in the Relations of England, France, and Russia, 1832–1841.* Urbana: University of Illinois, 1924.

Rogan, Eugene L. *The Arabs: A History.* London; Penguin, 2018.

———. "Sectarianism and Social Conflict in Damascus: The 1860 Events Reconsidered." *Arabica* 51 (2004): 493–511.

Root, Nina J. "Victorian England's Hippomania." *Natural History* 102 (1993): 34–38.

Roper, Geoffrey. "Christian Rassam (1808–72): Translator, Interpreter, Diplomat and Liar." In *Travellers in the Near East*, edited by Charles Foster, 183–200. London: Stacey International, 2004.

Rosen, Fred. *Bentham, Byron, and Greece: Constitutionalism, Nationalism, and Early Liberal Political Thought.* Oxford: Clarendon, 1992.

Rubenson, Sven. *The Survival of Ethiopian Independence.* London: Heinemann, 1976.

Said, Edward W. *Orientalism.* London: Routledge and Kegan Paul, 1978.

Saul, Norman. *Russia and the Mediterranean, 1797–1807.* Chicago: University of Chicago Press, 1970.

Schroeder, Paul W. *The Transformation of European Politics, 1763–1848.* Oxford: Clarendon, 1994.

Searight, Sarah. "A Naval Tourist, 1834–1840: Henry Byam Martin." In *Travellers in Egypt*, edited by Paul and Janet Starkey. London: I. B. Tauris, 1998.

———. *Steaming East: The Forging of Steamship and Rail Links between Europe and Asia.* London: Bodley Head, 1991.

Šedivý, Miroslav. "Metternich's Judgement on Islam: Modern Thinking?" *Acta Fakulty Filozofické Západočeské Univerzity v Plzni* 4 (2009): 155–62.

———. *Metternich, the Great Powers and the Eastern Question.* Pilsen, Czech Republic: University of West Bohemia, 2013.

Sedra, Paul. *From Mission to Modernity: Evangelicals, Reformers and Education in Nineteenth Century Egypt.* London: I. B. Tauris, 2011.

Seton-Watson, R. W. *Disraeli, Gladstone and the Eastern Question: A Study in Diplomacy and Party Politics.* London: Macmillan, 1935.

Shannon, R. T. *Gladstone and the Bulgarian Agitation, 1876.* 2nd ed. Hassocks, UK: Harvester, 1975.

Shaw, Stanford J., and Ezel Kural Shaw. *History of the Ottoman Empire and Modern Turkey.* 2 vols. Cambridge: Cambridge University Press, 1976–77.

Shepherd, Naomi. *The Zealous Intruders: The Western Rediscovery of Palestine.* London: Collins, 1987.

Shields, Sarah. *Mosul before Iraq: Like Bees Making Five-Sided Cells.* Albany: State University of New York Press, 2000.

Shupp, Paul F. *The European Powers and the Near Eastern Question, 1806–1807.* New York: Columbia University Press, 1931.

Simons, John. *Obaysch: A Hippopotamus in Victorian London.* Sydney: Sydney University Press, 2019.

Sinha, S. Prakash. *Asylum and International Law*. The Hague: Martinus Nijhoff, 1971.

Stanley, Brian. "'An Ardour of Devotion': The Spiritual Legacy of Henry Martyn." In *India and the Indianness of Christianity*, edited by R. Fox Young, 108–26. Grand Rapids, MI: William B. Eerdmans, 2009.

Stanley, Bruce E. "Berbera." In *Cities of the Middle East and North Africa: A Historical Encyclopedia*, edited by Michael R. T. Dumper and Bruce E. Stanley, 89–95. Santa Barbara, CA: ABC-Clio, 2007.

St. Clair, William. *Lord Elgin and the Marbles*. Oxford: Oxford University Press, 1983.

Stone, James. "Bismarck and the Great Game: Germany and Anglo-Russian Rivalry in Central Asia, 1871–1890." *Central European History* 48 (2015): 151–75.

Strathern, Paul. *Napoleon in Egypt: "The Greatest Glory."* London: Jonathan Cape, 2007.

Strong, Rowan. *Anglicanism and the British Empire, c.1700–1850*. Oxford: Oxford University Press, 2007.

Subaşı, Turgut. "Anglo-Ottoman Relations in the Nineteenth Century: Mustafa Reşid Paşa's Memorandum to Palmerston, 11 August 1839." *International Journal of Human Sciences* 8 (2011): 1732–46.

——. "The Apostasy Question in the Context of Anglo-Ottoman Relations, 1843–44." *Middle Eastern Studies* 38 (2002): 1–34.

Sylvest, Casper. "The Foundations of Victorian International Law." In *Victorian Visions of Global Order: Empire and International Relations in Nineteenth-Century Political Thought*, edited by Duncan Bell, 47–66. Cambridge: Cambridge University Press, 2007.

Talbot, Michael. *British-Ottoman Relations, 1661–1807: Commerce and Diplomatic Practice in Eighteenth-Century Istanbul*. Woodbridge, UK: Boydell, 2017.

——. "Divine Imperialism: The British in Palestine, 1753–1842." In *The British Abroad since the Eighteenth Century*, 2 vols., edited by Martin Farr and Xavier Guégan, 2:36–53. Basingstoke, UK: Palgrave Macmillan, 2013–14.

Taylor, A.J.P. *The Struggle for Mastery in Europe, 1848–1918*. Oxford: Oxford University Press, 1971.

Taylor, Miles. *The Decline of British Radicalism, 1847–1860*. Oxford: Clarendon, 1995.

Temperley, H.W.V. "British Policy towards Parliamentary Rule and Constitutionalism in Turkey (1830–1914)." *Cambridge Historical Journal* 4 (1933): 156–91.

——. *England and the Near East: The Crimea*. London, Longman, 1936.

Tennant, Bob. *Corporate Holiness: Pulpit Preaching and the Church of England Missionary Societies, 1760–1870*. Oxford: Oxford University Press, 2013.

Thompson, Jason. *Sir Gardner Wilkinson and His Circle*. Austin: University of Texas Press, 1992.

Thompson, J.R.F. *The Rich Manuscripts*. London: British Museum, 1963.

Tibawi, A. L. *American Interests in Syria, 1800–1901: A Study of Educational, Literary and Religious Work*. Oxford: Clarendon, 1966.

——. *British Interests in Palestine, 1800–1901: A Study of Religious and Educational Enterprise*. London: Oxford University Press, 1961.

——. *A Modern History of Syria, Including Lebanon and Palestine*. London: Macmillan, 1969.

Todd, David. *A Velvet Empire: French Informal Imperialism in the Nineteenth Century*. Princeton, NJ: Princeton University Press, 2021.

Toledano, Ehud. R. *The Ottoman Slave Trade and Its Suppression, 1840–1890*. Princeton, NJ: Princeton University Press, 1982.

——. *State and Society in Mid-Nineteenth-Century Egypt*. Cambridge: Cambridge University Press, 1990.

Traboulsi, Fawwaz. *A History of Modern Lebanon*. London: Pluto, 2007.

Tromans, Nicholas. "The Orient in Perspective." In *The Lure of the East: British Orientalist Painting*, edited by Nicholas Tromans, 102–25. London: Tate, 2008.

Trumbach, Randolph. *Sex and the Gender Revolution*. Vol. 1, *Heterosexuality and the Third Gender in Enlightenment London*. Chicago: University of Chicago Press, 1998.

Van den Boogert, Maurits H. *The Capitulations and the Ottoman Legal System: Qadis, Consuls and Beraths in the 18th Century*. Leiden: Brill, 2005.

Varouxakis, Georgios. "The Godfather of 'Occidentality': Auguste Comte and the Idea of the 'West.'" *Modern Intellectual History* 16 (2019): 411–41.

Vereté, Mayir. *From Palmerston to Balfour: Collected Essays*. Edited by Norman Rose. London: Frank Cass, 1992.

Walsh, Robert. *Account of the Levant Company; with Some Notices of the Benefits Conferred upon Society by Its Officers, in Promoting the Cause of Humanity, Literature and the Fine Arts*. London: J. and A. Arch, 1825.

Waterfield, Gordon. *Sultans of Aden*. London: John Murray, 1968.

Webster, Charles. *The Foreign Policy of Palmerston, 1830–41: Britain, the Liberal Movement and the Eastern Question*. 2 vols. London: Bell, 1951.

———. "Urquhart, Ponsonby, and Palmerston." *English Historical Review* 62 (1947): 327–51.

Wilson, K. M. "Constantinople or Cairo: Lord Salisbury and the Partition of the Ottoman Empire, 1886–1897." In *Imperialism and Nationalism in the Middle East: The Anglo-Egyptian Experience*, edited by Wilson, 26–55. London: Mansell, 1983.

Winder, R. Bayly. *Saudi Arabia in the Nineteenth Century*. London: Macmillan, 1965.

Windham, William. *The Windham Papers: The Life and Correspondence of William Windham, 1750–1810*. 2 vols. London: Herbert Jenkins, 1913.

Wood, Alfred C. *A History of the Levant Company*. London: Oxford University Press, 1935.

Wright, Denis. "Samuel Manesty and His Unauthorised Embassy to the Court of Fatḥ Ali Shah." *IRAN: Journal of the British Institute of Persian Studies* 24 (1986): 153–60.

Yapp, M. E. "The Establishment of the East India Company Residency at Baghdad, 1798–1806." *Bulletin of the School of Oriental and African Studies* 30 (1967): 323–36.

———. "Europe in the Turkish Mirror." *Past & Present* 137 (1992): 134–55.

———. *Strategies of British India: Britain, Iran and Afghanistan, 1798–1850*. Oxford: Clarendon, 1980.

———. "'That Great Mass of Unmixed Mahomedanism': Reflections on the Historical Links between the Middle East and Asia." *British Journal of Middle Eastern Studies* 19 (1992): 3–15.

Yaycioglu, Ali. *Partners of the Empire: The Crisis of the Ottoman Order in the Age of Revolutions*. Stanford, CA: Stanford University Press, 2016.

Yilmaz, Huseyin. "The Eastern Question and the Ottoman Empire: The Genesis of the Near and Middle East in the Nineteenth Century." In *Is There a Middle East? The Evolution of a Geopolitical Concept*, edited by Michael E. Bonine, Abbas Amanat, and Michael Ezekiel Gasper, 11–35. Stanford, CA: Stanford University Press, 2012.

Yurdusev, A. Nuri, ed. *Ottoman Diplomacy: Conventional or Unconventional?* Basingstoke, UK: Palgrave Macmillan, 2004.

Zahlan, Rosemarie Said. "George Baldwin: Soldier of Fortune?" In *Travellers in Egypt*, edited by Paul and Janet Starkey, 24–38. London: I. B. Tauris, 1998.

Zanou, Konstantina. *Transnational Patriotism in the Mediterranean, 1800–1850: Stammering the Nation*. Oxford: Oxford University Press, 2018.

Ze'evi, Dror. "Back to Napoleon? Thoughts on the Beginning of the Modern Era in the Middle East." *Mediterranean Historical Review* 19 (2004): 73–94.

Ziter, Edward. *The Orient on the Victorian Stage*. Cambridge: Cambridge University Press, 2003.

A NOTE ON THE TYPE

THIS BOOK has been composed in Miller, a Scotch Roman typeface designed by Matthew Carter and first released by Font Bureau in 1997. It resembles Monticello, the typeface developed for The Papers of Thomas Jefferson in the 1940s by C. H. Griffith and P. J. Conkwright and reinterpreted in digital form by Carter in 2003.

Pleasant Jefferson ("P. J.") Conkwright (1905–1986) was Typographer at Princeton University Press from 1939 to 1970. He was an acclaimed book designer and AIGA Medalist.

The ornament used throughout this book was designed by Pierre Simon Fournier (1712–1768) and was a favorite of Conkwright's, used in his design of the *Princeton University Library Chronicle*.